THE

Saturday Review

TREASURY

A VOLUME OF GOOD READING
SELECTED FROM THE COMPLETE FILES
BY JOHN HAVERSTICK AND
THE EDITORS OF THE SATURDAY REVIEW

Introduction by
Joseph Wood Krutch

SIMON AND SCHUSTER   NEW YORK   1957

PUBLISHED BY SIMON AND SCHUSTER, INC.

ROCKEFELLER CENTER, 630 FIFTH AVENUE

NEW YORK 20, N. Y.

FIRST PRINTING

LIBRARY OF CONGRESS CATALOG CARD NUMBER: 57-12407

MANUFACTURED IN THE UNITED STATES OF AMERICA

ACKNOWLEDGMENTS

THE MORAL ADEQUACY OF NATURALISM. From *The Genteel Tradition at Bay,* by George Santayana. By permission of Charles Scribner's Sons.

FOUR CARTOONS. All rights reserved to the artist, James Thurber.

PLAYS AND LANDSCAPES. By permission of Carl Van Vechten, Literary Executor of the Estate of Gertrude Stein, and by permission of Simon and Schuster, Inc.

TENDENCIES IN MODERN FICTION. By permission of A. Watkins, Inc., agents for the Estate of Edith Wharton.

ONE WAY TO WRITE NOVELS. By permission of Harcourt, Brace and Company, Inc.

THE STORY OF A NOVEL. By permission of Charles Scribner's Sons.

HOW I WRITE SHORT STORIES. By permission of the author.

THE SOURCES OF *ANTHONY ADVERSE.* Copyright, 1934, by Hervey Allen. By permission of Rinehart & Company, Inc.

FREUD AND THE FUTURE. From *Essays of Three Decades,* by Thomas Mann; translated by H. T. Lowe-Porter. Copyright, 1937, 1947, by Alfred A. Knopf, Inc. By permission of the publisher.

FASHIONS IN IDEAS. From *Philosopher's Holiday.* Copyright, 1938, by Irwin Edman. By permission of The Viking Press, Inc.

PLAY IN POETRY. From *Play in Poetry,* by Louis Untermeyer. Copyright, 1938, by Harcourt, Brace and Company, Inc.

THE FLOWER-FED BUFFALOES. From *Selected Poems,* by Vachel Lindsay. By permission of The Macmillan Company.

THE PIONEER. From *The Buck in the Snow & Other Poems,* published by Harper & Brothers. Copyright, 1925, by Edna St. Vincent Millay. Copyright renewed, 1953, by Norma Millay Ellis.

INVOCATION. From *Selected Works of Stephen Vincent Benét,* published by Rinehart & Company, Inc. Copyright, 1927, 1928, by Stephen Vincent Benét. Copyright renewed, 1955, 1956, by Rosemary Carr Benét.

SALUTATION. From "Ash Wednesday" in *Collected Poems 1909-1935,* by T. S. Eliot. Copyright, 1936, by Harcourt, Brace and Company, Inc. By permission of the publishers and of Faber and Faber, Ltd.

TRY TROPIC FOR YOUR BALM. From *Not Mine to Finish,* by Genevieve Taggard. Copyright, 1934, by Harper & Brothers.

CAPE HATTERAS. From *The Collected Poems of Hart Crane.* Copyright, 1933, by Liveright, Inc. By permission of Liveright Publishers.

FEAR. From *The Captive Shrew,* by Julian Huxley. By permission of Basil Blackwell & Mott, Ltd.

PRELUDE. Copyright, 1931, by Conrad Aiken.

HER POSTURE. From *Poems 1922-1947*, under the title "Inside and Out," by Allen Tate. By permission of Charles Scribner's Sons.

BAVARIAN GENTIANS. From *Last Poems*, by D. H. Lawrence. Copyright, 1933, by Frieda Lawrence. By permission of The Viking Press, Inc. and the Executors of the Estate of Frieda Lawrence.

TWO TRAMPS IN MUD-TIME. From *Complete Poems of Robert Frost*. Copyright, 1930, 1949, by Henry Holt and Company, Inc. By permission of the publishers.

SPAIN 1937. From *Another Time*. Copyright, 1940, by W. H. Auden. By permission of Random House, Inc. and of Faber and Faber, Ltd.

TO A YOUNG WRETCH. From *Complete Poems of Robert Frost*. Copyright, 1930, 1949, by Henry Holt and Company, Inc. By permission of the publishers.

THE MASK. From *Ruins and Visions*. Copyright, 1939, by Stephen Spender. By permission of Random House, Inc. and of Faber and Faber, Ltd.

READING TIME: 1 MINUTE 26 SECONDS. Copyright, 1939, by Muriel Rukeyser.

I HAVE SEEN THE MOUNTAINS. From *Poems 1930-1940*. Copyright, 1941, by Horace Gregory.

THE BOYHOOD OF THE WRIGHT BROTHERS. From *The Airmen*, published by Random House, Inc. Copyright, 1941, by Selden Rodman.

THE ORCHARD. Copyright, 1944, by Conrad Aiken.

SO YOU WANT TO BE A WRITER? By permission of Harold Ober Associates, Inc., Agents for the Estate of Sherwood Anderson.

HOW TO MARK A BOOK. All rights reserved to the author.

SOME POSTSCRIPTS TO OSCAR WILDE. All rights reserved to the author.

THE ARTIST AND HIS TIMES. From *The Yogi and the Commissar*, published by The Macmillan Company. Copyright, 1945, by Arthur Koestler.

THE IDEA OF HAPPINESS. From *The Making of Tomorrow*. Copyright, 1942, by Raoul de Roussy de Sales. By permission of Harcourt, Brace and Company, Inc.

UNLOCKING THE DOOR TO JOYCE. From *A Skeleton Key to "Finnegans Wake."* Copyright, 1944, by Joseph Campbell and Henry Morton Robinson. By permission of Harcourt, Brace and Company, Inc.

IN MEMORY OF GEORGE GERSHWIN. Copyright, 1944, by Bennett Cerf.

SHALL WE HAVE A WORLD LANGUAGE? By permission of the Estate of H. G. Wells.

MY STUDENT DAYS IN GERMANY. By permission of Katharine Newlin Burt.

THE GREAT FEUD. Mr. DeVoto's Charge: From *The Literary Fallacy*, published by Little, Brown and Company. Copyright, 1944, by The Trustees of Indiana University. Mr. Lewis' Reply: First published under the title of "Fools, Liars, and Mr. DeVoto." Copyright, 1953, by the Estate of Sinclair Lewis; Melville H. Cane and Pincus Berner, Executors.

WHY I REMAIN A NEGRO. From *A Man Called White*. Copyright, 1948, by Walter White. By permission of The Viking Press, Inc.

THE COMICS . . . VERY FUNNY! Copyright, 1948, by Fredric Wertham. By permission of James Brown Associates.

THE LIFE OF THE PARTY. From *The Vital Center*. Copyright, 1949, by Arthur M. Schlesinger, Jr. By permission of Houghton Mifflin Company.

AMERICAN TRAGEDY. From *Still Seeing Things*, published by McgrawHill Book Company, Inc. Copyright, 1950, by John Mason Brown.

WHERE THE SONG BEGINS. From *Lyrics*. Copyright, 1949, by Oscar Hammerstein II. By permission of Simon and Schuster, Inc.

WHAT DOES IT TAKE TO ENJOY A POEM? From *Mid-Century American Poets*, published by Twayne Publishers, Inc. Copyright, 1950, by John Ciardi.

BULWARKED AGAINST FATE. From *Like a Bulwark*. Copyright, 1949, 1956, by Marianne Moore. By permission of The Viking Press, Inc.

FOR AN ASSYRIAN FRIEZE. From *Terror and Decorum*. Copyright, 1948, by Peter Viereck. By permission of Charles Scribner's Sons.

THE LOVERS. Copyright, 1949, by Conrad Aiken.

THE TOWER. By permission of the Society of Authors as literary representative of the Estate of Walter de la Mare.

J.B.—THE PROLOGUE TO THE PLAY. Copyright, 1956, by Archibald MacLeish. By permission of the author and of Houghton Mifflin Company.

CATCH WHAT YOU CAN. Copyright, 1956, by Jean Garrigue.

NOTES FOR AN AUTOBIOGRAPHY. From *Albert Einstein: Philosopher-Scientist.* Copyright, 1949 and 1951, by The Library of Living Philosophers, Inc., Evanston, Illinois. By permission of the publishers and of the editor, Paul Arthur Schilpp. The excerpts here reprinted constitute less than half of the "Autobiographical Notes" appearing in the original volume. Translated from the original German by Dr. Schilpp.

THE PHILOSOPHER-IN-THE-MAKING. From *Contemporary American Philosophy,* by William P. Montague and George P. Adams. By permission of George Allen & Unwin, Ltd.

HOW MUSIC HAPPENS. From *A Composer's World: Horizons and Limitations,* by Paul Hindemith. Copyright, 1952, by The President and Fellows of Harvard College. By permission of the Harvard University Press.

THE NATURAL SUPERIORITY OF WOMEN. From *The Natural Superiority of Women,* published by The Macmillan Company. By permission of the author and the publisher.

IS OUR COMMON MAN TOO COMMON? From *Is the Common Man Too Common?* by Joseph Wood Krutch. Copyright, 1954, by the University of Oklahoma Press.

THROUGH HISTORY WITH J. WESLEY SMITH. Cartoon entitled "Don't take chances—call the humane society people" reproduced from *Through History with J. Wesley Smith,* by Burr Shafer. Copyright, 1950, by The Vanguard Press, Inc.

WASHINGTON, A.C.-D.C. From *The Book of Little Knowledge,* published by Simon and Schuster, Inc. Copyright, 1955, by Goodman Ace.

THE DAY AFTER WE LAND ON MARS. By permission of the author and the author's agents, Scott Meredith Literary Agency, Inc.

RANDOM THOUGHTS ON RANDOM DOGS. Copyright, 1955, by John Steinbeck.

WHAT MAKES A GENIUS? By permission of Mrs. Delbert Clark.

MOZART IN *THE MAGIC FLUTE.* All rights reserved to the author.

This book is dedicated to
AMY LOVEMAN
who gave so much of herself
to *The Saturday Review.*

CONTENTS

INTRODUCTION

Few written words justify the poet's boast and outlast "eternal bronze." As every journalist knows, all but an infinitesimal minority are writ in water instead.

Most of the time the journalist accepts this sad fact with a shrug. He would hardly be willing to adopt journalism at all if he didn't. Day by day he does his stint, fills his assigned space, and hopes for little more than that what he has written will hold the attention of the reader to the end. Tomorrow, next week, or next month there will be another issue. After all the very word "journalism" means "something written for the day."

Yet most journalists—or at least all who are any good—are pursued by a faint hope. Unlike the poet, they do not dream that every line is immortal. But they do hope, almost pathetically, that some few paragraphs, some sentence, some phrase even, will happen to have been somehow so right that it will be remembered for a year, a generation, or even a century; and that they, too, reading it again years later, will be able to say, "What a genius I had when I wrote that."

Here, then, in this substantial volume, is a selection of pieces published in The Saturday Review *which the editors believe to be for one reason or another—for subject matter, felicity of expression, or both—worth preserving for those who may remember them and for those who will be glad to make their acquaintance. Some of the pieces were published as much as a quarter of a century ago. Many are also reminders of time past, bringing back to life moods, situations, and issues which were in the foreground of thoughtful people's consciousness at one moment or another and which influenced the present even though they have now been half forgotten. The decisive criterion of selection has been interest and readability as of today.*

Before sampling the selection the prospective reader will perhaps be glad to be told something of the history, the aim, and the personality of the magazine in which these writings originally appeared and whose character they illustrate.

It all began when, in 1920, Henry Seidel Canby, then a professor at Yale, was invited by the New York Evening Post *to establish a literary supplement. The* Post *was one of the oldest and most respected—but decidedly not the most prosperous or most read—of the New York dailies. Dr. Canby assembled a most promising staff consisting of Amy Loveman and William Rose Benét as associate editors and, soon thereafter, the* Post's *own Christopher Morley as columnist. Though the literary supplement made a modest profit, someone had so successfully whittled away the* Post's *general circulation that in desperation the paper was sold to the Curtis Publishing Company of Philadelphia and the new operators decided to dispense with the supplement—partly, so the legend said, because one of them had watched Wall Street brokers automatically discard the supplement before opening the papers they took from the newsstands. Changing its name to* The Saturday Review of Literature, *the magazine moved into new quarters with support from Thomas W. Lamont and the promotors of another new magazine,* Time. *The first issue appeared on August 2, 1924, and though* Time *soon withdrew its support (and Mr. Lamont's tapered off),* The Saturday Review of Literature *had the solid support of an increasing circulation.*

For the founding of a new literary magazine the twenties offered an exceptionally favorable moment. We were just entering upon one of those phases during which literature gets an increasing amount of self-conscious public attention. Even among intellectuals the extent to which it does so varies greatly from time to time. Sometimes literature, consciously thought of as such, seems the most significant expression of the spirit of the age. Its condition, its problems, and its achievements are at the very center of the whole complex of thoughts, feelings, and ambitions of the era. At other times (as at the present moment) it is pushed from the center out to the periphery. That does not necessarily mean that fewer books are read or even that fiction or poetry or drama get less attention. But books are read less because one thinks of them as literature than for the sake of their immediate relevance to the social or political or moral attitudes which have come to occupy the central position in the consciousness of the majority of responsible people. Most of such people no longer think of a vital, original, or flourishing litera-ture as perhaps the most significant evidence of the status of a civilization.

You may, of course, call attention to the same situation by saying that 1920 was near the beginning of a publicly recognized literary renaissance in America when new and unfamiliar sorts of writing were appearing with unaccustomed frequency and were being promptly hailed with unaccustomed, sometimes uncritical, enthusi-asm. It was a moment when we had leisure for such a renaissance because the ghost of World War I seemed permanently laid and the Great Depression was undreamed of. But the other way of putting it seems to me even more illuminating in connection with the success of The Saturday Review of Literature *in its first avatar. Except for* The New York Times Book Review—*which explicitly defined itself as devoted to "news about books" rather than to criticism—there had been no major publication devoted exclusively to books considered as literature. There had, indeed, been no place for one. Now there was.*

Precisely what line should such a publication take? What function, other than that of giving news about books, was there for it to perform?

Twenty-five years later Dr. Canby was to state in SRL what his aims were and what, for the present-day (and shorter-named) The Saturday Review they have remained. Wrote Dr. Canby: "My own idea . . . was only the Jeffersonian belief in the necessity of education for a successful democracy. I wanted to go in for adult education in the value of books, foreign as well as native, but particularly the current books of our country. I wanted criticism to be first of all a teaching job." That Dr. Canby, in thinking of education for a democracy, should have thought first of "education in the values of books" and that he should have thought of belles lettres as a very important class of books, is itself an illustration of the tendency for the people of those times to think of literature as occupying a central rather than a peripheral position in a civilization.

Throughout its changing life—and that means not only changes in ownership and management but also certain changes of policy to meet a changed intellectual atmosphere—The Saturday Review has remained very strikingly itself and Dr. Canby's remark throws a good deal of light on what that self is. He thought of criticism as essentially educative in intention. This means, of course, not merely news about books. It means also a very broad conception of what criticism is, and that conception helps to explain why The Saturday Review has never been the organ of any of the various (and often dogmatic) "schools" of literary criticism. This, in turn, is why, after some thirty-three years, SR is still flourishing while half a dozen once-conspicuous "organs" of this or that group are gone and, for the most part, almost forgotten.

In the twenties the "new criticism" was Croceism as expounded by Professor Spingarn. The "new criticism" has, in the course of time, been successively various other things, though by now the phrase seems to be the permanent possession of a group no longer either very young or very new in its ideas. No group, I think, has ever been totally excluded from The Saturday Review's *pages. You can find in it Croceans, Agrarians, Pound-Eliot disciples, members of the history-of-ideas school, the "social significance" boys, and even, rarely, old-fashioned aesthetes. But its policy has always been education in the sense of a familiarity with the best that is being thought and said rather than in the sense of an indoctrination. Its editors have never assumed that they had got possession of the only road to truth about literary values or anything else. They did assume that their readers, like themselves, were pursuing an education—and that their subscribers were reading the magazine in the course of that pursuit rather than because it was an organ of some cult to which either editors or readers had given their allegiance.*

Such a policy runs certain risks. It may fall between the two stools of mass popularity and cult support. It will certainly be accused of obtuseness or worse by every cult. By the esoteric it will be called philistine, timid, and safe. And, of course, it will be labeled by the superior as middlebrow. What else can a journal devoted to criticism as education afford to be? After all only middlebrows are interested in education—except for others. Lowbrows don't want it and highbrows are certain they don't need it.

What, then, under such a conception as The Saturday Review *accepts, does constitute criticism? It is, I think, so many different things that it can only be described as including all relevant talk about books, whether that talk be historical, impressionistic, biographical, anecdotal, or talk concerned with the sort of rigid detailed analysis which now claims the only right to the label "serious criticism." It is any of the kinds of talk in which men with a deep interest in books and literature indulge. And every sort of such talk has in actual fact found its place in* The Saturday Review. *It has never been determined to be either conservative or avant garde —whatever that may mean—nor even determined nervously to be always right, and it has been willing instead to let the winds of doc-*

trine blow through. While it was still very young the woman editor of one of the best known of the more esoteric publications looked down her nose at me, a writer for SR, *and remarked that I, of course, was hampered by the fact that my audience was so miscellaneous. "We," she said, "have succeeded in whittling our circulation away until we reach only those who are seriously interested in aesthetics." A year later her magazine ceased publication entirely, and that, I suppose, she was prepared to regard as the ultimate success.*

The only major change in policy of the magazine occurred after 1939 when Norman Cousins became editor. A decade later the title of the magazine was shortened to The Saturday Review. *The change in title meant, first of all, simply a recognition of the fact that the field had already been broadened to take in arts other than literature —especially the theater, music, and broadcasting. But it meant something more. The Great Depression and the growing threat of World War II had intervened between 1939 and that earlier, perhaps happier, day when purely literary matters had been clearly at the center of the responsible citizen's concern with the state of his civilization.*

As time went on politics, economics, and foreign policy had demanded an increasing share of the citizen's attention. A different complex of attitudes and opinions and a different complex of subjects of dispute began to take precedence over purely literary matters, even in the minds of those who called themselves intellectuals. What ought we to do about the fact that we were now, fortunately or unfortunately, an indivisible part of a single human community? How should we use or not use the power which had made us the most powerful nation that had ever existed? What should we do about those inside and outside our own boundaries whom we could no longer call merely "the lesser breeds without the law"? To the editors of The Saturday Review *it seemed to have become impossible to separate the discussion of literature from the discussion of these other matters. And so* The Saturday Review of Literature *became*

The Saturday Review—*not only of literature but of all the things with which literature itself was now, willy-nilly, concerned.*

If there is one critical theory which the Review *was always inclined to reject out of hand it is that which maintains that literature, or at least literary excellence, has nothing to do with subject matter, moral attitude, reality, or even life itself. The nature of literature's relationship to all these things and the responsibility of literature toward man's various perplexities and problems will probably always be the subject of endless dispute. So, for that matter, will be the meaning of "reality" itself as well as the way in which literature can best deal with it. Symbolism, allegory, and metaphor; objectivity versus subjectivity; didacticism versus suggestion; external reality versus inner meaning—for all these methods a case can be made. So can it also for the individualist versus the social man and the public truth versus the private. But the fact that literature exists in the context of human life and of the universe in which that life is lived cannot be denied without rendering letters themselves irredeemably trivial.*

The selections which follow illustrate some of the most important areas of human concern with which the magazine has undertaken to deal. There is literary, theatrical, art, and music criticism in the narrowest sense of the term; there are reflective essays on literary and other topics; there are original poems by important poets, discussions of large political and social issues, also a sprinkling of the lighter treatment of all the topics more seriously discussed elsewhere. The constellation of novelists, critics, philosophers, essayists, and commentators on public affairs is impressive. Indeed, even such a necessarily incomplete selection as this reveals that an astonishing proportion of the most distinguished writers in every field have at one time or another contributed to The Saturday Review. *Here are, among the philosophers, George Santayana, Bertrand Russell, John Dewey, Albert Einstein, and Albert Schweitzer. Among the novelists: Edith Wharton, Ellen Glasgow, John Steinbeck, Thomas*

*Wolfe, W. Somerset Maugham, Thomas Mann, Sherwood Ander-
son, Arthur Koestler. Among the commentators: Elmer Davis,
Eleanor Roosevelt, Jacques Barzun, Arthur Schlesinger, Jr. Sui
generis: Gertrude Stein. And in addition, various members of the
past and present* Saturday Review *staff: Christopher Morley, Henry
Seidel Canby, Norman Cousins, Irving Kolodin, Bennett Cerf, and
others.*

*Nor is it only or even chiefly—as sometimes happens in anthologies
—merely a matter of names. In all these cases the important writer
is saying something which is important. H. G. Wells broaches one
of the largest of subjects, world unity. Thomas Mann traces the
relevance of Freud to his own fiction writing. Thomas Wolfe and
Somerset Maugham have interesting things to say about their own
creative processes. In one of the earliest of the pieces included
(1932) Elmer Davis analyzes the then new Red peril; in one of the
most recent (1956) Norman Cousins describes the greatest of
challenges to modern man. Bennett Cerf pays a tribute to his old
friend George Gershwin; Walter White tells why he chose to remain a Negro; Albert Einstein explains the origins of his theory
of relativity.*

*All these examples are chosen more or less at random. There
are many many more, though even an anthology of this size must
omit still other memorable pieces. A publication which from its
earliest days had a column signed with a pseudonym which stood
for the names of both Christopher Morley and William Rose Benét
was committed from the beginning to lighter comment also—to
pleasantries sometimes merely playful and sometimes carrying a
sting.*

Most of the original staff of the Post's *literary supplement continued to occupy positions on the magazine through the years and
the changes, until death claimed most of them one by one. No
doubt their loyalty has much to do with the fact that the publication they founded has, unlike so many long-lived publications,*

maintained down to the present its original personality. Apparently, and for the same reason, its old readers have tended to stay with it while new ones were recruited. Will the next quarter-century produce as much matter worth preserving for both old and new-found readers? We can only hope. Or perhaps not quite "only." A quarter of a century of performance gives grounds for somewhat more.

—JOSEPH WOOD KRUTCH

THE

Saturday Review

TREASURY

A NIGHT IN THE WHITE HOUSE

by Christopher Morley

In this intimate and nostalgic report that provides a backward glance at the literature and the politics of the twenties, a Saturday Review of Literature *writer who was also a famous novelist visits President and Mrs. Herbert Hoover, hears the President offer one small remedy for the Great Depression, and ends up playing medicine ball on the White House lawn.*

SEPTEMBER 24, 1932

"WHAT THIS COUNTRY needs is a great poem." This was Herbert Hoover speaking. *"John Brown's Body* was a step in the right direction. I've read it once, and I'm reading it again," the President continued. "But it's too long to do what I mean. You can't thrill people in three hundred pages. Three hundred words is about the limit. Kipling's 'Recessional' really did something to England when it was published. It helped them through a bad time. Let me know if you find any great poems lying around."

Perhaps because it was Leap Year, the goddess of Sudden Occasion had made me a bold suggestion. Might it be possible, she said, to print something about Herbert Hoover as the scholar, the man of culture, the lover of books? Here is a man who has given to his own university of Stanford one of the most unique collections in modern record, the Hoover War Library; who is possibly more widely interested in humane letters than any President we ever had. Why don't you write to your friend F. S., who is on the staff in Washington, and see if he won't send you a memorandum? I did so. And then one day, as I was innocently mulling over my desk, came the words of Gertrude, our delightful telephone operator, a little breathless. "The White House is calling you," she said, with a most delicate exclamation mark in her voice.

It was F. S. "The President likes your idea," he said. "I think perhaps something can be done."

"Fine," I said. "Will you send me a little story?"

"No," he said. "You and your wife had better come down and

I

spend the night at the White House. You can form your own opinions."

Often in fancy I had toyed with the notion of the Unknown Citizen and Mrs. Citizen visiting the White House to form their own impressions of the duty and dignity of government. But I always imagined it would be much more terrifying. A polite attendant met the travelers at the train gate in Washington. "Mr. Citizen?" he said, calling him by name. "From the White House," he stated, and led the way. The Redcap followed, greatly pleased. The shield of the United States was on the door of the waiting car, and the radiator cap had some sort of emblem of eagle's wings. The Citizen wanted to identify the make of car, but guests do not stare, and he was not smart enough. Mrs. Citizen was more acute in her own realm. "Sugar four cents a pound!" she exclaimed, seeing a Washington grocery sign. But they tried to sit steadfast and not peer about too much. A traffic policeman, recognizing the car, straightened up for a formal salute; then he saw it was not the President, and refrained.

"This is your Rose Bedroom," said the polite usher, "and there's an evening paper. Mrs. Hoover is engaged at the moment, but she will be expecting you for tea in about twenty minutes. If that clock is correct, as I presume it is, that will be at ten minutes to six. I will return for you at that time. The maid and the houseman will be here immediately."

Apparently the usher really believed that Citizen was going to sit down quietly and read the Washington *Evening Star*. I assure you he was much too excited to do that. There is no place in the world that an American citizen has a better right to be thrilled by than the White House. He wanted to see everything.

On the mantel was an ornate old marble clock, the one the usher correctly presumed correct, surmounted by a bronze Amazon drawing a bow, inscribed ANTIOPE. On the little table by the bed was a well-polished old bell-push, the three buttons of which were inscribed Maid, Buttons, Butler. On dressing table and center table were tall bunches of fresh flowers, roses and snapdragons. In the frames of the enormous windows were tucked little home-whittled wooden pegs, to prevent the sashes' rattling on stormy nights. There is nothing parvenu about the White House. It has much the righteous feeling of an ancient château which the Citizens once visited in France.

Mrs. Citizen, a person of better breeding, was a little shocked by her husband's inquisition into everything. He reported to her the titles of the books. On the center table were Lindbergh's *We;* Vandenberg's *The Trail of a Tradition* (which seemed to be a sort of biography of Alexander Hamilton); *The Miracle of Peille,* by J. L. Campbell; *The Changing Years,* by Norman Hapgood. In the smaller bedroom were one volume of a set called *The Library of Southern Literature* (with the President's own bookplate); Odum's *An American Epoch;* Glenway Wescott's *The Grandmothers;* Kathleen Norris' *Saturday's Child;* an odd volume of an old calfbound 16mo set of *Hudibras* (Edinburgh 1770, with the bookplate of David Steuart, Esq.) and *The Story of San Michele.*

The story is that the first night President Hoover spent in the White House not a readable book was to be found anywhere. Elderly accumulations of gifts had been transferred to the Library of Congress, and the new President had to send out and borrow a volume of history from the Secret Service to read himself to sleep. The White House having so much permanent character of its own it is surprising that it can also accommodate itself so flexibly to reflect the personality of its tenants. To those who like to analyze character by interests in literature it is at once evident that it is the dwelling of cultivated and scholarly curiosities. In one of the small drawing rooms there are solid elderly sets of Thackeray, Trollope, Dumas, the Waverley Novels, Hawthorne, Holmes, Stevenson, Richard Harding Davis, and the Historians' History of the World. In the colorful oval sitting room, where Mrs. Hoover served tea by an open fire (wearing her uniform as commander of Girl Scouts; she had just returned from one of their meetings) are two beautiful arched recesses of open shelves. These spaces had formerly been china cabinets for bric-a-brac, but Mrs. Hoover had them altered to house her own favorites in poetry and belles-lettres. The President's reticence in regard to his own private enthusiasms is well-known; unlike T. R., for instance, he does not tell the world when he discovers something that delights him. It would certainly startle him to have it suggested that there is a "story" in his interest in books: he takes books for granted as an essential part of life. Two years ago the American Booksellers' Association presented five hundred carefully chosen books to the White House library. The gift was a very welcome one, but as far as the President himself was concerned he had read most of those books long before.

The visitors were looking over these shelves, after tea, when a quiet step came down the corridor. It is well that White House boards have that tactful creak. "Here comes the President," whispered Mrs. Citizen, with just a pleasing touch of awe in her voice— very rare in wives. The Citizen turned from the shelf just in time. The President greets his guests very gently but he makes them feel instantly at ease. The Citizen was brought up among Philadelphia

Quakers, and there was something about the President's voice and intonation, a sense of power under shrewd control, that was memorably familiar. "Looking at the books?" he said. "If they sent those here to educate me, I'm afraid it was too late. I'd read 85 per cent of them before." There spoke the man of instinctive precision. Not "most of them" or "nearly all of them," but "85 per cent."

As the visitors returned to the Rose Bedroom to dress for dinner they could not help glancing through the open door of the President's study. Two large flags stood in the far corners, the Stars and Stripes and the dark blue Presidential flag. An easy chair of dark orange leather was drawn up near the desk, and beside it lay a newspaper tossed down after reading. A reading lamp shone brightly on the desk, on a large pen-stand ornamented with green elephants (a political symbol?) and a neat pile of small leather notebooks. A faint trail of cigar fragrance crossed the whiff of flowers in the corridor. It was just such a domestic interior as one might see in any wellordered home where the head of the house, returning from the office about six-thirty, sits down for a few moments in his favorite chair to look at the paper.

Here I have to encourage my friend Citizen to continue his observations. Is it too informal for him to say that nothing more endeared the President than the fact that his dress shirt, like yours and mine, tends to billow up under his chin? Or that, dining *en famille*, Mrs. Hoover calls him "Daddy"? It probably is. But even in that huge dining room of State, where over eighty can sit for an official function, one cannot be shy when one hears that oldest and kindest of names cross the table. The eye may be startled by an upward glimpse of the great silver chandelier overhead—as broad as the round table beneath it. The paneled walls, the blazing fire and a vaguely descried portrait above it, seem a long way off. But anything one might have been told about the severities of White House etiquette vanish under so cordial a spell. Even, for a fractional instant, the colored butler noiselessly appearing with a napkin-swathed bottle startled the renegade guest with a sudden secret amazement. It was only mineral water.

Dinner, served at eight o'clock, was satisfying and simple; there was something very American about it. A thick soup, fish, meat and vegetables, salad with cheese and crackers, a sweet, and fruit. Perhaps the most American feature was the promptness with which it was served. Somehow Citizen got the impression that the President has perhaps been put on a diet, and is glad to get past the temptations of the table as soon as possible, to escape to his study for coffee and cigars. He took no sweet, and Mrs. Citizen (who sat at his right) avers that he regarded hers with something of boyish wistfulness; exactly (she says) as U. C. himself does when he is hoping she won't finish something rather special but allow him to do so for her.

Perhaps there is a clue in this rapidity. The President is not much interested in food as a pastime, or in merely casual chat for the sake of casual chat. He is interested in Ideas. How well Mrs. Hoover understands this and plays team. At the table at first he said little, and Mrs. Hoover took the lead. But as soon as anything emerged that caught his imagination his chin came up from the bulge of his shirtfront, he caught Mrs. Hoover's eye and began to talk. His voice is low. One has to listen sharply. He talks with much humor, the humor of underemphasis which does not lend itself easily to quotation.

There were only three of us in the President's study after dinner. On the mantel a ship's clock from the former yacht *Mayflower* tingled nautical bells. The colored attendant lit the fire, and the President brightened it with great California pine cones. The inner walls are lined with glassed bookcases and rows of rather somber legal or official-looking volumes, including the writings of all the Presidents. On a low table was a large silver cigarette box engraved with facsimile autographs of the President's associates in the Commission for Relief in Belgium. Coffee was served.

By now the President's bookplate had been mentioned—a reproduction of a medieval mining print. He spoke with zest of the incunabula of science, and his collection of old mining treatises, and said that at the dawn of recorded history men had already discovered some of the technical processes still in use today. The Greek miners at Laurium, southeast of Athens, used the same means of separating silver from lead that the modern engineer does. "It would be interesting," he said, "to rewrite Greek history from the viewpoint of the engineer. It was the silver mines of Laurium that paid for the fleet with which Themistocles won the battle of Salamis—one of the great turning points of history. The first great orations of Demosthenes were arguments on cases of mining titles." He spoke of the expansion of the Roman Empire—mostly a search for sources of raw materials.

The second cigar was finished, the fire had burned low. The *Mayflower* clock chimed five bells—10:30. The President led the way to rejoin the ladies. And there, after a few minutes, "Well," he said, "there are some people in this house who have to get up early in the morning."

In bed the Unknown Citizen kept remembering what Mr. Hoover had said about the need of a poem. It would need courage to say in public anything so simply true. Among the shadowy walkers in that corridor was one tall homely wraith who would have understood the sooth of it; who in one prose poem of less than three hundred words said thoughts that have not perished from the earth.

The Unknown Citizen's final thought was a vote of confidence. The President is a good man, he said to himself. He pronounces *economics* correctly, with a long *e*. Beware of statesmen who call it *eck*onomics!

It is a rash impertinence to comment on any man's taste in reading, which is one of the few privacies left us; but the list the President's friend marked offers valuable comment on his character. He was not interested in wildcat mining, he does not care for wildcat literature. There is a strong sense of reality in his book choices. Hysterias and fantasticoes of postwar taste have mostly passed him by. His tastes in fiction were formed in the Golden Age of reading, the nineties. He sank his shafts deep into the solid ore of Balzac, Brontë, Cooper, Dickens, Dumas, George Eliot, Bret Harte, Hawthorne, Howells, Kipling, Meredith, Scott, Stevenson, Thackeray, Mark Twain. There is a word he is fond of which expresses his faculty: *empirical*. His intuitions are based on practical experiment. As a field geologist knows by the lay of the terrain what reefs are likely below, he knows what kind of book has precious metal for him. There is nothing austerely highbrow in his choice: he enjoyed the same thrillers and comedians that you and I were reared on a little later: Jules Verne, Conan Doyle, Rider Haggard, W. W. Jacobs, *Ruggles of Red Gap*. He seeks a good story, not whipped-cream fantasy or tinsel cynicism. When anyone remarks that he can find no leisure to read, consider this man of packed concerns who has found time for Arnold Bennett, Barrie, Donn Byrne, Conrad, Edna Ferber, Winston Churchill, Mrs. Deland, Jack London, Wells, Galsworthy, Frank Norris, O. Henry, Emerson Hough, Du Maurier, Weir Mitchell, W. H. Hudson. Though not a great zealot of the detective story he knows his Sherlock Holmes, Agatha Christie, Anna Katharine Green, Mary Roberts Rinehart, S. S. Van Dine. Among later American novelists his favorites seem to be Thomas Nelson Page, Tarkington, Edith Wharton, Stewart Edward White, Willa Cather, Harry Leon Wilson, Zane Grey. There can hardly ever have been a President who has read so much and said so little about it. His gusto is not narrow nor to be labeled in any conventional class. Among American novels he has enjoyed you will find such diverse titles as *The Honorable Peter Stirling, To Have and To Hold, A Certain Rich Man, Giants in the Earth, The Bridge of San*

Luis Rey, Vandemark's Folly, The Private Life of Helen of Troy. An intimate of his took the time to tick off for me on the American Booksellers' gift list those titles which Mr. Hoover had read in days when he had more leisure. In the section of Standard Fiction, for instance, out of fifty-six books he had read fifty. In the lists of Travel, History, Politics, and World Affairs, practically every title was marked. In books like Shakespeare, Dante, Tennyson, *Leaves of Grass,* Keyserling's *Travel Diary,* Wells's *Outline of History,* he had done as most of us have, "browsed."

The President was right: they *did* get up early. By seven o'clock he is ready, in leather jacket and old crumpled hat, for the morning game of medicine ball with a group of his official associates. It was a drizzling March morning, and the grass tennis court at the foot of the White House lawn showed broad slithers of mud in which a supreme court justice or a solicitor general can slide as impartially as an Unknown Citizen. The White House pets—a Norwegian elkhound and a big gray police dog—frolic on the outskirts of the play and follow the group back to an informal dining room in the basement where coffee and grapefruit are served. Weejee, the Norwegian elkhound, a lovable creature very like a husky, wears an ingenious leather moccasin on a crippled foot. He sat up in an empty chair next the President and shared his toast.

The medicine ball game is more exciting than the name sounds. It is played like deck tennis, with the massive leather sphere as missile and tennis scoring. Certain special rules have had to be made, the President remarked, on account of the unusual tallness of one of the frequent players, Dr. Ray Lyman Wilbur, Secretary of the Interior. The group have played this game every week-day morning for more than three years and are very adept; it involves a high competence of knack and strength and is fairly exhausting to the beginner. There is brisk masculine chaff among the others as they scramble to and fro (Mr. Justice Stone has a particularly deadly heave) but the President plays with more silent concentration. For the moment the game is the only thing in his mind. It is not just a game but also a means of keeping fit. Afterward he trots all the way back to the House, followed by the capering dogs. Passers-by outside the grounds perhaps only see in the distance a group of middle-aged men tossing a very heavy and muddy ball over a high net. Another might see in it a symbol of an even larger sphere which the courage and good will of men must keep in air. Occasionally it goes off the court and a point is lost. But they always bring it back.

There are fifteen minutes of coffee and talk round the basement

club table. The talk is casual and offhand, the coffee deliberated and
perfect. The regular breakfast is upstairs in a small cozy room with
a blazing fire. Grapefruit and hominy and bacon and eggs, and more
of that exquisite coffee. A curious hunk of brown woody substance
was put by the President's plate. Citizen thought it might be some
special tidbit for the dogs, who stay very close to the President's
chair. Mrs. Citizen imagined it some sort of gluten bread. It was a
burl (or knot) from a redwood tree; soaked in a bowl of water it
sends up delicate spires of baby redwood. This was for Mrs. Citizen
to take home to the children.

After breakfast the President walks across to his office, accompanied by Mrs. Hoover who always sees him cheerfully to his desk.
The President is always at work by eight-thirty.

THE MORAL ADEQUACY
OF NATURALISM

by George Santayana

The era's grand old man of philosophy, having settled down into retirement in Italy, sets forth a careful opinion concerning human behavior in an essay which smacks of The Saturday Review of Literature's *early days.*

JANUARY 17, 1931

SUPPOSE WE DISCOUNT as fabulous every projection of human morality into the supernatural: need we thereby relapse into moral anarchy? In one sense, and from the point of view of the absolute or monocular moralist, we must; because the whole moral sphere then relapses into the bosom of nature, and nature, though not anarchical, is not governed by morality. But for a philosopher with two eyes, the natural status of morality in the animal world does not exclude the greatest vigor in those moral judgments and moral passions which belong to his nature. On the contrary, I think that it is only when he can see the natural origin and limits of the moral sphere that a moralist can be morally sane and just. Blindness to the biological truth about morality is not favorable to purity of moral feeling: it removes all sense of proportion and relativity; it kills charity, humility, and humor; and it shuts the door against that ultimate light which comes to the spirit from the spheres above morality.

The early Greeks, who as yet had little experience of philosophers, sometimes invited their philosophers to legislate for them. Their problem was not so unlike that which confronts us today: in the midst of increasing bustle and numbers, the preponderance of towns, the conflict of classes, close and dangerous foreign relations, freer manners, new ideas in science and art. How did those early sages set to work? In one way, they didn't mince matters: the rule of life which each of them proposed for his city covered the whole life of the citizen, military, political, intellectual, ceremonial, and athletic: but on the other hand, for each city the rule proposed was different: severe and unchangeable at Sparta, liberal and variable at Athens; while the idealistic brotherhood of the Pythagoreans prescribed astronomy and sweet numbers for Magna Græcia. It was in quite other circumstances that Socrates and Plato, Moses and President Wilson came forward to legislate unasked, and for the universe.

I am afraid that even some of those earlier sages were not perfect naturalists. They did not merely consider the extant organism for which they were asked to prescribe, or endeavor to disentangle, in its own interests, the diseases or dangers which might beset it. A legislating naturalist would be like a physician or horticulturalist or breeder of animals: he would remove obstructions and cut out barren deformities; he would have a keen eye for those variations which are spontaneous and fertile, gladly giving them free play; and he would know by experience those other variations into which nature may be coaxed by grafting and watering. In all his measures he would be guided by the avowed needs and budding potentialities of his client. Perhaps some of those Greek lawgivers, the Pythagoreans, for instance, had something of the missionary about them, and while full of adoration for the harmonies of nature as they conceived them, conceived these harmonies idealistically, and felt called upon to correct nature by the authority of a private oracle. In this their philosophy, apart from some cosmological errors, may have proved its depths, and may have been prophetic of the revolution that was destined to undermine ancient society.

The only natural unit in morals is the individual man, because no other natural unit is synthesized by nature herself into a living spirit. The state is only a necessary cradle for the body of the individual, and nursery for his mind; and he can never really renounce his prescriptive right to shatter the state or to reform it, according to his physical and spiritual necessities. Even when his spontaneous fidelity causes him to forget or to deny this right, the force of fidelity is at that very moment exercising that right within him. Yet it was an intermediate and somewhat artificial unit, the ancient city, that was asking those early philosophers for counsel; and that counsel could not be good, or honestly given, unless it considered the life of the individual within the walls, and the life of the world outside, only as they might contribute to the perfection of the city.

Morality—by which I mean the principle of all choices in taste, faith, and allegiance—has a simple natural ground. The living organism is not infinitely elastic; if you stretch it too much, it will snap; and it justifiably cries out against you somewhat before the limit is reached. This animal obstinacy is the backbone of all virtue, though intelligence, convention, and sympathy may very much extend and soften its expression. As the brute unconditionally wills to live, so the man, especially the strong masterful man, unconditionally wills to live after a certain fashion. To be pliant, to be indefinite, seems to him ignominious.

Very likely, in his horror of dissipating his strength or deviating from his purpose, he will give opprobrious names to every opposite quality. His hot mind may not be able to conceive as virtues in others any traits which would not be virtues in himself. Yet this moral egotism, though common or even usual, is not universal in virtuous people. On the contrary, precisely those who are most perfect escape it: they do not need the support of the majority, or of the universal voice, in order to fortify them in some shaky allegiance. They know what they want and what they love: the evident beauty of the beautiful is not enhanced or removed by agreement. In its victorious actuality a man's work must be local and temporary; it satisfies his impulse in his day, and he is not forbidden to feel that in some secret sense the glory of it is eternal.

In this way aristocratic people, who are sure of their own taste and manners, are indifferent, except for a general curiosity, to the disputes of critics and pedants, and perhaps to the maxims of preachers; such things are imposing only to those who are inwardly wondering what they ought to do, and how they ought to feel. A truly enlightened mind is all the simpler for being enlightened and thinks, not without a modest sort of irony, that art and life exist to be enjoyed and not to be estimated. Why should different estimations annoy anyone who is not a snob, when, if they are sincere, they express different enjoyments?

Accordingly, a reasonable physician of the soul would leave his patients to prescribe for themselves, though not before subjecting them to a Socratic or even Freudian inquisition, or searching of heart, in order to awaken in them a radical self-knowledge, such as amid conventions and verbal illusions they probably do not possess. Evidently a regimen determined in this way has no validity for any other being, save in the measure in which, as a matter of fact, that other being partakes in the same nature and would find his sincere happiness in the same things. This is seldom or never exactly the case. Nothing is more multiform than perfection. No interest, no harmony, shuts out the legitimacy or the beauty of any other. It only shuts out from itself those qualities which are incompatible with perfection of that kind, there: as the perfect diamond shuts out the ruby, and the perfect ruby rejects the lovely color of the emerald. But from nature, in her indefinite plasticity, nothing is shut out *a priori;* and no sort of virtue need be excluded by a rational moralist from the place where that virtue is native, and may be perfect.

Perfection is the most natural form of existence, simply carrying out the organic impulse by which any living creature arises at all; nor can that impulse ever find its quietus and satisfaction short of perfection; and nevertheless perfection is rare and seems wonderful, because division or weakness within the organism, or contrariety without, usually nips perfection in the bud. These biological troubles have their echo in the conscience. The alternation between pride and cowardice, between lust and shame, becomes a horrible torment to the spirit; and the issue in any case is unhappy, because a divided soul cannot be perfected. This distress, grown permanent, probably infects the imagination. Mysterious half-external forces— demons and duties—are seen looming behind these contrary natural promptings; and fantastic sanctions, heaven and hell, are invented for the future, enormously exaggerating the terrors of the choice. Thus while on the whole the morality which men impose on themselves is rational, the reasons which they give for it are apt to be insane.

What is reason? There is a certain plasticity in some organisms which enables them to profit by experience. Instead of pushing forever against a stone wall, they learn to go round it or over it. This plasticity, even when not under pressure, may take to play and experiment; toys are made which may become instruments; and the use of sounds as signals may enable the talking animal to recall absent things and to anticipate the future. Moreover, many animals mimic what they see; they transpose themselves dramatically into the objects surrounding them, especially into other animals of the same species. This transposition gives a moral reality, in their own spirit, to all their instinctive coaxing, deceiving, or threatening of one another. Their mind begins to conceive and to compare mere possibilities; it turns to story-telling and games; life becomes a tangle of eager plans and ambitions; and in quiet moments the order of merely imaginary things grows interesting for its own sake. There is a pleasure in embracing several ideas in a single act of intuition so as to see how far they are identical or akin or irrelevant.

Such a power of intellectual synthesis is evidently the mental counterpart of the power of acting with reference to changing or eventual circumstances: whether in practice or in speculation, it is the faculty of putting two and two together, and this faculty is what we call reason. It is what the idiot lacks, the fool neglects, and the madman contradicts. But in no case is reason a code, an oracle, or an external censor condemning the perceptions of sense or suppressing animal impulses. On the contrary, in the moral life, reason is a harmony of the passions, a harmony which perceptions and impulses may compose in so far as they grow sensitive to one another, and begin to move with mutual deference and a total grace.

Such at least was the life of reason which the humanists of the Renaissance thought they discovered, as it were embalmed, in Greek philosophy, poetry, and sculpture. Socrates had expressed this principle paradoxically when he taught that virtue is knowledge—self-knowledge taken to heart and applied prudently in action. Not that spontaneous preferences, character, and will could be dispensed with: these were presupposed; but it was reason that alone could mold those animal components of human nature into a noble and modest happiness.

But is there anything compulsory in reason? Is there not still liberty for fools? Can reason reasonably forbid them to exist? Certainly not, if they like to be fools: I should be sorry to see reason so uselessly kicking against the pricks. But a naturally synthetic mind (and all mind is naturally synthetic) hates waste and confusion; it hates action and speech at cross purposes; and these instinctive aversions implicitly pledge all mind to the ideal of a perfect rationality. Nobody is forbidden to be mindless; but in the mindful person the passions have spontaneously acquired a sense of responsibility to one another; or if they still allow themselves to make merry separately—because liveliness in the parts is a good without which the whole would be lifeless—yet the whole possesses, or aspires to possess, a unity of direction, in which all the parts may conspire, even if unwittingly.

So far reason might be said to be prescriptive, and to impose a method on all moral life. Yet even where this method is exemplified in action, and life has become to that extent rational, nothing is prescribed concerning the elements which shall enter into that harmony. The materials for the synthesis are such at each point as nature and accident have made them; even in the same man or in the same nation they will be shifting perpetually, so that equally rational beings may have utterly disconnected interests, or interests hopelessly opposed. This diversity will be acceptable, so long as the parties are isolated, like China before the age of discoverers and missionaries; but where there is physical contact and contagion, the appeal must be to war, or to some other form of continued material pressure, such as industrial development or compulsory education: and in such a conflict both sides are apt to lose their original virtues, while the unthought-of virtues of the compound arise in their place.

In another direction the criterion of reason leaves the texture of life undetermined: the degree of unison requisite for harmony may differ in different rational systems. It is perhaps a classical prejudice that all happiness should be architectural. It might be simple and, like disillusioned Christian charity, alms for the moment. The finality of the incidental is more certain, and may be no less perfect, than the finality of great totals, like a life or a civilization. A good verse is much more unmistakably good than a good epic. Organization is everywhere presupposed, otherwise there could be no bodily life and no moral intuition: but where the level of intuition is reached, which is the supreme or spiritual level, the dead mass of the pyramid beneath that apex becomes indifferent. Reason cannot prescribe the girth of a man, or his stature; it can only reveal to his imperfect self his possible perfection. On this account I am not sure that the romantic temperament or art can be condemned offhand for not being organic enough. Why be so pervasively organic? A flood of details and an alteration of humors may possibly bring the human heart as near as it can come to the heart of things, which I suspect is very fluid; and perhaps the human spirit is not at its best in the spiderlike task of construction. Contemplation is freer and may be contemplation of anything.

Why is naturalism supposed to be favorable to the lower sides of human nature? Are not the higher sides just as natural? If anything, the naturalist, being a philosopher, might be expected to move most congenially and habitually on the higher levels. Perhaps the prejudice comes from the accident that when one element of human nature is reinforced by a supernatural sanction, and falsely assigned to a specially divine influence, the unsanctioned remainder alone retains the name of the natural. So Zola can come to be regarded as more naturalistic than Shakespeare, because more sordid in his naturalism, and less adequate; and Shakespeare can be regarded as more naturalistic than Virgil, although Virgil's feeling for things rural as well as for the cosmos at large was more naturalistic than Shakespeare's. Virgil is less romantic, playful, and vague: for the ancients poetized the actual surroundings and destiny of man, rather than the travesty of these facts in human fancy, and the consequent dramas within the spirit.

I think that pure reason in the naturalist may attain, without subterfuge, all the spiritual insights which supernaturalism goes so far out of the way to inspire. Spirituality is only a sort of return to innocence, birdlike and childlike. Experience of the world may have complicated the picture without clouding the vision. In looking before and after, and learning to take another man's point of view, ordinary intelligence has already transcended a brutal animality; it has learned to conceive things as they are, disinterestedly, contemplatively. Although intellect arises quite naturally, in the animal act of dominating events in the interests of survival, yet essentially intellect disengages itself from that servile office (which is that of its organ only) and from the beginning is speculative and impartial in its own outlook, and thinks it not robbery to take the point of view of God, of the truth, and of eternity.

In this congenital spiritual life of his, man regards himself as one creature among a thousand others deserving to be subordinated and kept in its place in his own estimation: a spiritual life not at all at war with animal interests, which it presupposes, but detached from them in allegiance, withdrawn into the absolute, and reverting to them only with a charitable and qualified sympathy, such as the sane man can have for the madman, or the soul in general for inanimate things: and of course, it is not only others that the spiritual man regards in this way, but primarily himself. Yet this gift of transcending humanity in sympathy with the truth is a part, and the most distinctive part, of human nature. Reason vindicates insights and judgments which, though overruling those of the world, overrule them within the human heart, with its full consent and to its profound peace and satisfaction. The disillusioned philosopher is (at least in his own opinion) happier than the fool: the saint is at least as human as the man in the street, and far more steadfast and unrepining in his type of humanity.

That the fruition of happiness is intellectual (or as perhaps we should now call it, esthetic) follows from the comprehensive scope of that intuition in which happiness is realized, a scope which distinguishes happiness from carnal pleasures; for although happiness, like everything else, can be experienced only in particular moments, it is found in conceiving the total issue and ultimate fruits of life; and no passing sensation or emotion could be enjoyed with a free mind, unless the blessing of reason and of a sustained happiness were felt to hang over it. All experience can of course never be synthesized in act, because life is a passage and has many centers; yet such a synthesis is adumbrated everywhere; and when it is partially attained, in some reflective or far-seeing moment, it raises the mind to a contemplation which is very far from cold, being in fact ecstatic; yet this ecstasy remains intellectual in that it holds together the burden of many successive and disparate things, which in blind experience would exclude one another: somewhat as a retentive ear, in a silence following upon music, may gather up the mounting strains of it in a quiet rapture. In raising truth to intuition of truth, in surveying the forms and places of many things at once and conceiving their movement, the intellect performs the most vital of possible acts, locks flying existence, as it were, in its arms, and stands, all eyes and breathless, at the top of life.

Reason may thus lend itself to sublimation into a sort of virtual omniscience or divine ecstasy: yet even then reason remains a harmony of material functions spiritually realized, as in Aristotle the life of God realizes spiritually the harmonious revolutions of the heavens. So it is with reason in morals. It is essential to the validity of a moral maxim that it should be framed in the interest of natural impulses: otherwise that maxim would be a whim or an impertinence. The human impulses to be harmonized should not be without a certain persistence and strength; they should be honest, self-renewing, and self-rewarding, so as not to prove treacherous factors in the method of life to be adopted; and this method in its turn, becoming a custom and an institution, should be a gracious thing, beautiful and naturally glorious, as are love, patriotism, and religion; else the passion for living in political and religious union, beyond the limits of utility, would be sheer folly. But there are fusions, transmutations, and self-surrenders in which a naturally social animal finds an ultimate joy. True reason restrains only to liberate; it checks only in order that all currents, mingling in that moment's pause, may take a united course.

As to conscience and the sense of imposed duty, we may suppose them to be the voice of reason conveyed by tradition, in words that have grown mysterious and archaic, and at the same time solemn and loud. In so far as conscience is not this, but really a personal and groundless sentiment, it may be left to cancel its own oracles. Those who have lived in Boston—and who else should know?—are aware how earnestly the reformed New England conscience now disapproves of its disapprovals. Positive blushes and an awkward silence fall on a worthy family of my acquaintance at the least mention of one of their ancestors, who once wrote a terrifying poem about the Day of Doom. Conscience is an index to integrity of character, and under varying circumstances may retain an iron rigidity, like the staff and arrow of a weather vane; but if directed by sentiment only, and not by a solid science of human nature, conscience will always be pointing in a different direction.

And in what direction exactly, we may ask, does conscience point so impressively in the American humanists, that they feel constrained to invoke a supernatural sanction for their maxims and to go forth and preach them to the whole world? I am at a loss to reply; because I can find little in their recommendations except a cautious allegiance to the genteel tradition. But can the way of Matthew Arnold and of Professor Norton be the way of life for all men forever? If there be really a single supernatural vocation latent in all souls, I can imagine it revealed to some supreme sage in a tremendous vision, like that which came to Buddha under the Bo-Tree, or to Socrates when he heard, or dreamt that he heard, the Sibyl of Mantinæa discoursing on mortal and immortal love. There is much in any man's experience, if he reflects, to persuade him that the circumstances of this life are a strange accident to him, and that he belongs by nature to a different world. If all the American humanists had become Catholics like Newman, or even like Mr. T. S. Eliot, I should understand the reason.

But can it be that all Latins and Slavs, all Arabs, Chinamen, and Indians, if they were not benighted in mind and degenerate in body, would be model Anglo-Americans? That is what British and American politicians and missionaries seem to believe: all nations are expected gladly to exchange their religion and their customs for the Protestant genteel tradition. I am myself an ardent admirer of the Anglo-American character. I almost share that "extraordinary faith in the moral efficacy of cold baths and dumbbells" which Mr. Bertrand Russell attributes to the YMCA. Sport, companionship, reading rooms, with an occasional whiff of religious sentiment to stop foul mouths and turn aside hard questions—all this composes a saving tonic for the simple masculine soul habitually in the service of Big Business; while for the more fastidious, or the more fashionable, I can see the value of the English public school and the Anglican Church, which Mr. Russell thinks mere instruments of oppression. To me—seeing them, I confess, at a more romantic distance—they seem instruments rather of a beautiful integration: none of those fierce darts of intellectual sincerity which Mr. Russell would like, but something voluminous, comfortable, and sane, on a political, conventional, and sporting level.

The senses, which we use successfully in action, distort the objects on which we act, yet do so harmlessly and poetically, because our bodies are quick to understand those perceptions before our minds have had time to consider them narrowly. In the same way understanding relieves a truly intelligent man from fussiness about social institutions and conventions: they are absurd, yet absurdity is not incompatible with their natural function, which may be indispensable. But in philosophy, when ultimately the spirit comes face to face with the truth, convention and absurdity are out of place; so is humanism and so is the genteel tradition; so is morality itself.

The commandment *Thou shalt not kill,* for instance, is given out on divine authority, and infinite sanctions are supposed to confirm it in the other world. Yet the basis of this commandment is not cosmic or supernatural, but narrowly human. It expresses the natural affection of kindred for one another, an affection surviving and woefully rebuking any rash murder; and it expresses also the social and political need of living, within a certain territory, in safety and mutual trust. In its human atmosphere, the thunder of that percept is therefore not hollow; the sharp bolts of remorse and ruin follow closely upon it. But in the cosmos at large, is killing forbidden? If so, the fabric of creation must be monstrous and sinful indeed. The moving equilibrium of things, so blind and inexorable, yet often so magnificent, becomes a riddle to be deciphered, a labyrinth of punishments and favors, the work of some devil, or at least a work of God so contaminated with evil as to be a caricature of the divine intentions. And not in human life only: the ferocity and agony of the jungle and the strange gropings of life in the depths of the sea, become perverse and scandalous; existence seems a disease, and the world a garden of poisons, through which a man must pick his way with fear and trembling, girded high, and dreading to touch the earth with his bare foot, or a fellow-creature with his hand. Had it been the Creator who said *Thou shalt not kill,* and said it to the universe, existence would have been arrested.

When therefore a tender conscience extends its maxims beyond their natural basis, it not only ceases to be rational in its deliverances, and becomes fanatical, but it casts the livid colors of its own insanity upon nature at large. A strained holiness, never without its seamy side, ousts honorable virtue, and the fear of so many enemies becomes the greatest enemy of the soul. No true appreciation of anything is possible without a sense of its *naturalness,* of the innocent necessity by which it has assumed its special and perhaps extraordinary form. In a word, the principle of morality is naturalistic. Call it humanism or not, only a morality frankly relative to man's nature is worthy of man, being at once vital and rational, martial and generous; whereas absolutism smells of fustiness as well as of fagots.

FOUR CARTOONS

by James Thurber

These cartoons about the plights of men who aspire to be writers were drawn for SRL during the thirties by James Thurber, a sporadic contributor who, being a writer himself, knew whereof he drew.

"Courting the Muse?"

DECEMBER 14, 1935

"The world crowds round the individual, leaving him no vista . . ."

OCTOBER 15, 1938

"He says Thomas Wolfe has no real stature."

APRIL 17, 1937

"There isn't room in this house for belles lettres and me both."

NOVEMBER 5, 1938

THE RED PERIL

by Elmer Davis

Way back in the early thirties a well-known political commentator, who was later briefly to become SRL's *editor (and later still chief of the nation's Office of War Information), set down his analysis of communism, especially as it related to a controversial literary work of the era, a novel entitled* Call Home the Heart *by Fielding Burke (the pen-name of Mrs. Olive Dargan).*

APRIL 16, 1932

EVEN IN THESE distressful times, it needs a lively imagination to see any serious danger (or hope, if you prefer) that America will go communist. What you read, and still more what you hear, among the intellectuals might lead you to think that the glorious day was at hand when, the awful summons hearing, the capitalist heaven and earth will pass away. But most of these ladies and gentlemen appear to have a somewhat vague notion of what communism is, in theory or practice, or why the ills we know not of are preferable to those we have. In fact, they would probably be among the first to be shot; when they saw communism in operation, in its early stages of gaining and consolidating power, they would be shocked; and being still under the influence of bourgeois ideology, they might give unguarded expression to their feelings before they realized that they were living in a new order which did not tolerate criticism.

However, they are not likely to be exposed to such a painful contrast between expectation and reality. The profit system as our ancestors knew it is apparently on the way out; the American economic order of the future, perhaps even the near future, will probably be something that would be unrecognizable to Alexander Hamilton or Commodore Vanderbilt. But unless a wholly improbable change occurs in the mentality of the American people, that order will be quite as alien to orthodox communism. Our Communist intellectuals virtually admit that fact when they write cheerfully of the rivers of blood (other people's blood) that must flow before the apostles of the enlightenment succeed in giving the American proletariat what is good for them.

There begin to be signs, however, that American literature is

22

going to have its Red peril, even though it is no more than a Red nuisance as yet. Germs that a healthy organism can throw off find a foothold in an enfeebled system, and while no part of American society looks any too vigorous at present, the intellectual group is about the sickest of the lot. In the nineteen twenties the intellectuals set up a great hullabaloo, most of which boiled down to the question, What is it all about? No satisfactory answer was found; and few intellectuals had sufficient sense of proportion or knowledge of history to realize that this misfortune was neither unprecedented nor necessarily fatal; to perceive that nobody has ever yet found a finally satisfactory answer but that somehow the human race has managed to worry along.

To admit that there are questions which even our so impressive intelligence is unable to answer, and at the same time not to despair of the ability of the human race to find, eventually, better answers than we can reach as yet—to recognize that there is nothing to do but keep on trying as well as we can, and to be as content as we can with the small gains that in the course of ages amount to something—that requires some courage and some balance; qualities which were not notably prevalent among the intellectuals of the twenties. Accordingly a good many of them have taken the easiest way out and yielded to the attraction of a system in which final and all-embracing truth is laid down in the sacred writings, to be authoritatively interpreted for the faithful by the communist church.

The merit of communism as an economic system is a technical question, requiring considerably more evidence than we now have before anybody can be sure of the answer. But so far as can be judged from their writings it is not communism as economics that has taken hold of the imaginations of its American intellectual converts; it is communism as a medicine for sick souls. Why not Catholicism, whose value as an anodyne has been proved by long experience? Well, for one thing because Catholicism is actually in operation in this country; a man who professed his conversion to Catholicism would be expected to behave as a Catholic and refrain from practicing the seven deadly sins and from writing novels about some of them. (Not all Catholic novelists so restrict themselves, but those who do not are apt to find themselves involved in arguments with their stricter co-religionists.) But a man who professes communism may continue, pending the dawn of the red millennium over these states, to enjoy all the advantages of capitalist democracy; not the least of which, for the intellectual, is the rare

felicity of being permitted to think what you like and say what
you think, in print.

That is not all of it, of course. The man or woman whose intellectual background is immediately rationalist and more remotely
Protestant has a subcutaneous emotional antipathy to Catholicism;
he is used to thinking of Catholicism as faith, whereas communism
is ostensibly a triumph of rationalism. That reason and faith are
blended in about the same proportion in each does not disturb
him; he takes them both at their face value. And finally a creed
which sets the attainment of perfect felicity in the hereafter is less
congenial to the contemporary spirit than one which (however recklessly) envisions the perfectibility of life on earth. People in whom
the judgment outweighs the emotions are likely to be skeptical of
the attainment of perfect felicity by the human race, at any rate
within the next million years; but those are not the people who are
looking around for a Rock of Ages.

Most of us are driven to strange shifts in these hard times, and the
bourgeois ideologist may doubt his right to condemn people who
save their emotional comfort at the expense of their capacity for dis-
interested thinking. They would deny, of course, that they pay any
such price. The art of reconciling faith with reason is an old one,
and the Communists follow respectable precedent if they accomplish it by subordinating reason to faith and holding, in the end,
that what appear as facts to the eye of the unsaved cannot be facts if
they contradict revelation. It may be that they are the heirs of the
future, but their inheritance cannot include very much of the stored
intellectual treasure of the past. They do not want it; it is "bourgeois," that is, it is hard to reconcile with the lately revealed truth;
and except in pure technology they are unfitted to grasp it exactly
in so far as they are good Communists. It is as true now as it ever
was that submission to religious dogma is poisonous to any attempt
at dispassionate thinking, or to intellectual appraisal of the ideas of
other men.

For proof of that you need go no farther than the analyses of international politics currently appearing in the editorials of *Izvestia*
and *Pravda*. The French General Staff and the American Farm
Board are allies in a foul conspiracy for an unprovoked assault on
proletarian Russia; if no such assault takes place, it is presumably
because vigilant Moscow editors have exposed the plot in time. The
Japanese adventure at Shanghai is only the first step in a joint attack on China by the imperialistic capitalist powers, to be followed
by the apocalyptically predicted crusade against the Soviet Union.
Yet at the same time, almost in the same issue, the Japanese adven-

ture in Shanghai is proof that the greed of the predatory capitalist powers is about to lead them into wars (also prophetically predicted) against one another. The bourgeois reader is likely to wonder if the men who concoct these theories are conscious liars or merely lunatics. They are neither, of course—only devotees of a dogmatic religion, frantically trying to twist the evidence to fit the sacred doctrines.

Or if you want an example nearer home, look at Mr. Dreiser's *Tragic America*. How sound Dreiser's communism may be, in the eye of the orthodox, I do not know; but it has evidently bitten deeply enough into him to rid him of the taint of bourgeois virtues. He used to be a good newspaperman, yet *Tragic America* is full of misstatements; in his novels he has analyzed character and motivated behavior as well as any man now writing, but his treatment of the character and motives of real people in *Tragic America* is often simply childish. Dreiser the artist knew a great deal about human beings; Dreiser the convert and missionary casts away the filthy rags of profane knowledge, and glories in the all-sufficient garment of faith.

This sort of thing is no doubt effective polemic, on the tabloid level; but people on the tabloid level are not going to take the considerable trouble involved in reading anything by Dreiser. There is plenty of valid evidence available for the indictment of a political and economic order which is not being very vociferously defended, at present, by anybody but Ralph Easley and Dolly Gann; and if Dreiser had confined himself to that evidence his argument would have more effect on the sort of people who would read a Dreiser book. But the appeal from reason to the passions seems, to the bourgeois critic, a pretty constant characteristic of Communist propaganda. The Communist denies that, of course. There is no truth, no beauty, but "proletarian" truth and beauty; *dæmonium cibus est sæcularis sapientia*. If communism gets the upper hand, all that has been thought and written in the past will be judged by new standards, and most of it condemned, as the church fathers judged the profane letters of Greece and Rome.

There is not much prospect of that misfortune overtaking America. But the Red infiltration into present-day literature is a nuisance because it imports alien and irrelevant values. It is like a conversation in two languages between people who do not understand each other. The Communist standard of truth and beauty is incommensurable with all other standards, past and present. It is a confusion of two things that do not mix; Communist art and Communist criticism are not what we call art and criticism at all. And a reader who is not persuaded that the past achievement of the human mind is one unrelieved mass of error finds himself increasingly annoyed by the intrusion into reviews and into creative writing of something that has, by our standards, nothing to do with the case.

Communist critics are only living up to their own creed when they review novels (as a good many of them have been reviewing novels lately) by this simple criterion: If it is not about the class struggle, or if it deals with personalities instead of masses, then it is not a good novel. *Omnis sapientia hominis in hoc uno est.* Some of these gentlemen show evidence of having had plenty of profane knowledge, and even taste, before their conversion; but they dutifully discard it now and measure everything by the foot rule of this new dispensation. This, perhaps, does not greatly matter, though I am old-fashioned enough to believe that the reader of a book review has a right to know something about the book, rather than about the theological opinions of the reviewer. But it is rather more serious when the frenzy of the devotee leads to the mutilation of a work of art, by the artist herself.

The recent *Call Home the Heart,* for instance, is, for the first half of its considerable length, one of the finest of American novels. It has pity, passion, elevation, a long list of characters clearly and plausibly realized; as you read it you are carried along on the current, completely surrendered to the illusion—and when you suddenly find yourself absorbing a Communist missionary sermon that lasts for eight solid pages you feel as if the second act of *Tristan* has been embellished with a long interpolation by a Salvation Army band. Thereafter the missionary sermons overshadow the story to such an extent that you are doubtful, for a while, whether this is Communist propaganda or a not very skillful parody of Communist propaganda. But it seems to be intended seriously; and it goes on and on till the very end, when the author, apparently not without shame for her weakness, permits herself a relapse into art. Her mountain heroine, descending into the plains and embracing the new faith, finally goes back to the mountains; her faith is firm, but she is too weak to labor in the vineyard; she can preach communism, but her blood revolts against physical contact with a Negress (and its corollaries in Communist doctrine). But despite this revulsion she seems able to swallow preachments that have wearied the reader long before.

The lady who calls herself Fielding Burke is an enthusiastic convert to the faith, but she cannot help looking backward occasionally toward the City of Destruction. She believes in the infallible Marxian Scriptures, and her criticism of truth is as strictly dogmatic as the most rigid of the faithful could ask; but when it comes to beauty she has some deplorable falls from grace. For she is an artist and she has not been able to rid herself altogether of an unregenerate weakness for bourgeois standards of beauty and proportion—even for bourgeois virtues. The chapters dealing with a Carolina mill town bring an authentic proletariat into the story; and Miss Burke commits the pretty nearly unpardonable offense of treating them as individual human beings and not as a mass. But her spirit is willing enough even if the flesh is sometimes feeble; she is ready to pluck out her right eye if it offends her, and the bourgeois reader can only be grateful that the left eye somehow escaped the same fate.

You will have to go a long way to find a more flagrant example of the disastrous consequences of a headlong collision between faith and art. The tolerant liberal will say, of course, that an author has a right to use her work as propaganda for her point of view. True enough; but the bourgeois ideology requires an author who does that to justify her faith by her works. A work of art aims at producing what may be called an illusion, in default of a better word; if the propaganda (or anything else) shatters that illusion, the novel has been spoiled by bourgeois standards of taste and the propaganda—also by bourgeois standards—becomes unconvincing.

So long as Miss Burke keeps her argument within the framework of the illusion and permits her doctrine to be inferred from what happens to the people in her story, the propaganda is powerfully effective. She knows her Carolina mill hands, and it may be presumed that she reports correctly what she has seen in a Carolina mill town. By mere presentation of what that means in its effect on the lives of human beings, she makes you feel that any social order which permits this sort of thing is self-condemned, that nothing could be worse.

If an artist who happened to believe in communism as the saving gospel had wanted to write propaganda for the faith that would be effective on the unconverted, she would have done this and no more. But nothing will satisfy her but drenching her later chapters in the sincere milk of the Word, and the unsaved will find that milk pretty sour. On those who are already true believers the last half of the book may have the stimulant effect of a revival meeting; but the people she is presumably trying to convert are not likely to be moved to any emotion more lofty than derision. Every claim made for communism of the ideal future is accepted as a present fact; any counterweight of practical difficulty in fulfillment of the program is serenely ignored. Even in arithmetic the bourgeois ideology is cast away and the hundred and fifty million Russians become, by proletarian computation, one sixth of the world's population.

As an artist Miss Burke is highly sensitive to pain and cruelty; as a Communist she knows that the only thing to do with people who disagree with her about the most effective method of improving the lot of the human race is to shoot them. Before the class struggle runs away with the story all the characters are realized with justice and insight; but the mill owner's wife is a figure from a comic strip and the professor who is set up as the intellectual champion of capitalism is a venal hireling aware of his own baseness and deliberately shutting his eyes to the true light. Moreover, Miss Burke is careful to give him only such arguments as could be knocked over by any bright pupil in a Communist kindergarten. And, true to the faith, she reserves her bitterest scorn for the socialists. The mill owner and his daughter, if not his wife, are permitted some trace of human decency; but there is no redeeming merit at all in the characters who happen to be Marxians of a schismatic sect.

This is not only bad art from a good artist, but ineffective propaganda from a writer who has shown that she can produce good propaganda. It can be rationally explained only on the theory that when the hallelujah urge gets hold of her Miss Burke forgets everything but the ecstasies of the sawdust trail. It is argument by assertion such as can be heard every Sunday from Fundamentalist pulpits, and it springs from the same state of mind; it would be unimportant if it were not the work of the remarkable woman who wrote the first two hundred pages of *Call Home the Heart*.

Christian mobs, in the fourth century, sometimes destroyed priceless statues because they happened to be images of pagan gods. There were no sculptors in the fourth century, Christian or pagan, capable of turning out priceless statues; but I do not doubt that here and there some sculptor, upon conversion, may have mutilated a work of which he himself at any rate had previously thought pretty well. There are Christian writers scattered all through the early centuries in whom love and hatred of profane learning are about as unstably balanced as they are in Miss Burke; but in the main, in those days, hatred got the upper hand.

Historical parallels are never quite parallel, and the obvious resemblance between contemporary communism and early Christianity, in their relation to world society, can easily be pushed too far. None the less, each of them professes to be a transvaluation of all previous values; in the case of Christianity the majority influence, for centuries, was against profane learning; and what the Church preserved of ancient truth and beauty, though it is pretty nearly all that was preserved at all, is considerably less than what Christianity destroyed. The present tendency of communism is in the same direction, and we are indebted to Miss Burke for furnishing, in the first and second halves of her book, an object lesson in the difference between bourgeois and proletariat art. If communism eventually gets the upper hand, what has hitherto been called literature is likely to be supplanted by something more on the order of the lives of the saints.

Christianity, of course, is not the only reason for the virtual disappearance of creative literature between the fourth and the eleventh centuries; they may both, ultimately, have been effects of the same cause, an unexplained alteration in the direction of the Mediterranean mind. None the less, the setting of human aspirations on the world to come and the constriction of human thought within the limits of dogma were powerful influences contributing to the repression of whatever literature the men of the Dark Ages might have been capable of producing. Eventually Christianity was humanized, as was Mohammedanism which began so fanatically; as communism no doubt will be when it passes out of the missionary phase. But it is not altogether pleasant to reflect that we may have a few centuries more of Dark Ages ahead of us, and that many of the enthusiasts who recently were busy freeing American literature from the last of the shackles imposed long ago by the Church are now so busy trying to replace the ineffectual tyranny lately thrown off by a new tyranny, which would be more jealously vigilant and more inflexibly dogmatic for generations to come.

I do not think that is going to happen, in this country; but it is to that event that Communist literature looks. Individual Communists can be artists, as Miss Burke proves in the first half of her book; but under present conditions they will be good artists—as artists have been defined for the past three thousand years—only to such extent as they are bad Communists. American literature, whether creative or critical, is not likely to profit much by the contribution of dogmatics whose standards of truth and beauty are as different from ours as were the standards of Orosius from those of Thucydides.

THE EARLIER LEWIS

by William Rose Benét

A long-time friend of Sinclair Lewis, SRL's poetry editor, the late William Rose Benét, recalls some youthful days in New York and California with the redheaded future Nobel Prize winner.

JANUARY 20, 1934

I FIRST HEARD of Harry Lewis, as he was called then—Sinclair being his middle name—when I was a Yale undergraduate. As he was in Yale College and I was in the Scientific School we had no occasion to meet. Second to the historic *Yale Literary Magazine* in those days there was another small literary magazine modeled somewhat upon Stone & Kimball's *Chap-Book,* known as the *Yale Courant.* Lewis was already drawing more books from the Yale library than, I believe, any undergraduate has before or since, and trying his prentice hand at writing, as he had doubtless done in school. It was quite natural that he quickly "made" both the *Lit* and the *Courant* and was elected to the chairmanship of the latter. This office he almost immediately resigned to devote his literary energies to the *Lit.* I stood second in the *Courant* competition and succeeded to his vacated office. Therefore, one afternoon, passing the precincts of the *Lit* in a basement passage of White Hall, on the way to my own editorial cubicle, I happened to espy the fellow of whose brilliance and independence I had already heard. A long, gangling youth with a conflagrate head of hair was stretched out on a high window seat smoking a pipe. He invited me in with a wave of the hand. We exchanged a few remarks, the usual "kidding," I think, of undergraduates.

But I am not going to dwell on Sinclair Lewis' undergraduate literary efforts. Henry Mencken, who professes a low opinion of poetry in general is, I believe, still trying to suppress any reappearance of his own early poetic efforts. As a matter of fact, "Red's" undergraduate verse was not at all bad for those days. I have some of it still, clipped from old *Courants.* He soon began to sell verse here and there to New York magazines. I remember a most rollicking stave he wrote about a priest, highly laudatory of this particular priest's convivial spirit and called "Father Kileen." It was modeled upon the late Richard Hovey's "Barney McGee." At that time there was another man of literary promise in Yale College, Allan Updegraff. He and Lewis were great friends and were associates later, I think, on *Transatlantic Tales* in New York, where they set themselves to translating foreign masterpieces of fiction. Updegraff has since become a well-known novelist.

I never saw Lewis again, that I remember, in college. It was after graduation, in California, that my best friend, Henry Hoyt (Elinor Wylie's brother), wrote me that he had run into "Red" in New York, found him a great scout, and that Lewis was coming to the Coast. I must meet him. At that time Henry and I had decided, with the arrogance of youth, that most people were bovine and that a soul could be discerned in very few. By that we meant, I suppose, that most people had very little independence of mind or spirit. "Red," however, quite evidently had.

I had lately come back from across the Pacific as deck yeoman on an Army transport, and I decided now to take a trip to Carmel, California, to meet this avatar. I arrived over a sandhill in a creaking buckboard of some sort to have a lanky individual, in corduroys and sweater or something of the kind, topped by the bonfire of his hair, hail me from the door of a shack. I lighted down, and "Red" introduced me to our mutual dwelling. As I remember it, we sat up all that first night discussing the Christian religion. I was quite conventional in my religious views at that time and Lewis proceeded to give me all the benefit of the higher criticism. On the other hand, I contributed a song I had learned from an Army officer, a nonsense song which "Red" immediately caught up and proceeded to troll lustily. It became one of his favorites.

We spent some time in Carmel together. We got to know the late George Sterling, drank his muscatel and ate his abalone. We wrote and wrote. I was writing pretty bad verse and Lewis was, at the time, writing short stories considerably under the influence of Edith Wharton whose work he intensely admired. He was acting at Carmel as secretary for Grace MacGowan Cooke and her sister Alice Mac-Gowan. Mrs. Cooke's daughter, Helen, whom we knew, later became the wife of Harry Leon Wilson. We were all great friends, even though Mrs. Cooke dubbed me "William the Silent," and "Red" somewhat annoyed Helen Cooke, solely out of his admiration for her, by chanting a most complimentary song about her which he had made up, entitled "A Fugitive Queen." "Red" and I swam in the Pacific, picnicked on the beach, took long walks, did our own cooking, and even tried experiments with our own laundry. I was amazed then, as I have been ever since, at the man's ability to reel off stories. On the way home from George Sterling's, through the Carmel woods, of a summer night, he would launch into some yarn that he had made up on the spur of the moment; and before we were back at our cottage—we had moved into better quarters due to the benevolence of a grand old lady who was then one of the leading spirits in Carmel—the whole story would have been completed in recitative. It was a marvelous performance, and apparently his fund of invention was inexhaustible. Also there were, as doubtless there are still—and as appears in *The Man Who Knew Coolidge*— the almost endless monologues in which he suddenly took on a character part, and the fantastic imaginings that would be worked out in the most intricate detail, till one almost screamed for surcease from the spate of words. From intense hilarity the man would also, at times, turn as grave and didactic as a Baptist minister and proceed to lay down the moral law, according to his own highly individual ideas, with an almost snarling earnestness that seemed to bode hell-fire for the unbeliever. It appeared as if Shelley himself could never have been more deeply stirred by the injustices and tyrannies of the economic order, or disorder.

My brain, to use Henry Hoyt's expression, was sometimes thoroughly "sandpapered" by the constant dissection of ideas, the questioning of every premise, the rovings of "Red's" insatiable curiosity concerning preconceived notions, and the constant challenge of his argument. And it did me a whole lot of good. This man was not content to stand and gaze at the horizon. He stalked forth immediately to crest the hill and find the next one. He may have come from Minnesota, but he was spiritually from Missouri, and had to be "shown." His intellect and his imagination were steaming up for the battle with life, and the ferment of young ambition in him shriveled up any "green sickness" of youth. The days of the making of a writer are days wonderful and absurd. "Red" himself has caught the yearning absurdity of such a period beautifully in his latest novel, *Work of Art,* in the grand Swinburnian poem that the youngster in Black Thread chants from a rooftop. We had great days—as they seem to me now—days of typewriter-pounding with "great thoughts." Nights of conviviality and tremendous conversations. Once we "hiked" a long way down the Coast together, camping out at night. Then the time at Carmel came to an end.

Lewis took a job on the San Francisco *Bulletin* and I went back to Benicia Arsenal, the Ordnance post of which my father was then in command. I had "Red" out to stay at the Arsenal and meet my family. He took an immediate strong liking for my father whose enormous reading, individual mind, humorous disposition, and liking for discussion exhilarated him. My father retained a deep fondness for one he would always speak of as "Harry" Lewis, as he had known him. He admired the questing intelligence and the spiritual integrity of the man. Naturally they were usually on opposite sides of an argument—but then my father enjoyed that. In fact it was a habit of his to take the opposite side. Otherwise there was no sharpening of wits, no arraying of the whole armament of opinion. This was right up "Red's" street, and they would sit up half the night in an intellectual duello that fascinated them both.

Lewis returned to the East, and soon I followed him. He got me a hall bedroom next to his own larger room on Van Nest Place in the middle of Charles Street. That was long before the days when, as now, Seventh Avenue cut a swath through that section of town. So we lived in Greenwich Village, "Red" being employed by the Frederick A. Stokes firm of publishers, I as a cub editor on the old *Century Magazine.* The youth of that period was chiefly interested in sociological matters. It was some years before the war, and after the war the more or less disillusioned youth of America seemed to turn, in the Scott Fitzgerald days, toward intense individualism and the "eat, drink, and be merry for tomorrow we die" attitude. Not so in that earlier time. Most of the young people were out to reform the world in one way or another—and, by Golly, the world was going to reform or know the reason why!

It was the day of the old *Masses* with Max Eastman and Floyd Dell as editors; of "The Working Girls' Home," namely the back room of O'Connor's old café on the corner of Greenwich Avenue and Sixth, where beer flowed freely and music had charms—the place where John Masefield himself once tended bar. It was the day of "The Old Grapevine," long gone, up Sixth Avenue a few blocks, where were checker players and bar philosophers and a cat that walked on the bar; it was the day of the Anarchist Ball, where I was introduced to Emma Goldman; it was the day when Frances Perkins, later a member of President Roosevelt's cabinet, was laying the foundation for a notable career in labor matters; when Edna Kenton lived not so far off; when Union Square was a veritable Hyde Park for soapbox orators; when "Red" came home one day with news of a new Stokes author who had just swum into their ken, by name Edna Ferber; when John Reed managed to get some of my poetry into the *American Magazine;* when Sinclair Lewis, on his way from Sauk Centre to Stockholm, pounded furiously at his typewriter, in his Van Nest Place room, lit by a tattered welsbach, composing lyrics for a comic opera he was sure he was going to sell to George M. Cohan. At the same time he had become fascinated by aviation and journeyed out to Mineola to renew acquaintance with Captain Paul Beck, one of the first Army fliers,

whom he had originally met in Benicia, California. He also took
time off from the office and wrote Stokes a boys' book, about a boy
aviator; and he was as busy as a bird dog doing a thousand and
one literary jobs and sitting up arguing till dawn.

Then "Red" wrote his first novel, *Our Mr. Wrenn,* and got married. His second novel, *The Trail of the Hawk,* reflecting his still
strong interest in flying—the conquest of the air took a strong hold
upon his vivid imagination—dealt in 1915 with a character in some
ways the prototype of Lindbergh. In fact, when "The Spirit of St.
Louis" did land at Le Bourget, taxiing to a stop with no casualties
in spite of the enormous onrushing crowd, it seemed to me as
though an early Sinclair Lewis novel had come true. He had called
the prophetic turn upon American history—I do not mean in exact
achievement, I mean in the spirit of American aviation. Charles
Lindbergh, with his upstanding liberal of a father, with his own
Minnesota background, and his own sturdy independence, would
have been just the sort of American "Red" could have novelized
with vehemence and enthusiasm.

In my first marriage my wife and I lived hardly a stone's throw
from the Lewises at Port Washington, Long Island. "Red" and I
commuted on the same train of a morning; but I regret to say that
his industry in that period quite put me to shame. While I was
content to loll in the smoker with a newspaper, "Red" was in another car, secreted from the conversation of commuters, writing
furiously upon a new book during the whole journey from Port
Washington to New York. Was that *The Trail of the Hawk,* or
could it have been *The Job?* At any rate, it was when he was still
being published by Harper's, before Alfred Harcourt had left
Henry Holt and Company to set up his own shop and to become
Sinclair Lewis' publisher. After jobs with *Adventure* and the Publishers' Newspaper Syndicate (under "Bill" Woodward, so well-
known now as a biographer) "Red" had become editor for George
H. Doran. He began to sell stories to *The Saturday Evening Post,*
and "The Innocents" and "Free Air" came along in their time. I
am not, however, sure of my dates here—and the rest is history: how
he took "time out" to write the novel Alfred Harcourt believed
would be his most vital, how he went to Washington to do it (where
Henry Hoyt and I once dropped in upon him at the room apart
from his home that he had rented for a workshop), how he produced
Main Street with only the motive of giving as true a picture of his
own Middle West as a scrupulous artist could give; and then, surprisingly to him, the fame and the fanfare.

The simile one instinctively thinks of first for Sinclair Lewis is "dynamo." He is the journalist *par excellence.* He has that absorbing curiosity about life without which no great writer was ever born. I was lucky to hear something of that curiosity stated in his earlier years, to be in contact for a while with that keen and searching mind, to have my lazy thinking questioned and exposed by that searchlight intellect. Conversation with him was always intensely stimulating. He could suggest a myriad new ideas in half an hour. And there is one incident I remember well because it seems to me the essential Lewis. Not Lewis the critic of his country, though he has been a badly heeded satirist of its institutions and the flame of his rage against our national stupidities has been a splendid cauterization.

We were dining together one night, and to our table came a stranger, a traveling salesman, whose conversation I thought a great bore and whose personality afflicted my intolerance. But "Red" plunged into conversation with him. Before he knew it the man was revealing all his characteristic ways of thinking and emoting, as well as giving us a good slice of his life. I can remember that I still maintained a rather annoyed attitude. The type didn't appeal to me. Then the man left and "Red" turned to me with a most quizzical smile. "Do you like that type of fellow?" I said—or words to that effect—believing my toplofty attitude to be inalienably the right one. "That's the trouble with you, Bill," said "Red" (or words to that effect), "you regard him as *hoi polloi,* he doesn't even represent the cause of labor or anything dramatic—but I understand that man—by God, I love him."

Of course this is misquoted after all these years; but what I am trying to convey is that Sinclair Lewis does love the essential humanness of people. He can be savagely against the ideas they may hold; just as he can scourge, and has scourged America, for many things. But when he said, as he did recently, that he loved this country, he said the truth. He is fundamentally an American. No other soil could have grown him. And he is a better thing than a humanist, he is a human-beingist. I think it is one of Fannie Hurst's titles— "Every Soul Has Its Song." That is what Sinclair Lewis fundamentally believes. And he can extort that song from even the queerest kinds of human beings. I'll bet he could easily extort it from the most laconic of red Indians! And that is why when two or three of us who have "known him when" are gathered together, though we may criticize him for this or that now and again, we usually end up by smiling into space at some particularly vivid reminiscence of him, and murmur to ourselves, "A great scout, 'Red'!"

PLAYS AND LANDSCAPES

by Gertrude Stein

An exile-extraordinaire *in Paris, the indefatigable Gertrude Stein formulates some ideas on the art of drama writing at a time when she was at the height of her glory.*

NOVEMBER 10, 1934

IN A BOOK I wrote called *How to Write* I made a discovery which I considered fundamental, that sentences are not emotional and that paragraphs are. I found out about language that paragraphs are emotional and sentences are not and I found out something else about it. I found out that this difference was not a contradiction but a combination and that this combination causes one to think endlessly about sentences and paragraphs because the emotional paragraphs are made up of unemotional sentences.

I found out a fundamental thing about plays. The thing I found out about plays was too a combination and not a contradiction and it was something that makes one think endlessly about plays.

That something is this:

The thing that is fundamental about plays is that the scene as depicted on the stage is more often than not one might say it is almost always in syncopated time in relation to the emotion of anybody in the audience.

What this says is this:

Your sensation as one in the audience in relation to the play played before you your sensation I say your emotion concerning that play is always either behind or ahead of the play at which you are looking and to which you are listening. So your emotion as a member of the audience is never going on at the same time as the action of the play.

This thing the fact that your emotional time as an audience is not the same as the emotional time of the play is what makes one endlessly troubled about a play, because not only is there a thing to know as to why this is so but also there is a thing to know why perhaps it does not need to be so. . . .

If you are taking part in an actual violent scene, and you talk

36

and they or he or she talk and it goes on and it gets more exciting and finally then it happens, whatever it is that does happen, then when it happens then at the moment of happening is it a relief from the excitement or is it a completion of the excitement. In the real thing it is a completion of the excitement in the theater it is a relief from the excitement, and in that difference the difference between completion and relief is the difference between the emotion concerning a thing seen on the stage and the emotion concerning a real presentation that is really something happening. . . .

I felt that if a play was exactly like a landscape then there would be no difficulty about the emotion of the person looking on at the play being behind or ahead of the play because the landscape does not have to make acquaintance. You may have to make acquaintance with it, but it does not with you, it is there and so the play being written the relation between you at any time is so exactly that that it is of no importance unless you look at it. Well I did look at it and the result is in all the plays that I have printed as Operas and Plays. . . .

The only one of course that has been played is *Four Saints*. In *Four Saints* I made the saints the landscape. All the saints that I made and I made a number of them because after all a great many pieces of things are in a landscape all these saints together made my landscape. These attendant saints were the landscape and it the play really is a landscape.

A landscape does not move nothing really moves in a landscape but things are there, and I put into the play the things that were there. . . .

While I was writing the *Four Saints* I wanted one always does want the saints to be actually saints before them as well as inside them, I had to see them as well as feel them. As it happened, there is on the Boulevard Raspail a place where they make photographs that have always held my attention. They take a photograph of a young girl dressed in the costume of her ordinary life and little by little in successive photographs they change it into a nun. These photographs are small and the thing takes four or five changes but at the end it is a nun and this is done for the family when the nun is dead and in memoriam. For years I had stood and looked at these when I was walking, and finally when I was writing Saint Therese in looking at these photographs I saw how Saint Therese existed from the life of an ordinary young lady to that of the nun. And so everything was actual and I went on writing.

Then in another window this time on the rue de Rennes there was rather a large porcelain group and it was of a young soldier giving alms to a beggar and taking off his helmet and his armor and leaving them in the charge of another.

It was somehow just what the young Saint Ignatius did and anyway it looked like him as I had known about him and so he too became actual not as actual as Saint Therese in the photographs but still actual and so the *Four Saints* got written.

All these things might have been a story but as a landscape they were just there and a play is just there. That is at least the way I feel about it.

Anyway I did write *Four Saints* an Opera to be Sung and I think it did almost what I wanted, it made a landscape and the movement in it was like a movement in and out with which anybody looking on can keep in time. I also wanted it to have the movement of nuns very busy and in continuous movement but placid as a landscape has to be because after all the life in a convent is the life of a landscape, it may look excited a landscape does sometimes look excited but its quality is that a landscape if it ever did go away would have to go away to stay.

Anyway the play as I see it is exciting and it moves but it also stays and that is as I said in the beginning might be what a play should do.

TENDENCIES IN MODERN FICTION

by Edith Wharton

During the thirties a lady novelist, the product of an older and more formal era of literature, looks somewhat down her nose at the spontaneous and less orthodox novelists of the time. When SRL *published this critique Mrs. Wharton, who is best remembered for her novels* The Age of Innocence *and* Ethan Frome, *was seventy-two. Three years later she died.*

JANUARY 27, 1934

THE MORAL AND INTELLECTUAL destruction caused by the war, and by its far-reaching consequences, was shattering to traditional culture; and so far as the new novelists may be said to have any theory of their art, it seems to be that every new creation can issue only from the annihilation of what preceded it. But the natural processes go on in spite of theorizing, and the accumulated leaf mold of tradition is essential to the nurture of new growths of art, whether or not those who cultivate them are aware of it. All the past seems to show that when a whole generation misses the fecundating soil stored for it by its predecessors its first growth will be spindling and its roots meager. So one waited; one hoped; one watched tenderly over every shoot that seemed to have sap in it.

This waiting has now lasted for nearly a generation. Enough time has elapsed for the critic to take stock of the new fiction, and for its creators to take stock of themselves; and it begins to look as though the rejection of the past—accidental, enforced at first, but now, it must be supposed, deliberate—had definitely impoverished the present. I believe the initial mistake of most of the younger novelists, especially in England and America, has been the decision that the old forms were incapable of producing new ones. No work based on the determination to be different seems to have a principle of life in it; genius is always "different" (that is, individual) in spite of itself; but never merely for the sake of being so.

For these reasons it is difficult, in judging the new tendencies, to find a common ground for criticism. The artist who rejects the past *en bloc* should at least offer some sort of new criterion, some view of life, some general conception of the validity of the creative act, by which his work may be measured. It is doubtful if such considerations have ever troubled the greater number; but, since the same sort of experiment necessarily leads to the same results, the new novelists have picked out of the ruins involving the older culture the odds and ends of some of the very principles they ignore.

In the early days of the art most of the characters in fiction were either "stylized" abstractions or merely passive subjects of experiment, or both. In the novels of character the figures were little more than the Lover, the Siren, the Miser, and so on; in the novel of adventure of the same period they were the Aunt Sallies of the village fair, perpetually set up to be knocked down by outward happenings. Both these sets of characters were virtually suspended in the void; their names were often reduced to initials, and the reader was at most allowed to know that the heroine had a brow of ivory, and the hero a frank, ingenuous eye. But presently someone—I suppose the merit is due first to Fielding and next to Scott—noticed the impact of surrounding circumstances on every individual life, the professional distortions, the religious and atmospheric influences, and those subtler differences produced by the then scarcely apprehended law of variability. The individual character burst the shell of the novelist's abstraction, and from the day of Scott and Balzac readers began to talk of this or that personage in a favorite novel as though he or she had been a living human being—as in the world of imagination, which is only a transposition of the other, they actually were.

This growth of individuality in the people of fiction led, about the middle of the nineteenth century, to the experimenting with new theories, perhaps necessary as a means of transition, though it turned out that they could never be more. The imagination, it was decided, was not a powerful enough medium; it was to be superseded by direct observation. The novelist exchanged his creative faculty for a kodak. Visible, palpable details of dress, of background, of bodily peculiarities, replaced the free drawing of character; statistics crowded out psychology. The "realists" had hit on a convenient device; they had discovered that it is much easier, whenever a given character appears, to put the same phrase on his lips, or to call the reader's attention to the same physical infirmity, a squint, a stammer, an odd pronunciation (a means of identification cruelly overused by Balzac), than to build up, stroke by stroke, the shape and growth of his soul. Whatever, as Henry James once put it, could be smelt, seen, tasted, or touched, was given precedence over mental and moral characteristics. But it remained to be discovered that this device led back, by another road, to the old stock types of the earlier fiction—save that the character who used to be merely the Miser was now the man whose left eyelid twitched, or the siren the young woman who was always preceded by a whiff of "White Rose."

Gradually the born novelists found that such short cuts did not lead them where they wanted to go, and the more gifted took another path, in the wake of the great Russians, while the feebler beat their brains out against the blank wall of "Naturalism." Transmutation is the first principle of art, and copying can never be a substitute for creative vision.

Many of our younger novelists seem innocently to have rediscovered the facile effects which Zola's generation had worn so threadbare; but in their opinion the generation which invented the "slice of life" had not the full courage of its method. Though the novelists of that day tore their slice from the lump, and served it up uncooked, they felt all the while the obligation to account for having chosen one particular slice and not another: and this obligation is precisely what the new novelists disavow. They profess (or would seem to) that any slice is equally to their purpose, if they do not scornfully reject any notion of a purpose. The mid-nineteenth-century group selected; the new novelists profess to pour everything out of their bag. Maupassant ended his "slices" with a climax (if this appalling metaphor may be forgiven); Katherine Mansfield tore hers off when they had filled so many pages—or so her imitators appear to believe. But every ending, as well as every beginning, is arbitrary and therefore selective. No bag has yet been found big enough to hold the universe, and the contents of the biggest bag is only, in the last resort, a selection. Yes; but it is, or would appear to be, an accidental selection; and as such it might be regarded, if only the creative intelligence were not always irresistibly sorting and rejecting. The experiments of the new novelists, and the comments of their docile interpreters, have proved, in spite of both, that any lasting creative work must be based on some sort of constructive system; the creator must have a conviction to guide him. The conviction of the new group is that there should be none; but this, too, is a system. And just as they have had to put together a sort of unconscious philosophy of life to support the fabric of their tales, so in method many of them have gone back to the "slice of life," and renamed it (perhaps because they did not know the experiment had already been made) the "stream of consciousness." Any such generalization must admit of notable exceptions; nevertheless the trend of the new fiction, not only in America and England, but on the Continent, is chiefly toward the amorphous and the agglutinative. The novelists most in view reject form not only in the structure of their tales but in the drawing of character. They reduce to the vanishing point any will to action, and their personages are helpless puppets on a sluggish stream of fatality. That many commit acts of violence does not disprove this: they drift into them like somnambulists, and the onlookers or participants are as spectral as the fugitive apparitions of a dream. The reader, at the moment, may be deceived by such artifices; but the book closed, he seems to stand on the scene of a drunken revel "whence all but he have fled"—so rapidly have the wraiths he has been reading about vanished from his memory.

To counteract this evanescence, the younger novelists attempt to give substance to their creations by an exaggerated physical realism, and by recourse to such superficial disguises as singularities of dialect and slang. To facilitate their realism, they naturally incline to situate their tales among the least developed classes; and in America, for instance, our young novelists are frequently praised for choosing the "real America" as the scene of their fiction—as though the chief intellectual and moral resources of the country lay among the poor whites of the Appalachians, or their counterparts in other regions.

Is there not some simpler explanation for this choice? It is obviously much easier to depict rudimentary characters, moved from the cradle to the grave by the same unchanging handful of instincts and prejudices, than to follow the action of persons in whom education and opportunity have developed a more complex psychology. For the same reason it is easier to note the confused drift of subconscious sensation than to single out the conscious thoughts and deliberate actions which are the key to character, and to the author's reason for depicting that character. I have often wished, in my "Sister Anne" watch for the coming great novelist, that these facilities did not so temptingly concord with the short cut in everything which is the ideal of the new generation, with the universal thirst to surpass the speed record in every department of human activity. The way of the young novelist used to be steep and difficult. The publishers rejected him, the public turned from him to names already known, and methods already familiar; the critic reviewed him in batches, as the "minor poets" are still dealt with. But nowadays all this is changed. Important prizes are offered for the "First Novel" (before it has even been tested by print), publishers advertise the work of the unknown as though being unknown were a quality and not merely a quantity; and every inducement is offered to seize the first short cut to notoriety and pecuniary benefit.

To a generation agreed that the past is not the soil of the future, such simplification of method was almost irresistible. The choice was probably unconscious, and the novelists left it to the critics to justify them, and to supply the key to a philosophy of art which did not yet exist.

Luckily the story-telling gift is a tough plant, and will survive the indiscriminate praise of the present day as it did the qualified approval of less accommodating critics. It will struggle through the chaos of present conditions in life and art, it will find out that difficulties are not meant to be avoided but to be mastered, it will develop the patience to explore and depict the enduring characters of human nature under the shifting surface of slang and sexuality, and it will gradually find methods of expression more pertinent to such a theme.

I have my white stone ready to mark the day when I see a young novelist slowly and doggedly rowing upstream instead of slipping down the current with the cheering crowd; for I believe that he is already training for the inevitable effort.

ONE WAY TO WRITE NOVELS

by Ellen Glasgow

A Southern writer, perhaps best known for her Pulitzer Prize-win-
ning novel The Romantic Comedians, *graciously contributes to*
SRL *a "highly personal statement" on her method of writing*
fiction.

DECEMBER 8, 1934

NOTHING, EXCEPT THE WEATHER REPORT or a general maxim of conduct, is so unsafe to depend upon as a theory of fiction. Every great novel has broken many conventions. The greatest of all novels defies every formula; and only Mr. Percy Lubbock believes that *War and Peace* would be greater if it were another and an entirely different book. By this I do not mean to question Mr. Lubbock's critical insight. *The Craft of Fiction* is the best work in its limited field, and may be studied to advantage by any novelist. In the first chapters there is a masterly analysis of *War and Peace*. Yet, after reading it with appreciation, I still think that Tolstoy was the best judge of what his book was about and of how long it should be.

This brings us, in the beginning, to the most sensitive, and therefore the most controversial, point in the criticism of prose fiction. It is the habit of overworked or frugal critics to speak as if economy were a virtue and not a necessity. Yet there are faithful readers who feel with me that a good novel cannot be too long or a bad novel too short. Our company is small but picked with care, and we would die upon the literary barricade defending the noble proportions of *War and Peace,* of *The Brothers Karamazov,* of *Clarissa Harlowe* in eight volumes, of *Tom Jones,* of *David Copperfield,* of *The Chronicles of Barsetshire,* of *A La Recherche du Temps Perdu,* of *Le Vicomte de Bragelonne.* Tennyson was with us when he said he had no criticism to make of *Clarissa Harlowe* except that it might have been longer.

The true novel (I am not concerned with the run-of-the-mill variety) is, like pure poetry, an act of birth, not a device or an invention. It awaits its own time and has its own way to be born, and it cannot, by scientific methods, be pushed into the world from behind. After it is born, a separate individual, an organic structure, it obeys its own vital impulses. The heart quickens; the blood circulates; the pulses beat; the whole body moves in response to some inward rhythm; and in time the expanding vitality attains its full stature. But until the breath of life enters a novel, it is as spiritless as inanimate matter.

Having said this much, I may confess that spinning theories of fiction is my favorite amusement. This is, I think, a good habit to cultivate. The exercise encourages readiness and agility while it keeps both head and hand in practice. Besides, if it did nothing else, it would still protect one from the radio and the moving picture and other sleepless, if less sinister, enemies to the lost mood of contemplation. This alone would justify every precept that was ever evolved. Although a work of fiction may be written without a formula or a method, I doubt if the true novel has ever been created without the long brooding season.

I have read, I believe, with as much interest as if it were a novel itself, every treatise on the art of fiction that appeared to me to be promising. That variable branch of letters shares with philosophy the favorite shelf in my library. I know all that such sources of learning as Sir Leslie Stephen, Sir Walter Raleigh, Mr. Percy Lubbock, Sir Arthur Quiller-Couch, Mr. E. M. Forster, and others less eminent but often more earnest, are able to teach me, or I am able to acquire. Indeed, I know more than they can teach me, for I know also how very little their knowledge can help one in the actual writing of novels. If I were giving advice to a beginner (but there are no beginners nowadays, there is only the inspired amateur or the infant pathologist), I should probably say something like this: "Learn the technique of writing, and having learned it thoroughly, try to forget it. Study the principles of construction, the value of continuity, the arrangement of masses, the consistent point of view, the revealing episode, the careful handling of detail, and the fatal pitfalls of dialogue. Then, having mastered, if possible, every rule of thumb, dismiss it into the labyrinth of the memory. Leave it there to make its own signals and flash its own warnings. The sensitive feeling, 'this is not right' or 'something ought to be different' will prove that these signals are working." Or, perhaps, this inner voice may be only the sounder instinct of the born novelist.

If this were a treatise on the art of writing, how simple it would be to pursue it to its logical end—to any end, indeed, except the one

that must begin the essay I am requested to write. But Dr. Canby*
did not ask for an article on prose fiction. He asked (intrepid
spirit!) for the "highly personal statement" which Mr. James Trus-
low Adams aptly describes as "a flagrant offense against modesty."
And immediately (though I am aware that my method, or the lack
of one, is not of the slightest interest to any human being but myself) the logical end becomes only a turning point, and the dignified
theory of fiction dwindles into the way I write novels.

The truth is that I began being a novelist, as naturally as I began
talking or walking, so early that I cannot remember when the impulse first seized me. Far back in my childhood, before I had learned
the letters of the alphabet, a character named Little Willie
wandered into the country of my mind, just as every other major
character in my novels has strolled across my mental horizon when
I was not expecting him, when I was not even thinking of the
novel in which he would finally take his place. From what or where
he had sprung, why he was named Little Willie, or why I should
have selected a hero instead of a heroine—all this is still as much
of a mystery to me as it was in my childhood. But there he was, and
there he remained, alive and active, threading his own adventures,
from the time I was three until I was eight or nine and discovered
Hans Andersen and Grimm's Fairy Tales. Every night, as I was
undressed and put to bed by my colored Mammy, the romance of
Little Willie would begin again exactly where it had broken off the
evening before. In winter I was undressed in the firelight on the
hearthrug; but in summer we moved over to an open window that
looked out on the sunset and presently the first stars in the long
green twilight. For years Little Willie lasted, never growing older,
always pursuing his own narrative and weaving his situations out
of his own character. I can still see him, small, wiry, with lank
brown hair like a thatch, and eyes that seemed to say, "I know a
secret! I know a secret!" Hans Andersen and the brothers Grimm
were his chosen companions. He lingered on, though somewhat
sadly, after I had discovered the Waverley Novels; but when I was
twelve years old and entered the world of Dickens, he vanished forever.

In those earliest formative years Little Willie outlined, however
vaguely, a general pattern of work. He showed me that a novelist
must write, not by taking thought alone, but with every cell of his
being, that nothing can occur to him that may not sooner or later
find its way into his craft. Whatever happened to me or to Mammy

---

* Henry Seidel Canby, who was then editor of *The Saturday Review of Literature*.

Lizzie happened also, strangely transfigured, to Little Willie. I learned, too, and never forgot, that ideas would not come to me if I went out to hunt for them. They would fly when I pursued; but if I stopped and sank down into a kind of watchful reverie, they would flock back again like friendly pigeons. All I had to do before the novel had formed, was to leave the creative faculty (or subconscious mind) free to work its own way without urging and without effort. When Dorinda in *Barren Ground* first appeared to me, I pushed her back into some glimmering obscurity, where she remained, buried but alive, for a decade, and emerged from the yeasty medium with hard round limbs and the bloom of health in her cheeks. Thus I have never wanted for subjects; but on several occasions when, because of illness or from external compulsion, I have tried to invent a theme or a character, invariably the effort has resulted in failure. These are the unnatural children of my brain that I should wish, were it possible, to disinherit.

It is not easy to tell how much of this dependence upon intuition may be attributed to the lack of harmony between my inner life and my early environment. A thoughtful and imaginative child, haunted by that strange sense of exile which visits the subjective mind when it is unhappily placed (and it is always, apparently, unhappily placed or it would not be subjective), I grew up in a charming society, where ideas were accepted as naturally as the universe or the weather, and cards for the old, dancing for the young, and conversation flavored with personalities for the middle-aged, were the only arts practiced. Several members of my family, it is true, possessed brilliant minds and were widely and deeply read; but all despised what they called "local talent," and my early work was written in secret to escape ridicule, alert, pointed, and not the less destructive because it was playful. There is more truth than wit in the gibe that every Southern novelist must first make his reputation in the North. Perhaps this is why so many Southern novelists write of the South as if it were a fabulous country. When a bound copy of my first book reached me, I hid it under my pillow while a cousin, who had run in before breakfast, prattled beside my bed of the young men who had quarreled over the privilege of taking her to the Easter German, as the Cotillion was called. Had I entered the world by way of Oxford, or even by way of Blooms-bury, I might now be able to speak or write of my books without a feeling of outraged reserve. And yet, in the very act of writing these words, my literary conscience, a nuisance to any writer, inquires if ideas were really free at Oxford, or even in Bloomsbury, at the end of the century, and if all the enfranchised spirits who babble of prohibited subjects nowadays are either wiser or better than the happy hypocrites of the nineties.

From this dubious prelude it might be inferred that I consider the craft of fiction merely another form of mental inertia. On the contrary, I agree with those writers who have found actual writing to be the hardest work in the world. What I am concerned with at the moment, however, is the beginning of a novel alone, not the endless drudgery that wrung from Stevenson the complaint, "The practice of letters is miserably harassing to the mind; and after an hour or two's work, all the more human portion of an author is extinct; he will bully, backbite, and speak daggers." For being a true novelist, even if one's work is not worth the price of a cherry to public or publisher, takes all that one has to give and still something more. Yet the matter is not one of choice but of fatality. Like the enjoyment of music, or a love for El Greco, or a pleasure in gardening, or the taste for pomegranates, or a preference for Santayana's prose, the bent of nature is either there or it is not there.

For my own part, and it appears, however far I stray, that I must still return to "the highly personal statement," the only method I have deliberately cultivated has been a system of constant renewal. If novels should be, as Sir Leslie Stephen has said, "transfigured experience," then I have endeavored, whenever it was possible, to deepen experience and to heighten what I prefer to call illumination, to increase my understanding of that truth of life which has never become completely reconciled with the truth of fiction. I do not mean by this that life should necessarily be eventful or filled with variable activities. Profound emotion does not inevitably bear "the pageant of a bleeding heart." Several of the most thrilling lives in all literature were lived amid the unconquerable desolation of the Yorkshire moors. Yet it is doubtful if either the exposed heart of Byron or the brazen trumpet of D. H. Lawrence contained such burning realities as were hidden beneath the quiet fortitude of Emily Brontë.

Because of some natural inability to observe and record instead of create, I have never used an actual scene until the impression it left had sifted down into imagined surroundings. A theme becomes real to me only after it is clothed in living values; but these values must be drawn directly from the imagination and indirectly, if at all, from experience. Invariably the characters appear first, and slowly and gradually build up their own world and spin the situation and atmosphere out of themselves. Strangely enough, the horizon of this real or visionary world is limited by the impressions or recollections of my early childhood. If I were to walk out into the country and pick a scene for a book, it would remain as flat and lifeless as cardboard; but the places I loved or hated between the ages of three and thirteen compose an inexhaustible landscape of memory. Occasionally, it is true, I have returned to a scene to verify details, though for freshness and force I have trusted implicitly to the vision within. And just as my scene is built up from fragments of the past, whether that past existed in fact or in a dream, so the human figures, though not one of them has been copied from my acquaintances, will startle me by displaying a familiar trait or gesture, and I will recognize with a shock some special blending of characteristics.

Frequently, these impressions have been buried so long and so deep that I have entirely forgotten them until they float upward to the surface of thought. Yet they are not dead but living, and recover warmth and animation after the creative faculty has revived them. In the same way, half-obliterated images, events, or episodes, observed in moments of intense experience, will flash back into a scene or a figure; and this is equally true of the most trivial detail my memory has registered. For example, in one of the tragic hours of my youth I looked out of a window and saw two sparrows quarreling in the rain on a roof. Twenty years or more afterwards, a character in one of my novels looks out of a window in a moment of heartbreak and sees two sparrows quarreling in the rain. And, immediately, light streamed back, as if it were cast by the rays of a lantern, into the unlit recesses of memory, and I felt the old grief in my heart and saw the rain fall on the roof and the two sparrows quarreling.

Because everything that one has seen or heard or thought or felt leaves a deposit that never filters entirely through the essence of mind, I believe that a novelist should be perpetually engaged in this effort to refresh and replenish his source. I am confident, moreover, that nothing I have learned either from life or from literature has been wasted. Whatever I have thought or felt deeply has stayed with me, if only in fragments or in a distillation of memory. But the untiring critic within has winnowed, reassorted, and disposed the material I needed.

Not until the unconscious worker has withdrawn from the task, or taken a brief holiday, and the characters have woven their own background and circumstances, does the actual drudgery of molding the mass-substance begin. Even now, after the groundwork is completed and the subject assembled, I still give time and thought (brooding is the more accurate term) to the construction. I try not to hasten the process and to leave the invisible agent to flash directions or warnings. The book must have a form. This is essential. It may be shaped like a millstone or an hourglass or an Indian tomahawk or a lace fan—but a shape it must have. Usually a novel assumes its own figure when it enters the world, and the underlying idea molds the plastic material to its own structure. More deliberately, the point of view is considered and selected, though this may, and often does, proceed naturally from the unities of time and place, or from one completely dominant figure. In *Barren Ground,* a long novel, I felt from the moment Dorinda entered the book that there could be but one point of view. From the first page to the last, no scene or episode or human figure appears outside her field of vision or imagination.

In *The Sheltered Life,* where I knew intuitively that the angle of vision must create the form, I employed two points of view alone, though they were separated by the whole range of experience. Age and youth look on the same scene, the same persons, the same events and occasions, the same tragedy in the end. Between these conflicting points of view the story flows on, like a stream in a narrow valley. Nothing happens that is not seen, on one side, through the steady gaze of the old man, seeing life as it is, and, on the other side, by the troubled eyes of the young girl, seeing life as she would wish it to be. Purposely, I have tried here to interpret reality through the dissimilar mediums of thought and emotion. I have been careful to allow no other aspects to impinge on the contrasting visions which create between them the organic whole of the book. This convention, which appears uncertain, when one thinks of it, becomes natural and even involuntary when the work grows, develops, pushes out with its own energy, and finds its own tempo.

While I am at work on a book I remain, or try to remain, in a state of immersion. The first draft of a novel, if it is long, will take two years, and still another year is required for the final writing. All this time the imaginary setting becomes the native country of my mind, and the characters are seldom out of my thoughts. I live with them day and night; they are more real to me than acquaintances in the flesh. In our nursery copy of *Gulliver's Travels* there was a picture which seems, when I recall it now, to illustrate my predicament in the final draft of a novel. Gulliver lies bound in threads while the Lilliputians swarm over him and hamper his struggles. So words swarm over me and hamper my efforts to seize the right one among them, to find the right rhythm, the right tone, the right accent. But here again intuition, or perhaps only a flare of organized memory, will come to my aid. Often, when I have searched for hours for some special word or phrase and given up in despair, I have awaked with a start in the night because the hunted word or phrase had darted into my mind while I was asleep.

Nevertheless, it is the act of scrupulous revision (the endless pruning and trimming for the sake of a sound and flexible prose style) that provides the writer's best solace even while it makes drudgery. Every literary craftsman who respects his work has, I dare say, this same feeling, and remains restless and wandering in mind until he has entered the right climate in the beginning and tracked down the right word at the end. Although my characters may develop traits or actions I had not anticipated, the scenes may shift and alter in perspective, and new episodes may spring out on the way, still the end shines always as the solitary fixed star above the flux of creation. I have never written the first word of the first sentence until I knew what the last word of the last sentence would be. Sometimes I may rewrite the beginning many times, as I did in *They Stooped to Folly,* and sometimes (though this has actually occurred but once) a shorter book like *The Romantic Comedians,* completely realized before pen was put to paper, may bubble over of itself with a kind of effortless joy. Yet in the difficult first chapter of *They Stooped to Folly* I could still look ahead, over a procession of characters that had slipped from my control, to the subdued scene at the end, while the concluding paragraph of *The Romantic Comedians* placed the tone of the entire book and accented the rhythm.

The final words to be said of any activity will always be, I suppose, was it worth what it cost? Well, the writing of fiction is worth, I imagine, exactly what digging a ditch or charting the heavens may be worth to the worker, and that is not a penny more or less than the release of mind that it brings. Although I may not speak as an authority, at least I can speak from long perseverance. I became a novelist before I was old enough to resist, and I remained a novelist because no other enterprise in life has afforded me the same interest or provided me with equal contentment. It is true that I have written only for the biased judgment within; but this inner critic has held an unattainable standard, and has infused a certain zest of adventure into what may appear on the surface to be merely another humdrum way of earning a livelihood. Still, to a beginner who is young and cherishes an ambition to be celebrated, I should recommend the short cut (or royal road) through the radio and Hollywood; and certainly more than one creative writer in search of swift economic security would do well to buy a new broom and to set out for the next crossing. But, incredible as it may appear in this practical decade, there are novelists so wanting in a sense of the best proletarian values that they place artistic integrity above the voice on the air, the flash on the screen, and the dividends in the bank. There are others who possess an unreasoning faith in their own work; and there are yet others endowed with a comic spirit so robust, or so lively, that it can find diversion anywhere, even in our national exaltation of the inferior. To this happy company of neglected novelists, the ironic art of fiction will reveal its own special delights, and may even, as the years pass, yield its own sufficient, if imponderable, rewards.

In looking back through a long vista, I can see that what I have called the method of constant renewal may be reduced to three ruling principles. Obedience to this self-imposed discipline has enabled me to write novels for more than thirty years, and yet to feel that the substance from which I draw material and energy is as fresh today as it was in my first youthful failure. As time moves on, I still see life in beginnings, moods in conflict, and change as the only permanent law. But the value of these qualities (which may be self-deluding, and are derived, in fact, more from temperament than from technique) has been mellowed by long saturation with experience—by that essence of reality which one distills from life only after it has been lived.

Among the many curious superstitions of the age of science there is the prevailing belief that immaturity alone is enough. Pompous illiteracy, escaped from some Freudian cage, is in the saddle, and the voice of the amateur is the voice of authority. When we turn to the field of prose fiction, we find that it is filled with literary skyrockets sputtering out in the fog. But the trouble with skyrockets has always been that they do not stay up in the air. One has only to glance back over the postwar years to discover that the roads of the jazz age are matted thick with fireworks that went off too soon. To the poet, it is true, especially if he can arrange with destiny to die young, the glow of adolescence may impart an unfading magic. But the novel (which must be conceived with a subdued rapture, or with none at all, or even with the unpoetic virtues of industry and patience) requires more substantial ingredients than a little ignorance of life and a great yearning to tell everything one has never known. When I remember Defoe, the father of us all, I am persuaded that the novelist who has harvested well the years, and laid by a rich store of experience, will find his latter period the ripening time of his career.

Transposed into an impersonal method, the three rules of which I have spoken may be so arranged:

1. Always wait between books for the springs to fill up and flow over.

2. Always preserve within a wild sanctuary, an inaccessible valley of reveries.

3. Always, and as far as it is possible, endeavor to touch life on every side; but keep the central vision of the mind, the inmost light, untouched and untouchable.

In my modest way, these rules have helped me, not only to pursue the one calling for which I was designed alike by character and inclination, but even to enjoy the prolonged study of a world that, as the sardonic insight of Henry Adams perceived, no "sensitive and timid natures could regard without a shudder."

THE STORY OF A NOVEL

by Thomas Wolfe

One of the most famous articles ever to appear in SRL's *pages was writer Thomas Wolfe's agonized account of his struggles in producing his first two novels. Here, as it originally appeared in the magazine, is "The Story of a Novel," a story which, he warns, is one "of sweat and pain and despair and partial achievement."*

DECEMBER 14, 1935

A GREAT EDITOR, who is also a good friend of mine, told me about six months ago that he was sorry he had not kept a diary about the work that both of us were doing, the whole stroke, catch, flow, stop, and ending, the ten thousand fittings, changings, triumphs, and surrenders that went into the making of a book. This editor remarked that some of it was fantastic, much incredible, all astonishing, and he was also kind enough to say that the whole experience was the most interesting he had known during the twenty-five years he had been a member of the publishing business.

I propose to tell about this experience. I cannot tell anyone how to write books; I cannot attempt to give anyone rules whereby he will be enabled to get his books published by publishers or his stories accepted by high-paying magazines. I am not a professional writer; I am not even a skilled writer; I am just a writer who is on the way to learning his profession and to discovering the line, the structure, and the articulation of the language which I must discover if I do the work I want to do. It is for just this reason, because I blunder, because every energy of my life and talent is still involved in this process of discovery, that I am speaking as I speak here. I am going to tell the way in which I wrote a book. It will be intensely personal. It was the most intense part of my life for several years. There is nothing very literary about it. It is a story of sweat and pain and despair and partial achievement. I don't know how to write a story yet. I don't know how to write a novel yet. But I have learned something about myself and about the work of writing, and if I can, I am going to try to tell what it is.

I don't know when it occurred to me first that I would be a writer. I suppose that like a great many other children in this coun-

54

try of my generation, I may have thought that it would be a fine thing because a writer was a man like Lord Byron or Lord Tennyson or Longfellow or Percy Bysshe Shelley. A writer was a man who was far away like these people I have mentioned, and since I was myself an American and an American not of the wealthy or university-going sort of people, it seemed to me that a writer was a man from a kind of remote people that I could never approach. I don't know how I became a writer, but I think it was because of a certain force in me that had to write and that finally burst through and found a channel. My people were of the working class of people. My father, a stonecutter, was a man with a great respect and veneration for literature. He had a tremendous memory, and he loved poetry, and the poetry that he loved best was naturally of the rhetorical kind that such a man would like. Nevertheless it was good poetry, Hamlet's Soliloquy, *Macbeth,* Mark Antony's Funeral Oration, Gray's "Elegy," and all the rest of it. I heard it all as a child; I memorized and learned it all.

He sent me to college to the state university. The desire to write which had been strong during all my days in high school, grew stronger still. I was editor of the college paper, the college magazine, etc., and in my last year or two I was a member of a course in playwriting which had just been established there. I wrote several little one-act plays, still thinking I would become a lawyer or a newspaper man, never daring to believe I could seriously become a writer. Then I went to Harvard, wrote some more plays there, became obsessed with the idea that I had to be a playwright, left Harvard, had my plays rejected, and finally in the autumn of 1926, how, why, or in what manner I have never exactly been able to determine, I began to write my first book in London. I was living all alone at that time. I had two rooms—a bedroom and a sitting room—in a little square in Chelsea in which all the houses had that familiar, smoked brick and cream-yellow-plaster look of London houses. They looked exactly alike.

As I say, I was living alone at that time and in a foreign country. I did not know why I was there or what the direction of my life should be, and that was the way I began to write my book. I think that is one of the hardest times a writer goes through. There is no standard, no outward judgment, by which he can measure what he has done. By day I would write for hours in big ledgers which I had bought for the purpose; then at night I would lie in bed and fold my hands behind my head and think of what I had done that day and hear the solid, leather footbeat of the London bobby as he came by my window, and remember that I was born in North Caro-

lina and wonder why the hell I was now in London lying in the
darkened bed, and thinking about words I had that day put down
on paper. I would get a great, hollow, utterly futile feeling inside
me, and then I would get up and switch on the light and read the
words I had written that day, and then I would wonder: why am I
here now? why have I come? I worked there every day with such
feelings as I have described, and came back to America in the winter
and worked here. I would teach all day and write all night, and
finally about two and a half years after I had begun the book in
London, I finished it in New York.

I should like to tell about this, too. I was very young at the time,
and I had the kind of wild, exultant vigor which a man has at that
period of his life. The book took hold of me and possessed me. In
a way, I think it shaped itself. Like every young man, I was strongly
under the influence of writers I admired. One of the chief writers
at that time was Mr. James Joyce with his book *Ulysses*. The book
that I was writing was much influenced, I believe, by his own book,
and yet the powerful energy and fire of my own youth played over
and, I think, possessed it all. Like Mr. Joyce, I wrote about things
that I had known, the immediate life and experience that had been
familiar to me in my childhood. Unlike Mr. Joyce, I had no literary
experience. I had never had anything published before. My feeling toward writers, publishers, books, that whole fabulous faraway
world, was almost as romantically unreal as when I was a child.
And yet my book, the characters with which I had peopled it, the
color and the weather of the universe which I had created, had
possessed me, and so I wrote and wrote with that bright flame with
which a young man writes who never has been published, and who
yet is sure all will be good and must go well. This is a curious
thing and hard to tell about, yet easy to understand in every writer's
mind. I wanted fame, as every youth who ever wrote must want it,
and yet fame was a shining, bright, and most uncertain thing.

The book was finished in my twenty-eighth year. I knew no publishers and no writers. A friend of mine took the huge manuscript—
it was about 350,000 words long—and sent it to a publisher whom
she knew. In a few days, a week or two, I received an answer from
this man saying that the book could not be published. The gist of
what he said was that his house had published several books like it
the year before, that all of them had failed, and that, further, the
book in its present form was so amateurish, autobiographical, and
unskillful that a publisher could not risk a chance on it. I was,
myself, so depressed and weary by this time, the illusion of creation
which had sustained me for two and a half years had so far worn

off, that I believed what the man said. At that time I was a teacher in one of New York's great universities, and when the year came to a close, I went abroad. It was only after I had been abroad almost six months that news came to me from another publisher in America that he had read my manuscript and would like to talk to me about it as soon as I came home.

I came home on New Year's Day that year. The next day I called up the publisher who had written me. He asked me if I would come to his office and talk to him. I went at once, and before I had left his office that morning, I had signed a contract and had a check for five hundred dollars in my hand.

It was the first time, so far as I can remember, that anyone had concretely suggested to me that anything I had written was worth as much as fifteen cents, and I know that I left the publisher's office that day and entered into the great swarm of men and women who passed constantly along Fifth Avenue at Forty-eighth Street and that presently I found myself at a Hundred and Tenth Street, and from that day to this I have never known how I got there.

For the next six or eight months I taught at the university and worked upon the manuscript of my book with this great editor. The book appeared in the month of October, 1929. The whole experience still had elements of that dreamlike terror and unreality that writing had had for me when I had first begun it seriously and had lain in my room in London with my hands below my head and thought why am I here now? The awful, utter nakedness of print, that thing which is for all of us so namelessly akin to shame, came closer day by day. That I had wanted this exposure, I could not believe. It seemed to me that I had shamelessly exposed myself and yet that subtle drug of my desire and my creating held me with a serpent's eye, and I could do no other. I turned at last to this editor who had worked with me and found me, and I asked him if he could foretell the end and verdict of my labor. He said that he would rather tell me nothing, that he could not prophesy or know what profit I would have. He said, "All that I know is that they cannot let it go, they cannot ignore it. The book will find its way."

And that fairly describes what happened. I have read in recent months that this first book was received with what is called a "storm of critical applause," but this really did not happen. It got some wonderful reviews in some places; it got some unfavorable reviews in others, but it unquestionably did have a good reception for a first book, and what was best of all, as time went on, it continued to make friends among people who read books. It continued to sell over a period of four of five years in the publisher's edition, and later in a cheaper edition, The Modern Library, it renewed its life and began to sell again. The upshot of it was that after the publication of this book in the autumn of 1929, I found myself with a position as a writer. And here one of the first of my great lessons as a writer began.

Up to this time I had been a young man who wanted to be a writer more than anything on earth and who had created his first book in the great blaze of illusion which a young writer must feel when he has no evidence except his hope to drive him on. Now, in a certain measure, this had changed. I had been a writer in hope and in desire before and now I was a writer in fact. I would read about myself, for example, as one of the "younger American writers." I was a person who, some of the critics said, was to be watched. They were looking forward to my future book with interest and with a certain amount of apprehension. Here, too, my education as a writer was increasing all the time. Now, indeed, I could hear myself discussed, and somehow the fact was far more formidable than I had dreamed that it could be. It worried me, confused me, gave me a strange feeling of guilt and responsibility. I was a young American writer, and they had hopes and fears about my future, and what would I do, or would it be anything, nothing, much, or little? Would the faults which they had found in my work grow worse or would I conquer them? Was I another flash in the pan? Would I come through? What would happen to me?

I let it worry me. I would go home at night and look around my room and see that morning's coffee cup still unwashed and books on the floor and a shirt where I had thrown it the night before and great stacks of manuscript and everything so common and familiar-looking and so disorderly, and then I would think that I was now a young American writer; that somehow I was practicing an imposture on my readers and my critics because my shirt looked the way it did and my books and my bed—not, you understand, because they were disorderly, common, familiar, but just because they looked the way they did.

But now another fact began to gnaw a way into my consciousness.

The critics had begun to ask questions about the second book, and so now I had to think about the second one as well. I had always wanted to think about the second one and the thirty-second one and the fifty-second one. I had been sure that I had a hundred books in me, that all of them would be good, that each of them would make me famous. But here again was a strange and jolting transition from wild hope and exultant conviction; and plain, blazing fact remained. Now that I had actually written one book and THEY, the actual readers and the critics who had read it, were looking for a second, I was up against it. I was not up against it the way I dreaded, I was just up against it cold and hard as one comes up against a wall. I was a writer. I had made the writer's life my life; there was no going back; I had to go on. What could I do? After the first book there had to be a second book. What was the second book to be about? Where would it come from?

This inexorable fact, although it became more and more pressing, did not bother me so much at first. Rather I was concerned with many other things that had to do with the publication of that first book, and, as before, I had foreseen none of them. In the first place, I had not foreseen one fact which becomes absolutely plain after a man has written a book, but which he cannot foresee until he has written one. This fact is that one writes a book not in order to re-member it, but in order to forget it, and now this fact was evident. As soon as the book was in print, I began to forget about it, I wanted to forget about it, I didn't want people to talk to me or question me about it. I just wanted them to leave me alone and shut up about it. And yet I longed desperately for my book's success. I wanted it to have the position of proud esteem and honor in the world that I longed for it to have—I wanted, in short, to be a suc-cessful and a famous man, and I wanted to lead the same kind of obscure and private life I'd always had and not to be told about my fame and success.

From this problem, another painful and difficult situation was produced. I had written my book, more or less, directly from the experience of my own life, and, furthermore, I now think that I may have written it with a certain naked intensity of spirit which is likely to characterize the earliest work of a young writer. At any rate, I can honestly say that I did not foresee what was to happen. I was surprised not only by the kind of response my book had with the critics and the general public, I was most of all surprised with the response it had in my native town. I had thought there might be a hundred people in that town who would read the book, but if there were a hundred outside of the Negro population, the blind, and the positively illiterate who did not read it, I do not know where they are. For months the town seethed with a fury of resent-ment which I had not believed possible. The book was denounced from the pulpit by the ministers of the leading churches. Men collected on street corners to denounce it. For weeks the women's clubs, bridge parties, teas, receptions, book clubs, the whole com-plex fabric of a small town's social life was absorbed by an outraged clamor. I received anonymous letters full of vilification and abuse, one which threatened to kill me if I came back home, others which were merely obscene. One venerable old lady, whom I had known all my life, wrote me that although she had never believed in lynch law, she would do nothing to prevent a mob from dragging my "big overgroan karkus" across the public square. She informed me further, that my mother had taken to her bed "as white as a ghost" and would "never rise from it again."

There were many other venomous attacks from my home town and for the first time I learned another lesson which every young writer has got to learn. And that lesson is the naked, blazing power of print. At that time it was for me a bewildering and almost overwhelming situation. My joy at the success my book had won mixed with bitter chagrin at its reception in my native town. And yet I think I learned something from that experience, too. For the first time I was forced to consider squarely this problem: where does the material of an artist come from? What are the proper uses of that material, and how far must his freedom in the use of that material be controlled by his responsibility as a member of society? This is a difficult problem, and I have by no means come to the bottom of it yet. Perhaps I never will, but as a result of all the distress which I suffered at that time and which others may have suffered on account of me, I have done much thinking and arrived at certain conclusions.

My book was what is often referred to as an autobiographical novel. I protested against this term in a preface to the book upon the grounds that any serious work of creation is of necessity autobiographical and that few more autobiographical works than *Gulliver's Travels* have ever been written. I added that Dr. Johnson had remarked that a man might turn over half the volumes in his library to make a single book, and that in a similar way, a novelist might turn over half the characters in his native town to make a single figure for his novel. In spite of this the people in my native town were not persuaded or appeased, and the charge of autobiography was brought against me in many other places.

As I have said, my conviction is that all serious creative work must be at bottom autobiographical, and that a man must use the material and experience of his own life if he is to create anything that has substantial value. But I also believe now that the young writer is often led through inexperience to a use of the materials of life which are, perhaps, somewhat too naked and direct for the purpose of a work of art. The thing a young writer is likely to do is to confuse the limits between actuality and reality. He tends unconsciously to describe an event in such a way because it actually happened that way, and from an artistic point of view, I can now see that this is wrong. It is not, for example, important that one remembers a beautiful woman of easy virtue as having come from the state of Kentucky in the year 1907. She could perfectly well have come from Idaho or Texas or Nova Scotia. The important thing really is only to express as well as possible the character and quality of the beautiful woman of easy virtue. But the young writer, chained to fact and to his own inexperience, as yet unliberated by maturity, is likely to argue, "she must be described as coming from Kentucky because that is where she actually did come from."

In spite of this, it is impossible for a man who has the stuff of creation in him to make a literal transcription of his own experience. Everything in a work of art is changed and transfigured by the personality of the artist. And as far as my own first book is concerned, I can truthfully say that I do not believe that there is a single page of it that is true to fact. And from this circumstance, also, I learned another curious thing about writing. For although my book was not true to fact, it was true to the general experience of the town I came from and I hope, of course, to the general experience of all men living. The best way I can describe the situation is this: it was as if I were a sculptor who had found a certain kind of clay with which to model. Now a farmer who knew well the neighborhood from which this clay had come might pass by and find the sculptor at his work and say to him, "I know the farm from which you got that clay." But it would be unfair of him to say, "I know the figure, too." Now I think what happened in my native town is that having seen the clay, they became immediately convinced that they recognized the figure, too, and the results of this misconception were so painful and ludicrous that the telling of it is almost past belief.

It was my experience to be assured by people from my native town not only that they remembered incidents and characters in my first book, which may have had some basis in actuality, but also that they remembered incidents which so far as I know had no historical basis whatever. For example, there was one scene in the book in which a stonecutter is represented as selling to a notorious woman of the town a statue of a marble angel which he has treasured for many years. So far as I know, there was no basis in fact for this story, and yet I was informed by several people later that they not only remembered the incident perfectly, but had actually been witnesses to the transaction. Nor was this the end of the story. I heard that one of the newspapers sent a reporter and a photographer to the cemetery and a photograph was printed in the paper with a statement to the effect that the angel was the now famous angel which had stood upon the stonecutter's porch for so many years and had given the title to my book. The unfortunate part of this proceeding was that I had never seen or heard of this angel before, and that this angel was, in fact, erected over the grave of a well-known Methodist lady who had died a few years before and that her indignant family had immediately written the paper to demand a retraction of its story, saying that their mother had been in no way connected with the infamous book or the infamous angel which had given the infamous book its name. Such, then, were some of the unforeseen difficulties with which I was confronted after the publication of my first book.

Month was passing into month, I had had a success. The way was opened to me. There was only one thing for me to do and that was work, and I was spending my time consuming myself with anger, grief, and useless passion about the reception the book had had in my native town, or wasting myself again in exuberant elation because of the critics' and the readers' praise, or in anguish and bitterness because of their ridicule. For the first time, I realized the nature of one of the artist's greatest conflicts, and was faced with the need of meeting it. For the first time I saw not only that the artist must live and sweat and love and suffer and enjoy as other men, but that the artist must also work as other men and that furthermore, he must work even while these common events of life are going on. It seems a simple and banal assertion, but I learned it hardly, and in one of the worst moments of my life. There is no such thing as an artistic vacuum; there is no such thing as a time when the artist may work in a delightful atmosphere, free of agony that other men must know, or if the artist ever does find such a time, it is something not to be hoped for, something not to be sought for definitely.

At any rate, while my life and energy were absorbed in the emotional vortex which my first book had created, I was getting almost no work done on the second. And now I was faced with another fundamental problem which every young writer must meet squarely if he is to continue. How is a man to get his writing done? How long should he work at writing? and how often? What kind of method, if any, must he find in following his work? I suddenly found myself face to face with the grim necessity of constant, daily work. And as simple as this discovery may seem to everyone, I was not prepared for it. A young writer without a public does not feel the sense of necessity, the pressure of time, as does a writer who has been published and who must now begin to think of time schedules, publishing seasons, the completion of his next book. I realized suddenly with a sense of definite shock that I had let six months go by since the publication of my first book and that, save for a great many notes and fragments, I had done nothing. Meanwhile, the book continued to sell slowly but steadily, and in February 1930, about five months after its publication, I found it possible to resign from the faculty of New York University and devote my full time to the preparation of a second book. That spring I was also fortunate enough to be awarded the Guggenheim Fellowship which would enable me to live and work abroad for a year. And accordingly at the beginning of May, I went abroad again.

I was in Paris for a couple of months, until the middle of July, and although I now compelled myself to work for four or five hours a day, my effort at composition was still confused and broken, and there was nothing yet that had the structural form and unity of a book. The life of the great city fascinated me as it had always done, but also aroused all the old feelings of naked homelessness, rootlessness, and loneliness which I have always felt there. During that summer in Paris, I think I felt this great homesickness more than ever before, and I really believe that from this emotion, this constant and almost intolerable effort of memory and desire, the material and the structure of the books I now began to write were derived.

The quality of my memory is characterized, I believe, in a more than ordinary degree by the intensity of its sense impressions, its power to evoke and bring back the odors, sounds, colors, shapes, and feel of things with concrete vividness. Now my memory was at work night and day, in a way that I could at first neither check nor control and that swarmed unbidden in a stream of blazing pageantry across my mind, with the million forms and substances of the life that I had left, which was my own, America. I would be sitting, for example, on the terrace of a café watching the flash and play of life before me on the Avenue de l'Opéra and suddenly I would remember the iron railing that goes along the boardwalk at Atlantic City. I could see it instantly just the way it was, the heavy iron pipe; its raw galvanized look; the way the joints were fitted together. It was all so vivid and concrete that I could feel my hand upon it and know the exact dimensions, its size and weight and shape. And suddenly I would realize that I had never seen any railing that looked like this in Europe. And this utterly familiar, common thing would suddenly be revealed to me with all the wonder with which we discover a thing which we have seen all our life and yet have never known before. Or again, it would be a bridge, the look of an old

iron bridge across an American river, the sound the train makes as
it goes across it; the spoke-and-hollow rumble of the ties below; the
look of the muddy banks; the slow, thick, yellow wash of an American river; an old flat-bottomed boat half filled with water stogged in
the muddy bank. Or again, it would be an American street with all
its jumble of a thousand ugly architectures. It would be Montague
Street or Fulton Street in Brooklyn, or Eleventh Street in New York,
or other streets where I had lived; and suddenly I would see the
gaunt and savage webbing of the elevated structure along Fulton
Street, and how the light swarmed through in dusty, broken bars,
and I could remember the old, familiar rusty color, that incom-
parable rusty color that gets into so many things here in America.
And this also would be like something I had seen a million times
and lived with all my life.

I would sit there, looking out upon the Avenue de l'Opéra and
my life would ache with the whole memory of it; the desire to see it
again; somehow to find a word for it; a language that would tell its
shape, its color, the way we have all known and felt and seen it. And
when I understood this thing, I saw that I must find for myself the
tongue to utter what I knew but could not say. And from the moment of that discovery, the line and purpose of my life was shaped.
The end toward which every energy of my life and talent would be
henceforth directed was in such a way as this defined. It was as if I
had discovered a whole new universe of chemical elements and had
begun to see certain relations between some of them but had by no
means begun to organize the whole series into a harmonious and
coherent union. From this time on, I think my efforts might be described as the effort to complete that organization, to discover that
articulation for which I strove, to bring about that final coherent
union. I know that I have failed thus far in doing so, but I believe I
understand pretty thoroughly just where the nature of my failure
lies, and of course my deepest and most earnest hope is that the time
will come when I will not fail.

At any rate, from this time on the general progress of the three
books which I was to write in the next four and a half years could
be fairly described in somewhat this way. It was a progress that began in a whirling vortex and a creative chaos and that proceeded
slowly at the expense of infinite confusion, toil, and error toward
clarification and the articulation of an ordered and formal structure.
An extraordinary image remains to me from that year, the year I
spent abroad when the material of these books first began to take on
an articulate form. It seemed that I had inside me, swelling and
gathering all the time, a huge black cloud, and that this cloud was

loaded with electricity, pregnant, crested, with a kind of hurricane violence that could not be held in check much longer; that the moment was approaching fast when it must break. Well, all I can say is that the storm did break. It broke that summer while I was in Switzerland. It came in torrents, and it is not over yet.

I cannot really say the book was written. It was something that took hold of me and possessed me, and before I was done with it— that is, before I finally emerged with the first completed part—it seemed to me that it had done for me. It was exactly as if this great black storm cloud I have spoken of had opened up and, mid flashes of lightning, was pouring from its depth a torrential and ungovernable flood. Upon that flood everything was swept and borne along as by a great river. And I was borne along with it.

There was nothing at first which could be called a novel. I wrote about night and darkness in America, and the faces of the sleepers in ten thousand little towns; and of the tides of sleep and how the rivers flowed forever in the darkness. I wrote about the hissing glut of tides upon ten thousand miles of coast; of how the moonlight blazed down on the wilderness and filled the cat's cold eye with blazing yellow. I wrote about death and sleep, and of that enfabled rock of life we call the city. I wrote about October, of great trains that thundered through the night, of ships and stations in the morning; of men in harbors and the traffic of the ships.

I spent the winter of that year in England from October until March, and here perhaps because of the homely familiarity of the English life, the sense of order and repose which such a life can give one, my work moved forward still another step from this flood tide chaos of creation. For the first time the work began to take on the lineaments of design. These lineaments were still confused and broken, sometimes utterly lost, but now I really did get the sense at last that I was working on a great block of marble, shaping a figure which no one but its maker could as yet define, but which was emerging more and more into the sinewy lines of composition.

From the beginning—and this was one fact that in all my times of hopelessness returned to fortify my faith in my conviction—the idea, the central legend that I wished my book to express had not changed. And this central idea was this: the deepest search in life, it seemed to me, the thing that in one way or another was central to all living was man's search to find a father, not merely the father of his flesh, not merely the lost father of his youth, but the image of a strength and wisdom external to his need and superior to his hunger, to which the belief and power of his own life could be united.

Yet I was terribly far away from the actual accomplishment of a book—how far away I could not at that time foresee. But four more years would have to pass before the first of the series of books on which I was now embarked would be ready for the press, and if I could have known that in those next four years there would be packed a hundred lives of birth and death, despair, defeat, and triumph and the sheer exhaustion of a brute fatigue, I do not know whether or not I could have found the power within myself to continue. But I was still sustained by the exuberant optimism of youth. My temperament, which is pessimistic about many things, has always been a curiously sanguine one concerning time, and although more than a year had now gone by and I had done no more than write great chants on death and sleep, prepare countless notes and trace here and there the first dim outlines of a formal pattern, I was confident that by the spring or the fall of the next year my book would somehow miraculously be ready.

So far as I can describe with any accuracy, the progress of that winter's work in England was not along the lines of planned design, but along this line that I have mentioned—writing some of the sections which I knew would have to be in the book. Meanwhile what was really going on in my whole creative consciousness, during all this time, although I did not realize it at the moment, was this: What I was really doing, what I had been doing all the time since my discovery of my America in Paris the summer before, was to explore day by day and month by month with a fanatic intensity, the whole material domain of my resources as a man and as a writer. This exploration went on for a period which I can estimate conservatively as two years and a half. It is still going on, although not with the same all-absorbing and fanatical intensity, because the work it led to, the work that after infinite waste and labor it helped me wonderfully to define, that work has reached such a state of final definition that the immediate task of finishing it is the one that now occupies my energy and interest.

In a way, during that period of my life, I think I was like the Ancient Mariner who told the Wedding Guest that his frame was wrenched by the woeful agony which forced him to begin his tale before it left him free. In my own experience, my wedding guests were the great ledgers in which I wrote, and the tale which I told to them would have seemed, I am afraid, completely incoherent, as meaningless as Chinese characters, had any reader seen them. I could by no means hope to give a comprehensive idea of its whole extent because three years of work and perhaps a million and a half words went into these books. It included everything from gigantic and staggering lists of the towns, cities, counties, states, and countries

I had been in, to minutely thorough, desperately evocative descriptions of the undercarriage, the springs, wheels, flanges, axle rods, color, weight, and quality of the day coach of an American railway train. There were lists of the rooms and houses in which I had lived or in which I had slept for at least a night, together with the most accurate and evocative descriptions of those rooms that I could write—their size, their shape, the color and design of the wallpaper, the way a towel hung down, the way a chair creaked, a streak of water rust upon the ceiling. There were countless charts, catalogues, descriptions that I can only classify here under the general heading of Amount and Number. What were the total combined populations of all the countries in Europe and America? In how many of those countries had I had some personal and vital experience? In the course of my twenty-nine or thirty years of living, how many people had I seen? How many had I passed by on the streets? How many had I seen on trains and subways, in theaters, at baseball or football games? With how many had I actually had some vital and illuminating experience, whether of joy, pain, anger, pity, love, or simple casual companionship, however brief?

In addition, one might come upon other sections under some such cryptic heading as "Where now?" Under such a heading as this, there would be brief notations of those thousands of things which all of us have seen for just a flash, a moment in our lives, which seem to be of no consequence whatever at the moment that we see them, and which live in our minds and hearts forever, which are somehow pregnant with all the joy and sorrow of the human destiny, and which we know, somehow, are therefore more important than many things of more apparent consequence. "Where now?" Some quiet steps that came and passed along a leafy nighttime street in summer in a little town down South long years ago; a woman's voice, her sudden burst of low and tender laughter; then the voices and the footsteps going, silence, the leafy rustle of the trees. "Where now?" Two trains that met and paused at a little station at some little town at some unknown moment upon the huge body of the continent; a girl who looked and smiled from the window of the other train; another passing in a motorcar on the streets of Norfolk; the winter boarders in a little boardinghouse down South twenty years ago; Miss Florrie Mangle, the trained nurse; Miss Jessie Rimmer, the cashier at Reed's drugstore; Dr. Richards, the clairvoyant; the pretty girl who cracked the whip and thrust her head into the lion's mouth with Johnny J. Jones Carnival and Combined Shows.

"Where now?" It went beyond the limits of man's actual memory.

It went back to the farthest adyt of his childhood before conscious memory had begun, the way he thought he must have felt the sun one day and heard Peagram's cow next door wrenching the coarse grass against the fence, or heard the streetcar stop upon the hill above his father's house at noon; and Earnest Peagram coming home to lunch, his hearty voice in midday greeting; and then the streetcar going, the sudden lonely green-gold silence of the streetcar's absence and an iron gate slamming, then the light of that lost day fades out. "Where now?" He can recall no more and does not know if what he has recalled is fact or fable or a fusion of the two. Where now—in these great ledger books, month after month, I wrote such things as this. Not only the concrete, material record of man's ordered memory, but all the things he scarcely dares to think he has remembered; all the flicks and darts and haunting lights that flash across the mind of man that will return unbidden at an unexpected moment; a voice once heard; a face that vanished; the way the sunlight came and went; the rustling of a leaf upon a bough; a stone, a leaf, a door.

It may be objected, it has been objected already by certain critics, that in such research as I have here attempted to describe there is a quality of intemperate excess, an almost insane hunger to devour the entire body of human experience, to attempt to include more, experience more, than the measure of one life can hold, or than the limits of a single work of art can well define. I readily admit the validity of this criticism. I think I realize as well as anyone the fatal dangers that are consequent to such a ravenous desire, the damage it may wreak upon one's life and on one's work. But having had this thing within me, it was in no way possible for me to reason it out of me, no matter how cogently my reason worked against it. The only way I could meet it was to meet it squarely not with reason, but with life.

It was part of my life; for many years it was my life; and the only way I could get it out of me was to live it out of me. And that is what I did. I have not wholly succeeded in that purpose yet, but I have succeeded better than I at one time dared to hope. And now I really believe that so far as the artist is concerned, the unlimited extent of human experience is not so important for him as the depth and intensity with which he experiences things. I also know now that it is a great deal more important to have known one hundred living men and women in New York, to have understood their lives, to have got, somehow, at the root and source from which their natures came than to have seen or passed or talked with 7,000,000 people upon the city streets. And what finally I should most like to say about this research which I have attempted to describe is this: That foolish and mistaken as much of it may seem, the total quality, end, and impact of that whole experience was not useless or excessive. And from my own point of view, at least, it is in its whole implication the one thing I may have to tell about my experience as a writer which may be of some concrete value to other people. I consider this experience on the whole the most valuable and practical in my whole life thus far as a writer. With all the waste and error and confusion it led me into, it brought me closer to a concrete definition of my resources, a true estimate of my talents at this period of my life, and, most of all, toward a rudimentary, a just-beginning, but a living apprehension of the articulation I am looking for, the language I have got to have if, as an artist, my life is to proceed and grow, than any other thing that has ever happened to me.

I know the door is not yet open. I know the tongue, the speech, the language that I seek is not yet found, but I believe with all my heart that I have found the way, have made a channel, am started on my first beginning. And I believe with all my heart, also, that each man for himself and in his own way, each man who ever hopes to make a living thing out of the substances of his one life, must find that way, that language, and that door—must find it for himself as I have tried to do.

When I returned to America in the spring of 1931, although I had three or four hundred thousand words of material, I had nothing that could be published as a novel. Almost a year and a half had elapsed since the publication of my first book and already people had begun to ask that question which is so well meant, but which as year followed year was to become more intolerable to my ears than the most deliberate mockery: "Have you finished your next book yet?" "When is it going to be published?"

At this time I was sure that a few months of steady work would bring the book to completion. I found a place, a little basement flat in the Assyrian quarter in South Brooklyn, and there I went about my task.

The spring passed into the summer; the summer, into autumn. I was working hard, day after day, and still nothing that had the unity and design of a single work appeared. October came and with it a second full year since the publication of my first book. And now, for the first time, I was irrevocably committed so far as the publication of my book was concerned. I began to feel the sensation of pressure, and of naked desperation which was to become almost maddeningly intolerable in the next three years. For the first time I began to realize that my project was much larger than I thought it was. I had still believed at the time of my return from Europe that I was writing a single book, which would be comprised within the limits of about 200,000 words. Now as scene followed scene, as character after character came into being, as my understanding of my material became more comprehensive, I discovered that it would be impossible to write the book I had planned within the limits I had thought would be sufficient.

. All of this time I was being baffled by a certain time element in the book, by a time relation which could not be escaped, and for which I was now desperately seeking some structural channel. There were three time elements inherent in the material. The first and most obvious was an element of actual present time, an element which carried the narrative forward, which represented characters and events as living in the present and moving forward into an immediate future. The second time element was of past time, one which represented these same characters as acting and as being acted upon by all the accumulated impact of man's experience so that each moment of their life was conditioned not only by what they experienced in that moment, but by all that they had experienced up to that moment. In addition to these two time elements, there was a third which I conceived as being time immutable, the time of rivers, mountains, oceans, and the earth; a kind of eternal and unchanging universe of time against which would be projected the transience of man's life, the bitter briefness of his day. It was the tremendous problem of these three time elements that almost defeated me and that cost me countless hours of anguish in the years that were to follow.

As I began to realize the true nature of the task I had set for myself, the image of the river began to haunt my mind. I actually felt that I had a great river thrusting for release inside of me and that I had to find a channel into which its floodlike power could pour. I knew I had to find it or I would be destroyed in the flood of my own creation, and I am sure that every artist who ever lived has had the same experience.

Meanwhile, I was being baffled by a fixed and impossible idea whose error at the time I did not fully apprehend. I was convinced at that time that this whole gigantic plan had to be realized within the limits of a single book which would be called "The October Fair." It was not until more than a year had passed, when I realized finally that what I had to deal with was material which covered almost 150 years in history, demanded the action of more than 2,000 characters, and would in its final design include almost every racial type and social class of American life, that I realized that even the pages of a book of 200,000 words were wholly inadequate for the purpose.

How did I finally arrive at this conclusion? I think it is not too much to say that I simply wrote myself into it. During all that year, I was writing furiously, feeling now the full pressure of inexorable time, the necessity to finish something. I wrote like mad; I finished scene after scene, chapter after chapter. The characters began to come to life, to grow and multiply until they were numbered by the hundreds, but so huge was the extent of my design, as I now desperately realized, that I can liken these chapters only to a row of lights which one sometimes sees at night from the windows of a speeding train, strung out across a dark and lonely countryside.

I would work furiously day after day until my creative energies were utterly exhausted, and although at the end of such a period I would have written perhaps as much as 200,000 words, enough in itself to make a very long book, I would realize with a feeling of horrible despair that what I had completed was only one small section of a single book.

During this time I reached that state of naked need and utter isolation which every artist has got to meet and conquer if he is to survive at all. Before this I had been sustained by that delightful illusion of success which we all have when we dream about the books we are going to write instead of actually doing them. Now I was face to face with it, and suddenly I realized that I had committed my life and my integrity so irrevocably to this struggle that I must conquer now or be destroyed. I was alone with my own work, and suddenly I knew that I had to be alone with it, that no one could help me with it now no matter how anyone might wish to help. For the first time I realized another naked fact which every artist must know, and that is that in a man's work there are contained not only the seeds of life, but the seeds of death, and that that power of creation which sustains us will also destroy us like a leprosy if we let it rot stillborn in our vitals. I had to get it out of me somehow. I saw that now. And now for the first time a terrible doubt began to creep into my mind that I might not live long enough to get it out of me, that I had created a labor so large and so impossible that the energy of a dozen lifetimes would not suffice for its accomplishment.

During this time, however, I was sustained by one piece of inestimable good fortune. I had for a friend a man who is, I believe, not only the greatest editor of his time, but a man of immense and patient wisdom and a gentle but unyielding fortitude. I think that if I was not destroyed at this time by the sense of hopelessness which these gigantic labors had awakened in me, it was largely because of the courage and patience of this man. I did not give in because he would not let me give in, and I think it is also true that at this particular time he had the advantage of being in the position of a skilled observer at a battle. I was myself engaged in that battle, covered by its dust and sweat and exhausted by its struggle, and I understood far less clearly than my friend the nature and the progress of the struggle in which I was engaged. At this time there was little that this man could do except observe, and in one way or another keep me at my task, and in many quiet and marvelous ways he succeeded in doing this.

I was now at the place where I must produce, and even the greatest editor can do little for a writer until he has brought from the secret darkness of his own spirit into the common light of day the completed concrete accomplishment of his imagining. My friend, the editor, has likened his own function at this painful time to that of a man who is trying to hang on to the fin of a plunging whale, but hang on he did, and it is to his tenacity that I owe my final release. Meanwhile, my creative power was functioning at the highest intensity it had ever known. I wrote at times without belief that I would ever finish, with nothing in me but black despair, and yet I wrote and wrote and could not give up writing. And it seemed that despair itself was the very goad that urged me on, that made me write even when I had no belief that I would ever finish. It seemed to me that my life in Brooklyn, although I had been there only two and a half years, went back through centuries of time, through ocean depths of black and bottomless experience which no ordinary scale of hours would ever measure. People have sometimes asked me what happened to my life during these years. They have asked me how I ever found time to know anything that was going on in the world about me when my life was so completely absorbed by this world of writing. Well, it may seem to be an extraordinary fact, but the truth is that never in my whole life have I lived so fully, have I shared so richly in the common life of man as I did during these three years when I was struggling with the giant problem of my own work.

For one thing, my whole sensory and creative equipment, my powers of feeling and reflection—even the sense of hearing, and above all, my powers of memory, had reached the greatest degree of sharpness that they had ever known. At the end of the day of savage labor, my mind was still blazing with its effort, could by no opiate of reading, poetry, music, alcohol, or any other pleasure, be put at rest. I was unable to sleep, unable to subdue the tumult of these creative energies, and as a result of this condition, for three years I prowled the streets, explored the swarming web of the million-footed city and came to know it as I had never done before. It was a black time in the history of the nation, a black time in my own life and, I suppose, it is but natural that my own memory of it now should be a pretty grim and painful one.

Everywhere around me, during these years, I saw the evidence of an incalculable ruin and suffering. And the staggering impact of this black picture of man's inhumanity to his fellow-man, the unending repercussions of these scenes of suffering, violence, oppression, hunger, cold, and filth and poverty going on unheeded in a world in which the rich were still rotten with their wealth left a scar upon my life, a conviction in my soul which I shall never lose.

And from it all, there has come as the final deposit, a burning memory, a certain evidence of the fortitude of man, his ability to suffer and somehow to survive. And it is for this reason now that I think I shall always remember this black period with a kind of joy that I could not at that time have believed possible, for it was during this time that I lived my life through to a first completion, and through the suffering and labor of my own life came to share those qualities in the lives of people all around me. And that is another thing which the making of a book has done for me. It has given my life that kind of growth which I think the fulfillment of each work does give the artist's life, and insofar as I have known these things, I think that they have added to my stature.

The early winter of 1933 arrived and with it, it seemed to me, the final doom of an abysmal failure. I still wrote and wrote, but blindly, hopelessly, like an old horse who trots around in the unending circle of a treadmill and knows no other end nor purpose for his life than this. If I slept at night, it was to sleep an unceasing nightmare of blazing visions that swept across my fevered and unresting mind. And when I woke, it was to wake exhausted, not knowing anything but work, lashing myself on into a hopeless labor, and so furiously at it through the day and then night again, a frenzied prowling of a thousand streets, and so to bed and sleepless sleep again, the nightmare pageantry to which my consciousness lay chained a spectator.

Such was the state my life had come to in the early winter of 1933, and even at that moment, although I could not see it, the end of my huge labor was in sight. In the middle of December of that year the great editor, of whom I have spoken, and who, during all this tormented period, had kept a quiet watch upon me, called me to his home and calmly informed me that my book was finished. I

could only look at him with stunned surprise, and finally I only
could tell him out of the depth of my own hopelessness, that he was
mistaken, that the book was not finished, that it could never be completed, that I could write no more. He answered with the same
quiet finality that the book was finished whether I knew it or not,
and then he told me to go to my room and spend the next week in
collecting in its proper order the manuscript which had accumulated during the last two years.

I followed his instructions, still without hope and without belief.
I worked for six days sitting in the middle of the floor surrounded
by mountainous stacks of typed manuscript on every side. At the end
of a week I had the first part of it together, and just two days before
Christmas, 1933, I delivered to him the manuscript of "The October
Fair," and a few days later, the manuscript of "The Hills Beyond
Pentland." The manuscript of "The Fair" was, at that time, something over 1,000,000 words in length. He had seen most of it in its
dismembered fragments during the three preceding years, but now,
for the first time, he was seeing them in their sequential order, and
once again his marvelous intuition was right; he had told me the
truth when he said that I had finished the book.

It was not finished in any way that was publishable or readable. It
was really not a book so much as it was the skeleton of a book, but
for the first time in four years the skeleton was all there. An enormous labor of revision, weaving together, shaping, and, above all,
cutting remained, but I had the book now so that nothing, not even
the despair of my own spirit, could take it from me. He told me so,
and suddenly I saw that he was right.

I was like a man who is drowning and who suddenly, at the last
gasp of his dying effort, feels earth beneath his feet again. My spirit
was overwhelmed by the greatest triumph it had ever known, and
although my mind was tired, my body exhausted, from that moment
on I felt equal to anything on earth.

It was evident that many problems were before us, but now we
had the thing, and we welcomed the labor before us with happy
confidence. In the first place there was the problem of the book's
gigantic length. Even in this skeletonized form the manuscript of
"The October Fair" was over a million words in length, which is
about twelve times the length of the average novel or twice the
length of *War and Peace*. It was manifest, therefore, that it would
not only be utterly impossible to publish such a manuscript in a
single volume, but that even if it were published in several volumes, the tremendous length of such a manuscript would practically
annihilate its chances of ever finding a public which would read it.

This problem now faced us, and the editor grappled with it immediately. As his examination of the manuscript of "The October Fair" proceeded, he found that the book did describe two complete and separate cycles. The first of these was a movement which described the period of wandering and hunger in a man's youth. The second cycle described the period of greater certitude, and was dominated by the unity of a single passion. It was obvious, therefore, that what we had in the two cyclic movements of this book was really the material of two completely different chronicles, and although the second of the two was by far the more finished, the first cycle, of course, was the one which logically we ought to complete and publish first, and we decided on this course.

We took the first part. I immediately prepared a minutely thorough synopsis which described not only the course of the book from the first to last, but which also included an analysis of those chapters which had been completed in their entirety, of those which were completed only in part, and of those which had not been written at all, and with this synopsis before us, we set to work immediately to prepare the book for press. This work occupied me throughout the whole of the year 1934. The book was completed at the beginning of 1935, and was published in March of that year under the title of *Of Time and the River*.

In the first place, the manuscript, even in its unfinished form, called for the most radical cutting, and because of the way in which the book had been written, as well as the fatigue which I now felt, I was not well prepared to do by myself the task that lay ahead of us.

Cutting had always been the most difficult and distasteful part of writing to me; my tendency had always been to write rather than to cut. Moreover, whatever critical faculty I may have had concerning my own work had been seriously impaired, for the time being at least, by the frenzied labor of the past four years. When a man's work has poured from him for almost five years like burning lava from a volcano; when all of it, however superfluous, has been given fire and passion by the white heat of his own creative energy, it is very difficult suddenly to become coldly surgical, ruthlessly detached.

To give a few concrete illustrations of the difficulties that now confronted us: The opening section of the book describes the journey of a train across the state of Virginia at night. Its function in the book is simply to introduce some of the chief characters, to indicate a central situation, to give something of the background from which the book proceeds, and perhaps through the movement of the train across the stillness of the earth to establish a certain beat, evoke a certain emotion which is inherent to the nature of the book.

Such a section, therefore, undoubtedly serves an important function, but in proportion to the whole purport of the book, its function is a secondary one and must be related to the whole book in a proportionate way.

Now in the original version, the manuscript which described the journey of the train across Virginia at night was considerably longer than the average novel. What was needed was just an introductory chapter or two, and what I had written was over 100,000 words in length, and this same difficulty, this lack of proportion, was also evident in other parts of the manuscript.

What I had written about the great train was really good. But what I had to face, the very bitter lesson that every one who wants to write has got to learn, was that a thing may in itself be the finest piece of writing one has ever done, and yet have absolutely no place in the manuscript one hopes to publish. This is a hard thing, but it must be faced, and so we faced it.

My spirit quivered at the bloody execution. My soul recoiled before the carnage of so many lovely things cut out upon which my heart was set. But it had to be done, and we did it. And so it went all up and down the line. Chapters 50,000 words long were reduced to ten or fifteen thousand words, and having faced this inevitable necessity, I finally acquired a kind of ruthlessness of my own, and once or twice, myself, did more cutting than my editor was willing to allow.

Such, then, were some of our major difficulties with the manuscript we had in hand, and although since its publication there have been many declarations to the effect that the book would have benefited by a much more radical cutting, the cutting we did do was much more drastic than I had dreamed was possible.

Meanwhile I was proceeding at full speed with the work of completing my design, finishing the unfinished parts and filling in the transition links which were essential.

This in itself was an enormous job and kept me writing all day long as hard as I could go for a full year. Here again the nature of my chief fault was manifest. I wrote too much again. I not only wrote what was essential, but time and time again my enthusiasm for a good scene, one of those enchanting vistas which can open up so magically to a man in the full flow of his creation would overpower me, and I would write thousands of words upon a scene which contributed nothing of vital importance to a book whose greatest need already was ruthless condensation.

During the course of this year, I must have written well over a half million words of additional manuscript, of which, of course, only a small part was finally used.

The nature of my method, the desire fully to explore my material, had led me into another error. The whole effect of those five years of incessant writing had been to make me feel not only that everything had to be used, but that everything had to be told, that nothing could be implied. Therefore, at the end, there were at least a dozen additional chapters which I felt had be completed to give the book its final value. A thousand times I debated this question desperately with my editor. I told him that these chapters had to go in simply because I felt the book would not be complete without them, and with every argument he had, he tried to show me that I was wrong. I see now that on the whole he was right about it, but at the time I was so inextricably involved in my work, that I did not have the detachment necessary for a true appraisal.

The end came suddenly—the end of those five years of torment and incessant productivity. In October I took a trip to Chicago, a two weeks' vacation, my first in over a year. When I returned I found that my editor had quietly and decisively sent the manuscript to the press, the printers were already at work on it, the proof was beginning to come in. I had not foreseen it; I was desperate, bewildered. "You can't do it," I told him, "the book is not yet finished. I must have six months more on it."

To this he answered that the book was not only finished, but that if I took six months more on it, I would then demand another six months and six months more beyond that, and that I might very well become so obsessed with this one work that I would never get it published. He went on to say, and I think with complete justice, that such a course was wrong for me. I was not, he said, a Flaubert kind of writer. I was not a perfectionist. I had twenty, thirty, almost any number of books in me, and the important thing was to get them produced and not to spend the rest of my life in perfecting one book. He agreed that with six months' additional work upon the book, I might achieve a certain finish and completeness, but he did not think that the benefit would be nearly as great as I thought it would be, and his own deep conviction was that the book should be published at once without further delay, that I should get it out of me, forget about it, turn my life to the final completion of the work which was already prepared and ready, waiting for me. He told me, furthermore, exactly what the nature of the criticism would be, the criticism of its length, its adjectives, its overabundance, but he told me not to despair.

He told me finally that I would go on and do better work, that I would learn to work without so much confusion, waste, and useless torment, that my future books would more and more achieve the unity, sureness, and finality that every artist wants his work to have, but that I had to learn in the way I had learned, groping, struggling, finding my own way for myself, that this was the only way to learn.

In January 1935, I finished the last of my revisions on the proof; the first printed copies came from the press in February. The book was released for final publication early in March. I was not here when it came out. I had taken a ship for Europe the week before, and as the ship got farther and farther from the American shores, my spirits sank lower and lower, reaching, I think, the lowest state of hopeless depression they had ever known. This, I believe, was largely a physical reaction, the inevitable effect of relaxation upon a human organism which had for five years been strained to its utmost limit. My life seemed to me to be like a great spring which had been taut for years and which was now slowly uncoiling from its tension. I had the most extraordinary sense of desolation I had ever known when I thought about my book. I had never realized until now how close I had been to it, how much a part of me it had become, and now that it had been taken away from me, my life felt utterly futile, hollow as a shell. And now that the book was gone, now that there was nothing more that I could do about it, I felt the most abysmal sensation of failure. I have always been somewhat afraid of print, although print is a thing I have tried so hard to achieve. Yet it is literally true that with everything I have ever written, I have felt when the hour of naked print drew nigh a kind of desperation and have even entreated my publisher not only to defer the publication of my book until another season, but have asked the editors of magazines to put off the publication of a story for another month or two until I had a chance to work on it some more, do something to it, I was not always sure what.

Now I had an overwhelming sense of shame greater than any I have felt before. I felt as if I had ruinously exposed myself as a pitiable fool who had no talent and who once and for all had completely vindicated the prophecies of the critics who had felt the first book was just a flash in the pan. It was in this frame of mind that I arrived in Paris on March 8, the day the book was to be published in America. I had come away to forget about it, and yet I thought about it all the time. I prowled the streets from night to morning, at least a dozen times in two short weeks I heard the celebration of Mass at Sacré Cœur, and then would walk the streets again and come back to my hotel at ten o'clock and lie upon the bed, and still I could not sleep.

After several days of this, I steeled myself to go to the office of the travel agency where a message might be waiting for me. I found a cablegram there. It was from my publisher, and it said simply: "Magnificent reviews somewhat critical in ways expected, full of greatest praise." I read it the first time with a feeling of almost intolerable joy but as I continued to read and reread it, the old dark doubt began to creep across my mind and by the time night had come I was convinced that this wonderful cable was just a sentence of doom, and that my editor, out of the infinite compassion of his spirit, had taken this means of breaking the news to me that my book was a colossal failure.

Three days passed in which I prowled the streets of Paris like a maddened animal, and of those three days I could later remember almost nothing. At the end of that time I sent a frenzied cablegram to that editor in which I told him I could stand anything better than this state of damnable uncertainty and pleaded with him to give me the blunt truth no matter how bitter it might be. His answer to this cable was such that I could no longer doubt him or the reception which the book had had at home.

This completes, as far as I can remember it, the story of the making of a book and what happened to its maker. I know it is too long a story; I know, also, that it must seem to be a story filled with the record of a man's blunders and ludicrous mistakes, but simply because it is that kind of story, I hope that it may have some value. It is a story of the artist as a man and as a worker. It is a story of the artist as a man who is derived out of the common family of earth and who knows all the anguish, error, and frustration that any man alive can know.

The life of the artist at any epoch of man's history has not been an easy one. And here in America, it has often seemed to me, it may well be the hardest life that man has ever known. I am not speaking of some frustration in our native life, some barrenness of spirit, some arid Philistinism which contends against the artist's life and which prevents his growth. I do not speak of these things because I do not put the same belief in them that I once did. I am speaking as I have tried to speak from first to last in the concrete terms of the artist's actual experience, the nature of the physical task before him. It seems to me that that task is one whose physical proportions are vaster and more difficult here than in any other

nation on the earth. It is not merely that in the cultures of Europe
and of the Orient the American artist can find no antecedent
scheme, no structural plan, no body of tradition that can give his
own work the validity and truth that it must have. It is not merely
that he must make somehow a new tradition for himself, derived
from his own life and from the enormous space and energy of
American life, the structure of his own design; it is not merely
that he is confronted by these problems; it is even more than this,
that the labor of a complete and whole articulation, the discovery
of an entire universe and of a complete language, is the task that
lies before him.

Such is the nature of the struggle to which henceforth our lives
must be devoted. Out of the billion forms of America, out of the
savage violence and the dense complexity of all its swarming, million-footed life; from the unique and single substance of this land
and life of ours, must we draw the power and energy of our own
life, the articulation of our speech, the substance of our art.

For here it seems to me in hard and honest ways like these we
may find the tongue, the language, and the conscience that as men
and artists we have got to have. Here, too, perhaps, must we who
have no more than what we have, who know no more than what
we know, who are no more than what we are, find our America.
Here, at this present hour and moment of my life, I seek for mine.

HOW I WRITE
SHORT STORIES

by W. Somerset Maugham

A noted English novelist and short-story writer explains the evolution of one of his most popular works, a story called "Rain" which was later to become a famous movie.

JULY 28, 1934

WHEN I BEGAN TO WRITE short stories I was fortunately in a position of decent independence and I wrote them as a relief from work which I thought I had been too long concerned with. Most of them were written in groups from notes made as they occurred to me, and in each group I left naturally enough to the last those that seemed most difficult to write. A story is difficult to write when you do not know *all* about it from the beginning, but for part of it must trust to your imagination and experience. Sometimes the curve does not intuitively present itself and you have to resort to this method and that to get the appropriate line.

I beg the reader not to be deceived by the fact that a good many of my stories are told in the first person into thinking that they are experiences of my own. This is merely a device to gain verisimilitude. It is one that has its defects, for it may strike the reader that the narrator could not know all the events he sets forth; and when he tells a story in the first person at one remove, when he reports, I mean, a story that someone tells him, it may very well seem that the speaker, a police officer, for example, or a sea-captain, could never have expressed himself with such facility and with such elaboration. Every convention has its disadvantages. These must be as far as possible disguised and what cannot be disguised must be accepted. The advantage of this one is its directness. It makes it possible for the writer to tell no more than he knows. Making no claim to omniscience, he can frankly say when a motive or an occurrence is unknown to him, and thus often give his story a plausibility that it might otherwise lack. It tends also to put the reader on intimate terms with the author. Since Maupassant and Chekhov, who tried so hard to be objective, nevertheless are so nakedly personal it has sometimes seemed to me that if the author can in no way keep himself out of his work it might be better if he put in as much of himself as possible. The danger is that he may put in too much and thus be as boring as a talker who insists on monopolizing the conversation. Like all conventions this one must be used with discretion.

In early youth I had written a number of short stories, but for a long time, twelve or fifteen years at least, occupied with the drama, I had ceased to do so; and when a journey to the South Seas unexpectedly provided me with themes that seemed to suit this medium, it was as a beginner of over forty that I wrote the story which is now called "Rain." Since it caused some little stir the reader of this article will perhaps have patience with me if I transcribe the working notes, made at the time, on which it was constructed. They are written in hackneyed and slipshod phrases, without grace; for nature has not endowed me with the happy gift of hitting instinctively upon the perfect word to indicate an object and the unusual, but apt, adjective to describe it. I was traveling from Honolulu to Pago Pago and, hoping they might at some time be of service, I jotted down, as usual, my impressions of such of my fellow-passengers as attracted my attention. This is what I said of Miss Thompson:

> Plump, pretty in a coarse fashion, perhaps not more than twenty-seven. She wore a white dress and a large white hat, long white boots from which the calves bulged in cotton stockings.

There had been a raid on the Red Light district in Honolulu just before we sailed and the gossip of the ship spread the report that she was making the journey to escape arrest. My notes go on:

> *W. The Missionary.* He was a tall thin man, with long limbs loosely jointed, he had hollow cheeks and high cheek bones, his fine, large, dark eyes were deep in their sockets, he had full sensual lips, he wore his hair rather long. He had a cadaverous air and a look of suppressed fire. His hands were large, with long fingers rather finely shaped. His naturally pale skin was deeply burned by the tropical sun. *Mrs. W. His Wife.* She was a little woman with her hair very elaborately done, New England; not prominent blue eyes behind gold-rimmed pince-nez, her face was long like a sheep's, but she gave no impression of foolishness, rather of extreme alertness. She had the quick movements of a bird. The most no-

ticeable thing about her was her voice, high, metallic, and
without inflection; it fell on the ear with a hard monotony,
irritating to the nerves like the ceaseless clamor of a pneu-
matic drill. She was dressed in black and wore round her
neck a gold chain from which hung a small cross. She told me
that W. was a missionary on the Gilberts and his district consisting of widely separated islands he frequently had to go
distances by canoe. During this time she remained at headquarters and managed the mission. Often the seas were very
rough and the journeys were not without peril. He was a
medical missionary. She spoke of the depravity of the natives
in a voice which nothing could hush, but with a vehement,
unctuous horror, telling me of their marriage customs which
were obscene beyond description. She said, when first they
went it was impossible to find a single good girl in any of the
villages. She inveighed against dancing.

I talked with the missionary and his wife but once, and with
Miss Thompson not at all. Here is the note for the story:

A prostitute, flying from Honolulu after a raid, lands at
Pago Pago. There lands there also a missionary and his wife.
Also the narrator. All are obliged to stay there owing to an
outbreak of measles. The missionary finding out her profession persecutes her. He reduces her to misery, shame, and re-
pentance, he has no mercy on her. He induces the governor
to order her return to Honolulu. One morning he is found
with his throat cut by his own hand and she is once more
radiant and self-possessed. She looks at men and scornfully
exclaims: dirty pigs.

The reader may have observed that in the original note of
"Rain" the narrator was introduced, but in the story as written
omitted. "Rain" was invented by the accident of my happening
upon persons here and there, who in themselves or from something
I heard about them, suggested a theme that seemed suitable for a
short story. This brings me to a topic that has always concerned
writers and that has at times given the public, the writers' raw material, some uneasiness. There are authors who state that they never
have a living model in mind when they create a character. I think
they are mistaken. They are of this opinion because they have not
scrutinized with sufficient care the recollections and impressions
upon which they have constructed the person who, they fondly
imagine, is of their invention. If they did they would discover that,
unless he was taken from some book they had read, a practice by

no means uncommon, he was suggested by one or more persons they had at one time known or seen. The great writers of the past made no secret of the fact that their characters were founded on living people. We know that the good Sir Walter Scott, a man of the highest principles, portrayed his father, with sharpness first and then, when the passage of years had changed his temper, with tolerance; Henri Beyle, in the manuscript of at least one of his novels, has written in at the side the names of the real persons who were his models; and this is what Turgenev himself says: "For my part, I ought to confess that I never attempted to create a type without having, not an idea, but a living person, in whom the various elements were harmonized together, to work from. I have always needed some groundwork on which I could tread firmly."

With Flaubert it is the same story; that Dickens used his friends and relations freely is notorious; and if you read the Journal of Jules Renard, a most instructive book to anyone who wishes to know how a writer works, you will see the care with which he set down every little detail about the habits, ways of speech and appearance, of the persons he knew. When he came to write a novel he made use of this storehouse of carefully collected information. In Chekhov's diary you will find notes which were obviously made for use at some future time, and in the recollections of his friends there are frequent references to the persons who were the originals of certain of his characters. It looks as though the practice were very common. I should have said it was necessary and inevitable. Its convenience is obvious. You are much more likely to depict a character who is a recognizable human being, with his own individuality, if you have a living model. The imagination can create nothing out of the void. It needs the stimulus of sensation. The writer whose creative faculty has been moved by something peculiar in a person (peculiar perhaps only to the writer) falsifies his idea if he attempts to describe that person other than as he sees him. Character hangs together and if you try to throw people off the scent, by making a short man tall for example (as though stature had no effect on character), or by making him choleric when he has the concomitant traits of an equable temper, you will destroy the plausible harmony (to use the beautiful phrase of Baltasar Gracian) of which it consists. The whole affair would be plain sailing if it were not for the feelings of the persons concerned. The writer has to consider the vanity of the human race and the *Schadenfreude* which is one of its commonest and most detestable failings. A man's friends will find pleasure in recognizing him in a book and though the author may never even have seen him will point out to him, especially if it is unflattering, what they consider his living image. Often someone will recognize a trait he knows in himself or a description of the place he lives in and in his conceit jumps to the conclusion that the character described is a portrait of himself. Thus in my story called "The Outstation" the Resident was suggested by a British Consul I had once known in Spain and it was written ten years after his death, but I have heard that the Resident of a district in Sarawak, which I described in the story, was much affronted because he thought I had had him in mind. The two men had not a trait in common. I do not suppose any writer attempts to draw an exact portrait.

Nothing, indeed, is so unwise as to put into a work of fiction a person drawn line by line from life. His values are all wrong, and, strangely enough, he does not make the other characters in the story seem false, but himself. He never convinces. That is why the many writers who have been attracted by the singular and powerful figure of the late Lord Northcliffe have never succeeded in presenting a credible personage. The model a writer chooses is seen through his own temperament and if he is a writer of any originality what he sees need have little relation with the facts. He may see a tall one short or a generous one avaricious; but, I repeat, if he sees him tall, tall he must remain. He takes only what he wants of the living man. He uses him as a peg on which to hang his own fancies. To achieve his end (the plausible harmony that nature so seldom provides) he gives him traits that the model does not possess. He makes him coherent and substantial. The created character, the result of imagination founded on fact, is art, and life in the raw, as we know, is of this only the material.

The odd thing is that when the charge is made that an author has copied this person or the other from life, emphasis is laid only on the less praiseworthy characteristics of the victim. If you say of a character that he is kind to his mother, but beats his wife, everyone will cry: Ah, that's Brown, how beastly to say he beats his wife; and no one thinks for a moment of Jones and Robinson who are notoriously kind to their mothers. I draw from this the somewhat surprising conclusion that we know our friends by their vices and not by their virtues. I have stated that I never even spoke to Miss Thompson in "Rain." This is a character that the world has not found wanting in vividness. Though but one of a multitude of writers my practice is doubtless common to most, so that I may be permitted to give another instance of it. I was once asked to meet at dinner two persons, a husband and wife, of whom I was told only what the reader will shortly read. I think I never knew their names.

I should certainly not recognize them if I met them in the street.
Here are the notes I made at the time:

A stout, rather pompous man of fifty, with pince-nez, gray-
haired, a florid complexion, blue eyes, a neat gray mustache.
He talks with assurance. He is resident of an outlying district and is somewhat impressed with the importance of his
position. He despises the men who have let themselves go
under the influence of the climate and the surroundings.
He has traveled extensively during his short leaves in the
East and knows Java, the Philippines, the coast of China
and the Malay Peninsula. He is very British, very patriotic;
he takes a great deal of exercise. He has been a very heavy
drinker and always took a bottle of whisky to bed with him.
His wife has entirely cured him and now he drinks nothing
but water. She is a little insignificant woman, with sharp
features, thin, with a sallow skin and a flat chest. She is
very badly dressed. She has all the prejudices of an English-
woman. All her family for generations have been in second-
rate regiments. Except that you know that she has caused her
husband to cease drinking entirely you would think her
quite colorless and unimportant.

On these materials I invented a story which is called "Before the
Party." I do not believe that any candid person could think that
these two people had cause for complaint because they had been
made use of. It is true that I should never have thought of the
story if I had not met them, but anyone who takes the trouble to
read it will see how insignificant was the incident (the taking of
the bottle to bed) that suggested it and how differently the two
chief characters have in the course of writing developed from the
brief sketch which was their foundation.

"Critics are like horseflies which prevent the horse from plough-
ing," said Chekhov. "For over twenty years I have read criticisms
of my stories, and I do not remember a single remark of any value
or one word of valuable advice. Only once Skabichevsky wrote
something which made an impression on me. He said I would die
in a ditch, drunk." He was writing for twenty-five years and during
that time his writing was constantly attacked. I do not know
whether the critics of the present day are naturally of a less ferocious temper; I must allow that on the whole the judgment that has
been passed on my own stories when from time to time a collection has been published in book form has been favorable. One
epithet, however, has been much applied to them, which has

puzzled me; they have been described with disconcerting frequency as "competent." Now on the face of it I might have thought this laudatory, for to do a thing competently is certainly more deserving of praise than to do it incompetently, but the adjective has been used in a disparaging sense and, anxious to learn and if possible to improve, I have asked myself what was in the minds of the critics who thus employed it. Of course none of us is liked by everybody and it is necessary that a man's writing, which is so intimate a revelation of himself, should be repulsive to persons who are naturally antagonistic to the creature he is. This should leave him unperturbed. But when an author's work is fairly commonly found to have a quality that is unattractive to many people it is sensible of him to give the matter his attention. There is evidently something that a number of people do not like in my stories and it is this they try to express when they damn them with the faint praise of competence. I have a notion that it is the definiteness of their form. I hazard the suggestion (perhaps unduly flattering to myself) because this particular criticism has never been made in France where my stories have had with the critics and the public much greater success than they have had in England.

The French, with their classical sense and their orderly minds, demand a precise form and are exasperated by a work in which the ends are left lying about, themes are propounded and not resolved and a climax is foreseen and then eluded. This precision on the other hand has always been slightly antipathetic to the English. Our great novels have been shapeless and this, far from disconcerting their readers, has given them a sense of security. This is the life we know, they have thought, with its arbitrariness and inconsequence; we can put out of our minds the irritating thought that two and two make four. If I am right in this surmise I can do nothing about it and I must resign myself to being called competent for the rest of my days. My prepossessions in the arts are on the side of law and order. I like a story that fits. I did not take to writing stories seriously till I had had much experience as a dramatist, and this experience taught me to leave out everything that did not serve the dramatic value of my story. It taught me to make incident follow incident in such a manner as to lead up to the climax I had in mind. I am not unaware of the disadvantages of this method. It gives a tightness of effect that is sometimes disconcerting. You feel that life does not dovetail into its various parts with such neatness. In life stories straggle, they begin nowhere and trail off without a point. That is probably what Chekhov meant when he said that stories should have neither a beginning nor an end. It is certain that sometimes it gives you a sensation of airlessness when you see persons who behave so exactly according to character and incidents that fall into place with such perfect convenience. The storyteller of this kind aims not only at giving his own feelings about life, but at a formal decoration. He arranges life to suit his purposes. He follows a design in his mind, leaving out this and changing that; he distorts facts to his advantage, according to his plan; and when he attains his object produces a work of art. He seeks to prove nothing. He paints a picture and sets it before you. You can take it or leave it.

GOD'S LITTLE ACRE

by Lawrence S. Kubie, M.D.

"Out of the modern temper . . . there has arisen a . . . group of books: one in which sex is treated frankly and seriously, and yet with a confused pattern of tension and distortion." In these words a noted psychiatrist prefaces his analysis of Erskine Caldwell's novel God's Little Acre, *an analysis that has become a classic of its kind.*

NOVEMBER 24, 1934

MEN HAVE ALWAYS known that the romantic picture of love and marriage is false. They have known that the eager yearnings of adolescence meet with strangely bitter disappointments in the effort to translate themselves into the realities of adult experience. Only recently, however, has any understanding come of why this is true, through the realization that, from childhood on, each step in Everyman's psychosexual evolution is taken in the face of opposing forces which threaten to drive him from the path of normal development. If then the impulse to write and to read bears any relation to human needs, it would seem to be inevitable that a struggle which begins in earliest years and continues throughout life must find insistent expression in literature. It is not strange, therefore, that novelists and readers have always been concerned with sex.

To meet the needs of different temperaments, however, literature assumes varied forms. The simplest and most childlike response to disappointment is to retreat into phantasies in which the frustrated yearnings are gratified. In this way simple people can console themselves with the adolescent and sentimental prevarications of the movies and the cheap magazines. Even the better forms of the romantic novel serve essentially the same simple need. Such writings might therefore be called the romantic and consolatory literature of sex.

More complicated temperaments cannot make use of this elementary device of phantasy and romance; but instead react to disappointment with bitterness and irony, which expresses itself in an effort to belittle that which is unobtainable. Much of the so-called "classical" erotic literature satisfied the needs of such readers; Ra-

belais and Casanova, Boccaccio and Cellini. But whether it be naïve
or sophisticated, romantic or ironical and bitter, all of this literature constitutes merely varying forms of literary escape. In neither
group is sex recognized as a serious, perplexing, and vital human
problem.

Out of the modern temper, however, there has arisen a third
group of books: one in which sex is treated frankly and seriously,
and yet with a confused pattern of tension and distortion. These
books form the great bulk of the so-called morbid modern literature, a literature which attempts not merely a safe and literary
escapade in sex, but rather a mirror of the moving realities of sexual
problems in all their intricacy.

Certainly a compelling drive to portray and solve the problems
of sexual unrest and dissatisfaction is not an obscene or morbid
purpose. Yet just as the problem play will be violently attacked
while the naked revue passes unmolested, so, too, the cheap and
"sexy" magazine, or the subtler waggery of classical erotica, will be
accepted unprotestingly by the very people who raise the cry that
these modern books are deliberately capitalizing the morbid and
perverse in human nature. In other words, an honest and vivid
literature, which is struggling to express the confused problems of
sex, arouses such hostile, uncomfortable, and suspicious feelings,
that it is attacked as dirty, obscene, sick, useless, ugly, etc. This is a
strange and paradoxical social phenomenon, the explanation of
which may lead to a deeper understanding of the psychological and
artistic significance of these books.

The most obvious point is that the protesting reader has been
made uncomfortable in a special and peculiar way. Furthermore,
not only is he uncomfortable, but he is resentfully aroused as well;
and it is out of this constellation of feelings that he throws up the
epithet "obscene."

To define what is meant by obscenity is impossible, because the
word does not carry quite the same implications to any two people.
Nor is there any one type of scene or phrase which will make all
people squirm. Yet the experience is almost universal, a feeling
which everyone has encountered and can recognize, even if its
effective stimulus varies from one human being to another. And
since it is universal, it must have some common underlying quality.

This experience might well be called the "sense of the obscene,"
and with regard to it we will take as our premise: (1) that a reader's phantasies, be they conscious or unconscious, arise from his personal needs; (2) that this angry, resentful sense of the obscene arises
when confused and troubling unconscious phantasies are stirred

into activity; (3) that this happens when such phantasies have been awakened in the reader by the vigor of the author's art.*

From what has been said already it should be clear that our search leads directly into the problem of psychosexual illness. The difficult lifelong struggle toward adult normality is pursued through a maze of infantile and childish impulses, which, though normal enough at their own levels, become disturbing if they persist with dominating force into adult life. It is inevitable, therefore, that in a literature which deals with a blind groping toward normal sexuality one should find much of the psychopathology of sex dramatized in literary expression. This will appear chiefly in descriptions of adult distortions of infantile impulses; and it is just here that the reader, either for lack of technical knowledge, or because of inner problems, is most likely to mistake the portrayal of distorted sexual development for the manifestations of a supernormal lustiness and release. Often enough the picture of sickness is taken for an example of a greater freedom. It becomes therefore a most difficult problem to estimate the esthetic significance of this confused borderland between sickness and health.

Since no problem in science or in art can be solved by generalizations alone, our first step must be to subject a typical example of this literature to a frankly psychoanalytic scrutiny. To do this one must use the tale and the people and their words as dreamlike products of imagination, dissecting the story for the conscious and unconscious content of the characters' minds or acts to see how much of sickness or of health lies within its pages.

For this purpose we have chosen the novel, *God's Little Acre*, by Erskine Caldwell, first published in the spring of 1933 by the Viking Press. It is an earthy and vivid story of Southern whites, who struggle in the land, and in town, and in their bodies to reach some kind of peace. And because here and there this struggle is infused with activity which is technically known as "perverted," the book drew upon itself the curiosity of all and the wrath of many.

In the tale, as in a dream, there are confused and kaleidoscopic shifts forward and backward between desolate farm land and a

---

* This statement can be misunderstood because it sounds as though I were denying that there is anything which merits the epithet "obscene." This is because I have not been concerned in my discussion with the deliberately obscene but rather with the angry defensiveness with which serious literature often is attacked on grounds of obscenity when it is, in fact, an effort to portray the confusion of the human spirit in dealing with its most complex instinctual process. The deliberately obscene exploits and titillates where the dedicated artist attempts gropingly to express and to illuminate.

turbulent strike-weary mill town; from deep pit holes in the red and yellow clay to hilly eminences, from swamp land to solid earth. Unlike an actual dream, however, the movement from scene to scene is carried along on a thread of story; whereas in a dream which has not been artificially elaborated the episodes would follow one another without even this pretense of conscious reason. To the analyst, therefore, the story serves as a rationalization, an effort to give an appearance of logical order to the sequence of free phantasies. This conscious elaboration of spontaneous phantasy succeeds in making the tale appear simple and realistic; but it also interjects elements which are extraneous to the fundamental dreamlike structure. It is necessary, therefore, to confine the analytic interpretation to the main outlines of the story, considering only the characters and their outstanding acts.

As in many dreams, one may recognize two groups of characters, those that are clear and those that are vague. There are some shrouded and ominous figures who hover dimly in the background, like those unseen persons in a dream whose presence one senses but never sees. There are others who stand out with all the hallucinatory vividness of the lions and tigers of a child's nightmare. Their clarity is a tribute to the author's skill, particularly because, despite their sharp outlines, they retain their fantastic and unreal quality; and when closely examined these figures fuse until they seem to become different aspects of a single human spirit, split up by a legitimate and effective literary artifice into the semblances of separate beings.

Among all the characters one finds no living mother in the book. Yet everywhere throughout the tale brood the spirits of unhappy, frustrated, and forgotten mothers, dimly seen, yet constituting the essential but unrecognized object of all the conflict which the story contains. The figures of women can be arrayed in order from the most dim to the clearest; and then one sees that the shadowy figures are the frank mother-images, and that as the figures of women become clearer the maternal role is distorted more and more toward perversion and prostitution. It is as if the book were saying that the only good woman is a dead and legendary mother—and that even there danger and sin may lurk.

First there is old Mrs. Walden, who, before the tale is begun, has died of heartbreak because her oldest son was ashamed of her. She is a dim phantasy of a good mother, dead and therefore forever unattainable. Then there is the witchlike figure of Gussie, supposedly diseased and hoarding gold, whom this oldest son had married and with whom he hid himself away. This is the "bad woman," "the sterile mother," no mother at all and yet more mother than wife, who is heard wandering eerily off-stage and who never appears directly in the action of the book.

The first woman to emerge even dimly from these shadows is Rosamond, Ty Ty Walden's oldest daughter, and the wife of Will Thompson. She remains vague in outline, but at least she is alive. She weeps in the background of the story, taking humbly and gratefully what Will has left over to give her, mothering him, feeding him, spanking him with her hairbrush when she catches him *flagrante delicto* with her younger sister, Darling Jill. Then she tries in a sudden rage to shoot him; but in the end she mourns his death in a paroxysm of grief.

And finally come the only two clear and vivid women in the tale, standing as the direct objects and instruments of primitive lusts. One is Griselda, the wife of Buck Walden, the daughter-in-law in the Walden family, no mother in spirit or in fact, but whose body stands to all the men as a perverse symbol for nursing. The other is Darling Jill, the youngest Walden daughter, who devotes her life to conquering men with her body, insatiable and destructive, tantalizing men, using them, throwing them aside, demanding pain as her only physical joy, and turning for peace at the last to the fat, infantile, and eunuchoid figure of "Pluto."

This much, then, can be safely concluded: that in this tale are found only certain limited conceptions of women. There are good mothers who are dead, good mothers who suffer, bad mothers who hoard their sustenance and will not share, mothers who breed and transmit disease, erotic mothers whose bodies exist to nurse men, and women who exist only to destroy. There is no image of a woman whose body is to be loved as an adult—genitally, confidently, happily, tenderly, reproductively. By some undefined magic of the moon, as Ty Ty Walden says, no act of intercourse in the book results in the conception of a child. In the confused and childlike phantasy, babies would seem to be conceived and born in some other manner; and, as we shall see, sex itself comes to mean either nursing or destruction.

It is the result of a deep inner logic then that the book is a story in symbolic language of the struggle of a group of men to win some fantastic kind of sustenance out of the body of the earth, the "body" of factories, and the bodies of women; and that the living women struggle through the mazes of a queer, disjointed, erotic travail to give sustenance or death to the bodies of men. Throughout the book the recurring themes are those of food (watermelons, hams, grits, and ice cream); or of biting, grabbing, sucking, and licking; and of haunted efforts to rend or tear or suck or bite out of the bowels of the earth a golden magical food. Furthermore, since in the tale nursing and intercourse have become confused and interchangeable yearnings, it is logical that the chief protagonists should chant obsessively the beauty of a woman's breasts, that the woman's body should always be described in unreal terms more applicable to a man's, and finally that the woman's body itself should be transformed into a fantastic well at which a man may slake his thirst, and ease with his mouth a torment of neurotic and perverse cravings.

But who are the men in this confused and fantastic tale, who play out their needs against these figures of women? First, there is Ty Ty Walden, an old man and a widower, seeking endlessly for gold by digging into the bowels of his farm, rendering his land sterile with mounds of earth from fruitless excavations. Despite his years he digs as a child might, because his "Daddy" told him there was gold in the ground, and because of the echoing rumor that Negroes have found nuggets. His gold fever is an obsession, which in his life has taken the place of women and drink. He is sensitive, visionary, a mute artist with an eye for beauty in painting and an ear for beauty in words; but he lives out his lusts and fears at a childlike level. With his words he arouses other men's fever equally to hunt for gold or to assault his daughter-in-law, Griselda. But, for himself, he is afraid of women, afraid that they "wear a man to a frazzle." He is willing to look at them but not to go too near them; and even when he looks upon Darling Jill in the very arms of Dave, he does not take in what he sees, but stands uncomprehending as a child. With his eyes he feasts on the body of his daughter-in-law, Griselda, yet he thinks of her and of his yearning for her as though she "were inside" him, as though his erotic impulses were "the rising up of something deep within" his own body. And he carries this feminine identification further by likening himself and Griselda "to a hen with a lone chick."

As an expression of these strange phantasies we find that his objective energy is directed solely toward tearing things out of the earth as if it were a human body; and that when the ground won't yield it up, he flails it like a reluctant living thing. Nor is it strange that he talks of science, yet resorts to a Negro "conjur," until finally he effects a confused compromise between the white man's science and the Negro's magic by capturing in a swamp the albino, Dave, to use him as his divining instrument, an all-white figure fashioned out of the black mud with which to combine white magic and black.

Furthermore, to Ty Ty the things of the spirit also lie within the body. His formulation of religion is that "God resides inside one," that "there are secret things hidden in every man," that "one hunts for the things that are inside and brings them to the outside." Thus it is clear that his gold hunt, his erotic obsession, and his religion are all part of one confused and largely unconscious system of obsessive phantasies. *He is fascinated and yet terrified by that which lies within the body.* Therefore he cannot approach the body; and though he is an old man, he is still a child, interested in the outside that he can see with his eyes, an aged Peeping Tom. Finally, and like a baby, he is concerned with the earthy products of the body, prizing that which other men discard, heaping mudpies while he hopes to find in the mud the seed of a supreme and golden treasure.

Will Thompson is Ty Ty's son-in-law, the husband of Rosamond. He is the effective instrument of Ty Ty's frustrated desires; for it is through Will that Ty Ty mates with both of his daughters and his daughter-in-law.

By trade Will is a weaver of cloth who lives and works in the town; yet it is his obsessive ritual to tear cloth into tiny pieces when he turns on the power in the mill; and similarly he must tear to pieces the garments of Griselda when he is about to attack her. For Will, then, intercourse, "to turn on the power," must be preceded by a rending or tearing or deflorating; whereas weaving is like repair and restitution. Will is thus portrayed as a violent man, a "male man" to the Negroes, the man whom all women seek and whom all other men hate and envy. With his own words, he likens himself to an almighty and omnipotent phallus. When aroused, his whole body plays this role. He compares his strength to that of "God Almighty." Yet all of this megalomanic phantasy of power can be punctured by a bullet; and in the end he is punished by death for his presumption, that is for his assault upon Griselda and his assault upon the mills.

Thus the bravado and pretended invulnerability of Will cover simple human weakness; and like all weak mortals he must restore himself with food, the most primitive of all restoratives. So Will is pictured as a hungry man who eats as the women wait upon him, and who is brought home by the lure of food; and in his final frenzy it is the mouth which becomes the focus of all his erotic desires. To Will, as to an infant, the most fundamental contact between bodies is through eating; and because his expressed phantasy of himself is of his whole body as a phallus his mouth becomes the instrument of the phantasy.

The other five male figures are less clear and less important fragments. Each of them is dominated by anxiety. None is in any true sense living. These figures of men nurse and dig and beat and threaten, or they peep and yearn and blush. They never love. They never procreate. Their women are either dim shadows of mothers out of the past, or destroying women of the vivid present. It is out of the stuff of phantasies such as these that sickness itself arises.

It is necessary to stress the elimination of the author from our study, because the book has frequently been spoken of as "sick," a characterization which might be taken as meaning that the author was sick as well. Such a deduction is not at all warranted on the basis of what is evident from the book. The relationship of an author to his work is always complex; and to judge of an entire man from an isolated fragment of his stream of conscious or unconscious thought would be both unscientific and unsound. We can speak with some measure of confidence only of that which we have in hand, namely the book itself, and draw no conclusions about the author.

Readers of the book can be observed directly, however, and one finds them to be variously affected. Some are carried away by the compelling picture of unchecked passion, finding in this a vicarious freedom from their own habitual restraints. Others react with violent and unhesitating aversion. More often, however, they are likely to be fascinated, repelled, and puzzled, all at the same time, hardly knowing whether to envy the characters for their unchecked and hypothetical lustiness, or to look down upon them as sick and bad. Thus we find the reader either caught by the lure of illness which masquerades as primitive power, or stirred by deeply buried impulses within himself which respond to the picture which is painted, or yet revolted at times and resentful of a note of arrogance which he may feel in the protagonists of the tale.

It is inevitable that a book which stirs deep and confused phantasies or feelings must exert a fascination upon the sensitive reader. Whether in any individual in whom such confused misconceptions are active, the inner turmoil will ever break out in active sickness is a matter which depends upon too many variable factors to allow of any generalizations. One can say with confidence, however, that among healthy readers it is unlikely that such a picture of illness could cause a serious disturbance, and that it is highly probable that anyone whose precarious balance could be upset by the book would have been shaken in any case by the pressure of his own sick inner needs. One need not feel too anxious, therefore, about the influence of the book upon the health of the reader; although one may deplore the confusion which the book may churn up within him.

And still, perhaps, the question remains, why such books are, or should be. To that the only answer possible is that they are because they have to be. As long as there is a group of people who cannot be fooled or consoled by romance, whether it be cheap and tawdry or delicate and sophisticated; as long as there are those who refuse to content themselves with the cold comfort of an ironical sneer; and as long as those who reject either of these escapes have courage and honesty, there will be a literature which seeks to write its way out of confusion and restraint into some pathway of passionate relief and happiness. It would seem to be inevitable that in all such literature the portrayal of illness must play a role.

For some readers one may be sure that there is achieved at times a therapeutic relief of feeling through the translation of inner problems into literary forms. For society at large, the question of the value of this literature is more difficult. On the one hand, such books to some extent inevitably break up bigoted and inhibited attitudes toward the body; but on the other hand, when, as in *God's Little Acre,* the values are confused, the book may seem to attempt to set up as standards of high normality forms of behavior which are in reality the expression of potential sickness. In all probability, with the passing of years, and with the deepening and clarifying growth of psychoanalytic knowledge, and the subjection of this new material to the needs of art, much of this confusion will gradually be eliminated. In the meantime it must be borne in mind that the search for beauty leads through strange fields; and that to touch deep chords in human nature, even those chords which are burdened with potential illness, may have subtler values than it is possible as yet to characterize.

THE SOURCES OF
ANTHONY ADVERSE

by Hervey Allen

*Far and away the best-selling novel of the early thirties was a com-
paratively unknown writer's historical romance entitled* Anthony
Adverse, *a book which boasted a total sale of more than a million
copies. In the Letters column of SRL one of the magazine's
readers pointed out some striking word-for-word similarities between Allen's novel and at least one widely known history of the
period, thereby inferring that Allen had been guilty of plagiarism.
The author's reply in defense of himself, here reprinted in its entirety, became one of the magazine's more unusual literary contributions.*

JANUARY 13, 1934

So MANY QUESTIONS have been asked in public and in private as to
the sources of *Anthony Adverse* that I feel it right to make a statement not only in behalf of my book but of historical romance in
general.

When *Anthony Adverse* was first published the question of providing it with an introduction and a bibliography was carefully
discussed. After careful consideration it was decided not to do so, for
reasons which I still feel to have been entirely pertinent and convincing.

In the first place, the book was already bulky, and there was also
the consideration that to furnish forth a huge romantic novel with
all the apparatus of historical introduction, notes, and a long bibliography would have been to give at first sight to reviewers, to the
book trade, and to the so important first readers a totally wrong
slant as to the nature of its contents. Considering that the author
was known in prose as a biographer, had his first novel appeared
disguised as an historical treatise or a scholarly dissertation upon
some historical period, with all references to authorities and sources
provided, it might have been taken for what it would have been
made to appear to be—a ponderous and erudite work upon an obscure and remote subject.

Furthermore, it is not the custom to provide novels with bibliographies and references to sources. Quite the contrary. To the general reader of fiction notes and the like are a nuisance and a stumbling block—and there was no more reason why they should be provided in the case of *Anthony Adverse* than in a thousand other cases.

At the time of publication no one, of course, foresaw that *Anthony Adverse* would have the enormous number of readers it has attained. Among them are many who have paid the novel the inadvertent compliment of taking it for actual history or biography. Indeed, there are some who insist that it is nothing but a mass of incidents and characters, taken piecemeal from books written during the epoch with which it deals and loosely strung together. There are even quite a few who assert that they are descended from, or related to, characters who appear in the book—and who are demanding further information about their relatives in no uncertain terms.

Now this is at once flattering, amusing, or annoying, as the case may be. For if the author takes the trouble to assure one of his correspondents, for instance, that someone in the novel is an imaginary character, his correspondent is both disappointed and angry and replies indignantly that he knows that this is not so. He has read about the original of the character, he has letters from him, he is living in a house built by him, etc., etc., etc.—and "P.S. We never knew Uncle was married. Did he have any children?"

Then there is the kind of person who is a small collector, a "great reader," or a specialist in some byway of time, who happens to have a copy of a book from which certain incidents in the novel are drawn. He can seldom resist writing the editor of the literary column that he *knows* just where the novel was taken from. "Plagiarism, by the gods! Put the author on the spot, Mr. Editor, and (incidentally) tell the world what a clever, erudite, and entirely right-minded man is Percy Q. Smith who watches thus over the annals of literature."

Among a million readers or so there are bound to be a number of Percy Q. Smiths. They do not realize that, if their basis of indignation were to be admitted, no more historical novels could be written, for there is only one way to write an historical novel and that is to use fully any material out of any book anywhere, always providing the material is reworked and reshaped into that new entity which is from the novelist's own mind.

After all, how do people who are given to grousing about the use of historical sources suppose that a novel like *Anthony Adverse* can be written? It is placed in time considerably over a century ago. The author, of course, was not alive then. Nor is there anyone left who was. Is the author, then, supposed to go into a trance and return with his story verbatim by some mystic intuition or "inspiration"? Or does he, like all the tribe of historical novelists before him, find that verisimilitude of the intricacy of incident in times past in the written records, the books, diaries, letters, and documents of the era which he is depicting? Of course he does—because he must.

So there is no doubt about the fact that many incidents in *Anthony Adverse* came from old books, etc. I should think that fact would have been too obvious to be seriously pointed out. The mere fact that *Anthony Adverse* is an historical novel *admits* it. People who make the "discovery" that there is old material in the book, and who solemnly insist upon pointing it out, are, of course, at liberty to do so. But they are also, I must be permitted to add, enormously naïve, and undertaking with a deal of pedantry to peddle no news and no scandal. They are simply elaborating the obvious. And the more elaborate the "proof" is, the more silly it becomes.

For the question is not whether material from certain sources was used, or even what was used, but *how* the material was used, and I propose at this time and in this place to be explicit about my use of source material for *Anthony Adverse*. I propose to tell where, in the main, it came from, what I did with it—and why.

In the first place, then, at least two thirds of the book is not immediately taken from any historical or literary source material at all. It came directly from my own imagination as the result of a lifetime of experience and general reading. It took shape in thought from a thousand events, people, places, and books that I can no longer trace myself, and which it is only ludicrous for me to see attributed to this or that printed source, as though everything in literature was always taken out of cold storage and nothing ever home-grown. There was not a great deal of formal research connected with the book. I did not haunt libraries to get up my subject, nor did I card-index my material. That is in this case nonsense. Only those who wish to be highly instructive go in for "creative research." I desired to amuse, and I began by amusing myself.

I began by making a story about an orphan. It was disjointed and tattered at first. I saw the last scene of his life plainly even before I was aware of many of the prior events. It is the scene where Anthony cuts down the tree, on page 1219 of the novel.

Then I saw that the beginning of my hero's life was vaguely like that of a real man whose biography I had once written, Edgar Allan Poe. There was also an old man, a Scotchman, in it, not the boy's father and yet in a strange paternal relation to him. I knew the old Scotchman's name was Bonnyfeather and that he was a Jacobite, because he said so himself when he was talking to various people in the dream scene in which I met him. I could tell what kind of person he was from the kind of room he lived in. But that room was at first in Florence, and that troubled me. For I could not understand just what an old Scotch Jacobite was doing in Florence during what seemed to be the days of the reign of the last of the Medici dukes. It did not fit historically. Yet I kept on trying to explain it to myself.

Then I had an argument with a British Colonial official one night at dinner at his home in Bermuda and was told I should at least read the life of Nelson if I intended to be dogmatic about the British Navy.

I took the hint and did so—and that, I think, is how *Anthony Adverse* really came to be written.

In the life of Nelson I read how he had evacuated the English from Leghorn, or Livorno, during the Napoleonic wars "where there were then many English factories and Scotch merchants of sorts." That, as I recall it, was the phrase that, as it were, "pulled the trigger."

For I saw instantly that Mr. Bonnyfeather had not lived at Florence at all but at Leghorn, and without any further trouble I instantly saw just why he lived there. I understood most of his life history. And that story, the first incident completed for the book, is the one Mr. Bonnyfeather tells Anthony in Chapter Fifteen.

It was not plain to me yet, however, how the orphan, whom, according to my plan, Mr. Bonnyfeather was to "father," had got into the old Scotchman's house. I had to invent the reason for that. I felt sure that once I could get my hero, as yet unnamed, into the old Scotchman's house, I should have him under the influence which would make his character and out of that nucleus the whole story would grow.

In order to bring about this meeting I invented the whole first book of the novel which contains the story of Anthony's conception and birth.

By this time I was already beginning to work with a rather careful chronology and I found that my young orphan was left at the convent on St. Anthony's Day. That is actually why I gave him the name of Anthony. I had no idea for some time what his last name was to be. I determined to let the story find that out for itself. For the tale had by this time begun to captivate me, and I was already beginning to look forward into Anthony's life and to foresee some of his adventures.

Little of this, of course, had been written down. Some of it was in the form of a few notes and character sketches on paper. The narrative thread, unfinished, remained wholly in my mind. But I had begun to know some of my people and I had started Anthony growing up.

I then wrote a sketchy chapter about the life of the child at the convent, which was a decided flop. But I consoled myself by going on and trying to reconstruct the life at the Casa da Bonnyfeather in Leghorn, with which I succeeded better. Whenever Mr. Bonnyfeather appeared all seemed to go well. I could see his house quite plainly. I used his room as I had first imagined it. I built the rest of the house around it, and the people, and began to read on Leghorn.

I read the history of the city. I got some old maps of the place and two old prints showing the waterfront. I obtained an Italian book by one Francesco Pera called *Curiosita Livornesi Medite o Rare* in which there was a mine of information biographical, literary, and historical, as well as many curious anecdotes and traditions. I had to labor over this with a dictionary because I do not speak Italian. But I culled several bits of information, some of them humorous, and I persisted also with another Italian book called *Epilogo Alfabitico dei Livornesi*. Then I found a veritable mint of information where no laborious translation was necessary: *Livorno, con 149 Illustrazioni*. This gave me a new idea as to the gathering of material for an historical novel and from then on I depended, whenever I could obtain them, upon contemporary pictures and prints. Before the book was finished, years later, I had seen or examined hundreds of old prints.

When the story again began to occur to me almost a year had passed. Meanwhile, I had been doing a great deal of reading. I read mostly at night, generally all night, and with complete absorption. Morning is always a surprise to me. I sometimes go through two fair-sized books in a night.

When I went to Bermuda in the autumn of 1927 I took with me several thousand volumes. Among them was a chest of old books that had come to me as a legacy from a great-uncle, one William Hervey Allen, a steamboat captain, who for years made the run regularly from Pittsburgh to New Orleans. He not only commanded but also owned the steamships *Norma* and *New Hampshire*.

Both he and his younger brother, George Allen, kept voluminous diaries, several volumes of which I have. They are beautifully bound and full of drawings and sketches, and abound with personal incident, anecdotes, and amusing biographical sketches of passengers and friends at various cities and plantation landings from Pittsburgh to New Orleans.

These diaries, which are now being edited by my sister, Mrs. Helen Hunt, constitute in an intimate but not explicit way the general background for much of the feeling of the age in *Anthony Adverse*. Through them I attained that sense of the importance of the city of New Orleans and of the Great River Valley of which it was "the head and capital," which feeling penetrates the ninth book of the novel.

In tracing literary sources too much stress is always put upon some particular incident that can be quoted and explicitly pointed out as having been suggested by one author to another. The sources to which one is really most indebted are those which give one a general grasp of the "time feeling" and a knowledge of how and why men acted and the fashion of manners that they employed at any given epoch. In that respect I must name as vital in the case of *Anthony Adverse* the diaries of my great-uncles.

My uncle's chest had not been opened for many years. All told there were nearly three hundred books with the remains of the "library" of the steamship *Norma*. I read them all with avidity; with nothing in mind but the pleasure of doing so and the personal contact it gave me with my great-uncle William whose notes filled many a margin. Many of these volumes were also annotated by passengers on the ship, in some cases by the authors of the books themselves, who had presented them to the captain en route. The books ranged from early American editions of Keats and other poets English and American through all kinds of obscure biographies and autobiographies of American and foreign travelers of the early nineteenth century. A number of these were books printed by local presses along the route. Among them was a *Life of Harman Blenner-hasset* issued at Cincinnati, and a number of books about Burr and his trial and his great conspiracy. I used them to some extent in the little section of the novel called "The Odyssey of Mrs. Udney," page 1116. About the same time that I was reading these books of my uncle, many of which dealt with New Orleans, I was led to reread Lafcadio Hearn's sketches of New Orleans which were first published in the newspapers of that city. These, it is true, dealt with a later period of the city, but the atmosphere was the same. I began vaguely to project a river story about New Orleans, and then my old story of the boy Anthony began to recur to me strongly.

I determined to bring him to New Orleans. It then occurred to me that in my great-uncle's chest was probably the material for much of the later life of my hero, who would, since he was born in the last quarter of the eighteenth century, live on well into the nineteenth.

I now began for the first time to read deliberately for the purpose of gathering material and with my own story in mind. I found among other books my uncle had collected Kendall's *Santa Fé Expedition*. From that I drew, introducing considerable differences and details from a great number of other books, principally histories of the Southwestern states and histories of Spain and New Mexico—all standard texts and available to anybody who can use a card index—the material used in the novel from Chapter Sixty-five on. For this section of the book I should also name as general sources General Pike's report to the War Department of his expedition in the Southwest. There are various versions of this. And a well-known piece of Americana called *Commerce of the Prairies* and the diary of my own grandfather, Colonel Edward Jay Allen, who crossed the plains at an early date. From all this data I used in particular the prison scene in Mexico City from the *Santa Fé Expedition* and the descriptions of early El Paso before the American occupation. The incident of the sled-riding grizzly bear came from a magazine article on grizzlies which I now cannot trace but distinctly remember. Many of the later scenes in the novel which take place at La Luz were provided from stories related to me by a Mrs. Sutherland of El Paso, Texas, who a good many years ago had lived at La Luz and was familiar with the strange sect of the Penitentes. I also read a good deal of the literature about them. In fact, I became thoroughly acquainted with Penitentes. The incident of the kettle mending on page 1217 was provided by Mrs. Sutherland. The last scenes of the novel take place on a mountain not far from El Paso, now called Cloud Croft, and well known to the people of that city. I visited it myself, and it must be remembered of all this Southwestern section depicted in the later pages of *Anthony Adverse* that I am personally familiar with it from my army experience on the Mexican border in 1916. I actually walked over much of the trail covered by Anthony.

It was thus that I now had the beginning and the end of my story thoroughly in mind. In mind, for very little of this was actually set down. I made a few notes and kept on collecting my narrative mentally.

But I had now come to several important conclusions about my story. I could see that in the first book of Anthony's birth I had a prelude. I had the end of my story in America. I then composed and actually wrote the epilogue almost as it now stands, for I had come to realize that my hero was to be a wanderer whose experience would cover several continents and I began also to realize him as a kind of epitome of the early American man whose origins were European and whose later life was lived in America after immigration.

And I also saw that all the men of the time were enthralled by business and that if I was going to give a true picture of the era I must involve my hero thoroughly in worldly affairs. For that purpose I went to the library and did my first piece of deliberate research. I read, in order to get a general glimpse of the epoch, a series of trade reports, piles of newspapers, and yearbooks from before the American Revolution to about 1842. I got the general grasp of the main economic trends of the early nineteenth century as seen by contemporary newspaper comment. I let the theorists alone.

The immense role of Napoleon in the economic history of the era was, of course, all along apparent. I felt inclined to involve my hero in Continental affairs and to take him to Paris near Napoleon. As the personification of thought in action, of the word "go" of which so much is made in the novel, I began to see Napoleon playing an important part in my story. He was to be the personification of the spirit of energy in the Occident, but as yet I was at a loss how to motivate my story to get Anthony to Paris. I continued my reading on various visits to America and began to buy reference books with my story in mind. Later, while I was writing the novel, I came across a portrait and part of the story of Mlle. Georges, the mistress of Napoleon, in Herbert Gorman's *The Incredible Marquis*. That first gave me the idea of having Angela turn up in Paris as Mlle. Georges and provided the impulse for much of the Parisian interlude.

Of my reading about this time I find the following notes: *Memoirs of William Hickey; The Diary of the Rt. Honourable William Windham; Memoirs of Napoleon Bonaparte,* by Bourrienne, his secretary; *Biographie Nouvelle des Contemporains, ou Dictionnaire historique et raisonné de tous les hommes qui, depuis la Révolution Française, ont acquis de la célébrité,* Paris 1820. Ouvrard, whose history fascinated me, finally led me to Spain. I had also become aware of the great role played by the house of Baring in the affairs of those days and I read practically all the biographical material connected with the members of that remarkable family.

The correspondence of Alexander Baring, later Lord Ashburton, led me by chance to the diary of the son of the Swiss banker Gallatin, Secretary of the United States Treasury. This is a charming diary and from the character of young Gallatin was suggested the temperament with which I wished to endow Anthony.

From a portrait published in the *Memoirs of William Hickey,* that of a certain Mr. Potts I think, I found the physical type I wished my hero to have.

I also note the following bits of reading: five or six volumes in theology, the "Ante-Nicene," "Nicene," and "Post-Nicene Fathers"; *Studies of Aryanism,* by one Gwatkin, M. A.; *The Education of Henry Adams; Mont-Saint-Michel and Chartres;* hymn written to the Virgin by Henry Adams shortly before he died.

From all these, in some curious way, came the idea of the Madonna, who, be it said, is not to be found in any museum as so many of my correspondents have inferred. I also read a whole shelf of volumes called the *Annual Biography and Obituary,* London, printed for Longman, Hurst, Rees, Orme, and Brown of Paternoster Row. It begins in 1817 and continues on into a delightful infinity of time and persons. Also a pamphlet by Sir Francis Baring, *Observations on the Establishment of the Bank of England,* London, 1797.

From all this material a good many things in the novel were later projected: Anthony's letters from London in Chapter Fifty-seven; part of the material about the House of Baring; the death of Anthony's wife at New Orleans. This tragedy had a double background. It was suggested to me by the great fire in the *Saga of Burnt Nial.*

In two old books which I found in my uncle's collection—*Fifty Years in Both Hemispheres* and *Captain Canot: or Twenty Years of an African Slaver*—I found a double thread of experience which covered the period I was working in and which provided the suggestion for one of my principal characters, Vincent Nolte.

I was first led to read Vincent Nolte's book from the fact that it began in Leghorn, upon which I had already assembled so much material. The great banking scheme upon which Nolte was engaged, bringing silver from Mexico through the United States and reshipping it to Napoleon, provided the material for the connecting link in my plot between Europe and America, and the same was true of Canot's slaving enterprise. *I combined the two stories in their main outlines* as a part of my narrative covering that portion of my hero's life from the time he left Italy until he got to Spain. The idea of taking him to New Orleans had already occurred to me. I found that Nolte's banking scheme would also serve to motivate that.

I was now at a crucial point in my story, none of which was really written down. It was as yet nothing but a dream. But I had a vast amount of material and the outline of a rather vague and wandering narrative which seemed to have about it a strange degree of vigor whose possibilities I was sure I had not yet tapped.

For I did not as yet really see what the story was "about." It was just a sort of composite biographical plot drawn from hundreds of sources—I have named only a few here—that might provide a rope of narrative upon which to hang a series of loosely constructed incidents.

I then sat down, in May 1929, and wrote out only the narrative of the story. Then I began to think over just how I would poise the whole book—what angle I would give it.

Three things became evident: First, I must have a well-integrated and complex plot by which to shape the enormous amount of material that constantly kept swarming into the narrative, for my mind was now working at great speed and concentration. Second, I must so poise or slant this story as to give it an acceptable and if possible valuable—shall I call it "philosophical"?—message to a modern audience. And third, I must make it, if possible, reasonably acceptable to the best critical thinking of my own time. Without a very distinct scheme which would serve to compress and shape the rather amorphous story of my hero's life as I had first conceived it in sheer narrative, I saw I should be lost.

I, therefore, invented the following scheme. It was rather arbitrary but it worked. In looking over my narrative I thought I saw three main themes running through it. I rearranged it on that basis. Then I took the hint of "three" and projected it further. I so planned my story as to write it on the basis of what I called "three times three." There were to be three novels, three books in each novel, and three themes running through the entire work. I also determined to present the development of each one of these three themes in three separate bits of imagery at crucial points in my hero's life on the basis that the arrangement of three gave me the chance to treat each theme with a beginning, a climax, and an end. The three various themes that ran through the book I called: The Vision of Light; the religious, or ethical, or philosophical theme, mystical if you will, shadowed forth by the Madonna; the Dionysian theme of the eating and drinking, the lusting and loving and hating, which, in contrast to the Madonna or spiritual theme, represented the things of the flesh and the lure of the world.

When I had once evolved this scheme and applied it to my material, the results were almost magical. The whole narrative resolved itself into a genuine new entity with shape and meaning. I saw the inherent slant of it. I began to envisage Anthony as a more universal type as well as an individual. I saw that my big story was not really romantic but rather classical in that it subordinated the individual to the whole. And I also found that it divided itself, under a logical plot treatment, into rather precise periods of a given length: to wit, "nine books." With my story now thoroughly ordered, I began to see the interplay of the characters who had already entered into it. And out of this interplay of personalities and events a great number of other characters developed themselves. I was now ready to sit down and actually begin to write the book. I had my narrative and critical abstract completely drawn out and set down on paper. In other words, I "knew" the story. I knew most of my people, and I felt the pressure of a thousand incidents constantly arising.

Something quite personal to the author, but also in a curious way vital to the book, now occurred. I was taken extremely ill and underwent an all but fatal operation. It took me weeks to recover, but in that time of quiet convalescence I had the complete leisure thoroughly to realize my story in all its details and meanings. I also had the time to consider whether it was really worth while to me. I felt an honest conviction that it was; that it might possibly, if I could ever finish it, mean a great deal to many people.

I emerged from the hospital prepared to face the labor of composition, determined to carry it through, and to leave behind me if possible a book that would have in it some of the richness and beauty, the enormous complexity, and yet something of the great and simple principles upon which I conceived life to be conducted. Above all, I desired to reassert some of the prime values which I had found in life.

Since these notes on the composition of the book are written after the event of publication, and may therefore have the appearance of an afterthought, I wish at this time to point out that this entire scheme for *Anthony Adverse* and the narrative of the plot were placed in the hands of my publishers four years before the book was completed. That scheme as then outlined was departed from only in a few minor particulars. The novel was to have been delivered in two years. Its composition required four.

Considerable discussion has arisen as to my use of certain material suggested above, namely, the book by Vincent Nolte and *Captain Canot: or Twenty Years of an African Slaver.* I shall answer that directly now.

In the first place, all the "fury" of discovery over the Nolte book is ridiculous. Vincent Nolte is one of the main characters in my novel. I have used ideas and facts from his book freely, which I had a perfect right to do. It is in the public domain and has been well known for years. Copies of it have been a drug on the old book market. There was nothing to prevent my publishing whole extracts verbatim from it if I had so desired. But I did not do so. In fact, in all of *Anthony Adverse* there are only a few phrases quoted directly from Nolte's book or from any other book. The main thing which I did use from Nolte's *Fifty Years in Both Hemispheres* was the outline of the story of the great financial plot in which Vincent was engaged. But even this in the novel *is not at all as related by Vincent Nolte.*

In fact, I soon discovered that for his own reasons Nolte in his autobiography—it is not a novel—was not to be relied upon as to what actually happened. The truth is, he was an old gossip who told his personal story with an unavoidable personal bias in favor of Nolte.

It was, therefore, necessary for me to restudy the banking operations of the entire Napoleonic era, to delve into the personal story of Ouvrard and his relations with the court of Spain and the French Empire, to dig into the history of the House of Rothschild, and to reassemble the material I had already gone over in regard to the Barings. In short, with infinite trouble and patience it was necessary thoroughly to familiarize myself with the whole economic history of the Napoleonic era. The truth, the story of what really happened, is enormously different from the small personal glimpse of the particular scheme in which Nolte, the real Nolte, was engaged only as a clerk or factor and as a very small cog in a big wheel. For his services he was later on given a pittance by the Barings and turned loose.

The real story of his later life is a painful one, full of poverty and failure, of desperate little shifts and rather shady enterprises. In real life he was an unimportant, enormously conceited, and quite a self-important man. Yet withal lovable I think, and with pleasant traits. Audubon in his diary mentions meeting him, and there exist some letters between Vincent Nolte and Lafayette.

Now in the novel I used neither the story of the Mexican financial venture as given by Nolte nor that of actual history. I used one which suited my own needs. It was a sort of combination of Nolte's story with what actually happened plus certain additions and vital changes of my own to suit the story I was telling. The whole date of the financial scheme was shifted back several years. The importance of Ouvrard as the originator of the whole was given due prominence and the entire French and Spanish sections of the novel grew out of that. For the Spanish section alone I read fifty or sixty books dealing with the reign of Charles IV, and a host of others about Spain. I shall name only a few of them later. With all of this Nolte had little to do. Indeed, his use, so far as my writing was concerned, was to put me on to a great deal of material that fitted into my plan.

Part of the apparent parallel of Vincent Nolte's book with *Anthony Adverse* arises undoubtedly from the fact that "Vincent Nolte" appears as the friend of Anthony Adverse in my novel. But the Vincent Nolte of my novel is *not* the Vincent Nolte of the autobiography. He is, in all but a few minor characteristics, an entirely different person. And I should like to make the point here that in the novel Vincent is a much finer, a more capable, loyal, and cultured type than his own memoirs indicate. In fact, I entirely, or almost entirely, discarded the life story of the real Vincent and presented him as a new man that I created myself with a larger role, a more ample stage in places other than those in which he actually appeared, and a more profound grasp of life. In short, except for a few minor incidents, I recreated him. The same is true of Ouvrard. I used some incidents from his true story, mostly financial, and recreated him as a character and as a type. In fact, I used Ouvrard (my character) to satirize certain types of modern bankers. I wish to insist upon this as the true test of how a novelist is using his material. It is of no use to point out that this and that incident is taken from Nolte or this and that person. Yes, the incident is taken occasionally, but it is always entirely reshaped. If a name is used, a new character is created to fit it.

Nolte mentions the fact that a Mr. Udney was British Consul at Leghorn. Out of that mere mention I developed the whole Udney family, with the complete story of Florence, Anthony's wife, the complicated character of her mother, and the story of Florence's first marriage to David Parish, which is all pure fiction. Parish himself is out of the whole cloth, except for one or two incidents. The real David Parish returned to Europe and later drowned himself in the Danube, after becoming involved in a contest with the Rothschilds. My David Parish dies of heart disease on the Ohio while on a purely imaginary quest, married to a woman who never existed. The whole French incident, in which the imaginary Nolte figures so largely at the House of the Wolf in Paris, is absolutely imaginary. The real Nolte had no such experiences whatever. The House of the Wolf was suggested by a paragraph in Lucas' *A Wanderer in Paris,* that mentions a similar place, and much of the rest of the incidents at Paris came from material on the life of Talleyrand or from data on the Rothschilds. I might also add that the character of the Rothschild partner given in the novel is largely imaginary. A few facts are elaborated upon. In all this kind of thing it would be wise if those who insist upon pointing out parallels between a novel and its sources should also be requested to mention the differences. I wish I could also convey the fact, in some way, that Dr. Terry Mitchell never existed. The several persons in both New Orleans and Philadelphia who think they are living in houses connected with him are mistaken. Neither did Edward Livingston of New Orleans come out of Nolte. He was a famous New Orleans character of the early days. The amount of material covered in my study of early New Orleans days precludes giving it in detail unless in a separate article. There again I was not following Nolte. Nor does Anthony's experience in New Orleans at all correspond to that of the real Vincent Nolte's. Not only are they not identical; they are enormously dissimilar. I should also like to add that all the letters in the novel were written by me. There is not even one sentence quoted from anywhere. Those who complain that I have in certain instances merged imaginary and historical characters as in the case of Angela and Mlle. Georges have no real complaint. Why pick on me? Dumas, Cooper, Scott, a thousand novelists have done just that. It is a device of fiction. If people are fooled by it that proves that it is effective. For one aim of a novel *is* to project a fictitious character as real.

Another small controversy has arisen over the fact that a considerable portion of the material used in the African section of *Anthony Adverse* was drawn from *Captain Canot: or Twenty Years of an African Slaver.* That is true. What of it? The material I used was entirely reshaped. This book is also in the public domain. It has long been known as a source book for the history of slavery on the West Coast of Africa and was recently republished. It has been used extensively, far more extensively than I used it, for writing the history of Liberia and the West Coast. I took some names, incidents, and considerable local atmosphere from it. Nor did I paraphrase. For instance, Canot mentions that at Regla in Havana lived a grocer by the name of Carlo Cibo who was a friend of his. He gives a few lines about him. Turn to Chapter Twenty-nine of the novel and you will see what has happened.

The same is true of the African incidents and the life about Gallegos which I created with the characters who lived there. It is a complete novel in itself. And I ask, what resemblance after all does it bear to Canot's story? An extremely remote one. About the same relation that the early chapters of *Henry Esmond* bear to Thackeray's source material.

Furthermore, Canot was *not* the principal source of my material for the African adventure in *Anthony Adverse*. The book I used persistently for facts and background is *Liberia,* by Sir Harry Johnston, with an appendix on the flora of Liberia by Dr. Otto Staff, with 28 colored illustrations by Sir Harry Johnston, 24 botanical drawings by Miss Matilda Smith, 402 black-and-white illustrations from the author's drawings and from photographs by the author and others, 22 maps by Mr. J. W. Addison, Capt. H. T. Pearson, and others (2 vols. London: Hutchinson. 1906).

Whether or not this provides a more fertile source of material than Canot I leave to anyone who cares to compare the two books. Nor was this all. I used *Wanderings in West Africa,* by Richard Burton: *An Essay on Colonization Particularly Applied to the West Coast of Africa,* by C. B. Wadström (London, 1794); also *The African Republic of Liberia and the Belgian Congo,* based on the observations made and material collected during the Harvard African expedition 1926-1927, which appeared while I was writing the novel, I think. I also referred frequently to a book called *A Transformed Colony, Sierra Leone,* by T. J. Alldridge (London, 1910), and of course to *The Golden Bough* for a general slant on the use of magic on the West Coast. Nor does this exhaust the books on Africa that I turned to. I made pages and pages of notes on African tribes and languages, on the flora and fauna, on the climate, and even on the prevailing winds. Altogether I must have consulted fifty or sixty books for the African background, and I repeat that to single out Canot as the only source or even the main source of the African adventure is simply to be mistaken. There was no more reason why I should give "credit" to him than to a lot of other books. And what would the reader have thought if a whole mass of technical references to source material or notes as to where I learned this or that fact had been printed in the novel? Also what possible harm can this use of material in my novel do to Canot's book or to anyone else's? I was not using any plots or stories created by anybody. I was supplying myself from the domain of history, biography, and technical literature with certain facts to fit into the background of a romance. Every novelist has done this since novels began. Is Defoe to be condemned because he used the narrative of Alexander Selkirk in *Robinson Crusoe?* If so, the writing of fiction is at an end.

For those curious about the Spanish section of the novel there still remains the discovery that I used quite extensively certain incidents from Théophile Gautier's *A Wanderer in Spain* and another famous book about Gypsies in Spain, which is well known to all those who read anything at all about Spain. I read the memoirs of Godoy, the Prince of the Peace, and used some incidents out of that, and a book about Spanish court etiquette, whose title I forget, and for a large part of the particulars about inns, streets, types of people, and remote and curious places I used a really great book, one that deserves to be much better known than it is, one from which the whole history of Spain can be drawn if one desires to do so. This is a *Guide Book to Spain* in two volumes, written during the early nineteenth century by an English don, one Mr. Richard Ford of humor whimsical and learning prodigious. Indeed, I was so captivated by Mr. Ford and his works that I not only used the material from his guidebook to guide me, but I put Mr. Ford himself right into my novel together with the gentleman to whom he dedicated his guidebook. And you will find them both introduced on page 1007. The fact that they were really mere boys in England when the incident of meeting Anthony at Burgos is supposed to have occurred is irrelevant and immaterial. It is as purely fictitious as the fishing expedition on which they go with Ouvrard and catch trout with an artificial worm made out of ravelings from the banker's stocking. The woman who was nursing the pig at her breast came out of Gautier, I think. But then most of the Spanish women in *Anthony Adverse,* including Neleta and Dolores, came out of Havelock Ellis who has an interesting study on Spanish female types in his book *The Soul of Spain.*

Last but not least, in fact the biggest "steal" of all, is the quotation from Rabelais, on page 28, from which the whole plot is taken! The dirge which the nuns sing as they leave New Orleans is a Latin version of one of the psalms. I took it from a Roman Catholic hymn book. Yes, sir, I printed it verbatim, and it was hard to get the printer to do it. The gentleman who recently asked me to give him the music to this "folk song" to dance to will, I am afraid, be disappointed.

Indeed, I am afraid that with a novel like *Anthony Adverse* there will never be an end of this clamor by the "discoverers" of the sources from which it was taken. I am awaiting the appearance of some Columbus among the infinite readers of Dickens who will rush forth into print with proof absolute that I have used Dickens' *Notes on Italy* for part of my material. Isn't the Villa Brignole at Genoa the very villa in which Dickens lived and wrote many of his notes? It is, my dear sir; go to the head of the class. And then, there are also all those other books on Italy which can be discovered one by one. There is *Old Etruria and Modern Tuscany,* by Mary Lovett Cameron, and there is *Life in Tuscany,* by Mabel S. Crawford, and *Florence and Northern Tuscany, with Genoa,* by Edward Hutton, and *Le Royaume d'Etrurie* (1801-1807), by Paul Marmottan, and for the English section there is Armstrong's *Actual Survey of the Great Post Road between London and Dover,* scale ½ inch to the mile, London, 1777. I used that a lot. And there is also *A Century of Swiss Alpine Coaches* issued, I think, by the Swiss post office authorities. And for the first part of the novel there are *Les Bulletins historique de l'Auvergne,* and *Essai sur la géographie de l'Auvergne,* by Leon Gobin—and a thousand more!

But I have forgotten to mention that great standby, the Encyclopaedia Britannica, and a hundred and one maps, and all the books about Napoleon, and the Court Memoirs of the reigns of Louis XIV, XV, and XVI, to say nothing of a careful little research into the life of Robespierre, the books on the different Roman Catholic orders that I read, Jesuits, Franciscans, and all the rest, and the legends about the Heavenly Twins.

Indeed, I admit I cannot remember them all. I shall simply have to leave them to be "discovered" by my readers, who have already discovered so much about everything under the sun in *Anthony Adverse.*

To the thousands of the public who have enjoyed *Anthony Adverse* as a novel, the best that the author could turn out under the circumstances in which he found himself, I wish to extend my gratitude. To the comparatively few who have found their principal enjoyment in the book as something to be dissected for the purpose of historical research, I extend my sympathy, and regret that their pleasure in literature is confined to curiosity. To the insignificant number who regard the ordinary processes of the writing of historical fiction as merely so much "second-story" work, I can only beg leave to part from them with the observation that they are confused in general and therefore wrong in particular.

FREUD AND THE
FUTURE

by Thomas Mann

One of the great novelists of the twentieth century, Thomas Mann, the author of The Magic Mountain *and of a tetralogy based on the Biblical story of Joseph, records how the psychoanalytical theories of Sigmund Freud proved true in Mann's conception of the character of Joseph.*

JULY 25, 1936

WHEN I BEGAN to occupy myself with the literature of psychoanalysis I recognized, arrayed in the ideas and the language of scientific exactitude, much that had long been familiar to me through my youthful mental experiences.

More than once, and in many places, I have confessed to the profound, even shattering impression made upon me as a young man by contact with the philosophy of Arthur Schopenhauer, to which then a monument was erected in the pages of *Buddenbrooks*. Here first, in the pessimism of a metaphysics already very strongly equipped on the natural-science side, I encountered the dauntless zeal for truth which stands for the moral aspect of the psychology of the unconscious. This metaphysics, in obscure revolt against centuries-old beliefs, preached the primacy of the instinct over mind and reason; it recognized the will as the core and the essential foundation of the world, in man as in all other created beings; and the intellect as secondary and accidental, servant of the will and its pale illuminant. This it preached not in malice, not in the anti-human spirit of the mind-hostile doctrines of today; but in the stern love of truth characteristic of the century which combated idealism out of love for the ideal. It was so sincere, that nineteenth century, that—through the mouth of Ibsen—it pronounced the lie, the lies of life, to be indispensable. Clearly there is a vast difference whether one assents to a lie out of sheer hatred of truth and the spirit, or for the sake of that spirit, in bitter irony and anguished pessimism! Yet the distinction is not clear to everybody today.

Now Freud, the psychologist of the unconscious, is a true son of the century of Schopenhauer and Ibsen—he was born in the middle of it. How closely related is his revelation to Schopenhauer's, not only in its content but also in its moral attitude! His discovery of the great role played by the unconscious, the Id, in the soul life of man, challenged and challenges classical psychology, to which the consciousness and the psyche are one and the same, as offensively as once Schopenhauer's doctrine of the will challenged philosophical belief in reason and the intellect. Certainly the early devotee of *The World As Will and Idea* is at home in Freud's admirable essay, "The Anatomy of the Mental Personality." It describes the soul-world of the unconscious, the Id, in language as strong, and at the same time in as coolly intellectual, objective, and professional a tone as Schopenhauer might have used to describe his sinister kingdom of the will. "The domain of the Id" he says, "is the dark, inaccessible part of our personality; the little that we know of it we have learned through the study of dreams and of the formation of neurotic symptoms." He depicts it as a chaos, a melting-pot of seething excitations. The Id, he thinks, is, so to speak, open toward the somatic, and receives thence into itself compulsions which there find psychic expression—in what substratum is unknown. From these impulses it receives its energy; but it is not organized, produces no collective will, merely the striving to achieve satisfaction for the impulsive needs operating under the pleasure-principle. In it no laws of thought are valid, and certainly not the law of opposites. "Contradictory stimuli exists alongside each other without canceling each other out or even detracting from each other; at most they unite in compromise forms under the compulsion of the controlling economy for the release of energy." You perceive that this is a situation which, in the historical experience of our own day, can take the upper hand with the Ego, with a whole mass-Ego, thanks to a moral devastation which is produced by worship of the unconscious, the glorification of its dynamic as the only life-promoting force, the systematic glorification of the primitive and irrational. For the unconscious, the Id, is primitive and irrational, is pure dynamic. It knows no values, no good or evil, no morality. It even knows no time, no temporal flow, nor any effect of time upon its psychic process. "Wish stimuli," says Freud, "which have never overpassed the Id, and impressions which have been repressed into its depths, are virtually indestructible, they survive decade after decade as though they had just happened. They can only be recognized as belonging to the past, devalued and robbed of their charge of energy, by becoming conscious through the analytic procedure." And he adds that therein lies pre-eminently the healing effect of analytic treatment. We perceive accordingly how antipathetic deep analysis must be to an Ego which is intoxicated by a worship of the unconscious to the point of being in a condition of subterranean dynamic. It is only too clear and understandable that such an Ego is deaf to analysis and that the name of Freud must not be mentioned in its hearing.

As for the Ego, itself, its situation is pathetic, well-nigh alarming. It is an alert, prominent, and enlightened little part of the Id —much as Europe is a small and lively province of the greater Asia. The Ego is that part of the Id which became modified by contact with the outer world; equipped for the reception and preservation of stimuli; comparable to the integument with which any piece of living matter surrounds itself. A very perspicuous biological picture. Freud writes indeed a very perspicuous prose, he is an artist of thought, like Schopenhauer, and like him a writer of European rank. The relation with the outer world is, he says, decisive for the Ego, it is the Ego's task to represent the world to the Id—for its good! For without regard for the superior power of the outer world, the Id, in its blind striving toward the satisfaction of its instincts, would not escape destruction. The Ego takes cognizance of the outer world, it is mindful, it honorably tries to distinguish the objectively real from whatever is an accretion from its inward sources of stimulation. It is entrusted by the Id with the lever of action; but between the impulse and the action it has interposed the delay of the thought process, during which it summons experience to its aid and thus possesses a certain regulative superiority over the pleasure principle which rules supreme in the unconscious; correcting it by means of the principle of reality. But even so, how feeble it is! Hemmed in between the unconscious, the outer world, and what Freud calls the super-Ego, it leads a pretty nervous and anguished existence. Its own dynamic is rather weak. It derives its energy from the Id and in general has to carry out the latter's behests. It is fain to regard itself as the rider and the unconscious as the horse. But many a time it is ridden by the unconscious; and I take leave to add what Freud's rational morality prevents him from saying, that under some circumstances it makes more progress by this illegitimate means.

After a sojourn in the world of Freud, how differently, in the light of one's new knowledge, does one reread the reflections of Schopenhauer, for instance his great essay "Transcendent Speculations on Apparent Design in the Fate of the Individual"? And here I am about to touch upon the most profound and mysterious point

of contact between Freud's natural-scientific world and Schopenhauer's philosophic one. For the essay I have named, a marvel of
profundity and penetration, constitutes this point of contact. The
pregnant and mysterious idea there developed by Schopenhauer
is briefly this: that precisely as in a dream it is our own will which
unconsciously appears as inexorable objective destiny, everything
in it proceeding out of ourselves and each of us being the secret
theater manager of our own dreams; so also in reality, the great
dream which a single essence, the will itself, dreams with us all, our
fate, may be the product of our inmost selves, of our wills, and
we are actually ourselves bringing about what seems to be happening to us. I repeat that I see in the mystery of the unity of the Ego
and the world, of being and happening, in the perception of the
apparently objective and accidental as a matter of the soul's own
contriving, the innermost core of psychoanalytic theory.

In Genesis we have talk of the bond (covenant) between God and
man, the psychological basis of which I have attempted to give in
the mythological novel *Joseph and His Brethren*. Perhaps my readers will be indulgent if I speak a little about my own work. It is
strange—and perhaps strange not only to me—that in this work
there obtains precisely the psychological theology that "the giver of
all given conditions resides in ourselves." Thus Abram is in a sense
the father of God. He perceived and brought Him forth; His mighty
qualities, ascribed to Him by Abram, were probably His original
possession. Abram was not their inventor, yet in a sense he was, by
virtue of his recognizing them and therewith, by taking thought,
making them real. God's mighty qualities—and thus God Himself
—are indeed something objective, exterior to Abram; but at the
same time they are in him and of him as well; the power of his own
soul is at moments scarcely to be distinguished from them, it consciously interpenetrates and fuses with them—and such is the
origin of the bond which then the Lord strikes with Abram, as the
explicit confirmation of an inward fact. The bond, it is stated, is
made to the interest of both, to the end of their common sanctifica-
tion. Need human and need divine here entwine until it is hard to
say whether it was the human or the divine that took the initiative. In any case the arrangement shows that the holiness of man
and the holiness of God constituted a twofold process, one part
being most intimately bound up with the other. Wherefore else,
one asks, should there be a bond at all?

The soul as "giver of the given"—yes, I am well aware that in the
novel this conception reaches an ironic pitch which is not author-

ized either in oriental wisdom or in psychological perception. But
there is something thrilling about the unconscious and only later
discovered harmony. Shall I call it the power of suggestion? But
sympathy would be a better word: a kind of intellectual affinity, of
which naturally psychoanalysis was earlier aware than was I, and
which proceeded out of those literary appreciations which I owed to
it at an earlier stage. The latest of these was an offprint of an article
which appeared in *Imago*, written by a Viennese scholar of the
Freudian school, under the title "On the Psychology of the Older
School of Biography." The rather dry title gives no indication of
the remarkable contents. The writer shows how the older and
simpler type of biography and in particular the written Lives of
artists, nourished and conditioned by popular legend and tradition,
assimilate, as it were, the life of the subject to the conventionalized
stock-in-trade of biography in general, thus imparting a sort of
sanction to their own performance and establishing its genuine-
ness; making it authentic in the sense of "as it always was" and "as
it has been written." For man sets store by recognition, he likes to
find the old in the new, the typical in the individual. From that
recognition he draws a sense of the familiar in life, whereas if it
painted itself as entirely new, singular in time and space, without
any possibility of resting upon the known, it could only bewilder
and alarm. The question, then, which is raised by the essay, is this:
can any line be sharply and unequivocally drawn between the
formal stock-in-trade of legendary biography and the characteristics of the single personality—in other words, between the typical
and the individual? A question negatived by its very statement. For
the truth is, that life is a mingling of the individual elements and
the formal stock-in-trade; a mingling in which the individual as it
were only lifts his head above the formal and impersonal elements. Much that is extrapersonal, much unconscious identification,
much that is conventional and schematic is nonetheless decisive for
the experience not only of the artist but of the human being in general. "Many of us," says the writer of the article, " 'live' today a biographical type, the destiny of a class or rank or calling. The freedom in the shaping of the human being's life is obviously connected with that bond which we term 'lived *vita*.' " And then, to my
delight but scarcely to my surprise, he begins to cite from *Joseph*,
the fundamental motif of which he says is precisely this idea of the
"lived life," life as succession, as a moving in others' steps, as
identification—such as Joseph's teacher, Eliezer, practices with droll
solemnity. For in him time is canceled and all the Eliezers of the

past gather to shape the Eliezer of the present, so that he speaks in the first person of that Eliezer who was Abram's servant, though he was far from being the same man.

I must admit that I find the train of thought extraordinarily convincing. The essay indicates the precise point at which the psychological interest passes over into the mythical. It makes it clear that the typical is actually the mythical, and that one may as well say "lived myth" as "lived life." But the mythus as lived is the epic idea embodied in my novel; and it is plain to me that when as a novelist I took the step in my subject matter from the bourgeois and individual to the mythical and typical my personal connection with the analytic field passed into its acute stage. The mythical interest is as native to psychoanalysis as the psychological interest is to all creative writing. Its penetration into the childhood of the individual soul is at the same time a penetration into the childhood of mankind, into the primitive and mythical. For the myth is the foundation of life; it is the timeless schema, the pious formula into which life flows when it reproduces its traits out of the unconscious. Certainly when a writer has acquired the habit of regarding life as mythical and typical there comes a curious heightening of his artist temper, a new refreshment to his perceiving and shaping powers which otherwise occurs much later in life; for while in the life of the human race the mythical is an early and primitive stage, in the life of the individual it is a late and mature one. What is gained is an insight into the higher truth depicted in the actual; a smiling knowledge of the eternal, the ever-being and authentic; a knowledge of the *schema* in which and according to which the supposed individual lives, unaware, in his naïve belief in himself as unique in space and time, of the extent to which his life is but formula and repetition and his path marked out for him by those who trod it before him. His character is a mythical role which the actor just emerged from the depths to the light plays in the illusion that it is his own and unique. Actually, if his existence consisted merely in the unique and the present, he would not know how to conduct himself at all; he would be confused, helpless, unstable in his own self-regard, would not know which foot to put foremost or what sort of face to put on. His dignity and security lie all unconsciously in the fact that with him something timeless has once more emerged into the light and become present; it is a mythical value added to the otherwise poor and valueless single character; it is native worth, because its origin lies in the unconscious.

Such is the gaze which the mythically oriented artist bends upon the phenomena about him—an ironic and superior gaze, as you can see, for the mythical knowledge resides in the gazer and not in that at which he gazes. But let us suppose that the mythical point of view could become subjective; that it could pass over into the active Ego and become conscious there, proudly and darkly yet joyously, of its recurrence and its typicality, could celebrate its role and realize its own value exclusively in the knowledge that it was a fresh incarnation of the traditional upon earth. One might say that such a phenomenon alone could be the "lived myth"; nor should we think that it is anything novel or unknown. The life in the myth, life as a sacred repetition, is a historical form of life, for the man of ancient times lived thus.

The Ego of antiquity and its consciousness of itself was different from our own, less exclusive, less sharply defined. It was, as it were, open behind; it received much from the past and by repeating it gave it presentness again. The Spanish scholar Ortega y Gasset puts it that the man of antiquity, before he did anything, took a step backward, like the bullfighter who leaps back to deliver the mortal thrust. He searched the past for a pattern into which he might slip as into a diving-bell, and being thus at once disguised and protected might rush upon his present problem. Thus his life was in a sense a reanimation, an archaizing attitude. But it is just this life as reanimation which is the life as myth. Alexander walked in the footsteps of Miltiades; the ancient biographers of Caesar were convinced, rightly or wrongly, that he took Alexander as his prototype. But such "imitation" meant far more than we mean by the word today. It was a mythical identification, peculiarly familiar to antiquity; but it is operative far into modern times and at all times is psychically possible. How often have we not been told that the figure of Napoleon was cast in the antique mold? He regretted that the mentality of the time forbade him to give himself out for the son of Jupiter-Amon, in imitation of Alexander. But we need not doubt that—at least at the period of his Eastern exploits—he mythically confounded himself with Alexander; while after he turned his face westward he is said to have declared: "I am Charlemagne." Note that: not "I am like Charlemagne" or "My situation is like Charlemagne's"—but quite simply: "I am he."

That is the formulation of the myth. Life, then, at any rate significant life, was in ancient times the reconstitution of the myth in flesh and blood; it referred to and appealed to the myth; only through it, through reference to the past, could it approve itself as genuine and significant. The myth is the legitimization of life; only through and in it does life find self-awareness, sanction, consecration. Cleopatra fulfilled her Aphrodite-character even unto death

—and can one live and die more significantly or worthily than in the celebration of the myth? We have only to think of Jesus and His life which was lived in order that that which was written might be fulfilled. It is not easy to distinguish between His own consciousness and the conventionalizations of the evangelists. But His word on the cross, about the ninth hour, that *"Eli, eli, lama sabachthani,"* was evidently not in the least an outburst of despair and disillusionment; but on the contrary a lofty messianic sense of self. For the phrase is not original, not a spontaneous outcry. It stands at the beginning of the Twenty-second Psalm, which from one end to the other is an announcement of the Messiah. Jesus was quoting, and the quotation meant "Yes, it is I!" Precisely thus did Cleopatra quote when she took the asp to her breast to die; and again the quotation meant "Yes, it is I!"

The Joseph of my novel is an artist, playing with his *imitatio dei* upon the unconscious string; and I know not how to express the feelings which possess me—something like a joyful sense of divination of the future—when I indulge in this encouragement of the unconscious to play, to make itself fruitful in a serious product, in a narrational meeting of psychology and myth, which is at the same time a celebration of the meeting between poetry and analysis.

I make bold to believe that in that novel so kin to the Freudian world, making as it does the light of psychology play upon the myth, there lie hidden seeds and elements of a new and coming sense of our humanity. And no less firmly do I hold that we shall one day recognize in Freud's life work the cornerstone for the building of a new anthropology and therewith of a new structure, to which many stones are being brought up today, which shall be the future dwelling of a wiser and freer humanity. This physicianly psychologist will, I make no doubt at all, be honored as the pathfinder toward a humanism of the future, which we dimly divine, and which will have experienced much that the earlier humanism knew not of. It will be a humanism standing in a different relation to the powers of the lower world, the unconscious, the Id: a relation bolder, freer, blither, productive of a riper art than any possible in our neurotic, fear-ridden, hate-ridden world. Call this, if you choose, a poet's utopia; but the thought is after all not unthinkable, that the resolution of our great fear and our great hate, their conversion into a different relation to the unconscious which shall be more the artist's, more ironic and yet not necessarily irreverent, may one day be due to the healing effect of this very science.

The analytic revelation is a revolutionary force. With it a blithe skepticism has come into the world, a mistrust which unmasks all the schemes and subterfuges of our own souls. Once roused and on the alert it cannot be put to sleep again. It infiltrates life, undermines its raw naïveté, takes from it the strain of its own ignorance, de-emotionalizes it, as it were, inculcates the taste for understatement—as the English call it—for the deflated rather than for the inflated word, for the cult which exerts its influence by moderation, by modesty—in almost the sense of the French *savoir faire:* to know how to do. May we hope that this may be the fundamental temper of that more blithely objective and peaceful world which the science of the unconscious may be called to usher in?

FASHIONS IN IDEAS

by Irwin Edman

In the late thirties the most popular—and best-selling—American philosopher was Professor Irwin Edman of Columbia University. Here, in a chapter from his then forthcoming collection of essays entitled Philosopher's Holiday, *Edman traces the course of some intellectual fads of the era—and finds some value in them.*

OCTOBER 15, 1938

THE PHILOSOPHER Alfred North Whitehead has, I believe, made current the phrase "climate of opinion" to describe the intellectual atmosphere in which people in a given period live. As I look back on what I hope is not more than half a lifetime spent mostly in New York, I become conscious of how much ideas are transmitted by a kind of osmosis, like those tricks of manner and even of voice that two people, long married, are said to catch from each other. Once long ago I had lunch with the editor of a New York monthly magazine, then distinguished, or just ceasing to be so, and now no longer independently existing. The editor was a bright, youngish man, too busy lecturing all around the country (and in the intervals editing his magazine and writing monthly homiletics for it) to read or to think. He made it a practice, he told me, to get his education at lunch. His teachers consisted of the people he talked to over the luncheon table in any given week, and, judging by the list he recited, he was shrewd in his choice of luncheon tutors. Nor was he a fool about picking up the essence of things whose details or whose foundations he would never have had the time, the industry, or the inclination to study, or to understand. Over the coffee once I recall giving him by request a *précis,* altogether sketchy, of Dewey's philosophy of education. He made quite a good article out of it, and showed the weak points of progressive education and experimental philosophy quite as well as if he had taken the trouble to understand its strong ones.

I was a little contemptuous of the method, and I am so still. But we all get our education partly at lunch or dinner. Certainly in New York the "climate of opinion" is compounded of the things that are said in the book reviews, and at the dinner tables and in the after-dinner conversation of those who live in the marketplace or among the suburbs of ideas. For the fact is that ideas among the talking literate have become a sublimated gossip. For a month or for a season, an idea or a theory spreads like a rumor or a scandal over the intelligentsia of New York. Soon it races, like a pulse or a song, over the whole country. One year it is the theory of the leisure class, another year technocracy; a season passes and it is abstractionism in painting, logical positivism in philosophy, Anglo-Catholicism (or Anglo-communism) in religion, the folklore of capitalism, or relativity in physics. Ideas painfully thought out in the study or worked out in the laboratory, or sometimes tossed off the top of some facile mind with a quick insight and a gift for phrase, become thinned down into the chit-chat of the salons. Einstein works years over his mathematical formulas, and on a sudden relativity becomes the gossip of the clubs, the studies, and the dinner tables. A sociological study might be made of the time lag between ideas and their popular or their snob appeal. Along with my contemporaries I have lived through many fashions of ideas: Dewey, Bergson, Freud, Marx, Einstein, T. S. Eliot, Liberalism, Progressive Education, Fascism, Communism, Neo-Thomism, Progress, Disillusion, Reform, Revolution.

When one is very young, the first fashion in ideas that one meets does not seem in the least to be simply a fashion. It seems most likely the sudden revelation of an eternal truth. For after all, how should one know, meeting one's first vogue for the first time, that it is a vogue? It is natural enough to mistake an epidemic for a norm; born during a whirlwind, one might think it the ordinary weather of the world.

In the years just before America entered World War I, Liberalism (which I am told is, but do not believe to be, dead) was the current fashion. How was a young man at college to know that Liberalism had some of the marks of a dying cause? It was in its origins the expression of a hopeful and expanding democratic and capitalistic world; it had its roots in a nineteenth-century England that itself was rapidly being transformed. The language and the hopes of the laboratory (as Joseph Wood Krutch pointed out in *The Modern Temper*) were being carried over to revive the hopes and certainly to stud the conversation of mankind, at least of the intellectuals in New York. Of course a good deal of mankind elsewhere was being slaughtered in large quantities by the discoveries of the laboratory. But that was, we believed, only a temporary setback, and we hoped optimistically that co-operative aspiration, engineered by intelligence, would give us a brave new world—a phrase which would not at the time, I think, have been used ironically. Walter Lippmann, after assisting Santayana at Harvard and being secretary to the Socialist Mayor of Schenectady, had written a gallant summons in *Preface to Politics.* He and all of us learned a lot from his teacher, Graham Wallas, who showed the workings of *Human Nature in Politics* and wrote another book on *The Art of Thought.* "Social psychology" had just about been discovered, and "behaviorism," too. H. G. Wells was pampering our hopes with *The Research Magnificent,* the image of a "House of Solomon" that was to remake mankind. *The New Republic* was founded, and in good prose on clear paper made weekly blueprints of a rational future. After a hundred weeks, as somebody remarked, it seemed a hundred years old. John Dewey had invented, and many mouthed as a slogan, "intelligent control"; James Harvey Robinson was pleading for the adult mind in place of the savage and child mind in the direction of human affairs; we must not have a sixteenth-century tradesman's mentality to control the twentieth-century motorcar that was modern civilization. Though it dated from an earlier time, Swinburne's line from his "Hymn to Man" might well have been the signature of the talk of the minds of the town: "Glory to man in the highest, for man is the master of things."

Even the pulpit was infected by the latter-day salvationism. Theology itself became a gospel of social reform. There was endless talk of Liberalism and the churches, and the Liberalism alluded to was touched with scientific hopes.

No one knows how long that fashion would have lasted had not the war intervened (though there is no great reason for believing that as a fashion it would have lasted more than any other). When ideas are used primarily as subjects of conversation, the subjects grow wearisome and new ones must be found. It was a shock to me to discover that this first climate of opinion I had ever known was temporary, almost as much a shock as the first time a young contemporary of my schooldays had died. One would not have thought that either would or could vanish. And like the memory of those whom one has known well and who have died young, those early imbibed ideas remain as controlling images. It is hard for me; it is hard, I suspect, for anyone who grew up during the fashion of prewar scientific hopes and liberal enthusiasms to believe that that vocabulary is quite outmoded or that the hopes which it expressed are dead. There are certainly good reasons for questioning that language, the naïve transference of the words of the physical laboratory to the passions and conflicts of men.

The first change I observed was right after the war, the period of disillusion. That has been discussed time and again, and its most reasoned and complete statement came in Joseph Wood Krutch's *The Modern Temper*. But the history of that book itself reflects the difference between *ideas* and the climate of ideas. The title, "The Modern Temper," is, I suppose, familiar to thousands. For a season, as was said later of technocracy, one would have had to walk into a soundproof room not to hear the name mentioned. Yet the book had a relatively small actual circulation and not many of those who swore by it as their negative creed of disillusion (though its theme was really rational skepticism) had the industry to read as well as talk about it. They read the reviews, or heard quotations from the reviews. A whole spate of writers, Aldous Huxley notably, in his pre-Buddhist days, fed the cult of spiritual weariness or contempt or revulsion.

For one of the ways in which ideas become fashionable is not through reasoned analysis, but through their being broached in novels and plays. Ideas, just beginning to fade in the seminars, appear, watered down, in the novels in the circulating libraries. Or they appear behind the footlights to people in evening dress who come as late to ideas as they come to the theater, as late, often, as the dramatists themselves. The ideas that found their tardy way into novels and plays constituted what Frederick Lewis Allen has called "The Credo of the Highbrows."

Religion and romantic love were both illusions; American life was dull and standardized; the liberal hopes had been rendered fantastic and foolish by the chaos of the postwar world; life could at best offer ironic gaiety and beauty, itself not to be taken too seriously. There was, it will be remembered, much talk about flaming youth, but nobody talked much about a hard, gemlike flame. One heard rather, from Edna St. Vincent Millay, about burning candles at both ends. The light was admitted to be lovely, but it would not last the night.

Meanwhile one had been hearing increasingly about Freud. Again it took me (it took many, I am sure) some little time to distinguish between the ideas themselves and their fashionable currency. It is hard to say how much good ideas have suffered from their modishness and been impeded by their very popularity. There is, I suppose, no serious writer on human affairs who would withhold tribute to the fundamental depths and importance of the psychoanalytic contribution to the understanding of human motives. Hardly any well-informed person (though there are a few) would contest the immense therapeutic value psychoanalytic treatment has afforded in vast numbers of cases. But the depths of the

ideas and their great curative possibilities are not what I mean
by psychoanalysis as a fashion. I mean the days, somewhat over
now, when a smattering of psychoanalytic terms studded all conversation everywhere, and even the gossip about friends and enemies had to take a psychoanalytic turn. One knew or one suspected
everybody's complexes. Where, earlier, people would have spoken of
brashness and rudeness, they spoke now of compensation and an
inferiority complex. One's friends were no longer unhappy, but
frustrated; castles in Spain gave place to wish fulfillments, and no
weekend was complete without an amateur psychoanalytic devastation of everybody not present and in turn of everybody there.

It is not easy to say just when it was that the vocabulary of the
dinner parties and the little groups began to change. Some say it
came with the depression, but I seem to remember noticing it a
little earlier. But suddenly it seemed (however gradual it may have
been) the talk had turned from sex to socialism. There was even
a revival, for a brief, frenzied period, of the ideal of a civilization
run by science, this time through the engineers. Technocracy was
the name of that short-lived epidemic. It seems incredible now that
for months that word to describe a civilization to be saved through
engineers and engineering (despite the failure of Herbert Hoover)
was the magic symbol, the shibboleth, that dominated the conversation of the intellectuals. There was a flood of books and pamphlets,
formulas and statistics; whole forests must have been destroyed to
provide the printed matter that nourished the fad. And in a few
months the whole forest of printed matter disappeared, and technocracy was as dead as Herbert Spencer.

This is not history but reminiscence, and I cannot say I remember exactly when Marxism first became, pro and con, a staple part
of the fashionable diet of ideas. Certainly Marxism to the literate
was not new; had we not been required in 1914 to read the *Communist Manifesto* as part of our reading in a regulation, though
exceptionally good, course in European history? But books on art
and metaphysics and novels and plays were not then discussed in
terms of their Rightness or Leftness; one heard little about the
Party Line, and Dialectic Materialism was unknown to most host-
esses, even as a label.

I am not speaking of serious students of Marxism, nor of the
importance of the Marxian understanding of history and politics.
I am speaking again of the fact that at a certain point in the history
of conversation among the articulates of New York, Marxism became the characteristic theme of conversation and almost a correct
standard of intellectual deportment. It cannot be attributed to the

Russian Revolution, for the Revolution had taken place in 1917 and between 1917 and 1929 there were many other fashions of ideas.

But it was some time before Marxism could be the comprehensive atmosphere in which all conversation was bathed. Even today, while the strategy of revolution is being discussed in one corner, and there are vivid debates as to how likely it is that the possessing classes will consent to be expropriated without violence, other choruses are sung in other corners. For a time it was relativity, although there was general agreement that nobody (save a dozen men whose names nobody remembered) could understand Einstein. That agreement, however, in which most discussions began, was no bar to talking about the Einstein theory, or even making diagrams of two trains moving at different speeds to illustrate how relative time was. Then there was the winter that Eddington's *Nature of the Physical World* was published, and Sir James Jeans revealed the philosophical mysteries of *The Mysterious Universe*. It is hard to remember now the easy way conversationalists had with the principle of indetermination, time-space, and quanta. If any one suggested that Jeans and Eddington were superimposing some very questionable—and old-fashioned—metaphysics upon their scientific researches, that Eddington remained fundamentally a Quaker who happened to be playing with quanta, such reservations were for one short winter not the mode.

In still another corner would be a young man who had discovered St. Thomas Aquinas, seven hundred years late, and found in the clear principles of that orthodox summit of Catholic orthodoxy the one way of life for a rational animal, and a most impressive vocabulary. Behaviorism and psychoanalysis had run their course, and it was years since anybody (save economic scholars) had mentioned Veblen, whose *Theory of the Leisure Class* and whose phrase "conspicuous waste" had once been in all literate mouths. Watson, the founder of behaviorism, had been forgotten and was now in the advertising business, and Bergson, whose lectures in French were attended by Frenchless fashionable ladies, was (most people believed) dead. Meanwhile, the free association prose, the introspective streams of consciousness of Proust and Virginia Woolf, began to be more than audible murmurs, "the cult of unintelligibility" began in poetry, and the breakdown of all familiar conventions in surrealist painting. In that time it was bliss to be alive, and to be young was heaven, a heaven filled with singular stars and strange colors, some of them resuscitated, like Aquinas, from a half-forgotten past, as if somebody should declare after looking at the pictures in the Pitti Palace in Florence that he had found the secret

of Raphael's blue, or that the methods of the Primitives were the
only techniques for modern painting to follow.

It is natural, living in New York, and moving among acquaintances generated by the writing and teaching profession, that I
should have been exposed in succession to all these modes. And
I discovered further when one left New York one heard the same
things, usually, that one had heard in Manhattan the previous
winter, in transformed farmhouses in Connecticut, in cafés in Paris,
on transatlantic steamers. What, I began to wonder, accounts for
these changes in fashions of ideas, so much more rapid in their succession among us than they are abroad? What is there that has made
many of these discussions so superficial that the term "intellectual,"
from being a term naturally enough taken to mean praise as an
adjective, has come to have the atmosphere of contempt about it as
a noun? I suspect one of the answers lies in the fact that the intellectuals are more interested in articulateness than in analysis, and
in themes for conversation than in objects for feeling and thought.
The parlor pink, the salon scientist, the drawing-room philosopher,
the teatime psychologist theologian, are not new in our era. They
were rampant in France in the eighteenth century. But the polite
world of learning was then a smaller world, and though it is still
small (the class of intellectuals is never as large as its fluency would
lead one to expect), it had then none of the devices of high-pressure
publicity that can rapidly make it as obligatory to have a certain
vocabulary as to wear certain kinds of clothes.

There is nothing heinous about the love of words for their own
sake. Was it not Plato himself who said that he would never write a
treatise on philosophy, that the latter must be acquired by conversation, the flame leaping from speaker to speaker "until the
soul itself caught fire"? "Education at lunch" may be a poor affair,
but everyone knows how out of a conversation new insights emerge
and one's old ones become clarified. But what one could see time
and again in New York was the love of words in the place of ideas,
and, even worse, simply the love of knowing and displaying the
words, clichés cherished for their snob values, or new and current
generalizations paraded like the latest fashions in ties or hats. Even
noble words standing for noble causes have in our time come to
be debased into such clichés. Antiwar and antifascism can become
mere labels and signals, and by the same token so can democracy
and socialism. The *Tyranny of Words* has itself, to borrow Mr.
Stuart Chase's stereotype, become a "stereotype," and the *Folklore
of Capitalism* itself a fashionable mythology.

Impatience with the talking intellectuals may thus easily bring the whole intellectual life into disrepute. I have heard talking fools dismiss the talkers time and again. It is easy enough for the stupid or the dull or the reactionary to mistake intellectual gossip for the intellectual life, and argue from the chatter, polysyllabic but trivial, of the salons that the intellect itself is to be condemned. Our current conservatives are not the first to identify all thinking with sophistry. Socrates himself was put to death partly because he was thought to be one of the glibly talking Sophists who had come to Athens and that, like them, he was teaching young Athenians to talk without knowing what they were talking about—which was what Socrates accused all Athens of doing. But the respectable suspicion of Socrates was plausible, for Socrates himself had become a fashion with the young wits of Athens. The dull and the conservative know only that there is a lot of talk going on, that it is dull to them, that what chiefly seems to recommend ideas (to those whose intellectual life is nearly all talk) is that they are new and that they can be talked about. To the man without a gift for conversation, or the passion for it, all conversation must seem so much chatter and not least so the conversation of the intellectuals. The intellectuals themselves have sometimes felt this about themselves. Every once in a while in New York, at some crowded cocktail party or at some dinner party of the well-fed, the well-clothed, and the well-informed, one hears the desire, usually well expressed, to get away from all the talk. The *"faux naïf"* itself becomes a fashion, and the silences and the simplicities become the theme of talk, and everyone moves to the country to continue the talk there in a barn made into a studio.

Yet the conservative and the dull are mistaken if they think the chatter that has been current in New York in the last two decades is unimportant. I suspect that the real grudge of the reactionary (rather than the dull) against the articulates is their shrewd perception that the chatter is symptomatic. They realize (what is true) that some of the modes of intellectual life which have become fashionable are symptoms of a deeper uneasiness (shared sometimes by themselves) and of a nervous search for values in place of those no longer adequate. Psychoanalysis may have become a theme for dinner-table conversation and a luxury for moneyed and leisured neurotics. But it never would have taken hold, its favorite terms would never have found their way almost into common speech, unless there had been a recognition of something fresh and important in them. Fascism and communism are terms to bandy about; one may sometimes, in New York, think they are *boutonnières* rather than banners. One may long to be among Vermont farmers who have scarcely heard of them (though one may be sure that the summer residents will have). But fascism and communism are not less serious because they, in certain mouths, become chit-chat.

There is any amount of loose talk about tight and subtle doctrines, which are in their own right of the greatest importance: Neo-Thomism over the cocktails, surrealism over the cigarettes, relativity while floating on a rubber mattress in a mountain pool on an August weekend! Like everybody else interested in words and ideas, I have participated in such goings-on. But let it be remembered that while leisured men and women in the eighteenth century were talking in the salons or the formal gardens, they were but the babbling surface of a deeper ferment. I think that is what the anti-intellectuals suspect and fear. It is not the intellectuals they are inveighing against, or loose talk, or the passion for novelty, or the forgetfulness of old important ideas, or the lack of discipline or exactness or responsibility in so much that passes for intellectual conversation. They would not, I think, mind these things so much, for such faults they share and can sympathize with. But the anti-intellectual prejudice is a prejudice against genuine intellection, actual thought. The anti-intellectuals know, correctly, that if the talk goes on long enough, new and disquieting ideas may get about, and the security of the world they know, and have a private interest in preserving, may be destroyed—for the illusions by which it is maintained will be punctured. There would be even more prejudice against real thinking than against conversational play with ideas; the anti-intellectualism of every reactionary regime in Europe illustrates the point.

One can be amused or bored by the talkers, but, as the entrenched and the smug know, *thinking* is cause for alarm. One can smile at the Sophists, but nothing less than execution will do for Socrates. The entrenched know also that what starts as a fashion may turn out to be a creed or a system of life or of politics. Christianity for a time seemed a harmless fashion among the more socially exalted ladies of Rome, and ideas are dangerous when they become endeared to the rich and the polite.

PLAY IN POETRY

by Louis Untermeyer

"Even while he scorns poetry, the ordinary man helps himself to its properties and symbols; his daily life is unthinkable without metaphor. Having slept 'like a log,' he gets up in the morning 'fresh as a daisy' or 'fit as a fiddle'; he 'wolfs down' breakfast, 'hungry as a bear,' with his wife, who has 'a tongue like vinegar,' but 'a heart of gold.' " Here poet, anthologist, and critic Louis Untermeyer writes of the fun and wonder of poetry—and of the ordinary man's natural feeling for it.

FEBRUARY 26, 1938

THE AVERAGE READER—who regards himself as a more than average critic—is the perfect dogmatist. Armed with impatience, predetermination, and six standard adjectives, he cuts his rapid way through the books of the dead and the literature of the living. He is particularly dogmatic about poetry, and that he seldom reads it makes his finalities all the more final. He has two conclusions about poetry, conclusions which are as complete as they are inconsistent. Poetry, he says, in the first place, is merely a tune without music, a melody without meaning, a set of soothing (and, sometimes, irritating) sounds without sense. And poetry, he inconsistently adds, is all too difficult because it is so full of hidden allusions, so intellectually condensed, so concentrated in meaning.

Actually poetry is neither an attempt to imitate music (except in such isolated cases as Sidney Lanier's) nor (except in the rhymed essays of Pope) an effort to rival the daily editorial in compact gravity and density. Poetry is often solemn, even somber, but more frequently it expresses the side-spring of fancy, the leap of the adventurous imagination, the surprising fantasia of the subconscious. I think it can be maintained that, on the whole, poetry is as playful as it is profound.

By "playful" I do not mean merely the outburst of high spirits or the formal lightheartedness of light verse. I mean the essential spirit which unites and intensifies the figures of speech, the hyperboles and similes, all of which represent the poet's varying use of

133

the invariable impulse to play. Poetry begins with metaphor, and the metaphorical power—the ability to see similarity in dissimilar things—is increased or decreased with the playfulness of the poet's mind. It is through metaphor that poetry achieves its rich suggestiveness, and becomes, as Robert Frost wrote half playfully, "the one permissible way of saying one thing and meaning another."

A metaphor is a game in which the wit of the writer and the wit of the reader are matched. The mind of the poet fastens on an object and then rushes halfway across the world to establish a relation between that object and some hitherto unrelated object. Although the objects are not in the least alike, the reader is quick to see the likeness at the point of comparison. My love, says the poet, is like—and, in the spirit of play, he looks about him for something resembling his lady as little as possible—like, he announces triumphantly, a red, red rose. To the solemn scientific eye there is no reasonable resemblance between the figure of a woman and the shape of a rose. But the reader is as little interested in laboratory realism as is the poet. It is an intellectual game, this saying one thing and meaning another, a verbal sportiveness; the poet points the way, and the reader's mind romps along.

No matter how long and deliberately the heart is studied, that variable organ would scarcely seem to be a thrush nesting in the willows, a tree bent down with apples, and a chambered nautilus rowing itself across the ocean—all at the same time. Yet the reader abandons deliberation; he forgets about the auricles and ventricles, the construction, the circulation, the position, even the function of that hollow, muscular organ. For the time being, at least, he is completely convinced when Christina Rossetti tells him:

> *My heart is like a singing bird*
>   *Whose nest is in a watered shoot;*
> *My heart is like an apple-tree*
>   *Whose boughs are bent with thick-set fruit;*
> *My heart is like a rainbow shell*
>   *That paddles in a halycon sea;*
> *My heart is gladder than all these*
>   *Because my love has come to me.*

Thus the metaphor is something more than an amusing literary device; it is a continual play of wit, an illuminating *double entendre,* a nimble magic in which writer and reader conspire to escape reality. Perhaps "escape" is the wrong word—the play of metaphor acts to enrich reality, even to heighten it. The average reader enjoys its intensification so much that he cannot help employing it. "My heart leaps," he says, knowing quite well that it contracts and expands quietly within the pericardium. Or, he declares still more mendaciously but earnestly, "my heart stood still." Even while he scorns poetry, the ordinary man helps himself to its properties and symbols; his daily life is unthinkable without metaphor. Having slept "like a log," he gets up in the morning "fresh as a daisy" or "fit as a fiddle"; he "wolfs down" breakfast, "hungry as a bear," with his wife, who has a "tongue like vinegar," but "a heart of gold." He gets into his car, which "eats up the miles," steps on the gas, and, as it "purrs" along through the "hum" of traffic, he reaches his office where he is "as busy as a one-armed paper-hanger with the hives." Life, for the average man, is not "a bed of roses," his competitor is "sly as a fox" and his own clerks are "slow as molasses in January." But "the day's grind" is finally done and, though it is "raining cats and dogs," he arrives home "happy as a lark."

What the Babbitt says in casual conversation is not so far removed from what the poet has to say to him. It is only a step from universal banalities to metaphorical ingenuities, an easy transition from the average man's colorless stereotypes to the colorful images of the Elizabethans. "You are a queen," says the young man breathlessly in the 1937 parked car, "a honey," "a knockout," "a riot!" Unconscious of the playfulness, the novel brilliance, the extravagant humor, of his metaphors, the hard-boiled youth would snort if you told him he was speaking poetry. Yet Robert Herrick said it not so differently nor less metaphorically three centuries ago.

> *You are a tulip seen today,*
> *But, dearest, of so short a stay*
> *That where you grew scarce man can say.*
> *You are a lovely July-flower,*
> *Yet one rude wind or ruffling shower*
> *Will force you hence, and in an hour.*
>
> *You are a full-spread, fair-set vine,*
> *You can with tendrils love entwine,*
> *Yet dried ere you distil your wine.*
> *You are like balm enclosed well*
> *In amber or some crystal shell,*
> *Yet lost ere you transfuse your smell.*

No reader can fail to recognize the play of fancy. "A tulip," "a July-flower," "a full-spread vine," "balm in a crystal shell"—the poet has gone somewhat far afield to compare his lady to these pastoral beauties. But it takes no less imaginative courage to draw metaphors from the prize ring and the turbulent streets in order to speak of the beloved as "a knockout" and "a riot."

Metaphors are so vital a part of our speech, so common and used so unconsciously, that they become, as William Empson has indicated, the normal mode of development of a language. And it is the incalculable reach of the image—the establishment of a kinship between unrelated objects, the combination of exactness and ambiguity—which is its charm and power. Poetry may rest on the success or failure to establish that precarious point of relation. The poet balances himself on this point, just as he vacillates continually between pure music and pure meaning. Blake cries:

> *Bring me my bow of burning gold!*
> *Bring me my arrows of desire!*
> *Bring me my spear! O clouds unfold!*
> *Bring me my chariot of fire!*

> *I will not cease from mental fight,*
> *Nor shall my sword sleep in my hand,*
> *Till we have built Jerusalem*
> *In England's green and pleasant land.*

To the wholly rational mind this is a statement so illogical as to be absurd. The logical mind pictures a man overburdened with a bow of burning gold, arrows (of desire!), a spear, and a sword, all of which he is, somehow, to wield not in physical combat, but in a "mental fight." And these implements of war suddenly become architectural tools, for they are to be used to build Jerusalem on the soil of England—an undertaking which is as difficult as it is, politically speaking, undesirable. But we do not read such lines as we read the report of the British Commission on Palestine. We read them and are excited by them because of the blend of visual and sensual effects, of prophecy and muffled heroism, of shifting images and fixed purpose, of precise statement and vague allusion —in short, because of the shifting play of exactness and ambiguity which affects us like a spell. A spell, an enchantment, for it was with enchantment, or incantation, that poetry began. It was an incantation, or invocation, a play of words and deeds between man and the gods; now it is a play between man and men.

In Vachel Lindsay, for example, the play was outspoken. His was a motley America, an America which impartially acclaimed Daniel Boone and William Jennings Bryan, Johnny Appleseed and John L. Sullivan, Andrew Jackson and P. T. Barnum—acclaimed them not as individual, isolated phenomena, but as a galaxy of demigods. Lindsay saw these disunited States finally united by a congress or a congregation of pioneers and baseball players, Presidents and movie queens; his "golden dream" was to be accomplished by a union of high idealism and the "higher vaudeville," by heroic endeavor and fantastic vision, by an earnest combination of beauty and ballyhoo. The humor was unashamed and explicit even when the purpose was most evangelistic; such poems as "The Congo," "General William Booth Enters into Heaven," and "John Brown" are both grandiose and comic; "The Daniel Jazz" is a grotesque extravaganza, "The Kallyope Yell," that glorification of noise

> *—the Gutter Dream*
> *Born of mobs, born of steam—*

is as uproarious as a football cheer, and "The Santa Fé Trail" is frankly labeled "A Humoresque." The conscious exhorter and the not too conscious humorist collaborate in performances where the Gospel is preached through a saxophone.

> *Booth led boldly with his big bass drum—*
> *(Are you washed in the blood of the Lamb?)*
> *The saints smiled gravely and they said, "He's come."*
> *(Are you washed in the blood of the Lamb?)*

The missionary and the minstrel are similarly combined in the rollicking opening of "The Congo," one of the wildest of contemporary fantasies, which the author gravely subtitled "A Study of the Negro Race":

> *Fat black bucks in a wine-barrel room,*
> *Barrel-house kings, with feet unstable,*
> *Sagged and reeled and pounded on the table,*
> *Pounded on the table,*
> *Beat an empty barrel with the handle of a broom,*
> *Hard as they were able,*
> *Boom, boom,* BOOM,
> *With a silk umbrella and the handle of a broom,*
> *Boomlay, boomlay, boomlay,* BOOM.

In Frost the humor is far more subtle; it is the humor of reservation, of philosophic banter, of understatement—the understatement of the most significant detail. In some of the poems the humor is instinctive and forthright. Even his titles betray his love of double meaning; "Mountain Interval" and "A Further Range" have the nature of puns and "North of Boston" turns a geographical direction into a spiritual suggestion. Humor invades the most serious and tragic of the poems; the very depth and intensity of "The Fear" are emphasized by its climactic anticlimax; "The Self-Seeker" pits the horror of its subject against a broad pungency of tone; "Mending Wall" is an extended piece of persiflage. Even "The Death of the Hired Man" half conceals its pathos in asides about self-respect and the way to build a load of hay, in differences as to the definition of "home" and the sheer fancy of the passage where the moon falls down the west, "dragging the whole sky with it to the hills." Perhaps "Birches" is the best example of this gravely quizzical humor. "Birches" begins with pure observation, but the angle of observation is a peculiar one; observation soon gives way to imagination, and the poem develops into a fantasy of trees arching in the woods

> . . . *trailing their leaves on the ground*
> *Like girls on hands and knees that throw their hair*
> *Before them over their heads to dry in the sun.*

Suddenly the poet interrupts himself in the midst of his fancies:

> *But I was going to say when truth broke in*
> *With all her matter-of-fact about the ice-storm . . .*

This, of course, is sheer play, the play not only of understatement but of contradiction. The poet has been dealing with anything but matters of "fact," and his truth is true only in the way that instinct and imagination are the truths of poetry.

In the lyrics the humor is still more marked. The sharply turned "Fire and Ice" is a sardonic epigram masking a speculation about that popular topic, the end of the world. Its grim conclusion etches itself in the mind:

> *I think I know enough of hate*
> *To say that for destruction ice*
> *Is also great*
> *And would suffice.*

It is revealing to compare Frost's brusque conclusion with Archibald MacLeish's treatment of the same theme. In MacLeish's sonnet, "The End of the World," the débâcle comes during a Breughel-like circus, while one set of freaks is performing for another, the top of the tent blows off, and there, overhead, there hung over

> *Those thousands of white faces, those dazed eyes,*
> *There in the starless dark, the poise, the hover,*
> *There with vast wings across the cancelled skies,*
> *There in the sudden blackness, the black pall*
> *Of nothing, nothing, nothing—nothing at all.*

MacLeish obtains irony with tension by a skillful accumulation of suspense and repetition; Frost achieves it by the concentration of philosophic undertones.

Elsewhere the effect is frankly comic, as in "The Cow in Apple Time," which begins:

> *Something inspires the only cow of late*
> *To make no more of the wall than an open gate—*

The humor is implicit in such a couplet, explicit in such a phrase as the mock-pedantic "of late." It is lightly ironic in "Plowmen," farcical in "Brown's Descent, or The Willy-Nilly Slide," politically Socratic in "Build Soil," critical in "The White-tailed Hornet," deliberately mocking in "Departmental, or The End of My Ant Jerry," bitterly satiric in "The Peaceful Shepherd":

> *If heaven were to do again,*
> *And on the pasture bars*
> *I learned to line the figures in*
> *Between the dotted stars,*
>
> *I should be tempted to forget,*
> *I think, the Crown of Rule,*
> *The Scales of Trade, the Cross of Faith,*
> *As hardly worth renewal.*
>
> *For these have governed in our lives,*
> *And see how men have warred!*
> *The Cross, the Crown, the Scales, may all*
> *As well have been the Sword.*

I stress, perhaps unduly, the humorous element, since Frost has been praised for almost everything but this quality. If I maintain that no poet in America has ever so effectively combined play and profundity it is only because it has usually been the critic's habit to appraise the latter and neglect the former. Frost has been praised for the unity of his thought, for the intellectual steadfastness which is not deceived by the schools and slogans of the moment. He has been applauded for the symmetry of his form and the shapeliness of his technique. He has been acclaimed as one who unearthed a new kind of poetry from old and stony soil, finding his material in what was "common in experience, uncommon in writing." It is not yet ascertainable by what name he will be labeled by the literary historian of the future. Contemporary theses have been written proving Frost to be a classicist, a symbolist, a humanist, a synecdochist (Frost's own half-serious classification), a centrist, and a glorified neighbor. All these designations are plausible, all have some justification, and none is an accurate measure of the man. He is actually far more radical than the extremists. But his is an old radicalism, not dependent on political shibboleths or technical eccentricities; it is highly personal radicalism, not unlike the individual insurgence of Thoreau and the quiet but thoroughgoing rebellion of Emerson. Frost has always questioned routines of thought, he has disguised his intransigence in raillery, in offstage whispers, in teasing circumlocutions, but his penetrations have been none the less thorough. If I were called upon to add to the categories, I would drop the classicist, the bucolic realist, and the political humanist. I would call him a revisionist. It is his power not only to restate, but to revise too easily accepted conclusions, a power which no contemporary has equaled.

But he is a revisionist who is also a humorist, if the term can be separated from its vaudeville implications and newspaper columnist connotations. In his introduction to Robinson's posthumous "King Jasper" Frost wrote, "The style is the man. Rather say the style is the way the man takes himself; and to be at all charming or even bearable, the way is almost rigidly prescribed. If it is with outer seriousness, it must be with inner humor. If it is with outer humor, it must be with inner seriousness. Neither one alone without the other under it will do." The sentences were written as a tribute to Robinson; essentially they are an almost perfect description of Frost himself. His style, so characteristic, so seemingly simple and yet so elusive, so colloquial and yet so elevated, has a way of uniting opposites. It combines fantasy with matter-of-fact; or, rather, it is not so much a combination as an alteration, an intellectual legerdemain in which fact becomes fancy and the fancy is more compelling than the fact.

That Frost is both a revisionist and a humorist must be apparent to those who closely examine the alternating play of inner and outer humor in the *Collected Poems,* but it is equally discernible in the highly playful "Wilful Homing," which appears here for the first time in print and has more than a little in common with Robinson's "Mr. Flood's Party." There is the same blend of uncertainty and determination, the same flicker of double meanings, the same shifts of mockery and tenderness. But no one can confuse the two inflections; slight though the poem is, its turns of phrase and idea make it indubitably Frost's. Here again is the quiet, careful humor of understatement.

WILFUL HOMING

It is growing late and time he drew to a house,
But the blizzard blinds him to any house ahead.
The snow gets down his neck in a chilly souse
That sucks his breath like a wicked cat in bed.

The snow blows on him and off him, exerting force
Downward to make him sit astride a drift,
Imprint a saddle, and calmly consider his course.
He peers out shrewdly into the thick and swift.

Since he means to come to a door he will come to a door,
Although so compromised of aim and rate;
He may fumble wide of the latch a yard or more,
And to those concerned he may seem a little late.

Such contrasting poetry transcends its material; it makes the reader aware of depths beyond the subject. The reader is grateful not because he has learned something, but because he has experienced something. He has drawn strength and serenity, but, perhaps most of all, he has fed on surprise. "Give us," wrote Frost, "immedicable woes—woes that nothing can be done for—woes flat and final. And then to play. The play's the thing. Play's the thing."

The teachers who tell us there must be a purpose in poetry are unquestionably right; no poet can escape his serious destiny. But, unless he can discard the leaping metaphor, the incalculable music, the free imagination, nothing can be done without play—"play's the thing"—especially when play has a purpose of its own.

TWO DECADES OF *SATURDAY REVIEW* POETRY

Some poems by the era's poets, ranging from Edwin Arlington Robinson to Conrad Aiken, are herewith reprinted from the pages of SRL.

AFTER THE WAR

by Edwin Arlington Robinson

AUGUST 2, 1924

Out of a darkness, into a slow light
That was at first no light that had a name,
Like one thrust up from Erebus he came,
Groping alone, blind with remembered sight.
But there were not those faces in the night,
And all those eyes no longer were aflame
That once he feared and hated, being the same
As his that were the fuel of his fright.

He shone, for one so long among the lost,
Like a stout Roman after Pentecost:
"Terror will yield as much as we dare face
Ourselves in it, and it will yield no more,"
He said. And we see two now in his place,
Where there was room for only one before.

THE ON-LOOKER
by Amy Lowell
FEBRUARY 14, 1925

Suppose I plant you
Like wide-eyed Helen
On the battlements
Of weary Troy,
Clutching the parapet with desperate hands.
She, too, gazes at a battle-field
Where bright vermilion plumes and metal whiteness
Shock and sparkle and go down with groans.
Her glances strike the rocking battle,
Again—again—
Recoiling from it
Like baffled spear-heads fallen from a brazen shield.
The ancients at her elbow counsel patience and contingencies.
Such to a woman stretched upon a bed of battle
Who bargained for this only in the whispering arras
Enclosed about a midnight of enchantment.

THE FLOWER-FED BUFFALOES
by Vachel Lindsay
MARCH 7, 1925

The flower-fed buffaloes of the spring
In the days of long ago,
Ranged where the locomotives sing
And the prairie flowers lie low;
The tossing, blooming, perfumed grass
Is swept away by the wheat,
Wheels and wheels and wheels spin by
In the spring that still is sweet.
But the flower-fed buffaloes of the spring
Left us long ago.
They gore no more, they bellow no more,
They trundle around the hills no more:—
With the Blackfeet lying low,
With the Pawnees lying low.

THE PIONEER

by Edna St. Vincent Millay

AUGUST 29, 1925

Upon this marble bust that is not I
Lay the round, formal wreath that is not fame;
But in the forum of my silenced cry
Root ye the living tree whose sap is flame.
I, that was fierce and valiant, am no more,—
Save as a dream that wanders wide and late,
Save as a wind that rattles the stout door,
Troubling the ashes in the sheltered grate.

The stone will perish: I shall be twice dust.
Only my standard on a taken hill
Can cheat the mildew and the red-brown rust
And make immortal my adventurous will.
Even now the silk is tugging at the staff;
Take up the song,—forget the epitaph.

INVOCATION

by Stephen Vincent Benét

JUNE 11, 1927

American muse, whose strong and diverse heart
So many men have tried to understand
But only made it smaller with their art,
Because you are as various as your land,

As mountainous-deep, as flowered with blue rivers,
Thirsty with deserts, buried under snows,
As native as the shape of Navajo quivers,
And native, too, as the sea-voyaged rose.

Swift runner, never captured or subdued,
Seven-branched elk beside the mountain stream,
That half a hundred hunters have pursued
But never matched their bullets with the dream,

Where the great huntsmen failed, I set my sorry
And mortal snare for your immortal quarry.

You are the buffalo-ghost, the broncho-ghost
With dollar-silver in your saddle-horn,
The cowboys riding in from Painted Post,
The Indian arrow in the Indian corn,

And you are the clipped velvet of the lawns
Where Shropshire grows from Massachusetts sods,
The grey Maine rocks—and the war-painted dawns
That break above the Garden of the Gods.

The prairie-schooners crawling toward the ore
And the cheap car, parked by the station-door.

Where the skyscrapers lift their foggy plumes
Of stranded smoke out of a stony mouth
You are that high stone and its arrogant fumes,
And you are ruined gardens in the South

And bleak New England farms, so winter-white
Even their roofs look lonely, and the deep
The middle grainland where the wind of night
Is like all blind earth sighing in her sleep.

A friend, an enemy, a sacred hag
With two tied oceans in her medicine-bag.

They tried to fit you with an English song
And clip your speech into the English tale.
But, even from the first, the words went wrong,
The catbird pecked away the nightingale.

The homesick men begot high-cheekboned things
Whose wit was whittled with a different sound
And Thames and all the rivers of the kings
Ran into Mississippi and were drowned.

They planted England with a stubborn trust.
But the cleft dust was never English dust.

Stepchild of every exile from content
And all the disavouched, hard-bitten pack
Shipped overseas to steal a continent
With neither shirts nor honor to their back.

Pimping grandee and rump-faced regicide,
Apple-cheeked younkers from a windmill-square,
Puritans stubborn as the nails of Pride,
Rakes from Versailles and thieves from County Clare,

The black-robed priests who broke their hearts in vain
To make you Guard in France or Guard in Spain.

These were your lovers in your buckskin-youth.
And each one married with a dream so proud
He never knew it could not be the truth
And that he coupled with a girl of cloud.

And now to see you is more difficult yet
Except as an immensity of wheel
Made of wheels, oiled with inhuman sweat
And glittering with the heat of ladled steel.

All these you are, and each is partly you,
And none is false, and none is wholly true.

So how to see you as you really are,
So how to suck the pure, distillate, stored
Essence of essence from the hidden star
And make it pierce like a riposting sword.

For, as we hunt you down, you must escape
And we pursue a shadow of our own
That can be caught in a magician's cape
But has the flatness of a painted stone.

Never the running stag, the gull at wing,
The pure elixir the American thing.

And yet, at moments when the mind was hot
With something fierer than joy or grief,
When each known spot was an eternal spot
And every leaf was an immortal leaf,

I think that I have seen you, not as one,
But clad in diverse semblances and powers,
Always the same, as light falls from the sun,
And always different, as the differing hours.

Yet, through each altered garment that you wore,
The naked body, shaking the heart's core.

All the day the snow fell on that Eastern town
With its soft, pelting, little, endless sigh
Of infinite flakes that brought the tall sky down
Till I could put my hands in the white sky

And taste cold scraps of heaven on my tongue
And walk in such a changed and luminous light
As gods inhabit when the gods are young.
All day it fell. And when the gathered night

Was a blue shadow cast by a pale glow
I saw you then, snow image, bird of the snow.

And I have seen and heard you in the dry
Close huddled furnace of the city street
When the parched moon was planted in the sky
And the limp air hung dead against the heat.

I saw you rise, red as that rusty plant,
Dizzied with lights, half-mad with senseless sound,
Enormous metal shaking to the chant
Of a triphammer striking iron ground.

Enormous power, ugly to the fool
And beautiful as a well handled tool.

These, as a memory of that windy day
On the bare hills, beyond the last barbed wire,
When all the orange poppies bloomed one way
As if a breath would blow them into fire,

I keep forever, like the sea-lion's tusk
The broken sailor brings away to land
But when he touches it, he smells the musk,
And the whole sea lies hollow in his hand.

So, from a hundred visions, I make one,
And out of darkness build my mocking sun.

And should that task seem fruitless in the eyes
Of those a different magic sets apart
To see through ice crystal of the wise
No nations but the nation that is Art,

Their words are just. But when the birchbark-call
Is shaken with the sound that hunters make
The moose comes plunging through the forest wall
Although the rifle waits beside the lake.

Art has no nation—but the mortal sky
Lingers like gold in immortality.

This flesh was seeded from no foreign grain
But Pennsylvania and Kentucky wheat,
And it has soaked in California rain
And five years tempered in New England's sleet

To strive at last, against an alien proof
And by the changes of an alien moon,
To build again that blue, American roof
Over a half-forgotten battle-tune,

And call unsurely, from a haunted ground,
Armies of shadows, and the shadow-sound.

In your Long House there is an attic-place
Full of dead epics and machines that rust
And there, occasionally, with casual face,
You come awhile to stir the sleepy dust,

Neither in pride nor mercy, but in vast
Indifference at so many gifts unsought,
The yellowed satins, smelling of the past,
And all the loot the lucky pirates brought.

I only bring a cup of silver air.
Yet, in your casualness, receive it there.

Receive the dream too haughty for the breast,
Receive the words that should have walked as bold
As the storm walks along the mountain-crest
And are like beggars whining in the cold.

The maimed presumption, the unskilful skill,
The patchwork colors, fading from the first,
And all the fire that fretted at the will
With such a barren ecstasy of thirst.

Receive them all—and should you choose to touch them
With one slant ray of quick, American light
Even the dust will have no power to smutch them,
Even the worst will glitter in the night.

If not—the dry bones littered by the way
May still point giants toward their golden prey.

SALUTATION

by T. S. Eliot

DECEMBER 10, 1927

The Hand of the Lord Was Upon Me:—*e vo significando.*

Lady, three white leopards sat under a juniper tree
In the cool of the day, having fed to satiety
On my legs, my heart, my liver and that which had been contained
In the hollow round of my skull. And God said
Shall these bones live? Shall these
Bones live? And that which had been contained
In the bones (which were already dry) said chirping:
Because of the goodness of this Lady
And because of her loveliness, and because
She honors the Virgin in meditation,
We shine with brightness. And I who am here dissembled
Proffer my deeds to oblivion, and my love
To the posterity of the desert and the fruit of the gourd.
It is this which recovers
My guts, the strings of my eyes, and the indigestible portions

Which the leopards reject. The Lady is withdrawn
In a white gown, to contemplation, in a white gown.
Let the whiteness of bones atone to forgetfulness.
There is no life in them. As I am forgotten
And would be forgotten, so I would forget
Thus devoted, concentrated in purpose. And God said
Prophesy to the wind, to the wind only for only
The wind will listen. And the bones sang chirping
With the burden of the grasshopper, saying

> Lady of silences
> Calm and distressed
> Torn and most whole
> Rose of memory
> Rose of forgetfulness
> Spattered and worshipped
> Exhausted and life-giving
> Worried reposeful
> The single Rose
> With worm eaten petals
> Is now the Garden
> Where all loves end
> Terminate torment
> Of love unsatisfied
> The greater torment
> Of love satisfied
> End of the endless
> Journey to no end
> Conclusion of all that
> Is inconclusible
> Speech without word and
> Word of no speech
> Grace to the Mother
> For the end of remembering
> End of forgetting
> For the Garden
> Where all love ends.

Under a juniper tree the bones sang, scattered and shining.
We are glad to be scattered, we did little good to each other.
Under a tree in the cool of the day, with the blessing of sand.

Forgetting themselves and each other, united
In the quiet of the desert. This is the land which ye
Shall divide by lot. And neither division nor unity
Matter. This is the land. We have our inheritance.

TRY TROPIC FOR YOUR BALM

(On the Properties of Nature for Healing an Illness)

by Genevieve Taggard

OCTOBER 13, 1928

Try tropic for your balm,
Try storm,
And after storm, calm.
Try snow of heaven, heavy, soft, and slow,
Brilliant and warm.
Nothing will help, and nothing do much harm.

Drink iron from rare springs; follow the sun;
Go far
To get the beam of some medicinal star;
Or in your anguish run
The gauntlet of all zones to an ultimate one.
Fever and chill
Punish you still,
Earth has no zone to work against your will.

Burn in the jewelled desert with the toad.
Catch lace
In evening mist across your haunted face;
Or walk in upper air the slanted road.
It will not lift that load;
Nor will large seas undo your subtle ill.

Nothing can cure and nothing kill
What ails your eyes, what cuts your pulse in two,
And not kill you.

IL NE REST QUE VOS PHOTOS

by Archibald MacLeish

OCTOBER 20, 1928

Since
And the snow since
And I have not heard
Leaf at the pane all winter
Nor a bird's wing beating as that was—

I have not dreamed
Not once
Not all this year
Your face again

Since I have never wakened but that smell
Of wet pine bark was in the room. . . .

CAPE HATTERAS

by Hart Crane

MARCH 15, 1930

The seas all crossed, weathered the capes,
the voyage done . . .
—WALT WHITMAN

Imponderable the dinosaur
    sinks slow,
        the mammoth saurian
           ghoul, the eastern
              Cape . . .
While rises in the west the coastwise range,
  slowly the hushed land—
Combustion at the astral core—the dorsal change
Of energy—convulsive shift of sand . . .
But we, who round the capes, the promontories

Where strange tongues vary messages of surf
Below grey citadels, repeating to the stars
The ancient names—return home to our own
Hearths, there to eat an apple and recall
The songs that gypsies dealt us at Marseille
Or how the priests walked—slowly through Bombay—
Or to read you, Walt,—knowing us in thrall

To that deep wonderment, our native clay
Whose depth of red, eternal flesh of Pocahontus—
Those continental folded aeons, surcharged
With sweetness below derricks, chimneys, tunnels—
Is veined by all that time has really pledged us . . .
And from above, thin squeaks of radio static,
The captured fume of space foams in our ears—
What whisperings of far watches on the main
Relapsing into silence, while time clears
Our lenses, lifts a focus, resurrects
A periscope to glimpse what joys or pain
Our eyes can share or answer—then deflects
Us, shunting to a labyrinth submerged
Where each sees only his dim past reversed . . .

But that star-glistered salver of infinity,
The circle, blind crucible of endless space,
Is sluiced by motion,—subjugated never.
Adam and Adam's answer in the forest
Left Hesperus mirrored in the lucid pool.
But the eagle that dominates our days, is jurist
Of the ambiguous cloud. We know the strident rule
Of wings imperious. . . . Space, instantaneous,
Flickers a moment, consumes us in its smile.

FEAR

by Julian Huxley

JANUARY 24, 1931

When I was a boy at school,
I was a coward and a fool;
And fool and coward I have stayed
All these years; I was afraid
Of pain and scornful boys; and then
Afraid of ridicule and men;
Afraid of drawing vital breath;
And I shall be afraid of Death.

BLUE CUIRASSIER

by Robert Penn Warren

JULY 11, 1931

Jay, flagrant and military,
Outrageous sergeant in the summer's rout,
Blatant and blue—plunge down the wind and harry
The golden tumble to its last redoubt,
Whip in the traitor leaves that scurry
From those green citadels you kept together,
And call, jay, in the blue weather.

Bright friend of boys and of the truant sun,
It is not long until your call's echo
Stops some old fellow trudging the first snow,
As once the boy, who with his dog and gun
Followed the rabbit's track long ago,
Stopped, hearing that brilliant call, and then
Caught wings that flashed into the red-haw thicket.
Blue cuirassier and summer's lost vidette,
Bright friend of boys, troubler of old men.

PRELUDE

by Conrad Aiken

AUGUST 8, 1931

But there were houses in the intermediate
Voyage from dark to dark, resting-places
Known to this homeless child that is the spirit,
Something remembered, something dearly loved,
The well-known door, the doorstep, the small
    window,
The face behind the window, the clock clacking
Comfortable time, time for sleep,
Time for the coming of the beloved's footstep,
Time for the firelight on the wall,
For the simple voice that says—

         Here I am,
Here is a letter from the other world,
Here is news from the land of everlasting,
Here is the yellow nasturtium picked in the garden,
    with purple
Bloodstains in its throat, the marks where the bee
Plunged in the pollen, remember these, take them
With you when you set out again, this flower
Will be your passport—

         And so this little room
With four walls and a ceiling and a floor,
A picturebook in which myself am picture,
The clock that strikes at a minute past the hour,
Moth in the carpet, corruption in the doorpost,
The visitor who comes and sits too long,
Angels who come too seldom, the little box
Worn down with affectionate use, and the air
So always, so particularly, in this place,
My own, my spirit's—

Come, it is time to move,
There are so many places we must see,
So many other houses we must visit,
Doorsteps and windows, so many faces too
Behind those windows, other clocks with other
Errors in time, other carpets, other chairs,
And we must hurry, or we will miss the ship
With clearance papers for the Milky Way—

Deluded sentimentalist, will you stay
In this one room forever, and hold only
One withered flower in your withered hand? . . .
This is the ship that goes to No Man's Land.

HER POSTURE

by Allen Tate

JANUARY 30, 1932

Now twenty-four or maybe twenty-five
Was the woman's age, and her white brow was sleek;
Lips parted in surprise; the flawless cheek;
The long brown hair coiled sullenly alive;
Her hands, dropt in her lap, could not arrive
At the novel on the table, being weak;
Nor breath, expunger of the mortal streak
Of nature, its own tenement contrive;

For look you how her body stiffly lies
Just as she left it, unprepared to stay,
Her posture waiting on the sleeping eyes,
While the body's life, deep as a covered well,
Instinctive as the wind, busy as May,
Burns out a secret passageway to hell.

BAVARIAN GENTIANS

by D. H. Lawrence

MARCH 18, 1933

Not every man has gentians in his house
in Soft September, at slow, sad Michaelmas.

Bavarian gentians, big and dark, only dark
darkening the day-time torch-like with the smoking blueness of
   Pluto's gloom,
ribbed and torch-like, with their blaze of darkness spread blue
down flattening into points, flattened under the sweep of white day
torch-flower of the blue-smoking darkness, Pluto's dark-blue daze.
black lamps from the halls of Dio, burning dark blue.
giving off darkness, blue darkness, as Demeter's pale lamps give off
   light,
lead me then, lead me the way.

Reach me a gentian, give me a torch!
let me guide myself with the blue, forked torch of this flower
down the darker and darker stairs, where blue is darkened on blueness
even where Persephone goes, just now, from the frosted September
to the sightless realm where darkness is awake upon the dark
and Persephone herself is but a voice
or a darkness invisible enfolded in the deeper dark
of the arms Plutonic, and pierced with the passion of dense gloom,
among the splendour of torches of darkness, shedding darkness on
   the lost bride and her groom.

TWO TRAMPS IN MUD-TIME

by Robert Frost

OCTOBER 6, 1934

Out of the mud two strangers came
And caught me splitting wood in the yard.
And one of them put me off my aim
By hailing cheerily "Hit them hard!"
I knew pretty well why he dropped behind
And let the other go on a way.
I knew pretty well what he had in mind:
He wanted to take my job for pay.

Good blocks of beech it was I split,
As large around as the chopping block;
And every piece I squarely hit
Fell splinterless as a cloven rock.
The blows that a life of self-control
Spares to strike for the common good
That day, giving a loose to my soul,
I spent on the unimportant wood.

The sun was warm but the wind was chill:
You know how it is with an April day:
When the sun is out and the wind is still,
You're one month on in the middle of May.
But if you so much as dare to speak,
A cloud comes over the sunlit arch,
A wind comes off a frozen peak,
And you're two months back in the middle of March.

A bluebird comes tenderly up to alight
And fronts the wind to unruffle a plume,
His song so pitched as not to excite
A single flower as yet to bloom.
It is snowing a flake: and he half knew
Winter was only playing possum.
Except in color he isn't blue,
But he wouldn't advise a thing to blossom.

The water for which we may have to look
In summertime with a witching-wand,
In every wheelrut's now a brook,
In every print of a hoof a pond.
Be glad of water, but don't forget
The lurking frost in the earth beneath
That will steal forth after the sun is set
And show on the water its crystal teeth.

The time when most I loved my task
These two must make me love it more
By coming with what they came to ask.
You'd think I never had felt before
The weight of an ax head poised aloft,
The grip on earth of outspread feet,
The life of muscles rocking soft
And smooth and moist in vernal heat.

Out of the woods two hulking tramps
(From sleeping God knows where last night
But not long since in the lumber camps).
They thought all chopping was theirs of right.
Men of the woods and lumber-jacks,
They judged me by their appropriate tool.
Except as a fellow handled an ax,
They had no way of knowing a fool.

Nothing on either side was said.
They knew they had but to stay their stay
And all their logic would fill my head:
As that I had no right to play
With what was another man's work for gain.
My right might be love but theirs was need.
And where the two exist in twain
Theirs was the better right—agreed.

But yield who will to their separation,
My object in life is to unite
My avocation and my vocation
As my two eyes make one in sight.
Only where love and need are one,
And the work is play for mortal stakes,
Is the deed ever really done
For Heaven and the future's sakes.

SPAIN

by W. H. Auden

MAY 22, 1937

Yesterday all the past. The language of size
Spreading to China along the trade-routes; the diffusion
   Of the counting-frame and the cromlech;
Yesterday the shadow-reckoning in the sunny climates.

Yesterday the assessment of insurance by cards,
The divination of water; yesterday the invention
   Of cartwheels and clocks, the taming of
Horses. Yesterday the bustling world of the navigators.

Yesterday the abolition of fairies and giants,
The fortress like a motionless eagle eyeing the valley,
   The chapel built in the forest;
Yesterday the carving of angels and alarming gargoyles.

The trial of heretics among the columns of stone;
Yesterday the theological feuds in the taverns
   And the miraculous cure at the fountain;
Yesterday the Sabbath of witches; but today the struggle.

Yesterday the installation of dynamos and turbines,
The construction of railways in the colonial desert;
   Yesterday the classic lecture
On the origin of Mankind. But today the struggle.

Yesterday the belief in the absolute value of Greece,
The fall of the curtain upon the death of a hero;
   Yesterday the prayer to the sunset
And the adoration of madmen. But today the struggle.

As the poet whispers, startled among the pines,
Or where the loose waterfall sings compact, or upright
   On the crag by the leaning tower:
"O my vision. O send me the luck of the sailor."

And the investigator peers through his instruments
At the inhuman provinces, the virile bacillus
   Or enormous Jupiter finished:
"But the lives of my friends. I inquire, I inquire."

And the poor in their fireless lodgings, dropping the sheets
Of the evening paper: "Our day is our loss, O show us
   History the operator, the
Organizer, Time the refreshing river."

And the nations combine each cry, involving the life
That shapes the individual belly and orders
   The private nocturnal terror:
"Did you not found the city state of the sponge,

Raise the vast military empires of the shark
And the tiger, establish the robin's plucky canton?
   Intervene. O descend as a dove or
A furious papa or a mild engineer, but descend."

And the life, if it answers at all, replies from the heart
And the eyes and the lungs, from the shops and the squares
    of the city:
"O no, I am not the mover;
Not today, not to you. To you, I'm the

Yes-man, the bar-companion, the easily-duped;
I am whatever you do. I am your vow to be
   Good, your humorous story.
I am your business voice. I am your marriage.

What's your proposal? To build the just city? I will.
I agree. Or is it the suicide pact, the romantic
   Death? Very well, I accept, for
I am your choice, your decision. Yes, I am Spain."

Many have heard it on remote peninsulas.
On sleepy plains, in the aberrant fisherman's islands
   Or the corrupt heart of the city,
Have heard and migrated like gulls or the seeds of a flower.

They clung like birds to the long expresses that lurch
Through the unjust lands, through the night, through the
    alpine tunnel;
  They floated over the oceans;
They walked the passes. All presented their lives.

On that arid square, that fragment nipped off from hot
Africa, soldered so crudely to inventive Europe;
  On that tableland seared by rivers,
Our thoughts have bodies; the menacing shapes of our fever

Are precise and alive. For the fears which made us respond
To the medicine ad and the brochure of winter cruises
  Have become invading battalions;
And our faces, the institute face, the chain-store, the ruin

Are projecting their greed as the firing squad and the bomb.
Madrid is the heart. Our moments of tenderness blossom
  As the ambulance and the sandbag;
Our home of friendship into a people's army.

Tomorrow, perhaps the future. The research on fatigue
And the movements of packers; the gradual exploring of all the
  Octaves of radiation;
Tomorrow the enlarging of consciousness by diet and
    breathing.

Tomorrow the rediscovery of romantic love,
The photographing of ravens; all fun under
  Liberty's masterful shadow;
Tomorrow the hour of the pageant-master and the musician,

The beautiful roar of the chorus under the dome;
Tomorrow the exchanging of tips on the breeding of terriers,
  The eager election of chairmen
By the sudden forest of hands. But today the struggle.

Tomorrow. For the young the poets exploding like bombs,
The walks by the lake, the weeks of perfect communion;
  Tomorrow the bicycle races
Through the suburbs on summer evenings. But today the
    struggle,

Today the deliberate increase in the chances of death,
The conscious acceptance of guilt in the necessary murder;
    Today the expending of powers
On the flat ephemeral pamphlet and the boring meeting.

Today the makeshift consolations: the shared cigarette,
The cards in the candlelit barn, and the scraping concert,
    The masculine jokes; today the
Fumbled and unsatisfactory embrace before hurting.

The stars are dead. The animals will not look.
We are left alone with our day, and the time is short, and
    History to the defeated
May say Alas but cannot help nor pardon.

TO A YOUNG WRETCH

by Robert Frost

DECEMBER 25, 1937

As gay for you to take your father's ax
As take his gun—rod—to go hunting—fishing.
You nick my spruce until its fibre cracks.
It gives up standing straight and goes down swishing.
You link an arm in its arm and you lean
Across the light snow homeward smelling green.

I could have bought you just as good a tree
To frizzle resin in a candle flame;
And what a saving 'twould have been to me!
But tree by charity is not the same
As tree by enterprise and expedition.
I must not spoil your Christmas with contrition.

It is your Christmases against my woods.
But even where thus opposing interests kill
They are to be thought of as conflicting goods
Oftener than as conflicting good and ill;
Which makes the war god seem no special dunce
For always fighting on both sides at once.

And though in tinsel chain and pop-corn rope
My tree, a captive in your window bay,
Has lost its footing on my mountain slope,
And lost the stars of heaven, may oh may
The symbol star it lifts against your ceiling
Help me accept its fate with Christmas feeling.

MASK

by Stephen Spender

APRIL 22, 1939

The face of the landscape is a mask
Of bone and iron lines where time
Has ploughed its character.
I look and look to read a sign,
Through errors of light and eyes of water
Beneath the land's will, of a fear
And the memory of a struggle,
As man behind his mask still wears a child.

READING TIME: 1 MINUTE 26 SECONDS

by Muriel Rukeyser

JULY 15, 1939

The fear of poetry is the
fear : mystery and fury of a midnight street
of windows whose low voluptuous voice
issues, and after that there is no peace.

That round waiting moment in the
theatre : curtain rises, dies into the ceiling
and here is played the scene with the mother
bandaging a revealed son's head. The bandage is torn off.
Curtain goes down. And here is the moment of proof.

That climax when the brain acknowledges the world,
all values extended into the blood awake.
Moment of proof. And as they say Brancusi did,
building his bird to extend through soaring air,
as Kafka planned stories that draw to eternity
through time extended. And the climax strikes.

Love touches so, that months after the look of
blue stare of love, the footbeat on the heart
is translated into the pure cry of birds
following air-cries, or poems, the new scene.
Moment of proof. That strikes long after act.

They fear it. They turn away, hand up palm out
fending off moment of proof, the straight look, poem.
The prolonged wound-consciousness after the bullet's shot.
The prolonged love after the look is dead,
the yellow joy after the song of the sun.

THREE POEMS

by Nym Wales

MARCH 2, 1940

JAPAN IN CHINA

A frog jumped
into an old pond
and made a magnificent ripple,
then all was quiet
and the butterflies came again.

RETRIBUTION

A Japanese Buddhist general
bought a flock of doves in the marketplace
and took them to a mountaintop
to set them free,
then he went back
and planted a cherry tree—
for he said that a good Buddhist
must give liberty
when liberty has been taken,
and create new life upon the earth
when life has been destroyed by him.

THE OLD CHINESE MANNER

To sleep but not to dream, and not to wake too soon,
to ask no questions that have no proven replies,
to spin your sorrows round you in a hard cocoon,
to let others unravel while the silkworm lies:
that was old China's simple way—take the long view,
change not the world, but let the world change you.

I HAVE SEEN THE MOUNTAINS

by Horace Gregory

AUGUST 10, 1940

Everything would have been better if I had not
seen the mountains;
not hills, but mountains with rocks as
big and naked as the side
of a reconditioned, bomb-proof dinosaur
that cannot come to life in a museum—
and near the top,
expensive people, dressed like rodeo

boys, leaping from expensive cars, shouting:
This scenery is beautiful,
this air is air you can't buy anywhere
but here, the mountains are
so big, so old, so everlasting,
so high, so deep.

The trouble is: mountains get in the brain,
growing against the sky, closing out the sun
until they seem to move behind your back
and suddenly are here where you are,
so big, so powerful, nothing can stop them now,
not even death, and the long, terrible pain
of waking up again with new arms like the branches of a tree,
or eyes like flowers, or hair like grass,
or body like a field of wheat, healthy and strong
in sunlight or in rain.

You might call it fate, the way I met the mountains,
the hope to get away from everywhere
into the sky as up a ladder in a dream,
head into heaven like a monument
of someone dead so many years
and is so famous that even children recognize his face
and mispronounce his name.

That is what I think I wanted, but could not get;
nobody wants mountains to follow him,
crowding him down into a corner of a room, against the wall,
moving as the short hand of a clock moves
until there is nothing left of him at all . . .

Perhaps it is all my fault to feel this way,
as though the flat sides of the city streets were mountains
until the walls and mountains seem the same,
to feel that darkness,
and that cold wind that seems to rise up from the ground,
making lights dim
and buildings, dockyards, tenements fall away
until each man feels night within himself,
and cannot speak,
knowing that power too great for any name.

THE BOYHOOD OF THE
WRIGHT BROTHERS

by Selden Rodman

SEPTEMBER 14, 1940

*Late in the autumn of 1878 our father came into the
house one evening with some object partly concealed
in his hands, and before we could see what it was, he
tossed it into the air. Instead of falling to the floor as
we expected, it flew across the room till it struck the
ceiling, where it fluttered a while, and finally sank to
the floor. . . .*

—FROM THE WRIGHT BROTHERS' ACCOUNT
OF THEIR FIRST FLIGHT.

That was in Cedar Rapids; their father, the Bishop, argued with his
 conscience, but decided
The expensive toy, though costing more than a Bible, would in-
 struct them; the boys
Laughing with delight, when they tired of watching it tumble to the
 floor, took it
Outdoors among the indignant bluejays, lost sight of it in sunlight,
 broke
The window of Dr. Wirds who broke it over his knee, built others
 by the dozen
Larger and larger; what baffled Cayley and Penaud baffled them:
The more bamboo and cork and rubber they added, the less it flew.

In Dayton, the boys flew kites. The city of the cash register and a
 thousand factories smiled
At the unskilled boys, but snickered the older and more expert they
 grew.
It was different at home. You were laughed at, but never because
 you tried.
Orville studied Rube Goldberg; Wilbur remembered Grandfather
 Koerner's lathe;

And the Bishop with his thousand books and liberal opinions could
never decide
Which made the better toys; but he gave them the run of the work-
shop and was full of pride.
That place the Bishop looked for all his life—where was that King-
dom?
Was it in organpipe that drowned despair? Chautauqua's median
grove
Whose deathly peace drove James to Buffalo's roaring freightyard?
Questions that neither Barnum nor the Browning Society tried to
solve
Came up outside the plateglass windows at the Bradley Martin's ball
—But was the curse of starving men the way to love?

The Bishop shook his head. It was too much for him. From the
distant shed
Came a noise like hundreds of skeletons fencing on roofs of lead.
Was it possible, he wondered, that Orville, that dreamer on his stilts,
Building his lathe, with marbles for bearings and a horse's bridle-
ring
And a sacred stone for the press-bed, and his calculating machine
of spools,
Was it possible that he, in his way—that he and Wilbur were find-
ing. . . .
Since the day when Wilbur returned, his mouth smashed by the
shinney-stick
And his ailing mother took care of him, and he, in his love, returned
that care,
Adding to the prowess of an athlete the touch of a hand that has
healed the sick,—
Is it possible that those delicate hands will shape this air?

Thousands are building; in by-ways and back-ways, unpressed by
profit, then bought by it,
The cold plow turns the land, the duplex telegraph says Yes and
No, the first
Web press and linotype machine convert the forests into what?
The burning plain is crossed by the refrigerator car; the voice from
a machine
Sings *Mary Had a Little Lamb;* the figure of a man upon a screen
Moves silently, flickering; the ears at the receiver hear;
And everywhere the frequencies of hope ask breathlessly whether
the brain

Has established communication between men, has conquered the
  ancient fear.

We ask too late. The inspired give. Acceptors, we expect
Them to solve everything. The Brothers in their bicycle shop are
  not busy with
Cosmic problems: assembling a tandem job from discarded parts,
  locating
That manufacturer's nightmare, the friction that makes a pedal
  wobble,
They repair the needle of a stopwatch with bicycle cement, discuss
The chance of winning Saturday's race, their stake the title "Most
  Skilled"
Or that item in yesterday's paper: LILIENTHAL, A GERMAN
  DAEDALUS IS DEAD
THE AIR UPHELD HIM IN SHORT HOPS BUT HE
  TEMPTED FATE TOO OFTEN AND WAS KILLED.

THE ORCHARD

by Conrad Aiken

OCTOBER 21, 1944

Taking our time by the compass
  our direction by the clock
under the celandine with the windfall
  bitten by frost and the squirrel
(through the jungle in which imagination
  says time is falling, time is falling,
the little jungle of crossed grasses
  and the green celandine of the fearful heart:)
who is it that steps with us like a leaf
  steps and then stops and then steps again
lifting the strand of cobweb over the door
  to one peril after another?
Who indeed but the whole world in the heart
  an apple full of seeds the dark seeds
waiting for the living to be dead
  and themselves dead to be awakened.

Morning is round as a blue globe
    on which no map has been painted
make a windmill of your arms
    and describe the bare circle
thus the tree knows with hard boughs
    the fatal fascination of sky
while the same secret design
    its roots grasp the terror of earth.
Nothing separates your footstep
    from the world it spurns and rejoins
you are both hurrying together
    to an indescribable assignation.
The sun might have been your brain
    the moon a drop of blood in your hand
turning to and fro in the tide
    of the Ceaseless Know-Nothing.

Let us square out a brief space here
    or have it round like a bird's nest
something to write a few words upon
    or a box in which to keep pencils
or a very small room with one window
    where we can watch the shadows
or a bed in which if we wish
    we can make believe to sleep:
something we can call for a moment
    known and familiar, our own:
a book opened at a passage
    of which the meaning is maybe
or a face whose eyes have come back
    from the magic peril of nightfall
a face whose eyes cannot hide
    their haunted love of forever.

ARISTOCRATIC REBELS

By Bertrand Russell

An English philosopher, essayist and Nobel Prize winner, one of the world's most unorthodox thinkers, analyzes the rebellion and the passion of the nineteenth-century Romanticists, as they were personified by the English poet, Lord Byron.

FEBRUARY 12, 1938

THE NINETEENTH CENTURY, in comparison with the present age, appears rational, progressive, and satisfied; yet the opposite qualities of our time were possessed by many of the most remarkable men during the epoch of liberal optimism. When we consider men, not as artists or discoverers, not as sympathetic or antipathetic to our own tastes, but as forces, as causes of change in the social structure, in judgments of value, or in intellectual outlook, we find that the course of events in recent times has necessitated much readjustment in our estimates, making some men less important than they had seemed, and others more so. Among those whose importance is greater than it seemed, I shall maintain that Byron deserves a high place. On the Continent, such a view would not appear surprising, but in the English-speaking world it may be thought strange. It was on the Continent that Byron was influential, and it is not in England that his spiritual progeny is to be sought. To most of us, his verse seems often poor and his sentiment often tawdry, but abroad his way of feeling and his outlook on life were transmitted and developed and transmuted until they became so widespread as to be factors in great events.

The aristocratic rebel, of whom Byron was in his day the exemplar, is a very different type from the leader of a peasant or proletarian revolt. Those who are hungry have no need of an elaborate philosophy to stimulate or excuse discontent, and anything of the kind appears to them merely an amusement of the idle rich. They want what others have, not some intangible and metaphysical good. Though they may preach Christian love, as the medieval communist rebels did, their real reasons for doing so are very simple: that the lack of it in the rich and powerful causes the sufferings of the poor, and that the presence of it among comrades

172

in revolt is thought essential to success. But experience of the struggle leads to a despair of the powers of love, leaving naked hate as the driving force. A rebel of this type, if, like Marx, he invents a philosophy, invents one solely designed to demonstrate the ultimate victory of his party, not one concerned with values. His values remain primitive: the good is enough to eat, and the rest is talk. No hungry man is likely to think otherwise.

The aristocratic rebel, since he has enough to eat, must have other causes of discontent. I do not include among rebels the mere leaders of factions temporarily out of power; I include only men whose philosophy requires some greater change than their own personal success. It may be that love of power is the underground source of their discontent, but in their conscious thought there is criticism of the government of the world, which, when it goes deep enough, takes the form of Titanic cosmic self-assertion, or, in those who retain some superstition, of Satanism. Both are to be found in Byron. Both, largely through men whom he influenced, became common in large sections of society which could hardly be deemed aristocratic. The aristocratic philosophy of rebellion, growing, developing, and changing as it approached maturity, has inspired a long series of revolutionary movements, from the Carbonari after the fall of Napoleon to Hitler's coup in 1933; and at each stage it has inspired a corresponding manner of thought and feeling among intellectuals and artists.

It is obvious that an aristocrat does not become a rebel unless his temperament and circumstances are in some way peculiar. Byron's circumstances were very peculiar. His earliest recollections were of his parents' quarrels; his mother was a woman whom he feared for her cruelty and despised for her vulgarity; his nurse combined wickedness with the strictest Calvinist theology; his lameness filled him with shame, and prevented him from being one of the herd at school. At ten years old, after living in poverty, he suddenly found himself a Lord and the owner of Newstead. His great-uncle, the "wicked Lord," from whom he inherited, had killed a man in a duel thirty-three years ago, and been ostracized by his neighbors ever since. The Byrons had been a lawless family, and the Gordons, his mother's ancestors, even more so. After the squalor of a back street in Aberdeen, the boy naturally rejoiced in his title and his Abbey, and was willing to take on the character of his ancestors in gratitude for their lands. And if, in recent years, their bellicosity had led them into trouble, he learnt that in former centuries it had brought them renown.

As an undergraduate, when for the first time he had an income of his own, he wrote that he felt as independent as "a German Prince who coins his own cash, or a Cherokee Chief who coins no cash at all, but enjoys what is more precious, Liberty. I speak in raptures of that Goddess because my amiable Mama was so despotic." He wrote, in later life, much noble verse in praise of freedom, but it must be understood that the freedom he praised was that of a German Prince or a Cherokee Chief, not the inferior sort that might conceivably be enjoyed by ordinary mortals.

In spite of his lineage and his title, his aristocratic relations fought shy of him, and he was made to feel himself socially not of their society. His mother was intensely disliked, and he was looked on with suspicion. He knew that she was vulgar, and darkly feared a similar defect in himself. Hence arose that peculiar blend of snobbery and rebellion that characterized him. If he could not be a gentleman in the modern style, he would be a bold Baron in the style of his crusading ancestors, or perhaps in the more ferocious but even more romantic style of the Ghibelline chiefs, cursed of God and man as they trampled their way to splendid downfall. Medieval romances and histories were his etiquette books. He sinned like the Hohenstaufen, and like the crusaders he died fighting the Moslem.

Calvinism, which he never shook off—to Shelley in 1816, he described himself as "methodist, Calvinist, Augustinian"—made him feel that his manner of life was wicked; but wickedness, he told himself, was a hereditary curse in his blood, an evil fate to which he was predestined by the Almighty. If that were indeed the case, since he *must* be remarkable, he would be remarkable as a sinner, and would dare transgressions beyond the courage of the fashionable libertines whom he wished to despise.

Byron, though he felt himself the equal of Satan, never quite ventured to put himself in the place of God. This next step in the growth of pride was taken by Nietzsche, who says: "If there were Gods, how could I endure it to be no God! *Therefore* there are no Gods." Observe the premise of this reasoning: "whatever humbles my pride is to be judged false." Nietzsche, like Byron, and even to a greater degree, had a pious upbringing, but having a better intellect, he found a better escape than Satanism.

The great man, to Nietzsche, is godlike; to Byron, usually, a Titan at war with himself. Sometimes, however, he portrays a sage not unlike Zarathustra:

> He who ascends to mountain tops, shall find
> The loftiest peaks most wrapped in cloud and snow;

He who surpasses or subdues mankind,
Must look down on the hate of those below.
Though high above *the sun of glory glow,*
And far beneath *the earth and ocean spread,*
Round *him are icy rocks, and loudly blow*
Contending tempests on his naked head,
And thus reward the toils which to those summits led.

Byron was not obliged to confine himself to the Levant and the
Middle Ages in his search for heroes, since it was not difficult to
invest Napoleon with a romantic mantle. The influence of Napoleon on the imagination of nineteenth-century Europe was very
profound; he inspired Clausewitz, Stendhal, Heine, the thought of
Fichte, and the acts of Italian patriots. His ghost stalks through
the age, the only force which is strong enough to stand up against
industrialism and commerce, pouring scorn on pacifism and shop-
keeping. Tolstoy's *War and Peace* is an attempt to exorcise the
ghost, but a vain one, for the specter has never been more powerful than at the present day. Just after Waterloo, Byron summed
him up:

> *Quiet to quick bosoms is a hell,*
> *And* there *had been thy bane; there is a fire*
> *And motion of the soul, which will not dwell*
> *In its own narrow being, but aspire*
> *Beyond the fitting medium of desire;*
> *And, but once kindled, quenchless evermore,*
> *Preys upon high adventure, nor can tire*
> *Of aught but rest; a fever at the core,*
> *Fatal to him who bears, to all who ever bore.*

During the Hundred Days, he proclaimed his wish for Napoleon's
victory, and when he heard of Waterloo he said "I'm damned sorry
for it." Only once, for a moment, did he turn against his hero: in
1814, when (so he thought) suicide would have been more seemly
than abdication. At this moment, he sought consolation in the virtue of Washington, but the return from Elba made this effort no
longer necessary. In France, when Byron died, "it was remarked
in many newspapers that the two greatest men of the century,
Napoleon and Byron, had disappeared almost at the same time."
Carlyle, who, at the time, considered Byron "the noblest spirit in
Europe," and felt as if he had "lost a brother," came afterward
to prefer Goethe, but still coupled Byron with Napoleon.

To Carlyle, Goethe and Byron were antitheses; to Alfred de Musset, they were accomplices in the wicked work of instilling the poison of melancholy into the cheerful Gallic soul. To Musset, it was only after Napoleon that Byron and Goethe were the greatest geniuses of the century. Born in 1810, Musset was one of the generation whom he describes as *"conçus entre deux batailles"* in a lyrical account of the glories and disasters of the Empire. In Germany, feeling about Napoleon was more divided. There were those who, like Heine, saw him as the mighty missionary of liberalism, the destroyer of serfdom, the enemy of legitimacy, the man who made hereditary princelings tremble; there were others who saw him as Antichrist, the would-be destroyer of the noble German nation, the immoralist who had proved once for all that Teutonic virtue can only be preserved by unquenchable hatred of France. Bismarck effected a synthesis: Napoleon remained Antichrist, but an Antichrist to be imitated, not merely to be abhorred. Nietzsche, who accepted the compromise, remarked with ghoulish joy that the classical age of war is coming, and that we owe this boon, not to the French Revolution, but to Napoleon. And in this way nationalism, Satanism, and hero worship, the legacy of Byron, became part of the complex soul of Germany.

Mary Shelley's *Frankenstein,* written under the inspiration of conversations with Byron in the romantic scenery of the Alps, contains what might almost be regarded as an allegorical prophetic history of the development of romanticism. Frankenstein's monster is not, as he has become in proverbial parlance, a mere monster: he is, at first, a gentle being, longing for human affection, but he is driven to hatred and violence by the horror which his ugliness inspires in those whose love he attempts to gain.

> My heart [he said of himself] was fashioned to be susceptible of love and sympathy; and, when wrenched by misery, and vice and hatred, it did not endure the violence of the change, without torture such as you cannot even imagine.
> . . . When I run over the frightful catalogue of my sins, I cannot believe that I am the same creature whose thoughts were once filled with sublime and transcendent visions of the beauty and the majesty of goodness. But it is even so; the fallen angel becomes a malignant devil. Yet even that enemy of God and man had friends and associates in his desolation; I am alone.

Robbed of its romantic form, there is nothing unreal in this psychology, and it is unnecessary to search out pirates or Vandal kings in order to find parallels. To an English visitor, the ex-Kaiser, at Doorn, lamented that the English no longer loved him. Dr. Burtt, in his book on the juvenile delinquent, mentions a boy of seven who drowned another boy in the Regent Canal. His reason was that neither his family nor his contemporaries showed him affection. Dr. Burtt was kind to him, and he became a respectable citizen; but no Dr. Burtt undertook the reformation of Franken-stein's monster.

It is not the psychology of the romantics that is at fault: it is their standard of values. They admire strong passions, of no matter what kind, and whatever may be their social consequences. Ro-mantic love, especially when unfortunate, is strong enough to win their approval, but most of the strongest passions are destructive —hate and resentment and jealousy, remorse and despair, outraged pride and the fury of the unjustly oppressed, martial ardor and contempt for slaves and cowards. Hence the type of man en-couraged by romanticism, especially of the Byronic variety, is vio-lent and antisocial, an anarchic rebel or a conquering tyrant.

This outlook makes an appeal for which the reason lies very deep in human nature and human circumstances. By self-interest man has become gregarious, but in instinct he has remained to a great extent solitary; hence the need of religion and morality to reinforce self-interest. But the habits of forgoing present satisfactions for the sake of future advantages is irksome, and when passions are roused the prudent restraints of social behavior become difficult to en-dure. Those who, at such times, throw them off, acquire a new energy and sense of power from the cessation of inner conflict, and, though they may come to disaster in the end, enjoy meanwhile a sense of godlike exaltation which, though known to the great mystics, can never be experienced by a merely pedestrian virtue. The solitary part of their nature reasserts itself, but if the intellect survives, the reassertion must clothe itself in myth. The mystic be-comes one with God, and in the contemplation of the Infinite feels himself absolved from duty to his neighbor. The anarchic rebel does even better: he feels himself not one with God, but God. Truth and duty, which represent our subjection to matter and to our neighbors, exist no longer for the man who has become God; for others, truth is what he posits, duty what he commands. If we could all live solitary and without labor, we could all enjoy this ecstasy of independence; since we cannot, its delights are only available to madmen and dictators.

The romantic movement is, in essence, a revolt of our solitary instincts against the difficult precepts of social co-operation. Such social relations as we share with gorillas—sexual love and family affection—are spared by the earlier forms of romanticism, because their hold upon our instincts is very strong, but other restrictions imposed by society are loosened one by one. First comes the revolt against etiquette and the formal manners of courts, the "return to nature" and the belief in the simple virtues of the peasant. With this (not from observation of peasants) goes the belief that sexual relations should be based on love and an attack upon the custom of making marriage an economic contract. At the same time there is admiration for pastoral scenery as opposed to that of Fleet Street, which Dr. Johnson preferred, and there is a revolt against artificial forms in art and literature. All this had happened before Byron's time, and since it attacked nothing essential to the social structure it was not open to serious criticism.

But, under the stimulus of the French Revolution and the Napoleonic wars, revolt went deeper. The change is typified by the change in scenery. Byron no longer writes of mossy glades and sylvan rivulets; he writes of deserts and Alps, of thunderstorms and shipwrecks:

> *O night*
> *And storm and darkness, ye are wondrous strong. . . .*
> *Far along,*
> *From peak to peak, the rattling crags among,*
> *Leaps the live thunder!*

All this, he says, is like "the light of a dark eye in woman"; love, for him, is not gentle, but violent like a thunderstorm. What Byron says of Rousseau is applicable to himself. Rousseau was, he says,

> *He who threw*
> *Enchantment over passion, and from woe*
> *Wrung overwhelming eloquence . . .*
> *yet he knew*
> *How to make madness beautiful, and cast*
> *O'er erring deeds and thoughts, a heavenly hue.*

But there is a profound difference between the two men. Rousseau is pathetic, Byron is fierce; Rousseau's timidity is obvious, Byron's is concealed; Rousseau admires virtue provided it is simple, while Byron admires sin provided it is elemental. The difference, though it is only that between two stages in the revolt of unsocial instincts, is important, and shows the direction in which the movement is developing.

Revolt of solitary instincts against social bonds is the key to the philosophy, the politics, and the sentiments, not only of what is commonly called the romantic movement, but of its progeny down to the present day. Philosophy, under the influence of German idealism, became solipsistic, and self-development was proclaimed as the fundamental principle of ethics. As regards sentiment, there has to be a distasteful compromise between the search for isolation and the necessities of passion and economics. D. H. Lawrence's story, "The Man Who Loved Islands," has a hero who disdained such compromise to a gradually increasing extent, and at last died of hunger and cold, but in the enjoyment of complete isolation; but this degree of consistency has not been achieved by the writers who praise solitude. The comforts of civilized life are not obtainable by a hermit, and a man who wishes to write books or produce works of art must submit to the ministrations of others if he is to survive while he does his work. In order to continue to feel solitary, he must be able to prevent those who serve him from impinging upon his ego, which is best accomplished if they are slaves. Passionate love, however, is a more difficult matter. So long as passionate lovers are regarded as in revolt against social trammels, they are admired; but in real life the love relation itself quickly becomes a social trammel, and the partner in love comes to be hated all the more vehemently if the love is strong enough to make the bond difficult to break. Hence love comes to be conceived as a battle, in which each is attempting to destroy the other by breaking through the protecting walls of his or her ego. This point of view has become familiar through the writings of Strindberg and D. H. Lawrence.

Not only passionate love, but every friendly relation to others, is only possible, to this way of feeling, in so far as the others can be regarded as a projection of one's own Self. This is feasible if the others are blood relations, and the more nearly they are related the more easily it is possible. Hence an emphasis on race, leading, as in the case of the Ptolemys, to endogamy. How this affected Byron, we know; Wagner suggests a similar sentiment in the love of Siegmund and Sieglinde. Nietzsche, though not scandalously, preferred his sister to all other women.

The principle of nationality, of which Byron was a protagonist, is an extension of the same "philosophy." A nation is assumed to be a race, descended from common ancestors, and sharing some kind of "blood-consciousness." Mazzini, who constantly found fault with the English for their failure to appreciate Byron, conceived nations as possessed of a mystical individuality, and attributed to them the kind of anarchic greatness that other romantics sought in heroic men. Liberty, for nations, came to be regarded, not only by Mazzini, but by comparatively sober statesmen, as something absolute, which, in practice, made international co-operation impossible.

Belief in blood and race is naturally associated with anti-Semitism. At the same time, the romantic outlook, partly because it is aristocratic, and partly because it prefers passion to calculation, has a vehement contempt for commerce and finance. It is thus led to proclaim an opposition to capitalism which is quite different from that of the socialist who represents the interest of the proletariat, since it is an opposition based on dislike of economic preoccupations, and strengthened by the suggestion that the capitalist world is governed by Jews. This point of view is expressed by Byron on the rare occasions when he condescends to notice anything so vulgar as economic power:

> *Who hold the balance of the world? Who reign*
> *O'er congress, whether royalist or liberal? . . .*
> *Who keep the world, both Old and New, in pain*
> *Or Pleasure? Who make politics run glibber all?*
> *The shade of Buonaparte's noble daring?*
> *Jew Rothschild, and his fellow Christian Baring.*

The verse is perhaps not very musical, but the sentiment is quite of our time.

To sum up:

The romantic movement, in which Byron was the most romantic figure, aimed at liberating human personality from the fetters of social convention and social morality. In part, these fetters were a mere useless hindrance to desirable forms of activity, for every ancient community has developed rules of behavior for which there is nothing to be said except that they are traditional. But egoistic passions, when once let loose, are not easily brought again into subjection to the needs of society. Christianity had succeeded, to some extent, in taming the ego, but economic, political, and intellectual causes stimulated revolt against the churches, and the romantic movement brought the revolt into the sphere of morals. By encouraging a new lawless ego it made social co-operation impossible, and left its disciples faced with the alternative of anarchy or despotism. Egoism at first, as in Frankenstein's monster, made men expect from others a parental tenderness; but when they discovered, with indignation, that others had their own ego, the disappointed desire for tenderness turned to hatred and violence. Man is not a solitary animal, and, so long as social life survives, self-realization cannot be the supreme principle of ethics.

SO YOU WANT TO
BE A WRITER?

by Sherwood Anderson

A veteran of the literary cocktail parties, the author of Winesburg, Ohio, *pokes a little fun at himself and at his vast non-reading public.*

DECEMBER 9, 1939

IN ANY GROUP of young writers you will inevitably find those who want to write and those who merely want to be writers. They want, it seems, what they think of as a kind of distinction that they believe comes with being a writer. It's an odd thing. I daresay a kind of distinction, always I fear a bit synthetic, does come to a few, but really there are so many writers nowadays. You meet them everywhere. You can't escape them.

Let us say you are a writer. You write and write and finally you get a book published and then another and another. You get your picture in the book section of *The New York Times* and in *The Saturday Review of Literature*.

So you go about. You meet people. You are probably thinking to yourself that everyone knows who you are. You forget that to be what is called famous as a writer only about one out of every 100,000 people need have ever even heard your name. The chances are that you have been associating a lot with others a good deal like yourself.

You have been seeking such people out and they have sought you out. You go about with so-called intellectuals. When your last book was published, your publisher, thinking it would boost your sales, has sent an advance copy of your book to a lot of other writers. He has said, "We are sending you by this mail an advance copy of Mr. Musgrave's new novel. We think it a great book. If you agree with us, please write." Or it may be a new novel by Miss Ethel Longshoreman. It seems women are nowadays writing our novels more and more. I guess they do it instead of getting married. It may be because of unemployment among the men. I don't know. Anyway it's a fact.

When it is put up to you, you do it. You think, "If I don't puff his or her book she or he won't puff mine." Very likely, however, you don't read the book. You get your mother-in-law to read it. Anyway that's my system.

The point is that you get to thinking everyone must know you. You have been about with other writers and they have said that your book is "just fine." They have said you have "a wonderful style" or something like that and you have paid them back by saying something nice about their last book and you have got rather to expecting it—I mean, you know, being something special, attracting attention wherever you go.

Then you get a jolt. Just when you want to be known, no one knows a thing about you. You have gone somewhere and have been introduced as an author. I knew a man, a manufacturer in Ohio. I was always meeting him in New York. He always had a blonde with him and always introduced her as a cousin. "Cousin Alice, meet my friend Sherwood Anderson, the author."

She always thought I was Maxwell Anderson or Robert Sherwood. She put me in the theater. She wasn't the kind that reads books.

"I just loved your last play."

Once I promised one of the man's cousins a part in one of my plays.

"I have just written a new play. You are just the type for it," I said.

His cousin became excited. I gave her Maxwell Anderson's address.

"You come to see me this afternoon."

It happens that I have never met Maxwell Anderson. I wonder if he is a strong man.

You are introduced as an author and at once someone is on the spot. You are introduced let's say to a doctor. He doesn't go about with a certain queer expectant light in his eyes, thinking that people who don't know all about him aren't cultured. He doesn't think that just because you haven't been to his office to get some medicine for your indigestion you are an ignoramus. He may even, up to the moment when he is introduced to you, have led an honorable, upright life. Like George Washington, he has never told a lie, but he tells one now. He thinks that, being an author, you are expecting it. He is like his wife who, when you once were invited to his house to dinner, rushed downtown and bought one of your books and put it on a table right in the middle of the living room, where no one could miss seeing it.

He says, "Oh yes. I have so enjoyed your books."

In a case like this, a man caught like this, in the company of an author he has never read, may try to get out of it by pretending he is a little deaf and hasn't heard when told you are an author, but he can't get away with that. It may be that you would let him get away with it, would be glad to, but someone is sure to pop up.

Let us say your name is Smith.

"How do you do, Mr. Smith. Glad to meet you," he says, and tries to make a getaway, but he is stopped.

"But this is Mr. Smith, the author," someone insists.

He gets a kind of hunted look on his face. There is a pleading look in his eyes. Please, if any of you who read this happen to become writers, when a thing like this happens to you, be kind. Don't press the man. Don't compel him to say, as he must say if you crowd him, that something happened just as he was becoming absolutely absorbed in your last book when his wife took it away from him and every time he tried to get it back she cried.

It is a good idea in such a case to help the man out. Don't force him to tell too many lies. Let's say you have written a novel about a banker. Of course, I know none of you, if you ever become writers, will be that foolish. No one ever writes novels about bankers. Writers can't even borrow money from bankers. You all know, or should know, that nowadays it isn't worth while writing novels about any class other than the proletariat. If you write novels about people of any other class the Communists will get you. They'll call you a bourgeois, and then where are you?

So you are face to face with the man who has not read your novel about the banker and who has made the mistake of pretending that he has. You should bear this in mind. The man who has made the bluff about reading your book, when he has only some five minutes earlier heard of you for the first time, really made the bluff out of kindness of heart. You ought to try in turn to be kind to him. Help the man out. Give him a lead. Say something like this, say, "I think the banker in my novel was a most unusual man, don't you?" That will let him know that the book is about a banker.

Then go a little further. Mention the name of the town in which the banker had his bank. That will be a help. And then, if your banker ran away with the wife of the cashier of the bank, mention that. Try to drag it in. You will find it worth while. Authors should occasionally do these little deeds of kindness. Oh, the glad look that will come into such a man or woman's eyes.

I remember once being at a party with Mr. Ring Lardner. It was down in the city of New Orleans. Ring had come down there with Grantland Rice and Grantland was afraid the people of New Orleans might not know Ring was there. So Rice had done a lot of free publicity for Ring. He had called up the Mayor, the president of the Chamber of Commerce, the Kiwanis Club, the Rotary Club, the Lions Club. There was a big party at some rich person's house, and Ring took me along. He said, "Come on, Sherwood, let's give them two authors. Let's see if they know which is which."

So we did go and they knew we were authors. Grantland had told them. He got there ahead of us. He pointed us out. "There they are. There they come," he said.

He did everything but tell them what books we had written. He slipped up on that. That was what raised the devil with them. A kind of dark shadow came over the assembly. People went about with troubled eyes. They gathered in little groups whispering to each other but finally, out of one of the groups, a woman emerged. She was, I remember, very determined-looking. She had that kind of jaw, that kind of eyes. She was a rather big woman, strong and muscular, who, had she been a man, might well have been a professional wrestler.

She came up to us. She had this do or die look on her face. She tackled me first. Someone had given her my name.

"Oh, Mr. Anderson," she said, "I'm so glad you are here. I have been so longing to meet you." She said that she felt she already knew me through my books. She got that off, and there was a pause.

"Oh that last book of yours," she said. She thought it was very, very beautiful and suddenly I had a vicious impulse.

"And what book do you mean? Name it. I dare you to," I wanted to say but I didn't say it. I kept still and there was another pause. It was the kind of pause that, if it had been pregnant, should have brought forth triplets. There was this terrible waiting time and then Ring, out of the fullness of his heart, helped her out.

"You mean of course *The Great Gatsby*," he said, and there was a look of joy and gratitude on that woman's face that I'll never forget. It was the kind of good deed on Ring's part that inspired other good deeds. It inspired me and I told the woman that Ring was the author of *Sister Carrie* and of course she ran about and told all the others. It made everything all right. It made an evening that had started to be a complete flop a great success.

A few years ago I was living in a certain town down in Virginia and I bought and ran for a time a country newspaper in the town. I don't know just why I did it. I guess I didn't want the people of the town to think of me as a writer. I figured that if they thought of me as a writer they would be afraid of me as they had a right to be. So I thought I'd get around them by being a newspaper publisher. And people have a right to be afraid. We writers, in certain moods will use anyone we can. We say to ourselves that we are after truth.

Once I did an unfair mean thing to a certain man in Ohio. He was my friend and I rather sold him out. He was angry. My name began to get up in the world and he threatened me. He said he was going to write telling just what kind of man I was.

"Please do," I said. "Rough it up. Send the whole story to me. I've half forgotten." I pointed out that I could do the job better than he could. I meant it too. I was a story-teller and I knew I could beat him telling the story.

There are certain men who are what I call "feeders." The story-teller loves such men. They go about telling little things that have happened to them. They cannot write the stories but they can tell them. Put pens into their hands and away fly the stories.

A man who worked for me on my farm was such a story-teller. What tales he told! There is a certain naïveté in such men. They look out upon life with clear eyes. They tell you the most wonderful tales of things they feel, things they have done, things that have been done to them. They tell everything very clearly. The man worked for me one summer and I cleaned up on him. I got several fine stories, heard them from his lips, while we worked together, or rather while he worked and I sat watching him, rushed at once into the house, put down the stories just as he had told them. Then I was a fool. At the end of the summer I told him what I had been doing and he grew afraid of me.

Or he thought I was getting too much for nothing. I should have kept my mouth shut. I lost a good feeder. Now the stories he might tell to many people through me are lost.

So there we are, we writers. We go about among people. We are presumed to be reading people as a man reads the pages of a book but most of the time we are doing nothing.

People keep coming up to a writer. "What are you at work on now?" they ask. He isn't working on anything. He has a tooth that needs filling and it hurts. He is wondering where he will get the money to buy a new car. He isn't at work on anything but he knows what is expected of him. It is expected that he will be at work on some big serious task. If he is wise he gives them what they expect. I do.

"I am at work on a history of the American Civil War," I say. It sounds dignified and scholarly. A look of awe and respect comes into the people's eyes.

"What a man!" they are thinking. It is wonderful. At times I almost convince myself that I am at some such great task.

We become self-conscious. That is what we have to fight against and it is sometimes a hard and bitter struggle. If we get up a little in the world people write about us. They put our pictures in newspapers and magazines. What we do about that is to send one taken when we were thirty, when our hair was thick yet, when our teeth were sound, when we had a fresh, cheerful look on our face.

Occasionally someone tells us that we are great.

It is so difficult not to believe and if you do convince yourself that it is all bunk you are miserable about that too.

So you want to be a writer?

Isn't it wonderful?

HOW TO MARK A BOOK

by Mortimer J. Adler

In 1940 one of the first of the now-burgeoning crop of self-help books appeared with the publication of Professor Mortimer J. Adler's How to Read a Book. *It was an immediate and continuing success. In* SRL *Professor Adler extended his practical guide for would-be better readers in the article reprinted here.*

JULY 6, 1940

You KNOW you have to read "between the lines" to get the most out of anything. I want to persuade you to do something equally important in the course of your reading. I want to persuade you to "write between the lines." Unless you do, you are not likely to do the most efficient kind of reading.

I contend, quite bluntly, that marking up a book is not an act of multilation but of love.

You shouldn't mark up a book which isn't yours. Librarians (or your friends) who lend you books expect you to keep them clean, and you should. If you decide that I am right about the usefulness of marking books, you will have to buy them. Most of the world's great books are available today, in reprint editions, at less than a dollar.

There are two ways in which one can own a book. The first is the property right you establish by paying for it, just as you pay for clothes and furniture. But this act of purchase is only the prelude to possession. Full ownership comes only when you have made it a part of yourself, and the best way to make yourself a part of it is by writing in it. An illustration may make the point clear. You buy a beefsteak and transfer it from the butcher's icebox to your own. But you do not own the beefsteak in the most important sense until you consume it and get it into your bloodstream. I am arguing that books, too, must be absorbed in your bloodstream to do you any good.

Confusion about what it means to *own* a book leads people to a false reverence for paper, binding, and type—a respect for the physical thing—the craft of the printer rather than the genius of the author. They forget that it is possible for a man to acquire the idea, to possess the beauty, which a great book contains, without staking his claim by pasting his bookplate inside the cover. Having a fine library doesn't prove that its owner has a mind enriched by books; it proves nothing more than that he, his father, or his wife, was rich enough to buy them.

There are three kinds of book owners. The first has all the standard sets and best sellers—unread, untouched. (This deluded individual owns woodpulp and ink, not books.) The second has a great many books—a few of them read through, most of them dipped into, but all of them as clean and shiny as the day they were bought. (This person would probably like to make books his own, but is restrained by a false respect for their physical appearance.) The third has a few books or many—every one of them dog-eared and dilapidated, shaken and loosened by continual use, marked and scribbled in from front to back. (This man owns books.)

Is it false respect, you may ask, to preserve intact and unblemished a beautifully printed book, an elegantly bound edition? Of course not. I'd no more scribble all over a first edition of *Paradise Lost* than I'd give my baby a set of crayons and an original Rembrandt! I wouldn't mark up a painting or a statue. Its soul, so to speak, is inseparable from its body. And the beauty of a rare edition or of a richly manufactured volume is like that of a painting or a statue.

But the soul of a book *can* be separated from its body. A book is more like the score of a piece of music than it is like a painting. No great musician confuses a symphony with the printed sheets of music. Arturo Toscanini reveres Brahms, but Toscanini's score of the C-minor Symphony is so thoroughly marked up that no one but the maestro himself can read it. The reason why a great conductor makes notations on his musical scores—marks them up again and again each time he returns to study them—is the reason why you should mark your books. If your respect for magnificent binding or typography gets in the way, buy yourself a cheap edition and pay your respects to the author.

Why is marking up a book indispensable to reading? First, it keeps you awake. (And I don't mean merely conscious; I mean wide awake.) In the second place, reading, if it is active, is thinking, and thinking tends to express itself in words, spoken or written. The marked book is usually the thought-through book. Finally, writing helps you remember the thoughts you had, or the thoughts the author expressed. Let me develop these three points.

If reading is to accomplish anything more than passing time, it must be active. You can't let your eyes glide across the lines of a book and come up with an understanding of what you have read. Now an ordinary piece of light fiction, like, say, *Gone with the Wind,* doesn't require the most active kind of reading. The books you read for pleasure can be read in a state of relaxation, and nothing is lost. But a great book, rich in ideas and beauty, a book that raises and tries to answer great fundamental questions, demands the most active reading of which you are capable. You don't absorb the ideas of John Dewey the way you absorb the crooning of Mr. Vallee. You have to reach for them. That you cannot do while you're asleep.

If, when you've finished reading a book, the pages are filled with your notes, you know that you read actively. The most famous *active* reader of great books I know is President Hutchins, of the University of Chicago. He also has the hardest schedule of business activities of any man I know. He invariably reads with a pencil, and sometimes, when he picks up a book and pencil in the evening, he finds himself, instead of making intelligent notes, drawing what he calls "caviar factories" on the margins. When that happens, he puts the book down. He knows he's too tired to read, and he's just wasting time.

But, you may ask, why is writing necessary? Well, the physical act of writing, with your own hand, brings words and sentences more sharply before your mind and preserves them better in your memory. To set down your reaction to important words and sentences you have read, and the questions they have raised in your mind, is to preserve those reactions and sharpen those questions.

Even if you wrote on a scratch pad, and threw the paper away when you had finished writing, your grasp of the book would be surer. But you don't have to throw the paper away. The margins (top and bottom, as well as side), the end papers, the very space between the lines, are all available. They aren't sacred. And, best of all, your marks and notes become an integral part of the book and stay there forever. You can pick up the book the following week or year, and there are all your points of agreement, disagreement, doubt, and inquiry. It's like resuming an interrupted conversation with the advantage of being able to pick up where you left off.

And that is exactly what reading a book should be: a conversation between you and the author. Presumably he knows more about the subject than you do; naturally, you'll have the proper humility as you approach him. But don't let anybody tell you that a reader is supposed to be solely on the receiving end. Understanding is a two-way operation; learning doesn't consist in being an empty receptacle. The learner has to question himself and question the teacher. He even has to argue with the teacher, once he understands what the teacher is saying. And marking a book is literally an expression of your differences, or agreements of opinion, with the author.

There are all kinds of devices for marking a book intelligently and fruitfully. Here's the way I do it:

1. *Underlining*: of major points, of important or forceful statements.

2. *Vertical lines at the margin*: to emphasize a statement already underlined.

3. *Star, asterisk, or other doodad at the margin*: to be used sparingly, to emphasize the ten or twenty most important statements in the book. (You may want to fold the bottom corner of each page on which you use such marks. It won't hurt the sturdy paper on which most modern books are printed, and you will be able to take the book off the shelf at any time and, by opening it at the folded-corner page, refresh your recollection of the book.)

4. *Numbers in the margin*: to indicate the sequence of points the author makes in developing a single argument.

5. *Numbers of other pages in the margin*: to indicate where else in the book the author made points relevant to the point marked; to tie up the ideas in a book, which, though they may be separated by many pages, belong together.

6. *Circling of key words or phrases.*

7. *Writing in the margin, or at the top or bottom of the page, for the sake of*: recording questions (and perhaps answers) which a passage raised in your mind; reducing a complicated discussion to a simple statement; recording the sequence of major points right through the books. I use the end papers at the back of the book to make a personal index of the author's points in the order of their appearance.

The front end papers are, to me, the most important. Some people reserve them for a fancy bookplate. I reserve them for fancy thinking. After I have finished reading the book and making my personal index on the back end papers, I turn to the front and try to outline the book, not page by page, or point by point (I've already done that at the back), but as an integrated structure, with a basic unity and an order of parts. This outline is, to me, the measure of my understanding of the work.

If you're a die-hard anti-book-marker, you may object that the margins, the space between the lines, and the end papers don't give you room enough. All right. How about using a scratch pad slightly smaller than the page size of the book—so that the edges of the sheets won't protrude? Make your index, outlines, and even your notes on the pad, and then insert these sheets permanently inside the front and back covers of the book.

Or, you may say that this business of marking books is going to slow up your reading. It probably will. That's one of the reasons for doing it. Most of us have been taken in by the notion that speed of reading is a measure of our intelligence. There is no such thing as the right speed for intelligent reading. Some things should be read quickly and effortlessly, and some should be read slowly and even laboriously. The sign of intelligence in reading is the ability to read different things differently according to their worth. In the case of good books, the point is not to see how many of them you can get through, but rather how many can get through you —how many you can make your own. A few friends are better than a thousand acquaintances. If this be your aim, as it should be, you will not be impatient if it takes more time and effort to read a great book than it does a newspaper.

You may have one final objection to marking books. You can't lend them to your friends because nobody else can read them without being distracted by your notes. Furthermore, you won't want to lend them because a marked copy is a kind of intellectual diary, and lending it is almost like giving your mind away.

If your friend wishes to read your Plutarch's *Lives, Shakespeare,* or *The Federalist Papers,* tell him gently but firmly, to buy a copy. You will lend him your car or your coat—but your books are as much a part of you as your head or your heart.

SOME POSTSCRIPTS TO OSCAR WILDE

by Frances Winwar

The nineteenth-century wit and playwright Oscar Wilde might have been both delighted and horrified by the statue of a nude and virile angel which was sculpted to mark his grave. But this was only one of the strange incidents which occurred after his death—and which added to the fascinating Wildean legend.

AUGUST 17, 1940

WHEN OSCAR WILDE WAS LAID in his grave on the morning of December 3, 1900, one might have hoped that he had at last found rest. But the concession which Robert Ross, his literary executor, had rented at the cemetery of Bagneux on the outskirts of Paris, allowed only temporary hostage to the man who had been variously known as convict C.3.3. and Sebastian Melmoth. Ten years later, after the devotion of Ross and the loyalty of other friends had restored to Wilde some of the fame that was rightfully his, it was thought fitting that his body be removed from its obscure grave to Père Lachaise, already tenanted by Chopin, Alfred de Musset, Balzac, and many another of France's great dead. Ross had raised money for the cemetery plot. Mrs. Carew, the mother of Sir Coleridge Kennard, donated the monument, the execution of which was entrusted to Jacob Epstein. It was all simple, beautiful, and noble. But the perverse fatality that pursued Wilde in life did not spare him after death.

During the month of June 1912, the Epstein sculpture, a nude, virile angel whose Sphinxlike face bore a distinct resemblance to Wilde's own, was exhibited in England before it was sent to Paris. No one had anything to say against it on the grounds of obscenity or of bad taste. When, however, it was transported to Père Lachaise in September, a minor revolution broke out. With appropriate irony, it was started by the proletariat. The employees at Père Lachaise, the masons, the gravediggers, and the custodians, saw nothing of art in the great flying Sphinx. They did see, however, that unlike the rest of the funerary sculptures, it was naked and decidedly unashamed. Accordingly, they made their complaints to the proper authority which proceeded to take what it considered adequate measures. Epstein himself, however, found them an offense to his art, and with his own hands, when he went to supervise the placing of his Sphinx, chipped off several kilos of plaster that had not been on the original.

For a time everything was quiet until one day in February 1913 Robert Ross received a letter from M. Delanney, Prefect of the Seine, informing him that the Epstein monument daily offended the sensibilities of the French people who went to the cemetery to meditate. Since Mr. Epstein had refused to make certain necessary modifications, and since the monument could not remain as it was, M. Delanney had the honor to warn Mr. Ross that unless something was done to remedy the situation, he would be obliged to remove the offending Sphinx at Mr. Ross's expense and at his risk "by virtue of Article 16 of the decree of the 23rd prairial, year 12." Moreover, the Prefect assured him, he was not alone in making the demand, but was supported by the Comité d'Esthétique de la Préfecture de la Seine.

All of Paris was up in arms. Who comprised this Esthetic Committee? And what was the Decree of the 23rd prairial? Upon investigation it was found that the committee consisted of more than a score of artists and sculptors, some of them members of the Institute. As for the decree—there it was, in black and white, among the archives of the first years of the Republic. The law showed a singular pudicity in a generation that had witnessed such outrages as those committed on the body of Mme. de Lamballe. Anyway, the article forbade the use of nudes as commemorative monuments in cemeteries unless such nudes were duly furnished with a *cache-sexe*.

In vain Wilde's friends circulated petitions and wrote letters to the newspapers. In vain Rémy de Gourmont made a public statement defending the statue and ridiculing the taste of the bourgeois with a pungency that had in it not a little of Wilde's manner. "I find nothing to object to in the monument. . . . What offends, believe me, is its originality. . . . It is the same with literature. Banality wins the day." In vain Aleister Crowley, that last shoot of the English decadence, unveiled the Sphinx in a gesture of defiance against the Paris authorities. Epstein's monument in the end had to submit to the adornment of a bronze fig leaf. "I should have much preferred," wrote the disheartened sculptor, "the monument to remain veiled until such time as the alleged improvements made against my express desires have been removed." During the years that followed zealous undergraduates took him at his word, and periodically one or another of them would appear in some public place wearing the bronze improvement round his neck. Today the winged Sphinx remains at Père Lachaise as the sculptor executed it except that some unknown hand has ended all controversy by mutilating the stone.

The same year that witnessed the furor over the Epstein monument released another sensation before its close. Ever since Wilde's death there had been persistent rumors that he was still alive and pursuing his existence incognito. Considering the myths sprung up during Wilde's life, it was no wonder the rumors were half believed by many who had swallowed whole the most preposterous inventions. What was to prevent the master of the pose, the arch-mystifier, from perpetrating another mystification?

George Sylvester Viereck, then a young newspaperman, found in the reports a core of plausibility, and out of his admiration for Wilde, wrote an article which he published in the *Critic*. The whole matter would have created only a mild stir were it not that the Paris correspondent of *The New York Times* took it up and promised to investigate it. Today, against the body of published source material, the testimony advanced seems weak, if not suspect. It hinges chiefly on the authority of a certain Arthur Craven Lloyd who claimed Oscar Wilde as his uncle by marriage. (Wilde's wife was Constance Mary Lloyd.)

On the 23rd of March, 1913—Mr. Lloyd is at least definite about the date—Oscar *redivivus,* fat, browned from his sojourn in sunny lands, and wearing a beard, came to look up his nephew in Paris. One might have thought that like Hamlet's father's ghost the very much materialized Oscar would have brought some startling message, pleaded for his vindication, or, to prove himself the real Simon Pure, uttered some memorable epigram. No. He merely quenched his thirst and said he was writing his memoirs. Nevertheless the Paris correspondent of *The New York Times* saw fit to declare by special cable on the eighth of November, that he almost believed "we shall see Wilde back in Paris some day." Robert Ross who had watched at Wilde's deathbed, Vyvyan Holland who had been called to the exhumation of his father at Bagneux, the remaining friends of Wilde who had been present at the funeral, maintained a disdainful silence. Only Henry Davray who had come to the wretched hotel room on the Rue des Beaux Arts before the coffin was nailed down cried in exasperated denial: "I have touched his corpse!" In spite of the hope of the Paris correspondent, the bearded Wilde never again appeared in the flesh. In the spirit world, however, he

leads an active life, to judge by the recorded Wildean epigrams of
the medium Lazar.

Works purported to be Wilde's began making their appearance
shortly after his death. Indeed, a translation of the *Satyricon of
Petronius,* and another of Barbey d'Aurevilly's flamboyant novel,
Ce Qui Ne Meurt Pas (What Never Dies) are still issued as genuine
Wildeana by publishers who may, or may not, be acting in good
faith.

What Never Dies appeared in Paris toward 1902 in an English
version attributed to Sebastian Melmoth. Wilde's most intimate
friends knew of no such work of his, but since the translation had
something of Wilde's style, and since they had no facts with which
to refute the assertion of the publisher, they could do nothing beyond wondering when Sebastian Melmoth had done his literary
hack work.

Robert Sherard, in *The Real Oscar Wilde,* quotes M. Dupoirier,
the landlord of the Hôtel d'Alsace, on Wilde's activities toward
the end of his life: "He used to work at night . . . all night long.
As a rule he used to come in at one o'clock in the morning and
sit down to his table, and in the morning he would show me what
he had written, and 'I have earned a hundred francs tonight,' he
would say."

What had Wilde been writing? Had he been doing work of which
he was ashamed and which therefore he kept secret from his friends?
Who would have paid him at the rate of a hundred francs for the
labor of a night? "At an important newspaper office," Sherard
writes elsewhere in his book, "I was told that he had been invited
to collaborate, regularly, [on] a weekly *chronique* at three hundred
francs the article." Had Wilde been writing part of such a *chronique?* Was that what he showed M. Dupoirier? Or, tortured by his
intellectual impotence which, with for once bitter humor he called
his *cacoethes tacendi,* was Wilde offering the simple Dupoirier hope
that the debts he owed him would be paid—by a pen that had been
broken in Reading Gaol? Whatever it was that kept him at his
table till morning, it was neither *What Never Dies* nor Petronius'
pagan banquet; for on an end-leaf in colored paper, inserted in
the edition of *The Picture of Dorian Gray* brought out in Paris in
1909 by Charles Carrington, there is a *nota bene* apprising the
reader that the publisher no longer offers the two translations as
the works of Sebastian Melmoth or Oscar Wilde.

Nevertheless short stories, poems, and other writings continued
to be thrust upon the public as newly discovered Wilde items.
There was a real stir in the literary world, however, when in 1922

the reputable house of Methuen of London which could boast of one of the finest editions of Wilde's complete works, included in the series *For Love of the King,* a Burmese masque, the existence of which came as a surprise to even such an authority as Christopher S. Millard who, under the pseudonym of Stuart Mason, had compiled in 1914 his extraordinary *Bibliography of Oscar Wilde,* one of the finest works of its kind ever produced.

"The very interesting and richly colored masque or pantomimic play which is here printed in book form, for the first time," an introductory note announces in *For Love of the King,* was invented sometime in 1894 or possibly a little earlier. It was written not for publication, but as a personal gift to the author's friend and friend of his family, Mrs. Chan Toon. . . . "

Who was this Mrs. Chan Toon? The same note offers enlightenment. "Mrs. Chan Toon, before her marriage to Mr. Chan Toon, a Burmese gentleman, nephew of the King of Burma and a barrister of the Middle Temple, was Miss Mabel Cosgrove, the daughter of Mr. Ernest Cosgrove of Lancaster Gate, a friend of Sir William and Lady Wilde, and herself brought up with Oscar and his brother Willie." A delicate little detail, this, of little Mabel Cosgrove growing up with the two Wilde boys. As all the persons mentioned could make no denial from the grave, Mrs. Chan Toon became her own authority for this infantile interlude. Still another question—Why had the masque not been published before?—was forestalled by the note which implied that out of a sense of delicacy Mrs. Chan Toon had not until then consented to see it in print, even though Robert Ross—also dead—had wanted to include it in his edition of Wilde's works. The public was further informed that Mrs. Chan Toon was now Mrs. Wodehouse Pearse, the nephew of the King of Burma having in the meantime joined his ancestors.

The weight, however, for the authenticity of the Burmese masque lay in the letter to Mrs. Chan Toon from Oscar Wilde which followed the introductory note. Unlike nearly all of Wilde's correspondence, it was carefully dated from Tite Street, November 27, 1894. In it he thanked Mrs. Chan Toon for the receipt of one of her books, advised her that he was sending her the fairy play "for your amusement," elaborated with unsubtle suggestion his meeting with "a Swedish Baron, French in manner, Athenian in mind, and Oriental in morals . . . " (not omitting the suspension points) and closed with remembrances from Constance "while I, who am bathing my brow in the perfume of water lilies, lay myself at the feet of you and yours."

In spite of much that would have roused the suspicion of anyone acquainted with the style of Wilde, *For Love of the King* was accepted by the reviewers, the critic of the *London Times Literary Supplement* alone wondering "whether Wilde would have cared to see this . . . solemnly put out among his collected works." There the matter might have ended had not Christopher Millard received a letter in June 1925 from Mrs. Wodehouse Pearse, offering him "six very interesting Wilde letters which for an immediate deal you can have at a bargain." Mrs. Wodehouse Pearse took the opportunity at the same time of reminding him that she was the owner of the original Burmese masque.

Needless to say, Millard, an ardent collector of Wildeana, leapt at the offer of six new letters, and immediately got in touch with Mrs. Wodehouse Pearse. Alas, even the most cursory examination convinced him that the letters were all forgeries. His suspicions thus confirmed, he wrote to Methuen the following day for permission to examine the original typescript of *For Love of the King*, with corrections in Wilde's handwriting, and also the Wilde letter printed with the masque, which no one but Mrs. Wodehouse Pearse had ever seen. After delay occasioned by the publisher's difficulty in obtaining the typescript, Millard had the opportunity of examining it. The corrections, he ascertained, were not in Wilde's handwriting. An expert whom he consulted went further: they were in the hand of Mrs. Wodehouse Pearse. The publisher, in absolute good faith, had been imposed upon by another ingenious hoax.

Acting on his knowledge, Millard exposed what he had no hesitation in calling "one of the most remarkable literary forgeries of recent years." But the masque still appears as the work of Oscar Wilde with the translation of *Petronius* and *What Never Dies.* Doubtless new forgeries will be perpetrated, other hoaxes be imposed upon a market in which the name of Oscar Wilde commands a high price.

THE ARTIST AND
HIS TIMES

by Arthur Koestler

The writer of timely novels faces his own peculiar problems, as the author of the political novel Darkness at Noon *herewith explains.*

ONE OF THE GREAT RUSSIANS—I think it was Turgenev—could only write with his feet in a bucket of hot water under his desk, facing the open window of his room. I believe that this position is typical for the novelist. The hot water bucket stands for inspiration, the subconscious, the creative source, or whatever you like to call it. The open window stands for the world outside, the raw material for the artist's creation.

Let us for once ignore the hot water bucket and assume that our novelist is a genuine artist, endowed with creative force; and let us instead concentrate on the open window and its influence on the man behind his desk.

The first and strongest temptation which the world outside the window exerts on the writer is to draw the curtains and close the shutters. Now this apparently so simple reaction has various interesting aspects. Perhaps the most dangerous one is that the gesture seems so natural. The writer needs concentration; his nerves are easily upset. He must make an immense and ever-renewed effort to bear the open window, to let those piercing screams into the room, the laughter, the groaning, and those ephemeral battle cries.

Another aspect of the temptation to close the window is that it does not at all resemble the traditional form of temptation, but rather the opposite. The tempter does not appeal to base mortal desires but to the loftiest regions of the spirit. His lures are: peace, beauty, perhaps even communion with God. The fiend does not ask you for your soul, he wants to make you a gift of it. He whispers: "Shut the window. The world is a hopeless case. Action is evil. Responsibility is evil. Draw the curtains, forget those savage battle cries, fill your ears with stillness, and bathe your smarting eyes in the dim light of eternity."

Behind the closed shutters strange and sometimes beautiful constructions come to life, the growths of the hothouse, plots and characters hatched in the hothouse. The ivory tower was only one passing form of closed-shutter-interior. There are others; for the decoration of the room with the drawn curtains is, strangely enough, subject to the fashion of the time, although fashion and time itself are supposed to be locked out. The ivory tower was an esthete's creation; others are modeled on ethic principles. Their inhabitants don't fiddle while Rome burns, they pray. The room with the drawn curtains may be changed into the nave of a cathedral where the bearded Russian novelist sings hymns of atonement for his revolutionary past; or a sort of introspective deep-sea-aquarium populated by monsters in phosphorescent light; or the padded cell of Maupassant and Gérard de Nerval. The latest transformation seems to be an exotic hermitage fit for Yogi exercises. It almost looks as if the Pink Decade were to be followed by a Yogi Decade. So much about Temptation No. 1.

In Temptation No. 2 the action of the open window on the novelist is experienced not in the form of pressure but of suction. The man behind his desk is tempted not to close the shutters but to lean right out the window. He is so fascinated by the events in the street that he begins to gesticulate, shout, and declaim. Before, we had the case of an unimpaired creative force, but no vision of reality; here we have the case of a boiling-hot vision undigested by the creative process. In leaning too far out the window our author has taken his feet out of the hot water bucket; in technical terms, he has ceased to be novelist and has become reporter. This seems to be the reason for the failure of many prose writers of the Pink Decade. It was a period in which novels read like dispatches by war correspondents from the fronts of the class struggle. The characters seemed to be flat, two-dimensional beings, fighting their shadow battles against a lurid background. People in the pink novel had a class-dimension (length) plus, say, a sex-dimension (width); the third, irrational dimension (depth), was missing or atrophied.

In the post-Pink or Yogi Decade the irrational dimension takes its revenge by outgrowing all others. The few authors who have survived the pink era are those who, even in the thick of the battle, never forgot the irrational dimension—e.g., Silone and Malraux. But they are exceptions.

Apparently it is very difficult to keep the window open and your feet in the hot water bucket at the same time. Therefore most novelists, past and present, adopt a compromise, and this compromise is the essence of Temptation No. 3.

In this case the window is neither open nor closed but left ajar, and the curtains are drawn in such a way as to expose only a limited section of the world outside while hiding the more painful and menacing sights from the author's eye. He may even push a telescope through a hole in the curtain and thus obtain an image with admirably sharp contours of a small and perhaps not very important fraction of the world. Works of incontestable merit can thus be produced in spite of the fact that they are made of fragments only of the phenomena outside—there is love without sex, work without sweat, class distinction without envy, melancholia without constipation. The telescope may also be focused in another direction, or the left window opened instead of the right—then we get sex without love and a sharp telescopic image of constipation, hatred, and sweat. And again works of merit have been produced with this fragmentary optic. Why then call this so-successful method a "succumbing to temptation" and why insist on the fully open window? Because the hole-in-the-curtain method may produce occasional masterpieces of technical virtuosity as in the Victorian novel or in the naturalistic novel, but inevitably leads to a dead end in the development of the novel as an art. Our admiration for Dickens or Zola always has a slight taint of benevolent indulgence.

Indeed, the term "temptation" presupposes the existence of a road leading to a certain end, a road to perfection from which the tempter tries to lure us to sidetracks. To yield does not necessarily involve artistic failure; but I do believe that there is a main road leading from *Eulenspiegel* and *Don Quixote* to *War and Peace, The Magic Mountain,* and *Fontamara.* And I also believe that *Tristram Shandy,* and *Wuthering Heights, Swann's Way,* and *The Waves* are masterpieces at dead ends.

To justify this apparently arbitrary distinction, let us return to our window and watch our fallen author at work. His curtains are closed, but he has made a tiny circular hole in the fabric, with a telescope pushed through, focused on a house and a garden, and a girl with a bunch of roses in her hands, waiting for her betrothed. She is not necessarily the wish-dream-girl of suburban circulating libraries—she may be a very sophisticated young lady with, in her free left hand, a volume of Proust. "Isn't she lovely?" asks our author—who may be a very good author recommended by the Book Society. "Isn't she *alive?* Her name is Sylvia." And indeed we must admit that house, garden, girl, and roses are perfectly lifelike in spite of the fact that they were produced by the hole-in-the-curtain

method. We watch them with admiration until about page twenty-
five; and then we horrify the author with the question: "Excuse us,
but haven't you forgotten the factory chimney in the background,
the splitting of the atom, Voronoff's apes, and the concentration
camps?" "Are you crazy?" retorts our author. "Do you expect me to
drag a German refugee into my picture, with scars on his back?"

The answer, of course, is no. We do not want him to *drag* anything into the picture, not even a chimney as background; that
would not help. But there is an alternative in our minds which does
require an answer if Sylvia is to be not a puppet but a real being,
living in this century, now and here. The alternative is this: either
she knows about the concentration camps and still goes on standing
there with roses in her hand, then this adds an important feature to
her character—not necessarily a derogative feature, but an important one. Or she has never heard or read about them, then this
again gives us a cue. And these cues are essential because they show
us her relations, or absence of relations, to the essential facts of her
time. But these essentials being shielded from the author by the
curtain with the one tiny hole—how can he show her to us in true
proportion? We do not miss the factory chimney in the picture—we
miss it in the author's mind.

The absence of background (not in the picture itself but in the
author's mind) makes the house, the garden, and Sylvia with her
roses, appear as a half-truth, a lie. It is the author's ignorance of
what is going on behind the veiled parts of the window which de-
prives the picture of its width and depth, of perspective and proportion, and which makes me feel that the longer we look at the
young lady in her garden, the more she resembles a wax figure at
Madame Tussaud's.

The perfect novel, then, indeed presupposes a totally open window, and that the author should have an all-embracing knowledge
of the essential currents and facts (including statistics), of the ideas
and theories (including the natural sciences) of his time. This
knowledge is not for actual use—that would produce an encyclopedia, not a novel. It is for use by implication. It has to act as a
catalytic agent, as the saliva in the process of creative assimilation.
Without it, the characters will be distorted and the story arbitrary,
like a Victorian plot. The act of creation presupposes omniscience.

But is not all this rather abstract? In hundreds of novels, with
some quite good novels among them, the young lady still stands
triumphantly in her garden and still clasps those roses in her out-
stretched hand. Our objection to her was that the author did not,
or did not want to, see her in the perspective of her environment,

the world of the split atom and the flame-throwers. But what if the narrow surroundings which conditioned her character bear in fact no relation whatever to those unpleasant events which we obstinately call the essentials? Do not millions of Sylvias exist unscorched by flame-throwers and the problems of their time? And is it not possible to write quite good books about them?

Let us imagine a human being living on an island isolated from the rest of the world, and with no knowledge of the rest of the world. His *real* character is of course conditioned by his immediate environment. Yet as a *novel* character the most interesting thing about him will be his ignorance of the essentials of his time, his (negative) relation to the background. We see him in the specific novel-perspective: that is, *we know more about him than he knows about himself*. We have included in our vision the background of the towns, mountains, and rivers unknown to him; and only by seeing him in proportion to these towns, rivers, and mountains did we give him novel-life. In other words: his novel-character is conditioned not by his narrow island-surroundings which condition his real life, but by distant surroundings with which he has no point of contact whatever. If I cut these distant surroundings out of my mind he will in reality be still alive, but for the novel he is dead. And are the concentration camps, the factory chimneys, and the flame-throwers less real or significant than the rivers and mountains?

The law of the novel-perspective prescribes that it is not enough for the author to create "real life," he must also locate its geometrical place in a co-ordinate system, the axes of which are represented by the dominating facts, ideas, and tendencies of his time; he must fix its position in an n-dimensional space-time continuum. The real Sylvia spins around the center of a narrow family vortex of conditioning factors, whereas the author, in promoting her to novel-life, places her in the center of a vortex formed by the great trade winds, typhoons, depressions, and hurricanes of her time. Of course he need not describe or even mention them. But implicitly they must be there.

Only this way, it seems, can the novelist keep on the main road, avoid the sidetracks and dead ends. His greatness is in direct proportion to the width and depth of his vision. His window has to be filled with an all-embracing view even if his subject is only a garden with a girl in it. His ears have to be filled with the harmonies and discords of the great symphony, even if his attention is concentrated on the voice of a single flute. "Where there is hope in the air he will hear it; where there is agony about he will feel it." (C. Day Lewis)

Being a contemporary of ours, what he feels will be mainly agony. In other periods it may seem that to care for politics is a temptation for the artist. In periods like the present the temptation is not to care for politics.

Yet whatever his convictions may be, any idea—political, philosophical, scientific—has novel-life and *raison d'être* only if assimilated by the characters of the novel. In the true novel, as opposed to reportage and chronicle, the main action takes place inside the character's skull and ribs. Thus both facts and ideas are conveyed only after a double process of digestion.

It is a strange and sometimes painful process. When I think of the species Novelist, I am always reminded of certain strange practices of the Australian white ant. The normal ants of this species are not able to benefit by the food within their reach owing to an insufficiency of their digestive apparatus. They would all die of starvation but for the existence of certain specialized workers who gather the harvest, select, devour and digest the food, and feed all the others, the queen, the workers, and the winged adults, with the contents of their stomach. In some species these workers never leave the nest; they hang head downward in the dark vaults and tunnels of the termitary, and in the absence of other receptacles become living reservoirs, cisterns, honey-pots—with enormous elastic, distended bellies into which the harvest is poured, to be pumped out when folk are hungry.

Hanging head downward in the dark vaults of our termitary, feeding warriors and winged adults with the assimilated products of a bitter and poisonous harvest, the artist of today is inclined toward rather sinister thoughts. At times he feels as if he were the only adult surrounded by beings still at the stage of befouling themselves. Hence his urge and duty in a world where nobody is well: *the duty not to accept.*

In fact all the temptations I mentioned have one common denominator: the temptation to accept. To close the window *pour embrasser l'absolu,* means to accept the madness outside as incurable, to shirk responsibility. To leave the window ajar and hide the more unpleasant sights means acceptance by complacency. Complacency is passive complicity, and in this sense all art is propaganda, by omission or commission. But only in this sense. Conscious propaganda means the artist's abdication and is only another form of escape—escape into the happy fields of dilettantism where all problems and difficulties are easily solved.

The artist is no leader; his mission is not to solve but to expose, not to preach but to demonstrate. "We make out of our quarrels with others rhetoric, but with our quarrels with ourselves, poetry," said Yeats. The healing, the teaching and preaching he must leave to others; but by exposing the truth by special means unavailable to them, he creates the emotional urge for healing.

Thus the writer has a definite social task and function to fulfill. When embarking on a novel the author is not unlike the captain of a vessel setting out on a voyage with sealed orders in his pocket. But when he opens the envelope after having put out to sea, he finds that the order is written in invisible ink. Unable to read it, he is yet constantly aware of a duty to perform. For he is a captain of a warship, not of a pleasure cruiser. The indecipherable yet imperative orders in his pocket fill him with consciousness of his responsibility. This is the greatness of the writer's mission; this is his predicament.

THE IDEA OF HAPPINESS

by Raoul de Roussy de Sales

*In Western history, the notion that man's chief end is happiness
is a comparatively new one. Here the origins of the notion are put
into proper historical perspective by a French scholar and essayist,
together with some interesting opinions of how the idea of happiness has affected the history of America.*

FEBRUARY 14, 1942

WHEN THE BLOODTHIRSTY, sinister, but intellectually superior friend
of Robespierre, the revolutionary Saint-Just, said: "The idea of
happiness is new in the world," he threw on his own time and on
the times to come one of those rare beams of light which, once in
a while, seem to illuminate the course of history.

For Saint-Just to speak of happiness as a new idea—he who had
sent so many to the guillotine and was to die on it himself at the
same time as Robespierre at the age of twenty-seven—may seem
paradoxical and even somewhat ironical. But Saint-Just, like all
fanatics, had flashes of insight which were totally irrelevant to his
actual behavior.

Approximately one hundred and forty years later, another fanatic
was to make another remark on the same subject which helps us
to appreciate the deep opposition between the French and the German revolutionary. "The era of personal happiness," said Hitler,
quoted by Rauschning, "is closed."

Thus, without knowing it, Hitler replied to Saint-Just and gave
him a denial as to the place of happiness in the world.

It would obviously be stretching the point to attribute to Saint-
Just the discovery that the era of happiness was beginning in his
time and to honor Hitler with the privilege of deciding that it is
now closed. But it is true that the French Revolution did launch
through the world the new notion that the aim of life was happiness, and that Hitler is doing his best to make this aim impossible by contending that the aim of life is merely the assertion of
power.

As it is always well-nigh impossible to imagine the outlook of
life of men living in past centuries, we have difficulty in conceiv-

206

ing today that for our forefathers the notion of happiness was not connected with this earth. Up to two hundred years ago, men placed their hopes in a life hereafter. Such had been the teaching of the Church since the Middle Ages and the pursuit of happiness on this earth was neither conscious nor encouraged. The whole moral outlook of the Western man was indeed based on the fundamental precept that the purpose of life was to deserve a place in Heaven, and that earthly ambition or satisfactions were more of a handicap than an asset to those who, one day, would have to appear before their Creator. Such was the conception of our forefathers, the "Theological Man."

The philosophical evolution that leads up to the eighteenth century and the great break of the French Revolution can naturally be traced back quite far. But the progress of rationalism was slow to penetrate the consciousness of the individuals. When Saint-Just declared that the idea of happiness was new in the world, he merely stated the fact that the reign of the theological man was at an end.

If one keeps in mind this concept of the theological man while reading the literature and memoirs of Western Europe previous to the eighteenth century, one cannot help being struck by the profound repercussions that this difference of point of view between ourselves and our forefathers had on the behavior of the individuals and on their whole conception of the world in which they lived.

For them—and more especially for those living before the Renaissance—the notion of the future was meaningless in terms of progress or happiness. The dogma of the Original Sin permeated all thinking. Man was born wicked and his only hope was for a better life after death. There was no concept that man considered as an individual, or as a succession of generations, could improve his lot on this planet. The future was not associated with any notion of betterment, except in so far as the promise of the advent of the Kingdom of God on this earth would be eventually fulfilled. Men were expecting the end of the world, sometimes in terror, sometimes in hope. They were not expecting that life on earth could ever be anything but miserable. To live was admittedly a punishment.

The Renaissance modified this pessimistic outlook to a great extent, but did not change the fundamental relation between the theological man and his environment. The discovery of the beauty, wisdom, and science of the ancient civilizations of Greece and Rome merely confirmed—on the secular plane—the religious belief in a

Paradise Lost. The men of the Renaissance found a new source of inspiration in the revelation that great cultural epochs had preceded them. But their admiration for these epochs, far from inciting them to look toward their own future, merely convinced them that the limit of perfection in art, thought, and knowledge had already been reached, and that they could do no better than to try and imitate and recapture it. With their eyes fixed on the glorious and fabulous mirage of past centuries, they walked backward into the future. If, in so doing, they were themselves equaling, and often surpassing their masters, they were not conscious of it.

Thus the Renaissance and the centuries that followed, in spite of the vast new fields that they opened to the curiosity and speculation of the Western mind, did not affect very rapidly or perceptibly the outlook of the generations of men to whom the notion that humanity as a whole could become *happier* on this earth through its own efforts, was still foreign. No doubt such men as Bacon and Descartes perceived that human reason could be utilized not only as an instrument of analysis of what was and what had been, but also as a means of elevating the status of mankind. But it is only in the eighteenth century that the concept of progress, such as we understand it today, became sufficiently clear to influence the course of history. The most important single fact in both the American and French Revolutions is probably the conscious will to create something *new*. For the first time in the history of the West, men deliberately turned toward the future and expressed the faith that the condition of mankind could be improved by human means.

The two Revolutions opened an era in which the whole philosophical nature of the Western man was to change with extreme rapidity and in such a way that nearly all the concepts of the past were to be abandoned. Society, instead of being merely a conglomeration of individuals each intent on his own personal salvation, became the medium through which the material as well as the spiritual welfare of these individuals could be gradually improved.

It is not necessary to dwell here on the various philosophical doctrines and scientific discoveries which, all through the nineteenth century, confirmed the modern man in his belief that he was definitely set on a new road, and that step by step he was advancing toward a better future.

The prestige of science and rational thinking as a means of solving ultimately all human problems was at its height at the end of the last century. The few thinkers who were beginning to doubt the limitless possibilities of science and were reverting to some sort of mysticism, made little impression on the public mind. The tangible and undeniable progress of applied science could only reinforce the popular faith in a philosophy of life, the truth of which every new discovery seemed to verify.

The religion of progress was universal, but nowhere did it find a more complete and harmonious expression than in the United States.

The philosophical and political concepts of the founders of the American republic, inspired as they were by English and French liberalism, adapted themselves perfectly to the expansion and growth of the American people. The whole history of America, in fact, appeared as a practical demonstration that these philosophical concepts were sound. Pioneering and the frontier spirit were the physical manifestations of the new faith of mankind in its own ability to reach happiness—or rather to create it by its own efforts.

That the pursuit of happiness often translated itself in the crudest kind of materialism cannot be denied. In America as elsewhere the tendency to identify happiness with wealth has been constant. In a nation where success is worshiped as a sign of superiority, and where the current measure of success is neither a title nor any distinctive honor, it is natural that wealth should be adopted as the universal standard of value.

But the remarkable thing is that the American faith in the principles of democracy as a means of distributing happiness to all should have survived the innumerable assaults of piratical groups, who all through American history have attempted to capture power for no other purpose than their own interests.

Many Europeans, from Karl Marx to Hitler, have been deluded by the so-called materialism of the Americans. It seems incomprehensible to them that in a country where there seems often to be only a difference of appreciation between the methods of the robber barons and those of the gangsters, the faith of the people as a whole in the validity of democratic ideals should remain intact. It is a fact that in no other civilized nation—and up to a very recent past—has the power of money given more impunity and caused more injustice than in America. But it is also a fact that in no other nation have these abuses caused less moral damage to the nation as a whole.

The reasons for this phenomenon are complex, but the main one seems to me to be found in the rocklike quality of what has been called the American dream. As long as the Americans believe in progress, in the pursuit of happiness on this earth, in the possibility of improving themselves and the rest of the human race both physi-

cally and spiritually by concerted efforts—as long as they believe
that democracy, both as a system of government and a philosophy
of life, offers them a means of achieving those ends—as long as
these political and moral truths are identified with the American
nation itself, such "heresies" as the purely materialistic enterprises
of some privileged individuals or minorities will be suppressed
periodically.

The conviction that man as an individual and as a species can become increasingly happy on this earth is so deeply rooted in the
American concept of life that it is not possible to consider any aspect of American activity without being struck by the realization
that progress is accepted as a law of nature, as rigid and as unfail-
ing as the law that governs the fall of Newton's apple. The possibility that progress, in the material sense, might not necessarily
bring with it more happiness, is not accepted and the whole trend
of American civilization is determined by the belief that happiness
is indeed a function of progress.

Without going into a futile philosophical or moral discussion
of what happiness means (the only word, said someone, that corresponds to nothing at all) it would appear that one of the great
achievements of American civilization is to have created and kept
alive the faith of the people in the practical possibility of achieving more happiness by a positive and constructive effort of the
community. In so doing they have also solved effectively the embarrassing problem which for so many centuries baffled the Christian world: the moral conflict arising from the incompatibility between the enjoyment of life and the pursuit of one's own salvation.
When President Hoover promised two cars in every garage, nobody
accused him of immorality. What did appear immoral in fact was
the failure of Mr. Hoover to make his promise come true. There is
room for any type of religious or moral reformer in America except one: Saint Francis of Assisi.

That the concept of happiness and that of progress have been
merged into one has had as a further consequence the nearly complete elimination of the opposition between the spiritual and the
material. According to the current American viewpoint, any material improvement entails automatically a spiritual one and vice
versa. The uncomfortable suspicion that although man can and
does improve his material surroundings and his body but does not
improve his mind, may trouble at times the sleep of the philo-
sophically minded, but such is not, by and large, the popular belief.

There are so many manifestations of this belief in everyday life
that I can give here only a few examples:

The American faith in the benefits of education as a means of collective and self-improvement is so absolute that it can be said that no other nation spends so much time per capita in trying to solve, through learning, some problems which in other times and other lands have been left to individual initiative or which have been left out of the field of education altogether. I am not referring here to the education given in the schools and colleges, but to the fabulous amount of books, magazine articles, lectures, radio talks, etc., which purport to teach the adults of both sexes such subjects as the art of being happily married, of making friends and influencing people, of becoming successful, of thinking, etc. Not that such pseudo-educational enterprise or quack advice is particularly harmful. But it is revealing of the belief of a very large public in the possibility of solving practically all conceivable human difficulties by the same methods as one gets a tooth filled or a car repaired. Extended to a larger sphere, it explains also and confirms the American faith in some political, social, and economic formula by which the ills of the world could be cured once and for all.

In another field, that of health, one recognizes the same tendency to believe that the progress of the human mind is intimately dependent on the improvement of health and hygiene. The old Latin saying *mens sana in corpore sano* is certainly part of the American credo, but it has been extended and improved in the sense that physical health and the outward perfection of the human body have become aims in themselves on the assumption that the mind and even the soul cannot but benefit indefinitely from a progressive elimination of the ills and imperfections which affect the human species.

The Greeks showed an analogous interest in health and beauty and in the athletic aspect of man. In fact, they deified the human body. But what is typical of the American point of view on this subject is that it is in no way pagan. There is no cult of human beauty nor even of health. What sustains the immense efforts made for the furtherance of medicine and the beauty parlor is not only the desire to alleviate suffering and to satisfy vanity, but the conviction of serving the future of the race as a whole. Here again we find a materialistic objective justified by and merged with a moral end.

The identification of the notions of happiness with the faith in progress has strengthened the belief that happiness on earth is not only attainable but that one can measure the advance toward this goal. Material progress can usually be computed in terms of statistics, and if it is assumed that more progress means more happiness, it follows that happiness can be weighed quantitatively. If fewer people die of pneumonia this year than last, if more people have radios this year than last, progress has been accomplished and this progress can be measured accurately. By inference the amount of happiness can also be measured, and although philosophers and moralists have argued for centuries to prove that individual happiness was totally independent of material circumstances, the American viewpoint and the American way of life formally deny their conclusions.

In regard to the present crisis and the war in particular, the American faith in constant improvement of mankind has produced many strange contradictions and insoluble mental conflicts. For instance, many spokesmen of public opinion have frequently expressed the idea, ever since the war started, that the reason why American opinion had been lethargic for so long in the presence of a recognized danger and so hesitant to make the necessary sacrifices to ensure victory, was the fear that the peace would not offer anything much better to humanity in general, and to the United States in particular, than had already been achieved. The Americans, it was argued, could not be convinced of the validity of this war until it could be demonstrated to them that they were fighting for a *better* world.

What this better world is to be varies according to individual ideas, but there appears to be a consensus that to defeat Nazi Germany is not enough. In the same manner as Wilson, in 1917, suggested a "peace without victory," which implied the triumph of a moral concept, contemporary Americans would like some sort of guarantee that this second world war has, as its ultimate purpose, not the defeat of the enemy, but the establishment of more justice and more prosperity for all (including the enemy). War, in other words, which means the conflict of force regardless of all considerations save defeat of one side by the other, cannot be accepted by the Americans for what it is. In spite of the realization that the very existence of America as a nation is at stake in this struggle, the waging of war must be presented as a means of furthering human progress, and not as a brutal necessity. War, in fact, must be integrated in the American concept of things, which implies that everything must, somehow or other, serve the progress of humanity.

Even the fatalists who believed that Hitlerism and the rise of German imperialism should not be resisted because this is the "wave of the future" did not renounce their fundamental American optimism. Quite the contrary. In fact their "fatalism" was bolstered up and justified by a firm belief that nothing can happen which does not eventually further the good of humanity and its happiness on earth. Thus the recommendation that one should abandon oneself to the "wave of the future," far from being the expression of a philosophy of nonresistance to a possibly dangerous fate, was merely a blind act of faith in the future. Those who adopted this attitude did not believe that Hitlerism was a good thing in itself. In fact they professed to loathe it. But being imbued by American idealism, they could not accept that even evil should not, by some obscure way, finally serve the cause of good.

WHAT I LEARNED ABOUT CONGRESS

by Norman Cousins

A willing pupil, the editor of SRL *takes a one-day course in Congressional behaviorism from the late Senator Taft, hears the Senate discuss the high price of hogs, waits breathlessly for the news of the first B-29 raid on Japan to filter through to the Senate floor, and draws a few conclusions of his own about the nation's chief legislative body.*

JUNE 24, 1944

THIS IS A REPORT of a visit to Washington for the purpose of learning about Congress at first hand from Senator Robert A. Taft, of Ohio. The trip grew out of a poem, "Recess for the Boys," by William Rose Benét, appearing in the Phoenix Nest of *The Saturday Review* (April 8, 1944). Senator Taft read the poem, which satirized absenteeism in Congress, then wrote to Mr. Benét, terming the criticism unreasonable and inviting the Pulitzer Prize poet to visit him for the purpose of learning just how Congress actually works.

This was the second time within a year that Mr. Benét had been tendered a distinguished invitation to learning. The first invitation came last summer from Thomas W. Lamont, head of the house of J. P. Morgan & Company, following a column by Mr. Benét on war profits. Mr. Lamont disagreed and offered to augment Mr. Benét's education in economics. The present invitation came from one of the most prominent and active Senators in Congress, son of a former President of the United States, and himself a "dark horse" possibility for the Republican Presidential nomination according to some political commentators.

The staff urged Mr. Benét to accept; clearly, solicitude for Mr. Benét's education was becoming a matter of considerable national importance.

But Mr. Benét found it impossible to accept. Other plans precluded even a one-day trip to Washington, and the keeper of the Phoenix Nest called upon me to pinch-hit. Needless to say, I jumped at the chance, conscious of serious education deficiencies of my own on Congress requiring expert attention. First, however, it was necessary to find out whether Senator Taft approved the change in the batting order. The Senator affably agreed, suggested a date —June 15—and supplied an advance outline of the following course of study:

> *Morning Classes*
>> 9 to 10 A.M. Senator's office, general routine, mail, organizing notes for committee meetings.
>> 10 to Noon. Observation in the theory and practice of a Senate committee.
>> Noon to 1 P.M. Observation in the theory and practice of the Senate itself. Vantage point: gallery.
>
> *Afternoon Classes*
>> 1 to 1:45 P.M. Refueling in the Senators' lunchroom. Instruction optional.
>> 1:45 to 3:00 P.M. Resumption of Senate theory and practice from the gallery.
>> 3:00 to 4:00 P.M. Parallel instruction at the House of Representatives. Gallery observation with the Senator.
>> 4:00 P.M. to as long as necessary. Summary lecture, at the Senator's office, the pupil to remain during visitors' calls.

As it actually turned out, the course was well planned, though somewhat intensive, and there was little deviation from the original outline. I arrived in Washington the evening of June 14, and set out early the next morning in high anticipation inevitably tinged with nostalgia at the prospect of going back to school. The scarcity of cabs, the heavy traffic, and my remarkable facility in getting lost within five seconds after entering any Government building, all combined to make me about twenty minutes late, something I had vowed to myself I would not let happen. I did not want to give the idea that Senators get to their offices any earlier or work any harder than editors of literary magazines. With profound chagrin, I learned that my mentor had arrived at 8:50 A.M., had asked for me, had worked for about fifteen minutes, then had stepped out of the office. While waiting for him to return, I became acquainted with Mr. I. Jack Martin, the Senator's secretary, a congenial, somewhat slight man of about 35, who was most co-operative in providing valuable basic orientation in office routine.

I learned from Mr. Martin that the Senator receives an average of 250 letters a day, though on peak days the number is so high

they don't even bother to count it; I learned, too, that many of the
letters or telegrams come from organizations and pressure groups;
that it is impossible for the Senator himself to read all the letters,
let alone answer them; that Mr. Martin screens through the most
important ones for the Senator's personal attention; that the others
are assorted, collated, tabulated, and filed after they are acknowledged—usually in the form of mimeographed letters. I learned that
the Senator is interested in the we-want-you-to-do-thus-and-so mail
but not dependent on it and generally uninfluenced by it. Even the
pressure telegram, talking at the top of its capital letters, must go
through the same processing as the less formidable regular correspondence.

I learned that the Senator is assisted by a staff of seven: a "Secretary" who is actually the office manager and special assistant; a
research or correspondence chief; and five secretarial stenographers
or typists. The research chief and a secretarial clerk work in an
additional office provided for Senator Taft in the Capitol itself,
within easy distance of the Senate Chamber and the Committee
rooms. Not all Senators enjoy these dual facilities, but Mr. Taft's
membership on seven important committees, as well as the fact that
his regular quarters in the Senate Office Building are somewhat
small, were responsible for the extra corner office in the Capitol.

My orientation was interrupted at this point by a young lady
who told Mr. Martin that the Senator had entered his office and
was waiting to see me. Senator Taft rose from his desk to greet me
as I walked in. He was as I had imagined him—a tall, somewhat
lean, fair-complexioned man of about fifty or fifty-five, with pleasant gray eyes, small nose, large, full mouth, and a small chin that
does not recede quite so much as it appears to in the newspaper
photographs. He is semi-bald and the effect is to give him a perhaps elongated and severe appearance from a distance, almost in
the manner of a Grant Wood portrait. But close up, his face becomes much softer, extremely youthful. His voice is well modulated,
his diction excellent, his choice of words simple yet effective. He
has a direct, pleasant manner and looks more like the head of a
chemistry department or economics department of a Midwest university than the popular conception of a Senator—broad beamed
fore and aft. He maintains an even composure, though he occasionally seems preoccupied.

Senator Taft began by discussing the general program for the
day, spoke about the morning's correspondence, ruffling through
the papers on his desk and coming up with a letter concerning
something that was said by the president of an Eastern university

at a Board of Directors' meeting of a large insurance company. The university president had been quoted as saying that he had just discussed the coming Republican National Convention with Senator Taft, who had confided to him that in all probability Governor Dewey would not be nominated on the first ballot, that there would be a deadlock between Dewey and Bricker, and that the plan was to break the deadlock by nominating Taft.

All this flabbergasted the Senator. He rang for a secretary and began dictating a letter. Politely but briefly, he told the university president that he was as surprised as he was bewildered, especially since the two hadn't seen each other for at least two years. But more important to him, he wrote, than the surprise or the bewilderment was the embarrassment. He had pledged his support to Governor Bricker and was prominent in organizing his campaign. References to his own candidacy, particularly when attributed to himself, might make it appear that he was only giving lip service to Governor Bricker and had plans and ambitions of his own.

Senator Taft finished the letter, sighed wearily, then smiled and said: "The old boy must be ga-ga."

I told the Senator that I myself had seen and heard numerous reports saying approximately the same thing. Surely there must have been some basis somewhere for it.

"If there is, this office has had nothing to do with it," he said. "I am not a candidate. The only thing I am getting ready to campaign about is for re-election as Senator from Ohio."

The phone rang. That gave me a chance to look around the office. It was furnished adequately, though somewhat mustily, with the heavy black leather fittings and glass-door bookcases that are as inseparable apparently from a Senator's office as franked envelopes. There was a generous assortment of family pictures. There was one of Mrs. Taft and several photographs of the four Taft boys, three of whom are now in military service. The largest picture in the room, standing on the floor and leaning against the fireplace, was a colorful sepia photograph of the Senator's father, President William H. Taft, snapped informally in his carriage as he lifted his hat to enthusiastic onlookers. Directly above it, on the mantel, was a brass statuette of President Taft. (Later I learned that Robert Taft idolized his father from early childhood and still does; that he goes out of his way to be nice to anybody who knew or has a kind word for his father.)

Next to the statuette on the mantel was a row of brightly jacketed books. I got up to examine the titles. Among them were

Pierre Van Paassen's *Forgotten Ally,* Louis Fischer's *Empire,* Philip
C. Nash's *World Order,* Ely Culbertson's *Total Peace,* Edward
Stettinius' *Lend Lease,* Carlos P. Romulo's *Mother America,* Philip
Kinsley's *The Chicago Tribune: Its First Hundred Years,* and
Horace Walpole, Gardenist, and David Dallin's *Soviet Russia's
Foreign Policy.*

Not a bad selection, I thought.

As I had looked over the books, the Senator had been observing
me—somewhat apprehensively, I thought. When his phone call was
completed, he spoke about the books with some anxiety. They had
been sent to him with the compliments of the author or the publisher, he explained. The books he read were in his library at home.
I made whatever mental adjustments were necessary.

By this time, it was past 10 A.M. and we were overdue at the
special committee meeting scheduled for that morning. Senator
Taft said that it was to be a closed meeting of the newly created
Senate Committee on Postwar Economic Policy and Planning, and
that he had arranged with Senator Walter F. George, the chairman, that I be permitted to sit in. On the way down to the committee room, he explained that the committee was currently working
on Senate Bill 1730, designed to cushion the shock of unemployment in the reconversion period immediately after the war.
The bill provided for what the sponsors believed was a comprehensive program of unemployment insurance.

We entered the committee room, there were brief introductions,
and I was seated on one side of the rim of a mammoth raised
horseshoe desk. The nameplate in front of me read "Claude E.
Pepper." The Senator from Florida, apparently, was unable to
attend. The Senators present, viewed left to right around the horseshoe from where I sat, were Scott W. Lucas, of Illinois; Alben W.
Barkley, of Kentucky, the Democratic majority leader; Senator Taft;
Carl Hayden, of Arizona; Walter F. George, of South Carolina,
the Chairman; Arthur H. Vandenburg, of Michigan; and Warren
R. Austin, of Vermont.

Under consideration was Senate Bill 1730. It sought to insure unemployment insurance programs of the individual states. Each
state has already enacted an unemployment insurance program,
ranging from benefits of $10 a week in some states to $22 a week in
Connecticut, over a period ranging from fourteen weeks in Arizona to twenty-four weeks in California. The states have established
funds with an aggregate total of some six billion dollars. Should
any state fail to meet its obligations under its own plan, the Federal
government would underwrite the deficit, according to the bill.

Most of the discussion concerned the relative advantages of the plan for one state as against another, for the small state as against the large, for the agricultural state as against the industrial, etc. It was apparent that two or three members of the committee were somewhat disturbed lest their own states suffer in relation to some hidden advantage held by another. After that, an inevitable brief dispute arose over States' rights vs. Federal powers, with Senator Taft championing the former and Senator Barkley the latter. Senator Taft then suggested that the Federal government make it possible for the states to extend the period of unemployment payments, when, as, and if necessary. Both sides seemed to think this suggestion reasonable.

After some further discussion on methods of collection and administration, Senator Taft signaled me to follow him.

Once outside, he explained that nothing new was likely to come up at his own meeting and asked whether I might care to attend a hearing of the Military Affairs Committee. The prospect intrigued me and the Senator phoned his secretary to serve as my escort. While waiting for Mr. Martin, I asked the Senator some questions. Unemployment insurance was fine as far as it went, but wasn't the basic problem one of creating a sound economy which in itself would provide against unemployment? Unemployment insurance was the least that Congress could do, but was it also the most that it intended to do?

The Senator replied that the Committee was proceeding on the basis of one thing at a time. The first problem to face the country at war's end, he said, would be the dislocations inherent in the demobilization, and the unemployment insurance was only an attempt to tide over the country until such time as reconversion and retooling could be accomplished. Moreover, he said, the Senate had already undertaken reconversion legislation.

And what about the longer range? What about the continuing problem of achieving a healthy economy? Consider the paradox: during war, we operate under a peak load with the bulk of the manpower drained off; during peace, we operate under a limited load with the bulk of the manpower available but largely unused.

The Senator acknowledged the problem, said he had certain ideas concerning a sound economy based on free enterprise. He said that free enterprise could never get going again under a continued policy of high Government spending, and that this policy could create a tremendous momentum for inflation. "We've got to put on the brakes," he said.

I asked him whether under certain circumstances it might not be impossible or inadvisable to put on such brakes. If free economy didn't start up by itself, wouldn't Government be compelled to help? Did not the Committee's own unemployment insurance act prove that the Government had to accept responsibility for economic dislocations? And what if the unemployed were still unemployed after twenty weeks or whatever the period of benefits might be?

In that case, said the Senator, he supposed there would have to be a period given over to work relief.

And if that wasn't enough?

"Then I guess we would have to keep men from starving by giving them checks outright," he said.

At that moment, the Senator's secretary arrived. Senator Taft arranged to meet me in the Senate gallery when Congress convened at noon, and he returned to his postwar committee.

When we arrived at the meeting of the Military Affairs Committee, I discovered that the same bill under discussion at the Postwar Committee session was also being considered here. After a half hour of approximately the same question-and-answer routine as the one I had just heard, with almost the identical considerations of States' rights, equality of benefits, administration costs, etc., I whispered to Mr. Martin, asking whether it was customary for Senate Committees to duplicate each other's work. His answer was that the Military Affairs Committee was at present studying demobilization and that this particular bill came within its purview. He added that subcommittees of both groups were to meet the following morning for the purpose of integrating their work and findings.

In any event, by this time, I had become reasonably aware of Senate Bill 1730 and I was eager to get over to the Capitol for the next step in my education. We got up and left. It was almost noon, time for the Senate to convene.

One of the most fascinating things about Washington is the underground passage between the Senate Office Building and the Capitol. The distance is perhaps no more than a quarter of a mile, but Senators are the most pathetic pedestrians in the world, so there is an electric car system operating by means of an overhead rail with only a single ground track on which the car is balanced. The vehicle looks like a cross between a mountain cable car and a tunnel-of-love contraption at Coney Island. It seats twelve people, strung out in pairs, with the operator in the center, and you go zipping along at a merry pace expecting the whole contraption to take off in flight at the first curve. Enchanted, I stayed on for an extra ride and I hope my official guide wasn't too embarrassed. All that was missing from the general get-up was a brass ring as you looped around the last turn.

If you are ever in Washington on one of those deadly summer days when the whole place feels like the black hole of Calcutta under a sun lamp, take my advice and stick it out in that cool cellar passage, every now and then shuttling back and forth on that breeze-blessed tram. If you rate temperature reduction above fragrance, then that ride is something out of this world. You don't have to be a Senator to get on, although you will be expected to give up your seat if the place suddenly becomes chock full of Senators and there isn't enough room. Another advantage possessed by Senators is that they can keep a car waiting for them even before they arrive simply by pressing a buzzer in the elevator on the way down. Sometimes a Senator may be fairly bursting to get over to the Capitol or back to his office, so he presses the buzzer three times. This is almost the equivalent of a four-alarm fire; and even if the tram has started on its way to the other side, it has to go into abrupt reverse to pick up its dashing cargo.

My cellar adventure resulted in my being five minutes late for the next class. The Senate had already convened when I entered the gallery with Mr. Martin, but it was difficult to know that by observing the men on the floor. Perhaps a half-dozen men were seated on the Democratic side of the chamber, a dozen on the Republican side, and men were walking up and down as well as in and out, and the chatter sent up a constant drone. The presiding officer, in the absence of Mr. Wallace, was Senator Guy M. Gillette, of Iowa, who was earnestly engaged in a side conversation with Senator Barkley.

Through it all came the overtones of some solid oratory. Someone was making a speech that I never would have believed had I not actually heard it. It seemed too typical to be true. It was about the virtues of the *great* American middle class, about how everyone was taking advantage of that *great* bulwark of American democracy, and how it was high time Congress recognized its tremendous responsibility to the *great* white class. Senator Barkley, quickly realizing that the speaker had intended to say "white collar class," politely tried to correct the blunder,* but that only served to stiffen the speaker, and he became more and more emphatic about less and

---

* The only other blunder of this type I was able to catch during the day was a reference to Iceland, instead of Finland, in connection with the regular payment on her debt.

less as he went along. What he had been leading up to so eloquently amounted to a demand for higher ceiling prices.

Another Senator chimed in to support the claim. He told about the ominous situation as it pertained to hogs and cattle and predicted a meat shortage in the near future. Two sentences later he was complaining about freight cars loaded with beef at sidings waiting futilely for buyers.

"Mr. Chairman," someone was saying, "this is the most outrageous situation I have ever heard of in my life."

Then someone said he wanted to pass along to the Senate a statement that had been told him in confidence about the cattle situation, but he was not at liberty to state the source of the information although he would be glad to divulge the source should anyone want to know it. This confidential information, he said, was that the cattle situation was the most confused it has been in years.

The matter of unfair hog prices was being aired with considerable gravity when an usher tapped my shoulder and told me that visitors were not permitted to take notes. Spying the press gallery at the other side, I thought it would simplify matters if I continued my notes from that section, only to discover that only representatives of the daily newspapers are entitled to work there. Not even weekly newspapers or news periodicals such as *Time* or *Newsweek* or *United States News* can use the Senate press gallery. This was an interesting curiosity and I asked the guard whether those magazines had tried to get the rule changed.

"Now don't start that war all over again," he said. "If you're from a magazine you'll have to rely on your memory."

When I returned to the gallery, Senator Taft came up to take me to lunch. He was accompanied by Senator John A. Danaher, of Connecticut, my own state, which I guess made me something of a constituent.

"We've got to cultivate the literary folk, now that elections are coming up," Senator Taft said.

On the way to the Senate restaurant, Senator Taft said he couldn't understand what all the noise was about that morning on the imminent shortage of beef, remarking that the present beef inventory was extremely high, yet only a few months ago the same scares were raised. I asked whether it was purely coincidental that the beef shortage scares were almost automatically followed with a proposal of higher prices. The Senator smiled.

The Senate lunchroom is as free of decorative ostentation as a cane chair. I don't suppose it has been redecorated since the last war. There is a large table in the center which can accommodate

perhaps fourteen or sixteen persons; the remaining tables are average sized and are spread alongside the walls. On the far side of the
room I observed Senator Robert La Follette sitting with his young
son, aged eight or nine. There was a generous sprinkling of women
around the room, most of them wives or daughters of Senators.

Whatever the situation may be around the rest of the country
with regard to runaway restaurant prices, the Senate menu certainly
indicates and justifies the existence of an OPA. For seventy-five
cents or a dollar you can order a meal unobtainable under a dollar
and a half in New York or under two dollars in any commercial
restaurant in Washington itself.

Most of the discussion at lunch was in the nature of shop talk
about mail, answered and unanswered, about long-distance telephone calls from irate constituents, about lobbyists, about legislation, about other Senators. I learned that the average Congressman
lives in constant dread of form letters sent over his signature to
people who ought to receive personal attention; that he never has
enough time to take care of his job properly; that what with committee meetings, Senate sessions, and the plaguing daily mail, he
keeps falling behind even though he may keep his office open three
or four nights a week.

Toward the end of the meal, someone rushed up and asked my
hosts to hurry back onto the floor. It seemed that Senator Bridges
was crying for help on some appropriations measure.

So far as I could see, the plea didn't make much of an impression.

"That type of thing gives me a pain in the neck," Senator Danaher said. "What makes him think I'd be of any help? What say,
Bob" (turning to Senator Taft) "let's get out there and vote the
other way—but only when we're good and ready."

Meanwhile, Senator Wherry, the party whip, was going from table
to table, in the Senate lunchroom, relaying Senate Bridges' call for
succor. If anyone got up promptly, I failed to notice it.

The conversation became more general after this. We got on to
the news, with cross-references to newspaper and magazine articles,
and I was both surprised and pleased to find Senator Taft quoting
with obvious relish from an item in *The New Yorker's* "Talk of
the Town." The subject of Wendell Willkie's series of newspaper
articles came up, and Senator Taft said that he agreed with the
piece on the Negro problem, but that all the other articles were
"the same old New Deal stuff all over again."

I suggested that perhaps that was why so many people seemed to
think so highly of them, and then pointed to the New York *Herald
Tribune* as a newspaper that could be opposed to the New Deal

and yet favor Mr. Willkie's articles. Senator Taft shook his head
to that, describing the New York *Herald Tribune* as a "Willkie
house organ."

After lunch, we returned to the Senate gallery, with Senator Taft
sitting alongside me and identifying the various members of Congress. I took this opportunity to confess my disappointment. A
debate on a supplementary appropriation bill was on the floor at
the time and we leaned forward to hear Senator Kenneth McKellar,
of Tennessee, as he orated on States' rights. At that moment, someone who had just come down the aisle whispered to Senator Taft,
who turned to me and said, simply:

"American bombers are over Japan."

Down below, on the floor of the Senate, young men rushed up
and down relaying the news. It was a dramatic moment.

Once the messengers left, there was nothing to indicate that anything exceptional had happened. Confusion and small talk. Senators strolling in and out. A handful of men in their seats. I had
the strange feeling that I was in a never-never land utterly removed
from the war. I thought of American planes over Japan, wondering
where they came from, wondering how many might never return.
And out of the mist of the strange world in which I found myself
words would come drifting up to me from the floor, words about
hogs and prices that ought to be higher, about items on appropriation bills that ought to be put in or left out, about States'
rights. . . .

*Wouldn't someone shut off the noise? Wouldn't someone raise the
curtain on reality if only for a moment by saying something about
what was happening in the world at that second?*

Finally, a dark man stood up in the far corner of the floor and
asked to be recognized. It was Senator Claude Pepper, of Florida.

"Mr. Chairman," he began, "word has just been received that
American B-29 planes have bombed Japan proper. I believe it is
only fitting that the Senate pause at this time both to pay tribute to
our aviators and to reflect upon the historic importance of this news.
It means that the theories of long-range, land-based aviation have
proven themselves. It means that the war will be brought home to
the enemy as never before. It means that America has come a long
way from the brink of chaos on which it found itself on the evening
of December 7, 1941. It means that . . ."

He was interrupted. Senator Clyde M. Reed, of Kansas, was asking a question.

"Did I understand the Senator from Florida to say that B-29
planes were the ones that did the bombing?"

Senator Pepper nodded.

"Well, then," sang out Senator Reed, "does everyone here know where those marvelous machines come from? They come from good old Kansas."

Thus saying, the Senator chuckled loudly and went back to his seat, obviously very happy with himself for having given his all for dear old Kansas.

After a momentary exposure to the face of reality, the Senate had snapped back into place.

I stepped outside for a breath of air.

Next stop was the House of Representatives. Senator Taft escorted me over. We didn't say much. Our minds were nine thousand miles away.

I confess that I was in no mood for the general pandemonium that burst upon me when I walked into the House gallery. I had expected confusion and disorder far beyond what I had witnessed in the Senate, since the House has more than four times as many members and physically is at least two or three times as large, but I was prepared for nothing like this. Let me try to give the picture as I saw it:

Perhaps one fifth of the Representatives were in their seats and were listening to the business at hand. The others were either clustered together in talkative little groups or were walking around chattering, or both. One of the Congressmen was bouncing a young child on his knee. Twice each minute the speaker had to rap for order; a comparative hush would follow the last rap of the gavel but would last perhaps five or ten seconds and the general commotion would start up all over again.

Since it is next to impossible to hear any Congressman from his seat, a microphone is set up at the rostrum in front of the Speaker's platform. A tall young-looking Congressman was speaking into the microphone at this time. The amplification system blared out his words but the combination of the over-all din and the poor acoustics made it difficult to snatch more than a phrase here and there. It was a curious and disturbing experience. People talking, talking. Hardly anyone listening. Now and then someone would ask to be heard, interrupting the speaker at the microphone. He would be recognized from the chair despite the general blur, and he would shout from his seat, but you couldn't hear anything. His lips would move, but that would be all. Or perhaps he would hurry down to say something in front of the microphone, but it only served to magnify the meaningless confusion.

With the feeling that I had aged at least ten years, I returned to Senator Taft's office for the concluding portion of the course. I sat alongside the Senator's desk while he carried on his regular business, the most conspicuous feature of which was its enforced lack of continuity. Unending interruptions by telephone calls, unexpected visitors, and office details reminded me somewhat of the editor's office of a magazine with which I have some familiarity.

There were telephone calls from Clarence Streit, the author of *Union Now,* who wanted the Senator to join him at dinner; from John D. M. Hamilton, who inquired on the progress of the Bricker campaign; from John T. Flynn, who wanted to show the Senator a statement he was preparing; from Alice Roosevelt Longworth, who extended a social invitation; and from several others from within the building.

So that my instruction would be as complete as possible, the Senator invited me to remain in his office while he received visitors. This may or may not have been disconcerting to the callers. It is possible that some of them left earlier than they had originally planned. At any rate, I took some comfort in the knowledge that I could reciprocate in some measure at least for the Senator's many favors.

It was now close to six o'clock, and I wanted to take up some general questions with the Senator that had occurred to me during the course of the day. First of all, I confessed my disappointment and apprehension at what I had seen on the floors of Congress. Even the Senate, for all its traditional dignity, seemed to be less a deliberative than an *adlib*erative body. So far that day I had heard nothing except jockeying around to favor one group or another at the expense of another. Was the Senate becoming nothing more than a sounding board for petty gripes?

"There's no place quite like this in the world," Senator Taft answered. "Anyone can get up at almost any time and talk about anything under the face of the sun. It makes for a good deal of confusion and a good deal of noise. There is a saying that the Senate gets its business done by unanimous consent or physical exhaustion. Sometimes you wonder whether anything at all is accomplished. But the surprise, actually, is how much really does get done despite all the appearance of disorder.

"When I first came here as a freshman Senator, it took me a year to get over my disillusion. Back in the State Legislature in Ohio everything was done with a sense of order and purpose. Here, I spent the first few months doing almost nothing except finding out where I was supposed to be and at what time, and trying to pick my way through the confusion. But after a while I got the hang of things and came around to the realization that, even if we do blunder through somewhat, the important thing is that free government is maintained—whatever its faults."

This seemed like the logical finale to my education on Congress, and I got up to leave. I expressed my gratitude to the Senator, whom I found to be an effective and engaging teacher, and he, in turn, extended an open invitation to me to return at any time for postgraduate work.

Returning on the train that night, I went over the day's lessons. Uppermost in my mind, of course, was Congress as I had actually seen it in action. I could still hear the bedlam, reminding me of an indefinite extension of the seventh-inning stretch at a ball game. I wish I could say I exaggerate. I wish I could say that so long as they blunder through, as Senator Taft put it, there is no point in bothering about it or even wondering about it.

True, I had been there at a bad time. Appropriation bills always make for chaotic and uninteresting sessions. Even so, I honestly can't help being bothered about it. I honestly can't help wondering about it. Yes; I know it is a thousand times better than a hall full of men whose minds click and keep pace just as do their heels. It is a thousand times better than hundreds of mouths chanting "Ja!" in unison. And if disorder and commotion are the price we have to pay for democratic institutions, then the price is utterly cheap and let the confusion reign supreme.

It hasn't always been this way. Congress hasn't always been a sounding board making big noises over small things. When De Tocqueville wrote his now-classic study of the American government more than a hundred years ago, he was impressed with the tremendous sense of responsibility and prestige of Congress. When Bryce wrote his *American Commonwealth* only fifty years ago, he, too, came away with a feeling of the towering dignity of the legislative branches of our government. But both writers also seemed to recognize that this magnificent framework had to be periodically strengthened; they seemed to recognize that the flexibility of the Congress could under certain circumstances become as great a disadvantage as it was an advantage.

It would be presumptuous of me to say what these "certain circumstances" are, but I should like to report my feeling that the blame cannot be placed upon the individual members of Congress or Congress itself as an institution. I agree with Jerry Voorhis, who asked people in a recent magazine article to "stop kicking Congress around." If Congress goes, we can kiss our democracy goodbye. The problem before us is to find out why and how it is that Congress has gotten this way, and then see if we can't help to restore something of an equilibrium.

What, then, is wrong with Congress? It isn't only the noise and the confusion, for those, after all, may be only external exercises which can be blotted out by a pair of sturdy earmuffs. But what troubles me is that the noise and confusion may be indicative of inner weaknesses.

In the first place, a Congressman's job is markedly different from what it was a generation or more ago. It is absolutely impossible for a Congressman today to meet all the demands upon him which are now inherent in the job. At one time, legislation was his chief concern. Today, legislation must take turns with dozens of other jobs, and this applies to Representatives and Senators both. The mail alone, if it is to be handled right, is a full-time job. There are at least twice as many letters today flooding in upon Congress as there were ten years ago. Personal calls from constituents are heavier than ever before, and a Congressman who wants to keep his job can't afford to turn away too many of them.

Then, too, the Congressman has inevitably become more of a lobbyist than he is a legislator. He is expected not only to vote but to use his influence in getting others to vote. He is expected to intercede for a business firm in his state or district which feels it is being discriminated against by a Government agency.

Most important, of course, is the matter of The Party. There are meetings and conferences and phone calls and letters, and sometimes hurried trips home to straighten out political snarls. There is no point in being falsely altruistic about this; a man who is interested enough to run for office in the first place is also interested in being re-elected.

What this all amounts to is that the largest part of a Congressman's time is almost inevitably taken up with activities which bear on his re-election. If this seems to be putting it too strongly, then we can at least say that the largest part of his time is taken up with activities that have little or nothing to do with a national legislative program. Certainly this is bound to reflect itself in the work of Congress as a whole. Men who are preoccupied with comparative trivia off the floor of Congress do not experience a revelation in high statesmanship the moment they step on the floor.

There is a disposition to excuse all this by saying that the real work of Congress is done in committee, and that most Congressmen keep up with current business by following *The Congressional Rec-*

ord. While I do not doubt that Congressmen have come to lean on the committees and *The Record,* I fail to see this as an adequate substitute. Otherwise, we shall have to admit that the floors of Congress are the greatest gymnasium for shadow-boxing in the world.

Still on the subject of time requirements, what about keeping well informed? That takes time, and plenty of it. I see no evidence to indicate that this particular demand has not frequently become an expendable. If wisdom depends upon knowledge, and knowledge upon information, and information upon time, one can readily understand how there is hardly time to be wise.

Faced with this drastic assortment of demands, the average Senator or Representative finds it impossible to attend the full daily session of his branch of Congress. Yet his name must appear on the roll calls; he must vote; occasionally he must make himself heard. Thus we have the peripatetic, or perhaps we should say perapathetic, Congressman who drops in and out, but who can never stay long enough to sink his teeth into any real legislative meat. Thus we have the noise and the confusion, which, as I said earlier, are actually and ominously indicative of deep-seated causes and strains.

Some members of Congress have protested that there has been afoot for the last few years an attempt to undermine not only the power but the prestige of Congress. If the institution of Congress has been weakened, then only Congress can answer for that. Only Congress can fix its own level. It can be as great or as inept as it chooses to be. It can play a vital part in the shaping of the peace or can trail meekly behind. It can be progressive or retrogressive, constructive or obstructive. There is no ceiling over its possibilities. But before these possibilities can be fulfilled, they must be recognized for what they are. A man who does not know where he wants to go is hardly likely to get there.

"COUNT NO COUNT"

by Phil Stone

The townsfolk laughed when he sat down to write, but today William Faulkner of Oxford, Mississippi is one of only five Americans who have won the Nobel Prize for Literature. Here Faulkner's friend, mentor, and townsfellow Phil Stone recalls how the novelist's early works were received in his home town.

SEPTEMBER 19, 1942

"COUNT NO COUNT" was the title by which he went in Oxford and at the University of Mississippi located here. His family was a noted one in this section of Mississippi beginning with his great-grandfather, William Cuthbert Faulkner—after whom he was named. The old man had been a prominent lawyer, had been a Colonel in the Confederate States Armies, had been politically influential, had built and operated a railroad, had traveled in Europe and had written a book about it, had written that news butch thriller *The White Rose of Memphis,* had been a most energetic, versatile, and successful man—and had accumulated a fortune.

The grandfather of William Faulkner, J. W. T. Faulkner, had also been a successful lawyer and had founded and been president for years of the First National Bank of Oxford. Bill's uncle had been a Circuit Judge and a successful lawyer and a member of the Board of Trustees of the state institutions of higher learning. Bill's father was Secretary and Business Manager of the University of Mississippi.

But he was just "Count No Count." True, his grandfather gave him a job in the bank for a while but he soon quit that. True, he would occasionally do an odd job of house painting or paperhanging or firing boilers. But he would work only a while and quit. True, too, it was said he wrote poetry and other things but none of them had ever been sold. He had an aristocratic, superior appearance—which most people considered an affectation—and an aloof reserve and an arrogant snappishness when someone tried to get familiar. So he was considered affected, peculiar, a crank, or a harmless ne'er-do-well. And thus he became "Count No Count."

The old families of Oxford tolerated him because, after all, he was a member of the Faulkner family. Also some of them had black

sheep in their own families. But they did not invite him to their
houses, as a rule, and my frequent statements that he was a writer of
ability and would one day be more famous than Stark Young (another native son) and would cause many people to come to Oxford
because it was the home of William Faulkner—such statements provoked guffaws from the general public and polite, derisive smiles
from the old families.

Even when he actually got a book published, there was no apparent change. (Some years ago at a party a lady member of one of
our most aristocratic families took pains to inform several groups
with studied casualness that Bill had just given her an autographed
copy of his latest book. I could not help but smile when I remembered that I still had at home her autographed presentation first edition copy of *The Marble Faun* for which I could not get her to pay
a dollar and a half when it was published.) Even the publication of
Soldier's Pay, Mosquitoes, Sartoris, Sound and Fury, and *As I Lay
Dying* did not budge them much. To be sure, some other people had
then said that he had ability but still he obviously had made no
money.

Then came *Sanctuary.* At first there were horrified whispers,
shocked surprise, and quick condemnation in Oxford. But all critics
everywhere began to acclaim. Stories by Faulkner began to appear in
the magazines. The movies began to seek him. The New York critics
had praised him and he had made money! Therefore he must be a
great writer after all.

David Cohn has asked me what the proletariat, the loafers around
the courthouse, now think of William Faulkner. (David, of all
people, should know that "proletariat" is not the word to describe
these highly individualistic Southern white people.) Well, the common people don't think of William Faulkner at all unless they happen to see him. They don't read his books, they don't read books at
all very often. And this may be the part of wisdom. When they think
of him they think of him with respect, respect for the fact that he is
articulate enough to write a whole book and for the fact he has
made money. The few of the common people who know him well
like him very much because he is a square, honorable, decent person,
and because they sense that social position is of no moment whatever
to him.

The aristocrats are somewhat in awe of him and somewhat silently
uneasy in his presence and he is invited now to more homes than he
goes. But they still faintly resent him and their awe and hospitality
will vanish if he gets to be less famous and does not continue to
make money. If he should completely lose out as a writer and should

cease to be a commercial success and should begin to write in a new vein—and a greater one? Well, until the New York critics should say that his new writing was greater than his old and until he made a lot of money thereby any claims for him would again be met by polite, derisive smiles.

MUST WE HATE
TO FIGHT?

by Eleanor Roosevelt

As her part in an SRL *debate during World War II the then First
Lady of the United States pleads for good will toward the individual citizens of the enemy countries.*

JULY 4, 1942

CAN WE KILL other human beings if we do not hate them? I suppose
the answer must come from those in our fighting forces. Some young
people will tell you that unless you hate the people of Germany and
Japan, you cannot possibly win. On the other hand, many a young
soldier going into the war will assure you that he cannot hate the
individuals of any race. He can only hate the system which has made
those individuals his enemies. If he must kill them in order to do
away with the system, he will do so, but not because he hates them
as individuals. If those who say that to win the war we must hate,
are really expressing the beliefs of the majority of our people, I am
afraid we have already lost the peace, because our main objective is
to make a world in which all the people of the world may live with
respect and good will for each other in peace.

If we allow the hate of other men as individuals to possess us, we
cannot discard hate the day we have won and suddenly become
understanding and co-operative neighbors.

There will be no victory if out of this war we simply develop
armed camps again throughout the world. We may in the interests
of self-preservation cut down the actual race to obtain guns, planes,
and battleships because no people will survive if it goes on, nor will
those who survive have the wherewithal for the decencies of life.
Even if we cut out all weapons of force, there can exist armed camps
in the minds of people, which express themselves through the economic systems which we set up and through all the barriers which
we set up between peoples to keep them from real understanding. If
we really do not mean that after this war we intend to see that
people the world over have an opportunity to obtain a satisfactory
life, then all we are doing is to prepare for a new war. There is no

excuse for the bloodshed, the sacrifices, and the tears which the world as a whole is now enduring, unless we build a new worth-while world.

The saving grace for most of us is that hope does spring eternal in the human breast. We do believe that just around the corner is that solution to our problems which we have long been looking for and that human beings will never give up till they find the answers.

I believe that the solution will be easier to find when we work together, and when all the plans, all the abilities of people the world over, are concentrated on finding positive solutions, but if we hate each other then I despair of achieving any ultimate good results.

I will acknowledge that it is easier to urge upon our people that they hate those whom we now must fight as individuals, because it is always easier to build up contempt and dislike for that which is making us suffer than it is to force ourselves to analyze the reasons which have brought about these conditions and try to eliminate them.

In small ways we see over and over again that the child who is badgered and punished in youth grows up to treat anyone weaker than himself in much the same way. That is probably what we will do to the people of our nation as a whole when we tell them that in fighting to stamp out cruelty and hate, dominated by force, they must hate. Somehow as a whole the thousands in our fighting forces must preserve a belief and a respect for the individual and a hate only of the system, or else we will go down ourselves, victims of the very system which today we are striving to conquer.

HOW TO SUFFOCATE
THE ENGLISH LANGUAGE

by Jacques Barzun

The junkman seemed to have usurped the lexicographer's easy chair back in the early forties, if historian and litterateur Jacques Barzun is to be believed—and the junkman may still be in possession of it.

FEBRUARY 13, 1943

LIKE FIVE MILLION other people I spend part of each day in a New York bus, and some of that time my eyes rest on the sign:

PLEASE REFRAIN FROM
CONVERSATION WITH OPERATOR
WHILE BUS IS IN MOTION

After some years of dumb staring, it has come over me that this foreign-language text means "Please do not talk to the driver between stops." But this knowledge does not make me sure that I shall ever understand that other sign, found in every shop, which reads: "Illumination is required to be extinguished before these premises are closed to business." Before it, I find I have only one thought: "WHOM is speaking?"

These public displays of literary ineptitude are not alarming in themselves. It is, as everyone knows, very hard to write even passably well, and the writing of inscriptions is the hardest genre of all. Consequently it is not faults of style as such that deserve comment, but the kind of fault. It so happens that in both the quoted examples, as well as in hundreds of others that strike the eye, and indeed in thousands of new speech forms that fall upon the ear, the fault is the same. It is love of the long word, circumlocution, flossiness, and pedantry.

The latest coinage that has come to my notice is *"definitize."* I can still remember what it means; it means "make definite." But I predict that if it takes hold, it will soon become a quasi-meaningless word-of-all-work. In the original context the proper word would have been "settle" or "decide": "Kindly definitize as to [why *as to?*] whether you will accept our suggestion of, etc." But very soon that same word will mean any of the following: inform, notify, choose, clinch ("is that business definitized yet?") discuss, arrange, conclude —and a dozen other ideas vaguely connected with these.

Not long ago the word-of-all-work was "clarify." Everybody was asking everybody else to clarify, or offering to do it. Such things as questions, answers, explanations, statements of policy, or corrections, went out of use. It was all clarification and the joke of it was that in almost every instance the word was ambiguous. When the President of Harvard, for example, said that the Deans of Medical Schools should clarify their requirements, it was not clear whether these gentlemen were to put order into their own heads or into those of others.

It is an accepted notion that the motive of vague, equivocal, and highfalutin language is either political or commercial. Verbiage, in short, is intended to dazzle and deceive. But this explanation fits only a part of the evidence. It will not account for *clarify* and *definitize*. Moreover it is an historical fact that during the last twenty-five years nearly everyone outside the criminal classes has been debasing the verbal currency with false issue of high denomination. And the counterfeiter's unmistakable mark has been the pseudo-educated ring of the coinage. Who, for instance, launched "basal" to compete with "basic"? Some of the so-called educators who teach teachers to teach. They were not content with a basic course or a basic text. That was a good many years ago, but example works better than precept, and we now find that it has influenced the officials who drew up the forms for the rationing of gasoline. If you want more than your [basal] allowance, you must apply for a *supplemental*.

Once upon a time American speech was known for its racy, colloquial creations—barnstorm, boom, boost, bulldoze, pan out, splurge, and so on. Now it is the flaccid polysyllable that expresses the country's mind. Pioneer has yielded to pedant, and one begins to wonder whether the German word order had better not be adopted to complete the system. True enough, when newspapermen were paid by the line, it was natural and even intelligent to use polysyllables, and we find Lowell making fun, in the *Biglow Papers,* of fires that were "conflagrations" and events that were "singular circumstances." Nowadays the excuse and the reason no longer hold. It is pure snobbery that breeds neglect of the simple words and impure education that creates the substitutes.

The abuse, incidentally, is not confined to American speech. Eng-

lish and French have been suffering from it too. In England, Mr.
A. P. Herbert, M.P., has formed a club to combat the evil and you
can read about it in his witty and depressing compendium, *What a
Word!* In France, André Thérive has been waging the same war in
the daily press, and the best of his columns have been collected
under the title *Querelles de Langage.* It, too, is a depressing collection, for French has long had the reputation of being a difficult
tongue to tamper with. It was thought simple and direct. Now you
can find a reputable sociologist discussing in print (I translate literally) "the social outcasts who practice a prostitutional existence."

The context in all these cases makes it clear that the writers are
educated. I beg your pardon, I mean semi-educated: here or abroad
they have had a college course and they can spell better than Shakespeare and Milton. But what is semi-education? I do not know. But it
so happens that I can point to a recent work which strikes me as the
embodiment of the semi-educated outlook upon life and language. I
refer to Mr. Eric Partridge's *Usage and Abusage.*

As its title suggests, this is a work, in dictionary form, that professes to teach the right and wrong use of English to people who do
not know it. The author, well-known for his great *Dictionary of
Slang and Unconventional English,* should be able—one would have
thought—to tell us the proper ways of conventional words. But
something in his training or temperament perverts his praiseworthy
intention and makes his advice downright dangerous. Already in his
Dictionary of Clichés, published two years ago, he had utterly confused idioms with clichés, and now he mixes every kind of true and
false rule concerning speech with prejudice and obtuseness. He has
learned, for instance, that "while" is frequently misused for "whereas," so every "while" becomes suspect. In quoting an English writer
who says "I can but suggest that while the form is logical, it is awkward" Mr. Partridge interposes the "whereas" that he has been
keeping up his sleeve and he asks us to read: "I can but suggest that
whereas this form is logical, it is awkward."

In column after column, this kind of pedantic nonsense parades
as superior knowledge. Mr. Partridge has moreover the lightness of
heart to patronize Dr. Johnson, as if Johnsonian prose were uniformly pompous and contemptible; he has the audacity to pat
Fowler on the shoulder and tell us that this writer is "not sufficiently
appreciated"; and—this will, I know, arouse the readers of *The
Saturday Review*—he has the bad judgment to take so many of his
examples from detective stories as to convey the impression that they
are worse written than other kinds.

I should add before saying more about the schoolmarmish mind
of Mr. Partridge, that Professor Cabell Greet, of Barnard College,

has added to the American edition of this monstrous work some notes which help to counteract its evil effect. But obviously Mr. Greet could not annotate every article, nor show by a steady stream of direct contradiction what he thought of his English colleague. Perhaps the clearest sign of the temper I am attacking is given in Mr. Partridge's comment on *ain't*: ". . . for *isn't* . . . is an error so illiterate that I blush to record it." There lies the whole trouble; or at any rate the whole difference between Mr. Partridge and me. I find "ain't" not only harmless but choice, expressive, sturdy, refined, beautiful, and elevating compared to some of the horrors that Mr. Partridge recommends and produces. He calls a book "sex-filled," he speaks of a "sad decline," considers someone "riotously happy," reproves another, "sadly and sternly," and suggests to a third "the solution of the stylistic crux." Throughout he waxes merry over those whom he pretends to correct. The book is full of ironic (!)s and (?)s. Writers' faults are introduced with elaborate minuetting, "in such and such a book I came upon the curious information that, etc." Consequently, when he has done crowing over the misuses of "between," it is a delight to come upon his article *"Cacao, coca, cocoa, coco (nut)*: Confusion is common between these."

A slip of this kind would be forgivable if one felt that in some one respect the author had dignity and sense. This makes me conclude that perhaps semi-education is simply an education, long or short, which, like the druggist's strong solutions, has been "for external use only." It has struck one, but none of it has been taken in and assimilated; none of it has gone into the formation of judgment: there is not a particle in this book. The author is a blind man who would lead the seeing. He cannot distinguish between the right and wrong kinds of "and which" clauses unprepared by a previous "which," even though Fowler explains the difference. He has a fantastic hope that we shall all reverse our habits and instead of saying "the man who, etc." shall say, *"that* man who says such things is not fit, etc." He uses bastard forms like "précis'd" for "outlined" or "synopsized." He wants us to give up saying "no use in" and "try and." He is bothered by ambiguities where none exist, as in "He died only yesterday," and "an excellent woman's college." He shows off by quoting French which he goes on to misinterpret. Then with sudden conciseness he gives out this mysterious advice: "the plural of *base* is *bases,* the plural of *basis* is *bases.*" But perhaps the choicest bit of ignorant fussiness is the shortest and the least likely to be caught up. It reads: "T.B., better Tb."—as if T.B. stood for the single word TuBerculosis. Shades of Fowler and Dr. Johnson! The lexicographer's easy chair has fallen into the hands of the junkman.

UNLOCKING THE DOOR TO JOYCE

by Henry Morton Robinson and Joseph Campbell

Two experts on one of the most experimental novels ever written in the English language present a skeleton key to James Joyce's monumental Finnegans Wake.

JUNE 19, 1943

RUNNING RIDDLE AND FLUID ANSWER, *Finnegans Wake* is a mighty allegory of the fall and redemption of mankind. It is a strange book, a compound of fable, symphony, and nightmare—a monstrous enigma beckoning imperiously from the shadowy pits of sleep. Its mechanics resemble those of a dream, a dream which has freed the author from the necessities of common logic and has enabled him to compress all periods of history, all phases of individual and racial development, into a circular design, of which every part is beginning, middle, and end.

In a gigantic wheeling rebus, dim effigies rumble past, disappear into foggy horizons, and are replaced by other images, vague but half-consciously familiar. On this revolving stage, mythological heroes and events of remotest antiquity occupy the same spatial and temporal planes as modern personages and contemporary happenings. All time occurs simultaneously: Sir Tristram and the Duke of Wellington, father Adam and Humpty Dumpty merge in a single percept. Multiple meanings are present in every line; interlocking allusions to key words and phrases are woven like fugal themes into the pattern of the work. *Finnegans Wake* is a prodigious, multifaceted monomyth, not only the cauchemar of a Dublin citizen but the dreamlike saga of guilt-stained, evolving humanity.

The vast scope and intricate structure of *Finnegans Wake* give the book a forbidding aspect of impenetrability. It appears to be a dense and baffling jungle, trackless and overgrown with wanton perversities of form and language. Clearly, such a book is not meant to be idly fingered. It tasks the imagination, exacts discipline and tenacity from those who would march with it. Yet some of the difficulties disappear as soon as the well-disposed reader picks up a few compass-clues and gets his bearings. Then the enormous map of *Finnegans Wake* begins slowly to unfold: characters and motifs emerge; themes become recognizable and Joyce's vocabulary falls more and more familiarly on the accustomed ear. Complete understanding is not to be snatched at greedily at one sitting; indeed, it may never come in its entirety. But the last state of the intelligent reader is certainly not bewilderment. Rather, it is admiration for the unifying insight, economy of means, and more-than-Rabelaisian humor which have miraculously quickened the stupendous mass of material. One acknowledges at last that James Joyce's overwhelming macro-microcosm could not have been fired to life in any sorcerer-furnace less black, less heavy, less murky than this, his incredible book. He had to smelt the modern dictionary back to protean plasma and re-enact the "genesis and mutation of language" in order to deliver his message. But the final wonder is that such a message could have been delivered at all!

The first clue to the method and mystery of the book is found in its title, "Finnegans Wake." Tim Finnegan is an Irish bricklayer who got drunk, fell off a ladder, and was apparently killed. His friends hold a death-watch over his coffin; during the festivities someone splashes him with whisky at which Finnegan comes to life again and joins in the general dance. On this comedy-song foundation, Joyce bases the title of his work. But there is more, much more, to the story. Finnegan the bricklayer is identifiable first with Finn MacCool, captain for two hundred years of Ireland's warrior-heroes, and most famous of Dublin's early giants. Finn typifies *all* heroes—Thor, Prometheus, Osiris, Christ, the Buddha in whose life and through whose inspiration the race lives. It is by Finn's coming again (Finn-again)—in other words, by the reappearance of the hero —that strength and hope are provided for mankind.

By his death and resurrection, bricklayer Finnegan comically re-figures the solemn mystery of the hero-god whose flesh and blood furnish the race with spirit-fructifying meat and drink. At the wake of Finnegan, the watchers eat everything that belongs to the dead hero. Not only do they devour all the edibles in the house, but they partake of his very body, as of a Eucharist. By its fall, the shell of the world-egg has been shattered, but the essential egg-substance has been gathered and served for the nutriment of the people "sunny side up with care."

Finnegan's fall from the ladder is hugely symbolic: it is Lucifer's fall, Adam's fall, the setting sun that will rise again, the fall of Rome, a Wall Street crash. It is Humpty Dumpty's fall, and the fall of Newton's apple. It is the irrigating shower of spring rain that falls on seeded fields. And it is everyman's daily recurring fall from grace. These various fallings (implying, as they do, corresponding resurrections) cause a liberation of energy which keeps the universe turning like a water-wheel, and provide the dynamic which sets in motion the four-part cycle of universal history.

But why a "four-part" cycle? This reference is to a conception of the eighteenth-century Italian philosopher Giambattista Vico, whose *La Scienza Nuova* provides the philosophic loom on which Joyce weaves his historical allegory. Essentially, Vico's notion is that history passes through four phases: theocratic, aristocratic, democratic, chaotic. The last phase is characterized (like our own) by individualism and sterility, and represents the nadir of man's fall. It is terminated by a thunderclap, which terrifies and reawakens mankind to the claims of the supernatural, and thus starts the cycle rolling again with a return to the primeval theocracy.

In Joyce's composition, the comical Finnegan episode is only the prologue to the major action. It is related to the later episodes as pre-history is related to history; or (to use a Viconian image) as the giants of the dawn-chaos are related to the patriarchs of orderly history. In *Finnegans Wake* the transition from the earlier to the later hero takes place on pages 24 to 29, where the company at the wake forcibly holds Finnegan down and bids him rest in peace. They tell him that a newcomer, his successor, has just sailed into Dublin Bay. The newcomer is HCE or, more specifically, Humphrey Chimpden Earwicker, who thereafter dominates the work.

As the tale unfolds, we discover that this H. C. Earwicker is a citizen of Dublin, a stuttering tavernkeeper with a bull-like hump on the back of his neck. He emerges as a well-defined and sympathetic character, the sorely harrowed victim of a relentless fate, stronger than yet identical with himself. Joyce refers to his protagonist under various names, such as Here Comes Everybody and Haveth Childers Everywhere—indications of his universality and his role as the great progenitor. Earwicker has wandered vastly, leaving families (that is, deposits of civilization) at every pause along the way: from Troy in Asia Minor (he is frequently called "the Turk") up through the turbulent lands of the Goths, the Franks, the Norse, and overseas to the green isles of Britain and Eire. His chief Germanic manifestations are Wotan and Thor; his chief Celtic, Manannan MacLir. Again, he is Saint Patrick carrying the new faith; again

Strongbow, leading the Anglo-Norman conquest; again Cromwell, conquering with a bloody hand. Most specifically, he is our Anglican tavernkeeper, HCE, in the Dublin suburb, Chapelizod.

As in *Ulysses,* the principal action takes place in Dublin and environs. We are introduced at once to Howth Castle, Phoenix Park, the River Liffey, Wellington Monument, Guinness' Brewery, and other important landmarks, all of which have allegorical significance. Phoenix Park, for example, is reminiscent of the Garden of Eden. And the product of Guinness' Brewery is the magic elixir of life, the immortal drink of heroes and gods. Many an allusion is clarified by consulting a detailed map of Dublin. For example, "the knock out in the park" (page 3) is Castle Knock at the west gate of Phoenix Park. The nearby hillocks are figuratively the upturned toes of the giant whose head is the Hill of Howth. This giant, whose belly is the city of Dublin itself, is none other than the prostrate comical hero-god of the wake. Indeed, all the living, loving, fighting, and dying of Dublin is precisely the hurly-burly of *Finnegans Wake.*

But to return to HCE. He is a man who has won his place in society, a place not of high distinction but of decent repute. He recently figured as candidate in a local election. Gossip, however, undid his campaign and his reputation as well.

It was in Phoenix Park (that Garden of Eden) near his tavern, that he committed an indecorous impropriety which now dogs him to the end of his life-nightmare. Briefly: he was caught peeping at or exhibiting himself to a couple of girls in Phoenix Park. The indiscretion was witnessed by three drunken soldiers, who could never be quite certain of what they had seen; from them it went out to the world. Earwicker's anxiety to justify himself riddles his every utterance with incriminating slips of the tongue, and contributes to his bulky presence a flavor of slightly rancid butter, exposing him to further gossip on every hand. The rumors grow. He is said to suffer from an obscure disease, suspiciously venereal, a physiological counterpart of his psychological taint.

Unquestionably his predicament is of the nature of Original Sin. He shares the shadowy guilt that Adam experienced after eating the apple. It is akin also to the bewilderment and confusion that paralyzes Hamlet, and is cognate with the neurotic disease of modern times. Stephen Dedalus, who suffers from an analogous malady in *Ulysses,* calls it the "agenbite of inwit," the incessant gnawing of rat-toothed remorse. Earwicker, suffering from this taint, yet aware of his claims to decency, is torn between shame and aggressive self-satisfaction, conscious of himself both as bug and as man (an earwig is a beetlelike insect, popularly supposed to creep into the human ear). Earwicker, worm before God, and giant among men, is a living, aching arena of cosmic dissonance, tortured by all the cuts and thrusts of guilt and conscience.

A very specific ramification of the guilt-motif crops out constantly in the "old-man, young-girl" situations sprinkled throughout the book. In the Swift-Vanessa, Daddy-and-Peaches Browning, Mark-and-Iseult episodes, graybeards are passionately fired with a half-incestuous, half-lyrical yearning for young love. Earwicker himself is troubled by a passion, compounded of illicit and aspirational desires for his own daughter, Isabelle, whom he identifies with Tristram's Iseult, and who is the sweet little reincarnation of his wife. Himself he envisions now as gallant Tristram and now as cuckolded King Mark.

Although Earwicker is a citizen of Dublin, he is resented by the populace as an intruder, even a usurper. Why? Well, springing from Germanic rather than Celtic stock, he typifies all the invaders who have overrun Ireland—Danes, Norsemen, Normans, and English. The clash of arms that resounds through the first pages of the book recalls the battles of all Irish history and furnishes a background to the battlefields of the tavern—and the battlefields of Earwicker's own soul.

The rumors about HCE are started by a native Dubliner smoking a pipe, who encounters Earwicker at midnight in Phoenix Park. This "cad with a pipe" asks HCE for the time, and is surprised when the great personage exhibits uneasiness and launches into an elaborate statement of self-defense. The cad goes home, broods over a bottle, and remumbles what he has heard. His wife, catching the suspicious words, communicates them to her priest, who, in turn, passes them on at the race track. Three down-and-outers pick up the tale, exaggerate it comically, and finally turn it into a scurrilous lampoon (the Ballad of Persse O'Reilly, page 44).

The rumor runs through the city like a virulent infection. Several pages (51 to 62) are devoted to round robins of public opinion. The plague of evil gossip that encircles the present Mr. H. C. Earwicker races back through the past—touches and contaminates every likeness of the unforgettable great citizen through all the annals, not only of Ireland, but of man. Thus the enquirer finds it impossible to distinguish between the tumultuous earwigging (gossiping) of the present and that of remoter days. The scandal-stew boils gloriously with ingredients from every moment of human time.

While the man in the street gossips, twelve stately citizens of the jury sit in formal though tipsy session. These twelve are, locally, the twelve constant customers of Mr. Earwicker's tavern. They are also leading mourners at Finnegan's wake. They are also the twelve signs of the zodiac. Their presence betrays itself with sonorous sequences of words terminating in "-ation"; as, for instance, on page 6, "all the hoolivans of the nation, prostrated in their consternation, and their duodisimally profusive plethora of ululation."

In addition, there are four slobberishly senile judges who remember and rehearse the anecdotes of old times. They are identified with the four winds, the Four Master Annalists of Ireland, the four Evangelists, the four Viconian Ages, and so forth. Their principal charge is to care for a donkey which, in its better moments, is revealed as an archaic incarnation of the Logos. Pages 383 to 399 are devoted largely to the recollections of the four. They themselves, in younger days, were protagonists of the great life-roles which they can now only regard and review. Life once stirred in them and shaped them; but it has moved on, so that they now are but cast-off shells. Crotchety, brittle crystallizations out of the past, they have only to await disintegration. Meanwhile, however, they sit in judgment over the living present.

A dim-witted policeman, crony of the four, arrests HCE for disturbing the peace and gives testimony against him (pages 62 to 63, and 67). But he has many of the traits of the hero himself—as have, indeed, all the male characters of the populace opposition. For, in the last analysis, the universal judgment against HCE is but a reflection of his own obsessive guilt complex; and, conversely, the sin which others condemn in him is but a conspicuous public example of the general, universally human, original sin, privately effective within themselves. Thus, throughout the work, there is a continual intermelting of the accused and his accusers. All these characters, moving around and against each other, are but facets of some prodigious unity and are at last profoundly identical—each, as it were, a figure in the dream-complex of all the others. One is reminded of Schopenhauer's wonderful image of the world in his essay "On an Apparent Intention in the Fate of the Individual." "It is a vast dream, dreamed by a single being; but in such a way that all the dream-characters dream too. Thus everything interlocks and harmonizes with everything else."

Earwicker has a wife, the psyche of the book—bewitching, ever-changing, animating, all-pervading. She appears typically under the name of Anna Livia Plurabelle, abbreviated to ALP. Just as Earwicker is metamorphosed into Adam, Noah, Lord Nelson, a mountain, or a tree, so ALP becomes, by subtle transposition, Eve, Isis, Iseult, a passing cloud, a flowing stream—the eternally fructive and love-bearing principle in the world. She is a little crone who goes about gathering fragments into a basket; Isis picking up the dismembered body of her brother-husband, Osiris. She is the widow who serves the feast at the wake: "Grampupus is fallen down but grinny sprids the boord" (page 7). Again, she is a little hen that scratches out of a dung heap the torn scraps of a bewitching letter (pages 110 to 111); a gossipacious letter; a letter which Major Thornton Wilder aptly describes as a missive revealing all the secrets of a woman's heart and the mystery of why the universe was set in motion. Only partially recovered, its life-riddle twinkles through every page of *Finnegans Wake;* in fact, the book itself is but a dreamlike emanation of this "untitled mamafesta memorializing the Mosthighest" (page 104), written (time and place unknown) by ALP herself.

But above all, Anna is a river, always changing but ever the same; the Heraclitean flux, which bears all life on its current. Principally, she is the River Liffey who runs through Dublin, but she is also the rivers of the world, the heavenly Ganges, the fruitful Nile, the teeming Irrawaddy, the mysterious Nyanza. She is the circular river of time, flowing past Eve and Adam in the first sentence of the book, bearing in her flood the debris of dead civilizations and the seeds of crops and cultures yet to come.

The circular course of the River Liffey illustrates her cycle of transformation. Her brooklet source in the Wicklow hills finds her as a young girl free, dancing gaily, a delicious nymph. Passing the Chapelizod of HCE's tavern, she is a comely, matronly stream. Still further on, flowing through the city of Dublin, she is an old haggard scrubwoman, carrying away the filth of the city. At last, she flows back to Father Ocean, from whence she rises again in mist, to descend in showers and become once more the sparkling mountain stream. Anna's cycle is a perfect example of the Viconian *corso* and *recorso*—the circular ground-plan on which *Finnegans Wake* is laid.

It is the role of the *younger* Anna to shatter HCE as the container of fixed energy. It becomes the function of the *older* Anna, the widow, to gather up the remains of her broken lord and consign them again to a fresh start. As Joyce says, "She puffs the blaziness on," converts past into future, and displays the female's typical concern for the future of her race. Among her younger manifestations are Earwicker's daughter and her twenty-eight little companions (the days of the month), seven beaming rainbow-color girls, and the two temptresses in the park. Among her older incarnations are the writer and receiver of the letter, and the garrulous housekeeper of the Earwicker establishment, Kate the Slop, "built in with the bricks." The roles are continually shifting and mingling into each other. Anna is ever the principle of vivid movement, ever setting in motion and ever keeping in motion the river-flow of time.

Earwicker and his wife have two sons, called in their symbolic aspect Shem and Shaun, and in their domestic aspect Jerry and Kevin. They are the carriers of a great "brother-battle" theme that throbs through the entire work. Just as HCE and ALP represent a primordial "male-female" polarity, which is basic to all life, so Shem and Shaun represent a subordinate, exclusively masculine "battle" polarity which is basic to all history. Opposing traits, which in their father were strangely and ambiguously combined, in these sons are isolated and separately embodied. As characters, therefore, these boys are very much simpler than their father, and, accordingly, the chapters of the work devoted to the delineations of their caricature-portraits (Book I, Section 7 for Shem; Book II, Sections I and II for Shaun) are comparatively easy reading; excellent places for trivial spins.

Shem (Jerry), the introvert, rejected of man, is the explorer and discoverer of the forbidden. He is an embodiment of dangerously brooding, in-turned energy. He is the uncoverer of secret springs and, as such, the possessor of terrific, lightning powers. The books he writes are so mortifying that they are spontaneously rejected by the decent; they threaten, they dissolve the protecting boundary lines of good and evil. Provoked to action (and he must be provoked before he will act) he is not restrained by normal human laws, for they have been dissolved within him by the too-powerful elixirs of the elemental depths; he may let loose a hot spray of acid; but, on the other hand, he may let loose such a magical balm of forgiveness that the battle lines themselves become melted in a bacchanal of general love. Such absolute love is as dangerous to the efficient working of society as absolute hate. The possessor of the secrets, therefore, is constrained to hold his fire. Nobody really wants to hear what he has to say: the shepherds of the people denounce him from their pulpits, or else so dilute and misrepresent his teachings as to render them innocuous. Thus Shem is typically in retreat from society; he is the scorned and disinherited one, the Bohemian, or criminal outcast, rejected by Philistine prosperity. Under the title of Shem the Penman he is the seer, the poet, Joyce himself in his character of misunderstood, rejected artist. His characteristic behavior is to take refuge in his own room, where, on the foolscap of his own body, he writes a phosphorescent book in a corrosive language which Shaun cannot understand.

The character of Shaun (Kevin), the folk-shepherd brother, the political orator, prudent, unctuous, economically successful favorite of the people, careful to preserve them from the causes and effects of immorality, policeman of the planet, conqueror of rebels, bearer of the white man's burden, is developed by Joyce elaborately and broadly. He is the contrapuntal opposite of Shem: the two brothers are the balanced ends of the human dumbbell. And if it is the typical lot of Shem to be whipped and despoiled, Shaun is typically the whipper and despoiler.

When he turns from making empires and preserving the peace of the world to the writing of best sellers, the favored son does not himself descend to those dangerous, obscene, and forbidden depths from which the other brings forth his mad productions; his works are never in danger of censorship and rejection; they are the censors and rejectors. Indeed, Shaun is not concerned with spiritual or esthetic matters except in so far as he can exploit them; the life of the flesh and senses is good enough for him. In a diverting passage beginning on page 429, Shaun addresses the little day-girls of St. Brigid's Academy, smiting their tender ears with admonitions of good counsel and very practical advice. "Collide with man, collude with money," is a typical Shaunian saw. In sum: Shaun is man naïvely and shrewdly outgoing, whereas Shem, his brother, has been touched by the "agenbite" which probes back again to the source. Shaun execrates Shem, maligns him, with the frank but not altogether unfearful disdain of the man of action for the man of thought. Under the title of Shaun the Postman, he delivers to mankind the great message which has been actually discovered and penned by Shem; but Shaun, who judges all things by their envelope, misdelivers the message. Yet he enjoys all the rewards of those who deliver good tidings.

Shem's business is not to create a higher life, but merely to find and utter the Word. Shaun, on the other hand, whose function is to make the Word become flesh, misreads it, fundamentally rejects it, limits himself to a kind of stupid concretism, and, while winning all the skirmishes, loses the eternal city.

HCE, the father of this pair, represents the unity from which their polarity springs. Compared with the rich plasticity of HCE, the boys are but shadow-thin grotesques. Their history plays like a strange mirage over the enduring core of the basic presence of HCE. The energy generated by their conflict is but a reflex of the original energy generated by the father's fall. Furthermore, antipodal as the brothers may be, they are both easily embraced by the all-inclusive love of their wonderful mother ALP. (See, for instance, the charming passages on pages 194 and 195).

Toward the close of the work (specifically, during the third section of Book III), the forms of the son-world dissolve and the everlasting primal form of HCE resurges. The all-father is reunited with his wife in a diamond-wedding anniversary, as if to demonstrate that behind the complexity of their children's lives they still continue to be the motive-givers. Together, they constitute the primordial, androgynous (man-woman) angel, which is Man, the incarnate God.

What, finally, is *Finnegans Wake* all about? Stripping away its accidental features, the book may be said to be all compact of *mutually supplementary antagonisms:* male-and-female, age-and-youth, life-and-death, love-and-hate; these, by their attraction, conflicts, and repulsions, supply polar energies that spin the universe. Wherever Joyce looks in history or human life, he discovers the operation of these basic polarities. Under the seeming aspect of diversity—in the individual, the family, the state, the atom, or the cosmos—these constants remain unchanged. Amid trivia and tumult, by prodigious symbol and mystic sign, obliquely and obscurely (because these manifestations are both oblique and obscure), James Joyce presents, develops, amplifies, and recondenses nothing more nor less than the eternal dynamic implicit in birth, conflict, death, and resurrection.

IN MEMORY OF
GEORGE GERSHWIN

by Bennett Cerf

"My people are American, my time is today," said the composer
of Rhapsody in Blue *and* Porgy and Bess. *Six years after Gershwin's death his old friend, publisher and* SRL *columnist Bennett Cerf, penned this tribute to an authentic genius.*

JULY 17, 1943

ON AN OPPRESSIVELY hot Sunday evening six years ago, a group of
people was gathered in a Bucks County remodeled farmhouse, engaged in various desultory pastimes. A spiritless bridge game was in
progress in one corner of the room; a bout of cribbage in another.
The host was tinkering aimlessly with the radio dials. Some of the
guests were splashing about in the pool outside, although there was
no moon, and the night was pitch black. The heat had everybody
down. Suddenly the clear voice of a news commentator came over
the air: "The man who said he had more tunes in his head than he
could put down on paper in a hundred years is dead tonight in
Hollywood. George Gershwin succumbed today at the age of thirty-
eight."

Everybody at that party was a close personal friend of George.
Two of them had collaborated with him on his brightest Broadway
hits. We had seen him within the month—joshed him on his complaint of recurring headaches (he had been telling us details of his
symptoms and disorders for years; nobody took them seriously) and
on a front-page report that a little French picture cutie had entrusted him with a gold key to her front door. His unbelievable
energy and vitality had astounded us for so long that we sat speechless at the thought that he was dead. Now, six years later, his music
is played so incessantly, stories about him spring so readily to
mind, it is still somehow unbelievable that he is gone. Because he
graduated from Tin Pan Alley, it has taken all these years to convince some critics that George Gershwin was a great composer—one
of the greatest we have produced in America. Because his monumental but strangely unobjectionable conceit encouraged his friends

249

to circulate hilarious anecdotes about him, some of them did not realize until he was dead how deeply they liked and admired him. The stories that I have gathered for this piece are set down in loving memory. George laughed at all of them himself.

George Gershwin was born in Brooklyn on September 26, 1898. He was the second of four children. Ira, whose sparkling lyrics were so perfectly attuned to George's music, was the oldest. Another brother, Arthur, followed George. The youngest was their sister Frances, happily married today to Leopold Godowsky. The family moved as a unit, a mutual admiration society that was completely unaffected by temporary failure or dizzying success. Mrs. Gershwin was adored by everybody. "You must meet my mother," George would tell anybody who called. "She's the most wonderful mother in the world." On further reflection, he would frequently add "and so modest about *me!*" The father, Morris, was one of those restless souls who embarked upon a new business career every year or so; the family was always ready to pull up stakes cheerfully at a moment's notice. George once figured that he lived in twenty-seven different houses before he finished school. Gershwin père was a lovable and loquacious soul whose accent lost none of its rich and indescribable flavor as the family fortunes rose. His son "Judge" was the apple of his eye. One day after the boys had hit the jackpot he was driving down Broadway in a roadster they had given him, when a cop flagged him for ignoring a red light. "But you can't do this to me!" he expostulated. "I'm Judge Gershwin's father!" "Oh, Judge Gershwin," said the copper, visibly impressed. "Pardon me for holding you up, sir!" New gadgets fascinated him. In the early days of radio, he came to George with an excited report about a new set that he wanted to order immediately. "Judge," he declared, "on this machine you could hear Havana, London, and China clear like a bell!" "London? China?" echoed George unbelievingly. "I'll settle for Havana," replied Mr. Gershwin hastily. When Professor Einstein published his paper on the theory of relativity, George commented, "Imagine being able to put the result of twenty years' study and research into three pages!" "But I'll bet it was very small print," said Mr. Gershwin.

When George was twelve, his mother bought a piano. The idea was for Ira to take lessons, but it didn't take long to discover that George was the one with music in his soul. At the High School of Commerce, he was pianist for the morning assembly exercises. At fifteen, he was a song plugger for the music publishing house of Jerome Remick. One of his chores took him to Atlantic City, where he pounded out Remick melodies at the local five and ten. Down the Boardwalk, Harry Ruby was doing a similar job for a rival outfit. At night the boys would dine together at Childs and dream of writing songs of their own.

His first song was published in 1916. It was called "When You Want 'Em You Can't Get 'Em," and it earned him an advance of five dollars. His next few numbers began to carry lyrics by Arthur Francis. That was brother Ira making his debut as a lyricist, using the first names of his other brother and kid sister as a pseudonym. His first real clicks came in 1919, when he did his first complete score for *La La Lucille* (remember "Nobody But You": "Billie Burke—Alice Joyce—none of them were my choice"?) and wrote a couple of numbers for the opening bill of Broadway's biggest movie palace of its time, the Capitol. One of the numbers was "Swanee," and I've heard it twice on the radio this very week.

Beginning in 1920, George wrote the music for *George White's Scandals* for five consecutive years. A few of the hits of these scores were "Drifting Along with the Tide," "I'll Build a Stairway to Paradise," and "Somebody Loves Me." Most of the lyrics were contributed by Buddy De Sylva, now head man at the Paramount Studios. In those days, White was the great Ziegfeld's only serious rival. Gershwin didn't meet up with Ziegfeld himself until 1929, when he wrote the score of *Show Girl.* Working with Ziegfeld was perfect training for a siege on Guadalcanal, but that's another story. After the contract with Gershwin was signed, Ziegfeld went to Carnegie Hall to hear *An American in Paris.* At the symphony's completion, Otto Kahn rose and made a brief speech in which he declared that George was well-nigh a genius. "In fact," said Kahn, "some day he will be a genius, but geniuses must suffer, and George hasn't suffered yet." Ziegfeld turned to Larry Hart, who was sitting next to him and said to him, with a sly wink, "He'll suffer!"

George became internationally famous in 1924, when Paul Whiteman introduced his *Rhapsody in Blue* at a concert in Aeolian Hall. By now the family was located in a private house on West 103rd Street, where George worked imperturbably amidst a hubbub that suggested Grand Central Station on the eve of a Fourth of July weekend. The *Rhapsody* was written there in exactly three weeks; George had to meet a deadline! That year saw, too, the first of seven musical comedies produced by Aarons and Freedley, with music by George and lyrics by Ira. Five of them made Broadway history. They were, in order, *Lady Be Good, Tip Toes, Oh, Kay, Funny Face,* and *Girl Crazy.* They made stars of Fred and Adele Astaire, Gertrude Lawrence, Ethel Merman, and Ginger Rogers. "Fascinating Rhythm," "Do, Do, Do," "Sweet and Low Down,"

"Embraceable You," "I Got Rhythm," and a dozen other wonderful songs followed one another in dizzy succession. In addition, *Of Thee I Sing*, written with George Kaufman and Morrie Ryskind, won the Pulitzer Prize in 1932. George moved to a Riverside Drive penthouse, which became headquarters for a series of wondrous Sunday evening delicatessen suppers that featured Barney Greengrass' sturgeon and attracted the greatest wits and socialites of the town. That's when the Gershwin saga really started. George, who loved to play the piano for hours on end, and naïvely—also justifiably—took it for granted that nobody wanted to hear anything but his own music, would finally suspend operations to seek refreshments. His place would be taken by a surly young man who played George's music just as well as the composer. His name was Oscar Levant.

Oscar likes to tell the story of the night he and George journeyed to Pittsburgh to play with the symphony orchestra there. George took it for granted that the lower berth of the compartment was his proper due. Before turning out the light, Oscar peered over the edges of the upper to see George sprawled complacently below, puffing on a huge cigar. "Do you know what this picture represents?" said George pleasantly, when he spied Oscar's face. "It's the difference between talent and genius!" One day, Oscar, George, Ira, and I journeyed up to Baker Field to see a Columbia-Navy football game. We were late, and I weaved in and out of the trolley poles on Sedgwick Avenue rather recklessly. "For God's sake, be careful!" cautioned George. "You've got *Gershwin* in the car!"

George loved to go to parties, and thought nothing of playing the entire score of a forthcoming musical for his friends. This practice irked his canny collaborator, George Kaufman. "If you play that score one more time before we open," Kaufman once told him, "people are going to think it's a revival." Kaufman also deplored Gershwin's genial habit of inviting everybody he met to sit in on rehearsals. Kaufman left one run-through with a deep scowl. "It's going to be a prize flop," he predicted. "What makes you say that? I thought it went beautifully," protested Gershwin. "Not at all," grumbled Kaufman. "The balcony was only half filled!"

I accompanied George on some wonderful vacation trips. They were a succession of hilarious adventures and beautiful girls. He banged out the Rhapsody once in the parlor of the Colonial Hotel in Nassau at seven in the morning to please a girl he had met on the boat, and was indignant when the manager made him stop. "I guess he didn't know I was Gershwin," he consoled himself. In Havana, a sixteen-piece rumba band serenaded him en masse at four in the morning outside his room at the old Almendares Hotel. Several outraged patrons left the next morning. George was so flattered that he promised to write a rumba of his own. He did, too. His "Cuban Overture" was played for the first time at the Lewisohn Stadium in August 1932. In Havana George reached his greatest height of indignation. A lovely Cuban miss failed to keep a luncheon date with him. Later that afternoon he spied her on the Yacht Club terrace, and exclaimed, "Hey, do you know that you stood me up today?" "Oh, I meant to phone and tell you I couldn't meet you," said the contrite maiden, "but do you know something? I simply couldn't think of your name!" George didn't recover for days. . . . He reserved one unpublished little waltz tune for affairs of the heart. "You're the kind of girl who makes me feel like composing a song," he would tell the enraptured lady of the moment, and lead her off to his suite. We would follow on tiptoe to hear him compose the familiar tune for her. "It will be dedicated to you," he would conclude soulfully. One day, I happened to remark that the score of one of his infrequent failures, *Pardon My English,* was below par. George demurred. All of us were sun-bathing in the nude; George insisted that we all go inside while he proved his point by going through the score from opening chorus to finale. I can still see him sitting at the piano, stark naked, playing the songs and singing them, too, at the top of his voice. George belonged at a piano. I have never seen a man happier, more bursting with the sheer joy of living, than George when he was playing his songs. He would improvise and introduce subtle variations, and chuckle with childlike delight when his audience exclaimed over them.

The work that George Gershwin loved best was *Porgy and Bess.* He composed it in eleven months and orchestrated it in nine. Its initial production by the Guild in 1935, a bit too stuffy and pretentious, was only moderately successful. When it was revived seven years later, it really came into its own, and its songs seem destined to become part of America's richest musical heritage; the tragedy is that George wasn't living to see that come to pass.

George moved to Hollywood in 1936. He wrote the music for the Fred Astaire-Ginger Rogers picture *Shall We Dance?,* which included one of his best songs ("Oh, No, You Can't Take That Away from Me") and "A Damsel in Distress." He was working on the Goldwyn Follies when he was stricken by a brain tumor.

The last years of Gershwin's life were almost equally divided between composing and painting. George took his painting very seriously, and indeed had a genuine talent for it. At a memorable dinner one evening he said, "A man told me today that I need never write another note; I could make a fortune with my palette and brush!" "Isn't it amazing," said one awed lady, "that one man should possess a genius for two of the arts!" "Oh, I don't know," said George modestly. "Look at Leonardo da Vinci!" At another dinner, apropos of nothing, George suddenly said, "Has anybody here seen my new cigarette case?" It was solid gold, and inscribed thereon were facsimile signatures of a score of famous men. It had been presented to him after a performance of his Concerto in F. The case was passed clear around the table. As George was putting it back into his pocket, his brother Ira produced a crumpled pack of Camels. "Anybody want a cigarette?" he inquired pleasantly.

But Ira, like everybody else who knew him well, adored George Gershwin. After his death, Ira wrote practically nothing for years. That he had lost none of his talent he proved, however, with the lyrics for *Lady in the Dark*. Now he is going to work on the screen biography of George Gershwin. The title role has not yet been filled, but Oscar Levant will play himself in the film.

George Gershwin expressed his credo in these words: "My people are American, my time is today. Music must repeat the thought and aspirations of the times." Six years after his death, his exciting songs are played more frequently than they were during his lifetime. One critic recently remarked, "George Gershwin brought to serious consideration a new idiom in American music, and forever changed its future direction." Last Tuesday twenty thousand people gathered in New York to hear a program dedicated to his memory. As the first familiar strains of the *Rhapsody in Blue* hushed the expectant audience, it was hard to believe that the composer had been dead for over six years. It seemed like yesterday that he had sat beside me in Cuba, listening to the same composition on the radio, and saying, "It *is* great, isn't it? But wait till you hear the one I'm working on now!"

SHALL WE HAVE A WORLD LANGUAGE?

by H. G. Wells

The world-famous novelist and author of The Outline of History
offers some dissenting reflections on a "short cut to global unity."

AUGUST 7, 1943

SOME RECENTLY REPORTED REMARKS made at a British Association
meeting have produced an inundation of typed and mimeographed
letters about Esperanto, Ido, and a whole series of well-meaning
experiments in language-making. The amiable idea inspiring all the
experiments is to find a short cut to human unity. A number of facts
and considerations go to show that this apparent short cut to unity
is really a blind alley, and that a practical solution of this very
urgent problem of world understanding is to be found in quite a
different direction.

Contemporary science is gradually clearing up the history of
speech, how the human being first talked, how he talked in his
primitive days, how little he talked, and why he talked. We know
within a few thousand years when it was that organized languages
appeared in the world and were written down and grammar descended upon mankind. Man, up to the beginnings of agriculture,
used gestures for communication and drawings for record as much
as or more than articulate speech. The simple association of bow-
wow with dog or hiss with snake is fairly obvious, but that is not
articulate speech.

Speech, indeed, is so specialized and localized that it seems highly
probable that the universal means of communication in the future
may involve a very scanty use of the spoken and written word. In
the past it was extremely difficult to make and multiply and dis-
tribute pictures. All that has been changed in a century. Instantaneous photography, color photography, microphotography, and air
transport make the most rapid and complete distribution not only
of facts, but, with a skillful use of diagrams and suchlike symbols,

of ideas, from end to end of the earth, possible. There is scarcely a fact spoken language can express which cannot be conveyed a thousand times as rapidly and completely through the eye. When we hear talk of re-educating the whole world for unity, the speaker must either have this new visual education in mind or he must be an impractical wishful thinker or altogether insincere.

The obdurate inadaptability of articulate speech to changes in sound or accent militates still more powerfully against the idea that the world may be de-Babelized. And there is also a perpetual shifting of the *meaning* of words. Consider such a word as "alibi." The other day I had a grossly insulting letter (anonymous, of course) declaring that my contempt for a "classical" training had led me to use "alibi" as an equivalent for "excuse," whereas it has no such meaning. The poor gentleman was scandalously ignorant of his Dickens and his Dictionary. Sam Weller gave a new twist to "alibi," and from the great Oxford English Dictionary my correspondent will learn that in the English language now, not only is this meaning for "alibi" as an "evasion" accepted, but that there is a verb, "to alibi," with various derivatives, carrying exactly the sense I gave it.

That is one instance of verbal depravity, a legal term that took the wrong turning. Directly one passes to more fundamental ideas, one finds in languages everywhere an endless array of false assumptions and the decaying metaphysics of a dead past. A number of scientific workers have developed a science of "semantics" or "significs" in a desperate attempt to cut this dead wood out of speech. I am not sufficiently versed in these studies to know the essential workers in this field or their order of importance, but the general reader will find an admirable debunking of language in *The Tyranny of Words,* by Stuart Chase (1938). Every language man has ever used is an ever-changing torrent with nothing whatever to keep it clear and clean. "Time, like an ever-flowing stream, bears all its sons away," but language has no ability to rid itself of its illegitimate and corrupt offspring.

This is true of the vocabulary of any language. The difficulty about the actual sounds of a language is equally insurmountable.

The professional philologist neglects George Bernard Shaw, and he is the one man best worth listening to in this matter. Would that he had stuck to philology. He took to other courses in early life, with most of which I disagree, and I have bickered with him ever since we became aware of one another; yet also I admire and like him very much. He has an exquisite ear for sound, and he has told us clearly and exactly what are the necessary preliminaries before you can dream of a world language. Until you take these preliminary steps, a world language remains a dream.

Manifestly, before you can think of a common language for the world, you must have a script that is universally readable. There are thirty-nine sounds requiring separate unambiguous letters. The vowel sounds are harder to fix than the consonants, but the range of variation can be reduced to the amount of difference between the vowel sounds of a Cockney and those of a Yorkshireman. With these thirty-nine letters and a few accents and indications of intonation, it would be possible to write down anything in any language, so that anyone totally ignorant of that language could nevertheless read it aloud and be understood by anyone using that language. But the letters for this universal alphabet must be freshly designed so as to be unambiguous. Such letter shapes as C O P, which in Russian would be read as S A R, must be suppressed altogether. Given such an alphabet, Ido or Volapuk become bare possibilities. Until you have it, they are impracticable dreams.

Nevertheless, when our utmost has been done with pictures and diagrams to convey fact and relationship, there still remain certain matters for which language must be used. There are the Universal Rights of Man and treaties generally. It is hard, for instance, to think of any pictorial method of prohibiting tyranny by the taking of hostages. Ogden, with his Orthological Institute, and his associates, have been experimenting therefore with the translation of the Universal Rights of Man into Basic English. ("Basic" English, Russian, or Italian is the minimum vocabulary necessary to talk understandably in any of these tongues.) The statement of the Rights has been simplified and universalized and written down in a great number of key languages, languages, that is to say, in which numerous books, pamphlets, and newspapers are printed, and into which textbooks and so forth are translated. Coupled with microphotography, "Basic" seems far more suitable for spreading ideas over the whole earth.

Gesture came long before the use of speech in the history of the human mind. Manifestly articulate speech was never adopted by man for the unrestrained broadcasting of what he had in his mind. Gestures, grunts, howls, and so forth conveyed one's feelings and intentions to everybody within sight and hearing, but spoken speech was a very convenient way of coming to an understanding with one's intimates while leaving the stranger present unaware of what was brewing. Most of us have passed through a phase in our adolescence when we invented languages. They were always *secret* languages, cants, back slang, "owhay oday ouyay" devices, designed to defeat the uninitiated listener and put authority at a disadvantage. The demand for a universal overriding speech is an innovation upon linguistic practice. Speech is used to conceal our thoughts much more frequently than it is used to express them. We go on using words at times, just as friendly savages hold up their hands, to show there is nothing in them.

So it is quite possible that the happy and united world which may be ahead of us will never have a universal speech, and any one of us revisiting the earth in a century or so may find a world of complete toleration and understanding with as many, if not more, spoken languages than there are now.

The various "Basics" may expand and pick up words from one another, and they seem likely to converge upon a sort of universal uninflected world "pidgin" speech with a vaster vocabulary of words in common than any languages have ever had hitherto. "Pidgin" will enable a traveler to get about, order accommodation, take a ticket and so forth, and remain as flat and unsuitable for poetic, intimate, and delicate expression as pidgin English is in China today.

No one will ever want to make love or describe a sonnet in a pidgin language. There is no Esperanto anthology. The first thing two lovers set about is the invention of new names for one another and a little language of their own. Every set and clique of friendship and conspiracy in the world devises its own slang and dialect, its nicknames and specialized interpretations. Nothing in the great times ahead is likely to abolish that.

It is hard to conceive of any form of poetic expression either in prose or verse that is either everlasting or translatable. Nor, in spite of the magnificence achieved by such a polyglot as Milton, can I believe that really lovely writing is achievable by anyone who is not saturated to an exclusive pitch by thinking, talking, and wringing the utmost expression out of his or her native tongue. William Shakespeare had little Latin and less Greek, and down the record of English literature to our own time the most clear, poetic, and delightful English has come from monoglots with a natural gift for verbal melody.

The Lord Chamberlain's company of actors and play-makers at the Globe Theatre, whose work is published under the name of "Shakespeare," knew everybody in town, laughed at most people, flattered when necessary, and had, I am convinced, not the slightest idea that all their chuckling fun, the shot-silk of the new-born Elizabethan language garment they made up for their shows, and their verbal serendipity would become the material for that solemn association, "Shakespeare and the Bible," and be handed out, castrated and annotated, for the affliction and perplexity of the immature.

Generation after generation of the English have undergone scholastic inoculation against the careless indelicacy of these Globe Theatre dramas. A wholesome tradition of gay derision has been replaced by a cultural cant. Ordinary English people dread Shakespeare as something far, far above them, something repulsive and improving. They lose a lot by that.

Most of that Globe Theatre accumulation seems to me to be shot not only with an unsurpassable starry beauty but with fun of the most wholesome grossness.

One gets flashes of the same quality in much English fiction, through a long succession which includes Sterne, that subtle artist, Dickens in his moments of honest happiness, down to such contemporaries as, for example, Christopher Morley. Jane Austen is one of my dearest aunts, Rebecca West when she is mocking and happy, another. My delight is the happiness one gets from talk in a gay and witty family which plays with words and associations. No literature is permanent, because no language is permanent; all literature is journalism and will pass away in this changing world. Language will change, ideas will change, there are no immortal works, and I count all "classics" dead and bores. We impose them on the innocent, who are too ashamed to confess how little they enjoy them. Even Chaucer, with all his route of pilgrims, is dead now, an affair for study and paraphrase, and epic and lyric poetry mere raw material for rebelliously disrespectful allusions from such lively spirits as have been subjected to them.

I am straying toward a critical disquisition that will take me, if I pursue it, far away from that Auxiliary Language. Possibly because I dislike and despise the idea and am glad of any excuse to get away from it. So I submit, melud the Public, I submit, melud, my case against this Auxiliary Language idea. What can be said for it, I cannot imagine. Perhaps some one will Esperant?

MY STUDENT DAYS
IN GERMANY

by Struthers Burt

*A well-known novelist recalls his experiences with schläger duel-
ing when he was a pre-World War I student in Germany.*

NOVEMBER 6, 1943

BEFORE I WENT to a German university I was told that I would
be challenged to a duel; several perhaps, one or two surely. And
then I was told what to do.

The tradition of how to behave when challenged to a duel had
been handed down from generation to generation of English and
American students. You looked very fierce, even if you wanted to
laugh at the insulting absurdity, then you began slowly peeling off
your coat, and when you had peeled off your coat, you adopted
the attitude of what was known as "the boxing." This, I was told,
never failed to work, as the German student, so keen about the
schläger and the saber, had a horror of fists. He considered them
ungentlemanly.

This, of course, was before the time of Max Schmeling, but I am
informed that even the example of that concentration-camp sports-
man did not altogether destroy the German dislike of close physical
contact, and there were moments in Schmeling's own career when
it looked as if he shared the prejudice. The German idea of man-to-
man fighting, I discovered, was to sweep aside suddenly, and without warning, a smaller opponent, especially if he wasn't looking,
by a straight-arm or a haymaker, and then to walk away rapidly
before the smaller opponent could get to his feet. I never saw this
done between men of equal size.

But when it came to dueling, an American or an Englishman
invariably, as the challenged party, had the advantage. His was the
choice of weapons, and why decade after decade this blind alley
had never occurred to the German mind, I don't know. Anyway,
decade after decade they had challenged, only to have to capitulate
at the cost of considerable national and spiritual discomfort. Occasionally the discomfort was physical—that was when the Englishman or American was really angry. There was the famous story,

260

for example, of the American varsity pitcher who chose baseballs —three, at thirty paces—to the initial amusement of his tormentors. The first ball whistled past his opponent's right ear, the second, past his left, the third knocked him senseless. And there was the equally famous story of the young Englishman, a crack shot, who chose pistols, and then, in the week preceding the duel, appeared casually in neighboring forests, and whenever he saw people approaching neatly clipped off a topmost pine cone, or something of the sort. On the day of the duel his opponent was ill in bed with a fever.

As most people know, there were, or rather, are, two kinds of German student dueling, forbidden under the recent republic, revived by Hitler who never fought a duel in his life. It is interesting to note that if the Fuehrer in his early days had challenged a student, or other civilian, the student or other civilian would have laughed at him, or if, in a moment of insanity he had challenged an officer, the officer, without ceremony, would have run him through. So far as that was the Fuehrer beneath the social plane of dueling.

Schläger dueling, the ordinary form of student dueling, was—is— a rite, a ritual, a code, and a perverted form of athletics. If you belonged to a fighting-verein, and practically all but the Catholic ones were fighting-vereins, you were supposed to fight at least three schläger duels before you were a member in good standing. Saber dueling was different—also baseballs and pistols. Saber dueling meant serious business and so was rare. If you were a foreigner, however, and a member of a fighting-verein, you were more or less excused. With unwonted broad-mindedness, it was admitted that young foreigners, for some strange and amusingly effeminate reason, did not like to go through life looking as if they had survived a good bout of unattended smallpox or a mild case of elephantiasis. As for yourself, the more scars you had, deliberately cultivated indented welts, the more famous you were. It was like being an All-American with your varsity letter tattooed on your face. When you entered a restaurant, peering about with truculent ice-blue eyes above swollen cheeks, everybody looked at you, and there was a hush, and then everybody whispered. And it was said that German maidens, with feminine willingness to trade masculine beauty for masculine achievement, found such scars irresistible. Virtue fell like ninepins before them.

I never understood the rationale of schläger dueling; it wasn't fun, and it wasn't sport, and it wasn't in the least hazardous, and it wasn't even very skillful. But then, I am a barbarian and a mem-

ber of a decadent democracy. It was supposed to train young men
to hardihood and the sight of blood, but it seemed to me with considerable less loss of time, and with none of the punctilio, the same
results could have been achieved by the mis-use of a safety razor,
and then the students could have gone out-of-doors to indulge in
some game requiring actual skill and courage. As to the blood
theory, if it be true, then butchers are the bravest of men.

The schläger is an immensely long, thin sword, not much wider
than a razor and ground to a razor's sharpness. It is slightly curved,
and has a blunt end and a basket hilt to protect your hand. When
you fight, you stand close together, one arm behind you, your
sword arm crooked and above your head, and all the action is with
the wrist. The object is to flick pieces of flesh from the scalp and
face of your opponent, and you mustn't give way an inch, or
grimace, and, under no circumstances, emit an "ouch!" or its German equivalent. The bouts take place in a hall, or cockpit, designed
for the purpose, and there are numerous spectators, most of them
members of the vereins involved. There is always a young surgeon
in attendance whose duty it is to stop the fight if there is too much
loss of blood, or between rounds, to sew up long wounds and
doctor small ones. He operates in as brutal a manner as possible in
order to further indoctrinate the young men in courage, also in
order that the scars may heal badly. This, naturally, is good for the
young surgeon, too—it teaches him not to be sentimental in his
future practice. If you achieve good wounds, you put salt in them
and keep them open to make spectacular scars.

Schläger dueling is an unbelievably gory spectacle. Foreigners
with weak stomachs have been known to vomit. And the tendency
to turn green is not helped by the foul air, the pipe and cigarette
smoke, and the smell of fresh or stale beer. But schläger dueling is
none the less fundamentally harmless, for your eyes are protected
by heavy goggles and all the rest of you above the waist, by heavy
quilted padding. Sometimes parts of your chest are left bare in
order, as suggested by *Simplicissimus* and other light-minded periodicals, to have something interesting to show your bride on her
wedding night.

My two duels, or rather, challenges, sprang out at me unexpectedly as I had been warned they would. I hadn't done a thing. And
both were important. They weren't schläger duels—my enemies
wanted to hurt me. The first time I had merely objected to a
drunken student, with a little round verein hat, leaning on my
shoulder—he hadn't even been introduced to me; and the second

time I had merely left word that I wasn't "at home" when a small, non-verein student, with a miniature female dachshund came for Sunday breakfast the sixth time without invitation to the apartment I shared with two other Americans—one studying painting, the other architecture—with whom I had gone to an American university. It wasn't my fault, anyhow. Being softhearted, or perhaps weak-minded, I might have let the student and the dachshund in, but the two other Americans said "no." They said, with considerable heat, that "they were goddamned if they were going to live with a German and a dog all the rest of their lives." So they instructed Hilda, our maid of all work, whose figure was becoming increasingly embarrassing to three young bachelors, due to the persistent attentions of a sergeant in the Bavarian army, to say that we "were out." Hilda did everything she was told, which perhaps accounted for her figure.

The big scarred student had come up to a long table in a beer-hall where I was sitting with some friends, also non-verein men. He recognized them graciously and they fluttered like doves at his condescension. Then he came over and, without a word, leaned on me. After a while I asked him in my bad German if he would mind not doing so. He looked down at me as if a hat rack had spoken, and resumed his conversation. I did, of course, the inevitable; I drew back my elbow and let him have it in his well-lined ribs. The results were dramatic; being not too well balanced, he slid across the floor and ended up against another table. As he was an extremely large young man, for a moment I was pleased, and then I realized I had done something serious. He gathered himself together, stood up straight, minced across the floor toward me, clicked his heels, and bowed, and said, "Come outside."

My non-verein friends were white and grave. Only one of them spoke, a man named Hans Reddig. I shall never forget him. "I shall act as your second," he said.

I followed the large student toward the vestibule, between what seemed unending tables filled with people who raised their heads and stared at me. Just a foot or so over my head fluttered an American eagle, a badly scared look in his eyes, and preceding him was a barred and starred flag that wavered considerably. Nobody saw these but me. Every foot we advanced the large student looked larger. We pushed through the revolving inner door of the vestibule and the large student clicked his heels again and bowed. He seemed unpleasantly sober.

"Your card," he said, and, reaching in his pocket gave me his.

I was fighting for time.

"Do you make a habit of leaning on strangers?" I asked in a weak voice.

"Do not be insolent," he said, "it will only make it worse for you. My second will call on you tomorow. The good Reddig has said that he will act as yours."

He should not have called me "insolent," and he should not have sneered at me—Germans always overdo things. Recollection flooded my brains like returning blood. "Very well," I said. "We'll fight here," and I began to take off my coat. No one except a small, slight man knows the exquisite pleasure of frightening a big one. There's hardly anything in the world just like it. And then the continuing pleasure of bullying him! For the most part small men never get a chance to bully anyone except smaller women.

"Oh, no!" said the huge scarred student, looking away from me, "Gentlemen do not fight that way!"

"English and American gentlemen do," I said, and advanced.

The situation was saved by the arrival of what seemed to me scores of other students, verein and non-verein men. The verein men, corps brothers of the large and drunken one, said he had broken all the rules by challenging me while drunk. He must apologize. I only hope I wasn't too eager . . . I'm likely to be when relieved.

My duel with the owner of the female dachshund was even simpler. I simply tore up his card and threw the pieces at his feet. By that time I was bored, old in the ways of duels, and hardened. The Monday morning after the Sunday on which Hilda had told him we "were out," the owner of the dachshund came up to me in the rotunda of the university, and clicked his heels, and bowed, and handed me his card. He was small and round and had dark curly hair and large round eyes, gentle as those of his dachshund.

"Why do you give me this?" I asked, looking at the card, although, of course, I knew. "I know your name already."

"I smelled you," he said. "I smelled all of you—you were eating breakfast. You lied to me, and insulted me. You smelled obviously."

He had told me that he was the only son of a rich and widowed mother.

I tore up his card and flung the pieces at his feet.

"Go away quickly," I said wearily, "or I will slap you." He went away, a look of heartfelt gratitude in his eyes.

When later, during the First World War, I heard, and many times, and on excellent authority, that the Germans, despite their immense courage, didn't like hand-to-hand fighting, I wasn't surprised.

THE GREAT FEUD

by Bernard DeVoto and
Sinclair Lewis

In the spring of 1944 the Pulitzer Prize-winning historian and critic Bernard DeVoto published in SRL *an article entitled "They Turned Their Backs on America," a chapter from his forthcoming book,* The Literary Fallacy. *He charged that since World War I American writers had misrepresented to the world the true character of the American people, and he named Nobel Prize-winning novelist Sinclair Lewis as one of those writers. DeVoto's charge provoked Lewis to pen a savage retort which was published in the following issue of* SRL *under Lewis' own title, "Fools, Liars, and Mr. DeVoto." The argument became a classic in the annals of the magazine. Here, as it originally appeared, is the famous DeVoto-Lewis debate.*

APRIL 8-15, 1944

Mr. DeVoto's charge:

THE NATION which came out of the war into the 1920s was hardly in any particular what the appraiser said it was. Our critics found it drab, cheerless, anemic, without hope, a decadent society. It was the most cheerful and energetic society in the world and, whether in envy or admiration, foreigners marveled that so much youth and so much hope could be left anywhere. At the very moment when literary critics were turning from us disgusted with industrial materialism and invoking the Russians as the only people who had a hopeful vision for mankind, with the most sedulous and imitative care the Russians were doing their utmost to reproduce the industrial materialism of America, in which they thought they had found the only hopeful vision for mankind. At the moment when criticism was describing America as a deadly uniformity of thought, belief, ideal, behavior, and social pattern, America was the most variegated and diversified society that the world had ever

265

seen. It was a welter of conflicting thought, beliefs, ideals, behavior, classes, interests, racial stocks, sectional sentiments, education, economies, social systems, philosophies, patterns, and culture. It was a heterogeneity so vast, so diversely composed, and in such rapid flux that no formula could express it, no generalization could contain it, and no system of ideas could subject it to control. At the very moment when literature was describing the Americans as dull, brutish, and slaves, they were the freest, the most colorful, and the most reckless people in the world.

As the 1920s came on, then, much that had been familiar and traditional in American life was either dead or dying. Much that was new, strange, and revolutionary was already upon us; more was on the way. Old energies had been accelerated, new energies had been released. In racial stocks, social and economic classes, interests, beliefs, cultures, this was a changed and changing nation. Innumerable old patterns had been broken, innumerable new patterns were forming. The nation had the greatest mechanical power, the greatest actual wealth, and very likely the greatest potential wealth in the world. It had the longest experience at self-government, the most flexible political institutions, incomparably the most flexible social institutions that history had ever seen. It had the greatest measure of democracy, the greatest freedom, the greatest social kindliness, the greatest degree of social justice, the greatest hope.

Also it contained many offenses, injustices, inequities, cruelties, and many possibilities that these would grow worse. Within it were conflicts, dislocations which grew graver, counterrevolutions, internal warfare of systems, exploitations, wastes, corruption. Many of the new energies were working evil and threatened to work worse evil. Much that was fine had been lost; the loss of more was possible. The continuity that had been preserved through fourteen decades of change was menaced, might possibly be destroyed. To these possibilities were added stresses from without, as old orders collapsed in Europe and new orders struggled to establish themselves there and in Asia.

It was a bewildering future—and an inspiring one. The nation was confused. But it was not dismayed—nor frightened—nor craven —nor decadent.

We may adopt the highest literary ground and remark that here was a challenge to writers. Our society greatly needed laborious study, patient exploration, sympathetic understanding. Furthermore, if literature likes variety, color, vigor, richness, intensity, flow and movement, the jewelry of lights and shifting patterns, here was perhaps the greatest wealth ever offered to it. Again if it is a function of literature to participate in the solution of common problems, to explain, to interpret—if, that is, literature has an organic place in culture—then surely here was its greatest opportunity in the American history.

We have seen the outcome. Study, patience, sympathy, and understanding were precisely the instruments which literature refused to bring to its job. An organic relationship with culture was precisely what literature refused to establish. Instead of studying American life, literature denounced it. Instead of working to understand American life, literature repudiated it. By voluntary act it withdrew from the very activity which it insisted was its proper business. Few will say that it accepted its responsibility or made use of its opportunity. Mr. MacLeish, Mr. Brooks, and innumerable penitents who have lately been tailoring sackcloth to their own measure acknowledge the failure. I have been discussing it as a betrayal, and yet the emphasis must not be on betrayal, for the generality of writers, as I pointed out, were moved by the highest idealism. The emphasis must be put on the inadequacy of means— on the ineffectiveness of purely literary ideas to make literary expression an organic part of culture.

It remains to speak briefly of the effect on literature itself. During the twenties and thereafter there were confusion and decay of values, there was anarchy of thought and feeling, in American life. But in our literature there were immensely greater confusion and decay of values, and the comprehensive word for it between wars is anarchy. The society was rugged, lively, and vital, but literature became increasingly debilitated, capricious, querulous, and irrelevant. Unquestionably many lives went down in despair but society never felt that it was futile, whereas literature came increasingly to confess its own futility. Even in the dreadful years of the early 1930s, when the most severe strains ever put on us made the nation face common failures new to the national consciousness, the generality of Americans felt no such despair as literature felt. It was writers, not the American people, who believed that the promise of American life had ended.

We must not permit ourselves the easy appeal to the last argument of kings. To escape into the rhetoric or the obscurantism of war emotions would be a species of literary trick. Yet it is invincibly true that danger brings clarification and that in this way war has an edge which cuts through unrealities. As the universal war drew nearer to the United States something fundamental, something eternally simple, became clear. The Americans have changed as their society has changed, but their vigor, their courage, and especially their faith had not changed in accordance with the literary repudiation. The nation had not doubted its strength, its greatness, or its future. And, oddly, literary people were suddenly saying so. It is with no idea of vindicating or disproving literary ideas that Americans have gone out to die in defense of our common ways of life, and in defense of the implicit faith that animates them—precisely as Americans had always done in the past which was held to be ignoble. It is not to reassure intellectuals that the nation has overturned the calculations of its enemies who knew that it was decadent, weak, and incapable of meeting the tests of the modern world. There was no such intention; the nation did not take the literary ideas into account and for the most part did not know that they existed. The point is that the literary ideas were wrong. The point is that the American people were not what their writers had believed them to be. The point is that only persons so lost in logic, dream, and theory that they were cut off from their heritage could have held those ideas.

Something final is said about the literature we have been discussing when we observe that it took a world war to reveal to writers truths about the culture they sprang from which had been the commonplace knowledge of every man of sense, the ordinary experience of everyone who lived in touch with the American realities. Never in any country or any age had writers so misrepresented their culture, never had they been so unanimously wrong. Never had writers been so completely separated from the experiences that alone give life and validity to literature. And therefore because separation from the sources of life makes despair, never had literature been so despairing, and because false writing makes trivial writing, never had literature been so trivial.

That, then, is where we come out. The characteristic literature of our age has not been serious, it has been a trivial literature. Despair is an automatic result of separation from the common life. Triviality is an automatic penalty imposed by that common life. In our time writers have been more widely read, more enthusiastically applauded, and rewarded with greater wealth and public honors than writers have ever had before. Nearly any writer could get an audience, nearly any writer could lead a coterie, nearly any writer could have had appurtenances of distinction, nearly any competent writer could be famous, and many writers became rich. In superficial public esteem, in publicity, in money, writers in our time have ranked higher than any writers before them anywhere. And yet there is no escape from a realization that, while bestowing all this on writers, the public has more than half-consciously degraded them to the status of entertainers. If a writer has not been equated with a movie actor or a baseball player, at least he has been understood to be a worker in the same field. If literature has been understood to differ from the crafts of illusionists, acrobats, and stripteasers, it has also been understood to be performing the same social function.

The public has been glad to reward its entertainers but has not supposed that literature was speaking for the American people. Fame writers might have, but authority they have been steadily denied. Mr. Mencken or Mr. Lewis has not been granted the authority that was freely accorded to Mark Twain. Neither Mr. Hemingway nor Mr. Brooks nor Mr. Jeffers has been granted the jurisdiction over the American spirit freely exercised by Emerson with the consent of his readers. Neither Mark Twain nor Emerson supposed that the Americans were the children of light or that America was the Kingdom of Heaven come upon earth. Both spoke rebukes to their countrymen so fundamental that anything said by writers in our time seems, by comparison, weak, captious, ephemeral, and a trifle effeminate. But both spoke with authority to a people who acknowledged their authority—because both spoke knowing whereof they spoke, and both spoke from within.

In the long arc of time when history comes to describe the culture of America between the two wars, it will not be American ideas or the American way of life that looks tawdry, cheap, empty, and base. It will be the half-bushel of writers who presumed to find them so on the basis of a blend of arrogance, ignorance, and beautiful ideas which would seem craven except that it is first of all ridiculous. Seeking for a phrase which will convey the quality of that literature, history may sum it up as the Age of Ignominy. "We must begin by thinking of American literature," the topic sentence may read, "not as functional in American life but as idle, dilettante, flippant, and intellectually sterile." The age of literary folly. The age of slapstick.

I should like to tell you that I hear the fiddles tuning all over America. I should like to promise you that a generation of writers of more seasoned intelligence, of greater wisdom, more serious, more deeply dedicated, are now laying the foundations on which at last will be erected a literature worthy of a great people. And in fact there is a haste of literary people to exalt democracy, to exult in the native grain, and even to inquire and examine and search out what these things may be. American literature is wearing jeans, eating grits and sidemeat, gathering at the crossroads store to take a stand on the preamble to the Declaration of Independence. The American writer has unbuttoned the collar of his flannel shirt, is grinding corn between two hand-smoothed stones, and has undertaken to re-create his personality with the proper proportions of Daniel Boone and Walt Whitman. His eyes have seen the glory of the coming of the Lord. O beautiful for spacious skies, for amber waves of grain, he sings with a loving and compassionate heart.

But I confess uneasiness. I am not yet an old man but already in my time I have seen this same eagerness and compassion expanded in many contradictory causes, this same literary personality dedicated to many disparate values with the same fervor. I cannot believe that ignorant love is more stable than ignorant contempt. The literary man loving freedom, who lately derided it as a superstition and a weakness of the plutocracies? The literary man praising the American way, who only a few hours back found in it nothing but absurdity? The literary man associating himself as with brothers of one heart with the democracy who yesterday were the boobs, the suckers, the fall guys, the Rotarians, the coarse-souled materialists of all the world? Well, maybe, but one long seasoned in folly may be permitted to add, probably not for long. The generality of writers of my time have suggested to me that the literary temperament is unstable and I must doubt if Almighty God has chosen the 1940s to make it over for all time. In some purple evening there will be another floodlighted opening at Grauman's Chinese Theater and worshipful thousands will discover that Miss Veronica Lake has let her hair down over her right eye. By noon the next day millions of girls will be looking at life with the left eye only and, the weary expectation is, resolute and one-eyed literary folk will once more be beholding the land of broken promises, inhabited only by inferior people who destroy individuality and break the Artist's heart.

Neither God nor nature has decreed ways in which books must be written. Literature is not subject to the laws which bring forth Mazzaroth in his season and guide Arcturus with his sons. It is subject to writers, mortal men all, men not notable for fixity of character, suffering much from neurosis, much given to whim, caprice, suggestibility, and mistaking the quirks of their emotions for the contours of objective fact. Books will continue to be written by writers. They will faithfully present the ideas and emotions of writers. When those ideas and emotions chance to be true or great, books will be true and great. When they chance to be childish or frivolous or silly, books will correspond. I cannot tell you what literature will be like when you have fought through the war and taken citizenship in the unpredictable world of the future. But, a literary man, I too can succumb to the persuasiveness of literary ideas—I can tell you a moral which the writers of my time have pointed out for the writers of your time. I can tell you what literature will have to do if it is to be what, in the faraway, expectant dawn of my era, it set out to be.

If literature is to be a dependable description of America, if it is to make a useful comment on America, then first of all it must know America. Knowledge is a slow growth, a long path beset with possibilities of error. Men are not given to know the nature of things by intuition. Authority is not born full-grown in any mind, nor can anyone come to it by staring into his own soul, or at his navel, or into the high priest's emerald breastplate. No one can know a country or a people, no one can know even the small portions with which most of us must be content, except by a long effort to know them, a refusal to be satisfied with the nobly vague, a distrust of the logically beautiful. Knowledge does not come from the matching up of myths, abstractions, and hypotheses that made the writers of the 1920s sure they were red to the shoulders with the blood of life when they were only watching the play of shadows across the screen of their own souls. Knowledge means sweat and doggedness, a realization that one can never know enough, and it comes from experience inappeasably sought after and tested with the most powerful reagents the mind can use. Writers must be content to hold their peace until they know what they are talking about. Readers must be willing to hold them to the job if they refuse to hold themselves. An uninstructed gentleness toward writers has been the mistake of readers in our time. Words like "fool" and "liar" might profitably come back to use. If literature is a trivial pursuit, folly and lying are of no particular moment, but if literature is to be serious then it cannot be permitted folly and lying and when they appear in it they must be labeled and denounced.

Yet knowledge can be come by. But first there is a fixed barrier which writers cannot cross except by virtue of a profound humility. The moral of our literature between the wars is that literature must come upon futility and despair unless it begins in fellowship from within. Rejection, the attitude of superiority, disdain of the experience of ordinary people, repudiation of the values to which the generality of a writer's countrymen devote their lives—the literature of my generation tried that path and found that the path ended in impotence and the courtship of death. The evils and abuses of society may be intolerable but my generation has proved that literature can do nothing whatever about them from outside.

It must enter in, it must speak its "Thou shalt!" as one who shares the dust and thirst. Cut the umbilical cord and what dies is not society but literature. Form coteries of the initiate, turn in abhorrence from the village square to the High Place, consecrate yourself to anything which the louts at the foot of the High Place cannot know, however fine or noble or beautiful it may be—and in the end you have only a group of the merely literary, speaking fretfully to one another in soft voices while the tides of the world sweep by.

Either literature deals honestly with the basic experiences in which all men may see themselves, or else it is only a mannered diversion practiced by the impaired and of interest only to the leisure moments of those who are whole. Either it is a man and a brother speaking to men and brothers, speaking of things which all share and are subject to, or else it is only a private titillation. Well over a century ago Ralph Waldo Emerson ordered the American writer to do his job—to the meal in the firkin, the milk in the pan. To know what it was that had appeared upon the earth, the new man, this American. To search his heart, his mind, his vision, his memory. Only in obeying that command has American literature ever found reality. Our literature can be true only as it is true of us, it can be great only as it comes to find greatness. All roots will be winter-killed and all the sweet green shoots will die except as they are warmed and fertilized by the common experience of Americans. That common experience is sufficiently wide and deep—literature has never yet drawn even with it and can never exhaust it. In it lies the future of American literature, possibly a great future, but only as the writers of the future, by their own wit or by the grace of God, may, as the writers between wars in the main did not, accept it as their own.

Mr. Lewis' reply:

IN LITERARY TREATISES it has not been customary to make one's points by yelling "Fool" and "Liar," but perhaps we have all been wrong. In his new volume, *The Literary Fallacy,* my old friend Mr. Bernard DeVoto—large D and no space before the V, apparently —has this pronouncement:

> Writers must be content to hold their peace until they
> know what they are talking about. Readers must be willing

to hold them to the job if they refuse to hold themselves. An uninstructed gentleness toward writers has been the mistake of readers in our time. Words like "fool" and "liar" might profitably come back to use. . . . If literature is to be serious then it cannot be permitted folly and lying and when they appear in it then they must be labeled and denounced.

Very well. I denounce Mr. Bernard DeVoto as a fool and a tedious and egotistical fool, as a liar and a pompous and boresome liar.

He is a liar in his statement of the purposes of *The Literary Fallacy,* and a fool in his repetitious announcements that he is the one authority on the American frontier, psychoanalysis, family life, the literature of geology, the technic of biography, the treatment of burns, and on Mark Twain, and all New England writers whatsoever.

The intrepid Mr. DeVoto rather fondles the offensive words. He writes, "Mr. Brooks's ignorance was for years a public instrument of literature. With its aid many writers . . . *lied* flatly about the people they were presuming to interpret." And: "As a mind Martin (Arrowsmith) suffers from arrested development, as a scientist he is a *fool.*"

Here is what, not very truthfully, Mr. DeVoto declares to be the thesis of his book. It is a four-barreled or machine-gun thesis. (1) There was a mysterious age of literature known as the twenties, confined to exactly ten years. [Upon whose completion, at 12:01 A.M., January 1, 1930, God sighed, "I'll never try anything like that again!" S. L.]

Mr. DeVoto admits that a few of the writers who exhibited in the twenties may have been born several months before them and a still smaller squad may go on existing in the 1940s, but he implies that their publishing books in the twenties miraculously made all these zombies exactly alike—for instance, Eugene O'Neill, Dale Carnegie, and Edith Wharton, perhaps?

(2) All of these scoundrels have maintained that a culture may best be understood by its books, and (3) such a belief in their own profession, like that of a priest, a soldier, a judge, or a teacher, is very naughty of them, and (4) to quote from *The Literary Fallacy*: "Never in any country or any age had writers so misrepresented their culture."

Now all of this makes up an obvious lie, but the double-lie comes in the fact that none of this actually belongs to Mr. DeVoto's thesis. What he really says in this booklet is merely that Mr. DeVoto is an incalculably wiser and nobler man than Mr. Van Wyck Brooks.

This is the third or fourth book, now, in which DeVoto has led a frantic one-man revolution with the slogan, "Brooks must go!" I do not believe that Mr. Brooks has ever answered or ever will answer. He is too gentle, too just, too scholarly—and perhaps too pitying.

My first encounter with DeVoto was on a train to Philadelphia, years ago. He timidly introduced himself as a teacher who was trying to write for *The Saturday Evening Post*. I had never heard of him but I was interested in that froglike face, those bright eyes, that boyish and febrile longing to be noticed. I was reasonably polite to him, and he was grateful. I saw him several times afterward, but his screaming, his bumptiousness, his conviction that he was a combination of Walter Winchell and Erasmus, grew hard to take, and it is a long time now since I have seen him. And I note that in the same way a good many reviewers find the growing noisiness and cocksureness of his books increasingly irritating.

The man must be studied. Like his fellow ornaments of New England, Lydia Pinkham, William Dudley Pelley, and Phineas T. Barnum, he has by brashness and self-advertisement pushed himself into notoriety, and since no serious critic, like Mr. Brooks or Mr. Carl Van Doren or Mr. Fadiman or Mr. Edmund Wilson, has thought it worth while to deflate him, many innocent and youthful believers still listen to him.

When his *The Year of Decision* appeared last year and we found that if he would but gag his babbling ego he could still write remarkably sound and unhackneyed history, many of us believed, however, that he still had a soul to save, and that the salvation might require nothing beyond a couple of miracles and twenty years of patience.

The Literary Fallacy is, aside from a few rather anxious introductory pages, composed of lectures delivered to the fortunate students of the University of Indiana in 1942-3. A foreword issued by the Patten Foundation of the University explains, "The purpose of this prescription (*sic*) is to provide an opportunity for members and friends of the University to enjoy the privilege and advantage of personal acquaintance with the Visiting Professor."

Let us not stray into speculation as to what the members and friends later thought about having had the privilege of personal acquaintance with the Visiting Professor.

This is a small, thin book, prosily dull, carelessly planned, presenting nothing but Mr. DeVoto's bellows about his own importance. Why then waste bombs on it?

I want to point the way to an adventure too beautiful for realization. What would happen if men like O'Neill and Hemingway, who have been too busy with living and writing to take time out for self-defense, should some day turn on such Talmudists as DeVoto, Howard Mumford Jones, Allen Tate, R. P. Blackmur, Yvor Winters, and Edmund Wilson—I wonder if it is an accident that Mr. Wilson's invariable nickname, "Bunny," so resembles Mr. DeVoto's "Benny"? Most of them are drier and more fastidious and responsible critics than DeVoto and much less given to shouting "Notice me—notice me," but they all have a kinship and it is their influence that has caused every college instructor now living to write, very badly, another book about Henry Adams, Henry James, T. S. Eliot, and William Faulkner.

It might be impossible to persuade Ernest Hemingway to spend even one hour in reading the pompousities of Benny and Bunny, but if he should ever see how easy it is to crush them at their own game, then God help those mincing messiahs.

Mr. DeVoto often seems to be taking a pose and waiting for a camera, any camera. He does so in the first pages of *The Literary Fallacy,* where he worries:

> Since ways of thinking are fairly constant, the fallacy which this book examines is likely to appear in some of the reviews of the book in literary periodicals. Readers who may want to see the fallacy in actual operation are advised to look for it there. The book . . . does not try to describe American literature during the 1920s completely, to tell the whole truth about it, or to pass judgment on it as a whole, but some reviewers may report on it in an understanding that it tries to do all three.

With only a passing wonder as to why DeVoto repeats a statement three times and then calls it three statements, and as to whether it is his personal knowledge of reviewing that makes him so jumpily apprehensive about the intelligence and honesty of his fellow-reviewers, let us note that for once he does tell the truth about this book.

It certainly is not a complete account of the literary crimes of the 1920s. In fact, it is nothing at all but a long-winded confession of DeVoto's obsession about Van Wyck Brooks, plus a few envious references to other contemporaries, and two essays, one on the geologist John Wesley Powell and the other on the medical treatment of burns. These essays, which are as original and definitive as a high-school theme, are supposed to indicate how many things we others failed to know and write about in the 1920s and to show how our

books would have been written if we had been so lucky as to have
Mr. DeVoto write them for us.

How it must irritate him to have to sit around year after year
waiting to find out what Van Wyck Brooks's next book will be, so
that he may know what *his* new book will be. If Brooks ever tackles
Proust or anything else east of Massachusetts or south of New Jersey,
then DeVoto is sunk for life.

Let us check all this.

Out of the 169 actually printed pages of this small book (on sale
for $2.50 at several book stores, if you want to pay that much), one
to four pages each are devoted to the sins of Dos Passos, Hemingway, Lewis, Wilson, Eliot, and Pound, and to the virtues of Frost
and Farrell. Other writers are disposed of more briefly. Mr. DeVoto
finds twenty-one lines quite enough to deal with Willa Cather, E.
A. Robinson, Sandburg, and Stephen Benét all put together, and
from five to fifty words each sufficient to finish up Mencken, Jeffers,
Hecht, Dreiser, Dell, Tate, Fitzgerald, Frank, Mumford, Tom Wolfe,
Carl and Mark Van Doren, MacLeish, Kazin, Beard, and Cabell.
How right you are, Mr. DeVoto. Your treatise cannot be accused of
completeness.

Indeed it is so far from that foible that, in an account of the
1920s, it does not even mention Booth Tarkington, eleven of whose
books appeared in the 1920s, Thornton Wilder, whose *The Bridge
of San Louis Rey* came out in 1927, Hergesheimer, Sherwood An-
derson, Flinor Wylie, Edna Millay, Upton Sinclair, Ellen Glasgow,
Edith Wharton, any dramatist whatever except O'Neill—whom De-
Voto hates—Hervey Allen, Conrad Aiken, Glenway Westcott, E. E.
Cummings, Ring Lardner, Evelyn Scott, Louis Bromfield, Hart Crane,
Zona Gale, or the Will Beebe who did for biology all that Mr. De-
Voto's Mr. Powell did for geology.

He may explain that he knows intimately and hates all of these
figures but that in his gay little sloop he simply hasn't room for
them.

But he does have room for seventy pages, seventy out of the total
169, for his attack on Van Wyck Brooks!

And he has room for the twelve pages of his medical treatise, the
purpose of which is to prove that he knows more about medicine
than Dr. Jacques Loeb, Dr. Paul de Kruif, and Dr. Martin Arrowsmith put together. And he can take ten pages for an account of
Powell, the actual purpose of which is revealed on page 133:

For this man (Major Powell) wrote . . . books, one of
which we must glance at, his *Report on the Lands of the Arid*

Region of the United States. Mr. Brooks has not heard about it, nor Mr. Mumford, Mr. Stearns, Mr. Lewisohn, Mr. Frank, Mr. Parrington, or Mr. Hicks, nor even Mr. Edmund Wilson or Mr. Kazin.

With all of his God-complex, Mr. DeVoto has never been so papal. Just how does he know what these men have heard of? I should think it likely that the late Vernon Parrington and the extremely learned Lewis Mumford, who have really inspired thought in America where DeVoto has merely done some inaccurate book-keeping on it, have heard a great deal about Major Powell. I doubt their ever having made a habit of running to Father DeVoto and reporting to him everything they have heard.

But suppose none of them had heard of Powell. So, as under any of his pen names Mr. DeVoto would write, what? It is the job of all historians to revive forgotten men of importance. They do it daily and, because it *is* their job, none of them except DeVoto would ever wind up an historical report with "Look at me! How much smarter I am than any of you! You never heard of that! Yah, yah, yah!"

That's how the yahoos got their name.

While we are on Powell, let us note Mr. DeVoto's acknowledgement to Wallace Stegner "for checking my account of Powell." Why he should need Mr. Stegner for that task, which any child with the extensive account of Powell in the Dictionary of American Biography before him could do in ten minutes, is a puzzle. For Wallace Stegner, author of *On a Darkling Plain, The Big Rock Candy Mountain, et al.,* is already one of the most important novelists in America, an incomparably better writer than DeVoto, and a number of us go daily to the cathedral and pray that he will get out of Harvard, get away from all the cultural quacks like Mr. DeVoto, go back to Utah and Iowa, and put on the mantle of greatness that is awaiting him.

It's a dull pamphlet, this *The Literary Fallacy,* and stumble-footed in style: On page 63 appears this example:

> "Literary climate" is a phrase of literary shorthand which stands for the moods and feelings and ideas of writers, the ways in which books are conceived and the daily excitements in which they are written, for literary associations, literary experience, the tones and shade and nuances and colorations of writers' minds in relation to their books and to literature in general—in short, for the whole sum of literary affect and effect.

The publisher's blurb says, "Mr. DeVoto makes his point with thoroughness, humor and truly brilliant phraseology." You can see that humor above, and the brilliance of the following must have brought the Indiana students right up out of their seats, cheering:

> It is not my finding but that of criticism itself that in its new occupations also it still finds frustration, that in fact it is not merely frustrated but ignominiously routed.

Thus powerfully does he show that the writers of the 1920s—say, Dorothy Canfield Fisher, George Kaufman, and James Branch Cabell—so lastingly corrupted our land as to have contaminated the entire 11,000,000 of our fighting forces today. Until he pointed it out, I didn't know we were that good.

Aside from its complaints about Mr. Brooks, the brochure contains two charges as specific and sensational as the remarks of a Senator who should reveal, "There are certain persons in a State which I shall not mention who have performed actions, or at least shown tendencies, that I can regard only as, if not sinister, then at least, beyond peradventure, pretty lousy." It is with this and no other courage and definiteness that Mr. DeVoto attacks his old literary buddies.

Says he on page 167—and don't forget the new rule is that Fool and Liar *must* be applied to writers who make dishonorable statements—"Never in any country or any age had writers so misrepresented their culture, never had they been so unanimously wrong (as in America in the 1920s). Never had writers been so completely separated from the experiences that alone give life and validity to literature."

Just whom do you mean, Mr. DeVoto? Do you mean Hart Crane or Dreiser or Miss Glasgow or Edgar Guest? Surely even you can't be such an undeviating fool as to hint that *all* of the hundred or two hundred writers, including a second-rate hack writer of fiction named Bernard Augustine DeVoto, were so precisely alike as to be "unanimous" about *all* great spiritual issues from 1920 to 1930? If you don't mean a hundred, or seventy-five, or fifty, whom do you mean? Just those whom you mention? You don't mean Tarkington, Wilder, Sherwood Anderson, Hergesheimer, Ring Lardner or Elinor Wylie, then? Or are you too important, too busy with pious thoughts of Van Wyck Brooks, to be interested in these last at all? For a Visiting Professor, who considers his lectures important enough to be preserved in a book, instead of just sighing and burning them up like the rest of us, you are rather unclear, Mr. DeVoto.

If the people you indict are those whom you have mentioned, let's hear more of them. Exactly what are the valid experiences that they have been so "completely separated from"?

From loving a red-headed girl, or being a grandmother, or serving in the navy, or committing a crime, or being converted to Episcopalianism, or reading Bernard DeVoto—which can be quite an experience, sometimes, I assure you. And just which writers lacked just which experiences?

You mean to say that you know all of this, Benny? You know what Waldo Frank thinks about war and God? You know the intimate family relationships, so revelatory of their philosophy, and the neighborhood friendships of Mencken and Jeffers and Mumford and Dos Passos?

If you don't, then you are a nebulous liar. If you do, for Heaven's sake write out all that rich stuff instead of a piffling little pocketbook about how much smarter than Van Wyck Brooks you are.

It is astonishing that, though he was bouncingly with us in the lethal twenties, DeVoto never saw how bad we were. Oh, he was there. There is no reason why any reader should remember them or even be able to give their titles, but he did publish novels in 1924, 1926, and 1928. He didn't notice then that most of his colleagues were assassins. In fact, it has taken him fourteen years to notice it.

I wonder if he could have been aroused from his sinful ignorance by the evangelical Mr. Archibald MacLeish who, for about ten minutes, took charge of the press of America and explained that he had to save our youth from the evil medicine we had brewed in the twenties.

MacLeish's doctrine was rather insulting to the millions of Americans whom he pictured as being so feeble-minded that we could utterly ruin them merely by saying that we considered service club luncheons and Americans on the Riviera dull. In other decades a like charge of infidelity has been attached to many other writers, to Dickens, Zola, Hawthorne, Tom Paine, and the Mark Twain who, unfortunately for his future reputation, has now been taken over by Mr. Bernard DeVoto as executor.

Just as fair—and just as unprovable—an assertion would be that the major writers of the twenties, men who so loved their country that they were willing to report its transient dangers and stupidities, have been as valuable an influence as America has ever known. DeVoto shouldn't have been so innocent as to take his doctrine from MacLeish who, through a large part of the beleaguered twenties, was living in France and reading T. S. Eliot and Ezra Pound.

Mr. DeVoto feels a good deal of agony over the inconsistencies of

Mr. Van Wyck Brooks, which appear to be very much like the inconsistencies of Mr. DeVoto who, in *Minority Report,* published only four years ago, so warmly liked some of the writers he now finds vile or watery that he rebuked other critics for underrating them. He scolds Mr. Brooks for not writing about Francis Parkman as Mr. DeVoto would have written, and presents a sample of his own method, which sounds very much like what Mr. John Fiske actually did write on that subject long ago.

Constantly busy with Brooks though Benny is, lately he has also been busy with writing a novel of his own. It is called *The Woman in the Picture,* and it was published only about a month before *The Literary Fallacy,* and by the same firm.

Not that *The Woman in the Picture* is signed by Mr. DeVoto. Certainly not. It is signed with his pen name, "John August," and a damn silly pen name it is, too. "Sardanapalus September" would have been much more convincing.

Its scholarly and strictly noncommercial publishers say of *The Woman in the Picture*: "Sophisticated romance and fast-moving adventure make this as exciting a tale as the author's last novel, *Advance Agent.* No more need be said."

Oh yes, Messrs. Little, Brown, a lot more need be said.

In *The Woman in the Picture,* Mr. Bernard DeAugust shows his belief in the people of these United States by depicting us as so dumb, softheaded, and ill-governed, with such idiotic police and F.B.I. and army and navy intelligence, that in the summer of 1942 a villain right out of the movies, one of these cold-eyed and non-alcoholic power-maniacs, was, with only half a dozen other plotters, going to take over and destroy our democracy.

The only thing that saved us was a liberal journalist, equally good at economic theorizing and at eye-gouging, assisted by an intellectual comic relief, who shows his training in Pareto and Emerson by constantly speaking with such humor as this: "You better buy a four-leaf clover. Yeah, get an asking price on rabbit's feet, too. So now what?"

Serious literature, Mr. DeVoto.

The hero has to drive the heroine halfway across the country, spending most of his time peeping at her bare legs and bosom, as enthusiastically reported by Mr. DeAugust, with a ten-year-old, behind-the-barn eroticism which has now been discarded by most of the pulps. There is also in the story the standard *B*-picture equipment of airplanes, automatic revolvers, telegraph codes, and gentlemen constantly getting themselves tied to logs, boxcars, telegraph poles, automobiles, Rocky Mountains, fences, statues of Ole Bull, coincidences, and lapses in the plot. But no cord can hold these guys, not when a serious writer who knows all about the literature of geology is creating 'em!

I wonder how much Visiting Professor DeVoto told the students at the University of Indiana about John August and his ideals and methods of work and his blessed freedom from any influence by Van Wyck Brooks? I hope he wasn't ashamed of John August; I hope he didn't keep silent about his jolly yarn, "The Woman Who Will Be Sold to the Pictures." Because in originality, in lucidity, in decent humanness it is much better fiction than *The Literary Fallacy*.

On pages 170-2 of *The Literary Fallacy*, Mr. DeVoto promises the dawn:

> There is a haste of literary people to exalt democracy, to exult in the native grain. . . . The American writer . . . has undertaken to re-create his personality with the proper proportions of Daniel Boone and Walt Whitman. His eyes have seen the glory of the coming of the Lord. O beautiful for spacious skies, for amber waves of grain, he sings with a loving and compassionate heart. . . . Books will continue to be written by writers. [Extraordinary! S. L.] They will faithfully present the ideas and emotions of writers. When those ideas and emotions chance to be true or great, books will be true and great. When they chance to be childish or frivolous or silly, books will correspond.

And with that, Mr. DeVoto yanks off the priestly robe, puts on a Hollywood jacket, and finishes *The Woman in the Picture,* the most childish, frivolous, and silly dime-novel, the most lacking in any beautiful for spacious skies, the least perceptive of the coming of the Lord, the most recreated with the proportions of Tarzan and M-G-M, that I have read for years.

Is he a liar? Perhaps not unintentionally. And fool? It is he who writes himself down a fool. And I quote again his, "Literature cannot be permitted folly and lying and when they appear in it they must be labeled and denounced."

Yet Mr. DeVoto is a fool of cleverness, not of malice. He really has done all the bumptious monkey-tricks I ascribe to him, yet at heart he loves books and streets and laboratories, he wants to be liked, and lets his glibness run away with him. Can't you be a good boy, Benny, and stop yelling "Liar!" at your little playmates? You see, they might answer you—more and more of them might answer you, Benny.

THE SINNER-SAINT
AS HOST

by Lawrence Langner

A well-known Broadway producer visits the great—and bearded —playwright George Bernard Shaw and discusses with him such interesting topics of the times as nudity, women's clothes, and divorce.

JULY 22, 1944

IN THE SUMMER OF 1927, my wife and I decided to take a trip through Northern Italy. I dropped a line to G.B.S. telling him we would be at Milan and would like to see him and Mrs. Shaw, and I asked, as usual, whether he had a new play ready. Shaw replied, as usual, on a picture postcard:

> I am not writing a play, the great book on Socialism not being yet finally disposed of. However, here we are; and here we are likely to be three weeks hence; so by all means run over to see us when you come to Milan: it is within easy distance; and we are always glad to see you and Mrs. Langner.

About the middle of August we arrived at Stresa on Lake Maggiore and put up at Shaw's hotel, the Regina Palace, an ornate, buff-colored, barracks-like structure overlooking the lake. G.B.S. had reserved our room for us, and greeted us on arrival.

"You must stay here for a few days," he said, and added, "but Americans are not very welcome here, on account of the Sacco-Vanzetti case." The populace was in a state of tremendous tension over whether Sacco and Vanzetti would receive the death penalty. Perhaps this was because they were inured to injustice in their own country but could not bear to believe that the same thing could happen in a democracy.

After settling comfortably in our room for the night, we were awakened at what seemed to be an unearthly hour by a loud knocking at our door.

"Come along, wake up!" cried Shaw from outside. "It's seven

o'clock, and if you want to come swimming with me, you'll have to hurry up! See you at breakfast!"

"Do you want to get up this early?" I remarked drowsily to Armina.

"Of course," she cried, leaping from her bed like a gazelle. "How often will you have an opportunity of swimming with G.B.S.?"

I was stumped. First of all, I didn't swim well—about fifty strokes, and I am winded. Secondly, it was blowing quite hard the night before, and I was sure the lake would be full of waves, which have an irritating habit of getting into my eyes, ears, and mouth and annoying me.

"Up you get," she cried, "you can't keep Shaw waiting for you!"

So I got up, protesting mildly, and down we went for breakfast. G.B.S. was waiting for us. It was his custom each morning to cross the lake in a motorboat, then moor this boat off the estate of Albert Coates, the conductor, swim for the shore, and end up with a sunbath on a grassy meadow which sloped down to the beach. We boarded the motorboat dressed in our bathing suits, crossed over toward the other side of the lake, and at what seemed to me to be an enormous distance from the shore, G.B.S. dived in off the side of the boat. As his head and shoulders emerged from the lake and he shook the water out of his white hair and beard, the sun caught his pink cheeks and blue eyes, and he looked for all the world like Father Neptune emerging from the waves.

"Come on in, it's fine!" he shouted.

Armina, like most California-bred girls, was somewhat of a mermaid, and in she dove, showing off with a very effective scissors stroke. I cautiously lowered myself down the side of the boat, looking nervously at the shore which seemed to be miles away. I suppose the motorboat will keep moving slowly behind us, I thought, throwing discretion to the winds and timidly striking out in the direction of Father Neptune and the Mermaid. I kept going for a while, as the waves waved wildly, and the other swimmers swam rapidly ahead of me toward the shore. I looked back to reassure myself that the motorboat was following me. It was not. The Italian boatman had stopped his engine and was settling down to a comfortable siesta. I was torn between the choice of drowning or calling for help. I called for help. The motorboat started up, G.B.S. and Armina swam back, and between the three of them I was heaved out of the water and ignominiously ferried to the shore. Some years later, when recounting this incident, G.B.S. remarked that it was the greatest compliment ever paid him.

"Lawrence Langner," he said, with a twinkle in his eye, "followed me to such an extent that, when I jumped into Lake Maggiore, he jumped in after me without being able to swim a stroke, evidently thinking that my mere presence would save him from drowning."

Arrived at Villa Intragnola, the estate of Albert Coates, G.B.S. disappeared behind some convenient bushes and returned a few moments later wearing what seemed to be an old pair of white underdrawers. By this time a young lady had appeared on the scene. She was Sylvia Ray, Mr. Coates's secretary, and she was in the habit of joining G.B.S. for his morning sunbaths.

Not unnaturally, since the aging philosopher was in a state of next-to-nudity, the question of modesty came up for discussion, since the Pope had recently forbidden all Italian women to enter churches in dresses without sleeves and skirts which did not cover the ankles.

"What on earth do priests know about morality!" Shaw asked impatiently. "The trouble with these men who try to adjudicate upon what is moral or immoral is that they really know nothing about the subject. Any man who attempts to decide that one style of clothing is seductive while another style of clothing is not, must know something about the art of being seductive, and priests who rail about the theme of women's costumes are obviously the very last persons to be in a position to express an opinion on the subject. I remember in my young days when women dressed in accordance with the dictates of the clergy, they were literally swathed in clothing so that they resembled feather mattresses more than anything else, and I may add the women who wore these clothes looked considerably more seductive than the half-clad girls of today. There are really only two competent judges of what is seductive in women's clothing, and they are the women who make it their business to be seductive because they study it, and playwrights like myself, because it is our business to *know* what women must wear in order to be seductive."

He thought the clergy, and playwrights too, might turn their attention from women's clothes to an abuse of marriage which he noticed had been growing recently:

"That is, the selling of husbands by their wives to wealthy women who, in return for the husbands, paid handsome sums by way of damages for alienation of affection. This new trade in husbands is gaining considerable headway."

He showed a good deal of interest in Eugene O'Neill. "Tell me all about him," he said. I did my best. "Is there any truth in the story that he drinks?" "That may have been true once," I said, "but he hasn't touched a drop for years." "Too bad," was the rejoinder, "he'll probably never write another good play again."

One morning I asked him if it was true that, on hearing of the death of Arnold Daly, he had remarked, "Death by spontaneous combustion is rare, but it sometimes occurs." This story had appeared on the front pages of the New York newspapers, a day or so after the tragic death by burning of this magnificent actor who had done so much to introduce Shaw's early plays to America. "In my opinion," I said, "you couldn't possibly have made such a cruel remark, so I've denied it." "You mustn't do that," he replied, "I actually did say it, and for a good reason. Arnold's death wasn't attracting much attention until I made this remark, intentionally, to bring the story into the headlines. Arnold loved publicity and, had he been alive, he would have thanked me for putting him on the front pages."

I thought of his remark about Ervine's leg. It was not callousness which motivated him, but a complete lack of sentimentality. His daily life in Stresa while we were there was living evidence of his very real kindness.

"Every afternoon," he said, "I go to Prince Troubetskoy's studio to sit for a statue of myself. It's very tiring but I have to do it."

"Why?" I asked.

"Well," he replied, "the Prince's wife died last spring, and he was very upset over her loss, so in order to get his mind off his troubles, I decided to commission him to make a statue of me, not that the statue isn't very good," he added.

Later on we met Prince Paul Troubetskoy, a tall, distinguished Russian who seemed very sad and serious. He was an old friend of Shaw's, and had done a very fine head of him some twenty years earlier. The Prince dined with the Shaws and ourselves at the hotel. He was an ardent vegetarian, and joined Shaw in his choice of soup and greens.

"If you are guest of my house," he said solemnly at dinner, in rounded Russian accents, "and you wish to eat lamb chops, I give you big knife and take you into garden and show you little lamb, and you can assassinate him!"

As I had no desire to assassinate a little lamb with a big knife, I was not a guest in his house. Still I felt I should defend my taste in lamb chops, so I ventured to remark that, but for our habit of eating lambs, they would probably have no existence whatever, and I instanced the fact that up to the time of their deaths domestic animals were fed, cared for, and relieved of all anxiety by their owners, who even supplied them with mates in order that succeeding generations of lamb chops might be perpetuated.

"I violently object," said Shaw, "to being a procurer for domestic animals. But," he added, "unlike the Prince, I don't advocate vegetarianism for anyone but myself. You see, I'm really a sort of Saint!"

"I tried vegetarianism, but had to give it up a long time ago," said Mrs. Shaw quietly to Armina. And then she whispered, "It's very bad for the teeth." I glanced sidewise in the direction of Mr. Shaw's teeth, but saw no evidence of any disastrous results. "Can anything about G.B.S. be false?" I asked myself, but I feared to carry the inquiry any further.

Prince Troubetskoy invited us to his studio, not to partake of lamb chops, but to see the statue for which G.B.S. was posing, and one fine afternoon we accompanied him and Mrs. Shaw down the lake on a small steamboat to the little village where the Prince made his home. I brought my 16mm. movie camera along with me, and had a field day taking pictures of G.B.S. posing for his statue. Then I asked him and Mrs. Shaw to allow me to take a picture of them walking together, and they both kindly obliged. As they approached the camera, G.B.S. suddenly embraced Mrs. Shaw and kissed her. Mrs. Shaw, taken by surprise, remarked, "What on earth did you do that for?" "Don't you know that every movie ends up in a clinch?" was the reply. And thus I came into possession of the only picture extant of Mr. and Mrs. Shaw kissing!

We took our departure soon after, but before leaving I asked G.B.S. whether I could not obtain a duplicate of the early Troubetskoy bust to place in the lobby of the Guild Theatre.

"I have two already," was the reply, "but there's no sense in my giving you one, because in a year or so, if you go on producing my plays, you'll be bankrupt and the Guild Theatre will fall into the hands of the Shuberts. My bust will be the chief asset of the Guild, and will be sold at public auction." However, Mrs. Shaw said she thought something might be arranged.

A month or so later I heard from Mrs. Shaw in reply to a suggestion that we might consider purchasing the bust:

> It was a great pleasure to get your letter. We have spoken of you both often lately and hoped we should get news for you said you would write when you got home.
>
> Also I am most grateful to Mrs. Langner for the little book. I have not yet studied it, but I shall, I will write to her and tell her what I make of it.
>
> . . . Now about the bust. You speak of purchasing—but, you know, at Stresa we had an idea of letting you have one of the two we had here! Of course, if there is any probability of the Theatre Guild *buying* it would not be right for us to come between Prince Troubetskoy and a sale! If that was to

come about you would have to write to him and ask him his price (Prince Paul Troubetskoy, Villa Cabranca, Suna, Lago Maggiore, Italy). But the other idea is this: G.B.S. does not want to give the bust unconditionally to the Theatre Guild. He says (ironically) "you never know what will happen in the theater—they may come to grips or . . . something may happen." I tell you what he suggests. He might lend the bust to *you,* and give you a free hand to do what you like with it; show it whom you like, or make what arrangements you think best: with the private arrangement between you and him that you put it up in the theater as long as the theater is in a satisfactory state. If it should ever happen that you wished to withdraw it from there—then you could arrange with us as to its future disposition: but you could have full power to withdraw it at any time, on your own private judgment.

I think we told you that the bust of G.B.S. as an old man has been accepted by the Tate Gallery and is now there—so it is the bust of the *young* man (the one that was in the far corner of the studio) that I am writing about.

We are looking forward greatly to getting the films—I will write about them later.

Much interested about *Doctor's Dilemma.*

Best remembrance to you both.

Arrived in New York in the summer of 1928, the bust of Shaw has remained in its place of honor in the lobby of the Guild Theatre ever since.

In November of that year, I wrote G.B.S.:

Your statue looks very well, indeed, in the Guild lobby. Unfortunately, however, a vendor of cigarettes has placed his stand underneath it so that you look for all the world like the patron saint of nicotine. I think we shall have to hang a card around the neck of the statue bearing the words, "Mr. Shaw does not recommend these cigarettes."

DUET ON A BUS

by Douglas Moore

The lady took her culture seriously and tried to explain to a visit-
ing Frenchman why it is that in America we sing Russian operas
in the language of the Italians. The author of this account, Doug-
las Moore, is the Pulitzer Prize-winning composer of the American
opera Giants in the Earth.

JANUARY 20, 1945

I OVERHEARD A BUS CONVERSATION the other day. It was a long one, lasting from Grant's Tomb to Forty-Second Street. A young French-man, recently arrived, was apparently being shown the city by a lady of middle age who took her culture as a heavy responsibility. I suspect she had been reading an article about American Opera which appeared in *Opera News*. It went something like this:

"I shall be happy to attend the opening of the Opera."

"Yes, it couldn't be nicer. *Faust,* you know."

"It will be amusing to hear *Faust* in English."

"Oh this won't be in English. All our operas are done in the original language."

"Why? Do American audiences understand French?"

"No, but it is much more artistic that way and the singers' French is usually so poor even French audiences wouldn't be able to understand them."

"The singers aren't French then?"

"Only one or two. Albanese will be Marguerite and Pinza Meph-istopheles. They are both Italian."

"What happens in the Italian operas? Are they sung by Italians?"

"Well, now let's see. In *Rigoletto* there's Tibbett, Kullman as the Duke, Antoine as Gilda, and Kaskas as Maddalena."

"They're all Americans, aren't they?"

"So they are. Well they sing Italian anyway. Isn't it wonderful so many of our best singers are American now."

"It is an amusing idea, operas in the original language. Is *Boris Godounov* sung in Russian?"

"No, that would be too hard except for Kipnis. He's Russian. The rest of them sing Italian."

"You mean at the same time?"

"Yes, most of them are not Italians but it seems a good language to use."

"Why?"

"Well, you see in the old days there were really two companies at the Metropolitan, the German and the Italian. I suppose when this opera came into the repertory the Italian wing sang it."

"Why don't they sing it in English? That is closer to the Russian in sound and the audience might understand it better."

"Well, we have tried some operas in English, but I don't believe the public likes it."

"Why not? Are they afraid they might catch a few words?"

"Well, you know those old operas often have very silly words. It is really more artistic just to ignore them."

"Well, of course, the modern operas often have more interesting libretti. I see that Weinburger, Montemezzi, Milhaud, and Hindemith all live here now. How are their new operas?"

"Are they opera composers?"

"Of course. Their operas are known everywhere in Europe. Very popular too."

"I do remember *The Love of Three Kings*. The music was lovely but the story mixed me up. I didn't have time to read the libretto before I went."

"It was sung in Italian?"

"Oh yes."

"Well, I suppose the European composers have little chance because all the new operas are written by Americans."

"Oh no. Americans don't write operas. At least not any more. We used to have one American opera a year at the Metropolitan but that was when Gatti-Casazza was director. He was a foreigner and he probably thought it would be polite to give American operas."

"Did the public like them?"

"I am afraid not very much. You see in those days the most popular singers were Italian and German and they sounded funny trying to sing English. When the American singers were used they didn't draw at the box office. I often think the public comes to hear favorite singers no matter what they sing."

"But you said your best singers are Americans now. Wouldn't the public come to hear Grace Moore, Swarthout, Peerce, and Tibbett in an American opera?"

"Possibly, but it is awfully risky trying out new works."

"Why not try them out in the other opera companies? Chicago or San Francisco?"

"Well, you see, those companies are really just the Metropolitan more or less moved out."

"Same operas, same casts?"

"Practically. You see, the people out there want only the best and it must be as much like the Metropolitan as they can make it."

"Well, why not try out the new operas in the provincial opera houses?"

"We really haven't any provincial opera. There are some touring companies, some of them even with Metropolitan stars. But there are the civic opera festivals."

"What are those?"

"Well, they are quite wonderful. The public-spirited citizens put them on with local talent. You know, organize something like a performance of *Aïda*."

"Is the idea of the festival to make money?"

"Heavens, no. It is all purely cultural and artistic. You know America is making great strides musically."

"And I suppose the way for these people to show it is to give an opera with a book everyone thinks is silly in a language no one can understand. Why don't they produce a new opera by some American composer? Aren't there any good American composers?"

"Of course. There are many American works played on our concert programs."

"Why not American opera then?"

"Well, I think it is the American composer's fault. If he could only write lovely melodies like those in *Carmen* and *Faust* and *Madame Butterfly* he would have an immediate success, the public would be at his feet."

"But all three of those operas were failures when they were first produced. It was only after a time that the public came to like them."

"I am afraid you don't understand our attitude about opera. You talk about it as if it were a form of entertainment."

"It has always been so regarded in Europe."

"Really. Well with us it is a cultural and educational experience. When we want entertainment, we go to the theater or the movies."

"What about Billy Rose's production of *Carmen?*"

"Oh that. Well, it had an all colored cast and they acted so well. I think the public liked it because the book was modern and they could understand the words."

"It was sung in English then?"

"Of course."

"But you wouldn't call it opera?"

"Well, after all it is *Carmen,* and it was very well produced in a theater where you could see and hear everything."

"But surely it could not have been successful with the public?"

"It has been playing for a whole year."

"Here we are at Forty-second Street. Let us go buy our tickets for *Faust.*"

GENIUS IN THE MADHOUSE

by Harrison Smith

*Here is the little-known story of how a young newspaper reporter
discovered a great American painter locked up in an insane asylum
—and managed to help set him free.*

MARCH 31, 1945

ONCE UPON A TIME the New York *Tribune* decided to brighten its
pages with colorful reporting of local events, so Mr. Reid bought
himself a young reporter or two whom he might otherwise have
kept off the payroll. I never saw Mr. Reid, but in the end he knew
I was there all right. The city editor was a nice, sarcastic, swearing
gentleman who was always asking me, what the hell kind of a place
did I think the *Tribune* was?

One Monday I got in on time, while most of the boys were busy
with hangovers, or catching up on their sleep, and was summoned
to the throne. "For God's sake, find out what this woman wants, I
don't know what the hell she is trying to say." I was introduced to a
middle-aged woman with glittering eyes and a fine neckpiece of rat's
fur around her throat. Her name was Mrs. Adams, and she said, "I
want to talk to someone about Ralph Blakelock."

I was just the man for Mrs. Adams. It so happened that I knew
about Ralph Albert Blakelock, born in 1847. He was one of our
greatest landscape painters, he had an immense canvas in the Met
with trees against a yellow sky and another one of a moonlit tree
that I thought had the edge on Corot's trees and moons. I seemed to
recall that Blakelock had died ages ago of whatever people die of,
or maybe of poverty. But I learned from this jumpy woman with
some kind of facial twitch that Blakelock was only artistically
dead, that his living remains were incarcerated in an insane asylum,
where his wife had placed him after he had burned up a hundred
dollars in the kitchen stove, because that was all he got for a painting for which he had been promised a thousand.

So Blakelock was alive, after all! In those days I had, or thought
I had, a scent for a front-page story. If I had been a bird dog, I

would have pointed at her, but, being only a reporter, prickles ran up my backbone. I looked in our morgue, where Ralph Blakelock's newspaper biography had ended years ago, though his paintings had come to life all over the country and had been sold for tens of thousands of dollars. He was a dead man to all intents and purposes, but he had never been officially buried. I poured all this in one long sentence into the ear of the city editor who looked at me as if I was offering him a dose of poison. But he scooped up a phone and called Middletown State Insane Asylum, still glaring at me.

Well, Blakelock was in Middletown all right, and I was on my way to him before the city editor put down the phone. They took me in to see him. Blakelock was in a room that might have belonged to one of the nicer cell blocks in Sing Sing. He had been sitting there, or in other rooms like it, for almost twenty years. He began to talk in a mild voice. He told me about the blue diamond of the Emperor of Brazil that somebody had stolen from him. If he had it now, he said, he would sell it and go somewhere and paint. The asylum had known nothing about him or his career, except that his name was Blakelock, and that he was mad. The reason why he jumped up from his chair as if someone had stuck a pin in him when I mentioned his canvases in the Metropolitan was because he was afraid he would be hydropathically punished if he talked about it. I looked at his frightened eyes, and I could hear a warden saying, "Blakelock, in 418, is talking about the Metropolitan Art Museum again, sir," and the director saying, "Take his temperature and give him a bath."

I stayed in the Middletown Asylum for four hectic and fascinating days. I had never been in an asylum before, and I made up my mind right then to maintain an appearance of sanity for the rest of my days. I was aflame with a kind of youthful ardor to make this old man's agony the story of the year, and, somehow, to make up for his neglect by the American people.

Middletown's director was of course charmed to discover that for all these years he and his predecessors had been sheltering a genius. It seems that he had had other geniuses there, nice quiet people, who were a credit to his institution. He thought that geniuses were naturally attracted to insane asylums. I liked him, all right, but he had a young daughter whom I liked a lot better, and I used to sit up with her in the kitchen after midnight when Pa had gone to bed. She had some lovely childhood recollections and one of the nicest was her remembrance of a night when she was chased around the very table I had my feet on by a lunatic, brandishing a carving knife. There was a dance one night and some female screwball who was skipping around took a fancy to the pink-striped shirt I wore and wanted me to take it off and give it to her. It was a good shirt so I kept it on.

One day the city editor phoned me at Middletown and asked me why the hell I didn't come home, and what the devil did I think I was writing, a front-page story? I said, Yes, I was going to write a front-page story, and I wanted two or three columns on the front page for Thursday night. He said, bitterly, "Are you crazy?" I said that I was, but that I was going to bring Ralph Blakelock back with me to New York with the director of the Asylum Thursday afternoon, that I wanted a suite for them at a grade-A hotel, and an unlimited expense account for myself for our lunch. "What in God's name is happening?" he screamed. "Look at your art page," I said, coldly, "and you will find a notice of a loan exhibition of Blakelock's paintings on Fifth Avenue near Forty-second Street."

There was a long deadly silence, but when he said, "Christ!" as if I had set fire to his coattails, I knew that I had him, that I had put it over. If I live to be a thousand, I will never experience a moment like that again.

Then he said bitterly, "But you can't write it yourself! I'll give you your two columns and a rewrite man." I said, "I will take the columns and shoot your rewrite man." There was another silence; then, "All right, but I don't believe you can do it." As a matter of fact, I didn't either.

Before we started for New York, I had a long talk with old Blakelock, who still looked nervous when he spoke about his own work. His mind was as clear as a bell about it, until the diamond of the Emperor of Brazil crept in. We talked about the Asylum as if it was a rest home in the country to which he had voluntarily retired. The warden sat beside me, smiling patronizingly at us, as if I were carrying on a conversation with one of his patients who thought he was Jesus or Napoleon. I asked Blakelock a silly question. Had he been able to do any painting in Middletown? He said that five years ago he had been given a child's paint-box, but it had been taken away from him, and that a long time ago he had discovered how to paint with ink. He showed me the brushes that he used. Brushes! They were made out of matchsticks, with the white hairs that he had pulled out of his head secured to the ends by rubber bands. I will swear on the Bible that this is true. And he diluted the ink, so that he could get, as he said, an almost infinite gradation of blue colors.

And so Blakelock, who seemed when we were finally on the train, to be less and less of a man, and more like a pale, long-fingered leprechaun, and the director, still inflated with this discovery of a genius who had been under his eyes for years, and my humble and frightened self rode to New York.

When Blakelock had left New York, it was a flat, brownstone city. He looked at the towering buildings on Fifth Avenue, and said mildly, "My, my!"

By this time I was really scared to death. I felt that I had made a damn fool of myself, that I had made the gesture of a D'Artagnan, without having any more courage than a rabbit, that I had put the boss and the whole noble outfit that was the *Tribune*, including Mr. Reid, in a spot they couldn't get out of. Also I knew that I was done for, and I could probably look forward to going back to Middletown—alone.

Well, we arrived at the big art gallery where Blakelock's work was on exhibition. It had been swept clear of visitors. A suave and nervous gentleman in a morning coat and a Van Dyke beard was there; also an experienced reporter from the *Tribune,* to take over in case I fainted, or something. Oh, no, the *Tribune* wasn't taking any chances on me! The gallery walls were lined with Blakelock's paintings, brought there from all over the country, a million dollar's worth, maybe. The effect on Blakelock was prodigious. He seemed to have gained a foot in height. Then I stopped looking at him because I didn't think I could take it any longer.

It turned into quite a story when I got downtown. I wrote it in a daze; it literally ran out of the typewriter by itself. The *Tribune* gave it the works, front page and all, and some weeks later a fund was raised to get the old painter out of the Asylum and put him in charge of the very Mrs. Adams who told me the story that morning in the office. Of course, Blakelock was graduated from Middletown, cum laude and all. He went to live in the Adirondacks. Four years later he died. Mrs. Adams came to see me after his death, twitching worse than ever and as mad as a hatter, I thought. She said that Blakelock had been murdered by the gang who had been forging his paintings. Maybe he had been. Certainly that afternoon in the gallery he had twice seized my arm and whispered in his precise voice, "I didn't paint that one." And then later, across the room, before another large canvas, "This one I had only started to paint." But that story was never printed. After all, Blakelock was supposed to be insane, wasn't he?

This, then, is the true story of the rediscovery of a great American painter. Even the Dictionary of American Biography omits the fact that he had been neglected and that his fate was known to only a few. It says mildly, "His health improved so distinctly that he left the asylum where his return to New York created much interest, not only owing to the signal appreciation of his pictures shown by high prices but because of sympathy for a man of attractive personality who had been overtaken by disaster at the high tide of his career." This is streamlined biography with a vengeance. It skips lightly over seventeen years of incarceration and forgets that he was not released because "his health improved" but because an aroused public restored him to life.

There used to be several ways of disposing of painters who were a nuisance while they were alive, but prospectively valuable ten years after they were dead. They could be starved in garret studios, knocked flat by critics, and neglected by commercial galleries who, nevertheless, kept stocks of their forgotten canvases in storage. To-day, if another Ralph Blakelock sprang into prominence, his work would be reproduced in six colors in *Life* and written up in *Time* and *Newsweek*. His mind would not be unhinged by lack of money. He would not be a dead genius while he was still alive.

Newspaper anecdotes do not need any point, but this yarn of the exhuming of Ralph Blakelock has one. It is good to know how far we have come in our willingness to recognize and reward the talents of artists in the last quarter of a century, a period about which so many calumnies have been written.

ADVENTURES IN STARTING A LITERARY MAGAZINE

by Henry Seidel Canby

The story of how a trusting professor of English literature at Yale University founded a literary magazine which became The Saturday Review of Literature.

OCTOBER 13, 1945

I BEGAN MY CAREER AS A LITERARY JOURNALIST in old downtown New York. From my window in an office building on Vesey Street I looked down on the ancient churchyard and across to the eighteenth-century belfry of St. Paul's, then ringed about with towers still the highest in New York. Broadway roared a block away, and to mingle in the sidewalk crowds of bankers' clerks, financiers, and journalists brushed off the scholar's cobwebs and gave a useful sense of responsibility to a large and indifferent world.

North a little way were the offices of all the great newspapers, except the *Times,* which had already gone uptown, and down toward the North River were narrow dirty streets under the elevated viaducts, with hole-in-the-wall restaurants, incongruous slums under million-dollar office buildings, and tiny shops for everything from ship models, trout flies, typewriter ribbons, patent medicine, old books to betting on the races. The ancient publishing house of Harper's was not far off, entered into by a broad flight of iron steps to a great semicircle of desks, from which cold eyes seemed to be looking down at the nervous contributor as he carried up his manuscript. Over by the East River was Walt Whitman's favorite eating place, and if the masts were all gone from the waterfront, the sea mist still blew in our windows, and the mournful blasts of liners' whistles were the undertones for the newsboys' shouts of extra, and the clatter of the elevators.

I had come to New York in 1920 to establish a literary supplement of high quality worthy of a long tradition for the old New York *Evening Post,* dean of American newspapers, but frequently

297

regarded as a dean *emeritus*. Alexander Hamilton had founded the *Post* to represent conservative interests in the young republic, and his ghost still walked the corridors, though it had a curious way of looking more like Thomas Jefferson. For the *Post* became what the English call a conservative radical. It represented the vested interests when they behaved themselves, and was proud of having the best financial section in New York. It was liberal, and progressive up to the point where the existing order seemed to be threatened. It was probably the best written, certainly the most scholarly paper in America, and in its subconscious was an impulse deeper than thought to oppose the majority whenever and however it came to power. The *Post,* under a different ownership, had been antiwar up to 1917. We were still anti to most of the current political and economic movements except world order and the League of Nations. It was a magnificent, a high-minded, a deeply responsible paper, but it was about as popular as the president of the anti-saloon league. There could have been no better foundation on which to erect an independent, scholarly, and responsible review of literature and current books.

The *Evening Post* gave me my only experience of newspaper journalism, and taught me more about co-operative endeavor than I had ever learned in a university. For an established newspaper, with a tradition behind it, is a corporate being in which a dozen trades, professions, skills are inseparably bound together in a common enterprise. The editorial writer, whose specialties may be pure milk, municipal politics, or the Missouri Valley, becomes conscious of his dependence upon the hard-knuckled thugs who get the paper distributed. The head of a literary section must learn a good deal about printing or be helpless when he is told that type lice have eaten up his overset.

I found a newspaper as rich in eccentrics as a university, and stuffed with personalities. We had an absorbed editor who never knew that he was to become a father until they telephoned him from the hospital. We had a temperamental typesetter who burst into tears whenever there was too much copy at the last moment, and had to be comforted by the lady assistants. There were the series of promotion men, all big-fisted, high-hearted fellows, who banged on the table and then went out to spend $100,000 on promotion, with no appreciable results. The wise and humorous Simeon Strunsky was at the head of our editorial council. At the darkest moments he could make us believe in the inevitable survival of virtue. These were the boom days, when Thomas W. Lamont, who had taken over the paper and many of the staff from

Oswald Garrison Villard, was abroad on affairs of the Peace, leaving his purse strings behind. He was a backer of good will and good works, never seeking his own advantage, and leaving us complete independence. I wish that before he left, he had taught us a little more about practical finance. There was too much belief on our staff in Tennyson's aphorism, "We needs must love the highest when we see it." The larger public simply couldn't see the *Post,* even if it was bristling with high standards. So those bad times came when everyone from the editor, Edwin F. Gay, an honest and able man, though not newspaper-minded, down to the office boys, was made to feel that the *Post* was an institution more important than private welfare, and that we must save it—and for a while we did.

My job in 1920 began in the boom days, but I was so accustomed to the parsimony of a university that it never occurred to me to ask for my share of the promotion money being spent so lavishly. My task was to organize a *Literary Review* to be published with the Saturday paper as a supplement—and when we came to the first printing, that was what we called it. Both time and place were propitious.

Before our regime, the *Nation* had been an organ of the *Post,* but it had declined into stodginess relieved only by occasional critical essays of great worth, written by the old guard, where erudition, however, did not always make up for their lack of contact with the oncoming age. It used to be told of the *Nation* of that day that it reviewed the Christmas gift books of one year in the following November. I doubt whether it mattered. The *Times* and the *Tribune* had fallen into the same rut together. Their leading articles on important books were competent and well written, but too often were designed to show how much more the critic knew about the subject than did the author. The book itself was buried by the review, and sometimes had no resurrection. The rest of the columns were entrusted to reviewers who could be expected not to say anything unpleasant. I hoped to kindle a new fire in these dry logs and brush heaps of criticism, and in addition I had my own private desire, which was to bring to the interpretation of new books for the intelligent reader the service of the erudition and trained thinking of scholarship in the universities.

And so I sharpened my pencil (a tool much more dear to me than pen or typewriter), organized my editorial staff, and set to work. Miss Amy Loveman, one of the ablest, certainly the kindest, assuredly one of the most useful women in New York, was my associate. William Rose Benét, poet and critic, was my literary adviser, a man of mingled fire and honey, whose concern was every human interest except his own. In a cubicle next door to my office, puffing pipe smoke at the hinges, was the columnist of the *Post,* Christopher Morley—a rusher in and out, bubbling ideas like a soda fountain, a wit, a wagster, an Elizabethan philosopher, with one of the few minds I have ever known that seemed to be continuously enjoying itself. Then I settled down to the first office job I had ever held, and though I could never learn to work happily in shirt sleeves and suspenders, and so was clearly not a congenital newspaperman, I spent engrossed and happy days.

Perhaps it is only in a small periodical in its formative years that one gets the sense of a gathering of a family of minds, so that when the magazine comes to maturity it has a personality of its own. Such a magazine was *Time* in its earliest years, when, for a while, our family group was associated with it. Such a magazine was this *Literary Review* of ours, which, if conceived in my brain, owed its vitality, and also its longevity (for the present *Saturday Review of Literature** is the same child grown up under another name) to a diverse group of like-minded editors. And it would seem that these earliest 1920s were by some literary astrology the right time for a corporate literary personality to be born. As I have said elsewhere, the columnists had been preparing an audience ready to support vitality and competence in either creative literature or in criticism. The success of a magazine like *The New Yorker* (born 1921) would have been impossible in, say, 1910. Whatever the cause, an editor who wished to give new books a chance to be read by the right people in the right way got plenty of support of the kind that cannot be bought.

This support came from the writers as well as from the audience. I was sure from past experience that if we gave good writers a chance to do what they wanted we should not (as indeed we could not) have to pay more than modest sums for their work. It is a fact that literary writing done for nothing is seldom good for much. Apparently the author who does not expect to be paid for his work loses his sense of audience and becomes too self-regarding. He writes just to please himself, which is a form of dilettantism. But if a payment is established, the amount has little relation to the excellence of the product provided it is all the editor can afford to pay. The editor's problem is to get the writer to work for him on subjects possible for his periodical or publishing house. The professional

---

* In 1952 the name of *The Saturday Review of Literature* was shortened to *The Saturday Review* and its scope was accordingly broadened to include the subjects of music, science, travel, and other not strictly literary content.

author will not write better for twice the money for he cannot. A fat purse is useful to an editor only in buying talent away from other editors or in priming the pump of a lazy mind. But a fat purse means a large circulation behind it, which means that the writer gets more money but a diluted audience, for whom often, though not always, it is impossible for him to write on the themes that interest him most. That is the vicious—but inevitable—circle. Fortunately, we were not seeking fiction or sensational news articles —the most expensive varieties of magazine literature—and yet we got, with a few exceptions, what we wanted for what we were able to pay. What we lacked in cash, however, had to be made up by double duty in the search for the right man for an appealing opportunity.

We believed that a literary supplement of a newspaper, which, however excellent, was local to one city, should have a subscription which was national even though small, and got permission to circularize among the right people, and soon had 8,000 to 10,000 subscribers strategically distributed all over the country. We believed that a literary magazine should be as carefully composed as was good literature itself. Carl P. Rollins, the typographer, helped us with our layout, in which we began by breaking two journalistic traditions. The leading article had only a one-column head, balancing the editorial essay on the other side, leaving the middle of the first page for a poem.

It was an audacious shifting of emphasis from the timely to attempts to present aspects of the eternal; and probably unwise, for there was often as much, or as little, of the eternal in the leading article as in an editorial. But I still like to look at that old first page. And it did represent something deep in my mind, which was that criticism written for the general intelligent reader should be liberal in its definition. It should include humor and wisdom and beauty also, as well as fact-finding and theory. The review was supposed to revolve around two planetary centers, with orbits interweaving in a harmony: the one, books under review for which the leading article beat the big drum; the other literary, in which creative comment on aspects of life and literature, interspersed with cartoon, caricature, and enlightened gossip about the authors who made the books, would relate our estimates of success or failure in the bookshops, with the long vistas of literary history.

We spent three months recruiting, balancing what we got, arranging a first number where everything was to swing into place like toy stars and planets in a model for a class in astronomy. The result was farcical, since it pleased everyone but the editor, who was

still too inexperienced to be anything but a perfectionist. This outline so interested the publishers that an actual storm of last-minute
advertising swept away the further reaches of our orbits with their
nice adjustments of minor constellations of criticism and comment
intended to complete the harmony of the whole. To change the
figure, the rear of the magazine became a billboard; and to change
it again, to my eyes, though fortunately not to others, the first number of the *Literary Review* looked like a man in a dress suit, with
the tails cut off, and patches visible on the seat of his trousers.

My colleagues developed abilities which they scarcely knew that
they possessed. Amy Loveman was soon more knowledgeable about
books and authors than anyone else in town. She had been trained
as an assistant on an encyclopedia, and heartily enjoyed escaping
from the dead to the living. William Rose Benét, already a poet of
distinction, proved to be a congenial columnist, and his wise and
witty comments on the human comedy of literary creation were
soon being widely quoted. His neighbor in the next cubicle, Christopher Morley, and he soon borrowed a name from the half legendary figure of Sir Kenelm Digby, which they shifted back and forth
as a shield behind which to shoot at all and sundry, including each
other. I was not only editor, but contact man in a large way. It was
my job to herd the great in name and experience into our little
clearing and milk them of what they could be persuaded to let
down of critical wisdom or scholarly erudition. It was surprising
how many came.

A magazine, I decided, must have either a policy or an idea, or
both, in which case the emphasis would be sure to fall on one or
the other. I had no objection to the policy magazine, as long as the
policy did not interfere with the job of making a good magazine.
The *New Republic,* once so brilliant, had been left sprawling by
the war and was seeking a line by which to pull itself together
again. The old, rather pedantic, *Nation* was turning leftward, with
new blood in its veins. The *New Masses,* a portent of the fanatic
ideologies and brutal politics in the storm clouds ahead, was all
policy, so much so that in the reviewing pages you could predict in
advance what they would say of any controversial book. It was a
valuable irritant, but bitterly unfair, and often stupidly ignorant
of any values not in its own ten commandments. Being a Quaker in
mood, tolerant, but passionately concerned for a more intelligent
world, I was better pleased by magazines with ideas rather than
dogmatisms behind them. I liked *The New Yorker* because it was
aware of the new sophistication of urban society, and made its own
very real idealism articulate by good-humored irony, whose cutting

edge just emerged like a safety-razor blade. I respected, though I did not always like, *Time,* because in an accelerating world it made the escape from provincialism easier.

My own idea was not original. Indeed it was only the Jeffersonian belief in the necessity of education for a successful democracy. I wanted to go in for adult education in the values of books—all kinds of books, foreign as well as native, but particularly the current books of our country. I wanted criticism to be first of all a teaching job. And, indeed, whether running a Freshman class, or editing the *Saturday Review,* or chairmaning the Book-of-the-Month Club, the inner impulse with me, and probably the chief value, has been the same, to teach.

Teaching is a delicate affair—a real art—and has to be separated from the more obvious tasks of critics, such as making and breaking reputations. I did some of that, but chose for my main task a series of weekly editorial essays whose purpose was a commentary on the ups and downs and ins and outs of the life of books, interpreting, prophesying when I dared, summarizing when I could, and never hesitating to swing from critical theory into nature descriptions (which I liked to write) if I felt that the cockneys were getting too far away from earth. They were true "assays," that is experiments in the search for values, leaving the working out of what I suggested to others, often to later and more ambitious efforts of my own.

And so the *Literary Review,* the parent of the *Saturday Review,* began to slide weekly from the presses. I took opinions as to its merits and demerits wherever I could get them, but the management of the *Evening Post,* on which, for all our independence, we were dependent for our existence, naturally looked to the publishers, whose support, or lack of it, could make or break us. They supported us, but they were by no means enthusiastic. I had thrown my nets widely for contributions, but most widely in the academic pool which I knew best. The magazine, so the trade thought, was unnecessarily erudite. And indeed it soon became more authoritative in its reviews of serious books than any other medium in America. It was the literary supplement of the *London Times,* and no periodical on this side of the water, which was held up to us as an example of a dignity and a scope to which we had not yet attained, and indeed I could well understand that publishers' salesmen and booksellers were at first inclined to regard the *Review* as just one more burden in their difficult business.

The inevitable day came when the *Evening Post,* staggering under its debts, was swallowed in one expensive gulp by the Curtis family organization, then at the height of its affluence. Henceforth, and for a little while our *Post* was to become a New York edition of a Philadelphia paper.

I came back from a brief Southern vacation to find a brisk managerial person in charge, who regarded our practical idealism (for our book section had made money) and our national circulation and influence as a string quartet playing irrelevantly in the corner of his three-ring circus. And so I wrote a final editorial headed, "And Twitched His Mantle Blue," guessing that the new proprietors would not know what was the following line in "Lycidas"— "Tomorrow to fresh woods, and pastures new."

The *Literary Review* itself became, first a hodge-podge, then a heading with a few reviews beneath it. But our friends would not let us die. With the support of Thomas W. Lamont and the co-operation of the editors of *Time,* two of whom had been students of mine at Yale, we migrated en masse—editors, columnists, poets, reviewers, critics, and commentators, with a baggage of ideas, and a somewhat dubiously acquired subscription list—left Vesey Street for good and all, and in three months launched the *Saturday Review of Literature,* which was the old *Literary Review* come of age, more humorous, more literary, broader in scope, better looking, but with the same will to further the cause of good thinking, good feeling, good writing, and good books.

New York and American literature were growing fast. The real end of the nineteenth-century era was close at hand. We were fortunate in our nearly five years of existence to have learned the hard way in financial restriction and by youthful experiment what could and could not be done before the new age brought new conflicts and new kinds of literature. I had shaken off some pedantic academicism, and no longer yearned to publish articles that only scholars could understand but almost no one, not even scholars, bothered to read. Much more important, our team had found their way to attics, studios, newspaper desks, Connecticut hilltops, and Greenwich Village hideouts, to libraries and universities, to selected minds in England, Ireland, France, and Germany, and recruited knowledge, perception, and good writing, often where no critical writing had been done before. Our friends came with us. I do not suppose that the Saturday edition of the *Post* in the New York area, which carried with it the *Literary Review,* ever had more than fifty or sixty thousand circulation, to which we added eight to ten thousand from our national, independent distribution. But we seemed to have found the right minds for our appeal, and they followed us to our new office uptown, above a factory, with floors reverberating from the machinery below in a new rhythm of a new age.

But most important and most interesting of all, we had lived intensely in what I have called a brief golden age of American writing before the boom and the burst and the preliminaries of war. We had become part of that literary scene which I still think was the first classical pausing moment of perfected art and summary achievements since the great days of the 1850s. And we had experienced what never can happen twice with the same excitement, an initiation into the curious swirl of the literary life around a young and creative magazine.

WHY I REMAIN A NEGRO

by Walter White

*"I am not white. There is nothing within my mind and heart
which tempts me to think I am. Yet I realize acutely that the only
characteristic which matters to either the white or the colored race
—the appearance of whiteness—is mine." In these words the late
president of the National Association for the Advancement of
Colored People prefaces his explanation of his own stand on the
race question.*

OCTOBER 11, 1947

THE SCENE was a New York duplex apartment. The people were
liberals, economically as well as intellectually well off. They were
discussing the race question. I had been invited to speak. One of the
women, listening, seemed agitated by something I had said. She
scribbled on a piece of paper and handed it to another woman, a
woman whose skin was reddish brown, a woman who was probably
colored. "Is Mr. White white or colored?" the message inquired.
The other scribbled an answer and passed it back. "I am Mrs.
White," the reply said. The white woman, reading it, became excited. Hastily she penciled a comment: "What a wonderful talk!
This is the first time I've had the opportunity to hear him."

I am a Negro. My skin is white, my eyes are blue, my hair is
blond. The traits of my race are nowhere visible upon me. Not long
ago I stood one morning on a subway platform in Harlem. As the
train came in I stepped back for safety. My heel came down upon
the toe of the man behind me. I turned to apologize to him. He
was a Negro, and his face as he stared at me was hard and full of
the piled-up bitterness of a thousand lynchings and a million nights
in shacks and tenements and "nigger towns." "Why don't you look
where you're going?" he said sullenly. "You white folks are always
trampling on colored people." Just then one of my friends came
up and asked how the fight had gone in Washington—there was a
filibuster against legislation for a permanent Fair Employment
Practices Commission. The Negro on whose toes I had stepped
listened, then spoke to me penitently.

"Are you Walter White of the NAACP? I'm sorry I spoke to you that way. I thought you were white."

I am not white. There is nothing within my mind and heart which tempts me to think I am. Yet I realize acutely that the only characteristic which matters to either the white or the colored race—the appearance of whiteness—is mine. White is the rejection of all color; black is the absorption of every shade. There is magic in a white skin; there is tragedy, loneliness, exile, in a black skin. Why then do I insist that I am a Negro, when nothing compels me to do so but myself?

Why did the white woman who listened to me speaking become flustered when the woman she chose for her question turned out to be my wife? What made her confused, bewildered, and incapable of direct and efficient communication? It was the enigma of a black man occupying a white body, the presentation in fact of a theory to which millions give lip service, never really believing it is so— that all men are brothers under the skin.

The lady's agitation was natural. Suppose the skin of every Negro in America were suddenly to turn white. What would happen to all the notions about Negroes, the idols on which are built race prejudice and race hatred? What would become of their presumed shiftlessness, their cowardice, their dishonesty, their stupidity, their body odor? Would they not merge with the shiftlessness, the cowardice, the dishonesty, the stupidity, and the body odor of the whites? Would they not then be subject to individual judgment in matters of abilities, energies, honesty, cleanliness, as are whites? How else *could* they be judged?

Many Negroes are judged as whites. Every year approximately 12,-000 white-skinned Negroes disappear—people whose absence cannot be explained by death or emigration. Nearly every one of the 14 million discernible Negroes in the United States knows at least one member of his race who is "passing"—the magic word which means that some Negroes can get by as whites, men and women who have decided that they will be happier and more successful if they flee from the proscription and humiliation which the American color line imposes on them. Often these emigrants achieve success in business, the professions, the arts and sciences. Many of them have married white people, lived happily with them, and produced families. Sometimes they tell their husbands or wives of their Negro blood, sometimes not. Who are they? Mostly people of no great importance, but some of them prominent figures, including a few members of Congress, certain writers, and several organizers of movements to "keep the Negroes and other minorities in their places." Some of the most vehement public haters of Negroes are themselves secretly Negroes.

They do not present openly the paradox of the color line. It is I, with my insistence, day after day, year in and year out, that I am a Negro, who provoke the reactions to which now I am accustomed: the sudden intake of breath, the bewildered expression of the face, the confusion of the eyes, the muddled fragmentary remarks—"But you do not look . . . I mean I would never have known . . . of course if you didn't want to admit . . ." Sometimes the eyes blink rapidly and the tongue, out of control, says, "Are you sure?"

I have tried to imagine what it is like to have me presented to a white person as a Negro, by supposing a Negro were suddenly to say to me, "I am white." But the reversal does not work, for whites can see no reason for a white man ever wanting to be black; there is only reason for a black man wanting to be white. That is the way whites think; that is the way their values are set up. It is the startling removal of the blackness which upsets people. Looking at me without knowing who I am, they disassociate me from all the characteristics of the Negro. Informed that I am a Negro they find it impossible suddenly to endow me with the skin, the odor, the dialect, the shuffle, the imbecile good nature. Instantly they are aware that these things are *not* part of me. Then they grope for the positive values of the race—genius at song, easy laughter, great strength, humility, manners. Alexander Percy said that the most polite people in the world are the American Negroes.

This shift to the virtues of the Negro is apt to be dangerous for me. Once a Southern lady, discovering my identity, entered into a long conversation with me, and suggested that I come to her home where we might enjoy a more intimate chat on race matters without being disturbed. She suggested a time. I said I would surely come, and that I would bring my wife, who would be equally interested in the discussion. The lady's attitude changed immediately. She did not break the date then, but later she telephoned and said that she would be unable to see us. What precisely she perceived in me of interest I do not know, but probably it was the sudden transformation of the faithful "darky" into a man covered with magic white skin which titillated her. Southern women have generally been more friendly toward the Negroes than Southern men—who are largely responsible for the chiaroscuro effects in the race—and she may have felt that in some way I represented her faith and efforts, rather than the infidelity of her ancestors. Or she may have thought, "Are you sure?"

I am sure. There can never be a doubt. I have seen Negroes, male and female, killed by mobs in the streets of Atlanta. I stood with my father, who was a mail carrier, and watched them die. The next night they came to the Negro section, perhaps five thousand of them. Our house was just outside the section, above it, on Houston Street. It was a neat, modest home, in which my father and mother raised a family of seven children. The whites resented our prosperity; so at times, did the Negroes. The Negroes resented our white skin, and the ethical standards which my parents maintained themselves and required of their children.

In the darkened house that night there were my mother and father, four of my sisters and myself. Never before had there been guns in our house, but that night, at the insistence of friends, we were armed. My father was a deeply religious man, opposed to physical violence. As we watched the mob go by, their faces weird in the light of the torches they carried—faces made grotesque and ugly by the hate which was twisting and distorting them—my father said, "Don't shoot until the first man puts his foot on the lawn; and then don't miss."

I heard a voice cry out, a voice which I knew belonged to the son of our neighborhood grocer: "Let's burn the house of the nigger mail carrier! It's too nice a house for a nigger to live in!"

In the flickering light the mob swayed, paused, and began to flow toward us. In that instant there opened up within me a great awareness; I knew then who I was. I was colored, a human being with an invisible pigmentation which marked me a person to be hunted, hanged, abused, discriminated against, kept in poverty and ignorance, in order that those whose skin was white would have readily at hand a proof of their superiority, a proof patent and inclusive, accessible to the moron and the idiot as well as to the wise man and the genius. No matter how low a white man fell, he could always be certain that he was superior to two-thirds of the world's population, for those two-thirds were not white.

It made no difference how intelligent or talented I and my millions of brothers were, or how virtuously we lived. A curse like that of Judas was upon us, a mark of degradation fashioned with heavenly authority. There were white men who said Negroes had no souls, and who proved it by the Bible. Some of these now were approaching us, intent upon burning our house. My father had told us to kill them.

It was a violence which could not be avoided. The white men insisted upon it. War was with them a business; war and pillage, conquest and exploitation, colonization and Christianization. Later, when I was older, I thought about this and I began to see why.

Theirs was a world of contrasts in values: superior and inferior, profit and loss, co-operative and non-co-operative, civilized and aboriginal, white and black. If you were on the wrong end of the comparison, if you were inferior, if you were non-co-operative, if you were aboriginal, if you were black, then you were marked for excision, expulsion, or extinction. I was a Negro; I was therefore that part of history which opposed the good, the just, and the enlightened. I was a Persian, falling before the hordes of Alexander. I was a Carthaginian, extinguished by the legions of Rome. I was a Frenchman at Waterloo, an Anglo-Saxon at Hastings, a Confederate at Vicksburg, a Pole at Warsaw. I was the defeated, wherever and whenever there was a defeat.

Yet as a boy there in the darkness amid the tightening fright, I knew the inexplicable thing—that my skin was as white as the skin of those who were coming at me.

The mob moved toward the lawn. I tried to aim my gun, wondering what it would feel like to kill a man. Suddenly there was a volley of shots. The mob hesitated, stopped. Some friends of my father's had barricaded themselves in a two-story brick building just below our house. It was they who had fired. Some of the mobsmen, still bloodthirsty, shouted, "Let's go get the nigger." Others, afraid now for their safety, held back. Our friends, noting the hesitation, fired another volley. The mob broke and retreated up Houston Street.

In the quiet that followed I put my gun aside and tried to relax. But a tension different from anything I had ever known possessed me. I was gripped by the knowledge of my identity, and in the depths of my soul I was vaguely aware that I was glad of it. I was sick with loathing for the hatred which had flared before me that night and come so close to making me a killer; but I was glad I was not one of those who hated; I was glad I was not one of those made sick and murderous by pride. I was glad I was not one of those whose story is in the history of the world, a record of bloodshed, rapine, and pillage. I was glad my mind and spirit were part of the races that had not fully awakened, and who therefore had still before them the opportunity to write a record of virtue as a memorandum to Armageddon.

It was all just a feeling then, inarticulate and melancholy, yet reassuring in the way that death and sleep are reassuring. Years later, when my father lay in a dingy, cockroach-infested Jim Crow ward in an Atlanta hospital, he put it into words for me and my brother.

"Human kindness, decency, love, whatever you wish to call it," he said, "is the only real thing in the world. It is a dynamic, not a passive, emotion. It's up to you two, and others like you, to use your education and talents in an effort to make love as positive an emotion in the world as are prejudice and hate. That's the only way the world can save itself. Don't forget that. No matter what happens, you must love, not hate." Then he died. He had been struck by an automobile driven by a reckless driver—one of the hospital doctors.

I have remembered that. I have remembered that when, sitting in the gallery of the House or the Senate, I have heard members of our Congress rise and spill diatribe and vilification on the Negroes. I have remembered it when the Negroes were condemned as utter failures in soldiering. I remembered it when, in the Pacific, where I went as a war correspondent, a white officer from the South told me that the 93rd Division, a Negro unit, had been given an easy beach-head to take at Bougainville, and had broken and run under fire. I collected the facts and presented them to him. Bougainville was invaded in November 1943. The 93rd was ordered there in April 1944. The first night it bivouacked on the beach, and motion pictures were shown.

I remembered it when I talked with my nephew for the last time, as he lay in a bitterly cold, rain-drenched tent on the edge of the Capodichina airfield near Naples. He was a Georgia boy, the youngest of four children. His father, like mine, was a mail carrier. He, like me, could have passed for a white man. By sacrifice and labor his parents provided him with a college education. He won a master's degree in economics, and the next day enlisted in the Army Air Corps, as a Negro. He went to the segregated field at Tuskegee, Alabama.

He hated war, he loathed killing. But he believed that Hitler and Mussolini represented the kind of hate he had seen exhibited in Georgia by the Ku Klux Klan and the degenerate political demagogues. He believed that the war would bring all of that hate to an end. He was a fighter pilot. He fought well. Over the Anzio beach-head he was shot down, bailing out and escaping with his right leg broken in two places. He was offered an opportunity to return home but he refused it. "I'll stick it out until the war is finished or I am," he told a friend. Later, returning from a bomber escort mission to Germany, his plane lost altitude over Hungary, was fired upon by anti-aircraft batteries, and was seen striking a tree and bursting into flames. That was the end of one of the men Senator Eastland of Mississippi described as "utter and dismal failures in combat in Europe."

It would be easy to grow bitter over such things, but in remembering my nephew and our last conversation, in which he asked me whether the war would really bring an end to prejudice and race hatred, I remember also the Negro corporal of an engineers unit, who said to me, "This is the only work they would give me, but I don't mind. We learn a trade; we do constructive work. The combat soldiers are taught how to kill. It will bother them. It will stick with them. It will have no effect on us. We will not have to unlearn it."

I could be sophisticated about the advantages of being a Negro. I am amused, for instance, at the fact that because it is considered remarkable that a Negro can write a book at all, a passing fair volume by one of my brothers is frequently hailed as a masterpiece. Everyone with the slightest sense is aware that genius has no color line. Everyone knows also that people generally choose friends and companions for their taste, manners, intelligence, and personality. Yet it does not occur to him that Negroes do likewise. Therefore he often mourns that we colored people cannot freely associate with whites, when it should be obvious that if we did have this privilege we would like no more of them for friends than he does. It is beyond the imagination of a white man to think that to a Negro he is dull.

Negro athletes and singers do not benefit from their color as do Negro scientists and intellectuals, for whereas the latter are considered wonderful if they attain mediocrity, the former are expected to surpass anything the whites can do. In the main, however, I have found it advantageous to be a Negro. My sense of humor is never without material, and I am easily able to judge the worth of white people by their reaction when they discover that I am not white. I am also able to add to my knowledge by pondering the fact that the people who turn away from me when they are told my identity are the most superior of all the peoples, for they look down upon those who are not afraid to be seen with me, and call them "nigger lovers."

Sometimes it is more enlightening not to insist that I am a Negro. Once on a subway going to Harlem I fell into conversation with a man who spoke with a marked German accent. "This used to be a pleasant line to ride on," he said. "But now there are too many Negroes. They have a distinctive smell." He wrinkled his nose.

"Suppose you and I had to do the same kind of work they do on the docks or over hot kitchen stoves," I said. "That is the kind of work Negroes are forced to do *because they are Negroes*. Would we be odorless—particularly if we lived in antiquated, crowded, segregated tenements, which we were forced to inhabit also because we were Negroes? Would we reek of lilies of the valley?"

He looked at me with amazement. "But Negroes *do* smell," he in-sisted.

I was tempted to paraphrase Dr. Samuel Johnson and tell him that "It is you who smell; they stink." But instead I quoted from the late James Weldon Johnson, who said, "Do you imagine the manufacture of deodorants is exclusively for a Negro market? I notice that the advertisements invariably feature a young and beau-tiful girl—a white girl."

The man shook his head. "I've lived in this country for thirty years," he said. "You're the first white man I've ever heard talk like that."

Looking at him I recalled an incident in Brooklyn during the early part of the war. A plant was manufacturing the famous and secret Norden bombsight. The plant refused to hire Negroes, but did hire persons of German descent. Most of these were loyal Ameri-cans, but a few were arrested by the F.B.I. for stealing the secret of the bombsight, and convicted. But it was too late. Germany got the information and passed it on to Japan. One of the officials of the company told a friend that, "I'd close down the plant rather than hire niggers."

Negro soldiers made a good record in this recent war. They have in previous ones. Yet I recall with uneasiness the grimness on a Negro soldier's face when he told me, one day in the Pacific, "Our fight for freedom will start the day we arrive in San Francisco."

It has indeed, and there are times when I have felt with a sweep of fear that the patience of the colored man is close to its end. I re-member the clamoring stillness and the blood heat of a day in Georgia. A lynching was prevented when a band of colored women walked with cans of kerosene toward the village store, a terrible calm upon their faces, an awful quiet in their silent stride. I remember how I felt when I stood beside my father and knew that the whites would not let me live, that I must kill them first and then be killed.

Yet I know, I know, I know that there is no reason for this kill-ing, this hatred, this demarcation. There is no difference between them. Black is white and white is black. When one shoots the other he kills his reflection. Only hate, the negative force, can separate them; only love, the positive force, can bind them together.

I am one of the two in the color of my skin; I am the other in my spirit and my heart. It is only a love of both which binds the two together in me, and it is only love for each other which will join them in the common aims of civilization that lie before us. I love one for the sins she has committed and the fight she has made to conquer them—and conquer them, in great degree, she has. I love the other for her patience and her sorrows, for the soft sound of her singing, and for the great dawn which is coming upon her, in which her vigor and her faith will serve the world.

Some of the members of the black race are passing over to the white race. It may be that I am one of these; that I am a member of a vanguard that in the millennium to come will transmute the great potentialities of the colored races into the civilizations which are to follow. I pray that those civilizations will be better and more virtuous than ours, and that the bridge which I and others are building will grow strong and be a highway for good.

I have a feeling that life is a rushing force, certain of its course and destination. Our bodies are its medium, and it shapes them to its use. As the social pattern of the Negro evolves, will his color change? Is it changing now? We do not know, and I, for one, am sure that it does not matter. I am white and I am black, and know that there is no difference. Each one casts a shadow, and all shadows are dark.

I DISCOVERED JAZZ
IN AMERICA

by Jean-Paul Sartre

*The chief exponent of France's postwar existentialist movement
visits Nick's bar in New York City's Greenwich Village and is mes-
merized by an indigenously American art form.*

NOVEMBER 20, 1947

JAZZ IS LIKE BANANAS—it must be consumed on the spot. God knows
there are recordings in France, and some sad imitators. But all they
do is give us an excuse to shed a few tears in pleasant company. Like
everyone else, I really discovered jazz in America. Some countries
have a national pastime and some do not. It is a national pastime
when the audience insists on complete silence during the first half
of the performance and then shouts and stamps during the second
half. If you accept this definition, France has no national pastime,
except perhaps auction sales. Nor has Italy, except stealing. There is
watchful silence while the thief works (first half) and when he flees
there is stamping and shouts of: Stop, thief (second half). Belgium
has its cockfights, Germany vampirism, and Spain its *corridas.*

I learned in New York that jazz is a national pastime. In Paris,
it is a vehicle for dancing, but this is a mistake: Americans don't
dance to jazz; they have instead a special music, heard also at mar-
riages and first communions, called: Music by Muzak. In apartments
there is a tap. It is turned on and Muzak musics: flirtation, tears,
dancing. The tap is turned off, and Muzak musics no longer: the
lovers and communicants are put to bed.

At Nick's bar, in New York, the national pastime is presented.
Which means that one sits in a smoke-filled hall among sailors, long-
shoremen, chippies, society women. Tables, booths. No one speaks.
The sailors come in fours. With righteous hate, they watch the
sharpies who sit in booths with their girls. The sailors would like to
have girls, but they don't. They drink; they are tough; the girls
are also tough; they drink, they say nothing. No one speaks, no one
moves, the jazz holds forth. From ten o'clock to three in the morning
the jazz holds forth. In France, the jazzmen are beautiful but dumb,

in flowing shirts and silk ties. If you are too bored to listen, you can always watch them and take a lesson in elegance.

At Nick's bar, it is advisable not to look at them; they are as ugly as the musicians in a symphony orchestra. Bony faces, mustaches, business suits, starched collars (at least in the early part of the evening), no velvety looks, their muscles bunching up their sleeves.

They play. You listen. No one dreams. Chopin makes you dream, or André Claveau. But not the jazz at Nick's. It fascinates, you can't get your mind off it. No consolation whatsoever. If you are a cuckold, you depart a cuckold, without tenderness. No way to take the hand of the girl beside you, to make her understand with a wink that the music reflects what is in your heart. It is dry, violent, pitiless. Not gay, not sad, inhuman. The cruel screech of a bird of prey. The musicians start to give out, one after the other. First the trumpet player, then the pianist, then the trombonist. The bass player grinds it out. It does not speak of love, it does not comfort. It is hurried. Like the people who take the subway or eat at the Automat.

It is not the century-old chant of Negro slaves. Nor the sad little dream of Yankees crushed by the machine. Nothing of the sort: there is a fat man who blows his lungs out in the weaving motion of his trombone, there is a pianist without mercy, a bass player who tortures the strings without listening to the others. They are speaking to the best part of you, to the toughest, to the freest, to the part which wants neither melody nor refrain, but the deafening climax of the moment. They take hold of you, they do not lull you. Connecting rod, horizontal shaft, spinning top. They beat, they turn, they crash, the rhythm surges forward. If you are hard, young, and fresh, the rhythm grips you and shakes you. You bounce in your seat, faster and faster, and your girl with you, in a hell-like round.

The trombone sweats, you sweat, the trumpet sweats, you sweat more, and then you feel that something has happened on the bandstand; the musicians don't look the same: they speed ahead, they infect each other with this haste, they look mad, taut, they seem to be searching for something. Something like sexual pleasure. And you too begin to look for something. You begin to shout; you have to shout; the orchestra has become an immense spinning top: if you stop, the top stops and falls over. You shout, they shriek, they whistle, they are possessed, you are possessed, you cry out like a woman in childbirth. The trumpet player touches the pianist and transmits his obsession in a kind of Mesmerism. You go on shouting. The whole crowd shouts in time, you can't even hear the jazz, you watch some men on a bandstand sweating in time, you'd like to spin around, to howl at death, to slap the face of the girl next to you.

And then, suddenly, the jazz stops, the bull has received the sword thrust, the oldest of the fighting cocks is dead. It's all over. But you have drunk your whisky, while shouting, without even knowing it. An impassive waiter has brought you another. For a moment, you are in a stupor, you shake yourself, you say to your girl: Not bad! She doesn't answer you, and it begins all over again. You will not make love tonight, you will not be sorry for yourself, you won't get really drunk, you won't even shed blood, and you will have undergone a fit of frenzy without issue, a convulsionary crescendo resembling a choleric and vain search for pleasure. You will leave a little worn out, a little drunk, but with a kind of dejected calm, like the aftermath of a great nervous exhaustion.

Jazz is the national pastime of the United States.

The foregoing article was translated from the French by Ralph de Toledano.

THE COMICS...
VERY FUNNY!

by Fredric Wertham, M.D.

A senior psychiatrist of New York City's Department of Hospitals deplores the frightening effects on the nation's children of today's cheapest literature, in an article which became one of the most widely read and debated ever to appear in SRL.

MAY 29, 1948

AN ANXIOUS MOTHER consulted me some time ago. Her four-year-old daughter is the only little girl in the apartment house where they live. The boys in the building, from about three to nine years old, hit her, beat her with guns, tie her up with rope whenever they get a chance. They hit her with whips which they buy at the circus. They push her off her bicycle and take her toys away. They hand-cuff her with handcuffs bought with coupons from comic books. They take her to a vacant lot and use her as a target for bow and arrow. They make a spearhead and scare her. Once, surrounding her in this way, they pulled off her panties to torture her (as they put it). Now her mother has fastened the child's panties with a string around her neck so the boys can't pull them down.

What is the common denominator of all this? Is this the "natural aggression" of little boys? Is it the manifestation of the sex in-stinct? Is it the release of natural tendencies or the imitation of unnatural ones? The common denominator is comic books.

I examine in the clinic a boy of eleven, referred because he fights in school and is inattentive. He says:

> I buy comic books every week. They kill animals, some-times they kill people. One of the girls is the best fighter. Sometimes they tie her up and sometimes they put her in a snake cave so that the snakes would kill her.

I examine a boy of fourteen referred to the clinic for stealing. I ask him: "Do you think your stealing had anything to do with the comic books?" He answers: "Oh, no. In the comic books it is mostly

murder." This is like the arguments used by the experts under sub-
sidy from the comic-book industry.

A boy of seventeen is referred to me by the Juvenile Aid Bureau
because in an argument he stabbed a boy of thirteen in the right
arm "with full intent." He says: "I don't read many comic books—
only about ten a week. I like crime comics. Sometimes they kill the
girl. In one of the books the girl wanted more money so they
stabbed her in the back." Was it "full intent," or was it perhaps
imitation that motivated him in his own actions?

A boy of thirteen is a problem at home and at school. He is a real
comic-book addict. He says: "They have some kind of guns that
shoot out a ray and kill a lot of people." Is that a natural fantasy?
Is that a penis symbol? Or is it a kind of reality that a lot of adults
dread now and which these kids will have to face sooner or later?

A boy of fifteen took a boy of twelve up a fire escape and threatened to push him down if he didn't give him a quarter. He says:
"I read two comic books a day." A thirteen-year-old boy is referred
to me by the State Charities Aid Association. He was caught stealing
five dollars. When asked why he took it he confided to me that the
older boys in school got up a gang and threatened him. If he did
not get them the money they would beat him up. So he stole the
money and gave it to them. (I verified this later.)

The experts of the comic-book industry tell us that what the
children read in comic books is pure fantasy. But when I examine
these many children and adolescents who tell me what they read in
comic books, I ask myself with Bernardo in *Hamlet:* "Is not this
something more than fantasy?"

Think of the many recent violent crimes committed by young
boys and girls. A twelve-year-old boy who kills his younger sister; a
twelve-year-old boy who kills his older sister; a thirteen-year-old
burglar who operates with a shotgun; a seventeen-year-old boy who
kills a thirteen-year-old boy and leaves a note signed "The Devil";
a public school in New York City where two police officers circulate
on the grounds and in the corridors to prevent violence; a mathematics teacher who has to give examinations with a policeman present in the classroom; a thirteen-year-old who shot a nurse and was
sent to a reformatory (where, incidentally, he will read more comic
books); a gang of adolescent bandits led by a fifteen-year-old girl;
two twelve-year-old boys and one of eleven stopping a man on the
street and shooting him with a semi-automatic; a fifteen-year-old
boy third-degreed as a suspect in a murder case; three sixteen-year-
old boys killing a fourteen-year-old "for revenge"; a New York City
school where the older pupils threaten the younger ones with

violence and with maiming them, robbing them of their money, watches, and fountain pens. The young victims don't dare tell the names of their tormentors. When two of them were asked by a teacher, they refused to answer: "We don't want our eyes cut out." Actually one sixteen-year-old boy in this school was beaten with a broken bottle from behind and cut so severely that seven stitches had to be taken around his eyes. Adults are horrified at this attack. They don't know that this is old stuff for comic-book readers. In one of the "good" comic books (*Classics Illustrated*) in a rendering of the novel by Eugene Sue, *The Mysteries of Paris,* there is a picture of a man tied down in a chair—a man whose eyes have been gouged out and whose blood runs down from beneath the bandage.

A twenty-year-old youth in New York City has just killed a policeman. Is that so astonishing when he can see anywhere a typical comic-book cover showing a man and a woman shooting it out with the police to the accompaniment of these words: "We'll give those flatfeet a bellyful of lead"? A nineteen-year-old youth has just been sentenced to the electric chair for the murder of a girl of fifteen, despite the jury's recommendation of clemency, by a judge who had previously disregarded a recommendation of mercy in the case of a sixteen-year-old participant in a holdup with a fatal shooting. There are recent cases where young men branded girls' breasts with burning cigarettes and carved initials into their flesh with a knife. A thirteen-year-old boy in Chicago has just murdered a young playmate. He told his lawyer, Samuel J. Andalman, that he reads all the crime comic books he can get hold of. He has evidently not kept up with the theories that comic-book readers never imitate what they read. He has just been sentenced to twenty-two years in jail; while the comic-book publishers who killed his mind with thoughts and methods of murder, and their experts who say his reading was good for him, continue as before.

All these manifestations of brutality, cruelty, and violence and the manner in which they are committed—that is the folklore of the comic books.

Comic books are the greatest book publishing success in history and the greatest mass influence on children. If I make the most conservative estimate from my own researches, one billion times a year a child sits down and reads a comic book. Crime does not pay, but crime comics do.

Recently I walked in one of the crowded sections of New York City and saw a sign: "Saturday Morning [which is the Saturday matinee for children] Comic Books Will Be Given Out Free to the First 500 Attending." I looked to see what was playing in that movie that morning. There were two horror films: *The Son of Franken-stein* and *The Bride of Frankenstein.* The posters calling attention to the movies showed girls in various stages of being overpowered. The movie was called the Ritz. As I stood there I was reminded of the story of the little boy who was asked what he wanted to be when he grew up and replied enthusiastically: "I want to be a sex maniac!"

There are two opinions about comic books. The one says they are very harmful to children; the other says they are good for the little kiddies. John Mason Brown has called comic books the "mari-juana of the nursery." The question can be put this way: Are comic books the marijuana of the nursery or the penicillin of a happy childhood? This difference of opinion is reflected also in the con-flict in the child's mind. Briefly summarized, it is a conflict between super-ego and sub-machine gun.

What is the case *for* the comic books? Seventeen points are ad-duced in favor of them. It is said:

1) That the children have their "own choice" in selecting this literature. (Go to any candystore or newsstand, and see what other books you can get for ten cents. The children are bombarded with at least sixty million comic books a month. That is seven hundred and twenty million of them a year. As far as their free choice is concerned, in a Chicago school recently the pupils collected and burned all the comic books and then went around in groups and persuaded the dealers in that neighborhood not to handle them any more. Other schools in Chicago followed their example.)

2) That they reflect the children's minds and if there is something wrong with them it must be the child's fault and the child must have been neurotic or disturbed or unstable in the first place. (That reminds me of the owner of the dog that had killed a rabbit, who claimed in court that the rabbit had started the fight.)

3) That it is good for children to find release for their aggressive desires. (Is there one sentence in Freud to indicate that it is ad-visable for children to see over and over again pictures of violence and torture?)

4) That they are educational. (Let's look at one of the much-vaunted "good" comic books again, for an example, those "good" comic books used as window-dressing for the whole industry. It would seem that no better choice could be made than the comic-book version of the novel by Charles Dickens: *Great Expectations.* The first nine pictures of this "educational" book show a gruesome, evil-looking man threatening a little boy with a big knife, and in one picture the little boy is crying out: "Oh, don't cut my throat,

sir!" Is this Charles Dickens speaking, or is it the circulation manager of a comic-book publishing firm?

(As for the claim that comic books lead children to read the
classics, many children whose confidence I have gained have told
me that when they have to make a book report in school they use
the comic-book version for their report so that they *won't* have to
read the book.)

5) That there are good comic books. (That reminds me of the
story of the polite clergyman who was asked about a bad egg which
he had just started to eat: "Isn't it good?" "Madam," he answered,
"parts of it are excellent.")

6) That the children identify themselves with the good figures
in the comic books. (That is like saying that the spectators in the
Grand Guignol who watch the rape, murder, and violence identify
themselves with the gendarme who breaks into the room a few
seconds before the curtain falls. There are comic books where girls
are bound and burned, sold as slaves, thrown to the animals, and
rescued only at the last moment by a good and faithful elephant.
Do the experts of the comic-book industry claim that the children
identify themselves with the elephant?)

7) That the children don't imitate these stories. (But the increase
of violence in juvenile delinquency has gone hand in hand with
the increase in the distribution of comic books.)

8) That comic books prevent crime and delinquency. (As a matter of fact, we are getting to the roots of one of the contributing
causes of juvenile delinquency when we study the influence of comic
books. You cannot understand present-day juvenile delinquency if
you do not take into account the pathogenic and pathoplastic influence of the comic books, that is, the way in which they cause trouble
or determine the form that trouble takes.)

9) That in comic books children are never threatened, killed, or
tortured. (But that happens in even "good" comic books. In one
comic book a little boy is stuffed into a sack with the following
dialogue: "Stop struggling, in you go." And the little boy: "No
. . . No . . . I want my mother!")

10) That they are good for reading. (But all the emphasis is on
pictures and not on printed matter, and good teachers know that
they have to get rid of comic books to make their children read
real books.)

11) That comic books make a lot of money. (They do!)

12) That when dealing with crime the comic books show the victory of law and order. (But what they really show is what Margaret

Osborn in her novel *The Ring and the Dream* called "the trapped destruction of some human prey.")

13) That comic books must be all right because they are so widespread. (That is like saying that infantile paralysis is all right because so many children have it.)

14) That comic books should be left as they are because curbing them would mean interference with free speech (as if censoring what adults read has anything to do with planning for children the kind of reading matter that will not harm them).

15) That the "experts" have approved of comic books so they must be all right. (But experts are not needed, only common sense.)

16) That comic books are socially harmless. (On the contrary, they immunize a whole generation against pity and against recognition of cruelty and violence.)

17) That comic books are a healthy outlet. (On the contrary, they stimulate unhealthy sexual attitudes: sadism, masochism, frigidity.)

It is pretty well established that seventy-five per cent of parents are against comic books. (The other twenty-five per cent are either indifferent or misled by propaganda and "research.") Since the comic-book industry enjoys second-class mailing privileges, the parents, as taxpayers, are paying for what they do not want. The apologists of comic books, who function under the auspices of the comic-book business (although the public is not let in on that secret), are sociologists, educators, psychiatrists, lawyers, and psychologists. They all agree that this enormous overstimulation of fantasy with scenes of sex and violence is completely harmless. They all rely on arguments derived from misunderstood Freud and bandy around such words as "aggression," "release," "vicarious," "fantasy world." They use free associations to bolster up free enterprise.

My own clinical studies and those of my associates of the Lafargue Clinic, the first carried out independently from the comic-book industry, and the first leading to their condemnation, have convinced me that comic books represent systematic poisoning of the well of childhood spontaneity. Many children themselves feel guilty about reading them.

The worst sector of comic books is increasing and the best, if there is a best, is getting smaller. The comic-book publishers seduce the children and mislead the parents. Their mass production is a serious danger to the production of good inexpensive children's books. The publishers of these good children's books, instead of fighting the experts of the comic-book industry and decoding their "codes," lie on psychoanalytic couches themselves, and delve into their own dreams instead of providing decent fare for the dreams of childhood.

When I recently conducted a symposium on the psychopathology of comic books I was blamed for not allotting more time to a representative of the comic-book business who was there. I am even more guilty than that: I once conducted a symposium on alcoholism and didn't invite a single distiller.

MY BROTHER,
SHERWOOD ANDERSON

by Karl Anderson

The aging brother of a great American writer (see page 182) sets down some interesting personal and literary memories of the author of Winesburg, Ohio.

SEPTEMBER 4, 1948

IN THIS ESSAY I shall attempt to give a picture of my brother, Sherwood Anderson, the natural story-teller, who by instinct built his tales with words of Biblical simplicity. As I begin I wonder: Can I put aside my long pride in my younger brother's accomplishment? Can I separate my impressions of one who shared my youth from my attitude toward the established author he later became? Should I, a painter, essay writing about *this* writer?

I was not quite three years old when Sherwood was born, on September 13, 1876, in a modest, two-family house in the small town of Camden, Ohio. Our father, Irving Anderson, was a harness maker and saddler, and the family moved about from one Ohio town to another, surrounded by the odor of leather and the hope of prosperity; one never left us and the other never came. Most of Sherwood's boyhood and mine, though, were spent in Clyde, a town of about 2,500 in the north-central section of the state and the hub of a cabbage-growing district.

The only abundance in our home, on Piety Hill—at the end of a straggling street that started pretentiously at Main Street and trailed away in a patch of weeds—was the ever-increasing number of children; their births came almost yearly until they numbered the magical seven.

In an environment tightly gnarled, among unimaginative folk, dependent upon agriculture for a living, it may appear surprising that the Anderson children should early have shown something of the fire of the poets; something also that could evaporate. I, the oldest, took up painting. Stella, who later became an occasional contributor to religious publications, was a year younger than myself. Next came Sherwood, then Irving, who had a youthful inclination to be an artist but became a businessman, then Raymond, who took up newspaper work, and Earl, who studied art in Paris. The youngest child, named Fern, died in infancy.

Sherwood, the exuberant one, was known as "the go-getter." He wanted to get on in the world. On Saturday afternoons he was on the streets selling the weekend edition of the *Cincinnati Enquirer,* a mishmash of news, scandal, adventure, and romance, to the farmers who came in town to do their shopping, and he was proud that he could sell more copies of the paper than any other boy in town. Once he boasted of his persuasiveness in inducing a farmer, in a barroom, to buy more than one copy of the *Enquirer.*

There was not a good library, public or private, in Clyde, with the possible exception of the schoolmaster's. There were but few books in our own home; I can remember only *Pilgrim's Progress* and Tennyson's *Poems,* and these chiefly for their fine illustrations. Sherwood, though, had the enterprise to borrow books; he was a great reader. However, I doubt that his preference was ever for the classics.

At school, Sherwood took no honors, but he was an effortless student. One day the principal of the school, the one man in town who owned books, a patriarch with a long, white beard, invited Sherwood and me to his house to discuss our futures. He appeared more interested in Sherwood than in me, and offered to try to get him a scholarship if he was interested in going to college. But Sherwood was somehow in a hurry for life, and he shrugged the idea off.

While attending school I had been apprenticed to a harness maker, for my father was insistent that I have a trade, and naturally favored his own. But I had other ideas: during my eighteenth year I left home to study at the Art Institute in Chicago. In later years Sherwood placed the blame for his having gone off to be a writer at my feet. "Your going off to study art," he said, "that set a bad example for me." I had been boarding with a family on the West Side of Chicago for about two years when Sherwood followed me there to share my room. He was twenty then, a callow youth of medium height. At once he captured the hearts of the family with whom we were staying by his good-natured assurance. He told everyone on the day of his arrival that he would first get a job as a grocery clerk, and then progress upward in a short space of time.

The following evening, Sherwood appeared at dinner with the exalted announcement that he, that day, had landed ten grocery jobs. "I'm to go to work at one of them tomorrow morning," he told us. "I haven't made up my mind which one. I'll flip a coin. See which fellow is to have my services."

As it turned out, Sherwood did not take any of the ten positions. A girl who happened to be visiting at the house that night was so impressed by his self-confidence that she took him to her father, the owner of a large cold-storage plant. Sherwood spent the next two years wheeling meat in and out of frigid vaults.

From this labor Sherwood escaped with light heart to go to the Spanish War. He wrote me in New York, where I had gone, and said, "I prefer yellow fever in Cuba to living in cold storage in Chicago." A girl Sherwood had written in Clyde told the town that he was planning to come home to enlist in the local militia, and Clyde's citizenry gave him a demonstration for which he was not prepared. The people were at the depot with a band to greet a patriot, a rudimentary hero. "Me, just to duck a rotten job, being made a fuss over—it was doggone embarrassing!" was the way he put it to me afterward.

Sherwood was in Cuba one year. He arrived there too late for the fighting and was detailed to police duty. Soon after he was mustered out of the Army, he came to me at Springfield, Ohio, where I was then employed as the resident artist for *Woman's Home Companion*. He was very thin, all skin and bones, and I could see that something was troubling him. Finally he confessed that he was in doubt about his future, and that he felt he should have a better education.

At the time I was boarding at "The Oaks," an establishment run by a Mrs. Folger, within strolling distance of Wittenberg College. Several Wittenberg professors lived at "The Oaks," and one of them became interested in Sherwood. Sherwood had attended high school at Clyde, but had never graduated, so it took a little doing on the part of the professor to prepare him to matriculate. Sherwood shared a room with me for two years, until I went to Europe to study art and visit the galleries.

In searching back in my mind now, I am inclined to believe that Sherwood's stay at "The Oaks" had no little to do with his deciding to become a writer. For the first time he was with people of quickened mentality who extended their interest beyond his mere geniality. With two of the friends he made—a teacher and a newspaperman—he corresponded regularly for many years.

During the next two years, while I was in Europe, a blank space existed in our intimate brotherhood. I returned to the United States and Chicago and Sherwood in 1902. Our mother had died. A year afterward our father married again; I never afterward saw him. The other members of the family had moved to Chicago, where

Sherwood was now working as a copywriter for an advertising agency.

One night, in the darkness of his apartment on the South Side, not far from the University of Chicago campus, Sherwood told me the story of his breakdown. He said he had left his first advertising job in Chicago to take charge of a failing mail-order business in Cleveland, with the understanding that he would receive an interest in the business if he put it on its feet again. By hard work he had increased the business 400 per cent, but the owners reneged on their agreement. He told me also of his marriage to a girl of much erudition, a former student at the Sorbonne.

From Cleveland Sherwood had gone to Elyria, Ohio, to start a factory making housepaint. Here he wrote some semi-autobiographical sketches which he had printed up in pamphlet form and distributed as advertisements. But his wife gave scant approval to his attempts at writing, he told me, because she felt him so poorly educated. He became so starved for intellectual companionship that he made a place in the business for Earl, our younger brother, simply so that on long walks in the evenings they might talk about writing and Earl could introduce to his mind unknown poets and novelists. He said the desire grew in him to write a story of his own, and he fixed an enclosure in his attic to be alone to write. After long hours in his office every day, he went to this boxed room and wrote deep into the nights upon a novel. He there wrote *Windy McPherson's Son*.

Now he came to the part of his story that was at variance from the account he later wrote. According to his writings, one day he suddenly walked out of his factory in such a way as deliberately to give the impression that he had lost his mind. Some critics have interpreted it as an act of brave escapism, a preconceived way of throwing aside the shackles of domesticity and business.

But as Sherwood told me about it that night, reluctantly, as one who would suppress even a recollection of his past weariness, there was nothing deliberate in the act. "I rose from my desk and walked through a door and beyond that door I have no remembrance. My mind was a blank until I found myself in a ward of a Cleveland hospital." A doctor told him he suffered from a loss of memory; said it was amnesia. The doctor advised him to take a rest and change his vocation. He rested several weeks, as long as he could afford such a luxury, then returned to Chicago and advertising.

It is not for me to decide which version of the incident Sherwood preferred or how others shall interpret them. For myself, the memory of that moment of listening to a hushed voice coming to me in the darkness of night is far too compelling to be denied.

It so happened, during an exhibition I gave in Chicago some time later, about 1913, that a newspaperwoman came to see my paintings —the wife of Floyd Dell, the brilliant and dogmatic young critic who was then assistant literary editor of the *Chicago Evening Post.* As she left the gallery, she invited me to a Sunday evening supper at her home, and I dared to ask the privilege of bringing Sherwood along. Masking her uncertainty of an unknown brother, she uttered a too declamatory, "Yes indeed!"

That Sunday Sherwood got on very well with the pugnacious and affirmative man, his host, Floyd Dell. For a period the two saw a great deal of each other, and it was through Dell that Sherwood met other members of the famous "Chicago group," including Theodore Dreiser, whom he came to consider his best friend.

Sherwood acknowledged to me that for a long time he had not the courage to tell Floyd Dell that he had written a novel. One evening in Sherwood's apartment, fortified by a few cocktails, he made his confession.

"Hell and damnation!" Dell exclaimed. "If I didn't like you, Sherwood, this would be the last straw. Come on, let's get it over with at once!"

Floyd Dell lay sprawled on Sherwood's bed that night and read *Windy McPherson's Son.* The next day he wrote an editorial for his paper to this effect: that he had read an unpublished novel by an unknown author with a gift of rare imagery—a man to be watched in American literature.

Credit has been given to many for helping Sherwood Anderson get a publisher; he himself chose to give Dreiser his greatest thanks. I do know that during the years the novel was in manuscript, it passed under many eyes and suffered numerous recommendations. Sherwood sent it to me to place in New York, but my acquaintances in literary commerce were few and, apparently, unperceptive. At last some woman in London who had read the book—my impression is that that woman was Rebecca West—told John Lane, the publisher, about it; gave her enthusiasm freely to him at a dinner party. In any event, Lane cabled his New York house to make a contract with Sherwood for it and his next book.

When *Windy McPherson's Son* was published in 1916, some critics said they detected in it marks of Henry Fielding, while others saw the influence of the Russians. The latter observation astonished Sherwood, so he told me, because he had not read, at the time, a single Russian writer.

The royalties of Sherwood's first four books—the fourth of them was *Winesburg, Ohio*—came to less than $400. (Later he was fond of saying, "I am the most talked about, most unread, most un-bought author in America.") It became necessary for him to go back to writing advertisements. Creation was his sideline; he com-posed stories in his mind during business hours, made notes on his cuffs, and wrote by night. He thought of himself as an amateur who could afford nonconformity. "I am damn well writing what I like!" he wrote me.

Winesburg, Ohio, was of course our boyhood town of Clyde. The characters in the book were suggested by certain personages in Clyde, but the stories were born of his imagination. Many critics and readers have taken Sherwood literally, have understood as au-thentic "Gospel truth" his own relating of himself and his ever-changing environment. They have ignored his warning on this. "I am destined," he once said, "to follow a crooked, unchaste path through the forest of my fancy"; and he also wrote, "I shall prob-ably never resort to exact truth of my people. . . . With me the spirit of people and the selection of my accounts of them is that which counts." I remember a visit Sherwood and Irving paid me, at my home in Connecticut, later in our lives. As we sat on the lower porch step in the spring sunlight, Sherwood related some incident that I had observed at first hand. I contradicted him on the exact-ness of his tale.

"Let him alone, Karl," Irving urged in an undertone. "I'd like to hear him tell it again to see what it would be like this time."

In the mid-twenties, Sherwood received $100 a week as a retainer from Horace Liveright, the book publisher, so he was secure finan-cially. It was later in the twenties that he wrote me, asking me to come to Ripshin, his home in Virginia. He needed my advice, he wrote. When I arrived, he told me he was thinking of buying two small newspapers in Marion, Virginia. I told him I thought he was foolish to consider tying himself down to such a demanding func-tion as that of country editor.

"But you know, Karl," he said, "that $100 a week of Liveright's worries me. I keep thinking about the damn check being on the way and about all the writing I'm not doing because of thinking about the check. I can write well only when I write to please myself."

I had nothing to say to that, of course.

Later, Sherwood sold the manuscript of one of his published books for $3,000 and used the proceeds as a down payment for the newspapers.

Often I have wondered why Sherwood did not write the story of our brother Earl, the queer one, who had shuttled between living with Sherwood and with me, then had suddenly declared his wish to be independent of us, a desire to be on his own. He walked out of our lives and nothing was heard of him, not a word, for the next thirteen years. Then he was picked up in a New York street, the victim of a stroke, but alive. Sherwood was in another part of the country then, and it was for me to tell him the tragic details of the finding of Earl. During Earl's last years, we were able to reconstruct the gap of thirteen years: he had been a sailor, an unsuccessful commercial artist, a helper in a bakery. He had been so proud that when he once saw Sherwood—then at the height of his fame—pass a few feet ahead of him on the street, he had scurried out of sight.

Years later, sitting in Sherwood's writing room, a one-room log cabin perched on the top of a mountain, at Ripshin, I asked him why he had never written the story of Earl, as I had told it to him, giving the words of my poor mining into his keeping. He did not answer. My mind brushed against the reason of his silence. Finally he rose and stood in the doorway, looking toward a range of far mountains, and from there drawled his low, dubious reply: "For a long time I've been mulling it over in my mind."

I sensed he did not want to talk about it. I got my answer a few days later. We were having breakfast in an open patio at his home, a stone house he had built at the foot of a mountain, by a racing stream. A number of Sherwood's friends were together there: Jim Boyd, Tom Wolfe, and a writer from Spain who had come to see about translating *Winesburg, Ohio,* into Spanish. Dogs were about our feet, and our conversation turned to their merits as companions.

Each man told his story, and I dared a factual tale of a red setter I once owned that never learned to heel. I told it not too well, I thought; so I was pleasantly surprised to have Sherwood say, "Karl, you managed to get perfect form in relating your story!"

Soon afterward the group dispersed, each man going to one of the small one-room shacks Sherwood had built for those of his guests who chose to write.

At midday we were again about the table, and I felt a lack of gaiety in Sherwood, as well as in the others, and I wondered at this. My brother sent a stern look my way and said, "Karl, that dog story of yours spoiled my morning for me."

"How come?" I asked.

"I tried to write it," he replied, with a wry smile of defeat.

Each man at the table acknowledged that he, too, had tried and failed.

For the first time I realized there was a difference between the spoken tale and the written one; that a writer wrote best of experiences and creations of his own. I knew then why Sherwood had never tried to write the story of Earl, as I had given it to him. More than that, it came to me that the queer characters dominant in the Winesburg tales came partly from Sherwood's preoccupation with his long departed brother. Throughout the lyrical perfection of the book was an undertone of remembrance. He *did* write about Earl. But Sherwood was not one to press within his being a withered flower of memory. Life, not death, was the essence of his being. Life was for him the great experience.

THE LIFE
OF THE PARTY

by Arthur M. Schlesinger, Jr.

What did it mean to be a Communist in the thirties and the forties? In this article the Pulitzer Prize-winning author of The Age of Jackson *analyzes the methods and the membership of the Communist party in the United States as they existed a decade and more ago.*

JULY 16, 1949

As a DISCIPLINED POLITICAL ORGANIZATION the Communist party in the United States would fill ex-Boss Hague with envy. Each candidate must be eighteen years old and duly certified by a member before he can be admitted to a local club. Cryptic communications bid the ten to fifty cell members to regular meetings for instructions and assignments. As a matter of course, members work as part of the Communist bloc in outside organizations and thereby help increase party influence far beyond the actual number of cardholders. The local clubs are the bottom of the chain of command, which stretches through county and state, or section and district, committees, to the National Committee and the National Secretariat, both housed in the Center, the smoky brick party headquarters on Twelfth Street in New York City, and finally to Moscow.

Why do people join the party in the United States? One can understand Communist strength in countries like China or South Africa, where cruel oppression affords little choice. But America has been through the longest period of liberal government in its history. The labor movement has never been so strong. Why should Americans submit themselves to the intolerable discipline of party membership? Yet even America has its quota of lonely and frustrated people, craving social, intellectual, and even sexual fulfillment they cannot obtain in existing society. For these people, party discipline is no obstacle; it is an attraction. The great majority of members in America, as in Europe, *want* to be disciplined.

It is hard work being a Communist in America, which is one reason the turnover is so great. But, once fully committed, the party

333

member finds that his world has become totally the world of the party. Communism fills empty lives. Surrender to the party gives a sense of comradeship in a cause guaranteed by history to succor the helpless and to triumph over the wealthy and satisfied. Ben Gitlow, for many years a Communist leader and twice Communist candidate for Vice President, describes concisely the impact of the organization on the individual member: "The party winds him up and keeps him going." One member explained why he had made the party the beneficiary of his insurance policy: "The reason I did that was, in the first place, I am not married and have nobody to leave anything like that to, and in the second place the Communist party is more in the world to me than anything else is." A pro-Communist novel, such as Isidor Schneider's *The Judas Time,* shows more clearly than any hostile tract ever could the implacability of Communist social life.

The total assimilation of the individual into the party creates for some a genuine selflessness and consecration. Like a platoon isolated behind enemy lines, the American Communists perform marvels of daring at their leaders' word, each acting as if he embodied the impersonal force of history. Their courage has impressed thousands of people with the invincible determination of their party. But the price of such intimate relations with history is the intensive personal supervision only to be duplicated in a religious order or a police state.

In the end they become so involved socially and psychologically that the threat of expulsion strikes them as ex-communication would a devout Catholic. It is enough to keep many in line long after they begin to develop intellectual doubts about the infallibility of Russia. When Granville Hicks left the party, a young woman wrote him, "So it all comes to this: that your whole life previous to this time . . . has gone up in a puff of smoke and lost its meaning. . . . What a pity to find one's life suddenly without meaning. What is left for you now?" And many, once they make the break, have become so dependent emotionally on discipline that, like Louis Budenz and Elizabeth Bentley, they rush to another form of discipline in the Roman Catholic Church, moving from one bastion to another in their frenzied flight from doubt.

In its own eyes the Communist party in the United States of America (CPUSA) has two main commitments: to support and advance the USSR, and to promote the establishment of communism in the USA. The second, of course has much the lower priority, since the preservation of the workers' homeland in Russia is indispensable to the triumph of communism anywhere else in the world. The consequent conflict between the requirements of Soviet foreign policy and the requirements of the American domestic scene has stunted the growth of the CPUSA. As the most impressive part of the Communist record in this country has been its courageous activity against local injustice and exploitation, so its least impressive has been its subservience to Soviet foreign policy. Yet the party leadership has had no choice but to stifle its grass-roots initiative and squander its grass-roots assets in order to whip up American backing for Soviet adventures abroad.

The policy of the CPUSA, of course, is a carbon copy of Soviet policy. For a long time, indeed, the party was billed as the American section of the Communist International. It has always received directives and in the past has received funds from Moscow. In the 1920s instructions flowed over the Moscow wire in such volume as to produce a wry joke among party members: "Why is the Communist party of the United States like the Brooklyn Bridge? Because it is suspended on cables." But Moscow's most effective control has probably been through Comintern representatives—the so-called "C.I. reps." In 1929, for example, when the party convention elected Jay Lovestone leader by a large majority, Moscow cables to the C.I. reps in attendance caused a reversal of the decision in favor of Earl Browder and William Z. Foster. From the famous John Pepper of Pogany in the twenties to Gerhart Eisler (Hans Berger) in the forties, inconspicuous foreigners in the background have made basic decisions for the American Communist party.

From the Moscow viewpoint, the American is clearly one of the expendable parties, so far as its political activity is concerned. Stalin and Molotov amuse themselves by making jokes about the CPUSA with non-Communist Americans; and the Comintern at no time has exerted itself to give the American party aid or to spare it embarrassment. No one in Moscow, for example, apparently ever dreams of giving the CPUSA a preview of an impending change in the party line; and every zigzag has caught the American leaders unprepared and red-faced.

The problem whether CPUSA operations are determined today by specific directives from Moscow or by New York attempts, through earnest reading of *Pravda* and *New Times*, to guess what such a directive would say is not important. The relation of Moscow to the CPUSA may be compared to that of a football coach to his team. The team has its quarterback to run it on the field, its set of plays and its general instructions. The coach will occasionally send in a substitute with new instructions or a new quarterback or an entire new team, but he is not likely to be giving play-by-play orders. (At times, though, it looks as if the Soviet Union had adopted the unlimited-substitution rule.) Since the team has complete confidence in the coach, it resents cracks from bystanders about taking orders from outside; after all, the players say, aren't the interests of the coach and team identical? As *Political Affairs,* the American party organ, recently put it, "The policies of the Soviet Union before, during, and since the anti-Axis war have corresponded to the best interests of the American people."

Jay Lovestone and Ben Gitlow were excommunicated for espousing various forms of the heresy of "American exceptionalism"—the heresy, that is, of arguing that special circumstances in the United States might justify occasional deviations from the Moscow line. Their disappearance signaled the Stalinization of the American party; it meant the extermination of the last flicker of independence. Thereafter, when Russia was militant, the CPUSA was militant. No more extreme document survives from the period of bellicosity than William Z. Foster's *Toward Soviet America* (1932). When Russia became the great advocate of the united front, the CPUSA precipitately stopped kicking liberals in the teeth and started to embrace them. When Russia opposed Nazism, America had no stouter defenders of collective security than Earl Browder; when Molotov signed up with Ribbentrop, no one took more delight in writing off the war in Europe as a "family quarrel of rival imperialisms."

Because the CPUSA has no mass following to take into account, local political realities do not restrain its passion to please Moscow. As a consequence, it has apparently won itself a low-comedy reputation in Comintern circles for always overdoing things—always jumping ten feet when the Comintern expects two. Thus in 1939 all Communist parties supported the Russo-German pact and denounced the British; but only the American party dropped its boycott of Nazi goods. Browder, in an article in *The Communist,* offered to shake hands with J. P. Morgan, who, having been dead for some months, was in no position to accept the invitation. Harry Bridges talked about the extension of the no-strike pledge far into the postwar world.

Browder had been leader of the party for fifteen years. He had steered it from anti-Roosevelt militancy to pro-Roosevelt popular frontism to anti-Roosevelt isolationism to pro-Roosevelt war unity, all without a quiver of distaste. But the experience of the wartime coalition seems to have given him the vision of an Americanized Communist party, working with its fellow American parties to solve the urgent questions facing the nation. He transformed the wartime tactic of national unity into a postwar strategy and argued the possibility that progressive capitalism, to save itself, would embark on policies favorable to the workers at home and to the Soviet Union abroad.

In April 1945, however Jacques Duclos of the French Communist party, published the celebrated repudiation of Browderism in *Cahiers du communisme*. The article lambasted Browder and commended William Z. Foster, quoting at length from Foster's criticisms of Browder within the Communist Central Committee—criticism which Browder had suppressed and which Foster not long before had sternly denied making.

The material in the article had clearly been handed over to Duclos by Moscow in order to announce the fundamental shift from the wartime policy of collaboration. It is likely that Moscow was simply using the CPUSA as a scapegoat in order to chart the new line for the somewhat more important Communist parties of Western Europe. Browder, receiving his copy of the *Cahiers du communisme* late in April, began to edge his way toward the new position. But the unexpected publication of Duclos's attack by the New York *World-Telegram* forced the Communists' hand. Overdoing things as usual, spurred on, in addition, by the personal hatred which many party functionaries, led by Foster, had developed toward Browder, his erstwhile followers ganged up on him and expelled him from the American leadership. Subsequent developments suggest that Moscow neither expected nor, probably, desired this result; at most, it doubtless intended a suspension of the kind that Harry Pollitt, the British Communist leader, received for his anti-Nazi deviation of 1939.

The events of the next few weeks show Communist methods in full swing—comic perhaps on the scale employed, but appalling in their implications if applied to an entire nation. In June 1945 the National Committee met to consider the case of Browder. With a vengeful Foster leading the attack, the members indulged in a three-day orgy of denunciation, while the unfortunate Browder, accused of such heinous offenses as "chronic tailism," slumped deeper and deeper in his chair, his head in his hands. The attacks were interlarded with confessions and avowals of penance on the part of the erring brethren attempting to explain how they had gone astray. Browder's speech in his own defense was subsequently suppressed by Foster lest it contaminate the membership—just as Foster's own criticism of Browder had been suppressed a year before.

There followed recriminations of intense bitterness. Browder retired into inactivity, but attacks continued upon him unabated; and soon the Westchester County (sic) section of the party was entertaining a motion for his expulsion from the party itself. In February 1946 the notice of expulsion appeared in the *Daily Worker*. Browder promptly accused the Secretariat of circulating charges against him which "ranged the whole gamut of social and political crimes excepting perhaps that of murder." One member of the National Board even proposed, according to Browder, that he be given the job of scrubbing floors in the National Office. "If there had been any evidence that there existed a real need for my services in this capacity, I would gladly have given them. However . . . I did not see fit to take the suggestion seriously." His refusal to give the National Board the names of all party members to whom he had spoken since the convention the summer before evidently precipitated his expulsion. Two months later he was on his way to Moscow.

The trip to Moscow was not unlike the pilgrimage made by Lovestone and Gitlow in 1929 after their repudiation by the Comintern. Both Lovestone and Gitlow were offered jobs if they promised to cease their opposition; both turned the propositions down. Browder accepted his offer and returned to America with a five-year contract as representative of Soviet publishing houses in the United States. He thus remains on the payroll in anticipation of a new shift in policy.

Since the war, one of the primary objectives of the Communists is what they call "mass organizations"—that is, groups of liberals organized for some benevolent purpose and, because of the innocence, laziness, and stupidity of most of the membership, perfectly designed for control by an alert minority. Sometimes the Communists start the organization themselves; sometimes—as in the case of the Independent Citizens Committee of the Arts, Sciences, and Professions in 1945 and 1946—they take over an existing organization. The Attorney General's list of subversive groups (whatever the merit of this type of list as a form of official procedure) provides a convenient way of checking the more obvious Communist-controlled groups. The list includes such outfits as the Civil Rights Congress, the Joint Anti-Fascist Refugee Committee, the Congress of American Women, and the National Council of American-Soviet Friendship. (The inclusion of such anti-Communist revolutionary groups as the Socialist Workers Party in the Attorney General's list seems to me foolish and unwarranted.) The Attorney General's list, however, leaves out organizations like PCA, which have a large proportion of non-Communist members, but rarely, if ever, oppose Communist objectives.

The infiltration into mass organizations is accompanied by a larger attempt to organize culture itself. During the thirties the party engaged in ambitious projects—the cult of "proletarian litera- ture" and the American Writers' Congress—by which they sought to establish firm control over the literary scene. These projects had a temporary success. But there seemed to be some basic incompati- bility in the relationship between the CPUSA and the creation of literature. The promising writers either broke with the party or abandoned serious writing in favor of Hollywood or disappeared entirely. Who can name today three "proletarian writers" of the early thirties?

Yet the party has not given up. Where it still has power, it has sought systematically to enforce the doctrine that writing must con- form, not to the facts, not to the personal vision of the author, but to a political line. Samuel Putnam, a disenchanted party-line au- thor, described in an article in the *New Leader* an instance which took place in 1946: "I had a book in press in which I set forth certain opinions that the party looked upon as unorthodox. No one, I take it, was supposed to know what the book contained ex- cept the author and his publisher; but somehow, doubtless through a loyal member somewhere along the line, the *Daily Worker* found out. . . . I was accordingly visited by a party functionary, who in- sisted that I discuss my book with him. This I declined to do; and just to see what his reaction would be, I quoted to him the words of Emerson that had stuck in my mind ever since high-school days: 'Speak what you think today in words as hard as cannon balls, and tomorrow, speak what you think in words just as hard though you contradict everything you said today.' 'That,' he replied, 'is a lux- ury you can't afford in times like these.' And I think it was then I finally realized what an unbridgeable gulf there was between us."

A *New Masses* controversy not so long ago displayed the exercise of party discipline in the literary field in rewarding detail. Albert Maltz, a former novelist who had become a Hollywood writer, sub- mitted an article to the *New Masses.* Communist critics, the author suggested in mild and tentative language, had perhaps employed political standards a trifle too mechanically in judging literary works. The *New Masses* itself, for example, had castigated *Watch on the Rhine* as a play but praised it as a film, the Nazi attack on Russia having intervened to transform the party line toward Ger- many. Writers like James T. Farrell and Richard Wright, Maltz went on, even though anti-Stalinist, might be able to write good novels. The political criterion, Maltz suggested, was fatal to artistic creation. "I know of at least a dozen plays and novels discarded in the process of writing because the political scene altered," he confessed, in a significant revelation of artistic methods in the Stalinist world. ". . . I even know of a historian who read Duclos and announced that he would have to revise completely the book he was engaged upon. . . . Obviously the authors in question were not primarily bent upon portraying abiding truths, either of character or of the social scene, but were mainly concerned with advancing a political tactic."

Isidor Schneider, literary editor of the *New Masses,* sent Maltz a note of approval and printed the article. Then all hell broke loose. Week after week in the *New Masses* and the *Daily Worker* the bush-league Zhdanovs—Howard Fast, Mike Gold, Eugene Dennis, even Foster himself—attacked Maltz in the most unrestrained manner. Maltz's subsequent performance was a pathetic demonstration of the power of Shigalovism. Capitulating completely, he even turned on sympathizers who had written to the *New Masses* objecting to the abusive tone in which correction had been administered. "What should be clear is that my article made fundamental errors," wrote the purified Maltz, as repentant as any Russian geneticist. ". . . A serious and sharp discussion was required."

As James T. Farrell pointed out in an article in the *Modern Review,* writers who accept easy social formulas may gain a superficial and temporary clarity about the world they live in; but they pay a price for allowing others to tell them what they ought to think and write. "They lose their own insights, and harden their talents. Many writers who take this path become cynical, and even abandon writing. They finally reach the point where they don't know their own problems, and are completely disoriented." The writer, it is clear, must have social perspectives—but they must be his own. The susceptibility to programs corrupts the artist by distorting and eventually superseding the personal truths by which he is nourished. Hence Balzac and Stendhal, whatever their politics, were more truly revolutionary than Victor Hugo or Eugène Sue; Henry James more than a party-line G. A. Henry like Howard Fast.

So direct political control either throttles the serious artist or makes him slick and false. Like Maltz, John Howard Lawson, Alvah Bessie, and Dalton Trumbo, the fellow-traveling, ex-proletarian writers go to Hollywood and become film hacks. Until, that is, they refused to own up to their political beliefs before a committee of Congress—in response to which the film industry, rearing itself in an unwonted spasm of moral nobility, turned them out into the storm. I do not wish to imply approval of the question asked by the Un-American Activities Committee. I suspect, however, that if the Committee had been asking witnesses whether they were members of the Ku Klux Klan, the Silver Shirts, or the Trotskyites, Mr. Lawson and his friends would be overflowing with indignation at the refusal to answer.

Hollywood, indeed, has turned out to have a particularly favorable climate for the spread of communism. The Hollywood writer, like the radio writer and the pulp fiction writer, tends to have a pervading sense of guilt. He feels he has sold himself out; he has abandoned his serious work in exchange for large weekly pay-checks; and he resents a society which corrupts him (it always seems to be society's fault in these cases). He has qualms of conscience, moreover, for making so much while others make so little. So he believes that he can buy indulgences by participating in the Communist movement, just as men in the Middle Ages bought remission for sins from wandering monks.

The result of the double corruption—first by the pay-checks, then by the Communists—is a corrupt criticism and a corrupt art. The larger result has been to create a dangerous inroad upon the moral fabric of American culture. Where direct political control cannot reach, the Communists and their friends have exerted their influence toward lowering and softening artistic standards in a pseudo-democratic direction. The wildly enthusiastic Communist claque for certain types of fake folk art is symptomatic. The vogue of "Ballad for Americans," for example, or for the incredible radio plays of Norman Corwin only results in betrayal of taste.

But these half-concealed exercises in penetration and manipulation represent only a part of the Communist mission in the United States. From the beginning, the party has had in addition an underground arm, operating apart from the formal organization of the CPUSA and working as the American section of the Soviet secret intelligence corps. Because clandestine operations of this kind are utterly foreign to American political life, many Americans dismiss them as wild fabrication. They are naïve to do so. Doctrine and experience have equipped the CPUSA for underground activity. Leninism sanctioned the use by the party of all methods in their war for survival against the American business classes; and the early history of the party—A. Mitchell Palmer and the meeting at Bridgman, Michigan—confirmed in the minds of the party leadership (both Foster and Browder were at Bridgman) an enduring psychology of clandestinity. Police raids, FBI penetration, and civil persecution have fortified the Communist belief that they are a small and ill-armed band, acting in a ruthlessly hostile environment, and justified in using any methods for their cause.

The underground arm of the party works through secret members and through fellow-travelers. Secret members report directly to a representative of the National Committee; they have no local affiliations, are exempt from the usual party discipline and are unknown to most of their party brethren. Their party cards usually are held in aliases, so that in the files they appear as "John Smith" with P.N. (party name) beside it. Fellow-travelers are those who for one reason or another wish to keep some elbow room but maintain relations practically as close as actual membership. A curious freemasonry exists among underground workers and sympathizers. They can identify each other (and be identified by their enemies) on casual meeting by the use of certain phrases, the names of certain friends, by certain enthusiasms and certain silences. It is reminiscent of nothing so much as the famous scene in Proust where the Baron de Charlus and the tailor Jupien suddenly recognize their common corruption; "one does not arrive spontaneously at that pitch of perfection except when one meets in a foreign country a compatriot with whom an understanding then grows up of itself, both parties speaking the same language, even though they have never seen one another before."

Far from being a threat to the status quo in America, the CPUSA has been a great ally of the American conservatives because of its success, for a season, at least, in dividing and neutralizing the Left. It is to the American Left that the CPUSA has presented an immediate political danger. And it is in the revival of the free Left, in America and through the world, that the answer to communism lies.

There can be no serious question that an underground Communist apparatus attempted during the late thirties and during the war to penetrate the United States government, to influence the formation of policy and even to collect intelligence for the Soviet Union. Though certain of the individual accusations, especially those of Elizabeth Bentley, are undoubtedly exaggerated, yet a substratum of truth survives in the stories told before the Federal grand jury.

These, then, are the proportions of the Communist movement in the United States: an organized party of 70,000 members, extending its influence by means of an underground apparatus and through the collaboration of fellow-travelers; controlling a political party, several trade unions, and a great many front organizations, and exerting a lingering power in cultural circles.

What kind of challenge does all this present to the United States? The espionage dangers, of course, are obvious and acute. No loyal citizen can underestimate these dangers, although there is probably little that he can do individually to grapple with them. All Americans must bear in mind J. Edgar Hoover's warning that counter-espionage is no field for amateurs. We need the best professional counterespionage agency we can get to protect our national security.

Beyond this field, however, it is hard to argue that the CPUSA in peacetime presents much of a threat to American security. In every area where Communist influence can be identified and exposed, the Communists have lost ground in the last two years. Does anyone seriously believe that even the Communist party is absurd enough to contemplate a violent revolution in the United States?

AMERICAN TRAGEDY

by John Mason Brown

Writers used to consider royal palaces the only proper settings for high drama—and kings the proper characters. Nowadays, however, tragedies are set in tenements and, instead of kings, their most heroic characters turn out to be prostitutes, alcoholics, or salesmen. In this article a drama critic of SRL *discusses the results of this trend.*

AUGUST 6, 1949

IT WAS THE YEAR of the Depression, though that had nothing to do with the depression which engulfed Joseph Wood Krutch when he was writing *The Modern Temper*. Mr. Krutch, one of the most penetrating and far-ranging of our critics—indeed, one of the few genuine critics we have in the big, proud sense of the word—contemplated Man, Love, Life, and Death. He was woeful then; woeful to such an extent that there were those who, in spite of their admiration, were forced to wonder if the apter title for his volume might not have been *The Modern Distemper*.

On no subject was Mr. Krutch more despairing than on the tragic fate which, as he saw it, had overtaken contemporary tragic writing *because* it had overtaken modern man. Mr. Krutch held tragedy, real tragedy, to be among the many good things which had vanished from the earth. He felt it to be an expression of the great ages, the Greek and the Elizabethan. For this very reason he would grant it no connection with our own. He saw the world in which he found himself a shrunken place. It had lost touch with the heroic. Its vision of life was not of that ample and passionate kind which had animated Shakespeare or Sophocles. According to Mr. Krutch, God and Man and Nature had somehow dwindled during the centuries since they had had their say. Mr. Krutch took as the measure of our littleness not the realistic creed of modern art which had led our writers to seek out mean people, but the meanness of the vision of life which had made such a credo acceptable. "A tragic dramatist," he observed, "does not have to believe in God, but he must believe in Man." One gathered that Mr. Krutch, like the modern dramatists he lamented, had misplaced his faith in both.

Mr. Krutch's lament, as I say, was uttered in 1929. Although it made its melancholy points brilliantly, it was guilty of a strange omission. Eugene O'Neill was not even mentioned. Had an historian of the New Deal or the war years written of them without referring to Roosevelt, the omission could not have been stranger. For O'Neill was already full-stream in his career as a tragic dramatist. Ten years had passed since the writing of *Beyond the Horizon;* eight since *The Emperor Jones, Diff'rent,* and *The Straw;* seven since *Anna Christie* and *The Hairy Ape;* five since *Desire Under the Elms;* four since *The Great God Brown;* two since *Strange Interlude,* and one since *Dynamo.*

No matter what our opinion may have been of this or that of O'Neill's dramas; no matter how small the biggest of them may have proved compared to the masterpieces of Shakespeare and the Greeks; no matter how tarnished most of them have become by mid-century, it was excitingly clear a quarter of a century ago when *Desire Under the Elms* was produced that in America, of all surprised and surprising places, a dramatist had emerged who was tormented and inspired by the truest sensing of the tragic which the modern world has known.

Few dramatists of his importance have written more unevenly than O'Neill. Few capable of rising as near to the heights as he has soared have sunk into the mire of more pretentious or deplorable mediocrity. Yet even the poorest of his dramas have been enriched by the courage of the man and by that fierce willingness to grapple with the imponderables which has made his best works memorable. What has enlarged the most unsatisfactory of his scripts, and made his career at once heartening and unique, has been the largeness of his concerns. No one, may I quickly add, has attested to this fact with greater warmth or discernment than did Mr. Krutch himself when, in a more cheerful mood, a short four years after his requiem for tragedy, he wrote a preface to a collection of O'Neill's plays welcoming their author to the select company of tragic dramatists.

Like Yank in *The Hairy Ape,* O'Neill's central characters have wanted to "belong." They have been visible cogs in the invisible machinery of the universe. Whatever the crimes into which their passions may have led them, they have cared passionately about the forces controlling their being and their undoing. Not only that, these forces have not been indifferent to them.

This high concern in play after play, regardless of its individual merits, has given to the body of O'Neill's work a significance at once solitary and touched with grandeur. Most dramatists in America and elsewhere during this past quarter of a century have at their

moments of greatest seriousness gone no further than to oppose
their characters to their neighbors or the social systems under which
they have lived. Not so Mr. O'Neill. The barricades his people have
assailed have been of a kind unfound in city streets. The altitude
of his reach has been the measure of his magnitude and more outstanding than any of his plays. It has set him apart, granted him a
deserved pre-eminence, left him lonely but a rallying point. For the
forces at war with his people or controlling their fates he has in
his evolution found various names—"the great angry eye of God,"
"the ironic life force," "Mother Dynamo," or "Christ the Crucified."
At his best, however, he has handled these elemental conflicts, un-
frightened by their savagery and equal to their passion.

To achieve the tragic view, O'Neill was compelled to outgrow the
surrenders to irony, crude melodrama, bathos, and pain for pain's
sake which cursed his fledgling efforts. Before he could write with
the high intensity attained in *Desire Under the Elms,* and even more
especially in the first two parts of *Mourning Becomes Electra,* he
also had to realize that outward naturalism—in other words, those
details devoted to documenting the physical life of the body—has
little to do with, and could only serve as impediments to, the interior and spiritual stuffs out of which true tragedy is wrought.

As early as 1922, two years before he wrote *Desire Under the
Elms,* O'Neill made for a Philadelphia paper an immensely revealing statement of his awareness of high tragedy as the Greeks and
Elizabethans had written it and of his attitude toward life and his
own works. "Sure I'll write about happiness," said he, "if I can
happen to meet up with that luxury, and find it sufficiently dramatic and in harmony with any deep rhythm in life. But happiness
is a word. What does it mean? Exaltation; an intensified feeling of
the significant worth of man's being and becoming? Well, if it
means that—and not a mere smirking contentment with one's lot—
I know there is more of it in one real tragedy than in all the happy-
ending plays ever written. It's mere present-day judgment to think
of tragedy as unhappy! The Greeks and the Elizabethans knew better. They felt the tremendous lift to it. It roused them spiritually
to a deeper understanding of life. . . . They saw their lives en-
nobled by it. A work of art is always happy; all else is unhappy.
. . . I don't love life because it's pretty. Prettiness is only clothes-
deep. I am a truer lover than that. I love it naked. There is beauty
to me even in its ugliness."

I have a reason for quoting this mention of the Greeks and the
Elizabethans, and the ennobling lift, the exaltation, the odd but
incontestable happiness created by true tragedy. My reason? Because

this statement appeared nine years before O'Neill, at the apex of his powers, was to write *Mourning Becomes Electra*. In it he chose not only to retell a Greek story in terms of Civil War New England but to house his Mannons in a great, chaste, Greek Revival home, columned as if it were a temple. In spite of his barroom, farmhouse, waterfront, or tenement backgrounds; in spite of his prostitutes, his stokers, outcasts, misfits, alcoholics, or sanitarium inmates, and the pungent Americanism of his dialogue, O'Neill did not have to wait for that setting in *Mourning Becomes Electra* to demonstrate that his best plays were Greek Revival in their spiritual architecture. The worthiest of them, and even some of the less successful such as *The Straw*, followed what in the great periods of the past has been the tragic blueprint.

Religions may change. God may pass under as many names as O'Neill has selected to identify the agents controlling his characters. Yet tragedy in the classic sense has always been, and remains, a kind of religion in its own right. It has sought to impose a pattern upon the patternless; to create an independent logic by relating cause and effect where actual living is most frequently illogical; and to wring ecstasy from misdeeds and tribulations.

Assuredly, tragedy is one of the strangest as well as the noblest of man's gropings for expression. Its subject is anguish, and anguish is the source of the pleasure it gives. No one can explain precisely what Aristotle meant by "through pity and fear effecting the proper purgation of these emotions." But everyone in the presence of an exalted tragedy has an intuitive comprehension of that elusive definition. For true tragedy, regardless of its subject matter, includes those who are adult enough to realize that all men, however happy, are doomed to die and that even a tranquil life, if survived long enough, is bound to be a shorn one.

Even so, tragedy is not concerned with the span of the years. In the vigorous or the old, it is concerned only with the intensity of the testing moments. It holds dying cheap and the death of its heroes and heroines a release for those who have achieved a certain tranquillity, a certain sublime and transfiguring peace, not merely from but because of the agonies they have endured. None of us would be cruel enough to stay their deaths or to deny them their final ecstasies and self-realization. We know that Death, when he at last appears to collect them, will have to be worthy of his conquests. In tragedy the body is almost an irrelevance; the spirit everything. This is why the wounds of the dying spill no blood. This is why, in the concluding acts of all the great tragedies (as once I tried to point out) no expiring character at the supremest moment of pain, whether he has stabbed himself or been stabbed, taken poison, fallen like a Roman on his sword, or been the victim of snakebite (more classically known as aspbite), has ever surrendered to the mortal luxury of an "ouch."

O'Neill's own tragedy, and ours, has been that though he possesses the tragic vision he cannot claim the tragic tongue. "The spirit of inquiry meets the spirit of poetry and tragedy is born," W. Macneile Dixon pointed out in as fine a book as has been written on the subject of tragedy. O'Neill's spirit has always been inquiring and protesting, but neither his inquiry nor his protest has led him to poetry. Although he has been able to feel and plan the great scenes, he has been unable to write the speeches which would have made them great. His poetry has been less than prose, his prose no substitute for poetry. Effective as his lines can be in the theater, they have little or nothing to say when taken out of context. They dramatize pain and exaltation without orchestrating either. The glorious and needed music of the Greeks and Shakespeare is lacking. The result is that, in spite of the attempts of his tragedies to soar, they fly with one clipped wing even when they are not earthbound. For O'Neill, like all of us, is a victim of an age of prose, and prose confronts the tragic writer with an almost insuperable obstacle.

Maxwell Anderson has been acutely aware of this. He, too, is mindful of the tragic blueprint, the example of the past, and the need for poetry. Indeed, poetry has found no more stalwart champion in the modern theater, fed as he holds it to be on a "starvation diet of prose," than Anderson. He has despised its deliberate inarticulateness and those climaxes in which the only eloquence has been a gesture or a moment of meaningful silence. Again and again, and unfortunately as if by rote, he has tried to escape from the strait jacket of contemporary realism. If his practice has not lived up to his theorizing, at least he has been haunted by the quickening dream.

Too often for his own good and the theater's, he has turned to the past in his verse plays, succumbing romantically to kings, queens, and costumes, especially Tudor. When he wrote *Winterset,* however, fourteen years ago, he tried to establish a new convention by seeking to do what "the great masters themselves" never attempted. This was "to make tragic poetry out of the stuff of their own times."

It was in *Winterset* that he came nearest to achieving the hopes and aims so eloquently stated in his prefaces. His contributions as a dramatic poet may be indifferent, but no one can deny that in theory the religion which is tragedy finds him among the faithful. This explains why he is so fond of likening the theater to a cathedral. To him as a thoughtful, sometimes despairing man, science is not enough. "It may answer a few necessary questions . . . but in the end science itself is obliged to say that the fact is created by the spirit, not the spirit by the fact." Anderson's faith, not a very positive or heroic one, is that man must have a faith. Perhaps his old rabbi in *Winterset* stated this belief for him most singingly when, just before the final curtain, he said:

> On this star,
> in this hard star-adventure, knowing not
> what the fires mean to right and left, nor whether
> a meaning was intended or presumed,
> man can stand up, and look out blind, and say:
> in all these turning lights I find no clue,
> only a masterless night, and in my blood
> no certain answer, yet is my mind my own,
> yet is my heart a cry toward something dim
> in distance, which is higher than I am
> and makes me emperor of the endless dark
> even in seeking!

If tragic times were alone required for the incubation of great tragedies, the years of the Depression, the war, and this unpacific peace would have yielded many of them. But, instead of aiding in the writing of tragedy in the older sense and on the older pattern, these tragic times have, if anything, added to the difficulties.

A period of realism and an age of prose are not the only hindrances. The lost or dwindling religious faith of many people; the encroachments of such a materialistic and earthbound theology as Marxism; an increasing uncertainty as to accepted or acceptable standards; our living with the threat of possible mass annihilation; great changes in the stresses and basic concepts of our economic and social life; the emergence of the "little man" as the new hero for hero worship; the shrinkage of the individual's importance under the pressures of superstates or ever-growing bureaucracies; indeed, not only the notion but the realization that the century belongs to the common rather than the exceptional man—all these are factors, widening or limiting, which have altered tragedy along with everything else. Because of them, one wonders if the tragic blueprint, cherished for so long as an ideal, has not, at least in part, become a glorious anachronism.

Not that tragedy is dead or will ever die. Or that Man has lost his touch with the heroic. No one who has watched men, women, and children rise to the terrible trials of these past years can maintain that Man has become mean. The bigness of the so-called "little man" in the face of such trials and of daily living is one of the most hopeful facts of recent history. It is simply that the heroic has become different in scale and kind, and for this very reason tragedy needs to be rediscovered for our own times and in our own terms.

We have come a long way since "gorgeous Tragedy in sceptred pall" came sweeping by. Thebes, Pelops' line, or the tale of Troy divine, and even the kings and courtiers of Shakespeare are not as close to all of us as they once were. But tragedy in the tenement rather than the palace, tragedy different as it may be in speech, action, and outlook, retains some of its old characteristics. It refuses to become merely a play with an unhappy ending. As Arthur Miller pointed out in some prefatory notes he prepared for *Death of a Salesman,* "tragedy implies more optimism in its author than does comedy. . . . Its final result ought to be the reinforcement of the onlooker's brightest opinions of the human animal."

This is why, much as we admire and are engrossed by such a play as Tennessee Williams' *A Streetcar Named Desire,* we deny it the name of tragedy. It is violent, powerful, and touching; written without mercy and without illusions. No study in disintegration to have come out of our theater has been more skillful or unflinching. But its people, though fascinating, are too small-spirited to be tragic. They do not grow by suffering; they merely decline. There is no exaltation in them.

There is, however, exaltation in *Death of a Salesman.* At first seeing it may be obscured by the bruising impact of this story of a "little man" who is sentenced to discover his smallness rather than a big man undone by his greatness. Yet the exaltation is there none the less, as the second or third seeing makes clear. It is not strong; it is not meant to be. The play, however, is far from being as negative as some have mistaken it to be. A positive belief in Man underwrites its compassion and lies behind its sorrows.

Willy Loman may be stupid, weak, and confused. He may ruin his life by never discovering who he is and by dreaming the wrong dream. But he has dreamed a dream, a dream he is willing to die by. He has, too, a kind of battered dignity. Small as he is, he is large enough for all of us to discover something of ourselves in him and in his plight. Moreover, Mr. Miller is unafraid of emotion and can release it in language which, though written in the idioms of daily speech, is poetic in mood and feeling.

What Mr. Miller's future will be, no one can say. We can only hope. But it is encouraging to have him divorce the pathetic from the tragic, in those same prefatory notes I have already mentioned, and to have him state his belief that "the common man is as apt a subject for tragedy in its highest sense as kings were." Our need for tragedies, written from and of our times, is great today. For, surely, never before have we so needed to be reminded of the dignity and worth of man the individual.

DON'T SHOOT
THE PIANIST

by Irving Kolodin

*The Horowitzes and the Rubinsteins are doing the best they can
in the madcap world of concert-giving, as this somewhat less than
serious article by* SRL's *music editor proves.*

SEPTEMBER 25, 1948

THE FOLKLORE OF MUSIC contains many old wives' tales, but none
so familiar as the one about oboe players being crazy. The basis
for this canard is the mechanism of the instrument—two thin vibrating reeds held in the mouth, operated by a compressed stream of
air from the player's lungs. Even a scientific basis has been ascribed
to the contention, the thesis being that long years of forcing air
through the reeds may induce high blood pressure, and, eventually,
might affect the player's mental faculties.

Note well the qualifying "may" and "might." The plain truth is
that much too much pity has been expended on such comparative
fortunates as oboists, and not nearly enough on their much less-
favored brethren of the keyboard. Have you ever heard of an oboist
failing to appear at a concert hall because of amnesia? Have you
ever read of a famous violinist pounding his left hand with a
hammer because it wouldn't respond as he desired? Or has it even
been necessary to post a warning: "Don't shoot the marimba player
—he's doing the best he can"? But all of these things are familiar
in the realm of those who devote their lives to the obviously impossible task of creating color from the black and white of the
piano keyboard.

Much of this I would attribute to the simplest source of unhappi-
ness known to man—sheer, mean, plain frustration. Merely to contemplate the huge bulk of a concert grand is to know what is meant
by an immovable object. Since no pianist has yet generated what
might be described as irresistible force, it is evident that the favorite
speculation of physicists will not be tested in music. The immovable
object shall and will prevail.

It is immovable to the extent, really, that virtually no pianist

352

actually performs on the instrument with which he practices. Can you imagine Heifetz practicing all summer on a Strad, then undertaking a tour in which he would play on fifty different violins in fifty different cities? Even the inside player on the last desk of the second-violin section (the orchestral equivalent of the Forgotten Man) tucks under his chin a possession which he fondles lovingly as his own —while a Serkin, or a Rubinstein, or a Casadesus operates on an instrument belonging to a piano company, which he knows only as a number.

For those of the uninitiate who may not know what the troubled life of the piano virtuoso is like, some explanation may be in order. Virtually the only famous artist who plays consistently on one and the same instrument is Vladimir Horowitz. He not only journeys about with it everywhere he plays, but allows no other virtuoso to use it between concerts, or when he is out of the country. Otherwise, most players, even of high rank, use one of the several hundred pianos the Steinway Company has cached in concert halls all over the country. If they are not Steinway users, they may be Baldwin users, a company which offers, as inducement, the transport of an instrument to some cities. But, even so, they will rarely have the same instrument all the time, or even the one on which they practice at home!

In the busy mill of concert-giving in New York, pianos are so much grist for the wheels, trundling back and forth between the warehouse, Steinway's basement, and the concert stages. "Picking a piano" is one of the delicate chores every recitalist performs before he plays, and in the underground cavern that occupies a full block from Fifty-seventh to Fifty-eighth Streets beneath the Steinway Building, as much tender care is expended as by a *sommelier* seeking out the perfect bottle of a rare vintage in the caves of Moquin.

On a clear day, when the wind is in the right direction, one can discern in the corner the Horowitz piano, blanketed like a stabled thoroughbred, clothed in silence. Around it in solemn rows stand the lesser public properties, to be tested and thumped, chorded and arpeggiated. Formally, they are known by numbers—something like 2547986D—and those who have favorites ask for them by number from year to year. But informally, among the inner circle, one hears whispers of the "Rubinstein" piano, the "Serkin" piano, the "Casadesus" piano. Some in the second rank of virtuosi have even been known to go to hear a rival play, not to appraise his art, or savor his interpretations, but merely to audition the piano.

While such gossip doesn't get into Winchell, the virtuoso set has its own rumor factory producing such juicy items as: "Did you know that Feigenbaum and 2547986 have phhft? This season he's using 2547985." Or they might pass along the story of the celebrated virtuoso who uses a Baldwin in public, but insists on a Steinway when he records.

Mention has been made of the second violinist who tucks his fiddle under his chin, proud in the possession of something indisputably his own. It is an additional source of frustration for a pianist that, virtually alone among the musical performers, he has no direct physical possession of his instrument. The singer, of course, is the most personal of all in this respect. His instrument is himself, and it accompanies him wherever he goes. It is as much a part of him as his nose or his kneecap, a thoroughly individual asset.

In descending order, there are the instrumentalists who have primary, secondary, or tertiary relations with the mechanisms they operate. The primaries I would nominate as violinists, cellists, or other string players who directly control the sounds they produce with little intervening metal. They have the feel of music in their hands, as the singer has it in his throat.

In secondary succession are the lip and finger performers—the winds of all sorts, from oboists to bass trombonists, who have one personal relationship with the instrument (the lips) and one impersonal one (the metal mechanism controlled by the fingers). Such a performer—especially hornists, trombonists, and clarinetists—are in equal proportion, artists, mechanics, and plumbers. They have the initial responsibility of functioning smoothly in any ensemble of which they are a part; they must keep their instruments oiled, greased, and otherwise friction-free, and the spittle that accumulates in tubes, valves, and pistons is a natural enemy of smooth execution.

At a degree removed from these are merely the finger and ear men—percussionists, cymbal players, xylophonists, even glockenspielers. The noisemakers with which these are concerned are wholly mechanized, but with some degree of individual control. The percussionist judges the pitch by applying his ear to the taut drumhead, absorbing some personal air contact thereby—and his corrections are made manually. The cymbalist has nothing more than two pot-covers in his hand, but he can damp their vibrations by pressing the instruments to his body.

Alone among all of these, the pianist has no more affinity with his instrument than a motorman with a streetcar. He applies pressure to a device, which in turn actuates another device, following which something contacts a taut string. If he seeks to limit the vibrations he has set in motion, he is reduced to the indignity of using his FEET, only a mere step away (and no sad kind of pun is intended) from the organist.

Is it any wonder, then, that the pianist is humbled to awkward, insipid, and thoroughly inartistic contortions? Lacking a true physical identity with his instrument, he must falsify it by chair adjustments, handkerchief wipes over the keyboard, solicitating sounding of chords. But once these preliminaries are disposed of, he is reduced to any manual means he can imagine to make the ugly, implacable thing a part of himself.

To my mind, among present-day pianists the most convincing technique for this belongs to Rubinstein. He betrays no fear of the ogre as he approaches it, rather a wary kind of self-dependence. He does not goad the keyboard, nor does he disdain it. Mindful that a barking dog will bite no one who displays a similar boldness, he pretends a confidence which, I am sure, he doesn't possess, intimidating both instrument and audience with his bland competence. But one can note in the tilt of his head, the arch of his eyebrows, that he is ever on guard against the untoward, prepared to abandon the whole thing the moment it threatens to explode in his face.

At a point 180° removed is such a virtuoso as Simon Barer, whose fabulous fingers have fathered more than one anecdote. Such as the one which concerns the Schumann Toccata. In his presence one day a phonograph repertory man was bewailing the nuisance that this piece was too short for a double-sided ten-inch disc, too long for a single-sided twelve-inch disc. "How much time for twelve-inch side?" he asked. "Four minutes, fifteen seconds," he was told. "Good," he responded. "I play it in four minutes ten seconds."

Lacking the sangfroid of Rubinstein or the perspired proficiency of Barer is the intense school of contemporary young pianists represented by William Kapell. Whether it is crowned by the crew cut of Eugene List or the aggressive cowlick of Kapell, this variety of performer seems to regard the piano bench as a mere airstrip from which to take off. The high-level approach to the keyboard is disdained in favor of a dive-bombing technique in which all the angles —both of approach and departure—are precipitous. One scarcely need be able to hear what is being played, for the visual representation, on the whole, is, of course, much more graphic.

Perhaps the most affecting figure of a pianist now before the public is the Chopin specialist Alexander Brailowsky. His frail body, as he assumes the attitude of attack, is hunched over the keyboard almost like a crescent, testifying to incredible weary man-hours of practice to precede his present perfection. But any suspicion of weakness is soon put at rest, as he plunges through etude after etude, prelude after prelude, books of polonaises, mazurkas, and impromptus, topped off by a sonata or two. Like the frail-looking Vernon Gomez, who threw the swiftest left-handed fast ball of his baseball era, Brailowsky has organized everything in his wispy body for one consuming purpose—to play the piano.

I have omitted such a pianist as Horowitz, since this article could scarcely encompass the massive spread of his two hands—like as many steam shovels—over the keyboard, or Oscar Levant, whose antipathy for the instrument is only exceeded by his urge to master it. Similarly, a complete catalogue would have to include Serkin, Arrau, Casadesus, Schnabel, and Moiseiwitsch, all of whom aspire, apparently, to make one believe that the mailed fist in the velvet glove is the one sure way to conquest of the keyboard.

As for the lady players, that is another whole subject, not to be included as an afterthought. This study, after all, is dedicated to pianists. The pianist is a separate breed, dangerous in its native lair, but suitable for domestication under some conditions. It may only be remarked, finally, that should the government ever get around to licensing musical performers, as has sometimes been suggested, there would have to be two categories established: owner-operators, such as violinists, cellists, clarinetists, and the rest—and mere musical chauffeurs of rented properties, such as pianists.

DOES OUR ART
IMPRESS EUROPE?

by James Thrall Soby

Back in the forties our country had produced no painter big enough to capture—and to hold—the world's attention. In this article SRL's art critic attempts to explain why.

AUGUST 6, 1949

SINCE THE FIRST DECADE of our century American art has tended, with notable regressions, to move out into the international mainstream, to join those swift contemporary currents which have originated most often in Paris, though sometimes in Germany, and once at least (futurism) in Italy. In 1910 Stieglitz held at his famous "291" gallery the exhibition "Younger American Painters," which Holger Cahill has called the first modernist group show in America; all the artists included were aware of advanced developments in Europe. In 1913 the immortal Armory Show brought to this country the full revolutionary impact of modern art abroad, and thereafter such foreign movements as abstraction and expressionism found recruits among some of the best American painters.

The First World War did not seriously interrupt a rising internationalism of style in American art. In 1916 the Forum Exhibition of modern American painters was held at the Anderson Galleries in New York. Many of the pictures shown—especially those of Andrew Dasburg, Arthur G. Dove, Marsden Hartley, Morgan Russell, and S. Macdonald-Wright—were as thoroughly "abstract" as anything being produced today by men like Baziotes, Stamos, Pollack, Rothko, and Motherwell. Indeed the importance of recognizable subject matter was flatly denied, and one of the Forum artists declared: "In conclusion I wish to say that I make no distinction as to the value of subject matter. I believe the representation of objective forms and the presentation of abstract ideas of form to be of equal artistic value." The artist's name? Thomas Hart Benton, later so vociferous a champion of regional accuracy and nationalistic sentiment.

The regionalists' reaction against advanced international styles began, in fact, soon after the *Saturday Review's* founding. In 1928

John Steuart Curry's "Baptism in Kansas" was shown at the Corcoran Gallery in Washington, evoking a divided response. A year or two later Grant Wood's "American Gothic" was exhibited at the Art Institute of Chicago and, in the words of the Institute's director, "the chief ikon of the [regionalist] movement was born." But regionalism was merely an exaggerated manifestation of a widespread return to realism and to native subject matter—the American scene. Yet the reaction against foreign-born innovation had barely got under way when a second wave of abstract art hit our shores, this time carrying with it the gaudy, brave barque of surrealism. The surrealists' use of precise techniques as a means of making the fantastic seem credible helped lead to a revival of "tight" painting for its own sake, and during the early 1940s some of our younger painters pushed to extreme limits the realist tradition which had, of course, never died out here. Today, however, by far the strongest tendency among the newer men is again toward abstraction, though now toward an abstraction imbued with symbolic meaning and referring, even if obliquely, to nature's forms.

Whether accepting or rejecting Europe's lead, American art has progressed rapidly over the past twenty-five years. At least this must have been the opinion of a number of our critics who replied in the spring of 1949 to a questionnaire sent out by the *Magazine of Art*. One of the questions asked was how well the critics felt that today's native art "stacks up against the Old World in quality of individual accomplishment and vigor of general activity." Twenty-five years ago most of the replies would have been defiant, envious, indecisive, or discouraging. Last spring, however, a majority of the critics declared that in their opinion American art now holds up very well against European, though several of them ruled out of the comparison the leaders of the original School of Paris—Matisse, Picasso, Braque, Rouault, and so on.

But are the American critics right or are they prejudiced? Certainly if the same question had been asked of a group of European authorities, the answer would have been very different. For no matter how much our art has grown in our own esteem, it has gained hardly at all in that of foreigners. This is a grave and puzzling matter. All over Europe our best writers are translated and admired, as in the past; in Italy alone Hemingway must have nearly as many disciples as in his own country. Our painters and sculptors, on the contrary, are for the most part unknown or condemned abroad, and only in architecture have we produced a name in the fine arts powerful enough to shake the European's faith in his continent's supremacy. I remember being asked by some Italian critics in Venice in 1948 why this great and vigorous nation did not now produce great and vigorous artists. "And Frank Lloyd Wright?" I asked. "Ah, yes," they said. "He is the first in architecture everywhere."

Perhaps Wright's armor in the battle for international prestige is the only invulnerable one: absolute genius as an artist. But this equipment, alas, cannot be won in any lottery except that of birth, and we have no one else to keep Wright's pace. Nor can the armor of final greatness be simulated, though some of our painters have made effective use of substitute materials—official rank in the case of Benjamin West, wit in that of Whistler, society and fashion for Sargent, courageous femininity in the case of Mary Cassatt. Nevertheless, we have produced in painting and sculpture no figure big enough to hold the eyes of the world on himself and also, inevitably, on those of lesser stature around him. Even so, we can take hope from a curious fact about giants in the arts: when you get one, the rest come more easily. We await our first in painting and sculpture, certain that he will appear and others after him.

Meanwhile, however, there are factors which have tended to restrict American art to a peripheral importance. One of these, with all due respect, has been the Parisian bottleneck. Since the seventeenth century Paris' supremacy in the arts has been so complete that it has been challenged seriously only by a few isolated foreigners like Tiepolo and Goya. No one, I think, can deny that Paris has produced or adopted more first-rank artists during the past 200 years than any other city—or country. But as part of the process alluded to above, the very stature of the great men in Parisian art has made those around them look larger rather than smaller. As a result, it has been extremely difficult in recent times for foreign artists of high but still secondary rank to crack the Parisian art front without going there to live and to become themselves Parisians. And if Paris has richly deserved its eminent place in the arts, it has sometimes taken advantage of it, exaggerating the abilities of its lesser men and underestimating artists from the outside.

In the late nineteenth century, for example, the Italian sculptor Medardo Rosso was ahead of Rodin in many respects. He was never allowed to become a formidable rival of Rodin in Paris. Similarly, most Parisian critics until very recently have given slight and grudging recognition to the Swiss-German Paul Klee—surely one of the finest and most personal masters of our time. It was Paris which first, or at any rate most damagingly, dismissed contemporary American painting as *l'École Frigidaire*. At the big display of our visual arts at the *Musée du Jeu de Paume* in 1937 Buster Keaton and Edward G. Robinson were far greater heroes of the day than

Winslow Homer or John Marin. Since that date there have been several attempts to interest the French in our newer painters. They have all ended in failure.

Today, however, Paris has lost to a great extent its role as international arbiter of fame and quality in the fine arts. This is not a statement to be made gleefully; it is something to be said with humility, in full recognition of Paris' magnificent achievement, with the knowledge that her place may never again be filled. But the fact remains that we may be at the beginning of an era in which the artists of the Western world will try to communicate from country to country instead of through the Parisian switchboard. In many European nations there is a decided curiosity as to what the younger American painters and sculptors are producing. These nations are anxious to see our art at first hand and to have us see theirs.

The difficulty, so far as our part of the exchange is concerned, is that our prosperity counts so heavily against us. Because of necessary restrictions on the expenditure of funds abroad, it is almost impossible for a European to buy or even to import for exhibition purposes the works of American artists. Moreover, as Lyonel Feininger points out, "what Europe can pay would not go far in our country." The prices of American paintings and sculptures are naturally related to the standards and cost of living in this country; they are on the average between two and four times higher than the prices of comparable works anywhere in Europe except England (where the great eighteenth-century era of collecting established art as an expensive commodity, where the nineteenth-century Pre-Raphaelites sold in their own time for staggering prices). Hence the dilemma of American artists. The one way in which most of them can have their art shown abroad is through dealers. And dealers are not interested in exporting works for which there is no likely market, though in a few prosperous cases we might expect them to be. The only possible solution to the problem of better international recognition for our painters and sculptors is Federal intervention—of which more later.

First, however, it might be well to consider the few cases in which modern American artists, as individuals, have been able to make at least an appreciable dent in European art consciousness. Quite likely the most effective procedure is more or less permanent expatriation—the tried and successful method of West, Copley, Whistler, Cassatt, and Sargent. Of all modern American painters, for example, possibly the best known in Europe has been Lyonel Feininger, who went to Germany in 1887 and remained abroad for fifty years, until his hatred of the Nazi regime forced him home. Feininger has never had a major standing in Paris, for the very reasons I have discussed above, but he played a vital part in the progressive movements of Central European art. By 1913 he was exhibiting with Klee, Kandinsky, Franz Marc, and others in the famous "Blue Rider" group. From 1919 to 1933 he was a leading figure on the staff of the Bauhaus—the most influential school for artists and designers which our century has produced thus far. In 1931 he was given a large retrospective exhibition at one of the great European museums, the National Gallery of Berlin. In short, he was recognized throughout Central Europe as one of the distinguished painters of our epoch.

A second procedure in attaining European recognition has proved workable in one conspicuous and exceptional case—that of Alexander Calder, whose fame extends to many of the capital cities of Europe, including Paris, and to those of Latin America as well. During his early career, from 1926 to 1932, Calder spent much of his time in Paris, and there became well known in art circles, first through his performances of a witty and beguiling miniature circus whose figures and properties he made out of commonplace materials, later through his abstract sculptures in motion, called "mobiles." In more recent years Calder has visited and exhibited in Europe periodically. A commuter rather than an exile like Feininger, he is the latter's most serious rival in foreign esteem. But his is a rare case, understandable only in relation to his vivid personality and to an imaginative ingenuity with mechanics which Europeans cherish as an American virtue.

The third procedure, oddly enough, is that of deliberate American nationalism in art. Here, too, the odds against European success are great, and we should remember that Winslow Homer, who consistently repudiated foreign influences, made little impression on the French at the *Jeu de Paume* exhibition of 1937, though he has long been regarded at home as one of our indisputable masters. In our own time, however, an artist far more thoroughly chauvinist than Homer is quite widely admired by Europeans. This is the late Grant Wood, already mentioned as a leader of the regionalist movement of the late 1920s. Wood's "Daughters of Revolution" was a hit in the London exhibition of American painting at the Tate Gallery in 1946, and I have heard his pictures praised by extremely critical authorities in Paris. For understandable reasons, Europeans occasionally like our art best when it looks least like their own, and "Daughters of Revolution," with its ambivalent humor and crisp intensity, confirms Europe's deeply rooted frontier romanticism toward this country, whereas more urbane manifestations of our culture do not.

If a few of our modern artists have been able to impress Europe in their separate ways, the fact remains that most of our best painters and sculptors are completely unknown abroad. Should this trouble us? I think it should—profoundly. Today we are engaged in a vital struggle to help the peoples of Europe regain their strength, to persuade them that we and they are committed to the same basic ideals. One of the most effective propaganda charges used against us in this struggle is that we are a rich, vast, powerful nation, but a nation not deeply concerned with the arts or with related spiritual values. On the political front, we are accused of "dollar diplomacy"; on the cultural front, the American movie is cited in its worst examples as an indication of our materialism.

In refuting propaganda of this kind we need every means of communication we can get. Our problem, unlike that of the Russians, is not to convince our own people of democracy's advantages. Americans with few exceptions are already convinced, and to regiment artists in a nationalist cause would be to destroy the character of the cause itself. Our problem is also very different from that of Mexico, where living artists have been a major factor both in asserting national pride and in atracting a badly needed foreign tourist trade. Our most pressing task is neither to inspire ourselves nor to bring in visitors from abroad. It is to show the peoples of other nations, in their own lands, what we are really like, without attempting to distort, to aggrandize, or to conceal. Our best writers and musicians, our finest movies, our few internationally known painters and sculptors are an immense asset toward foreign understanding.

We need more assets of this kind and, in the case of painting and sculpture, we are not likely to get them without Federal aid. Several years ago the State Department took the initiative by forming a courageous if incomplete and not wholly representative collection of modern American paintings. The collection was divided into sections and sent out on tours of the principal European and Latin-American cities. By majority account, the pictures were received with great interest, and seem to have done much to dispel the legend that our contemporary art is clumsy, cold, literary, over-realistic, and, above all, backward in style. At home, however, the collection was attacked as radical and possibly subversive, in any case a waste of the taxpayer's money. The paintings were hastily withdrawn from tour and sold.

The most plausible objection to the State Department's collection was the one least frequently heard: that it had been gathered and shown by an unsuitable Federal agency. Organizing painting and sculpture exhibitions is obviously not the direct concern of the State Department. It should be the concern of the Federal Department of Fine Arts. The Department of Fine Arts? We have none. And here, I think, we come upon a notable failure of American art over the past twenty-five years, for all the progress made. The steadily increasing public interest in the visual arts in this country has not yet resulted in the appointment of a Secretary of Fine Arts, whose first responsibility would be the elevation of the status of American art, past and present.

There would be terrible dangers in such an appointment, of course. In the hands of a reactionary, with no proven interest in the art of our own time, the job could become an instrument of repression or could be allowed to dawdle in the mires of academic dispute and political reward. I believe we should take our chances, and hope for every conceivable precaution against the wrong person being chosen. The danger, after all, was almost equally great when the various Federal art projects of the 1930s were launched, yet no one who studies their history carefully can deny that they made an extremely important contribution to the evolution of modern American art. The names of an impressive number of our present-day leaders in painting and sculpture were once listed with the Public Works of Art Project of 1933 and with the Federal Art Project of 1935.

One of the functions of a Secretary of Fine Arts would be to encourage the revival of Federal projects such as these. Another would be to promote an exchange of exhibitions with European countries. The benefit from these two activities would be very great. But an even greater good might be the gain in dignity and standing for the arts and for artists. In European countries, even when officialdom has been hopelessly inept, as has been often the case, artists have had a more encouraging climate in which to work than here, due to governmental recognition of their profession, at least in part. In France, for example, no one questions the absolute importance of art; it is only the relative quality of various kinds of art that is the point of dispute. The same cannot yet be said of this country, despite the protestations of those who claim to detest only one species ("modern"), when in reality they are suspicious of all. Federal recognition of the fine arts' place in our civilization might help immensely, as it did during the 1930s. It might even bring about here a symptomatic occurrence such as that described by the painter Stuart Davis. Arriving in France in 1928, Davis was stopped at customs because of his abstract pictures which he had brought from America. The chief inspector was summoned, and Davis explained that his paintings were related to those of the cubists. "Ah, cubism," the inspector said, "but of course"—and signed an immediate release.*

---

* Since this article appeared in 1949, a few contemporary American painters, notably the late Jackson Pollock and Willem de Kooning, have exerted a very considerable influence in England and on the Continent. Indeed, the new school of "Tachists" is quite widely considered to have been inspired by recent American painting.—EDITOR

THE STRANGE DEATH
OF EDGAR ALLAN POE

by Philip Van Doren Stern

On October 7, 1849, one of America's great poets, having been picked up unconscious in a saloon, died in a Baltimore hospital. Here is an account of the mysterious circumstances that surrounded Poe's death.

OCTOBER 15, 1949

THE NEED FOR SAVING fifty cents helped send Poe to his death. When he started out for Richmond in 1849 he had a choice of two routes between New York and Philadelphia. The most direct way was to go by ferry to Jersey City and take the New York and Philadelphia Railroad to Tacony, Pennsylvania, where a steamer carried passengers six miles down the Delaware River to their destination. The other way was to leave the Battery by steamer for South Amboy, the Eastern terminal of the Camden and Amboy Railroad, which ran across New Jersey to Camden, where passengers to Philadelphia were ferried over the river. Either trip required about five hours, but the Amboy route was fifty cents cheaper on the second-class cars. That is probably why Poe chose it, for, as always, he was desperately short of money.

He and his mother-in-law, Mrs. Maria Clemm, had left their Fordham home the day before and had spent the night in downtown Brooklyn, at the home of Mrs. Sarah Anna Lewis, a minor poetess whose husband had paid Poe to "correct" and publicize his wife's verses. Poe seems to have been in reasonably good spirits when he parted from Mrs. Clemm on the deck of the *John Potter*, the side-wheeler that took passengers to Amboy on its regular noonday run. But during the sail down the Bay something happened that aroused his latent insanity. Perhaps someone induced him to take a drink, or perhaps ships and the open water had a disturbing effect upon him. He was again to experience a strange sea-change three months later when he embarked at Richmond for the last water journey he was ever to undertake.

At South Amboy Poe caught the Philadelphia train, but before it reached Bordentown he was out of his mind. According to the story he told afterward to John Sartain, the Philadelphia artist, he was convinced that two men in the seat behind him were plotting to murder him. Fortunately, they got off the train at Bordentown, but by that time Poe was completely insane. He reached Philadelphia, but there he disappeared for several days. He told Sartain that he had been arrested for the "lying charge of theft of a $50 bill" and confined in Moyamensing Prison overnight. While he was in prison —if he actually was—he had a strange and horrible vision. When he related it to Sartain he said that he had seen a beautiful woman standing on the granite parapet, dressed in flowing robes.

> She showed me [he said] some of the terrible torments I would have to undergo. Ah! what a sight! Great caldrons of boiling liquor, steaming and fizzling in the moonlight. But I saw the trap set by the conspirators, and told her so, boldly. If I once faltered, down, down, she would plunge me to the chin in the burning brandy, there to squirm, like Tantalus, with parched throat, starting eyeballs, and agonies of pain. Then a pack of demons brought my *mother* to the caldron, chopped off her feet before my eyes, then her knees, her thighs, her arms, and at last plunged the poor, bleeding trunk into the reeking, bubbling caldron.

"By his mother," Sartain explained, recounting the episode to a roving Texas reporter in 1883, "Poe intended Mrs. Clemm. I do not know the precise relations which existed between them, but he once or twice referred to her as tempting him."

The next morning, still according to Sartain, Poe was recognized by the examining magistrate and released. He then went to Sartain's studio to seek help, for he was in a highly distraught state of mind, still babbling incoherently about the conspirators who wanted to kill him. He insisted on shaving off his mustache to disguise his appearance. Since Sartain was unwilling to trust Poe with a razor, he took a scissors and did the barbering himself. The demented man kept begging for laudanum to quiet his nerves, so Sartain gave him a small dose of opium and stayed with him that night while he slept quietly under the influence of the drug.

When he awoke in the morning he was no better. During the day he escaped from the studio to wander through the streets of the city where he had once lived happily with Virginia. By nightfall he was far out in the northern suburbs. He slept there in an open field, and the clean odor of the earth and grass, according to his own account, finally brought him to his senses. He returned to Sartain's studio in good enough shape to continue his journey. His money had been stolen, so some of his friends contributed ten dollars to send him on his way. Writing to Mrs. Clemm about his experiences in Philadelphia, Poe said:

> I have been *so* ill—have had the cholera, or spasms quite as bad, and can now hardly hold the pen. . . . I was never *really* insane, except on occasions where my heart was touched. I have been taken to prison once since I came here for getting drunk, but *then* I was not. It was about Virginia.

His valise had been "lost" during all this time, but he found it at the Philadelphia railroad station, where he had doubtless checked it on arrival. The manuscripts of two lectures he had intended to give in the South were missing—stolen, Poe insisted with insane conviction.

One of his friends put him on the train for Baltimore, where he took the steamer to Richmond and arrived there without further mishap. He immediately wrote to Mrs. Clemm, closing the letter by saying:

> I got here with two dollars over (from the ten dollars he had borrowed in Philadelphia)—of which I enclose you one. Oh, God, my Mother, shall we ever again meet? If possible, oh COME! My clothes are *so horrible,* and I am *so ill.* Oh, if you could come to me, my mother. Write instantly—oh *do not* fail. God forever bless you.

Five days later he again wrote to Mrs. Clemm, telling her that he was much better. Describing the attack he had had in Philadelphia, he said: "For more than ten days I was totally deranged, although I was not drinking one drop; and during this interval I imagined the most horrible calamities. All was hallucination, arising from an attack I had never before experienced—an attack of *mania-à-potu.*" Since mania-à-potu is the medical term that was then used for delirium tremens, it is hard to believe Poe was telling the truth about having had nothing to drink. But he was thoroughly frightened by what had happened to him—so frightened that he officially took the temperance pledge soon after his arrival in Richmond.

Richmond was the city of his youth. There his mother was buried, and there his sister Rosalie was still living. She had been adopted by a local family who did not tell her that she had a brother until she was nearly grown up. She was mentally subnormal, a strange and pathetic creature who now idolized her celebrated brother and annoyed him by following him everywhere he went. The sight of her must have been a sharp reminder to Poe of the dark strain he had inherited, for his father was reputed to have been a wastrel and drunkard, and his elder brother, William Henry Poe, had died of alcoholism and tuberculosis at the age of twenty-four.

Poe had friends in the city, but instead of staying with them, he took a room at the Swan Tavern near the Capitol. Knowing so many people in Richmond was unfortunate, for they kept inviting him to drink. After his second disastrous bout with liquor, a friendly doctor warned Poe that further indulgence would be fatal. That may have been what persuaded him to take the temperance pledge.

Much of his time was spent renewing old acquaintanceships, but he never lost sight of the main purpose of his visit—the raising of capital for his projected magazine, *The Stylus*. E. H. N. Patterson, a young newspaper publisher living in Oquawka, Illinois, had promised some financial support, but Poe needed more capital, and he wanted to obtain subscribers while he was in the South. He hoped to get some money by lecturing. Since he had arrived in Richmond penniless, he must have been living all this time on what he could borrow, probably promising to repay the lenders from his lecture receipts. The first lecture, "The Poetic Principle," was given in the concert room of the Exchange Hotel on the evening of August 17. It was well attended and favorably noticed in the newspapers, but with an admission price of twenty-five cents it could not have been very profitable. However, another lecture was scheduled for nearby Norfolk, and Poe was urged to repeat his appearance in Richmond.

Meanwhile, something happened that promised to solve permanently all the problems of Poe's tangled life. Years before when he was at the University of Virginia he had fallen in love with a Richmond girl, Sarah Elmira Royster. They had actually become engaged, but her father opposed the marriage and in true nineteenth-century style had intercepted Poe's letters to his daughter, so that she naturally thought her suitor had lost interest. At seventeen, she married Alexander B. Shelton, and the brief romance with Poe was over. Shelton died in 1844, leaving his widow an estate of about $50,000. Poe now met his former sweetheart and began to woo her again. She agreed to marry him, but their engagement—or "understanding" as she preferred to call it—was not made public.

However, the prospect of marrying a wealthy widow completely changed Poe's plans. At last he had in sight everything he had wanted—a woman to take care of him, an assured position in society, and, most important of all, financial independence with enough money at his command to put into effect his long-cherished plan for starting his magazine. He wrote to Mrs. Clemm announcing the forthcoming marriage and told her that he was going to bring her to Richmond for the ceremony. Meanwhile, since he was still in need of ready cash, he went ahead with his lectures. And when a Mr. St. Leon Loud, the husband of a Philadelphia poetess, offered him $100 to "edit" his wife's verses, Poe gladly accepted the proposal and agreed to stop off in Philadelphia to pick up the manuscript when he went north for Mrs. Clemm.

He spent the week of September 9 in Norfolk and its vicinity. On the fourteenth he lectured at the Norfolk Academy and then returned to Richmond at the end of the week. The receipts from this lecture were pathetic. Poe wrote that it brought him only two dollars above expenses, and the second Richmond lecture, given on September 24 with a fifty-cent admission charge, could not have been very successful either, since it is known that Poe was still borrowing from his friends.

A few days before the Richmond lecture Poe wrote to Mrs. Clemm announcing his intention to leave for Philadelphia and New York on September 25. The letter otherwise seems normal enough, but in it Poe shows his distrust of the world and displays his penchant for taking refuge behind an assumed name, for in asking Mrs. Clemm to write to him at Philadelphia he says: "For fear I should not get the letter, sign no name & address it to *E. S. T. Grey, Esqre.*"

He then went on to inform her that he might get married before starting—"but there is no telling." Four days later, Mrs. Shelton—probably under Poe's urging—also wrote to Mrs. Clemm. She mentioned her love for Poe but discreetly refrained from saying anything about their intended marriage on October 17.

For some unknown reason, Poe did not leave Richmond the day after his second lecture there, but stayed on for two more days. On Wednesday evening, September 26, he called on his fiancée for the last time.

He was not in good health when he arrived at Mrs. Shelton's home. Writing to Mrs. Clemm about his visit, she said:

> He was very sad, and complained of being quite sick. I felt his pulse, and found he had considerable fever, and did not think it probable he would be able to start the next morning [Thursday], as he anticipated. I felt so wretched about him all of that night, that I went up early the next morning to enquire about him when, much to my regret, he had left in the boat for Baltimore.

After leaving Mrs. Shelton, Poe went downtown to say farewell to his friend Dr. Carter. But when he left his office, he was so muddled that he took the doctor's malacca sword-cane with him instead of his own walking-stick. He then went to Sadler's Restaurant, only a few blocks away, for a late supper. There he met some friends, and they must have made a night of it, for when they brought Poe to Rockett's Landing, to put him on the steamer that sailed from there at 5:30 A.M., no one noticed that his baggage had been left behind.

If Mrs. Shelton was correct in saying that Poe departed from Richmond by boat on Thursday, September 27, he must have gone on the *Curtis Peck,* which was the only ship available that day. It arrived in Norfolk shortly after noon, in time for its passengers to catch the Baltimore Steam Packets that sailed daily from that port. The boat scheduled to leave that afternoon was the *Herald,* in charge of Captain Russell. It left Norfolk at 3:30 P.M. and arrived at Spear's Wharf in Baltimore at seven o'clock the next morning.

Poe must have been in bad shape by then, for he disappeared for five days. All sorts of rumors have been circulated about what he did during that time. From all this maze of rumor only one clear fact emerges: on the following Wednesday, a friend of his, a doctor and editor with whom he had often corresponded, received a note written in pencil on coarse paper. It is one of the most celebrated—and saddest—documents in American literature. It read:

> Baltimore City, Oct. 3d, 1849
>
> Dear Sir,—
>   There is a gentleman, rather the worse for wear, at Ryan's 4th ward polls, who goes under the cognomen of Edgar A. Poe, and who appears in great distress, & he says he is acquainted with you, and I assure you, he is in need of immediate assistance.
>   Yours, in haste,
>   Jos. W. Walker
> To Dr. J. E. Snodgrass

October third was dismal, cold, and rainy. And it was election day in a city that was noted for its political corruption. Members of Congress and the state legislature were up for election, and the Democrats and the Whigs were equally ruthless in their determination to win what appeared to be a close contest. There was no registry of voters in Baltimore then, and the local hoodlums used to capture and "coop" strangers and foreigners, fill them with whisky and drugs, and take them around to the various polling places to vote again and again for their ticket. The Whig coop was only two blocks from Cornelius Ryan's Fourth Ward polls, a saloon named Gunner's Hall. There is no certain proof, but nearly all of Poe's friends and relatives who left an opinion on the subject, believed that Poe had been "cooped." Since he was unable to take a single glass of wine without being violently affected by the slight amount of alcohol it contained, an overdose of whisky—and whisky that was probably drugged—must have worked like a poison on his already ravaged system.

When Snodgrass reached Ryan's saloon, he found Poe—according to his account written eighteen years later

> . . . in the bar-room, sitting in an armchair, with his head dropped forward. . . . His face was hagged [sic], not to say bloated and unwashed, his hair unkempt, and his whole physique repulsive. His . . . forehead . . . [was] shaded from view by a rusty, almost brimless, tattered and ribbonless palm leaf hat. His clothing consisted of a sack-coat of thin and slazy [sic] black alpaca, ripped more or less at several of its seams, and faded and soiled, and pants of a steel-mixed pattern of cassinette, half-worn and badly fitting, if they could be said to fit at all. He wore neither vest nor neckcloth, while the bosom of his shirt was both crumpled and badly soiled. On his feet were boots of coarse material, and giving no signs of having been blacked for a long time.

Since these were not the clothes in which Poe had left Richmond, his own apparel must have been stolen from him somewhere en route. Oddly enough, although unconscious by the time Snodgrass reached him, he was still clutching Dr. Carter's valuable sword-cane in his hand.

A carriage was called, and the dying poet was taken to the Washington College Hospital, where young Dr. J. J. Moran took him in charge. In a letter written to Mrs. Clemm about five weeks later, Moran describes the circumstances of Poe's death:

> When brought to the Hospital he was unconscious of his condition—who brought him or with whom he had been associating. He remained in this condition from 5. Ock. [sic] in the afternoon—the hour of his admission—until 3 next morning. This was on the 3rd Oct.
> To this state succeeded tremor of the limbs, and at first a busy, but not violent or active delirium—constant talking—and vacant converse with spectral and imaginary objects on

the walls. His face was pale and his whole person drenched in perspiration—We were unable to induce tranquility before the second day after his admission.

Having left orders with the nurses to that effect, I was summoned to his bedside so soon as conscious[ness] supervened, and questioned him in reference to his family—place of residence—relatives &c. But his answers were incoherent & unsatisfactory. He told me, however, he had a wife in Richmond (which, I have since learned was not the fact) that he did not know when he left that city or what had become of his trunk of clothing. Wishing to rally and sustain his now fast sinking hopes, I told him I hoped that in a few days he would be able to enjoy the society of his friends here, and I would be most happy to contribute in every possible way to his ease & comfort. At this he broke out with much energy, and said the best thing his best friend could do would be to blow out his brains with a pistol—that when he beheld his degradation he was ready to sink in the earth &c." Shortly after giving expression to these words Mr. Poe seemed to dose & I left him for a short time. When I returned I found him in a violent delirium, resisting the efforts of two nurses to keep him in bed. This state continued until Saturday evening (he was admitted on Wednesday) when he commenced calling for one "Reynolds," which he did through the night up to *three* on Sunday morning. At this time a very decided change began to affect him. Having become enfeebled from exertion he became quiet and seemed to rest for a short time, then gently moving his head he said "Lord help my poor Soul" and expired!

Some of Poe's relatives, who had been summoned to the hospital while he was still alive, but who had not been allowed to see him because of his condition, made arrangements for the funeral. He was buried the day after he died, at four o'clock on a rainy afternoon, when a single carriage followed his hearse to the First Presbyterian Church at Greene and Fayette Streets, where he was buried among the graves of his ancestors.

The local newspapers took little note of his death and none at all of his funeral. But two days after he died his self-appointed literary executor, Rufus Wilmot Griswold, with whom Poe had often quarreled, wrote a damaging obituary notice for the influential *New York Tribune*. This was widely reprinted, and it set the tone for the moralistic attitude with which Poe's Victorian contemporaries long continued to regard him.

These are the known facts in the case of Edgar Allan Poe. If he had been picked up dead, an inquest would have been held, but because he was alive when found, no official investigation was made. His friends and relatives followed up the case in a superficial way and then dropped it. Perhaps they were afraid of turning up more scandal, of bringing to light more unsavory incidents. There had already been enough. . . . Better to let the dead poet lie forgotten in the grave he had been unconsciously striving toward all his life.

The identification of the mysterious Reynolds, for whom the dying Poe kept calling, has always puzzled Poe's biographers. James A. Harrison, in his *Life and Letters of Edgar Allan Poe,* published in 1902, first brought forth the ingenious theory that it may have been J. N. Reynolds, an authority on South Sea exploration whose knowledge of the Pacific area was used as source material for the "Narrative of Arthur Gordon Pym," which Poe had written thirteen years before. It has always seemed a far-fetched theory, but biographer after biographer since Harrison has solemnly repeated it. The probable truth lies much nearer home. The names of the election judges at Ryan's Fourth Ward Polls that day were Richard Lilly, E. G. Starr, and—Henry R. Reynolds! It may have been to this Reynolds, who must have been a person of some standing to qualify as an election judge, that Poe made his last appeal for help. And since all sense of time vanishes in moments of delirium, Poe may still have been pleading with the shadowy election judge as death closed in. Some feeble remnant of the urge to live was probably stirring within him, trying to call him back to life. But he had reached his Samarra, where Death was waiting to collect his due, and there was no turning back.

The disaster that had always dogged Poe's footsteps did not end with his death. When Griswold edited his works and issued them in four large volumes, he included a biographical memoir which was even more damaging than the original obituary article he had written two days after Poe's death. Nor was Griswold content simply to rest his case on the facts; he vengefully falsified and even forged some of Poe's letters in order to do all the harm he could.

Meanwhile, the dead poet continued to lie in his unmarked grave. In 1855 Mrs. Clemm threatened to have his body moved to Greenwood Cemetery, Brooklyn, where friends had promised to erect a suitable monument. Nothing came of this, but in 1860, Poe's second cousin, Neilson Poe, ordered a tombstone made. A few days before it was to be put in place, a train ran off the track and plowed into the monument yard where the stone was standing. Other tombstones in the yard were damaged, but Poe's was the only one to be completely destroyed. The family made no effort to replace it, and years passed before another attempt was made to mark the grave. Then, in 1875, a group of Baltimore schoolteachers raised enough money to purchase an imposing marble monument. When Poe's body was exhumed that year for removal to the new site, the Baltimore *Evening News* printed an appropriately Poesque account of the opening of his grave.

> The coffin "was partially broken in at the sides, and the lid near the head was so much decayed that it fell in pieces to the ground. On looking through the aperture thus created . . . the *News* man beheld the skeleton of Poe. The flesh and funeral robes of course had crumbled into dust, and there was nothing left but the bare bones and a few clumps of hair attached to the skull, to tell that a body had once been there. The skeleton was in perfect condition, the arms lying as they were arranged in death, and the back and leg bones were in a natural position. The ribs had fallen out, but lay in order on either side of the coffin, and the skull had not moved in the least from its proper place. The teeth of the upper jaw must have been shaken out in the lifting of the coffin, for they lay scattered about the skull, but those of the lower jaw, which had fallen down from the rest of the "face," were perfect, not one being missing from either side. The teeth looked pearly white, and were in excellent preservation.

Mrs. Clemm had died in poverty in 1871 at the same hospital in which Poe had spent his last days. Her body was now dug up to be placed alongside her son-in-law's. An elaborate dedication ceremony was held on November 17, to which leading American and British poets were invited, but Walt Whitman was the only one who came. William Cullen Bryant sent a letter disapproving of the whole affair, saying that "there should be some decided element of goodness in the character of those to whose example a public monument directs the attention of the world." Nevertheless, the dedication of Poe's tombstone received far wider attention in the newspapers than his death had. His reputation was growing, and the press could no longer ignore him.

Virginia had been buried in Fordham in a vault owned by strangers. When this was torn down the same year her husband's monument was dedicated no one seemed to have thought of sending her remains to Baltimore to rest with his. Poe's early biographer,

William F. Gill, rescued her bones and kept them in a cardboard box under his bed for ten years, after which they were finally interred under the Baltimore monument.

There the unhappy little family still rests in the ancient burial grounds, where the dead of the early city lie under massive granite and marble monuments provided with gutters to keep off the rain water that ceaselessly gnaws away at the crumbling stone.

WHERE THE SONG BEGINS

by Oscar Hammerstein II

Which comes first, the words or the music? The fabulously success-ful co-author of such hit musicals as Oklahoma! *and* South Pacific *tells how he and Richard Rodgers write their popular show-stoppers.*

DECEMBER 8, 1949

IT TOOK ME YEARS to learn that I did not play the piano very well. I so enjoyed my own playing. I tackled everything—Victor Herbert, Verdi, Leoncavallo, George Cohan. What expression I could put into their music! What exaltation I felt! My mother thought I had "a lovely touch," she told her friends. But when I became fifteen or sixteen my own friends began to express less sympathetic reactions, and it became clear to me that they were not hearing the same music I thought I was hearing when I played. Remembering this illuminating and disturbing experience, I have misgivings right now as I embark on a discussion of lyrics. I am going to love it, but will you? The hunter gloats reminiscently over the last saber-toothed tiger he has brought back alive. So does the songwriter like to tell of how he has captured a refrain and imprisoned it safely behind thirty-two bars. Both are likely to overrate the spare time of their audience.

Almost every layman I have ever met exhibits a real curiosity about songs and how they are written. It is a standing joke among authors and composers that when they meet people the first question asked of them is "Which comes first, the words or the music?" Perhaps it is high time that one of us stopped laughing at the classic query and provided a sensible answer to it. There is nothing foolish about the question. A song is a wedding of two crafts, and it is a natural thing to wonder how they meet and live together.

There is, as a matter of fact, no invariable or inevitable method for writing songs. Sometimes the words are written first, sometimes the music. Sometimes two or more collaborators lock themselves in a room and write words and music at the same time. The kind of songs, the individuals involved, and the conditions under which they work dictate the process. Grand-opera scores are almost always set to texts already written by the librettists. In the case of the most famous of all comic-opera collaborations, it was the librettist, Gilbert, who wrote the words first. He would sometimes mail an entire act to Sullivan, who would then set music to his verses. On the other hand, the lyrics for most of the popular songs and musical comedies in our country today are written after the music. Up until my first collaboration with Richard Rodgers in 1943, I had always written this way. For twenty-five years, collaborating with Jerome Kern, Herbert Stothart, Sigmund Romberg, Rudolf Friml, and Vincent Youmans, I set words to their music. It would seem to most people —and I am one of them—that writing the words first would be a more logical procedure, music being the more flexible and less specific of the two mediums. Why then did I write in this upside-down manner for so long a time?

In the first decade of this century there were two factors which led songwriters into the custom of writing words to music. The best musical plays of that time were being created in Vienna. When they were imported, American librettists had to write translations and adaptations for melodies that had been set to another language. In those days we imported not only plays from Middle Europe, but many of the composers themselves came over here, settled down, and became American citizens. They embraced our democratic philosophy, but they found it much more difficult to get used to our language. Lyric writers who submitted verses to be set were horrified by the abortive accents written to their words, and they soon found it less trying on their nerves to let the foreign musician have his say first and then write a lyric to fit his melody.

The second influence was not foreign at all. It was distinctly an American one—the broken rhythm. First came ragtime, then jazz. For the purpose of creating these eccentric deviations from orthodox meters, it was better to let the composer have his head. Concomitant with the creation of these new rhythms came what we called, in 1911, "the dance craze." Dancing, once confined to ballrooms and performed mainly by the young, became a new international sport indulged in by all people of all ages in all kinds of restaurants and at all meal times, lunch, tea, dinner, and supper. The hit melodies of that time had to be good dance melodies. This being the most important consideration, it was better for the lyric writer to trail along after the composer and fit his words to a refrain written mainly to be danced to. Many lyrics of the period were about dancing. Irving Berlin wrote "Everybody's Doing It." (Doing what? The turkey trot!)

People were also, in other songs, doing the bunny hug and the grizzly bear. Not satisfied with writing lyrics describing dances already established by leading teachers and famous dancing teams, lyric writers set to work creating dances, giving them names, and hoping that the public would follow them.

I have conducted no exhaustive investigation of this subject, but these developments, as I remember them, seem to have been the chief influences which established the American songwriter's habit of writing the music first and the words later. It is a strange habit, an illogical one, but not entirely without compensating virtues. Writing in this way, I have frequently fallen into the debt of my composers for words and ideas that might never have occurred to me had they not been suggested by music. If one has a feeling for music—and anyone who wants to write lyrics had better have this feeling—the repeated playing of a melody may create a mood or start a train of thought that results in an unusual lyric. Words written in this way are likely to conform to the spirit of the music. It is difficult to fit words into the rigid framework of a composer's meter, but this very confinement might also force an author into the concise eloquence which is the very essence of poetry. There is in all art a fine balance between the benefits of confinement and the benefits of freedom. An artist who is too fond of freedom is likely to be obscure in his expression. One who is too much a slave to form is likely to cripple his substance. Both extremes should be avoided, and no invariable laws or methods should be obeyed. In our collaboration Mr. Rodgers and I have no definite policy except one of complete flexibility. We write songs in whatever way seems best for the subject with which we are dealing and the purposes of the song in the story which we are telling. Most often I write the words first, and yet in nearly all of our scores there are at least one or two songs in which he wrote the music first. When we first started to write together in 1943 we had no conversations on method. The first song we wrote was "Oh, What a Beautiful Mornin'," and the words were written first. I would like to tell you how this happened, because it furnishes a typical illustration of composer-author collaboration in the structure of a musical play.

Attacking the job of turning Lynn Riggs's *Green Grow the Lilacs* into what eventually became *Oklahoma!* the first serious problem that faced us involved a conflict of dramaturgy with showmanship. As we planned our version, the story we had to tell in the first part of the first act did not call for the use of a female ensemble. The traditions of musical comedy, however, demand that not too long after the rise of the curtain the audience should be treated to one of musical comedy's most attractive assets—the sight of pretty girls in pretty clothes moving about the stage, the sound of their vital young voices supporting the principals in their songs. Dick and I, for several days, sought ways and means of logically introducing a group of girls into the early action of the play. The boys were no problem. Here was a farm in Oklahoma with ranches nearby. Farmers and cowboys belonged there, but girls in groups? No. Strawberry festivals? Quilting parties? Corny devices! After trying everything we could think of, and rejecting each other's ideas as fast as they were submitted, after passing through phases during which we would stare silently at each other unable to think of anything at all, we came finally to an extraordinary decision. We agreed to start our story in the real and natural way in which it seemed to want to be told! This decision meant that the first act would be half over before a female chorus would make its entrance. We realized that such a course was experimental, amounting almost to the breach of an implied contract with a musical-comedy audience. I cannot say truthfully that we were worried by the risk. Once we had made the decision everything seemed to work right and we had that inner confidence people feel when they have adopted the direct and honest approach to a problem.

Now, having met our difficulty by simply refusing to recognize its existence, we were ready to go ahead with the actual writing. We had agreed that we should start the play outside a farmhouse. The only character on the stage would be a middle-aged woman sitting at a butter churn. The voice of Curley, a cowboy, would be heard off-stage, singing. Searching for a subject for Curley to sing about, I recalled how deeply I had been impressed by Lynn Riggs's description at the start of his play:

> It is a radiant summer morning several years ago. The kind of morning which, enveloping the shapes of earth—men, cattle in the meadow, blades of the young corn, streams—makes them seem to exist now for the first time, their images giving off a visible golden emanation that is partly true and partly a trick of imagination, focusing to keep alive a loveliness that may pass away.

On first reading these words I had thought what a pity it was to waste them on stage directions. Only readers could enjoy them. An audience would never hear them. Yet, if they did, how quickly they would slip into the mood of the story. Remembering this reaction, I reread the description and determined to put it into song. "Oh, What a Beautiful Mornin'" opens the play and creates an atmosphere of relaxation and peace and tenderness. It introduces the lighthearted young man who is the center of the story. My indebtedness to Mr. Riggs's description is obvious. The cattle and the corn and the golden haze on the meadow are all there. I added some observations of my own based on my experience with beautiful mornings, and I brought the words down to the more primitive poetic level of Curley's character. He is, after all, just a cowboy and not a playwright.

Let us take a case where the music was written first. The refrain of "People Will Say We're in Love" was a melody written by Richard Rodgers with the thought that it might serve well as a duet for the two lovers in *Oklahoma!* This procedure is the more usual approach to writing musical-comedy scores. The composer dreams up some melodies which suggest certain treatments. One might seem to him to be the love duet of the piece, the other a good comedy song or a good tune to dance to. Almost all composers have a reservoir of melodies which come to them at different times and which they write down in what they call a sketchbook. When they start work on a new musical play, they play over these previously written melodies for their collaborator, and it is decided which ones can be used in this particular score. They then write additional melodies as required. Dick Rodgers, however, does not work in this way. He writes music only for a specific purpose. Ideas for tunes seldom come to him while he is walking down the street or riding in taxicabs, and he doesn't rush to his piano very often to write a tune just for the sake of writing a tune. I don't believe that either Dick or I would be very successful essentially as popular songwriters—writers of songs detached from plays. We can write words and music best when they are required by a situation or a characterization in a story.

In all I have been saying, it will be noted that the composer and author work in very close collaboration during the planning of a song and the story that contains the song. This is an important point. It must be understood that the musician is just as much an author as the man who writes the words. He expresses the story in his medium just as the librettist expresses the story in his. Or, more accurately, they weld their two crafts and two kinds of talent into a single expression. This is the great secret of the well-integrated musical play. It is not so much a method as a state of mind, or rather a state for two minds, an attitude of unity. Musical plays, then, are not "books" written by an author with songs later inserted by a composer and a lyric writer. They are often written this way, but it is not a good way to write them and such plays seldom have a very long life. They are sure to lack form, and they cannot sustain a story interest when it is interrupted continually by songs that are of little value to the plot.

Let me say a few words now about the actual writing of lyrics once the subject matter of the song has been determined, and once it has been placed in its proper spot in the telling of the story. I am often asked if I use a rhyming dictionary. I do. I find it a great help and a time-saver. The one I like best is Loring's *Rhymer's Lexicon.* A rhyming dictionary, however, should be used as a supplement to one's own ingenuity, and not a substitute for it. I do not open mine until I have exhausted my own memory and invention of rhymes for a word. Attractive combinations of words to make double and triple rhymes are not found in rhyming dictionaries, nor are modern words or colloquialisms which can be used with humorous effect in a song. A rhyming dictionary is of little use and may, in fact, be a handicap when one is writing a song which makes a feature of rhyming. If you would achieve the rhyming grace and facility of W. S. Gilbert or Lorenz Hart, my advice would be never to open a rhyming dictionary. Don't even own one. While I, on occasion, place a timid, encroaching foot on the territory of these two masters, I never carry my invasion very far. I would not stand a chance with either of them in the field of brilliant light verse. I admire them and envy them their fluidity and humor, but I refuse to compete with them. Aside from my shortcomings as a wit and rhymester—or, perhaps, because of them—my inclinations lead me to a more primitive type of lyric. The longer I write, the more interested I become in expressing my own true convictions and feelings in the songs I write. When I was very much younger I thought that if ever I made all the money I needed out of writing musical comedy I would then sit back and turn to straight dramatic plays in which I could say whatever I wanted to say and state my reactions to the world I live in. Later on, however, I became convinced that whatever I wanted to say could be said in songs, that I was not confined necessarily to trite or light subjects, and that since my talent and training in the writing of lyrics is far beyond my attainments in other fields of writing, I had better use this medium.

If one has fundamental things to say in a song, the rhyming becomes a question of deft balancing. A rhyme should be unassertive, never standing out too noticeably. It should, on the other hand, not be a rhyme heard in a hundred other popular songs of the time, so familiar that the listener can anticipate it before it is sung. There should not be too many rhymes. In fact, a rhyme should appear only where it is absolutely demanded to keep the pattern of the music. If a listener is made rhyme-conscious, his interest may be diverted from the story of the song. If, on the other hand, you keep him waiting for a rhyme, he is more likely to listen to the meaning of the words.

After rhyming, I would place next in importance a study and appreciation of phonetics. Some words and groups of words that look beautiful in printed poetry are unavailable to one who is writing lyrics to be sung to music. There is an inexorable mathematics in music—so many measures in a refrain, so many beats in a measure, and they cannot be ignored. There is rhythm and tempo, and its continuity must be unbroken. The concessions with which a melody can favor words are limited. The larynxes of singers are limited. They must be given a chance to breathe after a certain number of words have been sung, and if they are building up to a high note at the finish, they must be given a good deep breath before they attack it. Both the lyric writer and the composer must worry about all these things. If a song is not singable, it is no song at all.

Lest at any point I seem to be laying down rigid rules, let me acknowledge quickly that there are no such things in my craft. Some of our most successful compositions stray far beyond the narrow borders that restrict the well-made refrain. "Star Dust" rambles and roams like a truant schoolboy in a meadow. Its structure is loose, its pattern complex. Yet it has attained the kind of long-lived popularity that few songs can claim. What has it got? I'm not certain. I know only that it is beautiful and I like to hear it. It is a mood-creating song. It has repose and wistfulness. It is something very special, all by itself. Anyone who tried to imitate it would be a fool.

"Begin the Beguine" is another rule-breaker—too long! It is what is known among professional songwriters as "a tape worm." It hasn't the cohesive and compact continuity of a popular song. But it is popular and has been for about twenty years. That's *very* popular. This is an "atmospheric" song. It transports you to places where palm trees wave across yellow moons and Spanish is spoken, which is exactly what Cole Porter wants it to do to you.

Songs like these, ignoring the orthodox principles, are freaks and anomalies. One doesn't learn much from anomalies. Common-sense solutions to normal problems are the first things to master. One very fundamental problem is the special use of certain words in songs. Some words, for instance, have lost their value through overuse. "Divine" is such a word. It occurs in "All the Things You Are." I didn't like this word when I submitted the song to Jerry Kern and, as I had anticipated, he didn't like it either. For many days I worked trying to find a substitute. I just couldn't. The last lines are: "Some day I'll know that moment divine, When all the things you are, are mine." I was trapped. "All the things you are," referred to poetically and romantically throughout the song, are certainly what I wish to be "mine." I could not surrender this finish. But it demands an "ine" rhyme. "Some day I'll know that moment . . ." What? Sign, line, fine, shine? Nothing served as well as the unwanted "divine." I never could find a way out. The song written in 1937 shows signs of being a long-lived standard ballad—but I shall never be happy with that word!

Rhyming, phonetics, semantics—all very important. But technique and professional polish do not make a song. They improve it and their absence might ruin it, but there is an element much less tangible that is the deciding factor in a song's life. One evening last summer I was on Arthur Godfrey's television program. He told me that he was continually besieged by young songwriters. He said that almost everyone seemed to have written his one song and wanted to find out how to get it before the public. I told Arthur that I'd had an entirely different experience. Most young songwriters or amateur songwriters of all ages who have approached me have told me that they had at least forty songs—sometimes 400 songs. Most of them make the point that they can rattle them off very quickly, one a day or as many as anyone would wish. "Songs just come to me," many people tell me. If I met a man with just one song, I would be more interested in him. I believe that anyone who stated sincerely what was deep in his heart could not only write a song, but could quickly get it published because it would be sure to be a good song. What actually happens in the case of practically all amateur writers is that they are imitating other men's songs. They are being, or trying to be, Irving Berlin or Cole Porter, or they are trying to imitate some of the songs currently on The Hit Parade. My observation about amateurs is that they are money-mad. The successful professional loves songs and loves songwriting. The amateurs want some quick money and think that songwriting is an easy way to get it. They want to believe that the main trick is to get to know some publisher, or a bandleader, or someone who will exploit their manuscript. But they don't spend enough time on each manuscript. They submit songs in their first draft. They don't go over them painstakingly as professional writers do, and they don't in the first instance dig it up out of their own brains and hearts.

The most important ingredient of a good song is sincerity. Let the song be yours and yours alone. However important, however trivial, believe it. Mean it from the bottom of your heart, and say what is on your mind as carefully, as clearly, as beautifully as you can. Show it to no one until you are certain that you cannot make one change that would improve it. After that, however, be willing to make improvements if someone can convince you that they are needed.

This sounds like simple advice, but no one knows better than I how hard it is to follow. The basic rules are always the hardest ones to observe, even though they seem the easiest. No beginner on the golf course or the tennis courts questions the good sense of his first lesson when he is told to keep his eye on the ball. This seems such an obvious thing to do, and yet no matter how many years you play these games your chief mistake remains taking your eye off the ball. This tendency to skip over the fundamental things and grasp the superficial is the tragedy of man's history from the beginning of time. I do not, therefore, place undue blame on misguided song-writers. They are merely keeping up the tradition of the stupidity of the human race when, instead of writing what they honestly feel, they invent fancy rhymes and foolish jokes and tricky titles and imitative phrases and lines that merely "fill in." I do not blame them if they spend their days trying to get to know someone who knows someone who is the brother-in-law of a publisher. I am just saying that all these things are a waste of time without a good manuscript. Get the right words and the right notes down on paper and, in some way, your song will reach the public. Publishers are looking for good songs. They often make mistakes and reject good ones and accept bad ones, but I do not believe that all the publishers will ever reject a really good song. Somebody will appreciate its quality. If a publisher doesn't, some record company will. The people who claim that the publishing and songwriting game is a tight ring into which beginners are not permitted are usually people with carelessly written manuscripts in their briefcases. The men who write the good songs haven't time for all this kind of talk. They are too busy writing and loving what they write before they show it to anybody else.

If I seem unfairly severe on the amateur songwriter, the source of my intolerance is my own history. When I first began writing I, too, made all these same mistakes, and I am frantically anxious to prevent others from making them. I used to write songs very quickly. A Long Island commuter, I prided myself that I could often write a refrain on one trip into New York, and the verse on the way back that night. Not many of these were good songs. I was too easily satisfied with my work. I was too often trying to emulate older and better lyric writers, saying things similar to the things they were saying. It would have been all right had I been content to imitate the forms of their songs, but the substance should have been mine and it was not. I know that insincerity held me back for several years, and I know that even after I'd had a period of success, it again handicapped me and caused me to have failures. Loathing all dishonest and sloppy work for the sorrows it has caused me, I loathe it in others as I would any poison, and if I can knock it out of anyone, I will.

WHAT DOES IT TAKE TO ENJOY A POEM?

by John Ciardi

The poetry editor of SR *discusses the difference between good and bad poetry—and offers some interesting clues for fuller appreciation of good poetry.*

DECEMBER 10, 1949

WHAT DOES IT TAKE to enjoy a poem?

Let us begin with a really difficult piece of symbolism:

> Hickory, dickory, dock,
> The mouse ran up the clock.
> The clock struck one,
> The mouse ran down,
> Hickory, dickory, dock.

Not really complicated you say? Consider these questions: What does it mean? Why a clock? Why a mouse? Isn't it fairly unusual for mice to run up clocks? What is the point of inventing this esoteric incident? And since the mouse ran up it and down again, the chances are it's a grandfather clock. What does that signify? And isn't it a fairly obsolete notion? Why did the clock strike one? (To rhyme with "down"? But is "down" a rhyme for "one," or is this another slovenly piece of modernism? Why didn't the poem make the clock strike three and the mouse turn to flee? It didn't, of course, but why?) What is the origin and significance of all these unexplained symbols? (A symbol is something that stands for something else. What is the something else?) Or is this simply nonsense verse? (I find that hard to believe.) And even as nonsense, what is there in this particular combination of sounds and actions (symbolic actions?) that makes this jingle survive a long word-of-mouth transmission in the English voice-box? Why mightn't the poem as easily have read:

> Thickery, thackery, tea,
> An owl flew into the tree.
> The tree's down,
> The owl's flown,
> Thickery, thackery, tea.

I submit: (a) that my parody is a bad poem, that the original is a good one, and that a serious and learned series of lectures might be devoted to the reasons why each is so; (b) that none of the questions I have raised are meaningless and that in fact many critics have made a career of asking this sort of question of less perfect poems, and (c) that neither you nor I know what the poem "means." I further submit that such considerations have frightened many readers away from good poems.

But—and this is the point—the child in whose babble the poem is immediate and alive has no critical theories and no troubles. He is too busy enjoying the pleasures of poetry. The moral is obvious: do not ask the poem to be more rational than you are. The way to read a poem is with pleasure: with the child's pleasure in tasting the syllables on his tongue, with the marvel of the child's eye that can really see the mouse run up the clock, be panic-stricken, and run down again, with the child's handclapping, rhythmic joy. In short, to read a poem, come prepared for delight.

But if a child can do it why can't you?

That question deserves attention, but before considering it, I should like to say one thing of which I am fairly certain: everyone writes poetry sometime in his life. Bad poetry is what we all have in common. Such poetry generally occurs in three categories: as invective, as obscenity, and as love-yelps.

The obscenity I assume everyone to be capable of documenting. Here is an example of invective:

> *Billy Billy, dirty coat*
> *Stinks like a nanny goat.*

And here is a fair example of the love-yelp:

> *Have you ever been in love?*
> *I ask you: have you ever been in love?*
> *Have you?*
>
> *I have . . . I know!*

"Billy Billy," you will recognize as a kind of "Georgie-Porgie puddin' and pie," but if you think it peculiar to your childhood or to grandfather's I urge you to look in the encyclopedia under *Fescennine* for an inkling of the antiquity of man's pleasure in jingling taunts at other men. "Billy Billy," as nearly as I know, was composed in our fourth-grade schoolyard by a former young poet now in the coal business and was used to taunt our local sloven, who has since washed up, cleaned up, grown up, and joined the police force. Almost inevitably it earned its young author a punch in the nose: a fair example of the way criticism operates in our society to kill the poetic impulse. The love-yelp, a reasonably deplorable specimen of its class, was submitted for the Tufts College literary magazine when I was an undergraduate assistant editor. Anyone who will take the trouble to be reasonably honest can almost certainly summon from himself examples of at least one of these forms he has attempted at one time or another, and enjoyed attempting.

If, then, the impulse to bad poetry is so widespread (though I insist that "Billy Billy" is not at all bad), why is it so few people enjoy reading what passes as good poetry? Why is it, for example, that in a nation of 146 million presumably literate people, the average sale for a book of poems is about 500 copies? Is it that the pleasures and outlets one finds in composing are purely private—that only one's own creation, good or bad, is interesting? Considering the variety of egos which has banded together to pass as the human race, that seems one reasonably good guess, but there is obviously more to it that is worth some speculation:

First, it seems fairly obvious that the process of growing up in a nuts-and-bolts world inhibits the poetry impulse in most people. Somewhere along the line, they learn to say, "Let's face it; we must be practical." Dickens' School of Hard Facts is with us all, and poetry, like poor Sissy Jupe, is still required to blush because it cannot define a horse as "Quadruped. Gramnivorous. Forty teeth, namely twenty-four grinders, four eye-teeth, and twelve incisive." So the literalist on his rostrum demands the rational: "What *does* hickory-dickory-dock *mean?* It *has* to mean *something.*" It does indeed, but not anything you can paraphrase, not anything you can prove. It means only what every child knows—delight. And delight is not a function of the rational mind. As Archibald MacLeish has written, "A poem must not mean, but be." Whereby, of course, it does mean, but not nuts and bolts. To see what it does mean, you need only go read Mother Goose to a child: you will then be observing a natural audience busy with the process of receiving poetry as it was intended to be received.

Point one, then, is delight: if you mean to enjoy the poem as a poem, stop cross-examining it, stop trying to force it to "make sense." The poem *is* sense. Or if you must cross-examine remember at least that the third degree is not the poem. Most poems do reveal themselves most richly after close examination, but the examination is, at best, only a preparation for reading the poem. It is never the reading itself.

More precisely put, an understanding of the rational surfaces of the poem (the prose part of the poem) may, in some cases, point a direction toward the poem. The poem is never experienced, however, until it is felt in the same complex of mind and nerve from which it arose—the subconscious. That experience sometimes happens immediately, and is sometimes helped along by our conscious (rational) perceptions. But to substitute rational analysis for the larger contact of the subconscious is to reject the poem. The kind of communication that happens in a poem is infinitely closer to that of music than to that of prose.

Second, poetry must never be read as an exercise in "reading-speed," that deplorable mental-mangle for increasing the rate of destruction of textbook English. The fastest reader is not the best reader any more than the best conductor of Beethoven is the man who gets the orchestra through the *Eroica* in the shortest elapsed time. Why not take a stop watch to the Symphony, if this is your measure? Obviously because music declares its own pace. But so does good poetry. By rhyme, by the word-values of the poem, by the sequence of syllables, and by all these taken together, good poetry contains its own notation. "We broke the brittle bright stubble like chaff" can no more be read at the same rate as "Bury the great duke with an Empire's lamentation" than *allegro vivace* can intelligently be played *adagio*.

Point two, then: leave your efficiency out of this and look for the notation within the poem. Every poem is in part an effort to reconstruct the poet's speaking voice. Listen for it. Listen to the poet on records and at public readings (but know the poems well before you do). You may discover more than you could have foreseen. In any case when reading a book of poems you must be prepared to linger. That thin volume will take at least as much reading as a detective story.

Third (and of course related to our second consideration): read it aloud. Few poems will come whole at one hearing. Few piano pieces will. But once you have *learned* either, their pleasure is always ready to repeat itself. Even difficult poems are meant to go into the voice-box. Put them there.

Fourth: there are still readers who must be specifically cautioned that twentieth-century poetry is not nineteenth-century poetry. That fact may seem rather obvious, but the point is not frivolously made. Your teachers and mine were products of nineteenth-century culture, and almost certainly the first poems you were given to read were nineteenth-century poems. I hasten to add that the nineteenth century was a great literary achievement, but it began with one dreadful flaw: it tended to take itself much too seriously. The mind of man seemed to suffer the illusion that it lived in a cathedral, and when man spoke he was not only too likely to pontificate, but he was pre-inclined to select from experience only the vast, the lofty, the divine-in-nature. The result was what Cleanth Brooks has called "the poetry of high-seriousness." Opposed to that tradition is the poetry of "wit," poetry in which the mind most definitely does not live in a cathedral but in the total world, open to the encounter of all sorts of diverse elements and prepared to take them as they come, fusing fleas and sunsets, love and charley-horses, beauty and trivia into what is conceived to be a more inclusive range of human experience. Judge the poet of "wit" by the standards of "high-seriousness" and he will likely appear crass and obnoxious; judge the poet of high-seriousness by the standards of wit and he will likely appear a rather pompous and myopic ass.

The point, then, is quite simple: judge the poet by his intent: if you tend to the illusion that you are on your way to church when you pick up a poem, stop off at the supermarket and watch man against his background of groceries for a while. The church is still next door, and I am quite sure that one of the things "modern" (whatever that is) poetry is trying to say, is that the cities of our life contain both church-spires and Wheaties, and that both of them, for better or worse, impinge upon man's consciousness, and are therefore the material of poetry.

A fifth consideration I can best present by asking a question: how do you, reader, distinguish between your responses to a very bad portrait of dear old Aunt Jane, and a very good one of Old Skinflint, the gentleman who holds your mortgage? The question is one that splits the reading audience straight down the middle: The tenacity with which the ladies of the poetry societies will hold on to Aunt Jane with a bluebird in her hair, and the persistency with which they reject all-that-is-not-bluebirds, reaches so far into the problem of a satisfactory approach to poetry (both reading and writing) that it has been necessary to evolve two terms: "poetry" for that which exists as an art form, "poesy" for that which exists as the sentimental bluebird in Aunt Jane's hair. Confusion is inevitable when these terms are not properly applied. The writers and readers of poesy always refer to their matter as poetry or true poetry, and defend it with as much violence as possible from "the ugly." Here is a piece of poesy—a sonnet of course:

THRENODY

Truth is a golden sunset far away
Above the misty hills. Its burning eye
Lights all the fading world. A bird flies by
Alive and singing on the dying day.
Oh mystic world, what shall the proud heart say
When beauty flies on beauty beautifully
While blue-gold hills look down to watch it die
Into the falling miracle of clay?

Say: "I have seen the wing of sunset lift
Into the golden vision of the hills
And truth come flooding proud through the cloud rift,
And known that souls survive their mortal ills."
Say: "Having seen such beauty in the air
I have seen truth and will no more despair."

This is a fair example of what I have learned to call "prop-room poesy." It fills the stage as a poem might, but it fills it with pieces discarded from other poems and left to gather dust in the prop room of tradition. It makes a stage of the stage, and brings the stage's own dust on as the play, rather than bring on the life outside the theater.

The result may look like a poem, but is really no more than a collection of poetic junk. For example: "golden sunsets far away" (question: have you ever seen a non-golden one nearby?), "misty hills," "burning eye," "fading world," "a bird flies by alive and singing" (question: have you ever seen a non-live one fly by?), "dying day," "the proud heart." . . .

I have tried many times to explain to the enthusiasts of this school that any reasonably competent craftsman could concoct such a poem in a matter of minutes, and with his tongue in his cheek. I said exactly that from a public platform once and claimed I could turn out such an illusion-of-the-sonnet in three minutes flat. I was challenged and given a first line to start with, but I failed: I discovered it is impossible, simply mechanically, to write off fourteen lines in three minutes. It took four minutes and eighteen seconds. The "sonnet" I have quoted above was the poem produced in answer to that challenge, and by way of further experimentation I sent it off to a magazine for "traditional" poetry and had it accepted for publication. In a moment of cowardice I withdrew the poem for fear someone I respected might see my name attached to it. I was wrong, of course; no one whose poetic opinion I could respect would have been reading that magazine.

The fact remains beyond all persuasion, however, that the devotees of poesy are violent in their charges against Modern Poetry (their capitals) as ugly, coarse, immoral, and debased (their adjectives). My good friend Geraldine Udell, business manager of *Poetry, A Magazine of Verse,* the oldest magazine of good poetry in America, once showed me thirty-four letters received in one day's mail accusing the magazine of debasing the pure tradition of English poetry, and enclosing pages of poesy from two magazines of "traditional poetry" as specimens of what should be printed.

It is, you see, Aunt Jane and Old Skinflint with a vengeance. Poesy (which is always anti-poetry) wants it pretty. It wants comfortably worn-out props to which comfortable and vague reactions are already conditioned. Everyone understands the bluebird in Aunt Jane's hair; the response to it is by now so stereotyped that it will do for a birthday card. Poetry, on the contrary, insists on battering at life, and on making the poem capture the thing seen and felt in its own unique complex. It does not repeat, it creates. Therefore, some willingness to dismiss preconception from the reader's mind is necessary if one is to partake of that vital process. One is also required to get himself and his own loose-afflatus out of the way of the poem.

The fifth point then is simple: poesy is not poetry.

A sixth and related consideration follows almost immediately: it concerns the preconception that demands moral affirmation of oneself from a poem, just as poesy demands a loose emotional affirmation of oneself. Consistently adhered to, this application of one's own morality as a test of the poem can lead to ridiculous ends. It would require, for example, the rejection of Milton by all who do not agree with his theology. It might reject beforehand all poems containing the word harlot, since harlots are immoral, and by that test we should have to reject such great lines as Blake's

> *The harlot's cry from street to street*
> *Shall weave Old England's winding sheet.*

Or, shifted to political concern, it might require a new Communist manifesto against any poem in which the lover is rich in his love, since it is bourgeois, decadent, and just plain indecent to be rich.

Similarly, I have observed many present-day reviewers to reject a poem because it seems cheerful ("withdrawal from reality"), because it does not ("defeatist and negativist"), because it is immediately understandable ("facile and slight"), and because it requires rereading ("obscurantist"). These are cartoons, of course, but they are cartoons of a real trend. The simple fact is that none of us can hope to be wholly free of preconceptions of one sort or another. I must confess, for example, that I still find Milton's theology a bit silly, and that my feeling prevents me from experiencing *Paradise Lost* as richly as I might. Even Milton's language creates blocks for me that he could not have intended and for which I am solely responsible. For whatever reason, I cannot read of Satan mounted on his "bad eminence" without an impulse to smile. I don't know why I want to smile at such a phrase, but I am sure the reason is within me and that it has nothing to do with the poem. I am being blocked in this case by a pre-set subjective response. I must, therefore, recognize the obstruction and try to allow for it. Unless I can do so, I am not permitting the poet his right to his own kind of vision and existence.

Point six, then: the poem does not exist to confirm moral, political, or religious prejudgments. The poem as a poem is in fact amoral. The poem, I say, not the poet. The poet may be the most moral of men, but when he writes poetry he is performing a ritual dance. He may even sermonize, but if the poem is to succeed as a poem, it must be a dancing sermon. What the poem says is always hickory-dickory-dock, that ineffable, wonderful, everlasting dance of syllables that moves the mouse and winds the clock over and over again, and sends the child to sleep among the swinging nebulae. Or perhaps it is hickory-dickory-God, but still what the poem says is what the child dreams: "Look, Universe, I'm dancing." There is no immorality more wretched than the habit of mind which *will* insist on moralizing that dance.

The last necessity for good reading that I shall discuss here is tradition. If you will grant me the existence of an unintellectualized basis for poetry upon which the responses of all readers may meet, we can probably agree that a fair example of such a response may be found in, say, Juliet on her balcony swooning into moonlight at the sound of Romeo's song rising from the shrubbery. Hers is certainly a non-intellectualized response. It is certainly a living response. And a worldwide one: Black Jade in her moony garden in Peiping will respond in an almost identical way to Pao-yii's serenade from beyond the garden wall.

But wait: let us switch singers. Now Pao-yii is in Verona under Juliet's balcony, and Romeo is in Peiping outside Black Jade's garden. Both strike up a song. Why is it that both girls now hear not a swooning love-cry but something closer to the sound of sustained gargling? The answer is—Tradition.

For the fact is we are being educated when we know it least. We learn simply by the exposure of living, and what we learn most natively is the tradition in which we live. But the response acquired effortlessly within one tradition will not serve us in another, any more than speaking pure Tuscan will help us in Peiping.

In order to read poetry, then, one must read poetry. One may of course have read only bad poetry, and in that case he will read badly. The criterion Matthew Arnold set forth as "the touchstone method" may well be applied here. This critical theory states simply that all poetry is judged by great poetry. Poetry may be called great only when it has been acclaimed by so many generations of different poetical taste that its merit and universality are beyond dispute. The way to come to a poem, then, is with the memory of great singing in one's inner ear.

Greatness, however, can be a dangerous measure, for it immediately implies rendering a verdict. I for one cannot lose the belief that it is more important to experience the poem than to judge it. Certainly there is real pleasure to be had from poetry no one will ever consider great or near-great. Certainly, too, every mental action implies a kind of judgment. Nevertheless, it seems to me more desirable in every way for the reader to conceive of himself as a participant in the action of the poem, rather than as a trial judge pondering its claim to immortality.

Time, of course, will hand down that verdict, and in a way from which there is no appeal. It may then happen that the verdict will be against modern poets, and against the principles on which they write. But until that verdict has been achieved, it would be well to bear in mind that the reader is as liable to error as the poet, and that when the poem fails to communicate, the failure may as reasonably be charged against the one as against the other.

POETRY: 1949-1956

Some poems by the era's poets, ranging from Marianne Moore to John Ciardi, are here reprinted from the pages of SR.

BULWARKED AGAINST FATE

by Marianne Moore

MARCH 19, 1949

Affirmed. Pent by power that holds it fast—
a paradox. Pent. Hard pressed,
   you take the blame and are inviolate.
Abased at last;
   not the tempest-tossed.
Compressed, firmed by the thrust of the blast
   till compact, like a bulwark against fate;
   lead-saluted;
   saluted by lead?
As though flying Old Glory full-mast.

FOR AN ASSYRIAN FRIEZE

by Peter Viereck

MARCH 19, 1949

"I, the great king, the powerful king, king of the world, King of Assyria, the king whose path was a cyclone, whose battle was a flaming sea, I am powerful, all-powerful, exalted, almighty, majestic, all-important in power."—INSCRIPTION OF 670 B.C.

Sometimes a lion with a prophet's beard
Lopes from a bas-relief to stretch his claws.
His bestial eyes are wonderfully sad.

Then he grows wings, the terrible king grows wings,
And flies above the black Euphrates loam,
Hunting for enemies of Nineveh.

His names are Shamshi and Adádnirari,
Tiglath-Piléser, Assurbanipal,
And the first Sargon of Dur-Shárukin.

"The day my chariots stormed the town, I waxed
My beard with oil of rose and waterlily,
And freed nine pearl-caged nightingales, and built

A pillar of skulls so high it stabbed the sun."
(Was that the tomb's voice, or the desert-wind's?
Or ours?—what ghost is still our roaring priest?)

The scribes shall say: his will outflew his wisdom.
The saints shall say: his was the sin of pride.
The skulls say nothing. And the lizards grin.

This is the rapture that the Gentiles feared
When Joshua made music masterful.
Each sinew is a harp-string crouched to twang.

The treble of such bloodlust if he pounced
Would shriek an anti-social kind of beauty
Like parrots in a gypsy carnival.

Then back to stone. In stone he sleeps the least.
It's not with love his brooding glitters so.
Earth spawns no gangrene half so luminous

As the contagion of those molten eyes.

THE LOVERS

by Conrad Aiken

MARCH 19, 1949

This painful love dissect to the last shred:
abjure it, it will not be solved in bed:
agony of the senses, but compounded
of soul's dream, heart's wish, blood's will, all confounded
with hate, despair, mistrust, the fear of each
for what the other brings of alien speech:
self-love, my sweet, no farther goes than this,
that when we kiss it is ourselves we kiss.

O eyes no eyes but fountains filled with tears,
O heart no heart but cistern of the years—
how backward now to childhood's spring we thrust
there to uncover the green shoots of lust:
how forward then to the bare skull we look
to taste our passion dead in doomsday book!
Self-love is all we know, my love, and this
breeds all these worlds, then kills them, when we kiss.

Yet would I give, yet would you take, a time
where self-love were no criminal, no crime:
where the true godhead in each self discovers
how the self-lovers are both gods and lovers:
O love, of this wise love no word be said,
it will be solved in a diviner bed,
where the divine dance teaches self-love this,
that when we kiss it is a god we kiss.

THE DARK PEOPLE
by William Rose Benét

MARCH 19, 1949

They are the traveling tent-folk, here and gone
Like Buttadeus they have wandered far;
From the five-waters-land in the world dawn
Trailing through Egypt under a falling star;
Tsingani of Persia, nomads of the Nile,
Those of the dark blood known in Muscovy
With their wild music, voices cleansed of guile
Varying, blending a melodious glee
Strangely alluring; these the ocean-tossed,
Sailing the broad black water to the isles,
Vivid at English fairs, whose palms were crossed
With silver, those with daggers in their smiles,
At pub or course to toss the cannikin
Or whistle a piebald from a farmer's field,
Their tawny women to *pen dukkerin*
Or proffer shawls and trinkets well-concealed.
They are God's cuckoos tolling in the grove,
The chaffering roguish birds whose souls are free,
Such thieving ones as bark-brown dryads love,
Scattering the patteran of Romany;
The Petulengros, Lovells fabulous,
Coopers and Hernes, Stanleys and Scottish Faas;
Anselo, Ursula, Tawno, Pyramus,
By dingle fires, on beds beneath the stars.
The van, the grazing *gry*, the tinker's trade,
The sorcerized cat-gut whipping fiddle-chords;
Bees in the marigold, saints in masquerade,
Horse-tamers, Pharaonic overlords
As were no Pharaohs of red desert noon!
Sunset and sealine all about the earth
From Northern Lights to Mountains of the Moon
Have known their clatter, melody, and mirth.

These the Word Master kenned, the Romany *rye,*
The philologue (and poor philogynist!)
Who fought the Flaming Tinman, and made sigh
Tall golden Isopel he never kissed.

He knew them in all humors. Tan and van
Were open to him. Many a bird-peaked eye
Gleamed with the hope his greeting "Sarishan!"
Meant "parl o pani, av' kushto mir' akai!"*
Carew, the cozener, was once their king.
Among their fires trod Wortley Montagu.
Bulwer abode their tents with youth at spring.
Their Romany *jib* Leland and Kester knew;
For Cairo's Rhagarin, who cast the shell
Of auspice, kinned the Indiana *chai*.
Apray the rom! Cry on Boro Duvel,
Lord of the Road! The world is rolling by . . .

Leaves on the pale weir-water drift to shade;
Brown faces pass, white teeth and glittering smiles.
Now a great orange moon surmounts the glade
Lighting the *gorgio* to more dusty miles;
Yet still the Magyar music that can swell
Where singers to the marvelous czardas move
Borne to ethereal heights or howling hell,
Makes all the night vibrate with gypsy love . . .

Bear-wards from Syria pass; then Kingston Fair
With thimblerig and drums and shouts and flags,
Cocoanut-shies, baskets and foreign ware,
Seems all about the traveler. He lags,
He kneels beside a rill to gulp with thirst
The clear leaf-shadowed water. Still he sees
Hop-poles in Kent, races on Molesy Hurst,
The scarf of some yet young Meg Merrilies.
The dark men have enthralled him, and their maids
Whose bell-like voices call from van and tan.
The moors, the furze, the hills, the moonlit shades
Throb forest yearning of the wild tzigane.
Far down the road the Egyptian pantherine
Writes in the dust. Her golden earrings gleam.
Even where ocean foams upon the dene
He hears the chuckling of a woodland stream.
Gramarye of all nature fills his mind.
The wandering ones have cast the ancient spell.
Till many a long dark league be left behind
The man goes charm-struck, though the end be well.

---

* "Come over the waters, O love, wherever you are!"

THE TOWER

by Walter de la Mare

MAY 20, 1950

There were no flowers among the stones of the wilderness:
I was standing alone by the green glazed tower,
Where among the cypresses winds went wandering,
Tinged now with gold-dust in the evening hour.

What goddess lingered here no tablet unfolded;
Birds wild with beauty sang from ilex and yew;
Afar rose the chasms and glaciers of mountains,
The snow of their summits wax-wan in the blue—

In the blue of the heights of the heavenly vacancy—
My companions the silence, the relics, the lost;
And that speechless, divine, invisible influence,
Remote as the stars in the vague of the Past.

GRASS

by John Holmes

FEBRUARY 18, 1956

Mouth down in the timothy,
Belly flat, knees dug
Into the dark earth,
Tastes more birth than death.
World green and wet,
Not with tears, rides up.
All grass pushes up
Under no one, no I.
Here for the lying on is
Green grown wild and always.

Give up to the grass.
It forgives you wholly.

Where your father drowned,
After all the men
Before him, and women,
You not last in that line,
Flung and gone down
To the grassy underlands,
You wash in that green,
That grass in your hands.

THE WINESHADE ESSENCE

by Norma Farber

MAY 5, 1956

In the arbor of my childhood,
green morning my roofage,
deep grapes like a midnight
sombered the leafage.

In the arbor where my childhood
afternooned and thirsted
for liquorlumpy fruitage
shadow-treated, dusk-frosted,

where clusterfall midnight
splashed the slatted arbor,
I ate gross purplings,
I drank vine-vapor.

In that arbor-calm childhood
I cut green capers
toward king-colored bunches,
to royal high purpose.

In a yard with an arbor,
those reap-ready seasons,
I sucked along of childhood
the wineshade essence.

RAIN

by Rosalind Levine

MAY 5, 1956

On the coast of my choice there are two rainfalls,
One of them flowers; umbrellas of hibiscus
Fold on the evening bush of August at
The drop of a sun. There are four seasons,

All of them summer. And the jacaranda
Drips blue, dissolves into November drizzle.
Poppies river the earthquake hills at Christmas;
Watches stop in a confusion of love.

Being no native daughter, I can remember
Torrents of Maine as well, diminishing
To a whisper of pine needles on an abandoned
Island, a walking of birds across the shingles.

And electric storms: Among the ninepin Catskills
I memorized the cataracts of lightning,
The rush of banisters down a wide front stair.
Rain speaks out; it is the living word

For the indefinable sorrow. Paul Verlaine
Knew this and the small child clasping a bucket
Under the wash-lines. Do you know the rain
Of Nevada, ample drops, well-spaced, that splash

Yellow on pavement, drying as they fall
Like paint on canvas, on the Truckee, shimmering
With broken promises of platinum
And placer gold, on dusty tennis courts

And swings of Wingfield Park, blue-green of Tahoe,
Sometimes the cottonwood's palpitating leaves?

AN ECHO SONNET
To an Empty Page

by Robert Pack

JUNE 16, 1956

Voice:	Echo:
How from emptiness can I make a start?	Start
And starting, must I master joy or grief?	Grief
But is there consolation in the heart?	Art
Oh cold reprieve, where's natural relief?	Leaf
Leaf blooms, burns red before delighted eyes.	Dies
Here beauty makes of dying, ecstasy.	See
Yet what's the end of our life's long disease?	Ease
If death is not, who is my enemy?	Me
Then are you glad that I must end in sleep?	Leap
I'd leap into the dark if dark were true.	True
And in that night would you rejoice or weep?	Weep
What contradiction makes you take this view?	You
I feel your calling leads me where I go.	Go
But whether happiness is there, you know.	No

FRIDAY SO SOON

by Winfield Townley Scott

AUGUST 4, 1956

There were many people on the island
Though, looking back at it now, it seems we were
Married with exile; we were allowed
The customary two weeks; the first
Floated like a slowed dream, like those boats
Windless and weightless and mirrored
Within folded lusters of air. The sea—
It is strange how at once on the island
You forget sea as the way of travel: others'
Continual arrival and disappearance

Enclosed us—safely, we thought, while
The sea-way which bore and must take us
Became God's moat to keep us.
We played in and out of it repeatedly.
Along shore that grass we almost sank in.
Weather spiraled from the full moon: storm
Shot rain and spray in salt horizontals
Three days. There was that too. Yet afterwards
The evening star like a pinwheel nail
Set all the galaxies awhirl until
Our island spun among them—
And then the sun with its wide quietness
Covered the sky and sea. The last days
Grew tense with being last: for instance,
Time and desire to swim nearly vanished.
We looked from sea at the grass and trees and flowers.
We were stilled by a recollected plan.
Sometimes I think it was all—but whose?—invention.
And yet how real you seemed when we ran with the sea.

TEXT FOR GRANDMA MOSES

by Ted Olson

AUGUST 11, 1956

All the clotheslines in America bannered
alike on Monday morning, gospel-white.
The sentry American eagle might have blenched,
thinking the whole land was surrendering.
Not a bit of it. This was ritual.
This was sacrament and absolution.
Godliness had had its day. The next—
likewise proudly, likewise prayerfully—
was vowed to cleanliness.
                I like to think
of America early on a Tuesday:
rinsed fresh, starched stiff, ironed shiny,
and only one day gone in sin.

SISTER

by Sydney Kessler

AUGUST 25, 1956

When ugliness meant so little,
It was easy to love the grotesque toy pig,
Difficult even to imagine the rutted wart
On an old man's nose.
Nor was it a matter of concern
That sister, a tom boy, was disliked
By most and always suspect of childhood's crimes.

In the end, more often than not,
She treated you meanly, which was expected
And guarded against, or loved you as a doll.
And always she was older and different from you.

But what I mean to say
Is that, with all of her flaws,
She was never ugly in any way, and this
Was apparent in everything, her movements,
Smile, apparent behind tirade and insult,
Grave bravado and utter thoughtlessness.

And what I am about, now, is that she grew
To be a sad and beautiful woman,
Was tormented no more or less than many,
Considerate to no great degree,
But beautiful.
                           It is that she died so recently
That I speak.
                 She is gone,
And there seems nothing between me, now,
And the wart on my nose, the pig grunting
Slothfully in the muddy patches of the mind.

"J.B." THE PROLOGUE TO THE PLAY

by Archibald MacLeish

SEPTEMBER 1, 1956

The following excerpt from Pulitzer Prize-winning poet Mac-Leish's full-length verse play, which is based on the Biblical story of Job, was first published in the pages of SR *more than a year before the play itself was given its first public presentation. In this excerpt, which serves as prologue to the finished play, the reader will have little difficulty recognizing the character named Mr. Zuss as Something-less-than-Zeus and the character named Nickles as Something-less-than-Old Nick.*

The scene throughout is a corner inside an enormous circus tent where a side show of some kind has been set up. There is a rough stage across the corner, on the left of which a wooden platform has been built at a height of six or seven feet. A wooden ladder leans against it. To the right is a deal table with seven straight chairs. There is a door-shaped opening in the canvas to the right rear. Above, a huge, slanted pole thrusts the canvas out and up to make the peak of the corner. Clothes that have the flimsy look of old costumes have been left about at one side and the other of the stage and the light at the beginning—such light as there is—is provided by bulbs dangling from hanks of wire. The feel is of a public place late at night, the audience gone, no one about but maybe a stage-hand cleaning up, fooling with the lights.

THE PROLOGUE

Mr. Zuss, followed by Nickles, enters from the dimness off to the left. They stop at the edge of the stage. Both wear the white caps and jackets of circus-vendors. Both are old. Mr. Zuss, who wears a bunch of balloons hitched to his belt, is large, florid, deep-voiced, dignified, imposing. Nickles is gaunt and sardonic: he has a popcorn tray slung from straps across his shoulders. Both betray in carriage and speech the broken-down actor fallen on evil days but nevertheless and always actor. Throughout the Prologue, from the moment when they mount the side-show stage, they jockey for position, ges-

ture, work themselves up into theatrical flights and rhetorical emotions, play to each other as though the little stage were real and they had an actual audience before them in the empty dark.

Mr. Zuss:	This is it.
Nickles:	This is what?
Mr. Zuss:	Where they play the play, Horatio!
Nickles:	Bare stage?
Mr. Zuss:	Not in the least.
	Heaven and Earth. That platform's Heaven.

They step up onto the stage together.

Nickles:	Looks like Heaven!
Mr. Zuss:	As you remember it?
Nickles:	Somebody's got to. You weren't there.
	They never sold balloons in Heaven—
	Not in my time.
Mr. Zuss:	Only popcorn.

Nickles shrugs a shudder of disgust, heaving his tray.

Nickles:	The two best actors in America
	Selling breath in bags . . .
Mr. Zuss:	and bags
	To butter breath with . . .
Nickles:	when they sell.
Mr. Zuss:	Merchandise not moving, Nickles?
Nickles:	Moves wherever I do—all of it.
	No rush to buy your worlds, I notice.
Mr. Zuss:	I could sell one to a . . .
Nickles:	. . . child!
	You told me. Where's the Earth?
Mr. Zuss:	Earth?
	Earth is where that table is;
	That's where Job sits—at the table.
	God and Satan lean above.

Mr. Zuss peers anxiously up into the canvas sky.

	I wonder if we'd better?
Nickles:	What?
Mr. Zuss:	Play it.
Nickles:	Why not? Who cares? *They* don't.
Mr. Zuss:	At least we're actors. They're not actors.
	Never acted anything.

Nickles:	That's right.

Nickles: That's right.
        They only own the show.
Mr. Zuss: I wonder . . .
Nickles: They won't care and they won't know.

His eyes follow Mr. Zuss's up to the dangling bulbs.

        Those stars that stare their stares at me—
        Are those the staring stars I see
        Or only lights . . .
                              not meant for me?
Mr. Zuss: What's that got to do with anything?
Nickles: Very little. Shall we start?
Mr. Zuss: You think we ought to?
Nickles: They won't care.
Mr. Zuss: Let's start . . .
                        What staring stars?
Nickles: They aren't.
        They're only lights. Not meant.
Mr. Zuss: Why don't we
        Start?
Nickles: You'll play the part of . . .
Mr. Zuss: Naturally!
Nickles: Naturally! And your mask?
Mr. Zuss: Mask!
Nickles: Mask. Naturally. You wouldn't play God in your
        Face would you?
Mr. Zuss: What's the matter with it?
Nickles: God the Creator of the Universe?
        God who hung the world in time?
        You wouldn't hang the world in time
        With a two-days' beard on your chin or a pinky!
        Lay its measure! Stretch the line on it!

Mr. Zuss stares coldly at Nickles, unhitches his balloon belt with magnificent deliberation, steps forward to the front of the wooden stage, strikes an attitude.

Mr. Zuss: "Whatsoever is under the whole
        Heaven is mine!"
Nickles: That's what I mean.
        You need a mask.
Mr. Zuss: *heavy irony*   Perhaps a more
        Accomplished actor . . .
Nickles: Kiss your accomplishments!

Nobody doubts your accomplishments—none of them—
The one man for God in the theater!
They'd all say that. Our ablest actor.
Nobody else for the part, they'd say.

Mr. Zuss: You make me humble.

Nickles: No! I'm serious.
The part was written for you.

Mr. Zuss: *gesture of protest*   Oh!

Nickles: But this is God in *Job* you're playing:
God the Maker: God Himself!
Remember what He says?—the hawk
Flies by His wisdom! And the goats—
Remember the goats? He challenges Job with them:
"Dost thou know the time of the wild goats?"
What human face knows time like that time?
You'd need a face of fur to know it.
Human faces know too much too little.

Mr. Zuss: *suspiciously*
What kind of mask?

Nickles: You'll find one somewhere.
They never play without the masks.

Mr. Zuss: It's God the Father I play—not
God the boiling point of water!

Nickles: Nevertheless the mask is imperative.
If God should laugh
The mare would calf
The cow would foal:
Diddle my soul . . .

Mr. Zuss: *shocked*
God never laughs! In the whole Bible!

Nickles: That's what I say. *We do.*

Mr. Zuss: *I* don't.

Nickles: *Job* does. He covers his mouth with his hand.

Mr. Zuss: Job is abashed.

Nickles: He says he's abashed.

Mr. Zuss: He should be abashed: it's rank irreverence—
Job there on the earth . . .

Nickles: On his dungheap . . .

Mr. Zuss: Challenging God!

Nickles: Crying to God.

Mr. Zuss: Demanding *justice* of *God!*

Nickles: Justice!
No wonder he laughs. It's ridiculous. All of it.
God has killed his sons, his daughters,
Stolen his camels, oxen, sheep,
Everything he has and left him
Sick and stricken on a dungheap—
Not even the consciousness of crime to comfort him—
The rags of reasons.

Mr. Zuss: God is reasons.

Nickles: For the hawks, yes. For the goats. They're grateful.
Take their young away they'll sing
Or purr or moo or splash—whatever.
Not for Job though.

Mr. Zuss: And that's why.

Nickles: Why what?

Mr. Zuss: He suffers.

Nickles: Ah? Because he's . . .
Not a bird you mean?

Mr. Zuss: You're frivolous . . .

Nickles: That's precisely what you do mean!
The one thing God can't stomach is a man,
That scratcher at the cracked creation!
That eyeball squinting through into His Eye,
Blind with the sight of Sight!

Nickles tugs himself free of his tray.

                                         Blast this   . . .

Mr. Zuss: God created the whole world.
Who is Job to . . .

Nickles: Agh! the world!
The dirty whirler of a world!

Mr. Zuss: *kicking savagely at the popcorn tray and the balloon*
belt to shove them under the platform

                                         What's
Wrong with the world, my friend?

Nickles: Wrong with it!
Try to spin one on a dungheap!

Nickles sits on a rung of the ladder, his elbows on his knees. After
a little he begins to sing to himself in a kind of tuneless tune.

I heard upon his dry dungheap
That man cry out who cannot sleep:
"If God is God He is not good,
If God is good He is not God;
Take the even, take the odd,
I would not sleep here if I could
Except for the little green leaves in the wood
And the wind on the water."

There is a long silence.

Mr. Zuss: You are a bitter man.

Nickles: I taste of the world!
I've licked the stick that beat my brains out:
Stock that broke my father's bones.

Mr. Zuss: Our modern hero! Our Odysseus
Sailing sidewalks toward the turd
Of truth and touching it at last in triumph!
The honest, disillusioned man!
You sicken me.

Nickles: All right, I sicken you.
No need to be offensive is there?
If you'd rather someone else . . .

Mr. Zuss: Did what?

Nickles: Flayed Job.

Mr. Zuss: What's Job to do with it?

Nickles: Job was honest. He saw God—
Saw him by that icy moonlight,
By that cold disclosing eye
That stares the color out and strews
Our lives . . . with light . . . for nothing.

Mr. Zuss: Job!
I never thought of you for Job.

Nickles: You never thought of me for Job!
What did you think of?

Mr. Zuss: Oh, there's always
Someone playing Job.

Nickles: There must be
Millions! Not with camels either:
Millions who suffer for no sin!
But where do I come in? Play the
Dungheap?

Mr. Zuss: All we do is start
Job will join us. Job will be there.

Nickles: I know. I know. I know. I've seen him.
Job is everywhere we go,
His children dead, his work for nothing,
Counting his losses, scraping his boils,
Discussing himself with his friends and physicians,
Questioning everything, the times, the stars,
His own soul, God's providence.
What do *I* do?

Mr. Zuss: What do *you* do?

Nickles: What do I do? You play God.

Mr. Zuss: I play God. I think I mentioned it.

Nickles: You play God and I play . . .

He lets himself down heavily on the rung of the ladder.

                             Ah!

Mr. Zuss: *embarrassed*   I had assumed you knew.

Nickles looks up at him, looks away.

Mr. Zuss: You see,
I think of you and me as . . . opposites.

Nickles: Nice of you.

Mr. Zuss: I didn't mean to be nasty.

Nickles: Your opposite! A demanding role!

Mr. Zuss: I know.

Nickles: But worthy of me? Worthy of me!

Mr. Zuss: I have offended you. I didn't mean to.

Nickles: Did I say I was offended?

There is an awkward silence. Nickles, his face in his hands, begins to hum the tune to his little song. Mr. Zuss looks up and around into the corners of the sky, his head moving cautiously. At length Nickles begins to sing the words.

      I heard upon his dry dungheap
      That man cry out who cannot sleep:
        "If God is God He is not good,
         If God is good He is not God;
         Take the even, take the odd,
         I would not sleep here if I could . . ."

Silence

      So I play opposite to God!

Silence

      Father of lies they call me, don't they?

Mr. Zuss does not answer. He is still searching the dark above. Silence. Nickles goes back to the song.

> "I would not sleep here if I could
> Except for the little green leaves in the wood
> And the wind on the water."

Silence. Then suddenly, theatrically, Nickles is on his feet.

	Who knows enough to know they're lies?
	Show me the mask!
Mr. Zuss:	What mask?
Nickles:	*attitude* My mask!
Mr. Zuss:	Are you sure you wear a mask?
Nickles:	Meaning what? That I don't need one?
Mr. Zuss:	Meaning are you sure it's here.
Nickles:	*They* never play without them. Certainly.
Mr. Zuss:	Yes but where?
Nickles:	In Heaven probably:
	That's where God and Satan meet:
	You told me that yourself. Remember?
Mr. Zuss:	Yes. . . . You wouldn't care to . . .
Nickles:	What?
Mr. Zuss:	Look for it?—for them?
Nickles:	In Heaven?
	Heaven is your department, Garrick.
Mr. Zuss:	Yes, I suppose it is. Here, hold this!

Nickles steadies the ladder. Mr. Zuss climbs warily, keeping his eye on the canvas darkness; heaves himself over the rail; rummages around on the platform; turns, holding out a huge white, blank, beautiful, expressionless mask with eyes lidded like the eyes of the mask in Michelangelo's Night.

Nickles:	That's not mine—not *his*. It's His.
	I've known that face before. I've seen it.
	They find it under bark of marble
	Deep within the rinds of stone:
	God the Creator . . . *(nastily)* of the animals!
Mr. Zuss:	*outraged* God of
	Everything that is or can!
Nickles:	Is or can—but cannot know.
Mr. Zuss:	There is nothing those closed eyes
	Have not known and seen.

Nickles: Except
        To see their sights: to know they've known it.
        Lions and dolphins have such eyes.
        They know the way the wild geese know,
        Those pin-point travelers who go home
        To Labradors they never meant to,
        Unwinding the will of the world like string.
        What would they make of a man, those eyelids?
Mr. Zuss: Make of him! They *made* him.
Nickles: Made him
        Animal like any other
        Calculated for the boughs of
        Trees and meant to chatter and be grateful!
        But womb-worm wonders and grows wings—
        It actually does. The cock-eyed things
        Dream themselves into a buzz
        And drown on windowpanes. He made them
        Wingless but they learn to wish.
        That's why He fumbles Job. Job wishes!—
        Thinks there should be justice somewhere—
        Beats his bones against the glass.
        Justice! In this cesspool! Think of it!
        Job knows better when it's over.
Mr. Zuss: Job knows justice when it's over.
        Justice has a face like that.
Nickles: Like blinded eyes?
Mr. Zuss: Like skies.
Nickles: Of stone.
        Show me the other.

*Mr. Zuss ducks away rummaging in the clutter on the platform;
turns again.*

Mr. Zuss: You won't find it
        Beautiful, you understand.

*Nickles has backed away from the foot of the ladder to enhance the
expected effect. He is very much the master of the situation.*

Nickles: I know that
        Beauty's the Creator's bait,
        Not the Uncreator's: his
        Is Nothing, the no-face of Nothing
        Grinning with its not-there eyes.
        Nothing at all! Nothing ever! . . .
        Never to have been at all!

Mr. Zuss turns, lifts the second mask above Nickles' preoccupation. This is large as the first but dark to the other's white, and open-eyed where the other was lidded. The eyes, though wrinkled with laughter, seem to stare and the mouth is drawn down in agonized disgust.

Mr. Zuss: Well?

Nickles is silent.

Mr. Zuss: *cheerfully*   That's it.

Silence.

> You don't care for it?
> It's not precisely the expression
> Anyone would choose. I know that.
> Evil is never very pretty:
> Spitefulness either. Nevertheless it's
> Him—you'll grant that, won't you?—the traditional
> Face we've always found for him anyway.
> God knows where we go to find it:
> Some subterranean memory probably.

Nickles has approached the ladder, staring. He does not reply.

> Well, if you won't you won't. It's your
> Option. I can't say I blame you.
> I wouldn't do it. Fit my face to
> That! I'd scrub the skin off afterward!
> Eyes to those eyes!

Nickles: *harshly*   You needn't worry.
> Your beaux yeux would never bear that
> Look of . . .

Mr. Zuss: No. I know.

Nickles: . . . of pity!
> Let me have it.

Nickles starts up the ladder, the mask in Mr. Zuss's hands above him.

> Evil you call it!
> Look at those lips: they've tasted something
> Bitter as a broth of blood
> And spat the sup out. Was that evil?

He climbs another rung.

> Was it?

Another

Spitefulness you say:
You call that grin of anguish spite?

He pulls himself over the rail, takes the mask in his hands.

> I'd rather wear this look of loathing
> Night after night than wear that other
> Once—that cold complacence . . .

Mr. Zuss has picked up the first mask again, lifts it.

Nickles: Horrible!

> Horrible as a star above
> A burning, murdered, broken city!
> I'll play the part! . . .
>   Put your mask on! . . .
> Give me the lines! . . .

Mr. Zuss: What lines?
Nickles: His!

> Satan's!

Mr. Zuss: They're in the Bible aren't they?
Nickles: We're supposed to speak the Bible?
Mr. Zuss: *They do . . .*

The light bulbs fade out, yellow to red to gone. A slow, strong glow spots the platform throwing gigantic shadows up across the canvas. Back to back the shadows of Mr. Zuss and Nickles adjust their masks: the masked shadows turn to each other and gravely bow. Their gestures are the stiff formal gestures of pantomime. Their voices, when they speak, are so magnified and hollowed by the masks that they scarcely seem their own.

God: WHENCE COMEST THOU?
Satan: FROM GOING TO AND FRO IN THE EARTH

There is a snicker of suppressed laughter.

> AND FROM WALKING UP AND DOWN IN IT. . .

A great guffaw. Mr. Zuss tears off his mask.

Mr. Zuss: Lights!

The spotlight fades out. The dangling bulbs come feebly on.

> Nobody told you to laugh like that.
> What's so funny? It's irreverent. It's impudent.
> After all, you are talking to God.

That doesn't happen every Saturday
Even to kitchen kin like you.
Take that face off! It's indecent!
Makes me feel like scratching somewhere!

Nickles painfully removes his mask.

Nickles: Do I look as though I'd laughed?
                If you had seen what I have seen
                You'd never laugh again! . . .

He stares at his mask.

                                    Weep either . . .
Mr. Zuss: You roared. I heard you.
Nickles: Those eyes *see*.
Mr. Zuss: Of course they see—beneath the trousers
                Stalking up the pulpit stair:
                Under the skirts at tea—wherever
                Decent eyes would be ashamed to.
                Why should you laugh at that?
Nickles: It isn't
                That! It isn't that at all!
                They see the *world*. They do. They see it.
                From going to and fro in the earth,
                From walking up and down, they see it.
                I know what Hell is now—to *see*.
                Consciousness of consciousness . . .
Mr. Zuss: Listen! This is a simple scene now.
                I play God. You play Satan.
                God is asking where you've been.
                All you have to do is tell him:
                Simple as that. "In the earth," you answer.
Nickles: *Satan* answers.
Mr. Zuss: All right—Satan.
                What's the difference?
Nickles: Satan *sees*.
                He sees the parked car by the plane tree.
                He sees behind the fusty door,
                Beneath the rug, those almost children
                Struggling on the awkward seat—
                Every impossible delighted dream
                She's ever had of loveliness, of wonder,
                Spilled with her garters to the filthy floor.
                Absurd despair! Ridiculous agony!

He looks at the mask in his hands.

> What has any man to laugh at!
> The panting crow by the dry tree
> Drags dusty wings. God's mercy brings
> The rains—but not to such as he.

Mr. Zuss: You play your part, I'll say that for you.
In it or out of it, you play.

Nickles: You really think I'm playing?

Mr. Zuss: Aren't you?
Somebody is. Satan maybe.
Maybe Satan's playing *you.*
Let's begin from the beginning.
Ready!

They take their places back to back.

> Masks!

They raise their masks to their faces.

> Lights!

The bulbs go out. In the darkness a distant voice:

> WHENCE COMEST THOU?

Mr. Zuss: That's my line.

Nickles: I didn't speak it.

Mr. Zuss: You did. Stop your mischief, won't you?

Nickles: Stop your own! Laughing. Shouting.

Mr. Zuss: Lights!

The spotlight throws the enormous shadows on the canvas sky.

God: WHENCE COMEST THOU?

Satan: FROM GOING TO AND FRO IN THE EARTH

. . . a choked silence

> AND FROM WALKING UP AND DOWN IN IT.

God: HAST THOU CONSIDERED MY SERVANT JOB
THAT THERE IS NONE LIKE HIM ON THE
EARTH
A PERFECT AND AN UPRIGHT MAN,
ONE THAT FEARETH GOD AND ESCHEWETH
EVIL?

*The platform lights sink, the masked shadows fading with them, as
a strong light comes on below isolating the table where J.B. stands
with his wife and children.*

CATCH WHAT YOU CAN

by Jean Garrigue

OCTOBER 13, 1956

The thing to do is to try for that sweet skin
One gets by staying deep inside a thing.
The image that I have is that of fruit—
The stone within the plum or some such pit
That gives the substance to a thing beyond.

Stay with me, mountain flowers I saw,
And battering moth against a wind-dark rock,
Stay with me till you build me all around
The honey and the clove I thought to sight
If lingering long enough I lived and got
Your intangible wild essence in my heart.
And whether that's by sight or thought
Or staying deep inside an aerial shed
Till imagination makes the heart-leaved vine
Out of damned bald rock, I cannot guess
The game is worth the candle if it's lit. . . .

A THOUSANDTH POEM TO DYLAN THOMAS

by John Ciardi

DECEMBER 15, 1956

Waking outside his Babylonian binge
        in the wet and cramp of morning stone, the sot
begins his daily death. A first stiff wince
        numbers his bones, each like a tooth of God.

Where did night end? Girlies in a red flame
        squeal through his broken memory like pigs:
Hell's barnyard burning or a zoo of days,
        stampeded shapes exploded from their skins.

He tastes again the ooze of a first sigh
    dead in his throat; his mouth, a rotten fig;
his sex, a broken glue-pot in the thighs;
    his breath, a shudder from below the will.

Sooner or later he must break an eye
    to look at what he sees of what he is.
An angel beating at the trap of time?
    A bird-heart pulsing in an idiot's fist?

Both. Either. Floated open from its muds,
    that moment in the clear, the sot's eye sees
as much as saints could bear of the fire-blood
    God's heart pumps in its seizure of the skies.

Then how the man could sing his meat to tears,
    there in God's eye and blood, for that lost place
where he was innocent, before his need
    changed to a thirst inside the worm of waste.

He pours his celebrations of regret,
    tormented joyous from the throat of mud,
hawk-hearted as Augustine in his sweat,
    dove-eyed as Francis' bridal with the wood.

It is the age of sots. Our holiness
    wakens outside the minareted fronts
of a jazzy, airless, and expensive Hell.
    He sings our wish. He drinks his death for us

who have no throats to die of or to sing.
    He is Saint Binge at death in his own meat,
the blaze meant in the char we make of things,
    our addict and our angel of defeat.

NOTES FOR
AN AUTOBIOGRAPHY

by Albert Einstein

At the suggestion of Dr. Paul Arthur Schilpp, professor of philoso-
phy at Northwestern University, Albert Einstein undertook the
writing of his memoirs, from which the following article is drawn.
Here the greatest scientist of modern times traces the course of
his intellectual growth, from his youthful success at proving the
Pythagorean theorem to his mature concern with the theory of
relativity—and beyond.

NOVEMBER 26, 1949

HERE I SIT in order to write, at the age of sixty-seven, something like my own obituary. I am doing this, not merely because Dr. Schilpp has persuaded me to do it, but because I believe that it is a good thing to show those who are striving alongside us how one's own striving and searching appear to one in retrospect. After some reflection, I felt how insufficient any such attempt is bound to be. For, however brief and limited one's working life may be, and however predominant may be the ways of error, the exposition of that which is worthy of communication does nonetheless not come easy —today's person of sixty-seven is by no means the same as was the one of fifty, of thirty, or of twenty. Every reminiscence is colored by today's being what it is, and therefore by a deceptive point of view. This consideration could very well deter. Nevertheless much can be lifted out of one's own experience which is not open to another consciousness.

Even when I was a fairly precocious young man the nothingness of the hopes and strivings which chase most men restlessly through life came to my consciousness with considerable vitality. Moreover, I soon discovered the cruelty of that chase, which in those years was much more carefully covered up by hypocrisy and glittering words than is the case today. By the mere existence of his stomach everyone was condemned to participate in that chase. Moreover, it was possible to satisfy the stomach by such participation, but not man in so far as he is a thinking and feeling being. As the first way out there was religion, which is implanted into every child by way of the traditional education machine. Thus I came—despite the fact that I was the son of entirely irreligious (Jewish) parents—to a deep religiosity, which, however, found an abrupt ending at the age of twelve. Through the reading of popular scientific books I soon reached the conviction that much in the stories of the Bible could not be true. The consequence was a positively fanatic orgy of free-thinking coupled with the impression that youth is intentionally being deceived by the state through lies; it was a crushing impression. Suspicion against every kind of authority grew out of this experience, a skeptical attitude towards the convictions which were alive in any specific social environment—an attitude which has never again left me, even though later on, because of a better insight into the causal connections, it lost some of its original poignancy.

It is quite clear to me that the religious paradise of youth, which was thus lost, was a first attempt to free myself from the chains of the "merely-personal," from an existence which is dominated by wishes, hopes, and primitive feelings. Out yonder there was this huge world, which exists independently of us human beings and which stands before us like a great, eternal riddle, at least partially accessible to our inspection and thinking. The contemplation of this world beckoned like a liberation, and I soon noticed that many a man whom I had learned to esteem and to admire had found inner freedom and security in devoted occupation with it. The mental grasp of this extra-personal world within the frame of the given possibilities swam as the highest aim half consciously and half unconsciously before my mind's eye. Similarly motivated men of the present and of the past, as well as the insights which they had achieved, were the friends which could not be lost. The road to this paradise was not as comfortable and alluring as the road to the religious paradise; but it has proved itself as trustworthy, and I have never regretted having chosen it.

What I have here said is true only within a certain sense, just as a drawing consisting of a few strokes can do justice to a complicated object, full of perplexing details, only in a very limited sense. If an individual enjoys well-ordered thoughts, it is quite possible that this side of his nature may grow more pronounced at the cost of other sides and thus may determine his mentality in increasing degree. In this case it is well possible that such an individual in retrospect sees a uniformly systematic development, whereas the actual experience takes place in kaleidoscopic particular situations.

The manifoldness of the external situations and the narrowness of the momentary content of consciousness bring about a sort of atomizing of the life of every human being. In a man of my type the turning-point of the development lies in the fact that gradually the major interest disengages itself to a far-reaching degree from the momentary and the merely personal and turns toward the striving for a mental grasp of things.

What, precisely, is "thinking"? When, at the reception of sense-impressions, memory-pictures emerge, this is not yet "thinking." And when such pictures form series, each member of which calls forth another, this, too, is not yet "thinking." When, however, a certain picture turns up in many such series, then—precisely through such return—it becomes an ordering element for such series, in that it connects series which in themselves are unconnected. Such an element becomes an instrument, a concept. I think that the transition from free association or "dreaming" to thinking is characterized by the more or less dominating role which the "concept" plays in it. It is by no means necessary that a concept must be connected with a sensorily cognizable and reproducible sign (word); but when this is the case thinking becomes by means of that fact communicable.

With what right—the reader will ask—does this man operate so carelessly and primitively with ideas in such a problematic realm without making even the least effort to prove anything? My defense: all our thinking is of this nature of a free play with concepts; the justification for this play lies in the measure of survey over the experience of the senses which we are able to achieve with its aid. The concept of "truth" can not yet be applied to such a structure; to my thinking this concept can come in question only when a far-reaching agreement (convention) concerning the elements and rules of the game is already at hand.

For me it is not dubious that our thinking goes on for the most part without use of signs (words) and beyond that to a considerable degree unconsciously. For how, otherwise, should it happen that sometimes we "wonder" quite spontaneously about some experience? This "wondering" seems to occur when an experience comes into conflict with a world of concepts which is already sufficiently fixed in us. Whenever such a conflict is experienced hard and intensively it reacts back upon our thought world in a decisive way. The development of this thought world is in a certain sense a continuous flight from "wonder."

A wonder of such nature I experienced as a child of four or five years, when my father showed me a compass. That this needle behaved in such a determined way did not at all fit into the nature of events which could find a place in the unconscious world of concepts (effect connected with direct "touch"). I can still remember —or at least believe I can remember—that this experience made a deep and lasting impression upon me. Something deeply hidden had to be behind things. What man sees before him from infancy causes no reaction of this kind; he is not surprised over the falling of bodies, concerning wind and rain, nor concerning the differences between living and non-living matter.

At the age of twelve I experienced a second wonder of a totally different nature: in a little book dealing with Euclidean plane geometry, which came into my hands at the beginning of a school year. Here were assertions, as for example the intersection of the three altitudes of a triangle in one point, which—though by no means evident—could nevertheless be proved with such certainty that any doubt appeared to be out of the question. This lucidity and certainty made an indescribable impression upon me. That the axiom had to be accepted unproved did not disturb me. In any case it was quite sufficient for me if I could peg proofs upon propositions the validity of which did not seem to me to be dubious. For example, I remember that an uncle told me the Pythagorean theorem before the holy geometry booklet had come into my hands. After much effort I succeeded in "proving" this theorem on the basis of the similarity of triangles; in doing so it seemed to me "evident" that the relations of the sides of the right-angled triangles would have to be completely determined by one of the acute angles. Only something which did not in similar fashion seem to be "evident" appeared to me to be in need of any proof at all. Also, the objects with which geometry deals seemed to be of no different type than the objects of sensory perception, "which can be seen and touched." This primitive idea, which probably also lies at the bottom of the well-known Kantian problematic concerning the possibility of "synthetic judgments *a priori*," rests obviously upon the fact that the relation of geometrical concepts to objects of direct experience (rigid rod, finite interval, etc.) was unconsciously present.

If thus it appeared that it was possible to get certain knowledge of the objects of experience by means of pure thinking, this "wonder" rested upon an error. Nevertheless, for anyone who experiences it for the first time, it is marvelous enough that man is capable at all of reaching such a degree of certainty and purity in pure thinking as the Greeks showed us for the first time to be possible in geometry.

From the age of twelve to sixteen I familiarized myself with the elements of mathematics together with the principles of differential and integral calculus. In doing so I had the good fortune of hitting upon books which were not too particular in their logical rigor, but which made up for this by permitting the main thoughts to stand out clearly and synoptically. This occupation was, on the whole, truly fascinating; climaxes were reached whose impression could easily compete with that of elementary geometry—the basic idea of analytical geometry, the infinite series, the concepts of differential and integral. I also had the good fortune of getting to know the essential results and methods of the entire field of the natural sciences in an excellent popular exposition, which limited itself almost throughout to qualitative aspects (Bernstein's *People's Books on Natural Science*, a work of five or six volumes), a work which I read with breathless attention. I had also already studied some theoretical physics when, at the age of seventeen, I entered the Polytechnic Institute of Zürich.

There I had excellent teachers (for example, Hurwitz, Minkowski), so that I really could have gotten a sound mathematical education. However, I worked most of the time in the physical laboratory, fascinated by the direct contact with experience. The balance of the time I used in the main in order to study at home the works of Kirchhoff, Helmholtz, Hertz, etc. The fact that I neglected mathematics to a certain extent had its cause not merely in my stronger interest in the natural sciences than in mathematics but also in the following strange experience. I saw that mathematics was split up into numerous specialities, each of which could easily absorb the short lifetime granted to us. Consequently I saw myself in the position of Buridan's ass, which was unable to decide upon any specific bundle of hay. This was obviously due to the fact that my intuition was not strong enough in the field of mathematics in order to differentiate clearly the fundamentally important, that which is really basic, from the more or less dispensable erudition.

Beyond this, however, my interest in the knowledge of nature was also unqualifiedly stronger; and it was not clear to me as a student that the approach to a more profound knowledge of the basic principles of physics is tied up with the most intricate mathematical methods. This dawned upon me only gradually after years of independent scientific work. True enough, physics also was divided into separate fields, each of which was capable of devouring a short lifetime of work without having satisfied the hunger for deeper knowledge. The mass of insufficiently connected experimental data was overwhelming here also. In this field, however, I soon learned to scent out that which was able to lead to fundamentals and to turn aside from everything else, from the multitude of things which clutter up the mind and divert it from the essential. The hitch in this was, of course, that one had to cram all this stuff into one's mind for the examinations.

This coercion had such a deterring effect (upon me) that, after I had passed the final examination, I found the consideration of any scientific problems distasteful to me for an entire year. In justice I must add, moreover, that in Switzerland we had to suffer far less under such coercion, which smothers every truly scientific impulse, than is the case in many another locality. There were altogether only two examinations; aside from these, one could just about do as one pleased. This was especially the case if one had a friend, as had I, who attended the lectures regularly and who worked over their content conscientiously. This gave one freedom in the choice of pursuits until a few months before the examination, a freedom which I enjoyed to a great extent and have gladly taken into the bargain the bad conscience connected with it as by far the lesser evil. It is, in fact, nothing short of a miracle that the modern methods of instruction have not yet entirely strangled the holy curiosity of inquiry; for this delicate little plant, aside from stimulation, stands mainly in need of freedom; without this it goes to wrack and ruin without fail.

Now to the field of physics as it presented itself at that time. In spite of all the fruitfulness in particular, dogmatic rigidity prevailed in matters of principles: in the beginning (if there was such a thing) God created Newton's laws of motion together with the necessary masses and forces. This is all; everything beyond this follows from the development of appropriate mathematical methods by means of deduction. What the nineteenth century achieved on the strength of this basis, especially through the application of the partial differential equations, was bound to arouse the admiration of every receptive person. Newton was probably first to reveal, in his theory of sound-transmission, the efficacy of partial differential equations. Euler had already created the foundation of hydrodynamics. But the more precise development of the mechanics of discrete masses, as the basis of all physics, was the achievement of the nineteenth century.

What made the greatest impression upon the student, however, was less the technical construction of mechanics or the solution of complicated problems than the achievements of mechanics in areas which apparently had nothing to do with mechanics: the mechanical theory of light, which conceived of light as the wave-motion of a quasi-rigid elastic ether, and above all the kinetic theory of gases: the independence of the specific heat of monatomic gases of the atomic weight, the derivation of the equation of state of a gas and its relation to the specific heat, the kinetic theory of the dissociation of gases, and above all the quantitative connection of viscosity, heat-conduction, and diffusion of gases, which also furnished the absolute magnitude of the atom.

These results supported at the same time mechanics as the foundation of physics and of the atomic hypothesis, which latter was already firmly anchored in chemistry. However, in chemistry only the ratios of the atomic masses played any role, not their absolute magnitudes, so that atomic theory could be viewed more as a visualizing symbol than as knowledge concerning the factual construction of matter. Apart from this it was also of profound interest that the statistical theory of classical mechanics was able to deduce the basic laws of thermodynamics, something which was in essence already accomplished by Boltzmann.

We must not be surprised, therefore, that, so to speak, all physicists of the last century saw in classical mechanics a firm and final foundation for all physics, yes, indeed, for all natural science, and that they never grew tired in their attempts to base Maxwell's theory of electromagnetism, which in the meantime was slowly beginning to win out, upon mechanics as well. Even Maxwell and H. Hertz, who in retrospect appear as those who demolished the faith in mechanics as the final basis of all physical thinking, in their conscious thinking adhered throughout to mechanics as the secured basis of physics.

It was Ernst Mach, who, in his *History of Mechanics,* shook this dogmatic faith; this book exercised a profound influence upon me in this regard while I was a student. I see Mach's greatness in his incorruptible skepticism and independence; in my younger years, however, Mach's epistemological position also influenced me very greatly, a position which today appears to me to be essentially untenable. For he did not place in the correct light the essentially constructive and speculative nature of thought and more especially of scientific thought; in consequence of which he condemned theory on precisely those points where its constructive-speculative character unconcealably comes to light, as, for example, in the kinetic atomic theory.

"Is this supposed to be an obituary?" the astonished reader will likely ask. I would like to reply: essentially yes. For the essential in the being of a man of my type lies precisely in *what* he thinks and *how* he thinks, not in what he does or suffers. Consequently, the obituary can limit itself in the main to the communicating of thoughts which have played a considerable role in my endeavors. A theory is the more impressive the greater the simplicity of its premises is, the more different kinds of things it relates, and the more extended is its area of applicability. Therefore the deep impression which classical thermodynamics made upon me. It is the only physical theory of universal content concerning which I am convinced that, within the framework of the applicability of its basic concepts, it will never be overthrown (for the special attention of those who are skeptics on principle).

The most fascinating subject at the time that I was a student was Maxwell's theory. What made this theory appear revolutionary was the transition from forces at a distance to fields as fundamental variables. The incorporation of optics into the theory of electromagnetism, with its relation of the speed of light to the electric and magnetic absolute system of units as well as the relation of the refraction coefficient to the dielectric constant, the qualitative relation between the reflection coefficient and the metallic conductivity of the body—it was like a revelation. Aside from the transition to field-theory, *i.e.,* the expression of the elementary laws through differential equations, Maxwell needed only one single hypothetical step—the introduction of the electrical displacement current in the vacuum and in the dielectrica and its magnetic effect, an innovation which was almost prescribed by the formal properties of the differential equations.

What rendered the insight into the essence of electromagnetic theory so much more difficult at that time was the following peculiar situation. Electric or magnetic "field intensities" and "displacements" were treated as equally elementary variables, empty space as a special instance of a dielectric body. *Matter* appeared as the bearer of the field, not *space*. By this it was implied that the carrier of the field could have velocity, and this was naturally to apply to the "vacuum" (ether) also. Hertz's electrodynamics of moving bodies rests entirely upon this fundamental attitude.

It was the great merit of H. A. Lorentz that he brought about a change here in a convincing fashion. In principle a field exists, according to him, only in empty space. Matter—considered as atoms —is the only seat of electric charges; between the material particles there is empty space, the seat of the electromagnetic field, which is created by the position and velocity of the point charges which are located on the material particles. Dielectricity, conductivity, etc., are determined exclusively by the type of mechanical tie connecting the particles, of which the bodies consist. The particle-charges create the field, which, on the other hand, exerts forces upon the charges of the particles, thus determining the motion of the latter according to Newton's law of motion. If one compares this with Newton's system, the change consists in this: action at a distance is replaced by the field, which thus also describes the radiation. Gravitation is usually not taken into account because of its relative smallness; its consideration, however, was always possible by means of the enrichment of the structure of the field, *i.e.*, expansion of Maxwell's law of the field. The physicist of the present generation regards the point of view achieved by Lorentz as the only possible one; at that time, however, it was a surprising and audacious step, without which the later development would not have been possible.

If one views this phase of the development of theory critically, one is struck by the dualism which lies in the fact that the material point in Newton's sense and the field as continuum are used as elementary concepts side by side. Kinetic energy and field-energy appear as essentially different things. This appears all the more unsatisfactory inasmuch as, according to Maxwell's theory, the magnetic field of a moving electric charge represents inertia. Why not then *total* inertia? Then only field-energy would be left, and the particle would be merely an area of special density of field-energy. In that case one could hope to deduce the concept of the mass-point together with the equations of the motion of the particles from the field equations—the disturbing dualism would have been removed.

H. A. Lorentz knew this very well. However, Maxwell's equations did not permit the derivations of the equilibrium of the electricity which constitutes a particle. Only other, nonlinear field equations could possibly accomplish such a thing. But no method existed by which this kind of field equations could be discovered without deteriorating into adventurous arbitrariness. In any case one could believe it possible by and by to find a new and secure foundation for all of physics upon the path so successfully begun by Faraday and Maxwell.

Accordingly, the revolution begun by the introduction of the field was by no means finished. Then it happened that, around the turn of the century, independently of what we have just been discussing, a second fundamental crisis set in, the seriousness of which was suddenly recognized due to Max Planck's investigations into heat radiation (1900).

My own interest in those years was less concerned with the detailed consequences of Planck's results, however important these might be. My major question was: what general conclusions can be drawn from the radiation-formula concerning the structure of radiation and even more generally concerning the electromagnetic foundation of physics?

Before I take this up I must briefly mention a number of investigations which relate to the Brownian motion and related objects (fluctuation-phenomena) and which in essence rest upon classical molecular mechanics. Not acquainted with the earlier investigations of Boltzmann and Gibbs, which had appeared earlier and actually exhausted the subject, I developed the statistical mechanics and the molecular-kinetic theory of thermodynamics which was based on the former. My major aim in this was to find facts which would guarantee as much as possible the existence of atoms of definite finite size.

In the midst of this I discovered that, according to atomistic theory, there would have to be a movement of suspended microscopic particles open to observation, without knowing that observations concerning the Brownian motion were already long familiar. The simplest derivation rested upon the following consideration. If the molecular-kinetic theory is essentially correct, a suspension of visible particles must possess the same kind of osmotic pressure fulfilling the laws of gases as a solution of molecules. This osmotic pressure depends upon the actual magnitude of the molecules, *i.e.*, upon the number of molecules in a gramequivalent. If the density of the suspension is inhomogeneous, the osmotic pressure is inhomogeneous, too, and gives rise to a compensating diffusion, which can be calculated from the well-known mobility of the particles. This diffusion can, on the other hand, also be considered as the result of the random displacement—unknown in magnitude originally—of the suspended particles due to thermal agitation. By comparing the amounts obtained for the diffusion current from both types of reasoning one reaches quantitatively the statistical law for those displacements, *i.e.*, the law of the Brownian motion. The agreement of these considerations with experience together with Planck's determination of the true molecular size from the law of radiation (for high temperatures) convinced the skeptics, who were quite numerous at that time (Ostwald, Mach), of the reality of atoms. The antipathy of these scholars towards atomic theory can indubitably be traced back to their positivistic philosophical attitude.

This is an interesting example of the fact that even scholars of audacious spirit and fine instinct can be obstructed in the interpretation of facts by philosophical prejudices. The prejudice—which has by no means died out in the meantime—consists in the faith that facts by themselves can and should yield scientific knowledge without free conceptual construction. Such a misconception is possible only because one does not easily become aware of the free choice of such concepts, which, through verification and long usage, appear to be immediately connected with the empirical material.

Reflections of this type made it clear to me as long ago as shortly after 1900, *i.e.,* shortly after Planck's trail-blazing work, that neither mechanics nor thermodynamics could (except in limiting cases) claim exact validity. By and by I despaired of the possibility of discovering the true laws by means of constructive efforts based on known facts. The longer and the more despairingly I tried, the more I came to the conviction that only the discovery of a universal formal principle could lead us to assured results. The example I saw before me was thermodynamics. The general principle was there given in the theorem: the laws of nature are such that it is impossible to construct a *perpetuum* mobile (of the first and second kind). How, then, could such a universal principle be found? After ten years of reflection such a principle resulted from a paradox upon which I had already hit at the age of sixteen: if I pursue a beam of light with the velocity c (velocity of light in a vacuum), I should observe such a beam of light as a spatially oscillatory electromagnetic field at rest. However, there seems to be no such thing, whether on the basis of experience or according to Maxwell's equations. From the very beginning it appeared to me intuitively clear that, judged from the standpoint of such an observer, everything would have to happen according to the same laws as for an observer who, relative to the earth, was at rest. For how, otherwise, should the first observer know, *i.e.,* be able to determine, that he is in a state of fast uniform motion?

One sees that in this paradox the germ of the special relativity theory is already contained. Today everyone knows, of course, that all attempts to clarify this paradox satisfactorily were condemned to failure as long as the axiom of the absolute character of time, *viz.,* of simultaneity, unrecognizedly was anchored in the unconscious. Clearly to recognize this axiom and its arbitrary character really implies already the solution of the problem. The type of critical reasoning which was required for the discovery of this central point was decisively furthered, in my case especially, by the reading of David Hume's and Ernst Mach's philosophical writings.

One had to understand clearly what the spatial co-ordinates and the temporal duration of events meant in physics. The physical interpretation of the spatial co-ordinates presupposed a fixed body of reference, which, moreover, had to be in a more or less definite state of motion (inertial system). In a given inertial system the co-ordinates meant the results of certain measurements with rigid (stationary) rods. (One should always be conscious of the fact that the presupposition of the existence in principle of rigid rods is a presupposition suggested by approximate experience, but which is, in principle, arbitrary.) With such an interpretation of the spatial co-ordinates the question of the validity of Euclidean geometry becomes a problem of physics.

If, then, one tries to interpret the time of an event analogously, one needs a means for the measurement of the difference in time (in itself determined periodic process realized by a system of sufficiently small spatial extension). A clock at rest relative to the system of inertia defines a local time. The local times of all space points taken together are the "time," which belongs to the selected system of inertia, if a means is given to "set" these clocks relative to each other. One sees that *a priori* it is not at all necessary that the "times" thus defined in different inertial systems agree with one another. One would have noticed this long ago, if, for the practical experience of everyday life light did not appear (because of the high value of c), as the means for the statement of absolute simultaneity.

The presupposition of the existence (in principle) of (ideal, *viz.*, perfect) measuring rods and clocks is not independent of each other; since a light-signal, which is reflected back and forth between the ends of a rigid rod, constitutes an ideal clock, provided that the postulate of the constancy of the light-velocity in vacuum does not lead to contradictions.

The above paradox may then be formulated as follows. According to the rules of connection, used in classical physics, of the spatial co-ordinates and of the time of events in the transition from one inertial system to another the two assumptions of

(1) the constancy of the light velocity

(2) the independence of the laws (thus specially also of the law of the constancy of the light velocity) of the choice of the inertial system (principle of special relativity)

are mutually incompatible (despite the fact that both taken separately are based on experience).

The insight which is fundamental for the special theory of relativity is this: the assumptions (1) and (2) are compatible if relations of a new type ("Lorentz-transformation") are postulated for the conversion of co-ordinates and the times of events. With the given physical interpretation of co-ordinates and time, this is by no means merely a conventional step, but implies certain hypotheses concerning the actual behavior of moving measuring-rods and clocks, which can be experimentally validated or disproved.

The universal principle of the special theory of relativity is contained in the postulate: the laws of physics are invariant with respect to the Lorentz-transformations (for the transition from one inertial system to any other arbitrarily chosen system of inertia). This is a restricting principle for natural laws, comparable to the restricting principle of the non-existence of the *perpetuum mobile* which underlies thermodynamics.

First a remark concerning the relation of the theory to "four-dimensional space." It is a widespread error that the special theory of relativity is supposed to have, to a certain extent, first discovered, or, at any rate, newly introduced, the four-dimensionality of the physical continuum. This, of course, is not the case. Classical mechanics, too, is based on the four-dimensional continuum of space and time. But in the four-dimensional continuum of classical physics the subspaces with constant time value have an absolute reality, independent of the choice of the reference system. Because of this [fact], the four-dimensional continuum falls naturally into a three-dimensional and a one-dimensional (time), so that the four-dimensional point of view does not force itself upon one as *necessary*. The special theory of relativity, on the other hand, creates a formal dependence between the way in which the spatial co-ordinates, on the one hand, and the temporal co-ordinates, on the other, have to enter into the natural laws.

Minkowski's important contribution to the theory lies in the following: before Minkowski's investigation it was necessary to carry out a Lorentz-transformation on a law in order to test its invariance under such transformations; he, on the other hand, succeeded in introducing a formalism such that the mathematical form of the law itself guarantees its invariance under Lorentz-transformations. By creating a four-dimensional tensor-calculus he achieved the same thing for the four-dimensional space which the ordinary vector-calculus achieves for the three spatial dimensions. He also showed that the Lorentz-transformation (apart from a different algebraic sign due to the special character of time) is nothing but a rotation of the co-ordinate system in the four-dimensional space.

First, a remark concerning the theory as it is characterized above. One is struck [by the fact] that the theory (except for the four-dimensional space) introduces two kinds of physical things, *i.e.*, (1) measuring rods and clocks, (2) all other things, *e.g.*, the electromagnetic field, the material point, etc. This, in a certain sense, is inconsistent; strictly speaking measuring rods and clocks would have to be represented as solutions of the basic equations (objects consisting of moving atomic configurations), not, as it were, as theoretically self-sufficient entities. However, the procedure justifies itself because it was clear from the very beginning that the postulates of the theory are not strong enough to deduce from them sufficiently complete equations for physical events sufficiently free from arbitrariness, in order to base upon such a foundation a theory of measuring rods and clocks. If one did not wish to forgo a physical interpretation of the co-ordinates in general (something which, in itself, would be possible), it was better to permit such inconsistency —with the obligation, however, of eliminating it at a later stage of the theory. But one must not legalize the mentioned sin so far as to imagine that intervals are physical entities of a special type, intrinsically different from other physical variables ("reducing physics to geometry," etc.).

We now shall inquire into the insights of definite nature which physics owes to the special theory of relativity.

(1) There is no such thing as simultaneity of distant events; consequently there is also no such thing as immediate action at a distance in the sense of Newtonian mechanics. Although the introduction of actions at a distance, which propagate with the speed of light, remains thinkable, according to this theory, it appears unnatural; for in such a theory there could be no such thing as a reasonable statement of the principle of conservation of energy. It therefore appears unavoidable that physical reality must be described in terms of continuous functions in space. The material point, therefore, can hardly be conceived any more as the basic concept of the theory.

(2) The principles of the conservation of momentum and of the conservation of energy are fused into one single principle. The inert mass of a closed system is identical with its energy, thus eliminating mass as an independent concept.

Remark. The speed of light c is one of the quantities which occurs as "universal constant" in physical equations. If, however, one introduces as unit of time instead of the second the time in which light travels 1 cm, c no longer occurs in the equations. In this sense one could say that the constant c is only an *apparently* universal constant.

It is obvious and generally accepted that one could eliminate two more universal constants from physics by introducing, instead of the gram and the centimeter, properly chosen "natural" units (for example, mass and radius of the electron).

If one considers this done, then only "dimension-less" constants could occur in the basic equations of physics. Concerning such I would like to state a theorem which at present cannot be based upon anything more than upon a faith in the simplicity, *i.e.*, intelligibility, of nature: there are no *arbitrary* constants of this kind; that is to say, nature is so constituted that it is possible logically to lay down such strongly determined laws that within these laws only rationally completely determined constants occur (not constants, therefore, whose numerical value could be changed without destroying the theory).

The special theory of relativity owes its origin to Maxwell's equations of the electromagnetic field. Inversely the latter can be grasped formally in satisfactory fashion only by way of the special theory of relativity. Maxwell's equations are the simplest Lorentz-invariant field equations which can be postulated for an antisymmetric tensor derived from a vector field. This in itself would be satisfactory, if we did not know from quantum phenomena that Maxwell's theory does not do justice to the energetic properties of radiation. But how Maxwell's theory would have to be modified in a natural fashion, for this even the special theory of relativity offers no adequate foothold. Also to Mach's question: "How does it come about that inertial systems are physically distinguished above all other co-ordinate systems?" this theory offers no answer.

That the special theory of relativity is only the first step of a necessary development became completely clear to me only in my efforts to represent gravitation in the framework of this theory. In classical mechanics, interpreted in terms of the field, the potential of gravitation appears as a *scalar* field (the simplest theoretical possibility of a field with a single component). Such a scalar theory of the gravitational field can easily be made invariant under the group of Lorentz-transformations. The following program appears natural, therefore: the total physical field consists of a scalar field (gravitation) and a vector field (electromagnetic field); later insights may eventually make necessary the introduction of still more complicated types of fields; but to begin with one did not need to bother about this.

The possibility of the realization of this program was, however, dubious from the very first, because the theory had to combine the following things:

> (1) From the general considerations of special relativity theory it was clear that the *inert* mass of a physical system increases with the total energy (therefore, *e.g.*, with the kinetic energy).

(2) From very accurate experiments (specially from the torsion balance experiments of Eötvös) it was empirically known with very high accuracy that the gravitational mass of a body is exactly equal to its *inert* mass.

It followed from (1) and (2) that the *weight* of a system depends in a precisely known manner on its total energy. If the theory did not accomplish this or could not do it naturally, it was to be rejected. The condition is most naturally expressed as follows: the acceleration of a system falling freely in a given gravitational field is independent of the nature of the falling system (specially therefore also of its energy content).

It then appeared that in the framework of the program sketched this elementary state of affairs could not at all, or, at any rate, not in any natural fashion, be represented in a satisfactory way. This convinced me that within the frame of the special theory of relativity there is no room for a satisfactory theory of gravitation.

Now it came to me: the fact of the equality of inert and heavy mass, *i.e.*, the fact of the independence of the gravitational acceleration of the nature of the falling substance, may be expressed as follows: in a gravitational field (of small spatial extension) things behave as they do in a space free of gravitation, if one introduces in it, in place of an "inertial system," a reference system which is accelerated relative to an inertial system.

If then one conceives of the behavior of a body, in reference to the latter reference system, as caused by a "real" (not merely apparent) gravitational field, it is possible to regard this reference system as an "inertial system" with as much justification as the original reference system.

So, if one regards as possible, gravitational fields of arbitrary extension which are not initially restricted by spatial limitations, the concept of the "inertial system" becomes completely empty. The concept "acceleration relative to space" then loses every meaning and with it the principle of inertia together with the entire paradox of Mach.

The fact of the equality of inert and heavy mass thus leads quite naturally to the recognition that the basic demand of the special theory of relativity (invariance of the laws under Lorentz-transformations) is too narrow, *i.e.*, that an invariance of the laws must be postulated also relative to *non-linear* transformations of the co-ordinates in the four-dimensional continuum.

This happened in 1908. Why were another seven years required for the construction of the general theory of relativity? The main reason lies in the fact that it is not so easy to free oneself from the idea that co-ordinates must have an immediate metrical meaning. The transformation took place in approximately the following fashion.

We start with an empty, field-free space, as it occurs—related to an inertial system—in the sense of the special theory of relativity, as the simplest of all imaginable physical situations. If we now think of a non-inertial system introduced by assuming that the new system is uniformly accelerated against the inertial system (in a three-dimensional description) in one direction (conveniently defined), then there exists with reference to this system a static parallel gravitational field. The reference system may thereby be chosen as rigid, of Euclidean type, in three-dimensional metric relations. But the time, in which the field appears as static, is *not* measured by *equally constituted* stationary clocks. From this special example one can already recognize that the immediate metric significance of the co-ordinates is lost if one admits non-linear transformations of co-ordinates at all. To do the latter is, however, *obligatory* if one wants to do justice to the equality of gravitational and inert mass by means of the basis of the theory, and if one wants to overcome Mach's paradox as concerns the inertial systems.

If, then, one must give up the attempt to give the co-ordinates an immediate metric meaning (differences of co-ordinates = measurable lengths, *viz.*, times), one will not be able to avoid treating as equivalent all co-ordinate systems, which can be created by the continuous transformations of the co-ordinates.

The general theory of relativity, accordingly, proceeds from the following principle: natural laws are to be expressed by equations which are covariant under the group of continuous co-ordinate transformations. This group replaces the group of the Lorentz-transformations of the special theory of relativity, which forms a subgroup of the former.

If anything in the theory as sketched—apart from the demand of the invariance of the equations under the group of the continuous co-ordinate-transformations—can possibly make the claim to final significance, then it is the theory of the limiting case of the pure gravitational field and its relation to the metric structure of space. For this reason, in what immediately follows we shall speak only of the equations of the pure gravitational field.

The peculiarity of these equations lies, on the one hand, in their complicated construction, especially their non-linear character as regards the field-variables and their derivatives, and, on the other hand, in the almost compelling necessity with which the transformation-group determines this complicated field-law. If one had stopped with the special theory of relativity, *i.e.*, with the invariance under the Lorentz-group, then the field-law $R_{ik} = 0$ would remain invariant also within the frame of this narrower group. But from the point of view of the narrower group there would at first exist no reason for representing gravitation by so complicated a structure as is represented by the symmetric tensor g_{ik}. If, nonetheless, one would find sufficient reasons for it, there would then arise an immense number of field-laws out of quantities g_{ik}, all of which are covariant under Lorentz-transformations (not, however, under the general group). However, even if, of all the conceivable Lorentz-invariant laws, one had accidentally guessed precisely the law which belongs to the wider group, one would still not be on the plane of insight achieved by the general principle of relativity. For, from the standpoint of the Lorentz-group two solutions would incorrectly have to be viewed as physically different from each other, if they can be transformed into each other by a non-linear transformation of co-ordinates, *i.e.*, if they are, from the point of view of the wider field, only different representations of the same field.

I must take a stand with reference to the most successful physical theory of our period, *viz.*, the statistical quantum theory which, about twenty-five years ago, took on a consistent logical form (Schrödinger, Heisenberg, Dirac, Born). This is the only theory at present which permits a unitary grasp of experiences concerning the quantum character of micro-mechanical events. This theory, on the one hand, and the theory of relativity on the other, are both considered correct in a certain sense, although their combination has resisted all efforts up to now. This is probably the reason why among contemporary theoretical physicists there exist entirely differing opinions concerning the question as to how the theoretical foundation of the physics of the future will appear. Will it be a field theory; will it be in essence a statistical theory? I shall briefly indicate my own thoughts on this point.

Physics is an attempt conceptually to grasp reality as it is thought independently of its being observed. In this sense one speaks of "physical reality." In pre-quantum physics there was no doubt as to how this was to be understood. In Newton's theory reality was determined by a material point in space and time; in Maxwell's theory, by the field in space and time. In quantum mechanics it is not so easily seen.

This exposition has fulfilled its purpose if it shows the reader how the efforts of a life hang together and why they have led to expectations of a definite form.

THE PHILOSOPHER-
IN-THE-MAKING

by John Dewey

*A famous American philosopher, who was largely responsible for
today's theories of progressive education, presents a step-by-step
history of his own intellectual development.*

OCTOBER 22, 1949

IN THE LATE SEVENTIES, when I was an undergraduate, "electives"
were still unknown in the smaller New England colleges. But in
the one I attended, the University of Vermont, the tradition of a
"senior-year course" still subsisted. This course was regarded as a
kind of intellectual coping to the structure erected in earlier years,
or, at least, as an insertion of the keystone of the arch. It included
courses in political economy, international law, history of civilization (Guizot), psychology, ethics, philosophy of religion (Butler's
Analogy), logic, etc., not history of philosophy, save incidentally.
The enumeration of these titles may not serve the purpose for
which it is made; but the idea was that after three years of somewhat specialized study in languages and sciences, the last year was
reserved for an introduction into serious intellectual topics of wide
and deep significance—an introduction into the world of ideas. I
doubt if in many cases it served its alleged end; however, it fell in
with my own inclinations, and I have always been grateful for that
year of my schooling. There was, however, one course in the previous year that had excited a taste that in retrospect may be called
philosophical. That was a rather short course, without laboratory
work, in physiology, a book of Huxley's being the text. It is difficult to speak with exactitude about what happened to me intellectually so many years ago, but I have an impression that there was
derived from that study a sense of interdependence and interrelated
unity that gave form to intellectual stirrings that had been previously inchoate, and created a kind of type or model of a view of
things to which material in any field ought to conform. Subconsciously, at least, I was led to desire a world and a life that would
have the same properties as had the human organism in the picture

of it derived from study of Huxley's treatment. At all events, I got great stimulation from the study, more than from anything I had had contact with before; and as no desire was awakened in me to continue that particular branch of learning, I date from this time the awakening of a distinctive philosophic interest.

The University of Vermont rather prided itself upon its tradition in philosophy. One of its earlier teachers, Dr. Marsh, was almost the first person in the United States to venture upon the speculative and dubiously orthodox seas of German thinking—that of Kant, Schelling, and Hegel. The venture, to be sure, was made largely by way of Coleridge; Marsh edited an American edition of Coleridge's *Aids to Reflection*. Even this degree of speculative generalization, in its somewhat obvious tendency to rationalize the body of Christian theological doctrines, created a flutter in ecclesiastical dovecots. In particular, a controversy was carried on between the Germanizing rationalizers and the orthodox representatives of the Scottish school of thought through the representatives of the latter at Princeton. I imagine—although it is a very long time since I have had any contact with this material—that the controversy still provides data for a section, if not a chapter, in the history of thought in this country.

Although the University retained pride in its pioneer work, and its atmosphere was for those days theologically "liberal"—of the Congregational type—the teaching of philosophy had become more restrained in tone, more influenced by the still dominant Scotch school. Its professor, Mr. H. A. P. Torrey, was a man of genuinely sensitive and cultivated mind, with marked esthetic interest and taste, which in a more congenial atmosphere than that of Northern New England in those days would have achieved something significant. He was, however, constitutionally timid, and never really let his mind go. I recall that, in a conversation I had with him a few years after graduation, he said: "Undoubtedly pantheism is the most satisfactory form of metaphysics intellectually, but it goes counter to religious faith." I fancy that remark told of an inner conflict that prevented his native capacity from coming to full fruition. His interest in philosophy, however, was genuine, not perfunctory; he was an excellent teacher, and I owe to him a double debt, that of turning my thoughts definitely to the study of philosophy as a life pursuit, and of a generous gift of time to me during a year devoted privately under his direction to a reading of classics in the history of philosophy and learning to read philosophic German. In our walks and talks during this year, after three years on my part of high-school teaching, he let his mind go much more

freely than in the classroom, and revealed potentialities that might
have placed him among the leaders in the development of a freer
American philosophy—but the time for the latter had not yet come.

Teachers of philosophy were at that time, almost to a man,
clergymen; the supposed requirements of religion, or theology,
dominated the teaching of philosophy in most colleges. Just how
and why Scotch philosophy lent itself so well to the exigencies of
religion I cannot say; probably the causes were more extrinsic than
intrinsic; but at all events there was a firm alliance established
between religion and the cause of "intuition." It is probably impossible to recover at this date the almost sacrosanct air that en-
veloped the idea of intuitions; but somehow the cause of all holy
and valuable things was supposed to stand or fall with the validity
of intuitionalism; the only vital issue was that between intuitionalism and a sensational empiricism that explained away the reality
of all higher objects. The story of this almost forgotten debate, once
so urgent, is probably a factor in developing in me a certain skepticism about the depth and range of purely contemporary issues; it
is likely that many of those which seem highly important today will
also in a generation have receded to the status of the local and
provincial. It also aided in generating a sense of the value of the
history of philosophy; some of the claims made for this as a sole
avenue of approach to the study of philosophic problems seem to
me misdirected and injurious. But its value in giving perspective
and a sense of proportion in relation to immediate contemporary
issues can hardly be overestimated.

I do not mention this theological and intuitional phase because
it had any lasting influence upon my own development, except
negatively. I learned the terminology of an intuitional philosophy,
but it did not go deep, and in no way did it satisfy what I was
dimly reaching for. I was brought up in a conventionally evangelical
atmosphere of the more "liberal" sort; and the struggles that later
arose between acceptance of that faith and the discarding of traditional and institutional creeds came from personal experiences and
not from the effects of philosophical teaching. It was not, in other
words, in this respect that philosophy either appealed to me or influenced me—though I am not sure that Butler's *Analogy,* with its
cold logic and acute analysis, was not, in a reversed way, a factor
in developing "skepticism."

During the year of private study, of which mention has been
made, I decided to make philosophy my life-study, and accordingly
went to Johns Hopkins the next year (1884) to enter upon that new
thing, "graduate work." It was something of a risk; the work offered

there was almost the only indication that there were likely to be any self-supporting jobs in the field of philosophy for others than clergymen. Aside from the effect of my study with Professor Torrey, another influence moved me to undertake the risk. During the years after graduation I had kept up philosophical readings and I had even written a few articles which I sent to Dr. W. T. Harris, the well-known Hegelian, and the editor of the *Journal of Speculative Philosophy*, the only philosophic journal in the country at that time, as he and his group formed almost the only group of laymen devoted to philosophy for non-theological reasons. In sending an article I asked Dr. Harris for advice as to the possibility of my successfully prosecuting philosophic studies. His reply was so encouraging that it was a distinct factor in deciding me to try philosophy as a professional career.

The articles sent were, as I recall them, highly schematic and formal; they were couched in the language of intuitionalism; of Hegel I was then ignorant. My deeper interests had not as yet been met, and in the absence of subject matter that would correspond to them, the only topics at my command were such as were capable of a merely formal treatment. I imagine that my development has been controlled largely by a struggle between a native inclination toward the schematic and formally logical, and those incidents of personal experience that compelled me to take account of actual material. Probably there is in the consciously articulated ideas of every thinker an overweighting of just those things that are contrary to his natural tendencies, an emphasis upon those things that are contrary to his intrinsic bent, and which, therefore, he has to struggle to bring to expression, while the native bent, on the other hand, can take care of itself. Anyway, a case might be made out for the proposition that the emphasis upon the concrete, empirical, and "practical" in my later writings is partly due to considerations of this nature. It was a reaction against what was more natural, and it served as a protest and protection against something in myself which, in the pressure of the weight of actual experiences, I knew to be a weakness. It is, I suppose, becoming a commonplace that when anyone is unduly concerned with controversy, the remarks that seem to be directed against others are really concerned with a struggle that is going on inside himself. The marks, the stigmata, of the struggle to weld together the characteristics of a formal, theoretic interest and the material of a maturing experience of contacts with realities also showed themselves, naturally, in style of writing and manner of presentation. During the time when the schematic interest predominated, writing was comparatively easy; there were

even compliments upon the clearness of my style. Since then thinking and writing have been hard work. It is easy to give way to the
dialectic development of a theme; the pressure of concrete experiences was, however, sufficiently heavy, so that a sense of intellectual
honesty prevented a surrender to that course. But, on the other
hand, the formal interest persisted, so that there was an inner
demand for an intellectual technique that would be consistent and
yet capable of flexible adaptation to the concrete diversity of experienced things. It is hardly necessary to say that I have not been
among those to whom the union of abilities to satisfy these two
opposed requirements, the formal and the material, came easily.
For that very reason I have been acutely aware, too much so, doubtless, of a tendency of other thinkers and writers to achieve a
specious lucidity and simplicity by the mere process of ignoring
considerations which a greater respect for concrete materials of experience would have forced upon them.

It is a commonplace of educational history that the opening of
Johns Hopkins University marked a new epoch in higher education in the United States. We are probably not in a condition as
yet to estimate the extent to which its foundaion and the development of graduate schools in other universities, following its example, mark a turn in our American culture. The eighties and
nineties seem to mark the definitive close of our pioneer period, and
the turn from the Civil War era into the new industrialized and commercial age. In philosophy, at least, the influence of Johns Hopkins
was not due to the size of the provision that was made. There was
a half-year of lecturing and seminar work given by Professor George
Sylvester Morris, of the University of Michigan; belief in the "demonstrated" (a favorite word of his) truth of the substance of German
idealism, and of belief in its competency to give direction to a life
of aspiring thought, emotion, and action. I have never known a
more single-hearted and whole-souled man—a man of a single piece
all the way through; while I long since deviated from his philosophic faith, I should be happy to believe that the influence of the
spirit of his teaching has been an enduring influence.

While it was impossible that a young and impressionable student,
unacquainted with any system of thought that satisfied his head and
heart, should not have been deeply affected, to the point of at least
a temporary conversion, by the enthusiastic and scholarly devotion
of Mr. Morris, this effect was far from being the only source of
my own "Hegelianism." The eighties and nineties were a time of
new ferment in English thought; the reaction against atomic individualism and sensationalistic empiricism was in full swing. It was

the time of Thomas Hill Green, of the two Cairds, of Wallace, of the appearance of the *Essays in Philosophical Criticism,* co-operatively produced by a younger group under the leadership of the late Lord Haldane. This movement was at the time the vital and constructive one in philosophy. Naturally its influence fell in with and reinforced that of Professor Morris. There was but one marked difference, and that, I think, was in favor of Mr. Morris. He came to Kant through Hegel instead of to Hegel by way of Kant, so that his attitude toward Kant was the critical one expressed by Hegel himself. Moreover, he retained something of his early Scotch philosophical training in a common-sense belief in the existence of the external world. He used to make merry over those who thought the *existence* of this world and of matter were things to be proved by philosophy. To him the only philosophical question was as to the *meaning* of this existence; his idealism was wholly of the objective type. Like his contemporary, Professor John Watson, of Kingston, he combined a logical and idealistic metaphysics with a realistic epistemology. Through his teacher at Berlin, Trendelenburg, he had acquired a great reverence for Aristotle, and he had no difficulty in uniting Aristoteleanism with Hegelianism.

There were, however, also "subjective" reasons for the appeal that Hegel's thought made to me; it supplied a demand for unification that was doubtless an intense emotional craving, and yet was a hunger that only an intellectualized subject matter could satisfy. It is more than difficult, it is impossible, to recover that early mood. But the sense of divisions and separations that were, I suppose, borne in upon me as a consequence of a heritage of New England culture, divisions by way of isolation of self from the world, of soul from body, of nature from God, brought a painful oppression —or, rather, they were an inward laceration. My earlier philosophic study had been an intellectual gymnastic. Hegel's synthesis of subject and object, matter and spirit, the divine and the human, was, however, no mere intellectual formula; it operated as an immense release, a liberation. Hegel's treatment of human culture, of institutions and the arts, involved the same dissolution of hard-and-fast dividing walls, and had a special attraction for me.

As I have already intimated, while the conflict of traditional religious beliefs with opinions that I could myself honestly entertain was the source of a trying personal crisis, it did not at any time constitute a leading philosophical problem. This might look as if the two things were kept apart; in reality it was due to a feeling that any genuinely sound religious experience could and should adapt itself to whatever beliefs one found oneself intellectually entitled to hold—a half unconscious sense at first, but one which ensuing years have deepened into a fundamental conviction. In consequence, while I have, I hope, a due degree of personal sympathy with individuals who are undergoing the throes of a personal change of attitude, I have not been able to attach much importance to religion as a philosophic problem; for the effect of that attachment seems to be in the end a subornation of candid philosophic thinking to the alleged but factitious needs of some special set of convictions. I have enough faith in the depth of the religious tendencies of men to believe that they will adapt themselves to any required intellectual change, and that it is futile (and likely to be dishonest) to forecast prematurely just what forms the religious interest will take as a final consequence of the great intellectual transformation that is going on. As I have been frequently criticized for undue reticence about the problems of religion, I insert this explanation: it seems to me that the great solicitude of many persons, professing belief in the universality of the need for religion, about the present and future of religion proves that in fact they are moved more by partisan interest in a particular religion than by interest in religious experience.

The chief reason, however, for inserting these remarks at this point is to bring out a contrast effect. Social interests and problems from an early period had to me the intellectual appeal and provided the intellectual sustenance that many seem to have found primarily in religious questions. In undergraduate days I had run across, in the college library, Harriet Martineau's exposition of Comte. I cannot remember that his law of "the three stages" affected me particularly; but his idea of the disorganized character of Western modern culture, due to a disintegrative "individualism," and his idea of a synthesis of science that should be a regulative method of an organized social life, impressed me deeply. I found, as I thought, the same criticisms combined with a deeper and more far-reaching integration in Hegel. I did not, in those days when I read Bacon, detect the origin of the Comtean idea in him, and I had not made acquaintance with Condorcet, the connecting link.

I drifted away from Hegelianism in the next fifteen years; the word "drifting" expresses the slow and, for a long time, imperceptible character of the movement, though it does not convey the impression that there was an adequate cause for the change. Nevertheless I should never think of ignoring, much less denying, what an astute critic occasionally refers to as a novel discovery—that acquaintance with Hegel has left a permanent deposit in my thinking. The form, the schematism, of his system now seems to me artificial to the last degree. But in the content of his ideas there is often an extraordinary depth; in many of his analyses, taken out of their mechanical dialectical setting, an extraordinary acuteness. Were it possible for me to be a devotee of any system, I still should believe that there is greater richness and greater variety of insight in Hegel than in any other single systematic philosopher—though when I say this I exclude Plato, who still provides my favorite philosophic reading. For I am unable to find in him that all-comprehensive and overriding system which later interpretation has, as it seems to me, conferred upon him as a dubious boon. The ancient skeptics overworked another aspect of Plato's thought when they treated him as their spiritual father, but they were nearer the truth, I think, than those who force him into the frame of a rigidly systematized doctrine. Although I have not the aversion to system as such that is sometimes attributed to me, I am dubious of my own ability to reach inclusive systematic unity, and in consequence, perhaps, of that fact also dubious about my contemporaries. Nothing could be more helpful to present philosophizing than a "Back to Plato" movement; but it would have to be back to the dramatic, restless, co-operatively inquiring Plato of the *Dialogues,* trying one mode of attack after another to see what it might yield; back to the Plato whose highest flight of metaphysics always terminated with a social and practical turn, and not to the artificial Plato constructed by unimaginative commentators who treat him as the original university professor.

The rest of the story of my intellectual development I am unable to record without more faking than I care to indulge in. What I have so far related is so far removed in time that I can talk about myself as another person; and much has faded, so that a few points stand out without my having to force them into the foreground. The philosopher, if I may apply that word to myself, that I became as I moved away from German idealism, is too much the self that I still am and is still too much in process of change to lend itself to record. I envy, up to a certain point, those who can write their intellectual biography in a unified pattern, woven out of a few distinctly discernible strands of interest and influence. By contrast, I seem to be unstable, chameleonlike, yielding one after another to many diverse and even incompatible influences; struggling to assimilate something from each and yet striving to carry it forward in a way that is logically consistent with what has been learned from its predecessors. Upon the whole, the forces that have influenced me have come from persons and from situations more than from books—not that I have not, I hope, learned a great deal from philosophical writings, but that what I have learned from them has been technical in comparison with what I have been forced to think upon and about because of some experience in which I found myself entangled. It is for this reason that I cannot say with candor that I envy completely, or envy beyond a certain point, those to whom I have referred. I like to think, though it may be a defense reaction, that with all the inconveniences of the road I have been forced to travel, it has the compensatory advantage of not inducing an immunity of thought to experiences—which perhaps, after all, should not be treated even by a philosopher as the germ of a disease to which he needs to develop resistance.

While I cannot write an account of intellectual development without giving it the semblance of a continuity that it does not in fact own, there are four special points that seem to stand out. One is the importance that the practice and theory of education have had for me: especially the education of the young, for I have never been able to feel much optimism regarding the possibilities of "higher" education when it is built upon warped and weak foundations. This interest fused with and brought together what might otherwise have been separate interests—that in psychology and that in social institutions and social life. I can recall but one critic who has suggested that my thinking has been too much permeated by interest in education. Although a book called *Democracy and Education* was for many years that in which my philosophy, such as it is, was most fully expounded, I do not know that philosophic critics, as distinct from teachers, have ever had recourse to it. I have wondered whether such facts signified that philosophers in general, although they are themselves usually teachers, have not taken education with sufficient seriousness for it to occur to them that any rational person could actually think it possible that philosophizing should focus about education as the supreme human interest in which, moreover, other problems, cosmological, moral, logical, come to a head. At all events, this handle is offered to any subsequent critic who may wish to lay hold of it.

A second point is that as my study and thinking progressed, I became more and more troubled by the intellectual scandal that seemed to me involved in the current (and traditional) dualism in logical standpoint and method between something called "science" on the one hand and something called "morals" on the other. I have long felt that the construction of a logic, that is, a method of effective inquiry, which would apply without abrupt breach of continuity to the fields designated by both of these words, is at once our needed theoretical solvent and the supply of our greatest practical want. This belief has had much more to do with the development of what I termed, for lack of a better word, "instrumentalism," than have most of the reasons that have been assigned.

The third point forms the great exception to what was said about no very fundamental vital influence issuing from books; it concerns the influence of William James. As far as I can discover one specifiable philosophic factor which entered into my thinking so as to give it a new direction and quality, it is this one. To say that it proceeded from his *Psychology* rather than from the essays collected in the volume called *Will to Believe,* his *Pluralistic Universe,* or *Pragmatism,* is to say something that needs explanation. For there are, I think, two unreconciled strains in the *Psychology.* One is found in the adoption of the subjective tenor of prior psychological tradition; even when the special tenets of that tradition are radically criticized, an underlying subjectivism is retained, at least in vocabulary—and the difficulty in finding a vocabulary which will intelligibly convey a genuinely new idea is perhaps the obstacle that most retards the easy progress of philosophy. I may cite as an illustration the substitution of the "stream of consciousness" for discrete elementary states; the advance made was enormous. Nevertheless the point of view remained that of a realm of consciousness set off by itself. The other strain is objective, having its roots in a return to the earlier biological conception of the psyche, but a return possessed of a new force and value due to the immense progress made by biology since the time of Aristotle. I doubt if we have as yet begun to realize all that is due to William James for the introduction and use of this idea; as I have already intimated, I do not think that he fully and consistently realized it himself. Anyway, it worked its way more and more into all my ideas and acted as a ferment to transform old beliefs.

If this biological conception and mode of approach had been prematurely hardened by James, its effect might have been merely to substitute one schematism for another. But it is not tautology to say that James's sense of life was itself vital. He had a profound sense, in origin artistic and moral, perhaps, rather than "scientific," of the difference between the categories of the living and of the mechanical; sometime, I think, someone may write an essay that will show how the most distinctive factors in his general philosophic view, pluralism, novelty, freedom, individuality, are all connected with his feeling for the qualities and traits of that which lives. Many philosophers have had much to say about the idea of organism; but they have taken it structurally and hence statically. It was reserved for James to think of life in terms of life in action. This point, and that about the objective biological factor in James's conception of thought (discrimination, abstraction, conception, generalization), is fundamental when the role of psychology in philosophy comes under consideration. It is true that the effect of its introduction into philosophy has often, usually, been to dilute and distort the latter. But that is because the psychology was bad psychology.

I do not mean that I think that in the end the connection of psychology with philosophy is, in the abstract, closer than is that of other branches of science. Logically, it stands on the same plane with them. But historically and at the present juncture the revolution introduced by James had, and still has, a peculiar significance. On the negative side it is important, for it is indispensable as a purge of the heavy charge of bad psychology that is so embedded in the philosophical tradition that is not generally recognized to be psychology at all. As an example, I would say that the problem of "sense data," which occupies such a great bulk in recent British thinking, has to my mind no significance other than as a survival of an old and outworn psychological doctrine—although those who deal with the problem are for the most part among those who stoutly assert the complete irrelevance of psychology to philosophy. On the positive side we have the obverse of this situation. The newer objective psychology supplies the easiest way, pedagogically if not in the abstract, by which to reach a fruitful conception of thought and its work, and thus to better our logical theories—provided thought and logic have anything to do with one another. And in the present state of men's minds the linking of philosophy to the significant issues of actual experience is facilitated by constant interaction with the methods and conclusions of psychology. The most abstract sciences, mathematics and physics, for example, have left their impress deep upon traditional philosophy. The former, in connection with an exaggerated anxiety about formal certainty, has more than once operated to divorce philosophic thinking from connection with questions that have a source in existence. The remoteness of psychology from such abstractions, its nearness to what is distinctively human, gives it an emphatic claim for a sympathetic hearing at the present time.

In connection with an increasing recognition of this human aspect, there developed the influence which forms the fourth heading of this recital. The objective biological approach of the Jamesian psychology led straight to the perception of the importance of distinctive social categories, especially communication and participation. It is my conviction that a great deal of our philosophizing needs to be done over again from this point of view, and that there will ultimately result an integrated synthesis in a philosophy congruous with modern science and related to actual needs in education, morals, and religion. One has to take a broad survey in detachment from immediate prepossessions to realize the extent to which the characteristic traits of the science of today are connected with the development of social subjects—anthropology, history, politics, economics, language and literature, social and abnormal psychology, and so on. The movement is both so new, in an intellectual sense, and we are so much of it and it so much of us, that it escapes definite notice. Technically the influence of mathematics upon philosophy is more obvious; the great change that has taken place in recent years in the ruling ideas and methods of the physical sciences attracts attention much more easily than does the growth of the social subjects, just because it is farther away from impact upon us. Intellectual prophecy is dangerous; but if I read the cultural signs of the times aright, the next synthetic movement in philosophy will emerge when the significance of the social sciences and arts has become an object of reflective attention in the same way that mathematical and physical sciences have been made the objects of thought in the past, and when their full import is grasped. If I read these signs wrongly, nevertheless the statement may stand as a token of a factor significant in my own intellectual development.

In any case, I think it shows a deplorable deadness of imagination to suppose that philosophy will indefinitely revolve within the scope of the problems and systems that two thousand years of European history have bequeathed to us. Seen in the long perspective of the future, the whole of Western European history is a provincial episode. I do not expect to see in my day a genuine, as distinct from a forced and artificial, integration of thought. But a mind that is not too egotistically impatient can have faith that this unification will issue in its season. Meantime a chief task of those who call themselves philosophers is to help get rid of the useless lumber that blocks our highways of thought, and strive to make straight and open the paths that lead to the future. Forty years spent in wandering in a wilderness like that of the present is not a sad fate—unless one attempts to make himself believe that the wilderness is after all itself the promised land.

THE PROBLEM OF ETHICS FOR TWENTIETH-CENTURY MAN

by Albert Schweitzer

A versatile philosopher, theologian, musician, and medical missionary to darkest Africa—who has been called "the greatest man in the world"—offers a modern interpretation of Christian morals.

JUNE 13, 1953

THE PROBLEM OF ETHICS in the evolution of human thought cannot of course be dealt with exhaustively within the scope of the present article. By singling out the main features of this evolution, however, we can perhaps appreciate all the more clearly the nature of the role which ethics has played in the history of man's thinking.

What we call "ethics" and "morality"—which are terms borrowed from the Greek and the Latin respectively—may be broadly defined as our good behavior toward ourselves and other beings. We feel the obligation to concern ourselves not solely with our own well-being, but also with that of others and of human society. It is in the notion of the scope of this solidarity with others that the first evolution to be observed in the development of ethics occurs.

For the primitive the circle of solidarity is restricted. It is limited to those whom he can consider as in some way related to him by consanguinity, that is to say, to the members of his tribe, which he regards as a larger family. I speak from experience. In my hospital I have primitives. When I have occasion to ask a patient of this category to render some small services to a bedridden fellow-patient, he will oblige only if the latter belongs to his tribe. If this is not the case, he will reply quite candidly, "This not brother for me." No amount of persuasion and no kind of threat will budge him from his refusal to do that unimaginable thing: putting himself out for a stranger. I am the one who has to give in.

However, as man begins to reflect upon himself and his behavior toward others, he comes to realize that man as such is his fellow and his neighbor. In the course of a long evolutionary process he sees the circle of his responsibilities widen until it includes all the human beings with whom he has any association.

This clearer knowledge of ethics was achieved by the Chinese thinkers—Lao Tse, born in 604 B.C., Kung Tsu (Confucius), 551-479 B.C., Meng Tsu, 372-289 B.C., and Chuang Tsu, in the fourth century B.C.—and by the Hebrew prophets Amos, Hosea, and Isaiah of the eighth century B.C. The idea enounced by Jesus and Saint Paul that man owes himself to every human being is an integral part of Christian ethics.

For the great thinkers of India, whether they belong to Brahmanism, to Buddhism, or to Hinduism, the idea of brotherhood of all human beings is contained in their metaphysical notion of existence. But they encounter difficulties in incorporating it in their ethics. They are unable, in fact, to abolish the dividing walls between men erected by the existence of different castes and sanctioned by tradition. Zoroaster, who lived in the seventh century B.C., was prevented from arriving at the notion of the brotherhood of men because he had to make the distinction between those who believed in Ormuzd, the god of light and good, whom he heralded, and the unbelievers who remained under the sway of demons. He required believers, fighting for the coming of the reign of Ormuzd, to consider unbelievers as enemies and to treat them accordingly. To understand this position one must remember that the believers were the tribes of Bactrians who had become sedentary and aspired to live as honest and peaceful tillers of the soil, and that the unbelievers were the tribes which had remained nomadic, inhabiting the desert regions and living by pillage.

Plato and Aristotle, and with them the other thinkers of the classic period of Greek philosophy, consider only the Greek human being —a free man who is not under the necessity of earning his livelihood. Those who do not belong to this aristocracy are regarded by them as men of inferior quality in whom one need not be interested.

It was only in the course of the second period of Greek thought, that of the simultaneous flowering of Stoicism and Epicureanism, that the idea of the equality of men and of the interest attaching to the human being as such was recognized by the representatives of the two schools. The most remarkable proponent of this new conception is the Stoic Panaetius, who lived in the second century (180-110 B.C.). He is the prophet of humanism. The idea of the brotherhood of men does not become popular in antiquity. But the fact that philosophy should have proclaimed it as a conception dictated by reason is of great importance for its future.

It must be admitted, however, that the idea that the human being as such has a right to our interest has never enjoyed the full authority to which it might lay claim. Until our day it has been and continues to be constantly compromised by the importance assumed by differences of race, of religious belief, of nationality which cause us to regard our fellow-being as a stranger to whom we owe only indifference, if not contempt.

On undertaking to analyze the development of ethics one is led to give one's attention to the influence exerted upon ethics by the particular conception of the world to which it is related. There is, in fact, a fundamental difference between these various conceptions.

The difference stems from the manner in which the world itself is appraised. Some view it as inviting an affirmative attitude, which means interesting oneself in the things of this world and in the life we lead in it. Others, on the contrary, advocate an extraordinary negative attitude. They recommend that we dissociate ourselves from everything which concerns the world, including the existence which is ours upon this earth.

Affirmation is in conformity with our natural feeling; negation is opposed to it. Affirmation invites us to make a place for ourselves in the world and to engage in action; negation commits us to live in it as strangers and to choose nonactivity.

Ethics, by its very nature, is linked to the affirmation of the world. It is a response to the need to be active in order to serve the idea of good. It follows from this that the affirmation of the world favorably influences the development of ethics and that negation, on the contrary, impedes it. In the former case ethics can offer itself for what it is; in the latter it must relinquish its claims.

The negation of the world is professed by the thinkers of India and by the Christianity of antiquity and of the Middle Ages; affirmation by the Chinese thinkers, the Hebrew prophets, Zoroaster, and European thinkers of the Renaissance and of modern times.

Among the thinkers of India this negative conception of the world is the consequence of their conviction that true existence is immaterial, immutable, and eternal, and that the existence of the material world is unreal, deceptive, and transitory. The world which we are pleased to consider as real is for them but a mirage of the immaterial world in time and in space. It is wrong for man to interest himself in this phantasmagoria and in the role he plays in it. The only behavior compatible with a true knowledge of the nature of existence is nonactivity. In a certain measure nonactivity has an ethical character. In detaching himself from the things of this world man renounces the egoism which material interests and vulgar appetite inspire in him. Moreover, nonactivity means nonviolence. It preserves man from the danger of doing harm to others by acts of violence.

The philosophers of Brahmanism, of Sankhya, of Jainism, like Buddha, exalt nonviolence, which they call "ahimsa" and which they consider the sublime ethics. Nevertheless, it is imperfect and incomplete. It allows man the egoism of devoting himself entirely to the salvation which he hopes to gain by leading a kind of life which conforms to the true knowledge of the nature of existence; it does not command him in the name of compassion, but in the name of metaphysical theories; it demands only abstention from evil and not the activity which is inspired by the notion of good. Only the ethics which is allied to the affirmation of the world can be natural and complete. If, then, the ethics of the philosophers of India should venture to yield to the promptings of a more generous ethics than that of ahimsa, it will be able to do so only by making concessions to the affirmation of the world and to the principle of activity. Buddha, who takes a stand against the coldness of the Brahman doctrine by preaching pity, has difficulty in resisting the temptation of emancipating himself from the principle of nonactivity. He succumbs to it more than once, unable to help committing acts of charity or recommending them to his disciples. Under the cover of ethics the affirmation of the world wages a hidden struggle in India through the centuries against the principle of nonactivity. In Hinduism, which is a religious reaction from the exigencies of Brahmanism, this affirmation succeeds in making itself recognized as the equal of nonactivity. The understanding between them is proclaimed and specified in the Bhagavad-Gita, a didactic poem incorporated in the great epic of the Mahabharata.

The Bhagavad-Gita admits Brahmanism's conception of the world. It recognizes that the material world has only a deceptive reality and cannot lay claim to our interest. It is only a diverting show to which God treats himself. Man may, therefore, with good reason believe himself to be entitled to take part in this spectacle only in the capacity of a spectator. But by the same token he has the right to consider himself called upon to play his role as an actor in the play. Activity is thus justified by the spirit in which it operates. The man who practices it with the sole intention of fulfilling the will of God pursues the truth, even as does he who chooses nonactivity. On the other hand, ingenuous activity, which interests itself in this unreal world and undertakes to carry out in it any purpose whatever, is wrong and cannot be justified.

This theory which legitimizes activity by a logic resting on the idea that the world is but a show staged by God for his own enjoyment can in no way give satisfaction to true ethics, to that ethics which asserts the need to be active. The theory, nevertheless, enabled ethics to maintain itself in the Indies at a period when its existence was threatened by Brahmanism.

In our day the philosophers of India make great concessions to the principle of activity by invoking the fact that it is to be found also in the Upanishads. This is correct. The explanation is that the Aryans of India, in ancient times, as the Veda hymns tell us, led an existence filled with a naïve joy of living. The Brahman doctrine of the negation of the world makes its appearance, alongside of the affirmation, only in the Upanishads, sacred texts belonging to the beginning of the first millennium before Christ.

The Christianity of antiquity and of the Middle Ages professes the negation of the world, without however drawing from it the conclusion of nonactivity. This peculiarity stems from the fact that its negation of the world is of a different nature from that of the philosophers of India. According to its doctrine the world in which we live is not a phantasmagoria, but an imperfect world, destined to be transformed into the perfect world of the Kingdom of God. The idea of the Kingdom of God was created by the Hebrew prophets of the eighth century B.C. It is this idea also which is at the center of the religion of Zoroaster in the seventh century.

Jesus announced the imminence of the transformation of the material world into the world of the Kingdom of God. He exhorted men to seek the perfection required for participation in the new existence in the new world. He asked man to detach himself from the things of this world in order to occupy himself solely with the practice of good. He allowed him to hold aloof from the world, but not from his duties toward men. In his ethics activity preserves all its rights and all its obligations. Herein is where it differs from that of Buddha, with which it has in common the idea of compassion. Because it is animated by the spirit of activity the ethics of Christianity maintains an affinity with affirmation of the world.

The transformation of the world into that of the Kingdom of God, which the first Christians regarded as near at hand, did not take place. During antiquity and the Middle Ages Christianity thus remains in the situation of having to despair of this world, without the hope of seeing the coming of the other—the hope which had sustained the first Christians. It would have been natural for Christianity then to come round to the affirmation of the world. Its active ethics made it possible for it to do so. But in antiquity and in the

Middle Ages there did not exist a passionate affirmation of the world which alone would have served its purpose. This passionate affirmation came into being with the Renaissance. Christianity joined forces with it in the course of the sixteenth and seventeenth centuries. Its ethics, along with the ideal of self-perfection which it derived from Jesus, henceforth embraced also the other, which consists in creating new and better material and spiritual conditions for the existence of human society. From this time on Christian ethics was able to give an objective to its activity and thus achieved its full development. From the union of Christianity and the Renaissance's passionate affirmation of the world was born the civilization in which we live and which we have to maintain and to perfect. The ethical conceptions of the Chinese philosophers and that of Zoroaster were from their origin linked with the affirmation of the world. They too bear within themselves the energies capable of producing an ethical civilization.

Having reached a certain level, ethics tends to develop depth. This tendency manifests itself in the need which it experiences to dedicate itself to the search for the fundamental principle of good.

Ethics no longer finds entire satisfaction in defining, enumerating, and recommending various virtues and various duties, but seeks to understand what they have in common in their diversity and how they flow from a single conception of good. It is thus that the great Chinese thinkers came to proclaim benevolence toward men as a fundamental virtue.

In Hebrew ethics, even before Jesus, emerges the question of the great commandment whose fulfillment is equivalent to that of the entire law. Jesus, in accord with the tradition of the Hebrew theologians, raises love to the rank of a supreme commandment.

In the first century of the Christian era philosophers of Stoicism following the path laid out by Panaetius, the creator of the idea of humanism, likewise came to consider love as the virtue of virtues; they are Seneca, Epictetus, and the Emperor Marcus Aurelius. Their ethics is essentially that of the great Chinese thinkers. They have in common with them not only the principle of love, but in addition —what is more important—the conviction that it stems from reason and is fundamentally reasonable.

In the course of the first and second centuries of the Christian era Graeco-Roman philosophy thus came to profess the same ethical ideal as Christianity. The possibility of an understanding between the ancient world and Christianity seemed to offer itself. No such development occurred. Ethical Stoicism did not become popular. Moreover, it also considered Christianity the worst of superstitions because it based itself on a divine revelation occurring in Jesus Christ, and because it awaited the miraculous coming of a new world. Christianity for its part despised philosophy as being merely the wisdom of this world. What separated the two also was the fact that philosophy adhered to the idea of the affirmation of the world, and Christianity to the idea of negation. No understanding was possible.

After a passage of centuries, however, such an understanding did occur. When in the sixteenth and seventeenth centuries Christianity began to familiarize itself with the passionate affirmation of the world which the Renaissance had bequeathed to European thought, it made acquaintance at the same time with ethical Stoicism and discovered with surprise that Jesus's principle of love had already been enunciated as a rational truth. It deduced from this that the fundamental ideas of religion must also be revealed truths subsequently confirmed by reason. Among the thinkers who at that time felt themselves to belong both to Christianity and to Stoicism the most remarkable were Erasmus of Rotterdam and Hugo Grotius.

Under the influence of Christianity the ethics of philosophy acquired an enthusiasm which it did not possess up to that time. Under the influence of philosophy the ethics of Christianity for its part began to reflect upon what it owed to itself and upon what it must accomplish in this world. Thus was born a spirit which could not permit the ethics of love to tolerate any longer the injustices, the cruelties, and the harmful superstitions which it had previously allowed. Torture was abolished, the scourge of sorcery trials came to an end, inhuman laws gave way to more human ones. A reform movement unprecedented in the history of humanity was undertaken and accomplished in the first enthusiasm of the discovery that the principle of love is taught also by reason.

To demonstrate the rationality of altruism, the love of others, eighteenth-century philosophers, including Hartley, the Baron d'Holbach, Helvetius, and Bentham, well-meaningly invoked the single argument of its utility. The Chinese thinkers and the representatives of ethical Stoicism had also brought forward this argument, but had advanced others as well. According to the thesis defended by these eighteenth-century thinkers, altruism could be regarded simply as enlightened self-interest, taking into account the fact that the well-being of individuals and of society can be assured only by the devotion men show toward their fellows. With this superficial thesis Kant and the Scots philosopher David Hume, among others took sharp issue. Kant, in his eagerness to defend the dignity of ethics, goes so far as to claim that its utility must not be taken into consideration. However manifest it may be, it must not be allowed as a motive of ethics. Ethics, according to the doctrine of the categorical imperative, commands in an absolute fashion. It is our conscience which reveals to us what is right and what is wrong. We have merely to obey it. The moral law which we bear within ourselves gives us the certainty that we belong not only to the world as it appears to us in time and space, but that we are at the same time citizens of the world as such, the spiritual world.

Hume, in order to refute the utilitarian thesis, proceeds empirically. He analyzes the motives of ethics and reaches the conclusion that it is above all a matter of feeling. Nature, he argues, has endowed us with the faculty of sympathy. The latter enables us and obliges us to experience the joy, the apprehensions, and the sufferings of others as our own. We are, according to an image used by Hume, like strings vibrating in unison with those which are played. It is this sympathy which leads us to devote ourselves to others and to wish to contribute to their well-being and to that of society. Philosophy since Hume—if we leave aside Nietzsche's venture—has not dared seriously to question the concept that ethics is above all a matter of compassion.

But where does this leave ethics? Is it capable of defining and of limiting the obligations of devotion to others and thus reconciling egoism and altruism, as the theory of utilitarianism attempted to do?

Hume hardly considers the question. Neither have suceeding philosophers judged it necessary to take into consideration the consequences of the principle of devotion through compassion. It is as though they sensed that these consequences might prove somewhat troublesome. And so indeed they are. The ethics of devotion through compassion no longer has the character of a law which we should like to continue to attribute to it. It no longer involves clearly established and clearly formulated commandments. It is fundamentally subjective, because it leaves to each one of us the responsibility of deciding how far he shall go in devotion.

Not only does the ethics of devotion cease to prescribe in a precise fashion; it becomes by degrees less disposed to confine itself to the realm of the possible, as the law must do. It is constantly obliging us to attempt the impossible, to push devotion to the point of compromising our very existence. In the dreadful times which we have lived through many such situations arose, and many were those who sacrificed themselves for others. Even in everyday life the ethics of devotion, if it does not go to the length of demanding this ultimate sacrifice, often requires each one of us to abdicate interests, and to give up advantages out of regard for others. But too often we manage to silence our conscience, which is the guardian of our sense of responsibility. How many are the conflicts in which the ethics of devotion abandons us to ourselves. Those who manage enterprises rarely have occasion to congratulate themselves on having, out of compassion, given employment to someone who urgently needed it instead of entrusting it to the most qualified. But woe to them if they should believe themselves warranted by experiences of this kind never again to take heed of the argument of compassion.

There is a final consequence to be drawn from the principle of devotion: it no longer allows us to concern ourselves solely with human beings, but obliges us to act in the same way toward all living beings whose fate may be influenced by us. They too are our fellow-creatures by the fact they experience as we do an aspiration to happiness, as well as fear and suffering, and like us dread annihilation.

The man who has preserved his sensibility intact finds it altogether natural to have pity for all living beings. Why can philosophy not make up its mind to recognize that our behavior toward them must form an integral part of the ethics which it teaches? The reason is quite simple. Philosophy fears, and rightly so, that this immense enlargement of the circle of our responsibilities will deprive ethics of the slight hope it still has of being able to formulate commandments in a way that is at all reasonable and satisfying. Indeed, concern with the fate of all the beings with whom we have to deal creates even more numerous and more troublesome conflicts for us than those of devotion limited to human beings. In respect to creatures we find ourselves constantly in situations which oblige us to cause suffering and to impair life. The peasant cannot let all the animals born in his flock survive; he can keep only those he can feed and which it will pay him to raise. In many cases we even face the necessity of sacrificing lives to save others. A man who picks up a stray bird finds himself obliged to kill insects or fish to feed it. In acting thus he is completely in the realm of the arbitrary. By what right does he sacrifice many lives in order to save a single life? In exterminating animals which he regards as harmful in order to protect others he likewise falls into the realm of the arbitrary.

It is, therefore, incumbent upon each one of us to judge whether we find ourselves under the unavoidable necessity of inflicting suffering and of killing, and to resign ourselves to becoming guilty by necessity. As for forgiveness, we must seek it by missing no

opportunity to succor living beings. How much better off we should
be if men would reflect on the kindness which they owe to creatures
and would abstain from all the harm they do them through heed-
lessness. The fight against the inhuman traditions and the inhuman
feelings which are still current in our day is one which our civilization must wage, if we have any concern for our self-respect.

Among the inhuman customs which our civilization and our
sentiment owe it to themselves no longer to tolerate I cannot refrain from naming two: bullfighting, with the kill, and stag-hunting.
Thus it is the requirement of compassion toward all living beings
which makes ethics as complete as it must be.

There has been another great change in the situation of ethics:
it is today no longer able to count on the support of a conception
of the world which can serve as its justification.

At all times it has been convinced that it was merely exacting
the behavior conforming to the knowledge of the true nature of
the universal will which manifests itself in creation. This is the
conviction on which not only religion but also the rationalist philosophy of the seventeenth and eighteenth centuries are based. But
it so happens that the conception of the world which ethics can
invoke is the result of the interpretation of the very world to which
ethics has offered, and still offers, itself. It attributes to the universal will qualities and intentions which give satisfaction to its
own way of feeling and of judging. But in the course of the nineteenth century the research which allowed itself to be guided solely
by concern for truth was bound to surrender to the evidence that
ethics can expect nothing from a true knowledge of the world. The
progress of science consists in an increasingly precise observation
of the processes of nature. These allow us to harness the energies
manifesting themselves in the universe to our own uses. But they
oblige us at the same time increasingly to give up any attempt to
understand its intentions. The world offers us the disconcerting
spectacle of the will to life in conflict with itself. One existence
maintains itself at the expense of another.

How can the ethics of devotion maintain itself without being
sustained by a notion of the world which justifies it? It seems
destined to founder in skepticism. This, however, is not the fate to
which it is dedicated. In its beginnings ethics had to appeal to a
conception of the world which would satisfy it. Having arrived at
the knowledge that its fundamental principle is devotion, it becomes fully conscious of itself and thereby becomes autonomous.

We are in a position to understand its origins and its basis by meditating on the world and on ourselves.

We lack a complete and satisfying knowledge of the world. We are reduced to the simple observation that everything in it is life, like ourselves, and that all life is mystery. Our true knowledge of the world consists in being penetrated by the mystery of existence and of life. This mystery becomes only more mysterious as scientific research progresses. Being penetrated by the mystery of life corresponds to what in the language of mysticism is called "learned ignorance," which at least has knowledge of the essential.

The immediate datum of our consciousness, to which we come back each time we desire to achieve an understanding of ourselves and of our situation in the world, is: I am life which wants to live, surrounded by life which wants to live.

Being will-to-life, I feel the obligation to respect all will-to-life about me as equal to my own.

The fundamental idea of good is thus that it consists in preserving life, in favoring it, in wanting to bring it to its highest value, and evil consists in destroying life, doing it injury, hindering its development.

The principle of this veneration of life corresponds to that of love, as it has been discovered by religion and philosophy which sought to understand the fundamental notion of good.

The term "respect for life" is broader and because of this more colorless than that of love. But it bears the same energies within it.

This essentially philosophical notion of good has also the advantage of being more complete than that of love. Love includes only our obligation toward other beings, but not those toward ourselves. One cannot deduce from it, for example, the quality of veracity, a primordial quality of the ethical personality along with that of compassion. The respect which man owes to his own life imposes upon him that he be faithful to himself by renouncing every kind of dissimulation to which he might be tempted to resort in a given circumstance.

Through respect for life we enter into a spiritual relationship with the world. All the efforts undertaken by philosophy which built up grandiose systems to bring us into relation with the Absolute have remained vain. The Absolute is so abstract in character that we cannot communicate with it. It is not given to us to put ourselves at the disposal of the infinite and inscrutable creative will which is the basis of all existence, by having an understanding of its nature and its intentions. But we enter into spiritual relationship with it by feeling ourselves under the impression of the mystery of life and by devoting ourselves to all the living beings whom we have the occasion and the power to serve. The ethics which obliges us solely to concern ourselves with men and society cannot have this meaning. Only that which is universal in obliging us to concern ourselves with all beings brings us truly into relationship with the Universe and the will which manifests itself in it.

In the world the will-to-life is in conflict with itself. In us, through a mystery which we do not understand, it wishes to be at peace with itself. In the world it manifests itself, in us it reveals itself. It reveals to us, among other things, that the world is our spiritual destiny. By conforming to it we live our existence instead of submitting to it. Through respect for life we become pious in an elementary, deep, and living sense.

HOW MUSIC HAPPENS

by Paul Hindemith

One of America's great classical composers explains how he trans-forms into symphonies the inner singing and ringing that bubbles up in any would-be musician's mind.

DECEMBER 29, 1951

THE WORD "IDEA" is a very vague term for what we really mean when we talk of the composer's creative imagination. The German word *Einfall* is the perfect expression needed in our situation. *Einfall,* from the verb *einfallen,* to drop in, describes beautifully the strange spontaneity that we associate with artistic ideas in general and with musical creation in particular. Something—you know not what—drops into your mind—you know not whence—and there it grows—you know not how—into some form—you know not why. This seems to be the general opinion, and we cannot blame the layman if he is unable to find rational explanations for so strange an occurrence.

Even many composers, although the rather prosaic labor of writing musical symbols on paper absorbs about 99 per cent of their work, look at the apparently unprompted appearance of their own ideas with amazement. They are in a permanent state of artistic narcissism, compared with which the harmless self-admiration of the original Narcissus is but child's play. They will tell you about their creations as they would about natural phenomena or heavenly revelations. You have the impression, not that they themselves did their composing, but that "it" composed within them almost in spite of their own existence.

Let us look with a somewhat more temperate attitude at the ideas, the *Einfälle* that populate our stage setup by musical space and musical time. When we talk about *Einfälle* we usually mean little motifs, consisting of a few tones—tones often not even felt as tones but felt merely as a vague curve of sound. They are common to all people, professionals and laymen alike; but while in the layman's mind they die away unused in their earliest infancy, the creative musician knows how to catch them and subject them to further treatment.

462

I know a scientist who said: "Everybody can have—and has—scientific ideas, but it takes a scientist to know what to do with them." I am very much inclined to include musical ideas in this statement. Who can be sure that the inner singing and ringing that any Mr. or Mrs. X feels bubbling up in a musically uncultivated mind is not, in its unshaped authenticity, at least as beautiful and satisfactory as—and perhaps even better than—the greatest composer's unshaped inner singing and ringing? It is exciting to know how primitive, commonplace, colorless, and insignificant the first ideas, the primordial *Einfälle,* of even extraordinary musical masters are. But it seems almost more exciting to recognize the specific talent with which those masters keep their ideas fresh and, despite all mutations, basically intact during the sometimes considerably long interval of time required for the treatment of these ideas. In this they are led by tradition, by the presumptive conditions of performance of the future piece, by its purpose and style, and, to a minor degree, by personal whims and fancies that may add certain flavors to the final form. Sometimes a composer may drive his musical material, on its way from the *Einfall* to its completion in a piece, through a tremendous barrier of frustrations which may suppress most of the aforesaid considerations and lead, even with the very first attempts at treating the basic material, to formulations of utter strangeness.

Although it is not possible to watch the source of the singing and ringing in other people's minds—it is not wholly easy even to analyze one's own mind far back into those remote regions of origin and creation—we can in some cases get glimpses of the early fate of musical ideas. To be sure, in order to be observable they must already have crossed the limitations of their first specterlike appearance and have gained some primordial form, either mentally by addition of the results of constructive conclusions, or even visibly in some jotted-down notes on paper. For the most part, only the mental form will exist, until a more extensive treatment brings the rudimentary material into some musically organized, yet still very primitive shape. Jotted-down notes can be regarded as the first steps away from the source, only if a composer's experience of many years has taught him to reduce the normally very long route from his brain to his writing hand. It is in the rare cases when composers of this kind have left us some of these first-step sketches that we can imaginatively trace these embryonic structures back to their still more elemental form, the original inner singing and ringing. Fortunately for our argument, one great composer left us a good many of these first-step sketches. I am referring to the sketch books of Beethoven.

In them we find many of the well-known themes which we are accustomed to think of as the most nearly perfect, the most convincing, the most suitable thematic creations: themes so homogeneous, so integrated, that they must have sprung up like the fully armed Minerva out of Jupiter's head. And yet we see them go through a process of transformation and conversion which sometimes gives us five or more intermediate steps from the first structural treatment to the final version. Some of the first versions are in quality so far below the final form, that we would be inclined any time to attribute their invention to Mr. X. And to watch the plodding through those many stages of development is oftentimes rather depressing: if that is the way a genius works, chiseling and molding desperately in order to produce a convincing form, what then is the fate of the smaller fellow? Perhaps it is always true that in working from the tiniest and almost imperceptible spark of structural invention up to an intelligible musical form a petty composer is very much like Beethoven. If only the work involved in reaching this goal really counted, there would be many a genius. The petty composer could do the same, technically, as the real genius did, and he would almost be justified in feeling godlike—as so many authors did and do—because he was able to turn his bubbling inner singing and ringing into music, which Mr. and Mrs. X could never do.

Does all this mean that the genius and the average producer of music are of the same stuff; that in reality there are no such things as musical imagination, ideas, *Einfälle;* and that by mere accident one individual happens to develop into a Beethoven while the other just as accidentally remains an unknown sixth-rate musician? No. It merely means that if we want to understand the power that animates the ideational personages on our scene of musical time and space, we must not ramble through the mental regions that are common to Mr. X, the untalented composer, and the genius. It means that the regions of genuine musical creation are so far beyond our everyday experiences, that Mr. X will never know what they are and the untalented composer will never enter their inner secrets. Mr. X may always have all the wonderful ideas necessary for an excellent work of art; the little fellow may possess the acutest technique, which permits him to develop the most rudimentary ideas into forms of sound. But what the genius has—and what is far beyond their reach—is vision.

What is musical vision?

We all know the impression of a very heavy flash of lightning in the night. Within a second's time we see a broad landscape, not only in its general outlines but with every detail. Although we could never describe each single component of the picture, we feel that not even the smallest leaf of grass escapes our attention. We experience a view, immensely comprehensive and at the same time immensely detailed, that we never could have under normal daylight conditions, and perhaps not during the night either, if our senses and nerves were not strained by the extraordinary suddenness of the event.

Compositions must be conceived the same way. If you cannot, in the flash of a single moment, see a composition in its absolute entirety, with every pertinent detail in its proper place, you are not a real composer. The musical creator, like any other creative individual, is permitted to share with the demiurge the possession of vitalizing visions; but it is the privilege of the demiurge to transform them into concrete existence without any interfering technical obstacle, whereas the creative musician, by reason of his earthly heritage, has to overcome many hurdles between them and their realization. If he is a real composer he will not feel disturbed or discouraged by this fact. Not only will he have the gift of seeing —illuminated in his mind's eye as if by a flash of lightning—a complete musical form (though its subsequent realization in a performance may take three hours or more); he will have the energy, persistence, and skill to bring this envisioned form into existence, so that even after months of work not one of its details will be lost or fail to fit into his photomental picture. This does not mean that any *f sharp* in the six-hundred-and-twelfth measure of the final piece would have been determined in the very first flash of cognition. If the seer should in this first flash concentrate his attention on any particular detail of the whole, he would never conceive the totality; but if the conception of this totality strikes his mind like lightning, this *f sharp* and all the other thousands of notes and other means of expression will fall into line almost without his knowing it.

In working out his material the composer will always have before his mental eye the entire picture. In writing melodies or harmonic progressions he does not have to select them arbitrarily, he merely has to fulfill what the conceived totality demands. This is the true reason for Beethoven's apparently more than philistine bickering with his material: a desire not to improve or to change any *Einfall* but to accommodate it to the unalterable necessities of an envisioned totality, even if with all his technical skill and experience he has to press it through five or more versions that distort it past recognition.

The half-gifted composer may have visions too; but instead of seeing them in the clarity of lightning, he perceives dark contours which he has not the divination to fill out appropriately. He may have lots of exciting and wonderful single ideas which he patches together in order to get a musical form that corresponds with his shadowy idea, after the formula: the greater the number of beautiful details, the more beautiful the over-all picture must be. For those gifted with flashlike visions, this hunting for beautiful details seems to be useless, since in fulfilling the demands of the vision they have no choice as to the kind and shape of building material; they can only try to obey these demands and find the sole suitable solution. If they should disregard them completely and consider a search for beautiful details justifiable, they would not be creative artists, any more than a philatelist is—or any other assembler of valuables, who with all his efforts succeeds merely in getting together a collection, never in creating an organism.

It is obvious that a composer, during the long period the notation of his work requires, is always in danger of losing the original vision of it. The flashlike picture may fade out, the outlines may dissolve, many details may disappear in darkness. One of the characteristics of the talent of a creative genius seems to be the ability to retain the keenness of the first vision until its embodiment in the finished piece is achieved. There is no doubt that this embodiment, if it is to appear as a true realization of the vision, can come to life only with the assistance of a great amount of technical skill. Skill can never make up for lack of vision, but on the other hand a vision will never receive its true materialization if a composer's technique does not provide every means toward this end. Yet, compositional technique can be acquired even by noncomposers, while clear visions are the privilege of real creative talent.

To acquire a decent technique in composition seems not to be too difficult. After all, there are a restricted number of rules of thumb concerning voice leading, harmonic progressions, tonal arrangements, and so forth, which are basically valid in all kinds of musical settings, regardless of style and purpose. The fact that after four or five years of study many so-called composers are leaving our schools with sufficient practical knowledge in the craft of putting tones together seems to prove this point. But the technique of composition, like the technique of any other art, is a deceptive thing. You may manage the few basic rules of construction with all their combinative possibilities pretty well, and yet the highest degree of subtlety, in which each technical item is in congruence with the respective part of the vision, again may be attained by no one but the genius. There are relatively few masterworks in which this ultimate congruence can be felt. Even in our stockpile of classical music, which by common agreement consists of works written by superior composers, not many pieces fulfill those highest requirements. True, there are many other great and excellent works, which in their artistic value are by no means less important. They may in their ability to speak as human creations to human beings be the closest to our hearts, but it is in those few uncontested masterpieces that we feel the breath of universality and eternity, because their particular kind of perfection, the absolute coincidence of intention and realization, is almost superhuman.

The fact that very few masterworks display this congruence of vision and materialization shows us that even the composer who possesses the greatest gift and the highest technical skill is not always able to reach this goal. A tremendous effort is necessary in order to work toward it; not merely a technical effort, but a moral effort, too—the effort to subject all considerations of technique, style, and purpose to this one ideal: congruence.

THE NATURAL
SUPERIORITY OF WOMEN

by Ashley Montagu

A noted anthropologist offers a serious, scientifically supported argument for the superiority of the fair sex as his part in a controversy that promises to continue for some time.

MARCH 1, 1952

OH, NO! I can hear it said, *not* superior. Equal, partners, complementary, different, but *not* superior. I can even foresee that men will mostly smile, while women, alarmed, will rise to the defense of men—women always have, and always will. I hope that what I shall have to say in this article will make them even more willing to do so, for men need their help more than they as yet, mostly, consciously realize.

Women superior to men? This is a new idea. There have been people who have cogently, but apparently not convincingly, argued that women were as good as men, but I do not recall anyone who has publicly provided the evidence or even argued that women were better than or superior to men. How, indeed, could one argue such a case in the face of all the evidence to the contrary? Is it not a fact that by far the largest number of geniuses, great painters, poets, philosophers, scientists, etc., etc., have been men, and that women have made, by comparison, a very poor showing? Clearly the superiority is with men. Where are the Leonardos, the Michelangelos, the Shakespeares, the Donnes, the Galileos, the Whiteheads, the Kants, the Bachs, *et al.,* of the feminine sex? In fields in which women have excelled, in poetry and the novel, how many poets and novelists of the really first rank have there been? Haven't well-bred young women been educated for centuries in music? And how many among them have been great composers or instrumentalists? Composers—none of the first rank. Instrumentalists—well, in the recent period there have been such accomplished artists as Myra Hess and Wanda Landowska. Possibly there is a clue here to the answer to the question asked. May it not be that women are just about to emerge from the period of subjection during which they were the "niggers" of the masculine world?

The Royal Society of London has at last opened its doors and admitted women to the highest honor which it is in the power of the English scientific world to bestow—the Fellowship of the Royal Society. I well remember that when I was a youth—less than a quarter of a century ago—it was considered inconceivable that any woman would ever have brains enough to attain great distinction in science. Mme. Curie was an exception. But the half-dozen women Fellows of the Royal Society in England are not. Nor is Lisa Meitner. And Mme. Curie no longer remains the only woman to share in the Nobel Prize award for science. There is Marie Curie's daughter, Irene Joliot-Curie, and there is Gerty Cory (1947) for physiology and medicine. Nobel Prizes in literature have gone to Selma Lagerlöf, Grazia Deledda, Sigrid Undset, Pearl Buck, and Gabriela Mistral. As an artist Mary Cassatt (1845-1926) was every bit as good as her great French friends Degas and Manet considered her to be, but it has taken the rest of the world another fifty years grudgingly to admit it. Among contemporaries Georgia O'Keeffe can hold her own with the best.

It is not, however, going to be any part of this article to show that women are about to emerge as superior scientists, musicians, painters, or the like. I believe that in these fields they may emerge as equally good, and possibly not in as large numbers as men, largely because the motivations and aspiration of most women will continue to be directed elsewhere. But what must be pointed out is that women are, in fact, just beginning to emerge from the period of subjection when they were treated in a manner not unlike that which is still meted out to the Negro in the Western world. The women of the nineteenth century were the "niggers" of the male-dominated world. All the traits that are mythically attributed to the Negro at the present time were for many generations saddled upon women. Women had smaller brains than men and less intelligence, they were more emotional and unstable, in a crisis you could always rely upon them to swoon or become otherwise helpless, they had little judgment and less sense, could not be relied upon to handle money, and as for the world outside, there they could be employed only at the most menial and routine tasks.

The biggest dent in this series of myths was made by World War I, when women were for the first time called upon to replace men in occupations which were formerly the exclusive preserve of men. They became bus drivers, conductors, factory workers, farm workers, laborers, supervisors, executive officers, and a great many other things at which many had believed they could never work. At first it was said that they didn't do as well as men, then it was grudgingly admitted that they weren't so bad, and by the time the war was over many employers were reluctant to exchange their women employees for men! But the truth was out—women could do as well as men in most of the fields which had been considered forever closed to them because of their alleged natural incapacities, and in many fields, particularly where delicate precision work was involved, they had proved themselves superior to men. From 1918 to 1939 the period for women was one essentially of consolidation of gains, so that by the time that World War II broke out there was no hesitation on the part of anyone in calling upon women to serve in the civilian roles of men and in many cases also in the armed services.

But women have a long way to go before they reach full emancipation—emancipation from the myths from which they themselves suffer. It is, of course, untrue that women have smaller brains than men. The fact is that in proportion to body weight they have larger brains then men; but this fact is in itself of no importance because within the limits of normal variation of brain size and weight there exists no relation between these factors and intelligence. Women have been conditioned to believe that they are inferior to men and they have assumed that what everyone believes is a fact of nature; and as men occupy the superior positions in almost all societies, this superiority is taken to be a natural one. "Woman's place is in the home" and man's place is in the counting-house and on the board of directors. "Women should not meddle in men's affairs." And yet the world does move. Some women have become Members of Parliament and even attained Cabinet rank. In the United States they have even gotten as far as the Senate. They have participated in peace conferences, but it is still inconceivable to most persons that there should ever be a woman Prime Minister or President. And yet that day, too, will come. *Eppure si muove!*

Woman has successfully passed through the abolition period, the abolition of her thralldom to man; she has now to pass successfully through the period of emancipation, the freeing of herself from the myth of inferiority, and the realization of her potentialities to the fullest.

And now for the evidence which proves the superiority of woman to man. But first, one word in explanation of the use of the word "superiority." The word is used in its common sense as being of better quality than, or of higher nature or character. Let us begin at the very beginning. What about the structure of the sexes? Does one show any superiority over the other? The answer is a resounding

"Yes!" And I should like this "Yes" to resound all over the world, for no one has made anything of this key fact which lies at the base of all the differences between the sexes and the superiority of the female to the male. I refer to the chromosomal structure of the sexes. The chromosomes, those small cellular bodies which contain the hereditary particles, the genes, which so substantially influence one's development and fate as an organism, provide us with our basic facts.

In the sex cells there are twenty-four chromosomes, but only one of these is a sex chromosome. There are two kinds of sex chromosomes, X and Y. Half the sperm cells carry X and half carry Y chromosomes. All the female ova are made up of X-chromosomes. When an X-bearing sperm fertilizes an ovum the offspring is always female. When a Y-bearing chromosome fertilizes an ovum the offspring is always male. And this is what makes the difference between the sexes. So what? Well, the sad fact is that the Y-chromosome is but an iota, the merest bit, of a remnant of an X-chromosome; it is a crippled X-chromosome. The X-chromosomes are fully developed structures; the Y-chromosome is the merest comma. It is as if in the evolution of sex a particle one day broke away from an X-chromosome, and thereafter in relation to X-chromosomes could produce only an incomplete female—the creature we now call the male! It is to this original chromosomal deficiency that all the various troubles to which the male falls heir can be traced.

In the first place the chromosomal deficiency of the male determines his incapacity to have babies. This has always been a sore point with men, though consciously they would be the last to admit it, although in some primitive societies, as among the Australian aborigines, it is the male who conceives a child by dreaming it, and then telling his wife. In this way a child is eventually born to them, the wife being merely the incubator who hatches the egg placed there through the grace of her husband.

The fact that men cannot have babies and suckle them nor remain in association with their children as closely as the wife has an enormous effect upon their subsequent psychological development. Omitting altogether from consideration the psychologic influences exercised by the differences in the hormonal secretions of the sexes, one can safely say that the mother-child relationship confers enormous benefits upon the mother which are not nearly so substantively operative in the necessary absence of such a relationship between father and child. The maternalizing influences of being a mother in addition to the fact of being a woman have from the very beginning of the human species—about a million years ago—made the female the more humane of the sexes. The love of a mother for her child is the basic patent and the model for *all* human relationships. Indeed, to the extent to which men approximate in their relationships with their fellow-men to the love of the mother for her child, to that extent do they move more closely to the attainment of perfect human relations. The mother-child relationship is a dependent-interdependent one. The interstimulation between mother and child is something which the father misses, and to that extent suffers from the want of. In short, the female in the mother-child relationship has the advantage of having to be more considerate, more self-sacrificing, more co-operative, and more altruistic than usually falls to the lot of the male.

The female thus acquires, in addition to whatever natural biological advantages she starts with, a competence in social understanding which is usually denied the male. This, I take it, is one of the reasons why women are usually so much more able to perceive the nuances and pick up the subliminal signs in human behavior which almost invariably pass men by. It was, I believe, George Jean Nathan who called woman's intuition merely man's transparency. With all due deference to Mr. Nathan and sympathy for his lot as a mere male, I would suggest that man's opacity would be nearer the mark. It is because women have had to be so unselfish and forbearing and self-sacrificing and maternal that they possess a deeper understanding than men of what it is to be human. What is so frequently termed feminine indecision, the inability of women to make up their minds, is in fact an inverse reflection of the trigger-thinking of men. Every salesgirl prefers the male customer because women take time to think about what they are buying, and the male usually hasn't sense enough to do so. Women don't think in terms of "Yes" or "No." Life isn't as simple as all that— except to males. Men tend to think in terms of the all-or-none principle, in terms of black and white. Women are more ready to make adjustments, to consider the alternative possibilities, and see the other colors and gradations in the range between black and white.

By comparison with the deep involvement of women in living, men appear to be only superficially so. Compare the love of a male for a female with the love of the female for the male. It is the difference between a rivulet and a great deep ocean. Women love the human race; men are, on the whole, hostile to it. Men act as if they haven't been adequately loved, as if they had been frustrated and rendered hostile, and becoming aggressive they say that aggressiveness is natural and women are inferior in this respect because they tend to be gentle and unaggressive! But it is precisely in this capacity to love and unaggressiveness that the superiority of women to men is demonstrated, for whether it be natural to be loving and co-operative or not, so far as the human species is concerned, its evolutionary destiny, its very survival is more closely tied to this capacity for love and co-operation than with any other. So that unless men learn from women how to be more loving and co-operative they will go on making the kind of mess of the world which they have so effectively achieved thus far.

And this is, of course, where women can realize their power for good in the world, and make their greatest gains. *It is the function of women to teach men how to be human.* Women must not permit themselves to be deviated from this function by those who tell them that their place is in the home in subservient relation to man. It is, indeed, in the home that the foundations of the kind of world in which we live are laid, and in this sense it will always remain true that the hand that rocks the cradle is the hand that rules the world. And it is in this sense that women must assume the job of making men who will know how to make a world fit for human beings to live in. The greatest single step forward in this direction will be made when women consciously assume this task—the task of teaching their children to be like themselves, loving and co-operative.

As for geniuses, I think that almost everyone will agree that there have been more geniuses for being human among women than there have been among men. This, after all, is the true genius of women, and it is because we have not valued the qualities for being human anywhere nearly as highly as we have valued those for accomplishment in the arts and sciences that we have out-of-focusedly almost forgotten them. Surely, the most valuable quality in any human being is his capacity for being loving and co-operative. We have been placing our emphases on the wrong values—it is time we recognized what every man and every woman at the very least subconsciously knows—the value of being loving, and the value of those who can teach this better than anyone else.

Physically and psychically women are by far the superiors of men. The old chestnut about women being more emotional than men has been forever destroyed by the facts of two great wars. Women under blockade, heavy bombardment, concentration camp confinement, and similar rigors withstand them vastly more successfully than men. The psychiatric casualties of civilian populations under such conditions are mostly masculine, and there are more men in our mental hospitals than there are women. The steady hand at the

helm is the hand that has had the practice at rocking the cradle.
Because of their greater size and weight men are physically more
powerful than women—which is not the same thing as saying that
they are stronger. A man of the same size and weight as a woman
of comparable background and occupational status would probably
not be any more powerful than a woman. As far as constitutional
strength is concerned women are stronger than men. Many diseases
from which men suffer can be shown to be largely influenced by
their relation to the male Y-chromosome. From fertilization on more
males die than females. Deaths from almost all causes are more frequent in males at all ages. Though women are more frequently
ill than men, they recover from illness more easily and more frequently than men.

Women, in short, are fundamentally more resistant than men.
With the exception of the organ systems subserving the functions
of reproduction women suffer much less frequently than men from
the serious disorders which affect mankind. With the exception of
India women everywhere live longer than men. For example, the
expectation of life of the female child of white parentage in the
United States at the present time is over seventy-one years, whereas
for the male it is only sixty-five and a half years. Women are both
biologically stronger and emotionally better shock-absorbers than
men. The myth of masculine superiority once played such havoc
with the facts that in the nineteenth century it was frequently
denied by psychiatrists that the superior male could ever suffer from
hysteria. Today it is fairly well known that males suffer from hysteria and hysteriform conditions with a preponderance over the
female of seven to one! Epilepsy is much more frequent in males,
and stuttering has an incidence of eight males to one female.

At least four disorders are now definitely known to be due to
genes carried in the Y-chromosomes, and hence are disorders which
can appear only in males. These are barklike skin (ichthyosis hys-
trix gravior), dense hairy growth on the ears (hypertrichosis), non-
painful hard lesions of the hands and feet (keratoma dissipatum),
and a form of webbing of the toes. It is however, probable that the
disadvantages accruing to the male are not so much due to what is
in the Y-chromosome as to what is wanting in it. This is well shown
in such serious disorders as hemophilia or bleeder's disease. Hemophilia is inherited as a single sex-linked recessive gene. The gene,
or hereditary particle, determining hemophilia is linked to the
X-chromosome. When, then, an X-chromosome which carries the
hemophilia gene is transmitted to a female it is highly improbable
that it will encounter another X-chromosome carrying such a gene;

hence, while not impossible, hemophilia has never been described in a female. Females are the most usual transmitters of the hemophilia gene, but it is only the males who are affected, and they are affected because they don't have any properties in their Y-chromosome capable of suppressing the action of the hemophilia gene. The mechanism of and the explanation for (red-green) color blindness is the same. About 8 per cent of all white males are color-blind, but only half of one per cent of females are so affected.

Need one go on? Here, in fact, we have the explanation of the greater constitutional strength of the female as compared with the male, namely, in the possession of two complete sex chromosomes by the female and only one by the male. This may not be, and probably is not, the complete explanation of the physical inferiorities of the male as compared with the female, but it is certainly physiologically the most demonstrable and least questionable one. To the unbiased student of the facts there can no longer remain any doubt of the constitutional superiority of the female. I hope that I have removed any remaining doubts about her psychological superiority where psychological superiority most counts, namely, in a human being's capacity for loving other human beings.

I think we have overemphasized the value of intellectual qualities and grossly underemphasized the value of the qualities of humanity which women possess to such a high degree. I hope I shall not be taken for an anti-intellectual when I say that intellect without humanity is not good enough, and that what the world is suffering from at the present time is not so much an overabundance of intellect as an insufficiency of humanity. Consider men like Lenin, Stalin, and Hitler. These are the extreme cases. What these men lacked was the capacity to love. What they possessed in so eminent a degree was the capacity to hate. It is not for nothing that the Bolsheviks attempted to abolish the family and masculinize women, while the Nazis made informers of children against their parents and put the state so much before the family that it became a behemoth which has well-nigh destroyed everyone who was victimized by it.

What the world stands so much in need of at the present time, and what it will continue to need if it is to endure and increase in happiness, is more of the maternal spirit and less of the masculine. We need more persons who will love and less who will hate, and we need to understand how we can produce them; for if we don't try to understand how we may do so we shall continue to flounder in the morass of misunderstanding which frustrated love creates. For frustrated love, the frustration of the tendencies to love with which the infant is born, constitutes hostility. Hatred is love frustrated. This is what too many men suffer from and an insufficient number of women recognize, or at least too many women behave as if they didn't recognize it. What most women have learned to recognize is that the much-bruited superiority of the male isn't all that it's cracked up to be. The male doesn't seem to be as wise and as steady as they were taught to believe. But there appears to be a conspiracy of silence on this subject. Perhaps women feel that men ought to be maintained in the illusion of their superiority because it might not be good for them or the world to learn the truth. In this sense this article, perhaps, should have been entitled "What Every Woman Knows." But I'm not sure that every woman knows it. What I am sure of is that many women don't appear to know it, and that there are even many women who are horrified at the thought that anyone can entertain the idea that women are anything but inferior to men. This sort of childishness does no one any good. The world is in a mess. Men, without any assistance from women, have created it, and they have created it not because they have been failed by women, but because men have never really given women a chance to serve them as they are best equipped to do—by teaching men how to love their fellow-men.

Women must cease supporting men for the wrong reasons in the wrong sort of way, and thus cease causing men to marry them for the wrong reasons, too. "That's what a man wants in a wife, mostly," says Mrs. Poyser (in *Adam Bede*), "he wants to make sure o' one fool as 'ull tell him he's wise." Well, it's time that men learned the truth, and perhaps they are likely to take it more gracefully from another male than from their unacknowledged betters. It is equally important that women learn the truth, too, for it is to them that the most important part, the more fundamental part, of the task of remaking the world will fall, for the world will be remade only by remaking, or rather helping, human beings to realize themselves more fully in terms of what their mothers have to give them. Without adequate mothers life becomes inadequate, nasty, and unsatisfactory, and Mother Earth becomes a battlefield on which fathers slay their young and are themselves slain.

Men have had a long run for their money in running the affairs of the world. It is time that women realized that men will continue to run the world for some time yet, and that they can best assist them to run it more humanely by teaching them, when young, what humanity means. Men will thus not feel that they are being demoted, but rather that their potentialities for good are so much more increased, and what is more important, instead of feeling hostile toward women they will for the first time learn to appreciate them at their proper worth. There is an old Spanish proverb which has it that a good wife is the workmanship of a good husband. Maybe. But of one thing we can be certain: a good husband is the workmanship of a good mother. The best of all ways in which men can help themselves is to help women realize themselves. This way both sexes will come for the first time fully into their own, and the world of mankind may then look forward to a happier history than it has thus far enjoyed.

IS OUR COMMON MAN
TOO COMMON?

by Joseph Wood Krutch

Millions of Americans live in a dream-world of soap operas, torch songs, and grade-B movies. Are these average citizens forcing their more intelligent compatriots toward a dangerous uniformity? A noted essayist discusses this question.

JANUARY 10, 1953

THE AGE OF THE COMMON MAN is not merely a phrase; it is also a fact. Already we are definitely entered upon it, and in all probability it is destined to continue for a long time to come, intensifying its characteristics as it develops in some of the directions which it has already begun to take.

Most people welcome the fact, but we have only begun to assess it or even to ask ourselves what choices are still open to us once the grand decision has been made, as by now it has. How common does the common man need to be? Does his dominance necessarily mean that the uncommon man will cease to be tolerated or that the world will become less suited to his needs, less favorable to the development of his talents, than it now is? Will excellence be looked upon as in itself unworthy or "undemocratic"? Can we have an Age of the Common Man without making it an Age of the Common Denominator? Do any dangers lie ahead?

One way to approach these questions is, of course, to ask what has happened already, what changes in attitudes have demonstrably taken place, how the culture of the first era of the Age of the Common Man differs from that which preceded it. What, in other words, is the culture of present-day America like, and are there aspects of it, directly traceable to the emphasis on the common man and his tastes, which are not wholly reassuring? And if there are, then to what extent are the defects corrigible, to what extent are they necessary consequences of the premises we have already accepted?

Unfortunately, but not surprisingly, there is no general agreement concerning the real nature of the situation at the present moment, though it does seem clear enough that most Americans judge both the present and the future a good deal more favorably than many observers from the Old World do.

Thus, in his recent book *The Big Change,* Frederick Lewis Allen summed up very cogently the case for contemporary American culture. Hundreds of thousands read the selections of the book club; hundreds of thousands more attend concerts of serious music; millions listen to debates, symphonies, and operas on the radio. Never before in the history of the world has so large a proportion of any population been so interested in and so alert to intellectual and artistic activities. Ours is the most cultured nation which ever existed.

Compare this with any one of the typical fulminations which proceed at regular intervals from European commentators and the result is both astonishing and disturbing. In Europe the prevalent opinion seems to be that this same civilization of ours constitutes a serious threat to the very existence of anything which can properly be called a culture.

We are told, in the first place, that for every American who does read the Book of the Month and attend a symphony concert there are a dozen who live in a vulgar dream-world induced by a perpetual diet of soap operas, comic books, torch songs, and "B" movies. Moreover, the material prosperity and political power of this majority of sick barbarians enable them to become, as no cultural proletariat ever was before, a threat to every civilized minority. They rule the roost, and they are becoming less and less tolerant of anyone or anything superior to them.

In the second place—and perhaps even more importantly—the culture of even the minority is described as largely an imitation. It consumes but does not produce art. The best of the books it reads and the music it listens to is imported. Its members are really only parasites feeding upon European culture, and their sterility will in time kill it completely. Even their power to "appreciate" is essentially shallow—the result of superficial education, propaganda, advertisement, and a general pro-cultural hoop-la, all of which produce something very different indeed from that deep, personal, demanding passion for Truth and Beauty which has always been the dynamic force in the production of any genuine culture.

Now it is easy enough to dismiss this European view as merely the product of ignorance, prejudice, and envy. But it is dangerous to do so. To look candidly at the two pictures is to perceive something recognizable in both of them. Nobody really knows what the American phenomenon means or what it portends. And the reason is that it is actually something genuinely new. Whether you call it the Dawn of the First Democratic Culture or call it the Triumph of Mediocrity, the fact remains that there is no obvious parallel in human history. Mr. Allen and those who agree with him are obviously right as far as they go. But the unique phenomenon which they describe can stand further analysis.

A college education for everybody and two cars in every garage are ideals not wholly unrelated. An even closer analogy can be drawn with the earlier, more modest ideal of universal literacy. America was the first country to teach nearly everybody to read. Whether we are quite aware of it or not, we are now embarked upon the pursuit of what is really an extension of the same ideal, namely, a minimum cultural literacy for all. There is a vast difference between being barely able to spell out a newspaper and being able to read in the full sense of what the term implies. There is a similar and probably no greater difference between, say, being able to get something out of the movie *The Great Caruso* or the latest volume dispatched to the members of a book club by editors who have trained themselves to understand the limitations of their average subscriber, and a genuine grasp of either music or literature. The term "literacy" covers a large area whether we are using it in its limited sense or extending it to include what I have called "cultural literacy." A few generations ago we pointed with pride to the fact that most Americans "could read"; we now point with pride to the fact that an astonishing proportion of them "read serious books" or "listen to serious music," and in both cases we take satisfaction in a mass capacity which exists only if we define it in minimum terms. In neither case does the phenomenon mean quite as much as those who celebrate it most enthusiastically sometimes seem to assume.

But, what, one may ask, is either disturbing or surprising about that? The minimum remains something more than any people as a whole ever before achieved. Is it likely that fewer people will read well just because a larger number can read a little? Is not, indeed, the opposite likely to be true? Is anything but good likely to come from the establishment of a broad base of even a minimum cultural literacy?

Any hesitation in answering "no" to the last question might seem at first sight to spring inevitably from nothing except arrogance, snobbishness, and a desire to preserve the privileges of an aristocracy. Yet a good many Europeans and an occasional American do seem inclined to take the negative position. The wide spread of our minimum culture does seem to them to constitute some sort of threat.

At least one fact or alleged fact they can cite as possible evidence on their side of the argument. So far, the number of recognized masterpieces produced by native-born Americans does seem disappointingly small when compared with the number of literate citizens we have produced. Is that because American art is inadequately recognized, or because we just haven't had time yet to mature? Or is it, perhaps, somehow connected—as some would say it is—with mass culture itself? Is the Good always the friend of the Best or is it sometimes and somehow the enemy? Is Excellence more likely to lose out to Mediocrity than it is to mere Ignorance or Nullity?

The line being taken in Europe today has a good deal in common with that of the American intellectual of the twenties. To some extent indeed it may have been learned from our post-World War I intellectuals; the disdainful European conception of American society is a good deal like Mencken's Boobocracy. At the present moment, however, the current of opinion at home is running in the opposite direction, and it is no longer unusual for the confessed intellectual to defend the culture which his predecessor of a generation ago despised and rejected. But complacency has its dangers too, and it may be worth while to examine a little further what can be said in support of the European's thesis.

This, he hears us say, is the Age of the Common Man. But we as well as he are not quite certain what we mean by that. In so far as we mean only the age of universal opportunity, what was once called simply "the career open to talents," nothing but good could seem to come of it. But many people do, sometimes without being entirely aware of it, mean something more. When we make ourselves the champion of any particular group we almost inevitably begin to idealize that group. From defending the common man we pass on to exalting him, and we find ourselves beginning to imply, not merely that he is as good as anybody else, but that he is actually better. Instead of demanding only that the common man be given an opportunity to become as uncommon as possible, we make his commonness a virtue and, even in the case of candidates for high office, we sometimes praise them for being nearly indistinguishable from the average man in the street. Secretly, no doubt, we hope that they are somehow superior, but we feel at the same time that a kind of decency requires them to conceal the fact as completely as possible.

The logical extreme of this opinion would be the conviction that any deviation in either direction from the statistical average is unadmirable; even, to take a concrete example, that the ideal man or woman could best be represented, not by an artist's dream, but

by a composite photograph of the entire population. And though
few would explicitly acknowledge their acceptance of this extreme
position, there is a very strong tendency to emphasize quantitative
rather than qualitative standards in estimating achievement. We
are, for instance, more inclined to boast how many Americans go
to college than to ask how much the average college education
amounts to; how many people read books rather than how good
the books are; how many listen to the radio rather than how good
what they hear from it really is.

Argue, as I myself have argued, that more can be learned about
almost any subject from ten minutes with a printed page than
from half an hour with even one of the better educational programs
and you will be met with the reply: "Perhaps. But so many *more*
people will listen to the radio." In a democracy quantity is important. But when the stress upon it becomes too nearly exclusive,
then democracy itself threatens to lose its promise of moving on to
higher levels. Thus the Good really can become the enemy of the
Best if one insists upon exclusively quantitative standards.

Certainly one of the striking—some would say one of the inevitable—characteristics of our society is its penchant for making widely
and easily accessible either substitutes for, or inferior versions of,
a vast number of good things, like the vile substitute for bread
available at any grocer's. That bread can be come by without effort,
and it may be true that fewer people are in want of bread of some
kind than ever were in want of it in any society before. But that
does not change the fact that it is a very inferior product.

Another and related tendency of this same society is its encouragement of passivity. A generation ago moralists viewed with alarm
the popularity of "spectator sports": the fact that people gathered
in stadia to watch others play games for them. But we have gone
far beyond that and today the baseball fan who takes the trouble
to make a journey to the Polo Grounds instead of watching the
game on his TV set has almost earned the right to call himself
an athlete. One wonders, sometimes, if the popularity of "discussion" programs does not mean very much the same thing; if most
people have not now decided to let others hold remote conversations for them—as well as play remote games—even though the
conversations are often no better than those they could hold for
themselves.

As John Stuart Mill—certainly no anti-democrat—wrote a century
ago: "Capacity for the nobler feeling is in most natures a very
tender plant. . . . Men lose their high aspirations as they lose their
intellectual tastes, because they have not time or opportunity for

indulging them; and they addict themselves to inferior pleasures, not because they deliberately prefer them, but because they are either the only ones to which they have access, or the only ones which they are any longer capable of enjoying."

In the history books of the future this age of ours may come to be known as the Age of Statistics. In the biological and physical as well as the sociological sciences, statistics have become, as they never were before, the most important tool of investigation. But as every philosophical scientist knows, the conclusions drawn by a science depend to a considerable extent upon the tools used. And it is in the nature of statistics not only that they deal with quantity but that they emphasize the significance of averages and medians. What usually exists or usually happens establishes The Law, and The Law is soon thought of as identical with The Truth. In all the arts, nevertheless, it is the exceptional and the unpredictable which really count. It is the excellent, not the average, which is really important. And there is, therefore, one aspect of the cultural condition of a civilization to which statistical study is curiously inappropriate.

No one, it may be said, needs to accept the inferior substitute or hold himself down to the average level. But simple and complete as that answer may seem to be, there are facts and forces which do tend to encourage an almost unconscious acceptance of mediocrity. One, of course, is that the inferior substitute—whether it be baker's bread or the movie show playing at the neighborhood house—is so readily accessible and so forced upon one's attention by all the arts of advertising as well as by the very way in which our lives have been organized. Another and more serious one is the tendency of the mass media to force out of the field every enterprise which is not based upon mass appeal. Whatever the reason may be, it is a generally recognized fact that it is becoming increasingly difficult, economically, to publish a book which is not a best seller or produce a play which is not a smash hit. More and more, therefore, artistic enterprise must be abandoned to the movies and to television where the mass audience is sufficient to defray the staggering cost.

Besides these economic reasons why the new media tend to concern themselves only with mass appeals, there is the additional technical reason why the two newest of such media tend to confine themselves to it. Since TV and radio channels are limited in number, all the arguments in favor of democracy as it is sometimes defined justify the existing fact that these channels should be used to communicate what the greatest number of people seem to want. That is the argument of the great broadcasting chains, and on the premise assumed it is a valid one.

The only mechanical instrument of communication which can make a reasonable case for the claim that it has actually served to increase the popularity of the thing communicated on its highest level of excellence is the phonograph, and it is significant that the phonograph is the only such device for communication which—especially since the invention of tape recording and LP—has found it economically feasible to cater to relatively small minorities. The fact that it does not cost much to produce a record may well have an incalculably great effect upon American musical taste.

What the question comes down to in the simplest possible terms is one of those which we asked at the very beginning of this discussion: Can we have an Age of the Common Man without having also an Age of the Common Denominator? That question has not been answered, probably cannot be convincingly answered, at the present moment. But it is a fateful question and the one with which this discussion is concerned.

One must not, of course, idealize the past to the extent of assuming that the best works were always, inevitably, and immediately the most popular. Two years ago James D. Hart's thorough and amusing *The Popular Book* (Oxford University Press) demonstrated conclusively that since Colonial times there have always been absurd best sellers. The year that Hawthorne earned $144.09 royalty in six months was the year his own publisher paid Susan Warner $4,500 for the same period and another publisher sold 70,000 copies of one of Fanny Fern's several works.

Neither, I think, should it be supposed that any society ever has been or ever will be so organized as to favor exclusively the highest artistic excellence. As a system, aristocratic patronage is absurdly capricious; capitalistic democracy tends to favor vulgarity; socialism would probably favor official mediocrity. The question here is not whether contemporary America provides ideal conditions for cultural developments on the highest level, but whether it renders such development unusually difficult instead of making it, as the optimists insist, almost inevitable.

Of the unfavorable influences which I have mentioned, it seems to me that the most serious is the tendency to confuse the Common Denominator with a standard of excellence. The mechanical and economic facts which tend to give the purveyors of mediocrity a monopoly—highly developed in the case of radio and TV, probably growing in the publishing business—may possibly be changed by new developments, as they have already been changed in the case of the phonograph. But to confuse The Best with the most widely and the most generally acceptable is to reveal a spiritual confusion which is subtle and insidious as well as fundamental. It could easily nullify any solution of the mechanical and economic problems created by the age of mass production.

How real and how general does this confusion seem actually to be?

More than one sociologist has recently pointed out that as technology integrates larger and larger populations into tighter and tighter groups the members of these groups tend inevitably to work, live, and recreate themselves in the same way and in accordance with the standardized patterns which the facilities provided for these various activities lay down. For ill as well as for good, "community living" becomes more and more nearly inevitable and individual temperament or taste finds less and less opportunity to express itself.

One result of this is that the natural tendency of the adolescent to practice a desperate conformity is prolonged into adult life and the grown man continues to want what his neighbors have, to do what his neighbors do, to enjoy what his neighbors enjoy. This is one of the things which the European may have in mind when he calls us a nation of adolescents, and commercial interests take advantage of our adolescent characteristics by stressing, through all sorts of publicity, the fact that this is the kind of cigarette most people smoke, the kind of breakfast food most people eat, and the torch singer or crooner most people like. The best-selling book is not only the one easiest to buy, but it is also the one we must read unless we are willing to be made to seem somehow inferior. What is most popular must be best. As a broadcast official recently said, to call the most popular radio programs vulgar is to call the American people vulgar. And that, he seemed to imply, was not merely nonsense but pretty close to treason. The voice of the people is the voice of God. God loves the common man. If the common man loves Bob Hope then God must love Bob Hope also. In musical taste as in everything else the common man is divine.

It is this logic which, unfortunately, the purveyors to the mass audience are very prone to follow. Undoubtedly, it leads them to the line of least resistance at the same time that it provides them with a smug excuse for both inanity and vulgarity. They are, they say, servants of the public and have no right to doubt that the people know not only what they want but what is good for them. The age of the common man has no place for any holier-than-thou attitude. It believes in government "by" as well as "for" the people. Totalitarianism is what you get when you accept the "for" but not the "by," and the attitude of, for example, the British Broadcasting Company, with its notorious Third Program, merely demonstrates that England has not yet learned what democracy really means.

No doubt the questions involved are too complicated to be discussed here. A few years ago, Charles A. Siepmann in his *Radio, Television, and Society* fully and impartially reported on both the policies and the arguments as they affect the media with which he was dealing. But at least one conclusion seems obvious. If there is any such thing as responsibility on the part of those most powerful and best informed toward those whose appetites they feed, then no provider of movies or records or television programs can escape the minimal duty of giving his public the best rather than the worst it will stand for. Mr. Mencken once declared that no one had ever gone bankrupt by underestimating the taste of the American public, but there is an increasing tendency to believe that, by dint of long trying, certain commercial exploiters of the mass media have succeeded only too well in underestimating it considerably.

What is obviously called for is a public opinion less ready than it now is to excuse the failure to meet even minimal responsibilities; but that public opinion is not likely to arise unless those responsible for public thinking play their own parts, and there is a tendency for them to yield rather than protest. Unfortunately, the fanatical exaltation of the common denominator has been taken up not only by the common man himself and by those who hope to profit by his exploitation but also and increasingly by those who are supposed to be educators and intellectual leaders. Instead of asking "What would a good education consist of?" many professors of education are asking "What do most college students want?"; instead of asking "What books are wisest and best and most beautiful?" they conduct polls to determine which the largest number of students have read with least pain. Examination papers are marked, not in accordance with any fixed standard, but in accordance with a usual level of achievement; the amount of work required is fixed by the amount the average student does; even the words with which the average student is not familiar are edited out of the books he is given to read. How, granted such methods, is it other than inevitable both that the average will seldom be exceeded and that the average itself will gradually drop?

As David Reisman and his collaborators pointed out two years ago in their brilliant analysis called *The Lonely Crowd* (Yale University Press), the ideal now persistently held before the American citizen from the moment he enters kindergarten to the time when he is buried under auspices of a recognized funeral parlor is a kind of conformity more or less disguised under the term "adjustment." "Normality" has almost completely replaced "Excellence" as an ideal. It has also rendered all but obsolescent such terms as "Righteousness," "Integrity," and "Truth." The question is no longer how a boy ought to behave but how most boys do behave; not how honest a man ought to be but how honest men usually are. Even the Robber Baron, who represented an evil manifestation of the determination to excel, gives way to the moneymaker who wants only to be rich according to the accepted standards of his group. Or, as Mr. Reisman sums it up, the American who used to be conspicuously "inner-directed" is now conspicuously "outer-directed."

According to the anthropologists, many primitive societies are based almost exclusively upon the idea of conformity and generate what are, in the anthropologist's meaning of the term, remarkable cultures. It may, of course, be argued that America and the whole world which follows in America's wake is evolving in the direction of this kind of culture. But if by "culture" we mean something more narrowly defined, if we mean a culture which is continuous with that of the Western world since the Renaissance, then it is my contention that it cannot flourish where the stress is as nearly exclusively as it threatens to become upon "adjustment," "normality," or any of the other concepts which, in the end, come down to mean that the Common Denominator is identical with the Ideal. Especially, it cannot flourish under those conditions if the result which they tend to produce is intensified by the fact that ingenious methods of mass production and mass propaganda help impose upon all the tyranny of the average.

Salvation, if salvation is possible, may be made so by technological developments like those in the phonograph industry which tend to break monopoly and permit the individual to assert his preferences and his tastes. But the possible will not become the actual if in the meantime the desire for excellence has been lost and those who should be leaders have willingly become followers instead. If the Age of the Common Man is not to become the Age of the Common Denominator rather than what it was originally intended to be—namely an age in which every man had the opportunity to become as superior as he could—then the cultural as well as the political rights of minorities must somehow be acknowledged. There is not really anything undemocratic about either the desire for, or the recognition of, excellence. To prove that ours is the most cultured nation which ever existed will constitute only a barren victory if we must, to prove our point, use nothing but quantitative standards and reconcile ourselves to the common denominator as a measure of excellence.

One might sum up the situation in a series of propositions. (1) The Age of the Common Man has begun. (2) Despite all the gains that it may legitimately claim, they are threatened by those confusions which arise when the common denominator is consciously or unconsciously allowed to function as a standard of excellence. (3) The dominance of mass media almost exclusively under the control of those who are little concerned with anything except immediate financial gain does tend to debase taste. (4) Ultimate responsibility for the future rests with the thinkers and the educators whose most important social task at the moment is to define democratic culture in some fashion which will both reserve a place for uncommon excellence and, even in connection with the largest masses, emphasize the highest rather than the lowest common denominator.

THE BIG LIBEL

by Cleveland Amory

*In the late forties the widely known newspaper columnist West-
brook Pegler accused author Quentin Reynolds of having "a yellow streak," "a mangy hide," and a "protuberant belly filled with
something other than guts." In reply to this and other attacks
Reynolds brought suit against the columnist for libel. Here is the
dramatic story of the Reynolds-Pegler legal battle.*

AUGUST 7, 1954

BURIED UNDER THE ARMY-McCARTHY HEARINGS during May and June,
and given only minor mention in the daily press (which dislikes
publicizing libel suits), there occurred an historic legal battle between two author adversaries. Both were first sports writers, later
war correspondents, and both are Roman Catholics. One, a Franklin
D. Roosevelt Democrat, is a big bearlike man whose chief talent is
making the sentimental story credible and yet not cloy; his weakness is an overbonhommous belief in everybody—witness *The Man
Who Wouldn't Talk,* which started out as nonfiction and ended up
as non-fact. The other, a James G. Blaine Republican, is a merchant
of venom whose chief talent is pouring the salty phrase on the old
wounds of live women, notably Eleanor Roosevelt, and dead men,
notably Heywood Broun; his weakness is, or rather was, his cherished
boast of never having been successfully sued for libel. "I love my
enemies," he once said. "I get spiritual satisfaction out of hate."

It all started five years ago, on November 29, 1949, when Quentin
Reynolds read a column by Westbrook Pegler in which Pegler said
Reynolds had "a yellow streak," "a mangy hide," and "a protuberant
belly filled with something other than guts." He said that Reynolds
"went nuding along the public road with his girl friend of the
moment" and he also added that Reynolds had proposed to Heywood Broun's widow on the way to Broun's grave. (The latter
turned out to be a particularly extraordinary accusation in view
of the fact that Monsignor, now Bishop, Sheen was also in the funeral car.) "After Pegler's charges appeared Quent looked out the
window for two days," says Mrs. Reynolds, "while I told him, 'For

489

once in your life get mad.' Finally he said, 'Do you mind if I sue?' 'Mind!' I said. 'I'll leave you if you don't!' "

Reynolds sought $500,000 in compensatory damages as well as punitive damages. He charged that he had sold 311 articles to *Collier's* before Pegler's attack and none since; he also charged Pegler had hounded him by calling up other speakers and VIPs at banquets, lecture platforms, etc., where Reynolds was to appear and intimating he was pro-Communist. In countersuit, since dismissed, Pegler charged that Reynolds, in reviewing Dale Kramer's *Heywood Broun,* had said that Pegler's attacks on Broun had so troubled Broun's last days (when he was dying) that Pegler was "morally guilty of homicide" and that this review had so provoked him (Pegler) that he had begun writing columns vs. Reynolds. So confident was the Hearst empire of inevitable victory that in answering Reynolds' charges they not only repeated their libels, they embellished them. Pegler and Hearst were alone involved; Reynolds could not afford to sue, in separate cities, the outside papers which still subscribe to Pegler's column.

It was the old anti-Army game. In McCarthy's book, if you attack McCarthy, you are a Communist. In Pegler's book, if you praise an enemy of Pegler, you are in for a large dose of the dirty-words-on-walls school of writing. The actual trial bore many similarities to the Army-McCarthy hearings. Like McCarthy, Pegler had little to lose except his face; his contract provides that Hearst will pay all damages. Like Stevens (instead of McCarthy), Reynolds (instead of Pegler) was really the man on trial. His character, not Pegler's, occupied the majority of the time in court. "I've got one piece of advice for everybody," says Reynolds. "You can't sue anybody unless you're clean as a whistle yourself." And, finally, there were physical similarities. McCarthy visited Pegler's home in Tucson, Arizona, just before the hearings began, and Pegler took the stand in New York the same day McCarthy took the stand in Washington. Here the similarities end. Reynolds proved a consistent and intelligent witness; his attorney, Louis Nizer, had a brilliantly prepared case which was unmarred by public cowardice or mistaken ideas of expediency.

Nizer's opponent, the Hearst lawyer, Charles Henry, was an elderly bachelor. "Remember," he said almost pathetically to Reynolds on one occasion, "we're adversaries, not enemies." By all odds the outstanding figure in court was Judge Edward Weinfeld, a magnetic man with a face like a prophet and a mind which anticipated everything several seconds before it happened. He went directly from high school to law school, was New York State's first housing com-

missioner, and, on becoming a judge, his first act was to find out
what prison life was actually like. At one time or another, and
through at least one meal, he has visited every Federal prison in
this country except two. "I'll get to those," he says quietly. "I want
to see every place I may be responsible for someone going." In such
a man's court there were no points of disorder. When the ex-
Communist Bella Dodd, a Pegler witness, failed to give evidence
she had ever seen Reynolds before, Judge Weinfeld summarily dismissed her from the stand.

To testify for Reynolds came three former *Collier's* executives,
William Chenery, Albert Winger, and Richard Chaplin, as well as
a Who's Who of Edward R. Murrow, John Gunther, Sidney Bern-
stein, Mrs. Heywood Broun, Patricia Broun, Mark Hanna, Lionel
Shapiro, Ken Downs, Walter Kerr, Jock Lawrence, and Harry
Butcher. There was a reference from Eisenhower, a letter from
Winston Churchill, depositions from Viscount Mountbatten and Sir
Walter Monckton, and even a message to Garcia from the Hon.
Clare Boothe Luce (although it arrived too late). To testify for
Pegler came, besides Miss Dodd, Mrs. Pegler, a Pegler nephew, one
Collier's ex-editor, a former Moscow priest, an ex-Canadian news-
paperman, the third wife of the late Harold Ross, and a Pepsi-Cola
executive. Not a single Hearst executive appeared to testify—a fact
of which the shrewd Nizer made much in his summation. "Do you
know why there is none here?" he asked, pointing to the empty
witness chair. "Because he would have had to say that Pegler had
a good reputation and I could have said to that empty chair, 'Mr.
Hearst Executive, I am going to prove that there is not in this whole
country a single writer with a *worse* reputation.'"

For most people the high point of the eight-week trial came when
Nizer cross-examined Pegler and made him admit 130 contradictions
of testimony given in pre-trial examination with his later statements under direct examination of his own counsel. At one point,
when Nizer read him a statement by an unnamed author, Pegler
branded it pro-Communist, then learned the author was Pegler. At
another time Pegler demanded Nizer show him something. When
Nizer handed it to him, Pegler raised his fist. "Get away from me,"
he snarled. Finally Pegler's manner, which varied from the four-
letter-word rambunctious to the coldly injured unctuous, was reduced to the breaking point. "I don't hate anybody," he sniffled.
"It's against my religion." At this even the jury laughed out loud.

The judge's charge to the jury was stern, slow, and scholarly; he
left no doubt that there were two distinct points of libel and that
the Pegler column was definitely defamatory. In order for Reynolds

to win anything, however, every member of the jury not only had to agree he should but also had to agree unanimously on the exact amount. (In a State court a 10-2 verdict is allowed, but not in a Federal.) Earlier the trial had been three weeks under way when one juror was dismissed for discussing the case out of court and fined $250; an alternate took his place and a Hearst legal assistant who knew about the juror's talking but had not brought it to the attention of the judge was severely reprimanded. The final group consisted of a sewing machine executive as foreman, a motion picture man, a pilot, a bookkeeper, a maintenance man, a garageman, two salesmen, and four housewives. For thirteen hours they deliberated; four times they filed back into the courtroom to clear up points. Finally, in the interest of arriving at a decision, the eight favoring high compensatory plus high punitive damages compromised their high compensatory to win high punitive. "It was like a tobacco auctioneer's convention," one later declared, "except for a guy who was so sleepy he kept his head on the table and kept mumbling, 'Aw, give 'im five thousand.'"

The verdict, delivered to a crowded courtroom at 1 o'clock on the morning of June 29, was for $175,000 punitive damages and $1 compensatory. It was the highest award in the history of American libel. For the Reynoldses it marked the end of a steady four-and-a-half-year-to-the-day fight. They were exhausted, financially and physically. Mr. Reynolds, dazed at first, thought the foreman said only $175. But Mrs. Reynolds heard it correctly. Dead tired, standing in her stocking feet, she burst into tears and then ran over to kiss one of the housewives.

THROUGH HISTORY
WITH J. WESLEY SMITH

Cartoons by Burr Shafer

The ubiquitous J. Wesley Smith has long illustrated for SR readers the eternal philistine's attitude toward great historical events. Here are six episodes in his odyssey through Western history.

"Don't take chances—call the humane society people."

"*I'm afraid little Nero will never set the world on fire.*"

"*Never mind why—we're moving to Florence and changing the name of the firm.*"

"*It's a nice enough picture of a boy, Mr. Gainsborough—but that ghastly blue!*"

"*And if you're not out by 12 o'clock, General Washington, I'll have to charge you for another day!*"

BOOK MARKS

by John T. Winterich

Few regular features of SR have proved more popular than the epigrams of John T. Winterich. Here are some of his best.

The more mediums of communication we develop the less we seem to have to communicate.

There are still novelists who think that when they make a character say *shure, uv, Wensday,* and *wimmen,* they are writing authentic dialect.

The function of punctuation is to lubricate the text—to make the sense slide easily into the reader's mind.

Can anything be ajar except a door?

Aren't there any thin-set people?

There are some novelists who are convinced that when they have given a member of the cast a cleft chin, meeting eyebrows, and a wen under the left ear, they have created an unforgettable character.

Not too common, these days, are books with illustrations by the author. We are lucky, in some quarters, to get even books with words by the author.

He who has read everything has read nothing.

WASHINGTON, A.C.–D.C.

by Goodman Ace

One of TV's highest-paid writers herewith bites the hand that feeds him, and, in addition, takes a pot shot at certain tendencies on the part of the White House today to make use of Madison Avenue advertising techniques.

JANUARY 23, 1954

THE NEW YORK TIMES recently carried an interesting account of what went on behind the scenes in preparation for President Eisenhower's two important television appearances—(1) the fifteen-minute Monday night commercial advertising his (2) Thursday afternoon State of the Union message before the Congress.

The White House staff, we are told, was augmented with advertising, public-relations, and Hollywood consultants to help establish contact with the voters through this newest of mass communications media. The preparation compared quite favorably to the chaos that goes into putting on a weekly run-of-the-mill television program.

The scripts; the rewrites; the teleprompter installed over the cameras so that the President could read his Monday night speech and yet appear to be speaking directly to the anxious citizens assembled in their living rooms; the special platform constructed in the chamber of the House so that when he read from his script the glare of the television lights would not bounce off his famous bald pate; the make-up girl who was sent over by CBS to dust with pancake make-up the face and head of the President; the party leaders, acting as directors, who advised him on the Monday night show to make full use of his friendly grin—

All these were there.

The President had some hard selling to do. His sponsors would be watching in the forty-eight states, and the hucksters gave it all their know-how to make certain the option would be picked up. The impact of television has been evaluated as three times that of radio.

Every move, every emphasis, every facial expression are as carefully noted as every spoken word. History is recorded on the spot in sight and sound not only for the present but for all posterity to see and hear.

Television comes a little late. The almost casual preparation for historic messages of a bygone day would have sent any TV producer scurrying around the corner of NBC to Hurley's Bar. With a slight anachronistic change of scene we set up our cameras for a remote telecast from the spot where another message is about to be delivered.

It's another Thursday. The date is November 19, 1863. Video men, audio men, directors, advisers huddle around Cemetery Hill, shouting at the fifteen thousand who have come to witness the telecast to keep off the cables and stand back from the cameras. The cameramen are setting up their shots for the speakers. The director comes briskly forward.

"Mr. President, you'll open up on camera two, that's this one. We're picking up Mr. Everett on camera one. When the red light comes on on camera two you can start your speech. Then we'll cut to a profile after we set up camera one—the red light will light on this one. You'll stand about here. Oh, I'll take that shawl, Mr. President."

"Well, there's a chill in the air and I—"

"But you're not going to do the show in that shawl, are you?"

"Yes, I am."

"Well I wish we'd have known—we could have had costume send one over. I'm afraid the lights are going to pick up all that fuzz around it. Oh, by the way, I'll get the make-up girl. We ought to trim that beard a little. It's kinda straggly and it might—"

"Oh, this is quite all right."

"But, Mr. President, this is television. At least we can touch up that right cheek. That mole is going to look like—"

"No, no, young man. It will be all right."

"But, Mr. President, you know you're following Mr. Everett. He's going to look quite distinguished with that white hair and that—oh, before I forget—your speech."

"My speech?"

"Yes, I'll have the boys run it off for the teleprompter. You can look right into the camera and read it, and it'll look like you're talking to the folks at home."

"No. I'll manage with this."

"With that! You're not going to read it off that envelope, are you?"

"Well, I had planned—"

"Okay, Mr. President. But Mr. Everett will steal the show. They'll come away talking about him. They'll little note nor long remember anybody else."

NEW YORK, C'EST FORMIDABLE!

by Art Buchwald

A less-than-serious observer sets down his notions of an average Frenchman's impressions of New York City. The author, Art Buchwald, is a Paris correspondent for the New York Herald Tribune.

APRIL 17, 1954

MONSIEUR FRANÇOIS DE PAUL,
235 Rue Faubourg St. Honoré,
Paris, France.

DEAR FRANÇOIS,

And so I have arrived in New York and am writing to you as you requested. My dear friend, New York is formidable. It is much larger than either one of us expected and the movies do not do it justice. I have had many adventures but I do not know where to begin. When I first arrived at Idlewild Airport I changed my francs into dollars at the official rate as I feared to get involved in the black market so early on my arrival.

Then I took a taxi into New York City making sure to check the meter as you advised me to do. The driver was very talkative and as soon as we started moving he said to me:

"What do you think the Dodgers will do this year?"

I told him I knew of no dodgers and he was very surprised. I explained I lived in France and he said, "Okay, we'll talk about France."

He knew everything about France. He said France had too many political parties and he was getting sick of having his money poured down the sewers of Europe, whatever that means. He said the trouble with the French is that they are always making love and sitting at sidewalk cafés and they never get down to work. He also told me his brother-in-law was in France for three months during the war, and his brother-in-law told him the French weren't serious people.

When we arrived at my hotel he told me that everyone gives him a dollar tip from the airport. I gave it to him but he did not say thank you. I discovered later that it is forbidden for a taxi driver in New York City to say thank you to his customers.

My hotel is located in the province of Manhattan. New York is divided into five provinces. There is the Bronx, Brooklyn, Queens, Staten Island, and Manhattan, where the seat of the government is. Most of the people in New York take the *métro* from the other provinces to go to work in Manhattan, where the Bourse is located.

But there is no *métro* connection with Staten Island and these people have to take a boat every morning and every evening. I understand that Staten Island is very primitive and has a Wild West atmosphere. I plan to go there if I can find a reliable guide.

New Yorkers have so many strange habits. You will be amused to hear that they eat enormous breakfasts including thick oats, strange wheat kernels, eggs, ham, bacon, large crepes called pancakes, and they put a thick sweet syrup on them. The coffee is just terrible and I would give anything for a good café filtre. I have also been unsuccessful in getting a brioche, but I was surprised to find things named after France that we do not have there. To name a few, French crullers, French toast, French dressing, and French bread (which has no resemblance to our bread at all).

Although they eat grand breakfasts they have hardly any lunch at all and the people eat in pharmacies. I don't think they take more than thirty minutes for lunch and it is criminal to see them shove the food in their mouths. It was only after I ate some pharmacy foods that I understood why they eat that way. It's better if you don't taste the food. You may not believe this, François, but I saw people drinking milk with their entrée. The first time I saw it I became sick, but now I am getting used to it.

The buildings in New York are almost as high as the Eiffel Tower but except for Central Park there are no trees or grass to be seen anywhere. The elevators work both ways and you don't have to walk downstairs as you do in Paris.

There are, unfortunately, no sidewalk cafés in New York and everyone must sit in dark drab bars if they wish to drink. The bars are very busy around 5:30 in the afternoon and people drink very fast and very much. Dinner is at 6:30, if that is not a laugh, but by then everyone is so drunk they do not know what they are eating anyway.

The theater is very good in New York and I saw two plays. One is called *Tea and Sympathy* and it is about a boy who is trying to prove he is not a homosexual. The other based on Gide is called *The Immoralist* and is about a man who is trying to prove he is one. So you see Broadway gives you both sides of every story.

A funny thing happened—someone, a lady, called me up one day and asked me to come on her television program and tell her all about France.

I went on like she wanted me to. The first question she asked me was "Will the French fight?" I do not remember what I answered but it made no difference because her second question was, "Why are all you Frenchmen Communists?" I said we weren't all Communists and she said that is not what she read in the papers. Then she said, "Why are prices so high in Paris?" but before I could answer she said, "And now let's hear from the sponsor." But there was no sponsor so she had to make the publicity herself. She was making publicity for a seasoning and she said it was the best seasoning you could buy anywhere. Then she asked me if the French used this seasoning and I said they did not, and so she said, "Well, if they did their food would taste much better." This is the truth, François, I swear it.

After the publicity she asked me what I thought of American women and I said they had very nice legs but they all looked alike. She did not like this and said American women are very beautiful, particularly those that used a certain kind of soap which she held up in her hand. She promised all the women in the audience that if they used the soap twice a day they would be loved by men. This is the truth, François. Then she asked me what I thought of American men and I said they were very nice. And she said the reason they were nice is because they drank fruit juice in the morning, and she held up a can of a certain kind of fruit juice and said that angry men become happy men when they drink this certain kind of fruit juice. She gave me a can of it and said, "And even Frenchmen like fruit juice, don't they?" I had to say yes.

Before the program was over I admitted that French floors would look better if they had a certain kind of house wax, that a certain California wine was as good as wines we have in France, that French couturiers received their inspiration from American fabrics, and that the French had no refrigerators to compare with one the lady commentator showed me. The program was over and they asked me to leave the studio immediately as they had to prepare for another show. I guess I did not leave fast enough because as I was looking for my coat two guards grabbed me by the arms and showed me to the door. I never found out the lady's name.

That is all, François. I wish I could tell you more about New York, but I'm sure you would not believe me anyway.

My affectionate sentiments,
PIERRE

THEY'RE SELLING
YOUR UNCONSCIOUS

by Lydia Strong

*Chances are that you don't know why your breakfast food crunches
or why you are encouraged to drink beer with your coat off. But
chances also are that an advertising motivational researcher knows
why, as writer Lydia Strong here explains.*

NOVEMBER 13, 1954

REMEMBER THE OLD CHESTNUT about the store that advertised: "We
stand behind every bed we sell"?

The advertiser is not just standing behind the bed today; he's
wired it for sound. Your dreams, your desires, and the rumblings
of your subconscious, formerly sacred to you and your analyst, have
been charted by advertising psychologists, eager to learn how you
buy and why you buy, and therefore how they can sell you many,
many more products.

Why do you smoke cigarettes, and is your favorite brand male or
female? How do you really feel toward your breakfast cereal? What
kinds of occasion make you think of beer? What does your new
car tell about your personality?

Don't try to answer these questions. The true answers, say the
motivational researchers, lie buried deep in your subconscious mind.
And the psychologists mining that area certainly have struck pay
dirt. Motivational research is the hottest trend on Madison Avenue.
The fatter the advertising budget, the greater the probability that
Freud helped write the copy. Firms pay huge fees to psychological
consultants for what *Business Week* has called bluntly "an effort
to pry off the top of the consumer's head" and to "find out what
makes him tick."

Social Research, Inc., an M.R. agency in Chicago, made a study
of attitudes toward cigarette smoking for *Chicago Tribune* advertisers. Psychiatric techniques were used to break through the "impersonal and objective attitudes" of the men and women tested.
They were shown pictures of people smoking and asked to make
up stories about them. They played the parts of total strangers and

talked as they thought these people would talk about situations involving cigarettes. Such tests are standard psychiatric procedure for pinpointing the emotional problems of individuals; here they were used, perhaps for the first time, to solve the merchandising problems of cigarette manufacturers.

One finding was that, although in blindfold tests most smokers could not tell brands apart, they nonetheless felt definite preferences based on unconsciously determined brand reputations. Cigarettes were felt to be masculine or feminine, strong or mild, ordinary or "classy." Camels and Luckies were considered masculine and "for ordinary people," while Chesterfields were both masculine and feminine and not tied to any special class. King-size and cork-tip cigarettes were considered most feminine and "classy."

Smokers seemed to want to strike a balance between the strongest cigarette (felt as evil) and the mildest (considered too prissy). Therefore few smokers would admit their brand was the strongest.

The seemingly casual gesture of lighting up was found to cover a tough struggle. Most smokers considered their habit morally and physically wrong; filthy and dangerous. Yet they felt compelled to smoke to prove their strength, sophistication, and sociability, to gain poise, to relieve tension, and experience pleasure. Hence the psychologists recommended that cigarette advertising should combine a promise of pleasure with a note of reassurance. Pall Mall's "Let your throat enjoy smooth smoking" and Camels' "Agree with more people than any other cigarette" seem to follow this advice.

Characteristics of smokers and nonsmokers will be probed in a psychological project announced by the Tobacco Industry Research Council. Perhaps the industry hopes to prove that many of its customers are neurotic individuals subject to psychosomatic strains. This could mean they are more likely than non-smoking types to develop cancer, even if they never light a cigarette.

Attempts to probe the consumer are not new. Since 1903, when Walter Dill Scott wrote his historic treatise on *The Psychology of Advertising,* a thriving industry has grown up in this field. But most of the research was confined to nose-counting surveys which showed, for example, that 79 per cent of native-born white housewives in six-room houses in East Cupcake, Illinois, wanted washing machines for Christmas, while 68.7 per cent of their sisters in Split Level, Oregon, preferred home harmonica lessons. These statistics were produced by asking the ladies what they wanted, a technique definitely old hat, though still used. Motivational research, based on the Freudian concept that action is determined by the subconscious, attempts to learn not what the consumer says he wants but what he really wants, and why he wants it.

The difference is shown in a story told by Dr. W. G. Eliasberg, a psychiatrist with industrial clients. A nail-polish manufacturer wanted to bring out red nail polish, then unknown. He had a market researcher do a "nose count" survey on the acceptability of such a product. The result was an overwhelming "No!" Red nails were rejected with disgust, called "degrading" by almost every woman polled. But the manufacturer trusted his hunch and brought out the product, with results that are highly visible today. Had he consulted a psychoanalyst, says Eliasberg, he would have learned that the very strength of the women's protest proved the strength of their desire.

Motivational research investigates conscious, preconscious, and unconscious feelings. Conscious material is readily available. The preconscious is half-forgotten, but can be recalled. But unconscious motivations are concealed from the conscious mind because they seem undignified, sinful, silly, or otherwise unacceptable.

Dr. Ernest Dichter, Viennese-born psychologist who has pioneered in this field, conducted an investigation for MandM candy. The company had assumed that their coated chocolate candies were bought mainly for their flavor. Dichter conducted a series of interviews in which he persuaded his subjects to relive and to report, step by step, occasions when they had eaten candy. He learned that, for many, candy was associated with doing a job they didn't want to do, using the sweet as a stimulus and a reward. MandM switched slogans in two test areas from "smooth, rich, creamy coated chocolate—everybody likes 'em" to "Make that tough job easier—you deserve MandM Candy." Sales ratios doubled in these areas.

In a subsistence economy hidden buying motives might not matter. A family with money only for bread and beans must by and large stick to bread and beans. But in the United States millions have more than satisfied survival needs. We have extra money with which to indulge our fancies, and depth psychology plays a large part in the battle for these "discretionary dollars."

Auto styling illustrates the change. Henry Ford's Tin Lizzie that got you there and brought you back sold well as long as other automobiles remained out of reach. But now that most families can own a car Fords must be as conspicuous and attractive as others if they are to sell.

Autos no longer represent just a means of transportation, a study by Social Research showed. They constitute definite symbols of social status, and each car has its own reputation. The purchaser buys the best car he can afford which expresses his approach to living.

Buyers of Ford, Mercury, Olds, or Lincoln, especially the two-tones and bright colors, may be expressing a trend toward modernism and individuality, the researchers say. Those who prefer to appear responsible, serious, and dignified lean toward Packard, Dodge, DeSoto, and Plymouth four-door sedans, dark, with a minimum of gadgets. A Cadillac may be purchased to tell the world that its owner can afford the best.

Buick headlined a recent ad: "It makes you feel like the man you are." Phrases like "a car that fairly breathes success," "command," "luxurious obedience," and "immediate mastery" were sprinkled lavishly through the copy.

A second, less publicized reason for depth research is the growing incredulity of consumers. Less than three persons out of ten believe most of the advertising they see, read, and hear, the Boston College School of Business Administration has reported. With resistance so strong at the conscious level, small wonder that advertisers try to sink a pipeline to the subconscious.

What techniques are used by the advertising analyst? Anything from a depth interview in which the respondent rambles on for hours to a hardware store where customers serve as unwitting guinea pigs. All methods have the same purpose: to secure reactions deeper and less guarded than the subject would express in a straightforward interview.

Dr. Dichter, at his Institute for Research in Mass Motivations, has organized a "psycho-panel" of several hundred families classified not only by income but by character. Dichter knows whether each member of each family is secure or insecure, resigned or ambitious, an escapist or a realist. Should a promoter of, let's say, correspondence courses want to learn primarily how to appeal to ambitious persons, persons of that type alone can be surveyed.

The depth interview is the most widely used M.R. technique. It lasts one to three hours and may seemingly cover a great many topics, gradually narrowing down to the actual topic under study. A psychologist interviewing a housewife about her preferences in buying bread might start out: "Do you remember what you did Monday?" She answers: "I went downtown—but I don't usually go downtown Mondays—it was just that . . ." As she continues, with the interviewer murmuring "Mhm" and "I see" at appropriate intervals, she reveals through words, gestures, and tone of voice how she really feels about housework. When this topic runs dry the interviewer may ask about shopping and meal planning. Again, the

actual foods bought and served tell more of her attitude toward nutri-
tion than she could tell if asked directly. The next question might
be: "How about your mother? What kind of cook was she?" If
this evokes wistful memories of Mom's superb, lavish cooking and
homebaked white bread it's possible, though by no means certain,
that the housewife would like to buy such bread for her family. If
the question calls forth a horrified "Mother's meals were so fatten-
ing!" this woman probably prefers a high-protein, low-starch loaf.
The interviewer may go on to ask about family food habits, thus
learning whose tastes are most consulted in the choice of bread.

Two hundred depth interviews with selected subjects will give
a bread-baking corporation a good idea of who its best customers
are and how to reach them; also whether to say "Just like mother's"
or "Only five calories per slice."

James M. Vicary, a New York City consultant to top-ranking ad
agencies, leans heavily on word-association tests. A word is given
and the subject responds as quickly as possible with another word
or string of words. These associations help Vicary to determine
possible reactions to a new brand-name or to words used in advertising, and also they indicate how people feel about a product.

Vicary advised a brewer to avoid the word "lagered" because
though some consumers knew it meant "aged before use" others
thought it meant tired, drunk, lazy, or dizzy. Words like *complaint,
co-operate,* and *voluntary,* he has warned, produce "a deep emotional disturbance with a sizable group." A study on "Chicago" for
the Commonwealth Edison Company showed that to the average
non-Chicagoan the name has more connotation of farming than of
industry. The power company, which was trying to bring more
industries into the city, responded with an advertisement stressing
the partnership of agriculture and industry in Chicago.

Procter and Gamble, after similar tests, dropped the word "concentrated" from soap advertising when they learned that 40 per
cent of housewives thought it meant "blessed by the Pope."

Picture tests are used widely. In such a test, borrowed directly
from the psychological clinic, the subject may imagine himself as
part of a pictured situation and may speak for one person in that
situation, or he may tell a story inspired by the picture. Either
way, he reveals his own feelings.

Weiss and Geller, ad agency for the Toni Company, conducted
picture tests with little girls before planning their campaign for
Tonette, a home permanent kit for children.

They showed each of their small subjects a series of pictures with
straight-haired and curly-haired girls. For each picture they asked

her to tell a story. Overwhelmingly, straight-haired girls were pitied because they were considered not only unattractive, but unwanted and unloved.

They asked the children to draw the figure of a person. One after another they drew figures with long, wavy hair.

Inspired by these findings, the agency's copywriters wrote a TV commercial with the wistful tagline: "All little girls dream of natural curls." It sold a good many Tonette kits.

Sentence completion tests as well as depth interviews were used by the Charles R. Rumrill company of Rochester, N.Y., in preparing copy for the Union Trust Company. They reported that the average potential customer subconsciously sees the bank as a parent, but at the same time feels afraid. He is haunted by fears that if he applies for a loan he may be turned down or treated discourteously, or his personal life may be investigated.

They used non-professional models and heart-to-heart copy to convince their readers that the bank was really concerned about their problems and wanted to do business with them. An ad headed "How I hated to open that door" told first hand of the cordial reception given a borrower.

A Chicago firm, the Ad Detector Research Corporation, straps consumers into a lie detector and flashes advertising copy before their eyes. The subjects talk about the copy while the lie detector measures what it does to their pulse, breathing, and blood pressure.

Alfred Politz, a researcher whose clients include DuPont, Chrysler, and Coca-Cola, has bought a large hardware store, location undisclosed, where he will try out on consumers the effects of differing sales approaches, displays and advertising policies. One of his objectives is to develop advertising copy that will sell products regardless of what the salesclerk says.

Politz has also devised a billboard which will spy on its spectators by taking pictures of them at three-second intervals. This can give a count of the persons attracted by a test poster, and an impression of their reactions to it.

Not every question is answered by actual tests. Social scientists are presumed to have expert knowledge of human reactions and motivations. On the crucial question: "What kind of TV salesperson is most effective?" Weiss and Geller assembled a team of eight eminent scientists (Gardner Murphy of the Menninger Foundation was one) and subjected them to thirteen and a half hours of straight TV while a stenotypist recorded their comments.

Often, when planning a campaign, a firm will consult experts on conscious and unconscious drives related to the specific product.

What are these basic drives which turn out to be helpful to the advertiser? Sex and sex-connected feelings probably head the list. A campaign for Luxite Lingerie played up narcissism or self-adoration. The campaign was based on a picture of a woman looking at herself in a mirror, with the slogan: "See yourself in Luxite."

A closely allied theme, exhibitionism, sparked the William Weintraub agency's successful series, "I dreamed I went walking (or stopped traffic—or was a lady editor) in my Maidenform Bra." In each ad the model appears partly undressed in public. The fact that this is only a dream makes it respectable and therefore all the more enjoyable.

Perfumes, soaps, creams, deodorants, and the other products guaranteed to make you smell better inside and out are routinely sold through sex promises.

But sex is not the only salesman. Other drives exert equal if not greater influence on buying. Many come under the general heading of security.

Relief of tension caused by frustration or hostility is one such drive. In a project for Wrigley, Weiss and Geller developed through depth interviews the hypothesis that people chew gum to relieve boredom and tension, and to work off hostility. A test area was selected, a mining region where living standards and literacy were low, frustrations high. The job was to convince consumers that they could relieve anxieties which they didn't even want to admit they had, by chewing gum. A series of comic strips was prepared, in which children and adults faced by everyday problems overcame their difficulties by chewing Wrigley's Spearmint Gum. The advertising used less space than previous ads, and all other promotion activities in the territory were suspended for the test period. Yet sales boomed.

Even so simple a product as breakfast food can appease hostility, according to E. L. Bernays, veteran publicist whose agency now offers M.R. services. The most successful breakfast cereals crunch, thus satisfying an aggressive desire to overcome obstacles, he points out.

The longing for social ease and equality is another drive tied to security. A series of depth interviews on beer drinking showed that people enjoy beer most when it makes some social event more relaxed and friendly. Discomfort was expressed over ads showing distinguished people drinking beer in rich surroundings. When they drank beer, the subjects said, they did not want to be reminded of people in situations that made them feel intensely discontented.

The conclusion, now followed by most beer advertisers, was that the ads should show family and friends in informal gatherings, should steer clear of rich people, "men of distinction" artists and intellectuals.

This hostility toward persons with pretensions of expertness or superior status is reflected also in consumer reaction to TV commercials. In a test by NBC a chef was shown pulling pastry out of the oven, and explaining how simple it was to make pastry with this mix. A second commercial showed a little girl, proud of the pastry she had made with the same product. The tot outpulled the chef, four to one.

According to the Weiss and Geller social-science panel, the most effective TV personalities are those which appear human and fallible—not too glib, not too expert, and just a bit vulnerable. This, they said, is one of the secrets of Arthur Godfrey's success. Women particularly resist other women who "know too much" and who remind them of nagging mothers telling them just what to do.

Many of us feel secretly more vulnerable than we could bear to admit. The desire for reassurance of virility was exploited by Dr. Dichter in a study for the Tea Council of the U.S.A. In this country, he said, tea carries a stigma of effeminacy. This unfortunate impression had been reinforced by Tea Council ads in pale colors, with such slogans as "Tired? Nervous? Try tea." On his advice the colors were switched to bright red, and the slogan to a dynamic "Make it hefty, hot and hearty, take tea and see." Tea sales rose 13 per cent in two years, even before zooming coffee prices forced millions more to "take tea and see."

Results of this sort have convinced many advertising executives that M.R is here to stay.

C. B. Larrabee, publisher of *Printers' Ink,* calls it the next great leap in market research, and a survey of leading advertisers has shown more than half of the big ones using M.R.

Even the admen come under the X ray. *Sponsor* magazine reported after extensive depth interviews that the choice of magazines, newspapers, and other advertising media is strongly influenced by irrational, unconscious drives. Among these influences are background (the adman clings to the media he knows best); job security (he's afraid to take a chance); personal bias; and the desire to make a big splash and impress prospective clients.

A few flies still buzz in the ointment.

Not all the depth research findings turn out to be useful. A Foote, Cone and Belding executive complained: "We had a facial soap . . . killed germs better than most other soaps. We wanted to know how we could best advertise it to teen-agers. . . . Well, we got a lot of talk about when a young girl uses soap it is to wash off the feeling of guilt that comes from newly awakened sexual desire. Where the heck do you go with that?"

Another firm employed a researcher to help determine attitudes of non-flying citizens. His major finding was that men who don't fly have a deep fear of plane crashes, but an even more devastating fear of sexual relationships with strange women. The information did not help sell plane tickets.

Nevertheless, the M.R. trend keeps growing. Will it develop to the point where we consumers have no further secrets and no defenses? Will we move in trance state, wallets wide open, toward the store?

Don't worry too much over this possibility.

Some thirty years ago Dr. J. B. Watson's theory of behaviorism was supposed to revolutionize advertising and selling. According to this doctrine all behavior, including buying, could be conditioned to take place in response to set stimuli. A dog is trained to jump through a hoop. In the same way, behaviorists reasoned, consumers could be conditioned to buy soap flakes. The craze swept the ad agencies, but the expected conquest of the consumer did not quite come off. We read the ads and we bought the soap flakes, but we simply refused to stay conditioned. Maybe too many people were trying to condition us at the same time.

Like microbes and other tough, low organisms, consumers are adept at developing new defenses against almost any form of attack. Perhaps we'll devise a subconscious to use as a kind of psychological storm cellar. Perhaps we'll resort to that Cinderella of psychology, the conscious mind. Either way, chances are that we'll survive.

OÙ EST LA SUNTAN OIL DE MA TANTE?

by Horace Sutton

Mon Dieu! Americans will undoubtedly be calling other Americans "mon vieux" and "mon petit chou," and things like that, unless lavish hotels like the Fontainebleau stop opening up in Florida's lush vacationland. Or at least so fears the author of this article, SR's *travel editor.*

JANUARY 8, 1955

WE HAVE BEEN DOWN to the white sands of Miami Beach to attend the opening of the Fontainebleau, a $14,000,000 hotel that seems destined to start a rash of parley-vous where even Berlitz wouldn't suspect it.

The vogue for French started by the Fontainebleau along the shores of Neon-sur-mer will render last year's animal kick *démodée, déclassée* and also dated. If you aren't *au courant* leave me tell you that a hupety-pupety motel called the Sahara is guarded by a pair of stuffed camels and a couple of stuffed Arabs. The Safari Motel is immediately recognized by a life-sized elephant on its lawn. The Desert Inn is marked by a team of horses pulling a covered wagon (you get the tie-in), and somewhere along the strip I found a stuffed zebra, although which hostelry it decorates fails me at the moment.

But this French flair, should it take hold—*Mon Dieu!* People will be calling people *"mon vieux," "mon petit chou,"* and like that. Already there are more fleur-de-lis in the Fontainebleau than *bois* in the Bois de Boulogne. This royalist emblem runs up and down the trim jackets of the waiters in the Fleur-de-lis Room. They are rampant on the pillow where you rest your head at night, and should you be a sheep-counter you will doubtless find them emblazoned on the mutton as they pass by.

On hand to open the Fontainebleau of Miami Beach, the largest chateau of chi-chi ever to be built on this reclaimed sandbar, was Senator H. Pajot, the mayor of Fontainebleau, France. He was a man of wispy hair, bearing a ready smile and a tree from the forest of Fontainebleau when he arrived at Idlewild Airport at New York. By the time he had gotten to Miami he had lost the tree to unromantic inspectors of the Agriculture Department, who impounded it. A red maple, no doubt.

The day was saved by an alert aide who removed a Christmas tree from a truck labeled Exotic Gardens, Miami, tied a red-and-blue ribbon about its scrawny trunk, and it was this tree that M. Pajot planted in the loam in front of this fifteen-story curved fortress that stands on the former Firestone estate. M. Pajot kissed M. Ben Novack, president of the hotel, on both cheeks and handed him a metal tablet on which these words were inscribed for posterity:

> . . . May the sun warm your day and the moon and the stars bring happy evenings . . .

The newsmen huddled in their collars and hoped so too, for the wind was whistling in the palms, and the thermometer was having trouble making the fifty-degree line. Despite the unseasonal California weather, there was no denying the *entente cordiale* that filled the air, put there no doubt by M. Leo Morrison, the American press agent who showed up in France's tricolor. His shirt was white and he wore a blue beret pulled sharply over one bloodshot eye.

M. Pajot was taken in tow by René Black, the famed *maître d'hôtel* who spent twenty years at the Waldorf carving Hoover's Thanksgiving turkey, tending the Duchess of Windsor's *soirées,* and serving everyone from Molotov to the Maharajah of Kapurthala. Said the mayor to the *maître,* the hotel was *épatant* and *formidable* and also *incroyable.* Moreover, he had some rather positive views about its architecture and design. "Outside," said Senator Pajot, "the building, very strong. But inside," his eyes bulged, "*bouilla-baisse!*"

Whether the interior of the roi-sized Fontainebleau will be *bouillabaisse* by the time it's completed remains to be seen. The architect, a Mr. Morris Lapidus, thinks not. While the first guests were arriving workmen were still stitching carpets with a curious whirring eggbeater, tiles were being laid in the dance floor, chandeliers were being hoisted into ceilings. When I leaned over the front desk long enough to ask for mail a carpenter began to build an inquiry window around me. In the Poodle Dog Bar workmen ripped the covers off tabletops, carpenters screwed in the legs, and waiters stood ready to spread tablecloths. It was one of the few places around where the guests and the walls were getting plastered at the same time.

On the third night it was in business; the partition that closes off the intimate Fleur-de-lis Room was removed, forming a gigantic ballroom. Some 1,600 people sat down for dinner by candlelight. The double-decker cabana colony itself covers five acres, and another four acres are still to be landscaped, reproducing the formal gardens of Fontainebleau and Versailles in France. Strollers can watch the mermaids bubble through the briny from subterranean windows.

As for the sleeping rooms, they are equipped with views of Paris, individually controlled air-conditioning, and knee-deep carpets at a minimum of $33 a day for one or two, no meals. If you have a spare $135 a day kicking around loose you can rent a two-room penthouse suite on the fifteenth floor with the most fabulous views of Miami Beach I have seen since the time I went to Hialeah in a helicopter. The old Firestone estate bulged out almost to the lagoon, forcing Collins Avenue into a giant bend. The Fontainebleau today sits inside the bend and Collins Avenue, canyon row of Miami Beach, seems to come right up to the front door when you look south. Northward you can scan the horizon clear up to Jacksonville if you have an unusual retina, for the land is flat, the days clear, the view unimpeded. Look down and you see the children's swimming-pool, shaped like a pussycat. Look up and you see a sky full of airplanes.

Supine on a padded redwood stretcher soaking up Vitamin D, one can look back on the great white curve of the hotel and view at one end a curious, bulbous, dome-shaped appendage which houses La Ronde, the night club. La Ronde is not only round but it is built dramatically in tiers rising, like a Greek theater, above an elevated stage. It can make room for 500 and the proceedings are lighted by a gigantic Scandinavian chandelier. A corner of the lobby is decorated with a gold-trimmed antique piano imported from France at the *fortissimo* price of $14,000. A quick check along the beachfront revealed it was the first piece of furniture more than four hours old ever brought to a Miami hotel.

THE JUKE MYTH

by Samuel Hopkins Adams

Everybody has heard of the classic down-and-out family of the schoolbooks, the Jukes. But few know that the clan never existed anywhere except in the imagination of a nineteenth-century amateur criminologist with whom novelist and essayist Samuel Hopkins Adams has at last caught up.

APRIL 2, 1955

No OTHER FAMILY in American annals is so well and unfavorably known as the Jukes. The name is a synonym for depravity. What the Rothschilds embody in finance the Jukes represent in misdemeanor. If there were an International Hall of Ill Fame they would get top billing.

And they never existed otherwhere than in the brain of an amateur criminologist. Richard L. Dugdale did not precisely invent them; rather, he compiled them from an assortment of human derelicts whom he collected after a method peculiarly his own, for the purpose of bolstering his theory of criminal heredity. He passed on his findings to posterity in his *magnum opus, The Jukes: A Study in Crime, Pauperism, Disease, and Insanity.*

This classic has permeated the sociology of nations. Geneticists like Giddings, East, and Walter have swallowed it whole. The New York State Prison Association sponsored it. Putnam's brought out three large editions, which were accepted as sociological gospel. Dugdale became the recognized authority on crime. His qualifications as an expert are peculiar. When the Dugdale family came to this country from England in 1851 Richard was ten years old. It was intended that he should go to college. After three years of schooling in New York something went awry in his education. He left school and became assistant to a sculptor. In the evenings he attended classes at Cooper Union, where he won something of a reputation as a debater on social topics.

His career, if such it were, was interrupted by the departure of the family to try farming in the Middle West. The venture was unsuccessful. The Dugdales returned to New York and Richard turned his hand to manufacturing. He was then twenty-three. The

515

business failed. Richard had a nervous breakdown and withdrew from active endeavor. "For four years I could neither earn nor learn," he records. Such was his technical equipment as a sociologist.

The Jukes came into his life quite by chance. He happened to be in a Kingston, N.Y., police court in 1873, where a youth was on trial for receiving stolen goods. Five relatives were present as witnesses. They came of a breed, to quote the incipient investigator, "so despised that their family name had come to be used generically as a term of reproach." They were alleged to live like haggards of the rock, in the caves of a nearby lake region. "Crime-cradles," our author calls the locality. He was a neat hand at a phrase.

He invented the name Juke for the clan.

The fact that the Juke at the bar of justice was acquitted in no wise discouraged young Dugdale. He made inquiries about the others present. An uncle of the accused is set down as a burglar. No proof is adduced. Two male cousins had been charged with pushing a boy over a cliff, one of whom was convicted. The remaining witnesses, two girls, he lists as harlots. By the Dugdale method, "under the heading of harlots are included all women who have made lapses, however seldom." This is fairly indicative of his standards of investigation and attribution.

With this auspicious start he canvassed the neighborhood for further specimens.

> With comparatively little inquiry [he writes], it was found that out of twenty-nine male adults, the immediate blood relations of the six, seventeen were criminals and fifteen others convicted of some degree of offense.

Impressed by this suggestive ratio—as who would not be by thirty-two out of a possible twenty-nine?—Dugdale went sleuthing back through the generations until he came upon an old Dutch reprobate who kept a turnpike hostelry in Orange County about the middle of the eighteenth century. Old Max appears to have been a sporting character. Several illegitimate children were imputed to him. He enjoyed a local reputation for drinking, gaming, and wenching, divertissements fairly general in those lusty pioneer days. He became Exhibit A in the Dugdale rogues' gallery, though nothing criminal appears in his record.

Max had two legitimate sons who married into a family of six sisters. With the discovery of the sisterhood Dugdale really hits his stride. The family line of the six is obscure; it "has not been absolutely ascertained," he admits. "One, if not all, of them were illegitimate," he surmises, on what grounds he does not explain. Delia is recorded as a "harlot before marriage," and Bell as a "harlot after marriage." Clara, he notes (presumptively with reluctance), was "reputed chaste." She did, however, marry a man who shot a neighbor. Effie's reputation was unknown to author Dugdale, which was certainly a break for Effie.

Another sister *circa* 1760 is Dugdale's prize specimen. "Margaret, Mother of Criminals," he calls her, although her name was Ada. Apt alliteration's artful aid again! To her goes the credit for "the distinctly criminal line of the family." But, what family? For all that he reveals Margaret-Ada, of unascertained parentage, may have been a Van Rensselaer, a Livingston, a Saltonstall, a Biddle, or the granddaughter of the original Joe Doakes. To be sure, he later characterizes the whole lot as "belonging to the Juke blood." Pure assumption. As their derivation was unknown and they were suspectedly illegitimate anyway, how could Dugdale or anybody else know anything of their ancestry?

As a "Mother of Criminals" Margaret (or Ada) hardly lives up to her name. Her daughter is designated as a harlot, but, by way of palliation perhaps, our author adds, "not industrious." One son was a laborer, "somewhat industrious." The other, a farmer, is stigmatized as having been "indolent" and "licentious in youth." The same might be said of some eminent non-Jukes, including Robert Burns and the Apostle Paul.

Margaret-Ada was married to one of old Max's sons. She had a son of her own, whom Dugdale holds to be co-responsible for the evil Juke inheritance. But this son was a Juke only in name. He was illegitimate. Dugdale says so.

Thus, the notorious criminal-Juke strain derives on one side from a progenitor who was not criminal (Old Max) and on the other from a line which was not Juke except by Dugdale fiat. (Margaret-Ada through her illegitimate son.)

It sufficed Dugdale. He had his theory; now he set out after supporting facts. He made a year's tour of prisons, almshouses, and asylums collecting Jukes. The result he published in 1875. It is still regarded by those who have not read it, and even by some who have, as an authoritative document. It established the Jukes as the type-family of degeneration.

Dugdale invented a terminology to go with his Jukes. His thesis is based, so he states, upon "Positive Statistics and Conjectural Statistics . . . Conjectural Statistics consists in Political Arithmetic

and the Theory of Probabilities." This recondite process "reduces
the method of study to one of historico-biographical synthesis united
to statistical analysis," which sounds as if it might have come out
of Lewis Carroll.

Applying this yardstick, Dugdale lists 709 alleged Jukes of whom
507 were social detrimentals. Such conventional crimes as murder,
arson, rape, and robbery, quite lacking in proof for the most part,
are cited. But there were not enough of them to support satisfactorily the Dugdale political arithmetic and theory of probabilities. So he fattens up the record with entries like the following:

> Reputed sheep-stealer, but never caught.
> Thief, but never caught.
> Petty thief, though never convicted.
> Guilty of murder, but escapes punishment.
> Unpunished and cautious thief.
> Bastardy prosecution.
> Supposed to have attempted rape.
> Cruelty to animals.
> Habitual criminal.
> Impossible to get any reliable information, but it is evident
> that at nineteen he was a leader in crime.

And such scattered attributions as "pauper," and "harlot,"
"brothel-keeper," "vagrant," "lazy," "intemperate," "drunkard,"
"immoral," "lecherous," etc., etc., etc. There was also a "contriver
of crime," and a hardened character who, in addition to frequent-
ing a saloon, was accused of breaking a deaf man's ear-trumpet.
Like the Juke who started it all, he was acquitted. It did not matter
to our investigator; the non-breaker of the ear-trumpet comes down
the ages, embalmed in criminal history.

All this might seem rather attenuated evidence on which to
indict an entire family. It sufficed Dugdale. He followed the long
and proliferating branches of the clan through the generations and
worked out a diagram as framework for the composite portrait.
This he calls "Leading Facts."

> In other words, *fornication* [the italics are his], either consan-
> guineous or not, is the backbone of their habits, flanked on
> the one side by *pauperism,* on the other by *crime.* The sec-
> ondary features are *prostitution,* with its complement of *bas-
> tardy,* and its resultant of miseducated childhood; *exhaus-
> tion,* with its complement, *intemperance,* and its resultant,
> unbalanced minds; and *disease,* with its complement, *extinc-
> tion.*

Consanguinity

		F		
C	Prostitution	O	Illegitimacy	P
		R		A
R		N		U
		I		P
I	Exhaustion	C	Intemperance	E
		A		R
M		T		I
		I		S
E	Disease	O	Extinction	M
		N		

Not Consanguineous

Dugdale's investigations into hygiene and morality are on a par with his criminological efforts. Insanity, epilepsy, deformity, impotency, and tuberculosis appear to have been as typical Juke phenomena as thievery, bastardy, and general lawlessness. Some of the evidence cited is calculated to astonish students of heredity. For example, it is recorded that the original Max went blind and transmitted the affliction to his posterity. As he lost his sight late in life, after his children were born, it is difficult to see how he can be held responsible for their blindness unless he poked them in the eye with a burnt stick.

Our author's figures on tuberculosis are confident, but where he found them is left a mystery. Nobody bothered to keep statistics in those days. Still more difficult would it have been to gather reliable data on venereal disease. Yet our conjectural statistician specifies, in one branch of the Jukes, forty harlots who contaminated 440 men, presumably eleven per harlot. In another genealogical line he states that 23½ per cent of the females were immoral. That ½ per cent is fairly awe-inspiring.

Not until long after the author's death did anyone rise to challenge his thesis. The late Thomas Mott Osborne, of prison-reform fame and at one time president of that same prison association which certified the Dugdale revelations, studied the Juke records with growing skepticism. Himself a practiced investigator, he raised questions about the Dugdale methods which that author might have found awkward to answer.

Whence, Mr. Osborne wished to know, did Dugdale derive those cocksure figures on disease, insanity, and death? Vital statistics at the time of his inquiry were practically nonexistent. How did he acquire his data on criminality when court records for the period were notoriously unreliable, if, indeed, they were available at all? What genealogical method did he use in tracing back the Juke line through the mazes of its prevalent bastardy, for a century and a quarter? Legitimate family lines, Mr. Osborne pointed out, were difficult enough to trace; illegitimate were flatly impossible, beyond a generation or two. Further, the objector indicated, a specially trained sociological investigator would have required at least three years to do the work which Dugdale completed in one.

Analyzing the indicated method of investigation, Mr. Osborne suggested that Dugdale based it on a formula of retroactive hypothesis as follows:

That every criminal was a putative Juke.

That every Juke was a presumptive criminal.

By the system which Dugdale employed in tracing down his Jukes, Mr. Osborne concluded, it would be possible to asperse the morality, sanity, and legitimacy of any family in America. As for the Jukes, they were "pure folklore."

Another dissident raised objections in *The Clinical Review* for April 1902. Was it credible, Edmund Andrews asked, that Old Max possessed "such a miraculous energy of vicious propagation that, by his sole vital force, he begat and transmitted the degeneracy of all the Jukes for five generations?" Each descendant in the fifth generation, the critic pointed out, had fifteen other progenitors. Why assign his or her lawless, shiftless, or bawdy habits to Max any more than to any other of the uncharted Jukes or Jakes or Jeeks or Jenkins? A sturdy breeder like Max might well be the ancestor of a couple of thousand great-great-grandchildren, 1,500 of whom, for all that Dugdale knew to the contrary, might have been missionaries.

"It is sheer nonsense," Mr. Andrews contends "to suppose that he (a fifth-generation Juke degenerate) got them all (his vicious proclivities) from that one lazy, but jovial old Rip Van Winkle, the original Juke."

These were but voices crying in a wilderness. To scotch a good, sturdy historical fake, once it has got its growth, is impossible. Nine-tenths of America devoutly believes that Robert Fulton invented the steamboat and that Abner Doubleday was the founder of baseball. So the Jukes will doubtless continue to furnish texts to trusting sociologists, and no great harm done.

But they are in the wrong category. The proper place of a Juke is not in criminology. It is in mythology.

THE DAY AFTER WE LAND ON MARS

by Robert S. Richardson

Now that the dizzying dream of traveling to Mars may prove a reality, an astronomer of the Mount Wilson and Palomar Observatories here offers a few tips for prospective interplanetary tourists.

MAY 28, 1955

MARS IS THE ONLY BODY aside from the Earth itself on which we have been able to detect evidence for life. The stars and nebulae present us with problems which in many respects make them more interesting objects for study than Mars, particularly in nuclear physics and related fields. A special interest attaches to Mars, however, owing to the fact that it may be the abode of life. There may be myriads of other stars besides our sun with planets revolving around them on which life has developed. We do not know. At present it seems unlikely that we will ever know. So far as life in the universe is concerned we are alone with Mars.

Doubtless men have always dreamed of traveling to far-off worlds more wonderful and (presumably) happier than their own. Until very recently the idea of travel beyond the Earth has hardly been more than a vague dream. Indeed few ever contended it could be anything else. Now suddenly the spectacular advances in rocketry and electronics have made space travel a possibility within our lifetime—within the next ten years, according to some. The prospect that unfolds before us is dazzling. The opportunities for discovery seem unlimited. And our enthusiasm for exploration in space unbounded.

In the excitement of the hunt we have paid little attention to the object of the chase. We have not bothered to question if the game is worth the candle. Or whether colonization of another world might lead to repercussions of a highly disturbing character. If we succeed in reaching Mars the total cost will run into the billions. It will be the biggest real-estate deal in history. What can we expect for our money? What kind of a world is Mars?

In appearance, at least, Mars is not so different from the Earth.

Many regions of the Earth must resemble Mars so closely that you could not tell which was which from a photograph. An artist friend of mine who has made a name for himself depicting planetary scenes tells me that Mars is his hardest subject. Editors balk at paying for a picture supposedly representing Mars when their readers are likely to mistake it for the country around Reno or Las Vegas. For Mars is practically all dry land and most of that land is desert. Mars is often referred to as a small planet, and it is true that its diameter is only about half that of the Earth's. But we must remember that three quarters of the Earth is covered by water and uninhabitable. When we compare the two globes on a dry-land basis Mars is found to be almost exactly the same size as the Earth.

On the Earth we immediately associate the word "desert" with "heat." On Mars, however, the situation is reversed. Over most of the planet the climate is similar to that of a cold high-altitude desert, such as the plateau of Tibet. Since Mars on the average is fifty million miles farther from the sun than the Earth we would naturally expect it to be considerably colder there, and actual measures with sensitive heat-detecting instruments confirm this. At noon in the tropics the average temperature is about 40° F. The atmosphere is so thin and dry that it has very little blanketing effect. Thus, the highest temperature comes near noon instead of about three o'clock in the afternoon as on the Earth. The temperature falls rapidly until at sunset it is 10° F. Since the unilluminated side of Mars is never turned directly toward the Earth we cannot measure the temperature at midnight, but it must be very low, say −20° F. A temperature of −90° F has been measured at the poles, and during the long polar night it may drop to −150° F. On the other hand, a temperature as high as 85° F was once recorded at a dark spot near the equator when Mars was close to the sun. For comparison, the highest and lowest temperatures ever recorded on Earth are 136° F in Tripoli and −90° F in Siberia.

Mars undoubtedly has a thin atmosphere of some kind as the familiar markings on the disc are often obscured by haze and clouds. On photographs taken in blue light which show only the outer atmospheric shell of the planet bright clouds often appear on the late afternoon side. In 1954 such a cloud formation was observed several times which bore a startling resemblance to the letter "W." The effect was the same as if someone had scrawled the letter on the side of the disc with a piece of chalk. (This is one of those "now it can be told" items. If astronomers had released this information in 1954 when Mars was closest there is no telling what the result might have been. Of course, if you turn the planet upside down the marking becomes an "M.")

Unfortunately, our knowledge of the constitution of the Martian atmosphere is mostly negative in character. We can only talk about what the atmosphere is *not*. For example, we know that it does *not* contain any oxygen; or, at most, less than 1 per cent of the amount in our atmosphere. The announcement in 1933 that observations taken with the 100-inch telescope on Mount Wilson had failed to detect oxygen in the atmosphere of Mars came as a blow to those who would like to have the planets inhabited by intelligent beings. Since oxygen is essential to all but the lowest forms of life it seems improbable that we will ever be destroyed by invaders from Mars. At present our best guess is that the atmosphere of Mars is made up of inert gases like those in our own atmosphere, but with the oxygen left out.

Water also is an exceedingly scarce article on Mars. Astronomers took about seventy-five years to establish the fact that oxygen is absent, but the evidence for water can be obtained almost at a glance. Among the easiest markings to discern on the disc are the white caps at the poles, which expand in winter and shrink with the approach of spring. The most natural explanation is that they consist of a thin deposit of frost and snow. For a while it was thought they might be frozen carbon dioxide or dry ice, but this idea has been abandoned. (The polar caps are too warm!) This deposit of snow at the poles appears to be the only source of water on the entire planet. To us it would seem pitifully inadequate. Long ago Professor H. N. Russell of Princeton illustrated the perpetual drought that prevails on Mars in a striking way when he remarked that all the water on the planet would hardly fill Lake Huron, a statement that has been repeated by practically every author who has written on Mars in the last thirty years.

Although it is hard to make out a case for animal life on Mars, the evidence for plant life is good. There are still a few dissenters, but I believe that most astronomers today are willing to admit the existence of plant life. The distinctive red color of Mars comes from the barren deserts in the northern hemisphere. But the southern hemisphere up to about latitude 40° is girdled by dark green areas called *maria*. As the name indicates, these areas were once thought to be actual seas, and not so long ago either. It seems incredible today that our grandfathers could have been so wrong. The *maria* show seasonal changes which suggest the growth and decay of vegetation. In winter they are dim and gray or brownish in tint. But as spring comes on and the polar cap begins to melt a "wave of quickening" proceeds toward the equator and the *maria* grow darker and turn to green. It seems almost certain that the *maria* must undergo regeneration each year, as otherwise they would have been obliterated after millions of years by the dust from the deserts.

The chief objection to the vegetation hypothesis is the absence of oxygen and the limited supply of water. Also, the sub-zero cold would rule out most types of plants. It is possible, however, that such extremely hardy plants as the lichens might be able to survive on Mars, as their adaptability to adverse conditions seems virtually unlimited. This does not mean of course that there are lichens growing on Mars. If the green *maria* consist of vegetation it is probably of a wholly different type from ours.

Let us look ahead to a time when space travel has become a reality. The journey to Mars is still hazardous and beset with difficulties, but it is no longer a major problem. However, the length of the trip is hard to specify at present; there are many uncertainties involved. One plan which has been worked out in detail puts the round trip at nearly three years. This includes a stay on Mars of 449 days. Even making liberal allowances for technical advances it appears that the time spent on the road will always be considerable. (Unless, of course, atomic fuel becomes available.)

By a stupendous effort a station of several hundred young unmarried men has finally been established on Mars. Needless to say, the personnel was selected with the utmost care to eliminate those with physical defects and undesirable personality traits. Transporting men from the Earth to Mars and back is an exceedingly expensive and difficult proposition. For this reason the men cannot be rotated as rapidly as is desirable. A man who volunteers for Mars must do so with the expectation of remaining a minimum of, say, five years on the planet.

To ensure a permanent supply of water the station should be located at one of the poles. We will put it at the north pole since this one has never been observed to disappear completely in summer. A steady water supply would also solve the oxygen problem, since oxygen could probably be obtained most easily on Mars by decomposing water into hydrogen and oxygen. Locating the station at the pole has the disadvantage of a long night with its frightfully low temperature. But it is going to be cold wherever you build on Mars. And it is doubtful if the men would be much less miserable at the equator.

If we are able to get to Mars in the first place we should be able

to build dwellings where the men can live in reasonable comfort
so far as their bodily needs are concerned. But it would be an unnatural artificial existence, as restricted as taking up residence in a
submarine. One could never step outdoors without suitable oxygen
equipment. Since the atmospheric pressure is probably from 10 to
20 per cent of that at the surface of the Earth an airtight spacesuit
would not be necessary. But even short trips would be dangerous
owing to accidents to the oxygen equipment, and the chance of
being caught outdoors at night without ample protection against
the cold. Exploring parties could probably make field trips by airplane despite the low density of the air, since gravity is only 37
per cent of that on the Earth.

Only a few of the men would work outdoors. Most of the men's
time would be spent inside the walls of the station. The work
would be of a monotonous character, analyzing and classifying data
secured on field trips, writing up reports, and transmitting the
results to Earth. A man would never be alone. Every hour would
be closely restricted and regulated. The discipline could never be
relaxed; the least slip might result in disaster. A man would lead
a precarious life, but it would lack the stimulation that comes from
exposure to imminent danger. It would be an endless war without
a truce or a victory.

Why should we risk lives and spend billions of dollars to reach
such a desolate world when there are vast regions so much closer
home that are still blank spots on the map? Because we will find
new elements or precious mineral deposits? Impossible. Because occupation of the planets will be useful for military purposes? Nonsense. Because we will find a type of intelligence far greater than
our own? The odds are overwhelmingly against it. Yet I feel confident in my own mind that if we attain the technical ability to
travel to the planets we will do it. Furthermore, we will do it
knowing perfectly well what to expect in advance.

Why?

Well . . . for no better reason than man's insatiable and restless
curiosity to see what lies beyond his horizon. Because there will
never be any peace for us until that challenging gap between the
Earth and Mars is bridged. We should quit trying to think up
logical, sensible reasons for space travel. *There are no such reasons.*
If we ever reach Mars it will be because we were lured there by
that same vague but irresistible urge that led men to make one
assault after another on Mt. Everest: "Because it's there."

In my opinion, the only valid reason for journeying to Mars is
pure scientific investigation. There is no question that a station on

Mars would add to our store of basic scientific knowledge. For instance, we would like very much to know about magnetic conditions
on Mars, or any planet for that matter. What is the strength of
the magnetic field? How does it vary over the surface and throughout the day and year? There are many other problems that would
be crying for study. The difficulty would be in trying to decide
which ones to do first. Whether the taxpayers would be willing to
foot a bill of $10,000,000,000 to learn that the magnetic axis of Mars
is inclined seven degrees to its axis of rotation is a question. My
hunch is they would not care particularly. Going to Mars would
be a lot of fun and excitement, a trip in which we could all vicari-
ously participate. Go ahead and spend the money.

The biologist would seem to have the biggest stake in such a
trip. If the *maria* consist of vegetation he would be in much the
same situation as Galileo with his first telescope—wherever he looked
he would be sure to make an important discovery. Imagine the
delight of a biologist able to study plant life that had originated
under extraterrestrial conditions. Biologists like to think of plant
succession, photosynthesis, and natural selection as fundamental
principles of life. But the fact remains that they have been studied
only under the conditions that prevail on the Earth, and their
universal nature can only be inferred. It would be a most striking
piece of evidence if such fundamental principles were also found
to hold true on Mars.

The nearest approximation we have to an outpost such as we
have visualized on Mars is the 5,000-man base which the United
States government has established at Thule, Greenland. Apparently
it is well equipped so that the men suffer no severe hardship. Yet
all reports tell of the boredom and monotony of the life, of the
conflicts arising from close contact with the same individuals day
after day, as well as a profound sense of depression that comes
from existence under such isolated and unnatural conditions.

But how much more intense would these sensations be to a man
confined on Mars! Regardless of how carefully the men were screened
beforehand, one wonders if any group of individuals could live for
long amid such alien surroundings without tensions building up
until they became intolerable. The sense of isolation would be
overwhelming in its intensity. The thought that they are the *only*
human beings in an entire world might drive men crazy. Worse
still would be the utter futility of escape from such surroundings.
At Thule the mere knowledge that civilization is always only a few
days away by airplane must be comforting even if one is unable
to make the trip. But on Mars civilization would be millions of

miles distant in space and years away in time. A man could not even stroll outdoors to seek solace in the bosom of nature without first having to don his oxygen equipment, check with the gate-keeper, etc.

In all the articles on space travel which I have read there is one aspect of the subject which has never been discussed or so much as even mentioned. Yet it is a problem that is certain to arise, especially if the planets are going to be inhabited mainly by normal, healthy young men. It strikes me that if we are going to talk about traveling to the planets on a realistic adult level at all we should take the problems out in the open and face them. There is sex.

Judging from what has been written so far for TV scripts men in space are not supposed to have women on their minds. It seems doubtful, however, if men on Mars will be so preoccupied with measuring the horizontal component of the planet's magnetic field, or in setting off artificial earthquakes, that they can be completely oblivious of their bodies. Although examples can be cited where men have lived together alone for long periods, few would contend that such an existence is normal or healthy. I am not a psychiatrist, and hence cannot speak on such matters with authority. But one hardly needs to be an expert to know that men and women were meant to live together, and that when compelled to live alone they undergo personality changes of an undesirable nature. Tensions would develop until they became explosive. Eventually a man would have to find some way to relax—to cut loose—to do something about the impulses and ideas that have been building up inside of him. The situation would not be so serious if the men could be rotated fairly rapidly, but space travel by its very nature makes this impossible.

If space travel and colonization of the planets eventually become possible on a fairly large scale, it seems probable that we may be forced into first tolerating and finally openly accepting an attitude toward sex that is taboo in our present social framework. Can we expect men to work efficiently on Mars for five years without women? Family life would be impossible under the conditions that prevail. Imagine the result of allowing a few wives to set up house-keeping in the colony! After a few weeks the place would be a shambles. To put it bluntly, may it not be necessary for the success of the project to send some nice girls to Mars at regular intervals to relieve tensions and promote morale?

We may ask further if men (and women) who travel to other worlds will not eventually develop moral attitudes quite at variance with those generally accepted at present? Our moral attitudes and religious customs are the product of thousands of years of life upon the Earth. They developed out of conditions that prevail upon one planet. Is it not conceivable that in an entirely alien environment survival will produce among other things a sexual culture—shocking on Earth—which would be entirely "moral" judged by extraterrestrial standards?

RANDOM THOUGHTS
ON RANDOM DOGS

by John Steinbeck

A famous novelist, the author of The Grapes of Wrath *and* Of Mice and Men, *offers a short treatise on some interesting aspects of man's best friend.*

OCTOBER 8, 1955

A VERY WISE MAN writing recently about the emergence and develop-ment of our species suggests that the domestication of the dog was of equal importance with the use of fire to first man. Through as-sociation with a dog, man doubled his perceptions, and besides this the dog—sleeping at dawn-man's feet—let him get a little rest un-disturbed by creeping animals. The uses of the dog change. One of the first treatises on dogs in English was written by an abbess or a prioress in a great religious house. She lists the ban dog, the har-rier, the dog from Spain called spaniel and used for reclaiming wounded birds, the dogs of "venerie," etc., and finally she says, "There been those smalle whyte dogges carried by ladys to draw the fleas away to theirselves." What wisdom was here. The lap dog was not a decoration but a necessity.

A dog has, in our day, changed his function. Of course, we still have hounds used for the chase and greyhounds for racing, and the pointers, setters, and spaniels for their intricate professions, but in our total dog population these are the minority. Many dogs are used as decorations but by far the greatest number are a sop for loneliness. A man's or a woman's confidant. An audience for the shy. A child to the childless. In the streets of New York between seven and nine in the morning you will see the slow procession of dog and owner proceeding from street to tree to hydrant to trash-basket. They are apartment dogs. They are taken out twice a day and, while it is cliché, it is truly amazing how owner and dog re-semble each other. They grow to walk alike, have the same set of head.

In America styles and dogs change. A few years ago the Airedale was most popular. Now it is the cocker, but the poodle is coming up. A thousand years ago I can remember when the pug was everywhere.

In America we tend to breed out non-working dogs to extremes. We breed collies with their heads so long and narrow that they can no longer find their way home. The ideal dachshund is so long and low that his spine sags. Our Dobermen are paranoid. We have developed a Boston bull with a head so large that the pups can only be born by Caesareans.

It is not wise to mourn for the apartment dog. His lifespan is nearly twice that of the country dog. His boredom is probably many times greater. One day I got in a cab and gave the address of an animal store. The driver asked, "Is it a dog you're after? Because I can let you have a dog. I got dogs."

"It's not a dog, but how is it you have dogs?"

"It's this way," the cabby said. "It's Saturday night in an apartment and a man and his wife were lapping up a scoop of gin. About midnight they get to arguing. She says, 'Your damn dog. Who has to clean up after him and walk him and feed him, and you just come home and pat him on the head.' And the guy says, 'Don't you run down my dog.' 'I hate him,' she says. 'O.K. Pal,' he says, 'if that's the way you want it. Come on, Spot,' and he and the dog hit the street. The guy sits on a bench and holds the mutt in his arms and cries and then the two of them go to a bar and the guy tells everybody there no dame could treat his pal that way. Well, pretty soon they close the bar and it's late and the liquor begins to wear off and the guy wants to go home. So he gets in the cab and gives the dog to the cabbie. It happens to me every Saturday night."

I have owned some astonishing dogs. One I remember with pleasure was a very large English setter. He saw things unknowable. He would bark at a tree by the hour, but only at one tree. In grape season he ate nothing but grapes which he picked off the vine, one grape at a time. In pear season he subsisted on windfall pears, but he would not touch an apple. Over the years he became more and more otherworldly. I think he finally came to disbelieve in people. He thought he dreamed them. He gathered all the dogs in the neighborhood and gave them silent lectures or sermons, and one day he focused his attention on me for a full five minutes and then he walked away. I heard of him from different parts of the state. People tried to get him to stay, but in a day or so he would wander on. It is my opinion that he was a seer and that he had become a missionary. His name was T-Dog. Long later, and 100 miles away, I saw a sign painted on a fence which said "T-God." I am convinced that he had transposed the letters of his last name and gone out into the world to carry his message to all the dogs thereof.

I have owned all kinds of dogs but there is one I have always wanted and never had. I wonder if he still exists. There used to be in the world a white, English bull terrier. He was stocky, but quick. His muzzle was pointed and his eyes triangular so that his expression was that of cynical laughter. He was friendly and not quarrelsome, but forced into a fight he was very good at it. He had a fine, decent sense of himself and was never craven. He was a thoughtful, inward dog, and yet he had enormous curiosity. He was heavy of bone and shoulder. Had a fine arch to his neck. His ears were sometimes cropped, but his tail never. He was a good dog for a walk. An excellent dog to sleep beside a man's bed. He showed a delicacy of sentiment. I have always wanted one of him. I wonder whether he still exists in the world.

WHAT MAKES A GENIUS?

by Delbert Clark

History's most promising candidates for the title of "genius" form an imposing group. But in this article a former Washington newspaperman has pared their number down to thirty-three. You may or may not agree with his nominations.

NOVEMBER 12, 1955

"JUST WHY," asked the law professor, with mock severity, "do you say that Rossini was a genius?"

"That's easy," replied the general, "he composed a wide variety of great music."

"That doesn't make him a genius," retorted the editor. "He has to have more than great talent and industry to qualify."

"Well," protested the general, "Thomas Wolfe said genius was 90 per cent energy and 10 per cent talent."

"Whoops!" whooped the professor. "That lets in E. Phillips Oppenheim and John Philip Sousa, to say nothing of Thomas Wolfe. You'll have to do better than that!"

"Seems to me," remarked the host, "that genius, as George says, is more than what we call talent, however prodigious. Genius adds something that wasn't there before."

At this point the hostess had found the right page in the dictionary.

"It says here," she put in, "that genius is 'extraordinary power of invention or origination of any kind.'"

"Freud had something to say on the subject, but I'm not sure I can quote him accurately," said the psychoanalyst, blushing a little. "As I recall it, he described a genius as something in the nature of one in an hypnotic state, who achieved great things without being really aware of it."

"Like Trilby?" inquired the professor. "I might go along with that in the arts, because I'm sure neither Beethoven nor Van Gogh nor Shakespeare, for example, ever said to himself: 'Now I'm going to create, now I'm going to perpetrate an act of genius.' But I'd want to qualify it a whole lot when you get into the laboratory sciences. It could be that some chemist has come up with a world-shaking discovery just by mixing stuff at random in a test tube, but I consider it more likely that he got only first-degree burns or a shockingly offensive odor. I'll bet Pasteur knew pretty well what he was doing and was quite aware of its importance."

The editor had been rummaging through his host's books.

"What about this?" he asked. "This man Amiel published a diary back in 1850, and he said: 'Doing easily what others find difficult is talent—doing what is impossible for talent is genius.' "

"Just what I said," said the host.

"It's clear enough," said the professor, "that not one of us, when the argument started, had more than the foggiest idea of what he meant by the word 'genius.' "

"Genius," continued the host, ignoring the interruption, "is creative; it goes beyond the talent, as Amiel said, and adds to the body of permanent knowledge in any field something of value which wasn't there before. It cannot be wholly derivative or purely accidental. And I think it's fair to narrow it down still more, and presuppose, generally, a continuous flow of creative thought and activity, even though the tangible results which can truly be classed as products of genius may be very few."

"Well, how many individuals in history of the world can you name to fit that description?" asked the hostess.

That's how it all started, and here is the list of thirty-two men and one woman that resulted. It is highly selective and highly explosive, the perfect overture to an interminable argument. It is notable for its unexpected inclusions and for its shocking omissions of traditional heroes. It certainly is not and does not pretend to be all-inclusive.

There is one name which seems not to live up to one of the conditions, but the stupendous nature of the achievement in this case appeared to justify a slight exception. There are only two names included solely for literary achievement, and only one musician. And, finally, no one is included whose existence is even in part legendary, or who has been generally credited with supernatural powers.

Alexander the Great	Cézanne
Archimedes	Copernicus
Aristotle	Curie (Marie)
Beethoven	Dante
Brunelleschi	Darwin
Buddha	Einstein
Caesar	Erasmus

Fleming	Michelangelo
Franklin	Napoleon
Freud	Newton
Giotto	Pasteur
Goethe	Praxiteles
Gutenberg	Saint Paul
Hannibal	Shakespeare
Hertz	Socrates
Leonardo da Vinci	Van Gogh
Machiavelli	

If this were a whodunit or a quiz program the reader would be asked at this point to write down his own appraisal of these thirty-three alleged geniuses, eliminating any that profoundly offended him, adding any others he is sure fit the definition, and giving his reasons. Well, here are the reasons, some of them possibly surprising, why these particular individuals have been labeled *genius*. Should any university consider giving posthumous honorary degrees on the basis of this appraisal it is free to use these capsule citations, with or without credit:

ALEXANDER THE GREAT (356-323 B.C.): Outstanding military genius and a poet who lived, not wrote, his epics. To quote a felicitous summation in the Encyclopaedia Britannica, "he was singular among men of action for the imaginative splendors which guided him, and among romantic dreamers for the things he achieved."

ARCHIMEDES (287-212 B.C.): Unsurpassed in the field of applied mathematics, he devised a method for measuring the circle, wrote a notable treatise which forms the basis of theoretical mechanics, and was responsible for many basic inventions.

ARISTOTLE (384-322 B.C.): Master of pure logic, founder of literary criticism, he exerted a deep influence on Christian dialectic.

LUDWIG VAN BEETHOVEN (1770-1827): Greatest and most creative of all musical composers, he brought polyphony to the highest stage of its development and, more important, reconciled it with the classic form which had dominated the art of his immediate predecessors. There is no composer in the Western world since Beethoven whose work he has not profoundly influenced. He opened up whole new vistas of composition, immeasurably enriching the literature of music.

FILIPPO BRUNELLESCHI (1377-1446): Most imaginative of the Renaissance architects, he "revived architecture" as an art. He was the first to apply the principles of perspective to building construction, and his great dome on the Cathedral of Santa Maria del Fiore in Florence served as a model for Michelangelo when the latter built St. Peter's in Rome.

GAUTAMA BUDDHA (536-483): Founder of an ethical system stressing non-injury, forgiveness of enemies, and friendliness to all, he laid the basis of a moral philosophy (including the "Golden Rule"), remarkably similar to the Christian philosophy enunciated five centuries later.

CAIUS JULIUS CAESAR (100-44 B.C.): Master political strategist and tactician, civil administrator, he combined with his political genius a military genius equaled by few in the history of the world. The two cannot in his case be viewed separately, for military capacity served primarily to implement his political plans.

PAUL CÉZANNE (1839-1906): One of two modern painters who made positive creative contributions to their art form, he achieved a synthesis of essential structure and surface appearances. Recognizing the existence of geometric forms in nature he contrived, by emphasizing planes, to give a greater logic to his colorful paintings.

NICOLAUS COPERNICUS (1473-1543): Outstanding among astronomers, he firmly established the heliocentric theory of the universe.

MARIE CURIE (1867-1934): With her husband she first discovered, then isolated, the metal radium as a powerful cure for some of mankind's worst ills, not to mention the infinitely varied and important industrial uses of the element.

DANTE ALIGHIERI (1265-1321): Universal poet, pioneer in the use of Italian as a literary language, he was authentic innovator of form in literature. He was, indeed, the literary pursuivant of the Renaissance.

CHARLES DARWIN (1809-1882): Through a lifetime of creative study and experimentation he established the doctrine of the origin of species through natural selection.

ALBERT EINSTEIN (1879-1955): On the basis of pure creative analysis he propounded new and fundamental theories of the nature of matter which have been generally accepted in his own lifetime, have added immeasurably to our knowledge of the external world, and have opened up limitless avenues of physical research and development, not the least of which is atomic fission.

DESIDERIUS ERASMUS (1466-1536): Great moral philosopher, apostle of common sense and rational religion, he was the greatest Renaissance humanist, and the philosophical father of the Protestant Reformation.

ALEXANDER FLEMING (1881-   ): Already distinguished for his research in the little-known field of antibiotics, he was led by curiosity and imagination to an analysis and understanding where others had been blind, and brought about the discovery of the curative properties of penicillin, first of a growing family of "wonder drugs."

BENJAMIN FRANKLIN (1706-1790): A many-sided philosopher and statesman, he established the identity of lightning and electricity, and propounded the basic theory of positive-negative electrical charges.

SIGMUND FREUD (1856-1939): Undisputed founder of psychoanalysis, and hence of an entirely new method of treating psychic disturbances. The sharp divergences among his pupils and associates as to the details of his theories did not impair their belief in the basic principles of psychoanalysis, and must not be permitted to discredit the importance of his contribution. Neither can it be discredited by the unscrupulous quacks who have sought to profit by the novelty of psychoanalysis and have thereby retarded public acceptance of Freud's discovery.

GIOTTO DI BONDONE (1267-1337): The great humanizer of painting, he brought natural action and natural feeling to his subjects, moving steadily away from the dead conventionalism of the past. He worked on the threshold of the Renaissance, as did Dante in literature, and opened the door to the astonishing versatility and realism which followed. It has been said that he "re-created" the art of painting; rather he gave it dimensions it had never had before.

JOHANN WOLFGANG VON GOETHE (1749-1832): One of the world's greatest imaginative and philosophical writers and outstanding in many areas of intellectual and practical activity, he foreshadowed Darwin in biological research and enunciated the law of organic evolution.

JOHANNES GUTENBERG (1397-1468): His invention of printing with movable type provided a mechanical extension for the mind of man which literally revolutionized human society.

HANNIBAL BARCA (247-183 B.C.): Greatest of all military geniuses, father of tank warfare, whose battles still serve as models, he was also an outstanding statesman and civil administrator.

HEINRICH RUDOLF HERTZ (1857-1895): He established the electromagnetic nature of light, laying the scientific basis for the development of wireless telegraphy and telephony, including radio broadcasting and television.

LEONARDO DA VINCI (1452-1519): Greatest of them all, there was virtually no field of human knowledge to which he did not make some notable contribution. Outstanding as painter, sculptor, architect, engineer, anatomist, he anticipated Dr. William Harvey's theory of blood circulation by two centuries, and laid down an aerodynamic basis for the Wright brothers 400 years later.

NICCOLO MACHIAVELLI (1469-1527): Building on the foundation of his own broad experience and penetrating analysis of the problems of government, he wrote a classic treatise which established him as the father of the modern science of politics.

MICHELANGELO BUONARROTI (1475-1564): Probably the greatest painter, sculptor, and architect of all times, he made great and lasting creative contributions to the arts in which he excelled.

NAPOLEON BONAPARTE (1769-1821): Ranking with Alexander and Caesar as military genius, he was at the same time a creative genius in statecraft and administration. His contributions of a peaceful character to France and the world are outstanding, but have been overshadowed by his military record; it can be only a matter for speculation what his position in history might have been had not virtually his entire adult life been devoted to warfare.

ISAAC NEWTON (1642-1727): Already famous for his work on the refraction of light and for his origination of differential calculus, he first fully understood and enunciated the law of gravity.

LOUIS PASTEUR (1822-1895): Discoverer of the cause of fermentation, he first positively associated bacteria with disease and opened up the whole field of immunization.

PRAXITELES (Fourth century B.C.): Greatest of the Attic sculptors, he was the originator of fully-rounded form and realism in sculpture, deeply influencing the work of all succeeding sculptors down to but not including the neo-primitives of our century. Credit for his creative contributions must be shared with his contemporaries Scopas and Lysippus, but the best available evidence points to Praxiteles as the great creator.

SAINT PAUL (64 A.D.): Master of organization and what has come to be known in twentieth-century trade jargon as "promotion," he assumed leadership of the confused and persecuted disciples of Jesus, formed what may, without disrespect, be termed the most effective "sales force" in history, and made the Christian faith a force to be reckoned with by the holders of temporal power.

WILLIAM SHAKESPEARE (1564-1616): Greatest and most versatile of dramatic writers, he left a body of literature which synthesized much of the wisdom of all time, and which remains after nearly four centuries the second greatest source book in the English-speaking world.

SOCRATES (470-399 B.C.): Before him philosophy in the Western world had been primarily interested in cosmology—speculation on the character of the universe. Socrates made the central problem of philosophy the formulation of a rule of life, which has remained its focus ever since. With the teachings of Socrates the "practical rule of reason" came into its own. In the words of Cicero, "He brought down philosophy from heaven to earth."

VINCENT VAN GOGH (1853-1890): Foremost among the so-called expressionists in the art of painting, as contrasted with the impressionists who preceded him. He could be called the first great emotional poet among painters, for as a poet uses words to convey his own private feelings, so Van Gogh, even in a landscape or a still life, employed selection and exaggeration of detail to convey a meaning not inherent in the objects themselves.

"Wait a minute!" cries an outraged voice. "You can't get away with that! What about Edison?"

"Where's Thomas Jefferson?"

"Where are Richard Wagner, and Bach, and Mozart, and Palestrina?"

"How about Keats and Shelley?"

"And Voltaire and Molière?"

"And Toscanini?'

Well, what about them, and many others? Why isn't Marconi in the list? And Ehrlich? And Hitler?

Let's take another look at our description of genius:

"Genius is creative; it goes beyond talent, and adds to the body of permanent knowledge in any field something of value which was not there before. Genius presupposes a continuous flow of creative thought and activity, even though the tangible results which can truly be classed as products of genius may be very few."

So what about Edison and Marconi and, for that matter, Henry Ford?

On that record the eminent achievements of these men, and many others who might be named in the same inventive category, were primarily derivative. Each built upon the pure research of others, and put it to practical use. They may not be included here unless you broaden the definition of genius.

Marconi, for example, applied to practical purposes the findings of Hertz and others—he did not invent wireless telegraphy.

Ford revolutionized manufacturing through his adaptation of mechanical methods and devices already in existence and, as a by-product of his one-man industrial revolution, brought equally radical changes in a wide range of other industrial practices.

Edison had a marvelous record of achievement in electronics, but it was a case of finding the most practicable method of putting to use the fundamental research of his predecessors.

In this sense none of these men was an *originator,* and it is not at all to their discredit to say so, any more than it would be a disparagement of Sarah Bernhardt to say she never wrote a play.

This brings us to Toscanini and a host of other performing artists. Interpretation, however great, cannot by our definition be classed as genius.

But Bach, Mozart, and Wagner, and Palestrina? Surely Wagner developed an entirely new music form? Didn't Palestrina virtually originate polyphonic composition, and didn't Bach teach us what the piano was good for? And certainly the great Mozart—how about Mozart?

Wagner didn't develop a new music form; rather he built on a foundation already laid, and a very imposing structure it was, but not creative in our sense.

Palestrina did not invent polyphony, but brought it to a high and intricate stage of development.

Bach certainly did things for the piano for which we should be eternally grateful, but this cannot be classed as creation. As for his wonderfully complex compositions in the classic, almost mathematical, form, parallel to the polyphony of Palestrina, but never meeting, it took Beethoven to marry the two forms and give new depth and dimensions to music.

Mozart? Did he really originate or did he, with towering talent and industry, build magnificent edifices of sound upon the firm foundation of form bequeathed to him by Bach and Haydn?

Of Voltaire, Molière, Keats, Shelley, and Lord knows how many other writers what can be said? Here is an extremely subjective, almost amorphous area of artistic activity, where each artist in a sense is a creator, breaking old molds and fashioning new ones at will. The definition all but breaks down. It seems as though Dante and Shakespeare qualify, but the others, even including Sophocles, are at least in doubt. For a subjective art there has to be a subjective appraisal, and if this be treason make the most of it!

As for Paul Ehrlich, he determined to do one thing—find a cure for a disease which was the traditional scourge of mankind. By dint of patient, protracted experimentation he came up with the right combination after 605 failures. Contrast this with Pasteur, with Fleming, who were working on the realm of the virtually unknown and blessed mankind with fundamental discoveries, not at all accidental, which formed the basis of remedies for not one disease alone, but for many.

Hitler? What did he devise, what create? Fascism? Nonsense! Mussolini was years ahead of him, and Mussolini's fascism was an obvious synthesis of Plato, Napoleon III, Julius Caesar, and probably many others. Someone objects that Hitler was capable of mass hypnosis, but so, no doubt, are some Indian fakirs and African witch doctors. So, they say, were Leon Trotzky, Billy Sunday, and Aimée Semple McPherson!

But Thomas Jefferson? That hurt! He was one of the first on the tentative list, but he fell victim of the very definition by which he had to be judged. Indeed, it may be said that he approached genius, but his political philosophy seems to have been entirely derivative. He was a great man in a great time, who was able to give living force and immediacy to the political thought of his predecessors.

One misguided friend ardently advocated the inclusion of Florence Nightingale as the "founder of modern hospital practice." Well, the record belies this. This mess in the Crimea was a major scandal back home in England and Miss Nightingale, who had considerable experience in the most up-to-date hospital methods in England and elsewhere, was sent out by the War Ministry to clean it up. In short she applied, and no doubt improved upon, methods already in practice.

Somone suggested Casanova, but it does not appear that he added anything new, other than assembly-line methods, to the oldest of the fine arts.

Finally, a bow in passing to several historical personages who lived, it might be said, on the fringes of genius, and who made it possible for many authentic geniuses to do their work. Outstanding in this category is Lorenzo the Magnificent of Florence. Lorenzo did for artists of every description what no one before him had ever done—he elevated them from the classification of servants, from the company of scullions, to the honorable status they had hitherto lacked. He was not concerned with their origins, whether base or noble, so long as they were artists.

For the statistical minded, five out of thirty-three—Alexander, Hannibal, Caesar, Napoleon, and St. Paul—were included primarily as men of action. Ten were selected for their contributions to one of the arts, including Leonardo, whose genius actually invaded nearly every field of activity. Six, including Goethe, who was also a literary artist, were set down for their work in medicine, biology, and allied sciences. Five, if one may include Machiavelli, the political scientist, are classed as philosophers. Seven were contributors to knowledge in the physical sciences.

Chronologically, eight lived and worked in the pre-Christian era; only one from the beginning of the Christian era through the twelfth century A.D.; nine in the period between the thirteenth and sixteenth centuries, embracing the Renaissance and immediate pre-Renaissance era; six in the seventeenth and eighteenth centuries, and nine in the nineteenth and twentieth centuries.

Anyone who tries to make something of these random statistics does so at his peril: however, it is interesting to note that no men in medical or allied fields occur before the nineteenth century; that the last philosopher on the list died more than four hundred years ago, and that the turbulence of the Renaissance and the twentieth century failed to contribute one primarily distinguished as a man of action.

All these appraisals, however presumptuous they may appear to be, are based upon undisputed facts. It would be amusing to include the unknown inventor of the wheel, the discoverer of the value of fire, the author of the Mayan calendar, and the genius who worked out the politico-social system of the Iroquois Indians. At any rate, the absence of Charles Lamb's Chinaman, who discovered the delights of roast pig by the accident of a house burning, is deliberate: this was the result of pure chance, and the limited supply of expendable houses makes the discovery of little practical worth!

MOZART IN
THE MAGIC FLUTE

by Bruno Walter

On January 27, 1956, the world celebrated the two-hundredth an-
niversary of the birth of Wolfgang Amadeus Mozart, thereby
prompting a famous orchestra conductor to discover the creative
personality of Mozart through one of the composer's best-known
operas.

JANUARY 28, 1956

GIVING THOUGHT to the coming celebration of the two-hundredth recurrence of the Mozart birthday has made me conscious of the obligation to pay a word of homage to the genius whose work, as musician, I have endeavored to serve throughout my life.

Above all, this word must be one of gratitude for the rare happiness with which the work of Mozart has brightened, indeed blessed, my life. To substantiate this feeling of gratitude in detail—that is, to indicate the beauty and greatness of the works with penetrating thoughts and words—seems to me superfluous in view of the copious and oftentimes excellent Mozart literature which exists. Also, I scarcely could hope, by so doing, to render him a better service than I have through my endeavors as an artist in opera and concert. However, on this solemn occasion I do believe that, through the medium of the word, I should single out a phenomenon upon which that otherwise so abundant literature sheds no light; a phenomenon, though, which seems to me worthy of the utmost attention, and one which, for a long time, has fascinated me in ever-growing measure.

Whereas perhaps the work of no composer is, today, so universally beloved and so dearly familiar as that of Mozart, his personality has remained strangely remote to the world. From the biographies, from the musicological and music-historical literature, from reports, letters, and anecdotes one learns a great deal about his works, about their origin and importance, and about the external course of Mozart's life. One hears of his words and of his actions, but the figure which emerges from all of this is scarcely to be brought into accord with that of the creative genius manifesting itself in the greatness, the profundity, and the overflowing wealth of his work.

The human personality of Beethoven stands clearly before our eyes, and is thoroughly convincing as that of a world-conqueror in the realm of the spirit. In the tearing-up of the dedication of the *Eroica* to Napoleon we recognize the same impetuous power which manifests itself in his tone-language. The Heiligenstadt Testament seems to us like a Beethoven's *adagio* in words. Indeed, actually everything known to us of Beethoven's personal nature and de-meanor, of his human relations, from his letters, from the accounts of his friends, his conversation-notebooks, his deep urge toward erudition and culture—everything demonstrates the mighty, inspired Promethean soul.

In his writings, Richard Wagner gave the world inexhaustible clues to his thoughts and feelings. To name but one example, from his treatise on Beethoven an all-embracing humanity streams to-ward the reader, which can be understood as the field of origin for his tremendous work. In the letters to Mathilde Wesendonck one feels the power for love of the heart to which the world owes the unique and everlasting miracle of *Tristan*. And the historical act of the creation of the Bayreuth Festivals supplemented the picture of a titanic nature.

But what do we know of the human personality of Wolfgang Amadeus Mozart? His letters give evidence of his upright, vivacious, kindly character, his open, trusting soul. He appears in them as a loving obedient son, a devout Catholic, an infatuated husband, and so on. Also, we see him as a musician who gives serious thought to the problems of his art, and as one fully conscious of his genius; and particularly frequently, as a high-spirited young Salzburger.

Still, neither in such personal documents, nor in the accounts of contemporaries, nor in the words and actions which have become known to us, does the master-creator of immortal symphonies and operas speak; the dramatist whose creative fantasy gave to the theater the most vital characters and proceedings. Actually, from nothing that we know of Mozart the man does Mozart the creator become believable; that creative man who, through the stentorian voice of the "Man of Stone" in *Don Giovanni* warned the sinner to think of eternity, the man who, in his sensitive emotional sym-pathy, so well knew how to give an ironical, yet kindly, understand-ing expression in his music to the vagaries of love in *Cosi Fan Tutte*. The man who, in the coloraturas of the Queen of the Night, conjured up a vision of the sparkling, starry nocturnal sky;

the man who expressed deepest love for humanity in the lofty message of Sarastro.

One might imagine one had discovered a similar incongruity between the human personality and its artistic greatness in the case of Bruckner, whose still more naïve—even primitive—nature stands in an equally enigmatic relationship to the might and significance of his creative genius. I confess that I do not see any possibility of comparison here. Bruckner was an absolute musician. His great soul did not need a wealth of worldly experience, intellectual life, or literary cultivation in order that he might compose his grandiose symphonies, full of transcendental content. They grew out of the impulses which his elemental musical creativeness received from his limitless powers of feeling, and the sublime visions of his soul. And in regard to his vocal compositions and masses, the word and sense of the religious works posed no problem to his pious, dogmatically believing heart.

Mozart, however, was, according to disposition and inclination, a dramatic musician. And no dramatic creation is conceivable without penetrating understanding of the hard-to-fathom human heart, of the many kinds of relationships between human beings, of the particularities of cultural circumstances. That is to say, such creation is inconceivable without a wealth of worldly experience and a knowledge of humanity, without an abundance of intellectual interest, without a many-faceted cultural background.

This conception of the dramatist is, to be sure, not forthwith applicable to the dramatic musician who intensifies and "de-realizes" through his music the action and the inner life of the characters of a libretto written by a foreign hand. But the figures of the Mozart libretti originally possessed scarcely more than shadowlike contours, and only from *his* imagination and dramatic vision did they receive their life-blood, their clear outlines, their outspoken characters. So may we rightly recognize Mozart, the genuine dramatist, in the musical characterization of the stage-events and such acting figures as the servile intriguer, Basilio, the clumsy Osmin, the boldsly Pedrillo; as Leporello, Masetto, Despina, and Dorabella, Monostatos and Papageno—all characters which have become clearly discernible, even personally familiar to us, through him.

Since one scarcely can succeed in building a bridge from the unpretentious although immensely lovable personality which emerges from the Mozart literature to the miracles of such works, the only course that remains is to attempt to build a bridge in the reverse direction: to seek an explanation of the true spiritual nature of Mozart in his works.

It seems to me that light is cast along this pathway by the appearance of a unique basic characteristic of Mozartean creation which manifests itself in two ways pointing to the same source: truthfulness becomes beauty, complexity becomes clarity. Every dramatic expression in tones, every musical characterization of people, feelings, moods, and events in Mozart's works for the stage, is elevated to a sphere of noble beauty without the loss of convincing truthfulness; the most vivid variety of dramatic happening is transformed into musical perfection of form. It is this beauty and this perfection of form which permits a deep glance into Mozart's nature. From it we may conclude that his heart was filled with a transcendental harmony which exercised a decisive influence upon his artistry. Everything that he created—his dramatic and vocal works as well as his absolute music (the latter, also, where it gave strongest expression to dissonant feelings)—preserved the overtones of an "otherworldly" consonance from a higher sphere. In the feeling of this inspiration ruling in Mozart's soul, one may well speak of a seraphic impulse which gave wings to his music and musicianship. (And perhaps here I may insert the personal avowal that I receive the rare happiness which I owe to my occupation with Mozart's works from that consonance of which his musical world gives ringing manifestation.)

While the fire and the might of a prophet often sound forth to us from Beethoven's works, while Bruckner's creations seem to us to give testimony of the inner world of a saint, in Mozart's music, in its beauty and perfection, its lofty kind of serenity and purity, an angelic sphere opens before us. This dominating, unearthly element in his nature can, perhaps, also explain that feeling of remoteness which tinges our picture of the personality of the creator of familiar works of art in such a strange and mysterious way. Yes, perhaps therein may even be revealed Mozart's intense capacity for penetrating human characters and emotions—a capacity which was not dependent upon a wealth of experience such as was required by more worldly natures. It is very much open to question whether Mozart was conscious of the higher nature which lent impulse to his music and of which this music gives evidence. However, in the later years of his short life he became fully aware of the growing harmony of his love-filled heart with the doctrine of Humanity and Brotherhood of the Freemasons. Out of the synthesis of the former, probably unconscious, impulse with the latter moral tendency originated the spiritual sphere which found its expression in *The Magic Flute*.

Thus, I believe, in this last, immortal opera of Mozart's we are allowed to come so close to his very nature that we perceive in it his first personal confession—in fact, the only one which allows us to look into the depths of his heart. Just as Shakespeare, after the lifelong anonymity of the dramatist who remains concealed behind the characters of his plays, appears himself in his last drama, *The Tempest,* in the person of Prospero, so, I believe, does the human personality of Mozart appear in *The Magic Flute.*

The original form of the book certainly would not have permitted such an appearance. The fairy tale which Schikaneder had written as an operabook for Mozart, based on a tale by Wieland, completely lacked those ethical motives which decisively determined the content and the course of action in the final version. It contained adventurous exploits, fantastic characters, merry and serious scenes from which the stage-wise Schikaneder could conclude that, coupled with Mozart's music, it was material to provide a great theatrical success. The part of Papageno, Schikaneder had reserved for himself, and one may well suppose that he had therefore planned the comic scenes as the main plot of the story. We do not know, and can only guess, which part of the alterations which led to the final version of the libretto was due to Mozart. I presume that it was primarily the introduction of Masonic ideas into the story—an alteration to which he could most easily persuade Schikaneder to agree, since the latter, like Mozart, belonged to that Order. In connection with this, before anything else, the most decisive change had to follow: namely, the character of Sarastro, which originally had been conceived by Schikaneder as an evil sorcerer, now had to be changed into that of a sage who was the noble leader of a brotherhood of priests.

That the introduction of high ethical ideals in the person of Sarastro was due to the demanding influence of Mozart may be concluded from the inconsistency of the final book—an inconsistency which originated through the alteration of the central figure, and which undoubtedly would have been avoided had the clever Schikaneder himself initiated this change. Then, too, there remains the disturbing incongruity that the evil Monostatos is in the service of the noble Sarastro, and is sent by the latter to act as jailer of the gentle Pamina.

Be that as it may, and despite its severe lack of dramatic cohesion, we must acknowledge that the libretto possesses not only theatrical vivacity, but also serious-meaningful features and poetic charms which have maintained their effect until today. No higher testimonial to its merits could be mentioned than the favor it found with Goethe, which inspired him to write a sequel entitled

The Magic Flute, Part II. This approval which the book enjoyed from so august a source may be well understood, since *The Magic Flute* with its adventurous phantasmagoria and its admixture of childish merriment and serious solemnity corresponded to an astonishing degree with the requirements which the author of *Faust,* in the Prelude on the Stage, has his Theatre Director and his Merry Person utter.

That Schikaneder contributed the book's elements of adventure and gaiety, and Mozart its solemnity—and perhaps a bit of the gaiety—may surely be assumed. The message of love for Mankind, of friendship, uplifting the glance to a "better land," gained so sublime and convincing a power through Mozart's musical setting that he thus made the Sarastro scenes the dominating ones of the plot, certainly very much contrary to Schikaneder's original intentions. Thus, therefore, we hear in the music of these scenes the beat of Mozart's heart, and may not doubt that he, as creator of the character of Sarastro, intended therein to set forth his human ideal.

With the transformation of the sinister Sarastro figure of Schikaneder into Mozart's radiant one the strivings of the youth Tamino to be accepted into the realm of Sarastro were given, of course, a corresponding higher meaning. If Mozart acquainted us, in the figure he created of Sarastro, with his thoughts on human greatness, wisdom, and the nearness to God, so may we recognize in Tamino (who is so irresistibly drawn to the world of Sarastro that he submits himself to all the trials which are imposed in order to be admitted) Mozart himself in his deep-felt longing for human purity. His love for Pamina, the beginning motive for his wandering, after the instruction of the priest, melts into the longing for initiation. Pamina, to whom the seeming loss of Tamino's love means death, and who accompanies him through fire and water without hesitation, represents his ideal of womanhood. And Papageno, the merry lad, the simple son of nature who loves to eat and drink well, and longs for pretty girls, who is he? What does his continuous presence as wayfaring companion and adventure-sharer mean in the course of a book which speaks so eloquently of Mozart's character?

Well, he accompanies Tamino everywhere because he, too, is Wolfgang Amadeus Mozart, because he, too, belongs to the Mozart character. For as in Faust's, so in Mozart's breast also dwelled two souls. He was the high-minded, striving one, like Tamino, full of ideals of noble humanity. At the same time he was the gay, true-hearted young Austrian whose mind was inclined to worldly pleasures. And, as in *The Magic Flute,* the Tamino in his soul was always superior to the Papageno, and censured the latter's weaknesses. The latter, however, occasionally showed himself obstinate to the moral admonitions of the former, and we may assume that the battle—not a very vehement one—never came to an end. But we know, also, that the comradeship with Papageno could not hinder our Tamino from pursuing the "path of virtue" with all determination.

For such a Pamina, though, as the one granted Tamino, Mozart longed in vain. His earthly pilgrimage did not gain him the ideal life companion, whose image dwelt within him. However, in Tamino's determination to undertake the journey filled with so many trials and tribulations, and in its victorious accomplishment, Mozart's belief in Freemasonic thought, which comes to expression here, becomes convincingly recognizable.

With a few words I should like to point to the musical style of the work, and to its difference from the earlier operas of the master. Never before in his creative work had he sounded a tone like that of the C minor fugato above the chorale of the two Men-in-Armor. The solemnity of the Overture, the comic-grotesque wildness of the aria of Monostatos, the high enthusiasm of Tamino's monologue before the picture of Pamina, the sparkling ornaments of the Queen of the Night, the streaming love for Mankind in Sarastro's E major aria, the mystic invocation of Isis and Osiris by the chorus of priests—all were new inspirations of the Mozartean genius and new colors on his palette.

With the exception of the Overture, and of the previously mentioned fugue, in *The Magic Flute* there is evident a definite simplification of orchestral language in comparison with that of earlier works. It is the simplicity of the highest maturity (as it is displayed, also, for instance, in Wagner's *Parsifal* as compared to his earlier music dramas), and one which testifies decisively to the ascent of the Mozartean genius to its ultimate mastery.

To me there is but one single instance of an actual personal word of Mozart which indicates those depths of soul to which his music bears testimony. This exception to the in-the-main so "worldly" content of his numerous letters, appears in one written to his father by the thirty-one-year-old Mozart, where he says:

> Since Death, strictly speaking, is the true end-purpose of our life, for several years I have made myself so familiar with this true, best friend of men that his image holds nothing frightening for me any more, but much that is calming and consoling. And I thank my God that He granted to me the blessing of providing me with the opportunity of recognizing in Death the real key to our true happiness. I never go to bed

without considering that perhaps, as young as I am, I may not see the next day dawn. And no one of all the people who knew me will be able to say that I was sullen or sad in my relationship toward anyone . . .

For this supreme joy, I thank my Creator every day, and wish it to every one of my fellow-men from the bottom of my heart.

So he thought daily of Death "with supreme joy." Herein becomes convincingly apparent the nearness to eternity, the unearthly harmony in his heart which rings through his music as a seraphic sound. Otherwise, the so-talkative, even gladly communicative man kept silent regarding the depths of his soul which, for a long time, perhaps, had only been known to him subconsciously.

At last in *The Magic Flute* he opened his lips, and poured out his heart in the tones and words of Sarastro and Tamino; and in the proclamations of the former the world may recognize Mozart's own spiritual will and testament.

To be sure, what was vouchsafed to Tamino—the glorious crowning of his strivings—was accorded to Mozart only *sub specie aeterni,* and long after his poverty-ridden time on earth had reached a sad end. But there was still one other wondrous analogy between his troublous earthly wandering and that of his hero in *The Magic Flute.* Just as they had to Tamino, so the "good gods" had given to Mozart the protection of music along the danger-fraught path of the journey. The music which had accompanied him on his earthly way gave him the courage, the noble serenity, the buoyancy of soul, of which not even the worst experiences of poverty, want, and sickness could deprive him.

And as the melodies of the magic flute bestowed their beneficent spell on Tamino through the trials of fire and water, as they also protected Pamina and Papageno, so still today—and maybe today more than ever—Mozart's music proves its helpful, blessing power on those to whom it speaks.

The foregoing article was translated from the German by Ruth and Thomas Martin, Beverly Hills, April 1955.

THE RISE AND FALL OF HORATIO ALGER

by Marshall Fishwick

For millions of poor but honest American boys of an earlier era the rags-to-riches stories of Horatio Alger, Jr. held out the hope of success with a capital S. Little did they know the story of Alger's real life, as here told by historian Marshall Fishwick.

NOVEMBER 17, 1956

> *Strive and Succeed, the world's temptations flee*
> *Be Brave and Bold, and Strong and Steady be.*
> *Go Slow and Sure, and prosper then you must*
> *With Fame and Fortune, while you Try and Trust.*
> —Horatio Alger, Jr.

SCRATCH THE GLISTENING SURFACE of the American dream and you will find, not far beneath, the American tragedy.

Many examples come to mind—none more poignant than that of the man who made the success story into a formula for millions but never understood it himself.

His name was Horatio Alger, Jr. His own story is more intriguing than any of his heroes', and reveals more about American life.* Born in 1832 of old Massachusetts stock, Horatio was the first son of a stern Unitarian minister who was a walking "blue law." Sunday after Sunday he damned human activities which lead to enjoyment and prescribed as remedies generous doses of self-denial. His son heard, and believed. At Gates Academy and Harvard College he became known as "Holy Horatio." He was definitely his brother's keeper.

His life at Harvard was filled with crises. The sin his classmates indulged in was not only original; it was unbearable. Even the Cambridge landladies contributed to his unrest. One winter evening his own landlady appeared at his front door in her negligee.

---

* The only full-length biography of Alger is Herbert R. Mayes' *Alger, A Biography Without a Hero* (New York, 1928).

"I might have seen her bare," he wrote in his diary, "but I did not look." He moved instead.

He was not a good student. Confused and unhappy, he persuaded his parents to let him spend a winter in Paris. There he learned things which had never been explored in his Massachusetts adolescence. He looked. His Paris diary contains two lines more worthy of immortality than all the others in the Alger canon:

> I was a fool to have waited so long. It is not nearly so vile as I thought.

With cold Massachusetts came sober sanity. He repented and decided to become a Unitarian minister like his father. Once again he was miserable and moody, and once again he headed for the Big City. This time it was New York, where in 1866 he took a job writing juveniles for William Adams ("Oliver Optic"). Basically intelligent and facile with words, Holy Horatio learned his trade quickly. He had not mastered life, but he would master words.

He learned how to capitalize on current political reputations. Alger's development can be followed in titles like *Webster: From Farm Boy to Senator; Lincoln: The Backwoods Boy;* and *Garfield: From Canal Boy to President.* The last of these was rushed through in thirteen days, so that the publisher could have it on the streets before Garfield died. Having proven his skill in this area, Alger turned to fiction, where he would be free of the tyranny of facts and research. He not only got into the new field of "self-made men" novels; he captured it.

In the next thirty years he turned out 135 novels which sold an estimated twenty million copies. The books were not carefully constructed, but they were readable. The literary critic scorned them, but the historian noted that, good or bad, they were becoming dicta for an America full of self-risers.

All of his stories are basically the same. They go something like this:

I am a sturdy lad. I know I can climb the golden ladder with only my talent and talons to sustain me. My hope rests with my pluck and luck. True enough, my father has been killed, and my dear mother takes in washing. As an honorable son, I sell papers in rain, sleet, and snow. Neighborhood bullies pick on me, but there's always a cheery gleam (not fostered by booze, you may be sure) in my blackened eyes when mother washes them at night. We

say our prayers together and wait—for we know there is always room
on top.

Yes, I could seek better prospects. But being a sturdy lad I can
never desert my ailing mother, who writhes in pre-penicillin pain.
Then the tide turns! One day, as I sell my papers, I find a wallet
which Rich Man has dropped. Shall I keep the money and buy
mother much-needed medicine? No. Innate honesty has its way, and
I take the wallet to Rich Man's house.

The door is opened by his lovely blue-eyed daughter. Could this
be love? Apparently not. For my clean (but ragged) clothes bring a
sneer to her imperial lips. Still, I know she is Good Beneath. One
day she will appreciate all three of us (me, my pluck, and my luck).

As I back away from the house (she must not see the patch in the
seat of my pants) her father and his walrus mustache come in. His
face lights with joy as he sees the wallet. The grin broadens as he
snatches it from my hand, counts the money, and finds it all there.
"You will be rewarded, young man," he says, putting a shiny new
dime in my hand. "Come by my office and we will see if we can
find a place for you at the Bottom of the Ladder."

Young Venus thaws a bit at this. In her mind my patch starts
to disappear. But I must be Steady and True. Reluctantly and
nobly I reply, "You are kind, sir, but I cannot come. My mother
is alone, sick. She needs me more than you."

She does not need me for long. Her gallant heart gives out over
the scrubbing board. She goes to her just reward knowing I have
been tried and true. With her last gasp she urges me to take Rich
Man's job. I do. As office boy I carry papers, trim pencils, and
yearn for the alabaster daughter. I am always on time, cheery, and
plucky. I move quickly up the Ladder.

My chief competitor is a flabby, foppish young man of Social
Position. He does not believe in the open marketplace. He wants
not only the junior partnership, but also the white goddess. My
job is to foil him.

So I watch him closely and discover (by pluck and luck) that he's
a secret swindler. At the climax, when he is cornered, he resorts to
fisticuffs, but in vain; for I live clean and he smokes. Rich Man's
fortune is saved and mine is won. I get the promotion and the girl.

She is something of a prig and a bore—but not nearly so priggish
as her husband. Now we are keepers of respectability and masters
of all we survey. I take over Rich Man's business. The stork brings
the necessary number of heirs. And we live Happily Ever After.

Ridiculous? Incredible? Many former Americans and some present ones do not think so (if, of course, the burlesqued version is told straight). Time has transformed but not destroyed the rugged image of the Self-made Man. Detractors have ridiculed him in vain. He still shouts "Invictus," clutches his Horatio Alger novel to his breast, and plunges into the big bull market. He is, and has long been, the nation's *beau idéal*. No hero has a more realistic grip on glory. It can be checked by any certified public accountant.

In the last third of the nineteenth century Alger's novels continued to appear, not in single volumes but whole series—the *Ragged Dick, Tattered Tom, Brave and Bold, Luck and Pluck, New World, Way to Success, Campaign, Atlantic and Pacific.*

Because he often wrote two books simultaneously Alger sometimes got his characters mixed up. Hence Grant Thornton disappears mysteriously from Chapter IX of *Helping Himself,* only to pop up and thrash a bully in Chapter XIII of *Hector's Inheritance.* Did Alger's readers mind? Not at all. To them an Alger novel was as much a part of the scheme of things as apple pie, corn-on-the-cob, and Republican depressions. He never let them down. Even as a novel was being written some real-life American of Alger's day would be living the legend the books glorified. Henry Ford was thinking of setting up his own shop; Buck Duke was peddling his first plug of tobacco; Thomas Edison was recalling how he had sold newspapers on the corner; John D. Rockefeller, after a period of unemployment, was lining up a job. The times not only made the novel, they also justified them.

Different readers meet Alger's stock hero in different guises. Two generations of boys got him via Tom Swift—Alger's Sturdy Lad with rockets on. In those balmy pre-atomic days, Tom promised Better Things for Better Living through Science. Urbanism and overproduction were no problems in his technological fairyland.

Among the many variations of the Tom Swift story is that of Sammy Glick. He is swifter than Swift: a human whippet chasing the mechanical rabbit, believing satisfaction is just around the bend. We understand the reverse side of the coin because we know what is on the front. Today's Sammy Glicks are Horatio Alger "Frankenstein's monsters."

Even more exotic and enduring is Tarzan, Alger's lad in leopard-skin. Holy Horatio himself could not have conceived of a better example of a self-made man. Suckled by a female gorilla, Tarzan quite literally exemplified survival of the fittest. His open market was filled with lions and alligators. Leopard-women, ant-men, and white renegades (Tarzan lived clean; they drank) could not overcome him. He was really the son of Lord Greystoke—and he had both pluck and luck.

Under his different guises the self-made hero is always the Cinderella of American society. He proves one of our favorite maxims: "I'm as good as the next feller." Performance, not birth, is the American yardstick.

This paragon is at his best in business and politics. In art, philosophy, music, and science we honor achievement, but do not claim that anyone who tries hard can rate it. The admiration we feel for Winslow Homer, John Marin, and Albert Einstein is different from that accorded to Sam Houston, Andy Jackson, or Abraham Lincoln. Geniuses are born, not made—but every boy can be President.

Or can he? The man who trumpeted so most loudly lived out the denial. None of the peaches and cream of his books spilled over into his own life. In fact, his career parodied them. He was so little appreciated in this grubby little corner that he sought recognition by pounding the bass drum in newsboys' parades, tipped the Astor House desk clerk so he would point out celebrities when they walked by. Horatio was as insecure as his heroes were certain.

Then came a violent affair with a married woman and estrangement from his family. His one refuge became chocolate candy bars, which he munched in the solitude of his own room in the Newsboys' Lodging House of New York City. Plump and balding, he was suspended somewhere between the myth he had created and the reality he confronted.

There was nothing to do except write steadily, desperately, trying to make the old formula work, writing for boys because he couldn't write for men. History closed in on him. He had nothing to say.

Finally even the Sunday-school teachers found it hard to read his glib little sagas with a straight face. Naturalism was coming into vogue. America was developing a style and poetry of her own. Walt Whitman had sounded his barbaric yawp over the rooftops of the world. Mark Twain was showing a river full of black violence, and Stephen Crane a red badge of courage. Who got a kick out of Alger's simple stuff?

A few months before the century ended Horatio Alger, Jr. died. On his desk was the outline of a story that would never be told. In his heart was another one. It would never be told either.

Years before he had playfully composed his own epitaph:

Six feet underground reposes Horatio Alger, Helping Himself to a part of the earth, not Digging for Gold or In Search of Treasure, but Struggling Upward and Bound to Rise at last in a New World—where it shall be said he is Risen from the Ranks.

Several decades later another, shorter epitaph was written for another pitiful fellow named Willy Loman. This would have served admirably for Alger:

"He never knew who he was."

MAN MAKES HIS
FIRST STAR

by John Lear

*For the first time in the history of the world men have been able
to place an artificial star in the sky—and make it stay. Here is the
story of that universe-shaking achievement as told by* SR's *science
editor.*

APRIL 21, 1956

THERE IS LIGHT IN THE SKY AT NIGHT, even when there is no moon.
Whence does it shine? All the stars together are not bright enough
to explain it. How, then, does it come to be there?

Generations of curious men have wondered at this riddle of the
heavens. A few of them have gone from wonderment to pondering.
Although their speculations have impressed most other people as a
foolish waste of time, this handful of intellectual adventurers has
slowly reasoned its way upward through the dark toward the mystery of "the air glow."

Little by little, with bits of knowledge that have been learned
about the light that reaches earth in the full sun-glare of day,
there have been pieced together theories of what must happen when
the sun "goes down" to the other side of our planet. By burning
fragments of the elements that make all things terrestrial, and
watching the fire through prisms, it is possible to measure each
differing shade of flame as simply as marking the widths of the
bands of a rainbow on a ruler held before your eyes. And when
these measured colors have been matched against the colors of the
light that comes down from the sky it has been no great feat to
identify the elements that float in the unplumbed sea of space
around us.

For a long time now it has been known that two of these space
dwellers are oxygen and nitrogen. And one of the popular theories
has been that oxygen and nitrogen constantly combine and separate
in smaller-than-firefly-size exchanges far apart miles away from us—
and that their ghostly twinklings are diffused through acres of
darkness to give the night sky its faint luminescence.

There is considerable difference, however, between being sure that something must be true and being able to prove that it is true. That's why the history books pay so much attention to Christopher Columbus, who found a new world he didn't expect in the course of proving that his familiar old world was what astronomers of his day were certain it was: round.

A small crew of cerebral space sailors at the Cambridge (Mass.) Center of the U. S. Air Force Research and Development Command recently had an experience somewhat comparable to that of Columbus. In trying to prove that "the air glow" came from chemical electricity emitted by oxygen atoms as these atoms combined with nitrogen into molecules, these men put the first artificial star into the sky.

Unlike Columbus, these armchair argonauts did not need to peddle their ideas from one palace door to another. The Air Force was already sold on exploration of the outer sky. In fact, it was hunting ideas as strenuously as it was recruiting men. One practical evidence of the vigor of the recruiting was that Dr. Murray Zelikoff, the physical chemist responsible for the explorations reported here, got his job virtually overnight. If he had caught the train he planned to take back home to Newburgh, New York—he had left there to study at New York University and the University of Illinois, and had gone to Cambridge to seek a fellowship at Harvard—another name would be posted at the head of this expedition. But Dr. Zelikoff missed the train, telephoned an old school chum, and accepted the friend's introduction to the laboratory where the Air Force was then just beginning to study atmospheric photochemistry.

That was six years ago. Ever since, Dr. Zelikoff and his little crew of New England scientists (Dr. Frederick Marmo, Jerome Pressman, Leonard Aschenbrand, Adolph Jursa) have been pursuing "the air glow" as one of many possible clues to the environmental aspects of the upper atmosphere. In everyday words, what they have tried to determine was: if man should succeed in traveling into space, what living conditions could he expect to find?

Rockets loaded with instruments had gone up beyond 250 miles and had come back with photographs, air pressure and temperature readings, reports on clouds, moisture and general weather conditions. Among other things, the rockets took accurate measurements of what scientists call "the ozone layer." This layer is like a blanket hanging in the sky, saturated with far more oxygen than the air we breathe here on the ground. The lower side of the blanket is fifteen miles above the surface of the earth, and the blanket itself is fifteen miles thick. If it were not for this blanket we would be

burned to a crisp in no time by the rays of the sun or, more probably, decomposed and blown away by the overpowering electricity
in raw sunlight.

A certain amount of invisible ultraviolet light comes through the
ozone blanket to give us sunburn in the summertime. But the ozone
absorbs all the ultraviolet at the extreme end of the spectrum,
where the rays carry intense heat and electricity. In the sky above
the blanket this extreme radiation acts on the air like a chemical
bath, breaking up molecules into their constituent atoms.

Once in possession of that information, Dr. Zelikoff and his crew
were about as ready as Columbus was when he got Toscanelli's
primitive map of the globe. Instead of building ships, the Cambridge explorers made an artificial sun: a gas-filled lamp with two
big bulbs, strong enough to generate ultraviolet light with photochemical properties. Next they made an artificial sky: a seamless
steel tank from which they pumped the air until the pressure inside
was a billion times less than that of the air we breathe. Then, one
by one, they purified the gases their theories told them must be
present in the upper atmosphere. This was necessary because the
tiniest impurity would cause a gas to behave differently than the
gas would behave if it were pure. And finally the gases were loosed
into the man-made sky and subjected to the light of the man-made
sun.

By measuring the widths of the bands of color in the rainbows of
light they saw in photographs of their "sky," the scientist concluded
that the photochemical ultraviolet rays of their "sun" were hitting
oxygen molecules and knocking the two atoms inside each molecule
apart. The force of the blow appeared to be such as to cause a
transfer in molecular energy: that is, the energy that binds one atom
to another (as distinct from atomic energy, which holds one atom
together). Each of the separated atoms seemed to carry along with
it a share of the electric charge that came from the shaft of the sun.

Later, when another gas, nitric oxide (its molecule has one atom
of nitrogen and one of oxygen), was introduced into the man-made
sky the sun-shocked atoms of oxygen were attracted to this new
molecule. And when an atom joined a molecule to form nitrogen
dioxide (one atom of nitrogen and two of oxygen) the electricity
that had been captured from the sun by the oxygen was freed again
into the heavens.

If the pyrotechnical display that Dr. Zelikoff saw in the laboratory were to take place close to earth, the sky would be alight
continuously. For our surface air is heavily populated with oxygen

and nitrogen molecules. Since, however, "the ozone layer" permits these fireworks only aloft, and since the molecular density there is exceedingly thin, the Cambridge scientists believed that the light they observed in their indoor sky might very well be the mysterious "air glow."

There was only one way to confirm the laboratory experiments. That was to pour an extra-large dose of nitric oxide into the night sky above the ozone blanket and see whether the air would glow more brightly than usual at that spot.

At 1:45 A.M., Mountain Standard Time, on the morning of Wednesday, March 14, 1956, an Aerobee rocket twenty-three feet long and eighteen inches in diameter was shot from the desert sands at Holloman Air Development Center, New Mexico, carrying in its belly two round glass bottles cocooned in piano wire. Leading from the bottles to two small holes in the rocket's shell were tiny tubes through which the nitric oxide could escape. Each tube was closed with a valve that could be opened automatically by a clock, or, if the clock failed, by a radio message from the ground.

Before the rocket was fired the alarm on the clock was set to go off two minutes and thirty-five seconds after the launching switch was pulled. Within that time, if all went well, the rocket would reach a height above 316,000 feet—sixty-two miles.

Dr. Zelikoff never saw what happened. He was indoors, eyes fastened on a radar screen, finger twitching on a button that would blow up the rocket and free the gas if all else failed. But observers waiting on a mountaintop sixty miles away saw a new star appear with nearly twice the brightness of the planet Venus. The glow was half as luminous as that of a full moon.

For ten minutes the star hung there, within easy sight of the naked eye, growing bigger and bigger and dimmer and dimmer until it measured three miles across and only instruments could detect its presence.

The star is still there. It will always be there, diffusing endlessly through space. For the nitric oxide that was released is not diminished by its repeated combinations with the oxygen atoms whose light it frees.

Is the mystery of the "air glow" finally solved, then?

Dr. Zelikoff will not say so. There may be gases other than nitric oxide which contribute to the eerie light.

One thing is certain. It is now theoretically possible for man to draw from the upper atmosphere itself power with which to propel or otherwise employ space vehicles if he once can push such vehicles high enough. The single rocket that hung man's first star carried eighteen and a half pounds of compressed gas. That gas generated a 50-to-100 kilowatt light, or more than 100 horsepower.

Laboratory experiments have shown that free oxygen atoms tend to be attracted to any surface. All man has to do, then, is build a machine that flies through space, draws in oxygen atoms as it goes, feeds the oxygen into a pool of nitric oxide and either frees the resulting energy immediately in the form of light (thus creating artificial moonlight for delayed crop harvests, for round-the-clock rescue or rehabilitation in disasters, for surveillance of trouble spots in maintaining peace), stores it in batteries or channels it off, perhaps back to earth. Centuries may be spent in perfecting such an engine, decades perhaps, or only years. Who knows?

Although it lacks the drama of star-making, another significant experiment has been performed with nitric oxide at high altitudes by Dr. Zelikoff and his fellow-explorers of space. This was done in the daytime, also by rocket, at a height of fifty-seven miles. In this case, the photochemical rays of the sun stripped an electron away from each molecule of nitric oxide. The free electrons then scattered over the sky to form an umbrella against which high-frequency radio, television and radar waves could be bounced back to earth.

By perfecting this artificial ionosphere (the real ionosphere is a natural blanket that hangs unevenly far up in the sky and turns only long-wave radio signals back to earth), man in time should be able to send TV pictures through the air whenever and as far as he wishes, instead of being limited, as he is today, to communication between points that can be sighted in straight lines by the eye.

THE FUTURE OF FORM IN JAZZ

by Gunther Schuller

A composer forecasts the riffs and the razor-sharp subtleties that will be found in tomorrow's jive.

JANUARY 12, 1957

IF THERE IS ONE ASPECT of present-day modern jazz that differentiates it from the jazz of even five years ago, it is its preoccupation with new musical forms. Jazz today, with its greatly enriched language, seems to feel the need for organization at a more extended level. Few musicians seem to find complete satisfaction in the procedure so prevalent even a few years ago of wedging a group of generally unrelated "blowing" solos and several choruses of "fours" between an opening and closing theme.

At a time, therefore, when one hears and reads terms such as "extended form" and "free form" almost every day, and because there seems to be very little agreement as to what is meant by these expressions, it might be interesting to examine these new tendencies, to see where they may be leading modern jazz, and to investigate what role composition is beginning to play in a music whose greatest contribution has been a renaissance of the art of improvisation.

I suppose the question will be raised: why new or extended forms? Why not continue with the same conventions and forms we associate with the main tradition of jazz? Obviously an art form which is to remain a legitimate expression of its times must grow and develop. As jazz becomes more and more a music to be *listened* to, it will automatically reach out for more complex ideas, a wider range of expression. Obviously too, more complex harmonies and techniques require more complex musical forms to support the increased load of this superstructure. The long-playing record, moreover, has emancipated jazz from its previous three-minute limitation, and the *forming* of tonal material on a larger scale has thus automatically become a main concern of the younger generation.

It would be dangerous, however, if the jazz musician were to be satisfied with complacently reaching over into the classical field and there borrowing forms upon which to *graft* his music. The well-known classical forms—such as sonata or fugue, for instance—arose out of and were directly related to specific existing conditions, musical as well as social; and their effectiveness in most cases has been greatly diminished to the extent that these conditions have changed.

For example, the sonata form, originally based upon the dominant-tonic relationship which governed diatonic music, obviously no longer applies in an atonal work. This has been amply proven by the discrepancy between musical material and form in many Schoenberg works, and by the progress made in this respect by Anton Webern and the young generation of composers following in his footsteps. It has become increasingly clear that "form" need not be a confining mold into which the tonal materials are poured, but rather that the forming process can be *directly* related to the musical material employed in a specific instance. In other words, form evolves *out* of the material itself and is not imposed upon it. We must learn to think of form as a verb rather than a noun.

Experience, moreover, has shown us that the borrowing of a baroque form such as the fugue—the most widely used non-jazz form at the moment—very rarely produces the happiest results. Even when successful, it is certainly not the ultimate solution to the problem of evolving new forms in jazz, mainly because jazz is a player's art, and the old classical and baroque forms are definitely related to the art of composing (Bach's ability to improvise complete fugues notwithstanding). Used in jazz these classic forms can, at best, produce only specific and limited results, but cannot open the way to a new musical order. Jazz, it seems to me, is strong and rich enough to find within its own domain forms much more indigenous to its own essential nature.

The idea of extending or enlarging musical form is not a new one in jazz. By the middle thirties Duke Ellington, the masterly precursor of so many innovations in common use today, had already made two attempts to break beyond the confines of the ten-inch disc with his "Creole Rhapsody" of 1931 and the twelve-minute "Reminiscing in Tempo." The latter work, written in 1935, took up four ten-inch sides, but the Columbia label blithely continued to call it a "fox trot." Its length, its advanced harmonic changes, its unusual asymmetrically coupled fourteen- and ten-bar phrases aroused angry reactions and cries of "arty," "pretentious" and "not jazz." In retrospect we find that it is a poem of quiet melancholy, evoking that special nostalgia which so consistently distinguishes the early Ellington from most of his contemporaries; and we see that it was a small, weak step forward to expand form in jazz. Ellington was simply trying to do two things: 1) to break away from the conventional phrase patterns based upon multiples of four measures (in "Creole Rhapsody" he had already experimented with a 16-bar phrase made up of a pattern of 5 plus 5 plus 4 plus 2); 2) to organize his musical material in a slightly more complex form, at the same time integrating solos within that form so that the entire work would produce a unified whole. The least ambitious but perhaps the most inspired of his large-scale works, "Reminiscing in Tempo," opened up a new vista on the jazz horizon.

And yet Ellington—in those days always years ahead of his colleagues—was to wait a decade to see his early experiments emulated by other musicians. Perhaps the intense commercialism of the swing era with its emphasis on polish (and too often slickness) led jazz temporarily in other directions; or maybe it was simply that jazz had reached a period of consolidation and gestation. Be that as it may, a new style began to crystallize in the early forties under the influence of Parker and Gillespie, a style which already embodied in an embryonic stage the considerable strides jazz has made in the last fifteen years.

It is impossible within the limits of this discussion to examine all the achievements that have led jazz to its present status. The genius of Charlie Parker, the important contributions made by the Miles Davis Capitol recordings, and the success of the Modern Jazz Quartet in popularizing a musical concept that combines classical organization with conventional jazz traditions—all these have already become a matter of history and require no further emphasis here.

More recently, serious contributions to the freeing of form have been made by an ever-increasing number of musicians. Among them (without attempting a complete listing) are: Teddy Charles (although he says most of what he and Hall Overton are doing is not jazz), Buddy Collette, Giuffre, Gryce, LaPorta, John Lewis, Macero, Mingus, the Phil Nimmons group in Toronto, George Russell, the Sandole Brothers, Tony Scott, and many others.

A closer look, however, at some outstanding representative examples may help to give a clearer idea of what solutions in the search for new forms have been found.

One of the more interesting uses of form has been developed by Charlie Mingus with what he calls "extended form." I think some of the confusion regarding this term arises from the fact that "extended form" can mean simply *that*—extending form in a general way—but also can mean a more specific idea as envisioned by Mingus. For him it means taking one part of a chord pattern, perhaps only one measure, and extending it indefinitely by repetition until the soloist or the "composer" feels that the development of the piece requires moving on to another idea. Actually, this procedure does not represent a new form as such, since it is simply a stretching or magnifying of a standard pattern. Its liberating possibilities, however, are considerable, as exemplified by Mingus' finest efforts in this direction, "Pithecanthropus Erectus" and "Love Chant."

Jimmy Giuffre made a giant step forward with his "Tangents in Jazz," the full implications of which may not be assimilated for years. Aside from his remarkable musical gift, his concern for clarity and logic, his economical means and direct approach indicate that Giuffre is already one of the most influential innovators in present-day jazz. Excellent examples of his concern for formal clarity, with actually extremely simple means, are his written pieces like "Side Pipers," "Sheepherder" and the moving "Down Home" with its Ellingtonish mood of quiet intensity.

"Down Home" makes me think of another earlier masterpiece with the same combination of formal perfection and mature musical sensitivity, namely John Lewis' "Django."

What can be done in terms of integrating musical substance with form is also beautifully illustrated by recordings of André Hodeir in France. In two albums, Hodeir not only incorporates some of the most recent compositional techniques of European 12-tone writing, but also indicates through them ways in which original forms can be derived from the very core of a musical idea.

Suffice it to cite one especially felicitous example, "On a Blues." Beneath an evenly sustained tenor solo of some length there appears, at first imperceptibly, a riff, which gradually increases dynamically and orchestrationally until it has overpowered and absorbed the improvised solo. The riff, moreover, is not simply repeated in its original form, but undergoes a gradual transformation, at first by means of changing registers, then by inversion, still later by increasingly complex harmonization, and finally through a kind of harmonic and rhythmic condensation of the original riff into a new shape. This building line of intensity, both dynamically and structurally, gives the piece a unique driving force and makes it swing beautifully.

Another remarkable instance of total musical organization (without sacrificing the essential vitality and spirit of jazz) is George Russell's "Lydian M-1," a swinging piece that moves with relentless drive and "quiet fury," to quote Teddy Charles. In a way which is rare in jazz, the entire piece grows tonally and formalistically out of a nucleus of thematic material which in turn is based on a principle which the composer calls the "Lydian concept of tonal organization."

An eighth-note figure of considerable length dominates the opening, and from this, as we shall see, emanates almost all that is to follow. This figure consists at first of a single repeated note divided into a ¾ pattern (against an underlying 4/4 rhythm set up by the drums), then breaks out into an ascending arpeggio-like pattern which sounds all the notes of the scale (in parenthesis) that determines the tonality of the work. As the thematic line continues, it descends gradually via a series of asymmetrically grouped rhythmic patterns (constantly shifting combinations of ⅜s and ⅔s) to its original starting point, but now grouped in a 3/2 pattern. (The emphasis on ternary rhythms is obvious.) This pattern extended over sixteen measures provides a sort of running commentary to chordal aggregates in the "horns," again derived from the thematic material by combining vertically (harmonically) what had previously been stated horizontally (melodically). Four bars of the original repeated-note figure provide a bridge to a sort of second aspect of the main theme, this time characterized by a blue-note motive which, however, still relates back to the original underlying modal scale.

During the course of the composition, unity is achieved through reference to this reservoir of material: a 3/2 pattern by the rhythm section contrasts vividly with a trumpet solo in quarter-note triplets; or chordal accompaniments retain the modality of the opening by being derived through transposition almost entirely from the blue-note motive; a recurring chord progression that frames the three improvised solos is based on the modal scale; and so on.

Above all, the over-all form of the piece is a direct natural product of its own tonal material, giving the whole a feeling of rightness and completeness which marks the work of art.

Now this high degree of integration—which should appeal to anyone admiring order and logic—is considered by many jazz musicians to be too inhibiting. They claim it limits their "freedom of expression" and they consider such music outside the realm of jazz. There is violent disagreement on this point—not without reason. It is a difficult point, usually beclouded by subjectivism and the intrusion of the ego, and it needs to be discussed.

The assumption that restrictions upon intuitive creativity (such as improvisation) are inhibiting is, I think, not tenable, as is demonstrated by all successful art. A great masterpiece, for example, grows out of the interacting stimulus of the constant friction between freedom and constraint, between emotion and intellect.

Charlie Parker seems to have known this. But he also sensed that his work would have been stimulated to even greater heights by the freedom inherent in a context more complex. The chord patterns of his day began to bore him; he said he knew every way they could be played. Many of his solos were so loaded—even overloaded —with musical complexities and razor-sharp subtleties that the implications of a more complex over-all structural level seem incontrovertible. That he did not live to realize the implications of his own style is one of the tragedies of recent music history.

In this connection, there is another point which needs to be aired. It is very much in vogue these days for jazz musicians to "put down" the classical or "legit" way of playing. They scorn the playing of written music (and therefore also composing), and exalt improvisation beyond all reasonable justification.

This is a delicate subject since it touches the very core of a musician's personality and his reasons for being a musician. The subject thus always arouses a defensive and subjective reaction—on either side. I think, however, certain *objective* facts can be stated regarding this controversy which may help to set things right.

Many jazz musicians claim that the classical musician's playing lacks spontaneity, that it has become dulled by repetition and by the very act of reproducing music rather than by creating it. Only those musicians who have actually played in a first-rate symphony or opera orchestra under an inspired conductor can know to what heights of collective spontaneity an orchestra can rise. After fifteen years of playing in such organizations, I can personally attest to this most positively. Admittedly it *is* rare, since it depends on many factors. But it does occur, and, I think, with more or less the same degree of frequency with which it occurs in jazz.

Listening to several sets on an average night by an average group at Birdland or at an all-night private session will bear this out. How often does a group *really* swing or *really* communicate at an artistic level? (After all, getting "knocked-out" by the beat of an average rhythm section is not yet communication at a very high level. I may respond to it—and I generally do—but that does not by itself make what I'm hearing great music.)

Moreover, is the batting average of a quartet playing "How High the Moon" for the umpteenth time any higher than a symphony orchestra doing its annual performance of the Beethoven *Eroica?* I humbly suggest that the average jazz musician is not in a position to answer that question since he has seldom, if ever, been to a symphony concert and even more rarely has he caught one of those inspired performances. Furthermore, the Parkers, Gillespies and Lester Youngs exist in the classical world too, only their names are Lipatti, Szigeti, and Gieseking, and *they are indeed just as rare.* Obviously, I do not mean musicians who can improvise like those first three, but soloists who are as highly trained and sensitive in their job of *spontaneously re-creating* a masterpiece as those jazz greats are in creating.

The illusion of spontaneous re-creation is a factual possibility, as we all know from great acting performances in the theater. At its highest level, it is an art as rare and as fine as improvisation at *its* highest level—no better, no worse; just different. If re-creating another man's music authentically and illuminatingly were all that easy, then every jazz trumpet player could play the trumpet part from the "Rite of Spring." Obviously what needs to be reiterated is that both ways of playing are highly specialized and require a different combination of skills.

Improvisation is the heart of jazz and I, for one, will always be happy to wait for that 5 per cent which constitutes inspired improvising, but is the average jazz musician prepared to look for that 5 per cent in classical music?

As for the purists who feel that the pieces under discussion here—and all those works that seem to be gravitating toward classical or composed music—do not qualify as jazz, one can only say that a music as vital and far-reaching as jazz will develop and deepen in an ever-widening circle of alternating penetration and absorption, of giving and taking.

Actually it matters little what this music is called; the important thing is that it is created and that it represents the thoughts and ways of life of its times. Let the academicians worry about what to label it. Seen in this light, the future of this music—jazz or not—is an exciting one. And a fascinating one, because exactly what shape this future will take will not become entirely clear until the next Charlie Parker arrives on the scene.

THINK OF A MAN

by Norman Cousins

Today man stands on the threshold of his greatest triumph—or of his most abysmal failure; for there is no human achievement and no thing of beauty which cannot be swept into void. In this article SR's editor-in-chief, the author of the famous editorial "Modern Man Is Obsolete," appeals to all who believe in the idea of progress to rise to the challenge of history's greatest hour.

AUGUST 4, 1956

YOU ARE ASKED to think of a man. Think of someone, living or dead, whose life has enriched your own. Think back for a moment on the name or names that have given history a forward thrust, a sense of direction, an infusion of important knowledge, an encounter with the beautiful. Names connected to great ideas or causes or deeds or works of art.

You are asked to do this because an intimate relationship, all at once, has come to exist between the life of such a man and your own. The turn of events has now made you the custodian of all his works. For it is now in your power—power on a scale never before possessed by human beings—to protect and fulfill those great works and ideas or to shatter them beyond recognition or repair. There is no achievement in human experience, no record, no thing of beauty that cannot now be rescinded and all its benefits and traces swept into void. It is this that distinguishes our generation from all previous generations: we possess total authority not only over our own time but over all the ages and works of man. Earlier generations have had the power merely to affect history; ours is the power to expunge it.

We have managed somehow to unhinge the permanent. Everything that has occurred in history until now has suddenly acquired interim status. The mammoth struggles and sacrifices, strung together over a period of centuries, that have reduced barbarism and released the human individual for creative purpose—all these struggles are now fragile and uncertain as though they had never been won. It is in this sense that our time has become a grand concourse for all the great causes and experiences of the race, six thousand years of them, suddenly made tentative and unresolved because of the new reach of modern man.

Think of a man. Begin in medicine. Think of the long procession of great theorists and researchers whose work has overturned the old vital statistics that condemned nine out of ten men to a lifetime under forty years. Think of the advances built on this work that now make possible great new expectations of sixty years or more for the average man in a large part of the world. But think, too, that the cures for the life-shortening diseases can now be nullified because of political diseases far more menacing to health and longevity.

More specifically, think of men such as Vesalius or Harvey who took medicine out of the dark ages by contributing so mightily to the working knowledge of the human structure in general and of the bloodstream in particular. But the principal dangers to bone and bloodstream today are far beyond the reach of the great men of medicine to combat or correct. For our age has devised a supremely efficient method of altering and damaging the balances in bone and blood. This is not difficult. Nor is it necessary to individualize the process. The blood of millions of human beings can now be altered by a political decision to throw a single switch.

If you are still thinking of warriors for better health, think of the famous microbe hunters like Koch or Van Leeuwenhoek or Pasteur or Ehrlich or Claude Bernard or Hideyo Noguchi, whose combined researches gave focus to the intricate nature of disease as well as the way to attack it. Here, too, it is important to reflect that something infinitely smaller than the bacillus or virus has become infinitely more dangerous. Neutrons released by radioactivity—visible not even to the microscope—can now surround man, piercing thick walls to get at him, shooting through every part of his being, causing his organs to function crazily or not at all. The neutrons are not hypothetical. They exist. As many as are required to twist all life out of shape can now be put to work without delay. The towering medical discoveries could be meaningless alongside this reality.

Or perhaps you have been thinking of men like Mechnikoff or Cohnheim who explored the world of the cells inside the human being—an ordered world with complex but stern requirements of its own. When excessive radiation enters this world it changes it and condemns it.

If the names that come to your mind have to do with preventive medicine, names like Jenner or Lister or Semmelweiss or Agramonte or John Enders or Jonas Salk, consider that, while countless thousands have been spared smallpox or diphtheria or yellow fever or pellagra or poliomyelitis because of these medical pioneers, there are countless millions today who are totally vulnerable to the fundamental and massive threats to their health and safety represented by the combination of grandeur in science and anarchy in the world.

The names of the giants are endless. Domagk and Waksman and Fleming and Dubos; Freud and Breuer and Jackson and Jung and Brill and Chisholm; Cannon and Selye and Hench and Beck and Blalock—men of our time who have used the creative and disciplined intelligence for freeing mind and body for a longer and more purposeful existence. But, whether with respect to antibiotics or mental health or synthetic hormones or new surgical techniques, the victories in these fields can only be held in escrow until the basic health of society is assured. For when civilization itself goes insane the diagnosis and treatment of an individual are valiant but incomplete.

Think of the men who have thought about the species of man— all the way from Aristotle and Bacon to Lamarck and Darwin and Wallace and Spencer. They tried to see man against the largest possible setting, which is to say, his natural one. And they were uninhibited in their approach. A question didn't have to have an answer, but if it was a good question it might produce three or four more questions related to it; and eventually a body of questions was formed which might add up to something.

The questions that Darwin asked had to do with the infinite variety of life but also with the basic similarities and relationships of living things. They led him to theories of change—generally change for the better, at least in terms of the need of life to adapt itself to changing needs or die. Life was a precarious enterprise because the means of sustaining it never quite remained the same. Different species might put in competing claims for the same means. It was natural that the species that developed sharper or more effective approaches to their changing environments would have a superior claim on survival. Natural selection, therefore, involved an upward drive or evolutionary process.

Darwin's ideas were generally accepted as a major contribution to scientific knowledge, but they were never proved. It is possible, however, that modern man may furnish proof of the Darwinian theory—in reverse. It may be entirely within the reach of man today to demonstrate the changeability of species—except that it may be devolution rather than evolution. This change may be away from higher or more selective development to less complex and cruder forms. Man may now be in a position to make a sudden descent biologically to a series of lower orders. Until now he could perform all sorts of assaults on himself; he could cheapen life, debase it, cripple it, and kill it. But he could not get at his own germ plasm, locked securely in the inner being of each of his cells. But now through radiation this last fortress of his physical integrity can be pierced. The radiation he himself is able to produce but is unable to control can violate his genetic purity by changing the structure of the human cell. If the radiation is sufficient the final barrier to a human mutation may be removed and the descent to the lower orders of life may proceed.

The theory of evolution, forecast by Buffon, speculated upon by Lamarck, and developed by Darwin and Wallace, had never been proved because in six thousand years of recorded history a major change from one species into another had never been scientifically observed. But life in various forms has existed on this planet for several hundred million years and our knowledge is confined to a puny fraction of that period. As it concerns the history of man himself we have only the vaguest ideas about his age on earth, whether it covers a million years or considerably more or less.

At any rate, even without proof, Darwin's carefully assembled ideas have seemed reasonable enough to the scientific intelligence to be accepted as a working theory. Though this is sheer speculation, it is possible that there can be, and probably has already been, retrogression of the species. Man may have gone up and down the ladder of evolution several times during his hundreds of thousands or millions of years on earth. It is at least theoretically possible that he has built other civilizations as complex as our own and suffered the same inability to operate them. He may have surged as far ahead in his inventiveness as we have done, but may have been just as deficient in creating the basis for sanity in the relations between the various groupings into which he was divided. No one can say that our generation is the first that has played with nuclear energy or that there may not have been earlier uncontrolled situations in which radioactivity brought about a whole reshuffling of species.

If onrushing knowledge and applied science can create an environment in which man's basic existence is threatened, he may respond or adapt by sinking far enough in the order of intelligence so that science is beyond his reach, whether for good or evil. The tendency of nature may be to push the forms of life upward through a process of natural selection, as Darwin argued, but it may also be true that man has co-operated in this natural process only up to a point. That point in the past, as it seems to be in the present, may be a point of maximum power and maximum opportunity from which he abruptly veered away, turning his power on himself and the essence of his being.

Whether the lower orders have descended from man or vice versa, or whether there has been a combination of both, depending on the causes and circumstances, it becomes important for our generation to comprehend the nature of the power at our disposal and its full meaning. And here we come to the most startling fact of all about our own time. The nature of the power available to modern man and its implications are hardly understood by the people in whose name it will be used and on whom it will have its effects. The major governments which are producing the nuclear explosives have failed to make a distinction between the legitimate need to preserve secrecy with respect to the size and nature of the respective stockpiles and the moral obligation to inform the people fully concerning the nature of those weapons and their effects. Meanwhile large-scale experimentation has proceeded without adequate laboratory knowledge concerning the extent of danger of the tests themselves. Only now do laboratory studies show that the threat of genetic damage to humans from excessive radiation is at least ten times greater than what had earlier been supposed.

When you think of the theories of the great naturalists, therefore, think also of the new reversing power man now possesses over nature and its drive toward higher forms of life.

But it is not only in medicine or the sciences of life that the present generation can cancel out great gains or ideas. All the fields that add up to progress for man are involved, whether with respect to the arts of man or the rights of man.

Think of the men who proved that the human being need not be condemned to the life of the drone. Here were the men who worked on the frontier of human uniqueness, expressing the need to create beauty and enabling other men to respond to it. What they did gave a necessary extra dimension to life.

One thing their works had in common, quite apart from the power to convey rhythm or harmony or a state of esthetic grace or expressive power in general. Whether with respect to great paintings or songs or poems or books or edifices, these works stand above time. It is not only that they appeal to all ages; they were created independent of time itself. A work of art took as long to produce as was necessary to make it a work of art. A Greek temple took a lifetime or more to build. The Taj Mahal was a generation in the making. The paintings in the Dome in Milan were spaced out over a period of centuries. The massive religious sculptures and carvings at Borodudur, Indonesia, were worked on for five hundred years. Kyoto and Nara, Japan, were neither pressed for time nor obsessed by fears of time when these cities devoted themselves to the cause of beauty and the permanence of beauty.

Only a second is now required to knock down all of it.

Nor is the nullifying power of modern man over time and its relationship to beauty confined to the big objects that are so easily swept aside. A Giotto fresco, a window at Chartres, a poem by Aeschylus or Blake or Iqbal, a tragedy by Euripides or Shakespeare, a sermon by Donne or Tagore, an etching by Rembrandt or Turner or Hiroshige, a quartet by Mozart or Haydn or a symphony by Beethoven—all are now equally vulnerable. It is no longer true that no force can kill a book or a work of art. Obliteration can do it. Ultimate power that fulfills itself in an instant can do it. And if the force cannot find art to destroy it man can lose it by losing his own awareness of beauty. This inner loss, too, is now within his reach.

Now think of the men who were identified with great causes. Think of the men who fought to establish the most revolutionary principle in all history; namely, that the purpose of the state was to serve the cause of the individual. Think of Solon, the great law-giver of early Greece who championed the sovereignty of the individual, beyond the reach of authority of the nation. Or Pericles, calling for equal justice toward all and arguing that public discussion, far from being a stumbling block to workable government, was an "indispensable preliminary to wise action."

Think of the men who continued and enlarged this cause, frequently at the cost of their lives. These were the leaders who believed that the act of being born carried with it a long list of natural and basic rights—political, spiritual, social. Erasmus, Milton, Harrington, Cowley, Locke, Spinoza, Montesquieu, Voltaire, Garibaldi, Mirabeau, Alfieri, Manzoni, Hume, Woolman, Penn, Fox, and the American revolutionary leaders—Franklin, Washington, Samuel Adams, John Adams, John Dickinson, Jefferson, Madison, Paine, Wilson, Hamilton, Freneau. Only a partial list but enough to serve as focus for purposeful thought about the relationship of the individual citizen to the nation. These men believed in the independence of the nation and in self-government—not as an abstraction or as an end in itself but as a specific way of protecting individual man and assuring his right to participate in the shaping of his society.

When a man like Jefferson or Madison thought about government the things that came to mind were not concerned with grandiose political machinery or master operational plans for the control of a nation. Each idea about government had something to do with people. Would this feature of government help a man to grow? Would that aspect of government help force errors into the open by government itself? Would this provision of government make it possible for a man to pick his own church or books or newspaper or friends? Was there any danger that government would arrogate to itself an official conscience that would seek to displace the conscience of the individual or limit its range? How could a man be fortified with rights so that overblown functionaries could not barge into his home at will just to make him squirm?

It was natural that a Jefferson would think of these things for he knew that the tendency of a state was to collect power far beyond its needs, just as it was the tendency of the men at the top to try to make a permanent acquisition of the government itself. What counted most was not the sovereignty of the state but the sovereignty of the individual. The great cause, therefore, was the cause of the individual against the state.

The cause has come a long way. If it is in danger today, however, it is not only because of the perpetual threats from dictators or ambitious men who constantly scheme to gain supremacy over the laws. The cause of individual man is in danger today because the sovereign state itself is no longer an adequate instrument for safeguarding the individual or underwriting his freedom. The sovereign state no longer represents the solid outer rim of security for its citizens. Indeed, it is the state itself that has become the core center of insecurity in the modern world. It is so busy fending for itself in the great open arena where nations come into contact with each other, jostling or preening or jockeying for position, that all other functions become secondary. And the insecure state tends to bolster its position by doing things that add to the insecurity of the individual. It does this through standing armies or increased taxes or a prodded economy or internal security measures that reflect and increase the very tensions they try to eliminate.

If the states live in anarchy the individual citizen pays the price of anarchy. Law and order within the state are no protection against the larger violence and injustice outside the state. Whatever the intermediate forms of protection afforded to man in his daily life, the major threats to his well-being and future find him open and exposed.

All this the state does in the name of security. But what kind of security is it that condemns the unborn, pursues the innocent through generations to come, diminishes and deforms man, and poisons air and earth? If this is what total sovereignty has come to mean, then it is a monstrous thing and man has the duty to replace it with the higher and saner means that will come into conflict with neither nature itself nor his own natural rights.

No matter how hard today's sovereign state tries to pursue security through power, the power is never quite enough. For other states are increasing their power too. The state and its people are thus trapped in their own sovereign coils. To have no power when other nations are becoming more powerful could be an invitation to attack and disaster. But the pursuit of power means the pursuit of superior power, hard to define and even harder to create.

The dilemma is especially acute for free peoples. They have been vulnerable to aggressors in the past precisely because their freeness makes for openness. And, even as they now accept the need to become brawny in the cause of self-preservation, they become involved in something beyond their control—a massive competition in potential terror the very nature of which pulls them inexorably toward a showdown.

For the dictator state the world condition of tension and uncertainty offers a natural habitat. The presence or prospect of an outer threat lends weight to the internal controls. But even if the dictatorship faces the stark need for changes inside itself; even if it is willing to denounce or renounce its own tyrants and the products of the tyranny; even if it is willing to modify its ideological ambitions for large dominion—even if it does all these things the mountain of its sovereign statehood still stands. The sovereignty precedes the ideology and survives it. And in its sovereign role the dictator state sticks to its last. It may make concessions, it may permit deviations, but it will not surrender its position above the law. As it concerns the ultimate question of national sovereignty, it insists on the unlimited and unfettered development and mobilization of its own power.

This power need not be applied in order to inflict hurt. Just the act of flexing it has a bruising reality all its own. Already a single bomb is three hundred times more powerful than the bomb which has so far accounted for 230,000 lives in Hiroshima, according to official estimates. Neither science nor technology stands in the way of a bomb three thousand times or thirty thousand times more powerful still. While high-altitude detonations can reduce the amount of dirt and debris sucked up into the upper altitude, thus decreasing the quantity of dangerous fallout, there remains a vast potency in radioactivity over a large area. A modest-sized hydrogen bomb, for example, has a danger zone of 2,500 square miles.

Some questions: How much more radioactivity can be pumped

into the upper atmosphere before the fallout of strontium becomes menacing to life far outside the areas supposedly under control? How much official study has so far been given to the possible connection between the nuclear tests already conducted and the extreme weather manifestations that have already taken lives, wrecked crops, and washed out cities? The conviction grows that the tests are proving mainly how dangerous they are, yet they continue—proof of the grim fascination with which the nations race each other to be the first to devise the means for an ultimate attack on the planet itself.

If increasing experimentation represents increasing danger—not only to the contestants in the nuclear competition but to all people —on what basis are the tests to be stopped? More important still, on what basis are the existing stockpiles of the big explosives to be reduced or eliminated? Each side has talked about the desirability of some control, but neither side has yet faced up to the need for the compulsory measures that will be essential—measures involving not only inspection but actual enforcement binding on individuals. Nor has either side yet accepted the essential connection between the control of weapons and the control of war itself. The dance is still on the periphery; there have been no bold steps toward the working center where basic causes can be recognized and the responsibility for dealing with them accepted.

For the United States, then, true security need not be a thing of fits, starts, and reciprocal terrors. It need not confine us to a choice of evils. It can have the mark of good sense on it and the solidity of affirmative appeal.

True security begins with the advocacy of a large idea that singularly fits the problem not only of the American people but of all people. The problem is how to create abundance on earth and use it for greater good; how to eliminate or control the situations that lead to war, whether with respect to predatory assault or the injustice that is worse than war itself. And, if we cannot do all this, how to keep the large idea alive so that the job of the next generation can be something more inspiring than clearing away the meaningless rubble left by mighty but mediocre men.

In advocating the large idea, we can offer our pledge that we will take no measures in the cause of our own protection that will jeopardize the safety of the world community—and call upon others to do the same. We can pledge our fullest moral and material support in developing the responsible powers of the world organization so that it can truly enforce the peace—and call upon others to do the same.

The central objective is a new relationship of the states to each other as part of the specific machinery of a world organization responsible directly to people instead of to governments. It would require some pooled strength, at least to the extent of being able to stand behind its control both of the massive weapons of war and the situations that could result in war.

Built into it would have to be the principles and agencies of justice, without which it could become irresponsible, arbitrary, overbearing. It would have to be limited in its authority to those matters which concern the human community as a whole, whether with respect to dangers or needs. In all other respects the states must retain authority and jurisdiction over their own peoples and cultures. Indeed, a primary function of the world organization should be to underwrite this kind of sovereignty and help in every way to make it meaningful.

The spirit in which such an enterprise is advocated is no less essential than the plan itself. If the spirit is one of deep affirmation and vitality, if it views the present as the rich and proper moment for the greatest forward surge in human history, then we will not invite the dangers of a purely mechanical approach to peace. Such a spirit might well be expressed in a statement of human interdependence, in which the lack of geographical or physical barriers in the world is fully recognized; in which man's right to his genetic integrity is declared; in which unity and diversity are both recognized and assured—unity in terms of the basic oneness of man, diversity in terms of his cultures or groupings or purposes; in which the natural rights of man are redefined and placed beyond the state; and in which air and earth are declared the natural assets and possessions of the world's people, to be utilized for the common good and to be kept free from assault or corruption by human agencies.

It is not necessary for the Soviet Union and the United States to merge or create a political unity between them in order that sanity and safety may exist on this earth. It is necessary only that each give up the specific rights and the means to upset the vital balances which make human life on this planet possible, on condition that the world community itself develop the workable mechanisms of law in which both can have confidence and in which both can participate for the greater good of all the earth's people.

If there is any other hope, then those who profess it have the obligation to define it and advocate it. Far better to have a debate on world law and its alternatives than to continue a state of moral anesthesia and global anarchy which accepts any explosive situation so long as the fuse is not actually spluttering. The big opportunity, of course, is represented by a United Nations which can be developed fully and dramatically into the kind of world organization that the age requires and that the institution of man deserves.

Finally, then, let us think about ourselves. If our purposes are frail, if the value we attach to the idea of progress is small, if our concern for the next generation is uninspiring, then we can bow low before the difficulty, stay as we are, and accept the consequences of drift. But if we have some feeling for the gift of life and the uniqueness of life, if we have confidence in freedom, growth, and the miracle of vital change, then difficulty loses its power to intimidate.

No greater fallacy exists in the modern world than that the individual in a free society is helpless. If anything, he exercises his power without being aware of it. Vast sums are spent to find out what he thinks or is likely to think. No major move can be made without him. Great designs are giving ground to great hesitations out of fear that he might not favor difficult but necessary steps. The result is not a heroic effort in behalf of a better tomorrow but a preoccupation with the glories of the short term. Hence the paradox: the fully sovereign state is unable to act effectively in the world arena in behalf of the very individual whose support it so zealously courts and whose opinion it so ardently seeks on questions for which government itself has failed to provide adequate information.

Certainly the individual is not helpless. The question for him is not whether he possesses any power but how to use the power he possesses. He will receive information if he demands it. He can appraise information if he will give time to it. He can think, he can talk, he can write, he can associate, he can make his opinions known. He need not wait to be asked for his views. He can free himself from the daily trivia that soak up his time and energies and he can apply himself to what is important. Nor need he fear that this is an academic or futile undertaking. The act of informed dedication is a power by itself.

The individual can consult other individuals; he can also consult history. He can tap the experience of the race. He can find out something about the great causes he is now asked to protect. And he can think about the great spiritual leaders in human history and ask himself what their response would be to the forces of man that now jeopardize the estate of man. He can think about the prophets of the Old Testament and their emphasis on respect for the individual design and their insistence on justice. He can think about the purity, simplicity, and grandeur of the morals and ideals and teachings of Jesus, and the power of dedication of the Apostles. He can think about the reforming zeal and desire for spiritual emancipation of Mohammed. About the Deities of the Veddas, with their seamless and poetic continuity between life and the universe. About Buddha's concern for the individual in stress and suffering and the higher reality of which he is part and which knits him together. About Baha'ullah and his efforts to provide a basis for spiritual and social unity among all men. About the ethics and restraint and service to humanity of Confucius.

It should not be difficult for the individual to determine what the spiritual leaders would say in the present situation. They would say that it is not enough for man to profess oneness with other men; he must act it out. Not enough to wear the garment of religious identification; he must accept its ethical and moral obligations and glory. Not enough to lay claim to personal sacredness; he must bind himself to it through respect for it and sensitivity to it. Not enough to boast of the gift of a rational intelligence; he must nurture it, work it, apply it, defend it. Not enough to prate about justice; he must create a basis for it in the world itself.

INDEX